WordPerfect®:
The Complete Reference

WordPerfect®:
The Complete Reference

Karen L. Acerson

Osborne **McGraw-Hill**
Berkeley, California

Osborne **McGraw-Hill**
2600 Tenth Street
Berkeley, California 94710
U.S.A.

For information on translations and book distributors outside of the
U.S.A., write to Osborne **McGraw-Hill** at the above address.

A complete list of trademarks appears on page 1077.

WordPerfect®: The Complete Reference

1234567890 DODO 898

ISBN 0-07-881266-6

Nancy Carlston, Acquisitions Editor
Don LaVange and Jennifer Nelson, Technical Reviewers
Lyn Cordell, Project Editor
Bay Graphics Design Associates, Cover Design

To my parents, Richard and Mary Jane Cozzens,
for teaching me the value of hard work

CONTENTS

Part Three: Printing

FIVE — Laser Printers   751

SIX — Printer Specifics   781

SEVEN — Printer Program   973

One morning in August 1983, I was in Dan Lunt's office (Dan is VP of Marketing at WordPerfect Corporation). We were feeling sorry for ourselves because we wanted to hire a certain person away from IBM and knew we couldn't afford her (WordPerfect was then a small company of about 30 employees). As I stepped out of Dan's office, I saw a young woman waiting in the lobby who looked like she had just stepped out of an IBM sales brochure.

After talking with her long enough to find out that she was a secretary at Brigham Young University and was helping professors learn WordPerfect (not many people knew the program well at the time), I ushered her into Dan's office and we offered her a job on the spot.

We never regretted the decision. Karen started as our third Customer Support employee and, because of her enthusiasm for and knowledge of all WordPerfect products, she quickly became the designated demonstrator and trainer for large and important accounts. When she wasn't traveling, she worked in almost every department of the company. When motherhood nudged her into semi-retirement, she helped the Publications Department write product documentation, then accepted a position as Manager of the Customer Support Department. We reluctantly accepted her resignation when she left to have a second child. Although she is no longer an "official" employee, Karen continues to be heavily involved with the company.

Karen probably knows WordPerfect better than anyone else (except me) and has an almost fanatical devotion to the product. I heartily recommend her book to anyone who wants to learn more about WordPerfect.

W. E. Pete Peterson
Executive Vice-President
WordPerfect Corporation

ACKNOWLEDGMENTS

Many thanks:

To my husband Jeff and our children Mark and Kimberly, for their love and patience.

To Jennifer Nelson, Don LaVange, and Pete Peterson for editing. Their suggestions were invaluable, and helped to make this book as accurate as possible. Special thanks to Pete Peterson for his advice and encouragement.

To those at WordPerfect who have taught me: Alan Brown, Derrick Shadel, Kevin Crenshaw, Terry Brown, Layne Cannon, John Dance, Daron Bradford, Stan Mackay, Terry Owens, Chuck Middleton, Stuart Smith, Reese Bastian, Kent Russell, and many, many others. My gratitude also goes to Scott Echols, Steve Sullivan, and Shannon Cotton for their help with research.

To Nancy Carlston, Lindy Clinton, Lyn Cordell, Madhu Prasher, and Marcela Hancik at Osborne/McGraw-Hill, who were responsible for the completion of this book.

Above all, I am grateful to Bruce Bastian and Alan Ashton for creating WordPerfect; without it, I could not have written this book.

This book is for all WordPerfect users: those who are making a transition from a previous version, a typewriter, or another word processor, as well as those who have used the program for many years. It is a comprehensive reference guide that gives users the basics as well as the most up-to-date technical information available. It has been written because of a need for more thorough explanations, details, and practical applications.

If you are a new WordPerfect user, refer to Chapters 1 through 3. When you are ready to learn about specific features and acquire new skills, refer to individual WordPerfect topics in Chapter 4. There you'll find information on keystrokes and applications, along with hints for easing your mastery of each feature.

Advanced users who are ready for more detailed information will find answers to the most technical questions as well as tips and specialized macros throughout the book.

What This Book Contains

The following summarizes the information contained in each part and chapter of this book.

Part One: Introduction to WordPerfect

Chapter 1, "Getting Started," answers questions you might have about DOS, your computer, your printer, and how all three work with WordPerfect.

Included are basic rules and helpful tips for installing WordPerfect on your system. Even if WordPerfect has already been installed, you might want to read this chapter so that you can make any necessary changes.

Chapter 2, "WordPerfect Basics," gives new users the necessary information to begin using WordPerfect and also serves as a refresher for those who are more experienced. It leads you through the steps of creating, editing, formatting, checking for correct spelling, printing, and filing a document.

Also included is a question and answer section that addresses some common questions from new users.

Chapter 3, "The Next Step," introduces you to macros, possibly WordPerfect's most valuable feature. This chapter also gives you advice about customizing WordPerfect to fit your personal needs.

Part Two: Reference

Chapter 4, "Commands and Features," which makes up the bulk of this book, is a comprehensive reference that provides information for every key, feature, and command in WordPerfect. Each entry includes a description, the keystrokes involved, hints, suggested applications, and related entries for the feature.

Part Three: Printing

Chapter 5, "Laser Printers," discusses fonts, printing envelopes or legal-size documents, and other special features unique to laser printers.

Chapter 6, "Printer Specifics," gives you the information that will enable you to get the most from your particular printer. Character tables and attributes for each font, proportional spacing and Line Draw information, printer limitations, and sheet feeder information are included for dozens of printers.

Chapter 7, "Printer Program," covers changing or creating printer definitions. Sheet feeder definitions and tips for creating a character table are also included.

Part Four: Integration

Chapter 8, "Software Integration," introduces you to other software programs that are compatible with WordPerfect, including several from WordPerfect Corporation. Details about sharing data between WordPerfect and other programs are also included.

Appendixes

Appendix A is a table of ASCII characters and their decimal values.

Appendix B, "Terminology Reference," compares the terms used in WordStar, MultiMate, Microsoft Word, and Display-Write to those used in WordPerfect. A glance at the tables found in this appendix will give you some idea as to the differences in concepts and language among popular word processing programs.

Appendix C is a macro library that lists several macros and the keystrokes necessary to define each one.

Conventions

The following conventions have been used throughout this book to let you know which keys to press.

Instruction	Procedure
Type **SINCERELY,**	Type the boldfaced text (upper or lower-case is acceptable).
Enter **WP**	Type the boldfaced text and press ENTER. (If the computer does not act on a command, it is probably waiting for you to press the ENTER key. Note, again, you may type upper- or lowercase letters.)
Press Bold (F6)	Press the F6 function key (*not* F then 6 on the regular keyboard).
Press Center (SHIFT-F6)	Hold down the SHIFT key and press the F6 function key. Keys that should be pressed at the same time are connected by a dash.
HOME,↑	Press the HOME key, then the UP ARROW key. Keys that should be pressed in succession (not simultaneously) are separated by commas.

More information about specific keys on your keyboard is found in Chapters 1 and 2.

WordPerfect: The Complete Reference
Supplementary Disk Order Form

All the macros, files, forms, and menus mentioned in this book are available on disk for $15. You can order the disk by calling the toll-free number below:

1-800-222-9409

VISA, MasterCard, and C.O.D. orders are accepted. Utah residents can call 1-801-224-4000.

If you prefer to order the disk with a bank check or money order, complete the following form and mail it to the address below:

WordPerfect: The Complete Reference
Supplementary Disk Offer
329 North State Street
Orem, UT 84057

Please mail the supplementary disk to:

_____

_____

_____

_____

Osborne/McGraw-Hill assumes no responsibility for this offer. This is solely the offer of Karen L. Acerson and not of Osborne/McGraw-Hill.

Introduction to WordPerfect

This section is especially important for new WordPerfect users and for those who have never used a computer.

Chapter 1, "Getting Started," tells you how to use your computer and how to work with its *disk operating system* (DOS). You are taught how to format and copy disks, how to create directories and organize a hard disk, and how to create batch files. This chapter explains how your system is set up, and gives you the knowledge necessary to install WordPerfect.

Chapter 2, "WordPerfect Basics," teaches you the fundamentals of word processing with WordPerfect. You'll learn how to start WordPerfect and create basic documents. A section at the end of the chapter answers common questions.

Chapter 3, "The Next Step," gives you directions for moving forward. You are introduced to Macros, a feature that will save you time and keystrokes. This chapter also teaches you how to customize WordPerfect to fit your specific needs.

P
A
R
T

O
N
E

Getting Started

This chapter is for readers who are new to personal computers and word processing. It tells you what you need to know about your computer and printer so that you can use Word-Perfect effectively. As you read, you will also become acquainted with several keys that are not found on a regular typewriter or dedicated word processor.

The sometimes mysterious world of DOS (the disk operating system) is also explained. This information will be a valuable reference when you are working with WordPerfect and other programs. This chapter introduces you to several DOS commands and explains how WordPerfect and DOS work together.

Those who already have experience with computers and DOS can skip to Chapter 2.

Your Computer and Printer

There are three basic parts to your computer: the system unit (containing the central processing unit, disk drives, and other accessories), the keyboard, and the monitor (see Figure 1-1).

The central processing unit, or CPU, is where information is processed and either stored on disk or sent to the screen or printer.

The keyboard is used to send instructions, text, or other information to the CPU. The CPU can also receive information from a mouse, through a network, or via a modem.

The monitor displays information and lets you move through text by means of a *cursor*, a small, usually blinking,

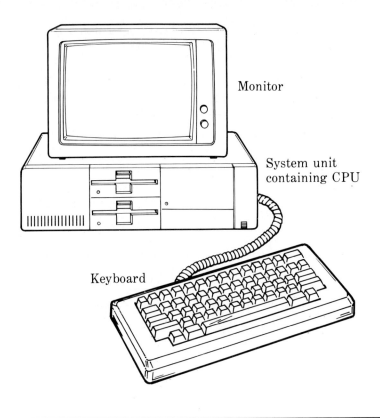

Figure 1-1.   System unit, monitor, and keyboard

symbol. You can use the cursor to move around the screen
when making changes or additions. The monitor may have
an on/off switch, and brightness and contrast controls. If you
are having problems with the display, check these controls or
refer to the user's guide for more information.

How Your Computer Stores Information

All computers have a certain amount of *memory*, or information storage area, in the CPU. This is usually referred to as RAM or *random access memory*. The notation "256Kb" means your system has the ability to hold 256,000 bytes of information in memory. A *byte* is a unit of information roughly equal to one alphanumeric character.

Computers can access RAM quickly; therefore, most programs and text are loaded into memory from a disk. But programs and other information cannot be kept permanently in RAM because of space limitations and because RAM is erased when you turn your computer off. To keep documents you create, you will need to save them on a disk.

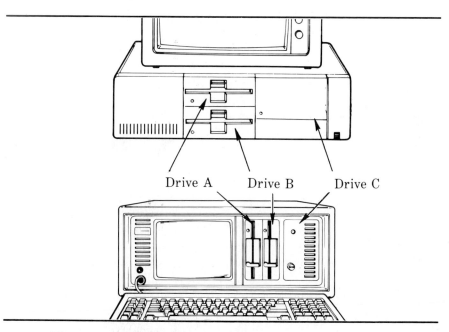

Drive A   Drive B   Drive C

Figure 1-2.   Disk drive options

All or part of a software program can be loaded into memory so there is little disk access during its operation. (You can also think of the text that appears on your monitor as being in memory.) With some programs, the length of your document is limited by the amount of RAM you have. WordPerfect uses all the machine memory that is available, then begins using temporary overflow files on a disk; thus, a document is limited only by the amount of available disk space.

Disk Storage

Depending on your system, you might have one or two floppy disk drives and a hard, or fixed, disk. The floppy disk drives are usually referred to as drives A and B, while the hard disk is referred to as drive C. Even if you have only one floppy disk drive and a hard disk, the hard drive is still called drive C. Figure 1-2 shows how the drives are typically arranged.

Some computers, such as the IBM PC AT, have two types of floppy disk drives. One accepts regularly formatted disks, while the other can be used for high-density disks that hold more information.

Ports: Where Your Printer Comes In

The back of your system unit will look something like the one shown in Figure 1-3. Notice the two ports on the right side. A *port* connects a cable to the system unit. Information is transferred through the cable to other computers or to a printer.

There are two kinds of ports: parallel and serial. A parallel port is often a female connector while a serial port is a male connector. The main difference between parallel and serial is in the way the bits that make up each character are arranged for transfer. They can either travel parallel to each other or follow each other in a series, or serial. You will need a parallel or serial cable, depending on whether your printer is a parallel or serial printer. A parallel cable is usually thicker than a serial cable.

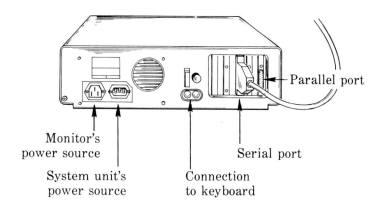

Figure 1-3.   Rear view of a system unit showing ports

When you tell WordPerfect what type of printer you have, you will need to know the kind of port it uses. Most programs refer to parallel ports as "LPT" while "COM" identifies serial ports. If you have a serial printer, you must provide WordPerfect with some special information, such as the baud rate (speed at which information is sent), parity (used for error checking), character length (number of data bits that make up the character), and stop bits (the number of bits that separate each character). Table 1-1 shows the options available for each of these settings.

The printer manual or computer dealer that sold you the equipment should be able to give you more information about your particular printer. (See Chapter 6 for additional tips.)

The Keyboard

Your keyboard will probably look like one of those shown in Figure 1-4, with the function keys either at the left or across the top.

Setting	Options Available
Baud	110, 150, 300, 600, 1200, 2400, 4600, 9600
Parity	None, Odd, Even
Character length	7, 8
Stop bits	1, 2

Table 1-1.   Options for Serial Printers

Other types of keyboards might have a larger RETURN or ENTER key, CTRL (control) and ALT (alternate) keys on both the left and right side of the keyboard, or keys such as the ESC (escape) key or backslash (\ ) in different locations.

There are some specific keys on your computer's keyboard that you should be familiar with. As you read the following, refer to Figure 1-4 for their location on the keyboard.

Function Keys (F1-F10)

On a dedicated word processor such as a Wang, the function keys are named with words that indicate their use, such as Delete, Copy, Move, and so on. On a personal computer, the function keys are numbered so that they can be used differently by different programs. Each program assigns roles to the function keys to fit its particular needs. A template (plastic overlay) that labels the function keys is included with WordPerfect so you will know which function key does a specific task.

ENTER

The ENTER or RETURN key is used to send a command to the computer or to go to a new line. If you are asked in this book or the WordPerfect manual to *enter* a command, you should

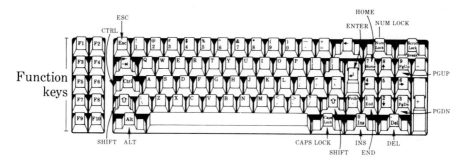

IBM PC Keyboard

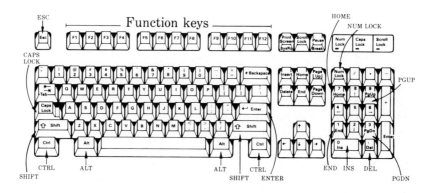

IBM PC AT Keyboard

Figure 1-4.   Location of keys on two types of IBM keyboards

type the command, then press the ENTER key. If you find yourself waiting for the computer to do something, it is probably waiting for you to press ENTER.

When entering text while in WordPerfect, you can press ENTER to add blank lines or move down to a new line. However, you cannot use the ENTER key exactly as you would use the return key on a typewriter. The ENTER key cannot be used to move over text; instead, press the DOWN ARROW (↓) to move the cursor down through existing text. Pressing the ENTER key inserts blank lines in the text rather than moving the cursor through the text. If you insert blank lines, you can delete them by immediately pressing the BACKSPACE key.

SHIFT

The SHIFT key lets you type text in uppercase or capital letters. When using WordPerfect, you can hold down the SHIFT key and press a function key to execute the functions printed in green on the WordPerfect template.

CTRL

The CTRL key has no function if pressed alone. It has an effect only if you hold it down while pressing another key. In WordPerfect it can be used with the function keys to execute the commands printed in red on the WordPerfect template.

If you press CTRL with another character, it usually creates a *control character* such as ^C or ^D. Control characters are used by some programs such as WordStar to mark text for boldface or underlining, move the cursor, or delete text. WordPerfect uses control characters to control information that is to be merged into a document, including such things as the current page number, date, or fields from a data file. For more information on control characters see *Merge* in Chapter 4, "Commands and Features," which provides a complete, alphabetical reference to WordPerfect.

You can also "map" special characters to a CTRL-key combination using CTRL and a letter from A through Z. For instance, the Greek character β is not found on most keyboards, so WordPerfect lets you assign that character to a CTRL-key (or ALT-key) combination. You could use CTRL-B to display the β if that is easiest for you to remember. Special Characters in Chapter 4 gives step-by-step instructions.

ALT

The ALT key is similar to the CTRL key. It has no function of its own, but is used with the function keys for those features printed in blue on the WordPerfect template. This might be a little confusing to those who have an IBM-enhanced keyboard, because the ALT key is printed in green. However, you can use the stick-on colored dots included with WordPerfect to "change" the green to blue.

As with the CTRL key, you can use the ALT key in conjunction with a letter from A through Z for mapping special characters.

A valuable feature of WordPerfect is its *macro* capability, which lets you store text and commands that can be recalled with just a few keystrokes. You can use ALT-key combinations (ALT and a letter from A through Z) to name macros, then recall them just by pressing the ALT-key combination again. As you can see, the ALT-key combination can be used both to map special characters and name macros. However, if the same combination is used for both purposes, it is not as easy to execute a macro. See "Using Macros" in Chapter 3 for more information.

ESC

The ESC key usually cancels a command. In WordPerfect it is also used as a counter and will repeat a command or keystroke a specified number of times.

DEL

The DEL key deletes text at the cursor. If you continue to press the DEL key, it deletes text to the right or ahead of the cursor, while the BACKSPACE key deletes text behind or to the left of the cursor.

INS

When pressed, the INS key toggles between inserting and replacing text. WordPerfect has been preset to insert characters as they are typed, pushing existing text to the right as characters are entered. If you press the INS key, "Typeover" appears at the bottom of the screen and characters to the right of the cursor are replaced with new text as you type.

CAPS LOCK

CAPS LOCK is similar to the SHIFT LOCK key on most typewriters and will type letters in uppercase without having to continually press the SHIFT key. Unlike SHIFT LOCK, however, CAPS LOCK on a computer keyboard works only for letters (A-Z). For instance, if you want the # symbol and you have CAPS LOCK on, you will still need to press a SHIFT key to get that character. Another difference is that if you press SHIFT and a letter (A-Z) while CAPS LOCK is on, the letter is typed in lowercase rather than in uppercase.

NUM LOCK

The numeric keypad is used for two purposes: moving the cursor and entering numbers. In WordPerfect, these keys will normally move the cursor. If you press NUM LOCK, the numeric keypad is used to enter numbers. If you are trying to move the cursor but get numbers instead, you have most likely pressed the NUM LOCK key by accident. Press it again to turn it off.

HOME, PGUP, PGDN, and END

In WordPerfect, HOME, PGUP, PGDN, and END are used to move the cursor through larger sections of text. These are explained in more detail in Chapter 2.

Using DOS

Among other duties, the disk operating system (DOS) allows your computer to use and communicate with disks. The IBM PC, XT, and AT use PC-DOS, while compatibles use a version of MS-DOS. Both do essentially the same tasks, using similar commands.

Starting Your Computer

Every computer comes with a DOS *system disk* that contains system files including COMMAND.COM. These files are used to start (or *boot*) the computer. If you have one or two floppy disk drives, place the DOS disk in drive A, then turn on the computer. If you are using a hard disk, it has probably been prepared (formatted) by the computer dealer. If so, the computer should start up automatically without a floppy disk. In the unlikely case that the hard disk hasn't been formatted, start your computer with the DOS disk in drive A.

If you try to start your computer with a disk that does not contain the COMMAND.COM file, you will get the error message

    Non-System disk or disk error
    Replace and strike any key when ready

If this happens, place a disk containing COMMAND.COM in drive A (the DOS disk will have the necessary files) and strike any key. If you have a hard disk, remove the disk from drive A allowing the computer to boot from its hard disk.

See "Formatting Disks" later in this chapter to learn how to copy COMMAND.COM and other system files onto a disk.

When the computer finds the files it needs, it will beep and start up. The more RAM your system has, the longer it will take to start because the memory is checked for possible errors.

Date and Time

When the computer is started, you may be prompted to enter a new date as shown in the following illustration.

```
Current date is Tue   1-01-1980
Enter new date:
```

If you have a real-time clock in your computer, the date and time are inserted automatically.

You can use a slash (/) instead of a hyphen (-) to separate the month, day, and year. You can also press ENTER to accept the current date displayed. After you enter the new date, you are prompted for the time.

```
Current date is Tue   1-01-1980
Enter new date:   11-25-87
Current time is 10:42:45.09
Enter new time:   13:30
```

To accept the current time shown, press ENTER. To enter a new time, type the hour and minutes. You can enter seconds and even hundredths of seconds if you desire. The time command uses a 24-hour clock, so if it is 2:30 P.M., you should enter 14:30. If you enter 2:30, the system will assume it is 2:30 A.M. Hours and minutes should be separated with a colon.

It is important to enter the correct date and time for two reasons. First, it is easier to manage your files because each file is "stamped" with the current date and time when it is created or edited. Second, WordPerfect has a Date function which inserts the current date and time. If you enter or accept an incorrect date and time, WordPerfect's Date function will use that incorrect date and time.

If you want to change the date or time in DOS after the computer has already been started, use the DOS commands DATE or TIME (enter **DATE** or **TIME** at the DOS prompt) and enter the new information as shown in Figure 1-5.

```
A>date
Current date is Fri  1-02-1987
Enter new date:   11-25-87

A>time
Current time is 10:42:45.09
Enter new time:  10:17
```

Figure 1-5.   DATE and TIME DOS commands

The DOS Prompt

The next thing you will see on the screen is the DOS prompt. It is called a *prompt* because it is waiting or "prompting" you for a command. The prompt usually displays the current drive being used, followed by the > character as shown here.

```
Current date is Tue  1-01-1980
Enter new date:  11-25-87
Current time is 10:42:45.09
Enter new time:  13:30

A>
```

You can use either uppercase or lowercase letters when entering a DOS command. To distinguish them from Word-Perfect commands, DOS commands are in capital letters; boldface indicates that a command or any other text is to be typed into your computer.

When you enter a command, it will read from the displayed drive (the *default drive*) unless you specify another. For example, if you want to see a directory listing for the files on the default drive, enter **DIR**. If drive A is the default drive, enter **DIR B:** to see the list of files on drive B. If the list of files scrolls off the screen, press CTRL-S to stop it temporarily. Press any other key to continue listing the files.

If you have a hard disk, you will probably divide it into different sections or *directories* (see "Directories," "Pathnames," and "Paths" later in this chapter). The preset DOS prompt displays only the drive, without the name of the current directory (for example, C>). To avoid having to enter DIR each time you want to find out the name of the current directory, you can customize the DOS prompt so it will show the name of the directory automatically.

Enter the DOS command **PROMPT $P $G** to get a prompt that looks like the following:

```
A>prompt $p $g
A:\ >
```

PROMPT is the name of the DOS command used to set a new prompt. The dollar sign ($) is used to separate parameters. The P parameter displays the current directoryname while G displays a > (right angle-bracket or greater-than character). There are many other options available. See your DOS manual for more details.

You can enter the PROMPT command each time you start your computer or store it in a *batch file* so it will be executed automatically (see "Batch Files" later in this chapter).

To change drives (and the DOS prompt), you would type the drive letter followed by a colon. If you want to change to drive B, enter **B:**. B> would then appear as the DOS prompt. Entering A: would return you to drive A.

Formatting Disks

A computer can read from or write to only disks specifically formatted for that type of computer. For instance, a disk formatted for an Apple computer cannot normally be read by an IBM PC.

The DOS FORMAT command is found on the DOS disk and is named FORMAT.COM. If you are using a system with two disk drives, place the DOS disk in drive A and the disk to be formatted in drive B.

Warning   Remember that the FORMAT command will automatically *erase* a disk and should be used with care.

Because the FORMAT command is found on the DOS disk in drive A and the target disk is in drive B, you would enter the following command at the A> DOS prompt:

A>FORMAT B:

You are asked to insert a diskette (which you have probably already done) and press a key. After the disk has been formatted, information about the disk is displayed which tells you the amount of space available on the disk and whether there are any damaged places or "bad sectors" found on the disk. You are then asked if you want to format another disk. Continue by following the instructions on the screen.

As mentioned before, you can format a disk so that it can be used to start your computer. You usually cannot just copy the COMMAND.COM file to a disk, because there are actually three files that make up the DOS "system" (two of the filenames do not show up when you look at a directory on the disk). To copy these DOS system files onto a disk as it is formatted, type /S (meaning format "with the system") after the drive letter, as shown below:

A>FORMAT B:/S

Because of the disk space used by the DOS system, you would want to format a disk with /S only if you were going to use it to start your computer. If you format a disk with the /S option and copy the files for a program such as WordPerfect onto the disk, you can then use that disk rather than the DOS disk and the program disk to start the computer and bring up WordPerfect.

If your hard disk has not yet been formatted, you need to use the FDISK command to prepare it for use with DOS first.

Warning   If your hard disk has already been formatted, it is best not to experiment with FDISK or with the FORMAT command. You could erase the hard disk or damage the current setup.

To prepare an unformatted hard disk for formatting, put the DOS disk in drive A and enter

    A>FDISK

You would usually choose the first option to create a DOS partition. You should then answer yes or no to the question, "Do you wish to use the entire fixed disk for DOS?" You would usually answer yes. If the disk has already been prepared, entering the FDISK command will display the current setup and allow you to make changes.

After the hard disk has been prepared using this command, it is ready to be formatted. With the DOS disk in drive A, enter

    A>FORMAT C:/S

The system files are automatically copied onto your hard disk so that you can start your computer without a disk in drive A.

You will need to copy the FORMAT.COM file from your DOS disk onto the hard disk should you want to use your hard disk to format a disk in one of the floppy disk drives. With the DOS disk in drive A, enter the following command.

    >COPY A:FORMAT.COM C:

Filenames

Most computer programs, including WordPerfect, use the DOS method to name files. You are allowed to enter up to eight characters and an optional extension with up to three characters. A period (.) is used to divide the extension from the rest of the name.

You could use the optional extension for a client's initials, month abbreviations, or to indicate a type of document. Some examples of filenames are LETTER.DRT (letter to David Robert Thomas), CONTRACT.12 (contract for apartment #12), EXPENSES.FEB (expenses for the month of February), or CAR (notes on problems with a car).

The following characters cannot be used in a filename.

$* + = [ ] '' < > ? | ,$

You should give careful attention to the way you name files so that they help you remember the contents of the files. However, WordPerfect lets you "look" into a file to see the document without retrieving it and provides a "word search" feature that searches through files in a directory for a word or string of words (see *Word Search* in Chapter 4, the alphabetical reference). This feature helps you locate a specific file by searching for words that are unique to that file.

Copying Files

Some DOS commands are found in the COMMAND.COM file which is loaded into memory when your computer is started. COPY (as well as DATE, TIME, and PROMPT) is a DOS command held in memory and does not require the DOS disk, while the FORMAT command requires the use of the DOS disk (or other disk containing the FORMAT.COM file).

You can use the COPY command to copy one file, several files, or an entire disk. For example, you can copy files from the hard disk to a floppy, from floppy to floppy, or from one directory on the hard disk to another. To do this, enter **COPY**, the location and name of the file to be copied (source), and the drive or directory to which it will be copied (target).

You can save a few keystrokes by noting the default directory before copying files. Some examples follow.

A>COPY CHAPTER.1 B: copies the file CHAPTER.1 from drive A to drive B. Notice that you did not have to type A: before CHAPTER.1 because drive A is the default drive.

C:\WORK >COPY C:\TAXES\ASSETS.87 copies the file ASSETS.87 from the TAXES directory on the hard disk to the WORK directory. You do not have to type C:\WORK as the target because it is the default directory.

C:\WORK >COPY A:SMITH.LTR B:NEW.LTR copies the SMITH.LTR file from drive A to drive B and names the copied file NEW.LTR. Both drive names were typed because the command was entered from "C:\WORK," which was not involved in the copy procedure.

Wildcard Characters

When you are copying more than one file, the *wildcard* characters (∗ and ?) are useful. You can use these characters to copy all files or selected files. The asterisk (∗) can stand for any number of characters and the question mark (?) can stand for a single character. If you want to copy all the files from one disk to another, you can enter

A>COPY ∗.∗ B:

In this example, you type a period and asterisk to include all those files that have an extension.

If you give similar files a common extension, you can use this to your advantage when copying files. To copy all the files for David Robert Thomas (having the extension .DRT), enter

A>COPY ∗.DRT B:

To copy all the files containing information about your stocks for the entire year, enter

A>COPY STOCKS.* B:

The following command would copy all the files having an extension that indicates the years from 1970 to 1979.

A>COPY *.7?

Remember that a question mark indicates a single character.

DISKCOPY is a command that can also be used to create an exact duplicate of a disk. At times, it is advantageous to use this command, because the target disk can be formatted during the procedure and the system files can be copied from the source disk without using the FORMAT /S command. However, if there are any bad sectors on the source disk, they will be copied to the new disk. To copy a disk using this command, enter **DISKCOPY**, followed by a space, the drive letter of the source disk, a space, then the drive letter of the target disk. The example below would copy the contents from the disk in drive A to the disk in drive B.

A:\ >DISKCOPY A: B:

Directories

In the previous examples, you learned that a hard or fixed disk can be divided into several sections or directories. You can also divide a floppy disk into directories. This section uses a hard disk as an example.

If you have a newly formatted disk (hard or floppy), you will have only one directory, called the *root directory*. The root directory is indicated by a single backslash (\). If you entered PROMPT $P $G, as suggested earlier, the DOS prompt for the root directory will look like

C:\ >

Dividing the hard disk into directories is similar to having many floppy disks. You will want to create directories for better organization and to make more room for files. The root directory will store only 112 files regardless of size, while a directory can hold an unlimited number. If you work with many small files on a floppy disk and reach the limit of 112 files but still have plenty of disk space available, you can make a directory on the floppy disk for more file storage. (The 112-file limit may vary depending on the operating system used.)

To make a new directory, you would enter the DOS command MD (or MKDIR) and the name of the new directory. The command MD LETTERS would make a directory called LETTERS. You could then save all your letters in this directory.

The CD (or CHDIR) command will change to a specified directory. If you make a new directory, you are not automatically placed in it. Enter **CD \LETTERS** to change to the LETTERS directory. You do not have to leave a space between the CD command and backslash; **CD \LETTERS** is also correct. The backslash is included so that DOS will return to the root directory, then search for the named directory. While in the LETTERS directory, the DOS prompt would appear as

    C:\LETTERS >

To return to the root directory, enter **CD **. (Remember, the root directory is indicated only by a backslash.)

You can divide directories even more for better organization. However, dividing a directory is not always necessary and can even slow down the operating system slightly because it has to go through several levels to find a file or command. If you want to divide a directory, change to the directory to be divided (called the *parent directory*), then enter the MD command to make a new directory. Your hard disk could be structured in the following way.

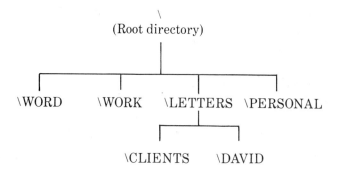

If you were in the subdirectory called DAVID, the DOS prompt would appear as

C:\LETTERS\DAVID >

Notice that a backslash (\ ) divides each directory and helps show the level and organization of directories.

If you want to see the organization of your hard disk, you can enter the DOS command TREE from any directory. All directories and subdirectories are displayed. (The TREE command is machine specific and might not work with your computer.)

Pathnames

While using WordPerfect or another program, you might be asked for a pathname. The pathname indicates the location of the file. The pathname is a string beginning with the drive, the directory, and the filename (each of these is divided by a backslash). When you save or retrieve files, you can just enter the filename; the default directory is automatically used. If you want a file to be saved to or retrieved from a different directory, you will need to enter the full pathname. For instance, if you wanted to save a file named BUDGET to a directory named PERSONAL, you would enter the pathname

C:\PERSONAL\BUDGET

A backslash is used to separate the filename from the name of the directory.

If WordPerfect cannot find a program file, such as the thesaurus file (TH.WP), for example, it will ask you for the full pathname. You would then enter the drive and directory where it is found *and* the name of the file.

You might also need to enter a pathname when giving DOS a command. For example, if you have two floppy disk drives and want to use drive B as the default drive for file storage and drive A for the WordPerfect program disk, you make drive B the default drive, then tell DOS where to find WordPerfect.

A>B:
B>A:WP

These commands make drive B the default drive, but will look in drive A for WordPerfect.

Paths

As mentioned before, when you enter a DOS command, the system will search the current (or default) directory for the command or file. You can use the PATH command to tell DOS to search in more than one directory so you do not have to change directories before giving a command.

A path is a list of directories that DOS will search for a command. The PATH command can be put in the AUTO-EXEC.BAT file or it can be entered each time you start your computer (discussed under "Batch Files" in this chapter).

DOS version 2.1 or earlier does not let you enter a command with the directory where it is found. You have to use the PATH command so it can find the correct directory. If you are using DOS version 3.0 or later, however, you can enter the full pathname (directory and command) and don't have to worry about a path. For example, type **\WP\WP** to start WordPerfect from the WP directory instead of using a path.

To enter a DOS PATH command, type **PATH** followed by the list of directories, each separated by a semicolon. A sample PATH command would be

C:\ >PATH C:\;C:\WP;C:\PROGRAMS;C:\UTIL;A:\

Note that you can also include other drives as well as directories. The directories are searched in the order that they are entered in the PATH command. In the interest of speed, it is best to place the most commonly used directory first in the list.

After creating a path, you can enter a command from any directory. This means that you can change to the directory to be used for saving and retrieving files and execute WordPerfect from there.

Miscellaneous DOS Commands

The DOS commands DEL or ERASE delete files. Type **DEL** or **ERASE** (depending on your preference), a space, then the filename (DEL NOTES, for example). Remember to enter the full pathname if the file is not found in the current drive or directory. You can also delete more than one file using the wildcard characters (* and ?).

REN or RENAME lets you rename files while in DOS. Enter **REN** or **RENAME** (again depending on your preference), the name of the file to be renamed, followed by a space and the new name. For example, enter **REN A:APPLES ORANGES** to rename the APPLES file on drive A to ORANGES. The pathname only needs to be specified with the original filename. The newly named file will remain in the same directory.

You can use COPY to copy a file to another disk or directory and rename it at the same time. For instance, COPY A:APPLES B:ORANGES would copy the APPLES file from drive A, leaving the original as it was, to drive B and rename it ORANGES.

TYPE is another DOS command you should be familiar with. This command will display the contents of a file on the screen. Although it works best for a DOS (ASCII) file that contains no codes, you can display any file in one form or another. If you type a WordPerfect file, you will see all the symbols used for formatting commands with the text.

Batch Files

This chapter has covered most of the DOS commands necessary to effectively use your computer with WordPerfect and other programs. Some of these commands, such as DATE, TIME, PROMPT, and PATH, are mose useful if they are entered each time your computer is started.

If you don't want to enter these commands each time, you can put them in a file named AUTOEXEC.BAT. This is a file holding a "batch" of DOS commands that will be automatically executed each time your computer is started. You can also create other batch files so you don't have to enter the same commands again and again.

Enter **CD ** to go to the root directory where the AUTO-EXEC.BAT file needs to be stored. You should first check to see if an AUTOEXEC.BAT file already exists. The DOS command TYPE will display the contents of a DOS file, so enter

C:\>TYPE AUTOEXEC.BAT

If the file is not found, "Bad command or file name" will appear on the screen. If the file exists, you will see the commands that are already in the file, some of which you might not have learned in this chapter, but which may be very important to your system. The existing file is probably sufficient. If you want to make changes, you should print the commands or write them down so you can reenter them in the new file.

The following steps will create an AUTOEXEC.BAT file. Note, however, that they also replace the AUTOEXEC.BAT file that already exists.

To create an AUTOEXEC.BAT file, enter

```
C:\ >COPY CON AUTOEXEC.BAT
```

This command tells DOS to copy whatever is entered from the CONsole (keyboard) to a file named AUTOEXEC.BAT. When you press ENTER, you are placed on the next line. The DOS commands you enter will be stored in that file. A suggestion for commands for this file might be as follows:

```
DATE
TIME
PROMPT $P $G
PATH C:\;C:\WP
```

Of course you would want to list more (or different) directories in the path and add any commands you found in a previous AUTOEXEC.BAT file if applicable. If you have a clock in your computer, you can skip the DATE and TIME commands, but should include the command used by your clock to set the time (AUTOTIME or ASTCLOCK are examples).

When finished, press F6 or CTRL-Z. A ^Z is displayed, marking the end of a DOS file. Press ENTER and "1 Files copied" will appear. This indicates that the file has been successfully created.

When you turn on the computer or reboot, the file is executed. The previous example would pause and let you enter the date and time (or display the correct date and time if you have a clock), set the prompt as shown previously, and create the path.

If you want to see the results, enter **AUTOEXEC** at the DOS prompt or press CTRL-ALT-DEL at the same time (see Figure 1-6). This is sometimes referred to as a *warm boot* or *soft boot* and is like turning your computer off and on again.

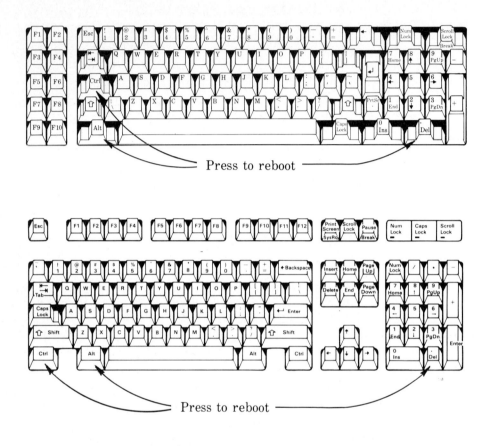

Press to reboot

Press to reboot

Figure 1-6.   Pressing CTRL-ALT-DEL to restart your computer

However, it doesn't take as long for the computer to come up because the memory is not checked for errors.

Another example of a batch file follows.

```
C:\>COPY CON MIKE.BAT
CD \MIKE
WP
^Z
```

This batch file, named MIKE, will change the default directory to MIKE, then start WordPerfect. To start the batch file, enter **MIKE** at the DOS prompt.

You can create other batch files, each with a name consisting of up to eight characters and the extension .BAT. Avoid using the same command used to execute a program such as WP.BAT because WP is used to start WordPerfect and you might create a loop that will lock up the computer.

To execute a batch file, you only need to enter the name of the file without the .BAT extension. You should be in the directory where the batch file is stored when you start the batch file, or have that directory as part of the path so the batch file can be found.

WordPerfect and DOS

WordPerfect and DOS work very closely together. WordPerfect uses the DOS method of naming files (eight characters and an optional extension) and uses directories to help organize the files.

WordPerfect's List Files feature helps you do many DOS commands without ever leaving WordPerfect. You can look at a directory, delete, rename, or copy files, change directories, and even make a new directory by choosing options from the menu. To do the same things from DOS, you would use the DIR, DEL, REN, COPY, CD, and MD commands.

You can even do several things from List Files that you cannot easily do in DOS. As previously mentioned, you can look at a file to see its contents without retrieving it and search through the listed files for a word or word pattern to help locate a specific file.

While in WordPerfect, you can leave the current document in memory, press a key to go to DOS, then return to your document in WordPerfect right where you left it. This type of feature allows you to execute any DOS command, such as FORMAT, COPY, or DEL (delete).

DOS helps WordPerfect send text to the printer. While in DOS (or WordPerfect), you can press SHIFT and PRTSC at the same time to send the contents on the screen directly to your printer. This might not work if you have a serial printer (serial printers need a MODE command to redirect the print screen output from the parallel port to the serial port). If your printer prints the contents of the screen when you press SHIFT-PRTSC, you know that the printer is able to accept commands from the computer and WordPerfect should also be able to print successfully.

Another way of testing your printer is to copy a file to the port used by your printer. WordPerfect includes a file called README that can be used for this test. Place the Learning disk in drive A if you have a hard disk or drive B if you are using two disk drives. Enter **COPY A:README PRN** (or **B:README PRN**) at the DOS prompt if you have a parallel printer. If you have a serial printer, enter **COPY A:README COM1** (or **B:README COM1**). If it does not print, you might need to try COM2, COM3, or even COM4 if you have more than one serial port.

If your printer will not print with DOS, it will not print with WordPerfect. Any problems with the connection should be corrected before trying to print in WordPerfect. Check to make sure the cables are secure and the printer is on line. See "Printer Selection" later in this chapter or Chapter 6, "Printer Specifics," for more information.

Installation Tips

Now that you have learned about DOS, you can install Word-Perfect or better understand how your system has been set up. Please keep in mind that these are only suggestions. Feel free to make adjustments that will best use the capabilities of your system and fit your personal needs.

If you have forgotton how to do a DOS command such as FORMAT or COPY, return to the appropriate section in this chapter.

WordPerfect comes with six disks, labeled WordPerfect, Speller, Thesaurus, Learning, Printer 1, and Printer 2. Table 1-2 shows the files that are included on each disk.

Two Disk Drives

Use the DOS disk to format enough disks to make copies of the WordPerfect program disks and a few extra (at least seven). Remember to format one disk with the /S option for the WordPerfect program files so it can be used to start your computer.

The formatted disks will be used to make copies of the WordPerfect disks. You should never use the originals. Remember to label each disk properly. Extra disks could be labeled "Personal," "Work," or any other name of your choosing.

You should then put the WordPerfect program disk in drive A and a newly formatted disk in drive B. If you formatted a disk with the /S option, use that disk for the Word-Perfect program. Copy all files from drive A to drive B, using the command COPY A:*.* B:. Continue until you have made a backup copy of all the disks. Store the originals in a safe place so you can copy them again if your copies become damaged.

Place the newly made copy of the WordPerfect disk in drive A and create the AUTOEXEC.BAT file. You can use the following suggestion or make necessary changes.

```
A>COPY CON AUTOEXEC.BAT
DATE
TIME
B:
A:WP
^Z
```

Place the WordPerfect disk in drive A and a blank disk in drive B. If you created an AUTOEXEC.BAT file, restart your computer (you can use CTRL-ALT-DEL) or enter **AUTOEXEC**.

Disk	File	Description
WordPerfect	WP.EXE	WordPerfect program
	WPRINTER.FIL	Contains selected printer defintions
	WPFONT.FIL	Contains corresponding character tables
Speller	LEX.WP	Dictionary containing 115,000 words
	SPELL.EXE	Spell program used to customize main dictionary
Thesaurus	TH.WP	Thesaurus file
Learning	WPHELP.FIL	Help information for function keys
	WPHELP2.FIL	Help information for letters A through Z
	TUTOR.COM	Tutorial program
	*.TUT	Files used in the Tutorial
	*.LRN	Files used in the Learning section of the WordPerfect manual
	*.MAC	Macros used in the WordPerfect manual. Two macros, FONTTEST.MAC and FNTTEST1.MAC, are used to simplify the testing of character tables (fonts)
	*.TST	Printer test files
	CONVERT.EXE	Convert program for converting documents for use with other software programs
	CURSOR.COM	Cursor program that lets you customize the style of the cursor
	WP.TBL	File to be used with TopView
	MAC.MEX	Macro information for the Macro Editor
	README	File used to test the printer
Printer 1	WPRINT1.ALL	Contains printer definitions from A through N

Table 1-2.   WordPerfect Disks and Their Corresponding Files

Disk	File	Description
	WPFONT1.ALL	Contains corresponding character tables
	WPFEED.FIL	Contains sheet feeder definitions
	PSCRIPT.PS	Used with PostScript printers such as the Apple LaserWriter. The file was once named LASERWRT.PS. It is automatically copied to a disk/directory when the Apple LaserWriter printer definition is selected
	INITLWRT.PS	File to be copied to Apple LaserWriter *once* to change the protocol from XON/XOFF to hardware handshaking. See Chapters 5 and 6 for more information
Printer 2	WPRINT2.ALL	Contains definitions from O through Z and limited support printers
	WPFONT2.ALL	Contains corresponding character tables
	WPFEED.FIL	Contains sheet feeder definitions (same as file on Printer 1 disk)
	PRHELP.EXE	Printer help program for more printer information
	PRINTER.EXE	Printer program used to create or modify printer definitions, character tables, or sheet feeder definitions
	XONXOFF.PS	File used to change the Apple LaserWriter from hardware handshaking back to XONXOFF

Table 1-2.   WordPerfect Disks and Their Corresponding Files
(continued)

If you did not create the AUTOEXEC.BAT file, enter

```
A>B:
B>A:WP
```

WordPerfect is started. You will see an introductory message on the screen. After reading this message, press any key to enter the program. Continue with the instructions in "Printer Selection."

Hard or Fixed Disk

You should first create or edit the AUTOEXEC.BAT file. It should include the PROMPT command. Use the suggested PROMPT $P $G or a PROMPT command of your own. You should also include the PATH command. You can list the names of directories not yet created. The following is a sample that can be changed to fit your needs.

```
C>COPY CON AUTOEXEC.BAT
DATE
TIME
PROMPT $P $G
PATH C:\WP;C:\
^Z
```

Next, create the directories for the WordPerfect program and your personal work files. Use the MD command to make at least two directories. Suggested directory names might be WP and PERSONAL. If you plan to use the learning files and the tutorial, you might consider making a third directory called LEARNING. If you use these suggestions, you would enter MD WP, MD PERSONAL, and MD LEARNING at the root directory.

Place the original WordPerfect disk in drive A and copy all the files into the WP directory by entering

```
COPY A:*.* C:\WP
```

Continue with the Speller and Thesaurus disks. (Hint: To avoid retyping the COPY command for each disk, press the F3 function key to repeat the last command entered.)

You will probably not want all the files from the Learning disk to be copied to the WP directory. However, you should at least copy WPHELP.FIL, WPHELP2.FIL, and CONVERT.EXE if you plan to use the Convert program (see Chapter 8), and CURSOR.COM if you want to change the configuration of the cursor. All other files on the Learning disk can be copied to a separate directory, such as Learning. Later, after you finish the lessons and tutorial, you can erase those files and remove that directory from the hard disk.

You will not want to take up disk space by copying all the files from the Printer 1 and Printer 2 disks. You will learn how to copy the printer definitions to your hard disk later in this chapter in "Printer Selection."

Use the CD command to change to the directory that is to be used to store your files (for example, CD \PERSONAL). Next, enter **WP** and the WordPerfect program should be started. If it does not start and you see the message "Bad command or file name," you probably did not create a PATH command and the WordPerfect program files cannot be found. Enter the PATH command **PATH C:\WP** (or the name of the applicable directory), then enter **WP**. If you have DOS version 3.0 or later, you can enter **\WP\WP** instead of using a PATH command.

You might want to create a batch file that will execute these commands for you each time you start WordPerfect. It might be similar to the following:

```
>COPY CON W.BAT
CD \PERSONAL
PATH C:\WP
WP
^Z
```

When you enter W at the DOS prompt, the commands will be executed automatically. Of course you could use a different name, such as WORK or START, rather than W.

Printer Selection

When WordPerfect is started for the first time, you will see an introductory message. You will continue to see this message each time you start WordPerfect until you select a printer. After you read the message, press any key to continue. You will then see a blank screen with a status line in the lower right-hand corner.

WordPerfect allows you to choose from hundreds of printers. Each printer, whether it is a dot matrix, letter quality, or laser printer, has different capabilities. WordPerfect has been preset to use a standard printer definition and assumes that your printer is connected to the first parallel port (LPT1). Even though you might be able to print with this type of setup, you should select a printer definition so that all the printer's features can be used to your advantage.

If you find during this selection procedure that your printer or sheet feeder is not among the selections, you can either try a printer definition that is similar to yours (see Chapter 6 for suggestions) or you can read Chapter 7 for more information about defining a printer yourself.

WordPerfect allows up to six different printer selections. You do not have to have six different types of printers to use all six selections. For example, one printer could be used for hand-fed paper and another for continuous paper, but both would use the same printer definition. If you have a laser printer, you could use a different printer selection for each cartridge (up to six).

If you have not already done so, place the template included in the WordPerfect package over the function keys. Two types of templates are included; use the one that matches your keyboard.

Use the following steps to select a printer definition. If you have a laser printer, see Chapter 5 for additional information.

1. Press Print (SHIFT-F7).

2. Type **4** for Printer Control.

3. Type **3** to select Printers. Two printer definitions are listed: Standard Printer and DOS Text Printer. The

Standard Printer definition is used for printers 1 through 5 and the DOS Text Printer is used for printing to disk with printer 6.

4. Press PGDN to see more printer definitions. You will see the following message.

```
Can't Find Printer Files...

    Place a WordPerfect Printer Diskette
    in any floppy disk drive other than drive C:

    (If you don't have another floppy disk drive, you must
    install WordPerfect properly on your system before you
    can select printers.  See the "Getting Started" section
    of your WordPerfect manual for help with this.)

Press Drive Letter When Ready:
```

Two printer disks are included with WordPerfect. The Printer 1 disk contains the printer definitions from A through M in a file named WPRINT1.ALL. The font information for those printers is saved in a file named WPFONT1.ALL. The Printer 2 disk uses the files WPRINT2.ALL and WPFONT2.ALL for the printer and font definitions from N through Z as well as a few limited support printers. *Limited support* means that WordPerfect Corporation has a third printer disk available upon request for all limited support printers.

Place the printer disk that you think contains your printer definition into the floppy disk drive (use drive B if you have a two-disk-drive system) and type the letter of the drive.

Continue to press PGDN until you see your printer among those on the list. If you need to use the second printer disk, press Exit (F7) to return to the Printer Control menu, replace the first disk with the second, and repeat this step.

5. Enter the number for the correct printer definition. The printer and corresponding font information are copied to the WordPerfect disk (or hard disk) into the files WPRINTER.FIL and WPFONT.FIL, respectively.

6. Type the number corresponding to the port. Remember that LPT is used for parallel printers and COM is used for serial printers. Since you usually have only one parallel or serial port, you would normally type **0** for LPT1 (parallel) or **4** for COM1 (serial). Option 8 is used to specify a filename when printing to disk or to a different device (applicable when using a network).

If you choose a serial port, you are asked to supply the baud rate, parity, stop bits, and data bits. This information is available in your printer manual. You can also check Chapter 6 for the settings commonly used for your particular printer.

7. Select the type of forms that will be used. If a printer such as an IBM Quietwriter or laser printer has a paper tray, it is usually considered to be a continuous feeder rather than a sheet feeder.

If you type **3** for a sheet feeder, you are asked to answer the questions in Figure 1-7. Check the "Sheet Feeder" section in Chapter 4 if you are not sure of the proper settings. If you still have questions, leave the set-

```
Sheet Feeder Information
      Number of Extra Lines Between Pages (12 LPI):   24
      Column Position of Left Edge of Paper (10 Pitch):   26
      Number of Sheet Feeder Bins (1-3):  1

Sheet Feeder Type

    1 Apple LaserWriter               2 BDT LetterMate I,II,III
    3 BDT MF-830 6 bin Laser Feeder   4 BDT MF-830 6 bin La (continued)
    5 BDT MF-850 3 bin Laser Feeder   6 BDT MF-850 3 bin La (continued)
    7 Brother HR-15/HR-25/HR-35       8 Canon A1
    9 Diablo Single/Dual/Envl        10 Epson LQ-1500 Single/Dual
   11 HP LaserJet 500+               12 HP LaserJet 500+     (continued)
   13 IBM 5218 Dual Bin/Envl Feed    14 IBM Pageprinter 3812
   15 NEC 3515/5515/7715 Single/Dual 16 NEC 3550 Single/Dual
   17 Qume Single Bin                18 Rutishauser Dual Bin
   19 Texas Instruments 2015         20 Xerox 2700 Laser
   21 Ziyad PaperJet 400             22 Ziyad PaperJet 400  (continued)



 Selection: 1        (Use the PRINTER program to define a new sheet feeder)
```

Figure 1-7.   Sheet Feeder menu

tings as they are and adjust them later if you experience problems.

Do not select a sheetfeed option marked "continued" (see options 4, 6, 12, and 22 in Figure 1-7). When you select the first option with the sheet feeder name, the "continued" selection is automatically copied with it.

If you do not see your sheet feeder among the selections, press Cancel (F1) until the screen returns to the type of forms. Try selecting the continuous type of forms and do a test print to see if it will work before defining a new sheet feeder.

8. Continue selecting as many printer definitions as applicable. If you have a laser printer, select definitions for all the cartridges you have without regard to printer number. You can select up to 32 printer definitions, although only six can actually be assigned to the six printers. If you have WordPerfect running on two disk drives, however, be aware that the space on the Word-Perfect disk is limited.

9. When the printer definitions are copied, they are assigned a new number on the screen. Use the arrow keys to change the printer number (1-6) in the lower left corner of the screen and see which definition is being used for each. If you selected more than six printer definitions, you will most likely want to reassign the six most commonly used.

If you are using two different types of forms, such as continuous and hand-fed, you can assign the same printer definition to two different printer numbers. The only difference between the two definitions would be the type of forms selected. Select the type of forms most commonly used for printer 1. When sending a print job to the printer, you can decide with Print Options which printer (continuous or hand-fed) should be used.

10. Press Exit (F7) when finished. You'll be returned to the Printer Control menu. If you make a mistake during the process, press Cancel (F1) to ignore the changes. You can continue to make changes to the printer definitions later, if necessary.

11. While in the Printer Control menu, type **2** to see which printers have been selected, the type of forms being used, and the character tables for each font. Only printers 1 through 3 are shown. Usually the same character table is used for all eight fonts; however, there is sometimes a special Line Draw font defined for printing lines and boxes.

If you have a dot matrix printer, a different characteristic or style (such as expanded, italics, compressed, draft, or letter quality) is assigned to each font. This information is not displayed on this screen. See the following page for information about PRHELP that lists the attributes assigned to the eight fonts. If you have a daisy wheel printer, each font is usually assigned to a different print wheel.

12. Press any key to see printers 4 through 6. Press any key to return to the Printer Control menu.

Testing the Printer

WordPerfect provides two documents that can be used to test the capabilities of your printer and let you know how the fonts have been defined. Turn your printer on and place the WordPerfect Learning disk in drive A if you have a hard disk, or drive B if you have two disk drives.

You should still be in the Printer Control menu. If not, press Print (SHIFT-F7), then **4** for Printer Control.

1. From the Printer Control menu, type **P** to print a document and enter **A:PRINTER.TST** (or **B:PRINT-ER.TST** if the disk is in drive B).

2. Press ENTER to print all the pages of the document.

3. Repeat the steps to print the second document, entered as **PRINTER2.TST**.

4. If you are using hand-fed paper or a daisy wheel printer, remain in the Printer Control menu so you can press **G** to send the printer a "go."

More Printer Information

A valuable tool included on the Printer 2 disk is the Printer Help program. It is listed on the disk as a file named PRHELP.EXE.

1. To use the PRHELP program, you first need to exit WordPerfect. If you are still in the Printer Control menu, press ENTER to return to the screen. Press Exit (F7), type **N** (assuming you don't have a document to be saved), then **Y** to exit WordPerfect.

2. Place the Printer 2 disk in drive A and type **A:PRHELP** at the DOS prompt. A list of printers appears.

3. Use the arrow keys to move to the desired printer or type the name of the printer and the cursor will move to that section.

4. When you reach the desired printer, press **ENTER**. A screen similar to the one shown in Figure 1-8 appears.

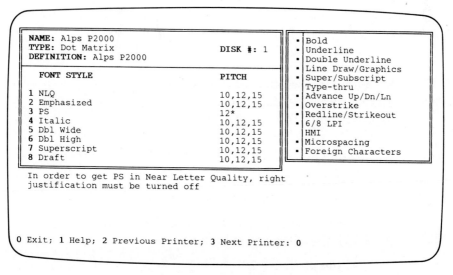

Figure 1-8.   More printer information found by using the PRHELP program on the Printer 2 disk

The printer name, type, specific printer definition to be used, and the printer disk that contains the definition are shown. Also shown are the attributes and pitch assigned to each of the eight fonts, the WordPerfect features supported 100 percent (marked with a ■), and other related notes.

5. Press **2** or **3** to move to the previous or next printer, respectively. PGUP and PGDN will also work. If you need more help or explanation, press **1**.

6. When finished, type **0** to exit or press Exit (F7) until you return to DOS.

Special Characters

This section will help you find out exactly what characters are defined for your printer.

Even though a font is usually the print style, WordPerfect also refers to a character table as a font. As mentioned before, the fonts listed when you choose option 2 in the Printer Control menu to Display Printers and Fonts are actually the character tables being used. Different printers print different characters, depending on the print wheel installed or the character set included within the printer.

WordPerfect includes a macro to help you print the characters in each font so you can see which characters your printer supports. The following steps provide a guide to using the Font Test macro.

1. Start WordPerfect if it has not already been started.

2. Place the Learning disk in drive A if you have a hard disk or drive B if you have two floppy disk drives.

3. Press List Files (F5), =, then **A:** or **B:**, depending on which drive contains the Learning disk. Press ENTER to change the default to that drive. If you follow this step, you don't have to copy the three files involved (FONT-TEST.MAC, FONT.TST, and FNTTEST2.MAC) to the default drive on the hard disk.

4. Press Cancel (F1) to avoid entering the List Files menu.

5. Press Macro (ALT-F10) and enter **FONTTEST**. Follow the instructions displayed on the screen.

6. After you have selected all the fonts that have a different name, press Cancel (F1) to stop the macro.

7. Press Exit (F7) and type **N** twice to clear the screen.

8. If you have a dot matrix or laser printer, the font tests should print automatically. If you have a daisy wheel printer and need to change print wheels for each font, or if you are hand feeding the paper, press Print (SHIFT-F7), then **4** for Printer Control. Follow the instructions displayed by installing a new print wheel, if applicable, pressing **G** to send the printer a "go."

Figure 1-9 is a sample of the font test printed with the IBM Quietwriter. As you can see, every character is supported. The numbers above and to the left show you which number has been assigned to a character for that particular character table.

See *Special Characters* in Chapter 4 or "Character Tables" in Chapter 7 for more information about printing special characters.

WordPerfect Library

WordPerfect Corporation makes a product called WordPerfect Library that lets you put WordPerfect on a menu. The advantages to using this program are that you don't have to type the same commands again and again, create batch files to change the default directory, find the WordPerfect program, or enter other start-up options. Figure 1-10 shows a sample menu that lets you type the letter **A** to start WordPerfect (you could customize the menu to use another letter, such as **W**). Figure 1-11 shows the setup information that can be entered for a menu option.

See Chapter 8 for more details on using WordPerfect Library.

This prints all characters:

```
        0                   1
        0 1 2 3 4 5 6 7 8 9 0 1 2 3 4 5 6 7 8 9

000       ☺ ☻ ♥ ♦ ♣ ♠ · ◘ ○ ◙ ♂ ♀ ♪ ♫ ☼ ► ◄ ↕ ‼

020     ¶ § ▬ ↨ ↑ ↓ → ← └ ↔ ▲ ▼   ! " # $ % & '

040     ( ) * + , - . / 0 1 2 3 4 5 6 7 8 9 : ;

060     < = > ? @ A B C D E F G H I J K L M N O

080     P Q R S T U V W X Y Z [ \ ] ^ _ ` a b c

100     d e f g h i j k l m n o p q r s t u v w

120     x y z { ¦ } ~   Ç ü é â ä à å ç ê ë è ï

140     î ì Ä Å É æ Æ ô ö ò û ù ÿ Ö Ü ¢ £ ¥ ₧ ƒ

160     á í ó ú ñ Ñ ª º ¿ ⌐ ¬ ½ ¼ ¡ « » ▓ ▒ ▓ │

180     ┤ ╡ ╢ ╖ ╕ ╣ ║ ╗ ╝ ╜ ╛ ┐ └ ┴ ┬ ├ ─ ┼ ╞ ╟

200     ╚ ╔ ╩ ╦ ╠ ═ ╬ ╧ ╨ ╤ ╥ ╙ ╘ ╒ ╓ ╫ ╪ ┘ ┌ █

220     ▄ ▌ ▐ ▀ α β Γ π Σ σ µ τ Φ Θ Ω δ ∞ φ ε ∩

240     ≡ ± ≥ ≤ ⌠ ⌡ ÷ ≈ ° · · √ ⁿ ² ∎ (end)

        0 1 2 3 4 5 6 7 8 9 0 1 2 3 4 5 6 7 8 9
        0                   1
```

This is a test of footnote numbers[234].

---

[234]This is footnote 234!

Figure 1-9.   FONT.TST printed on an IBM Quietwriter

```
┌─────────────────────────────────────────────────────────────────────┐
│ ┌─────────────────────────────────────────────────────────────────┐ │
│ │ WordPerfect Library          Wednesday, November 25, 1987, 11:52am│ │
│ ├──────────────────────────────┬────────────────────────────────────┤ │
│ │ A - WordPerfect              │                                    │ │
│ │                              │                                    │ │
│ │ B - PlanPerfect              │                                    │ │
│ │                              │                                    │ │
│ │ C - Calculator               │                                    │ │
│ │                              │                                    │ │
│ │ D - DOS Command              │                                    │ │
│ │                              │                                    │ │
│ │ E - Calendar                 │                                    │ │
│ │                              │                                    │ │
│ │ F - File Manager             │                                    │ │
│ │                              │                                    │ │
│ │ G - NoteBook                 │                                    │ │
│ │                              │                                    │ │
│ │ H - Program Editor           │                                    │ │
│ │                              │                                    │ │
│ │ I - Macro Editor             │                                    │ │
│ │                              │                                    │ │
│ │ J - Beast (Game)             │                                    │ │
│ └──────────────────────────────┴────────────────────────────────────┘ │
│  1 Go to DOS; 2 Clipboard; 3 Change Dir; 4 Setup; 5 Memory Map:  (F7 = Exit) │
└─────────────────────────────────────────────────────────────────────┘
```

Figure 1-10.   WordPerfect Library's shell menu

```
┌─────────────────────────────────────────────────────────────────────┐
│                         Program Information                           │
│  Menu description:  WordPerfect                                       │
│                                                                       │
│  Program name:  c:\wp\wp.exe                                          │
│                                                                       │
│  Default directory:  c:\work                                          │
│                                                                       │
│  Clipboard  Filename:                                                 │
│            End-Of-Line Macro Name:  EOLW.SHM                          │
│                                                                       │
│  Startup options:  /r/b-15                                            │
│                                                                       │
│  Prompt for startup options?  NO                                      │
│                                                                       │
│  DOS command or batch file?  NO                                       │
│                                                                       │
│  WordPerfect Corp. Program?  YES                                      │
│                                                                       │
│  Start resident?  NO                                                  │
│                                                                       │
│     Enter the message you want displayed on the shell menu for        │
│     this program.                                                     │
│                                          (F7 = Exit, F3 = Help)       │
└─────────────────────────────────────────────────────────────────────┘
```

Figure 1-11.   Screen showing the WordPerfect Library setup
options and how WordPerfect can be configured

WordPerfect Basics

This chapter teaches you how to use WordPerfect by explaining the word processing concepts used by the program rather than by teaching you exact keystrokes. If you are already familiar with WordPerfect, you might want to review this chapter quickly and move on to Chapter 3 for information about using macros and customizing WordPerfect to fit your needs.

If you are just beginning to use WordPerfect and have questions, check the section at the end of this chapter for answers to common questions from other new users.

Template and Keystrokes

There are several keys in addition to those covered in Chapter 1 that you should be familiar with before learning the basics of WordPerfect.

As mentioned previously, a template (plastic overlay) fits over the function keys to label them with WordPerfect features, as shown in Figure 2-1. Four functions are assigned to each key. These functions are printed in black, blue, green, and red on the template. When you want the feature printed in black, press the function key by itself. The functions printed in green require that you hold down the SHIFT key and press a function key. The SHIFT keys on your keyboard might be labeled with an arrow pointing upward instead of with the word "SHIFT." Functions printed in blue use the ALT key, while those printed in red use the CTRL key.

In each case, hold down the SHIFT, ALT, or CTRL key, but press or tap the function key lightly. This light touch is

Enhanced Keyboard Template

Shell	Spell	Screen	Move	Text In/Out	Tab Align	Footnote	Print Format	Merge/Sort	Macro Def
SUPER/SUBSCRIPT	<-SEARCH	SWITCH	->INDENT<-	DATE	CENTER	PRINT	LINE FORMAT	MERGE E	RETRIEVE TEXT
Thesaurus	Replace	Reveal Codes	Block	Mark Text	Flush Right	Math/Columns	Page Format	Merge Codes	Macro
Cancel	Search->	Help	->Indent	List Files	Bold	Exit	Underline	Merge R	Save Text
F1	F2	F3	F4	F5	F6	F7	F8	F9	F10

Ctrl + Function Key
SHIFT + FUNCTION KEY
Alt + Function Key
Function Key alone

WordPerfect 4.2 Template (IBM Layout)

F1	**Shell** SUPER/SUBSCRIPT Thesaurus Cancel	**Spell** <-SEARCH Replace Search->	F2
F3	**Screen** SWITCH Reveal Codes Help	**Move** ->INDENT<- Block ->Indent	F4
F5	**Text In/Out** DATE Mark Text List Files	**Tab Align** CENTER Flush Right Bold	F6
F7	**Footnote** PRINT Math/Columns Exit	**Print Format** LINE FORMAT Page Format Underline	F8
F9	**Merge/Sort** MERGE E Merge Codes Merge R	**Macro Def** RETRIEVE TEXT Macro Save Text	F10

Ctrl + Function Key
SHIFT + FUNCTION KEY
Alt + Function Key
Function Key alone

Figure 1-2.   Two types of WordPerfect templates used to label function keys (courtesy of WordPerfect Corporation)

necessary because all the keys (except SHIFT, ALT, and CTRL) are *repeating* keys. If you see messages or menus flash on and off, you have held a function key down too long. To demonstrate this, hold down the INS key found below the numeric keypad. "Typeover" will flash on and off in the lower left corner of the screen. Press a function key as you would any other key when typing and it will turn on or off just once.

In earlier versions of WordPerfect, the keys along the top of the keyboard were used with the ALT and CTRL keys to access the various functions. The features assigned to these keys have been duplicated on the ten function keys, but have been retained for early users. If you press one of these keys accidentally, you can press Cancel (F1) to back out of a menu or prompt.

Two very important keys found on the WordPerfect template are Help (F3) and Cancel (F1). Other important and commonly used keys are explained in "Creating Documents" later in this chapter.

Help

There are two ways of using Help. When you press Help (F3), you will see the message shown in Figure 2-2 that tells you how to choose which of the two types of help you need at the time. If you see a message at the bottom of the Help screen telling you that the help files are not found, place the Learning disk in one of the floppy disk drives and type the letter of that drive. If you are using drive A for the WordPerfect disk, insert the Learning disk in drive B.

You can see an alphabetized list of WordPerfect features, along with their corresponding function keys, by typing a letter from A through Z. This is especially useful because not all features are listed on the template. If you cannot find a feature listed on the template (such as Margins), press Help (F3), then the letter for that feature (M in this case). As shown in Table 2-1, all the features beginning with "M" are listed along with the function key used to invoke each feature and the name that WordPerfect has assigned to that function key. (Note: Some non-IBM-compatible computers will show the feature and key name but not the exact keystrokes.)

```
Help                                    WP 4.2   11/25/87

   Press any letter to get an alphabetical list of features.

      The list will include the features that start with that letter, along
      with the name of the key where the feature is found.  You can then
      press that key to get a description of how the feature works.


   Press any function key to get information about the use of the key.

      Some keys may let you choose from a menu to get more information
      about various options.  Press HELP again to display the template.


   Press the Enter key or Space bar to exit Help.
```

Figure 2-2.   Initial Help screen

```
Function Key      Feature                          Key Name

Alt -F10          Macro                            Macro
Ctrl-F10          Macro Definition                 Macro Def
Shft-F8           Margins                          Line Format - 3
Alt -F5           Mark Text                        Mark Text
Alt -F7           Math Definition                  Math/Columns - 2
Alt -F7           Math On/Off                      Math/Columns - 1
Ctrl-F9           Merge                            Merge/Sort
Alt -F9           Merge Codes                      Merge Codes
Shft-F9           Merge E - End of record          Merge E
F9                Merge Return - End of field      Merge R
Ctrl-F4           Move                             Move
```

Table 2-1.   List of Features Beginning with M in Help screen

After pressing Help, you can also press a function key that you want to learn more about and you will see a short description of the feature. You can continue pressing function keys (or letters) and reading the help message for each without ever leaving Help. When finished, press ENTER or the SPACEBAR.

Cancel

Cancel (F1) is used for two purposes: to cancel a procedure or restore deleted text.

If you are in a menu or a feature is in process (search, merge, or a macro, for instance), press Cancel (F1) to leave the menu or cancel the procedure. You may have to press the Cancel key more than once to return to your text. If you see "Macro Def" flashing in the lower left corner of the screen, Cancel won't work; press Macro Def (CTRL-F10) to turn it off.

If you are not in a menu, Cancel will restore any or all of the last three deletions. When you press Cancel (F1) to "undelete" text, the last deletion is shown in reverse video (highlighted) at the cursor and a message appears at the bottom of the screen (see Figure 2-3).

Type **1** to restore the deleted text or **2** to show the previous deletion. Up to three deletions can be displayed. If you decide not to restore the deletion, press Cancel or ENTER.

Miscellaneous Keystrokes

Other keys that have special features are listed at the bottom or side of the template. The following descriptions of those features and the keystrokes that invoke them will help familiarize you with their functions. You can find more detailed information about each item in Chapter 4, "Commands and Features."

In the following descriptions, two keys separated by a hyphen (-) are to be pressed together. If the keys are sepa-

```
        State of New Hampshire shall be entitled to choose three,

    Massachusetts eight, Rhode-Island and Providence Plantations one,

    Connecticut five, New York six, New Jersey four, Pennsylvania

    eight, Delaware one, Maryland six, Virginia ten, North Carolina

    five, South Carolina five, and Georgia three.

        When vacancies happen in the Representation from any State,

    the Executive Authority thereof shall issue Writs of Election to

    fill such Vacancies.

        The House of Representatives shall choose their speaker and

    Officers; and shall have the sole Power of Impeachment.

        Section 3.  The Senate of the United States shall be

    composed of two Senators from each state, (chosen by the

Undelete: 1 Restore; 2 Show Previous Deletion: 0
```

Figure 2-3.   The screen after pressing CANCEL

rated by a comma (,) the second key is to be pressed after the first.

Hard Page Break (CTRL-ENTER)

WordPerfect automatically inserts a page break (referred to as a *soft-page*) at the end of each page as you type. If you want to force a page break, press CTRL and ENTER together. A double dashed line appears, marking the designated break to a *hard page* rather than the single dashed line indicating a soft page break. See "Hard and Soft Codes" later in this chapter to read more about the difference between a hard and soft page break.

Delete Word (CTRL-BACKSPACE) and (HOME,BACKSPACE)

Pressing CTRL and BACKSPACE deletes the word at the cursor. If you continue pressing these keys together, words to the right of the cursor are moved over and deleted.

Pressing HOME, then BACKSPACE (one after the other, not together) also deletes the word at the cursor. If you continue to press HOME, then BACKSPACE, words to the left of the cursor are deleted.

Delete to the End of Line (CTRL-END)

Press CTRL and END (number 1 on the numeric keypad) together to delete text from the cursor to the end of the line.

Delete to the End of Page (CTRL-PGDN)

To delete text from the cursor to the end of the page, press CTRL and PGDN. You are asked to confirm this type of deletion.

Word Left/Right (CTRL ←) and (CTRL →)

You can move to the previous or next word by pressing CTRL and the left (←) or right (→) arrow, respectively.

Screen Up/Down (−) and (+) or (HOME,↑) and (HOME,↓)

Press − (found on the numeric keypad) to move to the top of the screen and + (also on the keypad) to move to the bottom of the screen. If you continue to press the key, the cursor moves through the text one screen at a time. Pressing (HOME,↑) and (HOME,↓) will also move through the document one screen at a time.

Page Up/Down (PGUP) or (PGDN)

These keys move the cursor to the previous or next page.

Home (HOME)

The HOME key is used with other keys to move through large sections of text. Press HOME and any arrow key to move to the outside edges of the text on the screen. For example, you would press (HOME,↑) to go to the top of the screen or (HOME,←) to go to the left side of the screen.

To move to the extreme edges of the document, press HOME *twice*, then the appropriate arrow key. Thus, (HOME, HOME,↑) takes you to the beginning of the document, (HOME, HOME,↓) moves to the end of the document, and, if your margins are wider than the screen, pressing (HOME,HOME,→) or (HOME,HOME,←) moves the cursor to the far right or left margins.

Go To (CTRL-HOME)

When you press CTRL and HOME together, "Go to" appears on the lower left of the screen. Enter a number, and the cursor moves to the top of that page. If you enter a nonexistent page number, the cursor moves to the top of the last page.

After pressing Go To, you can type a character instead of a number and the cursor moves to the next occurrence of that character. You can also press the SPACEBAR, a period, or ENTER to move by word, sentence, or paragraph, respectively, because the cursor finds the next occurrence of a space, period, or hard return. A beep will sound if the key entered is not found.

Pressing Go To *twice* moves the cursor to its previous location. You could use this feature if you moved to page 20, for example, then decided you wanted to go back to your original location (but forgot where it was).

When you are working with multiple text columns, Go To is used with → and ← to move from column to column.

Escape (ESC)

As in most programs, ESC is used to "escape" from a menu or situation. If you are in a WordPerfect menu, pressing ESC will also return you to your text. However, if there is not a menu on your screen, ESC performs a different and useful function. When you press ESC, the message "n = 8" appears in the lower left corner of the screen. You can press any key and it will repeat eight times. You can enter another number to replace the eight, repeating the new key that many times. For instance, you can press ESC, 20, then ↑, to move up 20 lines. You can also repeat a macro *n* number of times (see *Macros* in Chapter 4, "Commands and Features," for more information).

You can change the default from eight to any other number during an editing session by pressing ESC, the number, and ENTER. See *ESC Key* in Chapter 4, which contains a complete, alphabetical reference to WordPerfect and "Customizing WordPerfect" in Chapter 3 for changing the default permanently.

Left Margin Release (SHIFT-TAB)

Pressing SHIFT and TAB together moves the cursor back to the previous tab. If you are already at the left margin, this option works as a left margin release, moving the cursor to a tab setting in the left margin.

When working with the Outline feature, TAB is used to go to the next level and SHIFT-TAB returns to the previous level in the outline.

Soft Hyphen (CTRL--)

When WordPerfect hyphenates words for you or assists in hyphenating words, it inserts a *soft hyphen*. If, after additional editing, the word no longer needs to be hyphenated, the hyphen does not appear on the screen. If you type a word that might need to be hyphenated, or WordPerfect inserts a hyphen in the wrong location (a small percentage of error exists), you can insert a soft hyphen at the exact location where you want the hyphen to occur. WordPerfect would then use this hyphen rather than suggesting a soft hyphen of its own. With the automatic hyphenation provided by WordPerfect, however, it is unlikely that you will ever need to use this feature.

Starting WordPerfect

If you have not installed WordPerfect, or if you do not understand DOS, please refer to Chapter 1.

Two Disk Drives

Start your computer. It is suggested that you use drive A for WordPerfect and drive B as the default for storing and retrieving files. With the WordPerfect disk in drive A and a disk for files in drive B, enter the following commands.

```
A>B:
B>A:WP
```

This makes drive B the default drive for storing and retrieving files, then looks to drive A for the WordPerfect program. When you save or retrieve files, you will only need to enter the name of the file; you do not have to type B: at the beginning of the filename each time.

If you have not already done so, you can create a batch file that will enter these commands for you. See Chapter 1 for more information.

Hard Disk

If you have the WordPerfect program installed as suggested in Chapter 1, you should change the default directory from the root directory to the one where the files are to be stored; then enter WP as in the example below.

```
C:\ >CD PERSONAL
C:\ PERSONAL >WP
```

If you have not entered the PATH command telling DOS where to search for the WordPerfect program files, you will also have to enter the directory name. If you have the Word-Perfect program files in a directory called WP and have

DOS version 3.0 or later, enter WP\WP. However, it is best to put the PATH command in an AUTOEXEC.BAT file. See Chapter 1 for details about creating batch files.

Error Messages

If you have a power or system failure while running Word-Perfect, or if you shut the machine off without using Exit (F7), you will see the message, "Are other copies of WordPerfect currently running? (Y/N)" when trying to start Word-Perfect. Each time you start WordPerfect, it attempts to create temporary files. If it finds that the temporary files already exist (they weren't closed properly using the Exit key), you are asked this question. To start WordPerfect normally, type **N** for no and WordPerfect will be started.

If you are on a network system, or want to have more than one copy of WordPerfect in memory, answer **Y**, then specify which directory should be used for the new set of temporary files. Those on a network system are not usually asked this question because their passwords are used to create unique temporary files.

Previous versions of WordPerfect displayed a message, "Overflow files exist." If you see this message, choose option 3 and the overflow files will be replaced.

If you had the timed backup feature on during a power or system failure (see Chapter 3 about setting "Backup Options"), you will probably want to retrieve the backup file (named {WP}BACK.1 or {WP}BACK.2). Regardless of whether or not you retrieve the backup file, the following message appears when WordPerfect attempts to make the first backup.

```
Old backup file exists. 1 rename; 2 delete:
```

Type **1** to rename the old backup file and enter the new name, **2**, to delete it, or Cancel (F1) to return to your text and retrieve the file.

Status Line

When you first enter WordPerfect, you see a status line at the bottom of the screen as shown here.

```
                                    Doc 1  Pg 1  Ln 1        Pos 10
```

The status line tells you the current location of the cursor (blinking dash in the upper left corner of the screen). "Doc" displays "1" or "2" depending on which document you are editing (you can have two documents in memory at once), "Pg" indicates the page number, "Ln" tells you the line on the page, and "Pos" tells you how far the cursor is from the left edge of the page.

You can use Switch (SHIFT-F3) to switch between two documents. Press these two keys together and the document number on the status line will change from "Doc 1" to "Doc 2" or vice versa.

The page number ("Pg") changes when you reach a soft page break (usually at line 54) or after you press Hard Page (CTRL-ENTER) to force a page break.

The line indicator ("Ln") changes when you press ENTER to create a new line or press ↓ to move down through lines. You cannot move down using ↓ if there is no text to move through.

The position of the cursor ("Pos") changes as you type text or press the SPACEBAR. "Pos" is also used to indicate if the CAPS LOCK key is on ("POS" is shown in uppercase) or NUM LOCK is on ("Pos" flashes on and off temporarily). The position number is displayed in bold if bold is on (Pos **10**), underlined if underlining is on ("Pos 10"), or bolded and underlined if both are on ("Pos **10**"). For those with a color monitor, the number is shown in a different color. See *Colors* in Chapter 4 or "Colors" in Chapter 3 for more information on changing the color for these and other items.

Although the left margin is at column 10, the cursor appears at the far left of the screen so you can see as much text as possible. WordPerfect version 4.1 displays text away from the left side of the screen, but horizontal scrolling is not as efficient. If you prefer the 4.1 method, press Left Margin Release (SHIFT-TAB) twice and BACKSPACE twice.

When working with text columns, "Col" is added to the beginning of the status line to indicate the column in which the cursor is located. You can have as many as 24 text columns.

If you have saved and named a document, the status line also shows the full pathname of the current document (drive, directory, and filename) in the lower left corner of the screen. This area is also used to display messages, warnings, and one-line menus.

Word Processing Concepts

This section introduces you to some of the word processing concepts used by WordPerfect and should help you understand more about the program.

You should use the tutorial found on the Learning disk provided with the WordPerfect package to reinforce these concepts. Because it is an on-screen, interactive tutorial, it can teach you exact steps much better than if you were to read the same steps in a book.

To use the tutorial, insert the WordPerfect disk in drive A and Learning disk in drive B, enter **B:**, and then enter **LEARN** at the B> DOS prompt. If you are using a hard disk, copy the files found on the Learning disk to a separate directory and enter TUTOR from that directory. See *Tutorial* in Chapter 4, "Commands and Features," for more detailed information.

Clear Screen

There is no "main menu" when first entering WordPerfect. With other word processors, you usually have to "open" a document and name it. WordPerfect lets you create a document, check the spelling, print it, then clear the screen without ever having to name or save it. This saves steps and disk space for short notes, memos, and letters that don't need to be saved for future use.

If you are accustomed to seeing a list of files as the opening menu, press List Files (F5) and ENTER upon entering WordPerfect. Among many other options, this menu lets you highlight a file and retrieve it to the screen. If you press List Files and do not retrieve a document, press Exit (F7) to leave the menu and begin working on a new document.

Because of WordPerfect's clear-screen approach and few menus, it might seem hard to find a feature or know what features exist. Even after working with WordPerfect for some time, you might not realize all that it can do for you because the features may seem hidden.

One of the easiest ways of finding out what features are

```
Page Format

        1 - Page Number Position

        2 - New Page Number

        3 - Center Page Top to Bottom

        4 - Page Length

        5 - Top Margin

        6 - Headers or Footers

        7 - Page Number Column Positions

        8 - Suppress for Current page only

        9 - Conditional End of Page

        A - Widow/Orphan

Selection: 0
```

```
Document to be Saved:
```

Figure 2-4.   Function keys can produce a full-screen menu (top) or a prompt that requests information (bottom)

available, as well as which function keys invoke the features, is to take some time pressing each key. Some function keys act as on/off keys (such as Bold (F6) or Underline (F8)). Other function keys show a full-screen menu or prompt you for more information (see Figure 2-4).

As mentioned before, you cannot harm your computer by pressing keys. Cancel (F1) will return you to your document from any menu without invoking a feature. The only way you can destroy files already saved on the disk is by pressing List Files (F5), pressing ENTER to view the directory, highlighting a file, typing **2** to delete it, and typing **Y** to confirm the deletion. These five steps are necessary to delete a file; the last one is even a confirmation step. You could also replace a file on the disk by attempting to save another document with the same filename. However, because you cannot have two files with the same name, you are asked if you want to replace the previous file with the new one. This question helps to protect your documents and gives you an opportunity to enter a different filename.

WordPerfect Codes

As you type a WordPerfect document, you will see the text on the screen much like it will appear when it is printed. You will not see dot commands and control characters cluttering the screen or misaligning text.

Each key you press is recorded either on the screen or "behind the scenes." The codes used to format a document are hidden so they don't clutter the regular text on the screen. They are sent to the printer along with the document to give the printer instructions for formatting the document.

You can reveal the codes and the regular text with Reveal Codes (ALT-F3) as shown in Figure 2-5. A reverse-video ruler bar showing current margins and tabs divides the screen. The upper half of the screen displays the regular text while the lower half shows the location of codes in the text.

Most of the codes used by WordPerfect are easy to interpret. In Figure 2-5, "[Spacing Set:2]" indicates double spacing, "[B]" shows where bold was turned on, "[b]" shows where bold was turned off, and [HRt] indicates a hard return. The

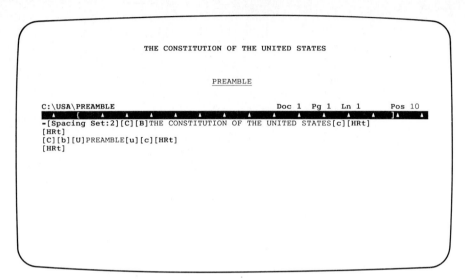

Figure 2-5. Text and embedded codes displayed by pressing Reveal Codes

blinking "–" shows the current location of the cursor. Some functions, like bold and underline, use an on/off code while others indicate where a format change takes place.

You can move through the text and codes using the cursor keys and can delete both text and codes with BACKSPACE or DEL. Pressing any key other than a search, cursor movement, or deleting key returns you to normal editing.

If, while in the normal editing screen (not Reveal Codes), you are using BACKSPACE or DEL, you might see a message such as "Delete [Bold]? (Y/N) N" displayed in the lower left corner of the screen. This message is telling you that you have run into a code and wants to know if it should be deleted. If you want to delete the code, type **Y**. If you don't want to delete the code (or don't understand the message), press any other key (even the DEL key) and the cursor will skip over the code rather than delete it.

The easiest way to delete codes is to press Reveal Codes (ALT-F3), move the cursor next to the code, then press BACKSPACE or DEL, depending on whether the code is before or after the cursor. When you delete codes using this method, you are not asked to confirm the deletion.

After you become accustomed to WordPerfect, you will

be familiar with the location of the codes without having to use Reveal Codes, especially since you were probably the one who inserted them (unless you are editing someone else's document). Some codes, such as Center, Bold, and Underline, give an indication as to their location on the screen.

If you are using → and ← to move the cursor and run into a code, the cursor does not appear to move on the screen but is actually moving over the code. If you go to the beginning or end of a word that is shown in boldface or underlined, you can watch the "Pos" number while moving the cursor. It will also be shown in bold or underline when the cursor moves over the code. Then, depending on which side of the code the cursor is on, you can use BACKSPACE or DEL to delete the code and type **Y** to confirm the deletion.

Hard and Soft Codes

In WordPerfect, a return that you insert is usually referred to as a *hard return*. This term is used to differentiate between the Hard Return code [HRt] that is inserted when you press ENTER (RETURN), and the Soft Return code [SRt] that is automatically inserted during word wrap.

If you type a document and press ENTER at the end of each line and later want to add or delete text, the document will not reformat correctly because of the [HRt] codes inserted. Instead, when you type, you should let WordPerfect wrap the text to the next line for you. When text is edited, soft returns are removed if they are no longer needed.

WordPerfect inserts a soft page break [SPg], indicated by a dashed line across the screen, when it reaches line 54 (see Figure 2-6). This setting allows for 1-inch top and bottom margins on a letter-size page. If you have page numbers, headers, footers, and/or footnotes, WordPerfect will automatically subtract the number of lines needed for these features and insert a page break at the appropriate place.

A page break that you insert manually is referred to as a hard page [HPg]. If you type a page that has a small amount of text, such as a title page, you can press Hard Page (CTRL-ENTER) to immediately go to the next page rather than pressing ENTER until you reach line 54. A hard page is indicated by a double dashed line on the screen (see Figure 2-7).

```
direct.  The Number of Representatives shall not exceed one for
every thirty Thousand, but each State shall have at Least one
Representative; and until such enumeration shall be made, the
State of New Hampshire shall be entitled to choose three,
-----------------------------------------------------------------------
Massachusetts eight, Rhode-Island and Providence Plantations one,
Connecticut five, New York six, New Jersey four, Pennsylvania
eight, Delaware one, Maryland six, Virginia ten, North Carolina
five, South Carolina five, and Georgia three.

      When vacancies happen in the Representation from any State,
the Executive Authority thereof shall issue Writs of Election to
fill such Vacancies.
      The House of Representatives shall choose their speaker and
C:\USA\CONST                          Doc 1  Pg 2  Ln 47     Pos 15
```

Figure 2-6.   A soft page break

```
                            PREAMBLE

      We the people of the United States, in Order to form a more
perfect Union, establish Justice, insure domestic Tranquility,
provide for the common defense, promote the general Welfare, and
secure the Blessings of Liberty to ourselves and our Posterity,
do ordain and establish this Constitution for the United States
of America.
=======================================================================
ARTICLE I.
      Section 1.  All legislative Powers herein granted shall be
vested in a Congress of the United States, which shall consist of
a Senate and House of Representatives.
C:\USA\CONST                          Doc 1  Pg 2  Ln 1      Pos 10
```

Figure 2-7.   A hard page break

Like soft returns, soft pages are automatically readjusted during editing. Hard returns and hard pages remain in their exact location until you manually delete them using BACKSPACE or DEL.

Pagination

WordPerfect is document-oriented rather than page-oriented. You can see text across page breaks rather than having to "put a page away" before retrieving another. The repagination step that is required by most word processors is also eliminated.

You can change the length of the page (up to 108 lines) and WordPerfect will continue to break the page automatically.

You can move across page breaks easily using ↑ and ↓. If you want to move one page at a time, use PGUP or PGDN. To go to a particular page, press Go To (CTRL-HOME), then enter the number of the page.

Default Settings

When you enter WordPerfect, you can start typing immediately because the format settings (such as margins, tabs, and page length) have been preset. You can change the format as many times as you want in a document. When you make changes to the format, codes are inserted and saved with the document. When you clear your screen to begin work on a new document, the standard defaults are once again in effect.

The defaults for some of the more common format settings are listed in Table 2-2. You can choose your own defaults with the WordPerfect Setup menu (see "Customizing WordPerfect" in Chapter 3).

Format Item	Default Setting
Margins:	
Left	10
Right	74
Top	1 inch (12 half-lines)
Bottom	1 inch
Tabs	Every 5 spaces
Spacing	Single spacing
Pitch	10 pitch
Right justification	On
Page length	66 lines for the form length, 54 lines of single-spaced text
Page number	None

Table 2-2.   Default Settings

WordPerfect Menus and Prompts

Although WordPerfect does not use a main menu to guide you through the process of creating a document, other menus appear when you press certain function keys. Each option on a menu is numbered or lettered so that you can type the number or letter without pressing ENTER to make your selection.

There is also a default answer for each menu option. Even though you can always use Cancel (F1) or Exit (F7) to leave a menu, you can also press any key other than the numbers or letters listed on the menu to leave the menu. For example, if you have a menu listing six choices, you can press any key other than those from 1 through 6 to leave the menu. Depending on your preference, you might find it easiest to press ENTER or the SPACEBAR to leave a menu rather than Cancel or Exit.

WordPerfect will prompt you to answer yes/no questions. When this happens, you will see "(Y/N)" followed by the default answer. WordPerfect displays the "safest" answer for each situation rather than always displaying a Y or N as the default. For instance, if you press Exit (F7), you will see

```
Save Document? (Y/N) Y
```

Notice that Y is the default. You can press *any* key other than N to save the document. Even if you do type N, you can press Cancel (F1) to return to the document without exiting.

WordPerfect will sometimes display a filename, path-name, or search string when saving a document, listing files, or searching. When this happens, you can enter new characters, edit the displayed name, or press ENTER to accept what is already displayed. For example, if you press Save (F10) and you have previously saved the document, the current filename will appear. You can press ENTER to accept that name, enter a new name, or edit the displayed name. The name C:\WORK\MINUTES.JAN could be changed to C:\WORK\MINUTES.FEB by moving the cursor to the J, deleting JAN, and entering FEB.

A common mistake new users make is to type **Y** rather than press ENTER to accept the displayed name. If you do this, you can probably find a lost file under the name of Y on your disk.

What You See Is What You Get

WordPerfect is not a "graphics" program, but rather displays each character in a fixed *pitch*. This means that each character has a set amount of space, so WordPerfect cannot show proportional spacing, superscripts, right justification, or italics during normal editing. With this design, however, WordPerfect is much faster when creating and editing documents.

To compensate, WordPerfect has a Preview feature that

shows right justification, headers/footers, footnotes, page numbers, and line numbering on the screen.

Virtual Memory, Document Size, and Switching Disks

At some time, you might see a question or statement regarding WordPerfect's *overflow files*. These are temporary files that are automatically created on the disk each time you start WordPerfect and are closed when you exit WordPerfect. Table 2-3 shows the temporary files created during the operation of WordPerfect.

As you learned in Chapter 1, the document that you see on your screen is in memory. When memory is filled, the document spills into overflow files on disk. As a document increases in size, so will these *virtual files*. Any text above the cursor that needs to be stored is kept in the top virtual file and the text below the cursor is stored in the bottom virtual file. The names for these files are {WP}.TV1 and {WP}.BV1 for document 1, and {WP}.TV2 and {WP}.BV2 for document 2.

Overflow files, along with other temporary files (those beginning with {WP}), are stored on the same drive/directory as the WordPerfect program file WP.EXE. See Chapter 3 under "Options for Starting WordPerfect" for information on storing these overflow files elsewhere.

Because of the virtual memory design, the size of a document is limited only by memory size and the amount of disk space available. Although it is recommended that you work with smaller files, you can increase the size of documents by adding more memory or disk space. If you have two floppy disk drives, not much memory, and you have not redirected the overflow files to a disk other than the one containing WordPerfect, the size of your documents will be limited. This is true because there is limited space on the WordPerfect disk—especially if it contains DOS system files.

When using two floppy disk drives, you should always leave the WordPerfect disk in its drive (usually drive A). However, you can change disks in the other drive. If you plan to use the spelling dictionary or thesaurus, you will need to

File	Description
{WP}.TV1	Top virtual file for document 1. Text above the cursor is stored in this overflow file if needed
{WP}.BV1	Bottom virtual file for document 1. Text below the cursor is stored in this overflow file if needed
{WP}.TV2	Top virtual file for document 2. See {WP}.TV1 above
{WP}.BV2	Bottom virtual file for document 2. See {WP}.BV1 above
{WP}.CHK	Keeps track of the overflow files
{WP}SYS.FIL	WordPerfect system file containing user-definable attributes such as colors and key mapping for special characters
{WP}.SPC	Contains special information such as the version number, network information, and a few error messages. Also used to reserve space on the disk in the case of a disk-full error
{WP}0.UND	Contains the most recent deletion
{WP}1.UND	Contains the second most recent deletion
{WP}2.UND	Contains the third most recent deletion
{WP}LEX.SUP	Supplementary dictionary containing user-added words
{WP}BACK.1	Backup file for document 1 (if backup is specified)
{WP}BACK.2	Backup file for document 2
{WP}.Q	Printer queue, which lists the documents waiting to be printed
{WP}.#	When printing from the screen rather than disk, files are given a temporary number instead of the filename being used

Table 2-3.   Temporary Overflow Files

replace the data disk with the Speller or Thesaurus diskette at the appropriate time. If you have enough memory available (at least 320Kb), you might consider loading WordPerfect into memory. You can then remove the WordPerfect diskette and use that drive for the speller or thesaurus. See "Options for Starting WordPerfect" in Chapter 3 for more information.

If you have a RAM drive, you can copy the speller or thesaurus files to the RAM drive to make them run faster and eliminate disk switching. See *RAM Drives* in Chapter 4, "Commands and Features," for details.

Creating Documents

This section presents the basic steps in creating a WordPerfect document.

Entering Text

As you enter text, remember that WordPerfect is designed to do most tasks for you automatically. If you attempt to do the same things manually, you will find yourself having to do extra work with a document after even small editing changes have been made.

The first basic rule is that you should not press ENTER unless you want to end a paragraph, make a short line, or create a blank line. WordPerfect will wrap text to the next line when you reach the right margin. If you accidentally press ENTER, you can immediately press BACKSPACE to delete the effect of the ENTER key.

WordPerfect will insert text as you type. Any text after the cursor is pushed to the right and reformatted as the new text is added. If you want to type over existing text, press INS and "Typeover" will appear on the status line. Press it again to return to inserting text.

You can also retrieve other documents (or parts of documents, as explained later in this chapter) at the cursor's location. If you know the name of a document, press Retrieve

(SHIFT-F10) and enter the name of the document. If the file is not in the default drive/directory, enter the full pathname (drive, directory, and filename). If you don't know the filename, press List Files (F5) and ENTER to see an alphabetized listing of the files in the default drive/directory. Move the cursor to the file you want to retrieve and type **1**. If you retrieve a file and you happen to have a file on your screen at the time, they will be combined. If you don't want this to happen, be sure to have a clear screen before retrieving another file.

The following features are commonly used in word processing. Other features such as decimal tabs, superscripting, double underlining, using the thesaurus, footnotes, text columns, and inserting the current date and time are explained in detail in Chapter 4, "Commands and Features."

Centering

WordPerfect will, upon your command, automatically center titles and headings between the left and right margins. While at the left margin, press Center (SHIFT-F6), type the heading, then press ENTER to turn off centering and move to the next line.

If you want to center text that has already been typed, move the cursor to the beginning of the line and press Center. If the text is not centered immediately, insert a hard return by pressing ENTER at the end of the line.

Indenting

There are several ways of indenting text (see Figure 2-8). You can use the TAB key to move the cursor to the next tab stop (tabs have been preset every five spaces). The TAB key on your keyboard might be labeled with two arrows facing in opposite directions (⇄). This key can be used to indent the first line of a paragraph or when you want to move to a specific tab stop.

Pressing Indent (F4) indents and wraps each line to a tab stop until you press ENTER. You could use this option for

```
        AMENDMENT 1  Congress shall make no law respecting an
    establishment of religion, or prohibiting the free exercise
    thereof; or abridging the freedom of speech, or of the press; or
    the right of the people peaceably to assemble, and to petition
    the Government for a redress of grievances.


        AMENDMENT 2  A well regulated Militia, being necessary to
    the security of a free State, the right of the people to
    keep and bear Arms, shall not be infringed.


        AMENDMENT 3  No Soldier shall, in time of peace be
    quartered in any house, without the consent of the
    Owner, nor in time of war, but in a manner to be
    prescribed by law.

        AMENDMENT 4  The right of the people to be secure in their
        persons, houses, papers, and effects, against unreasonable
        searches and seizures, shall not be violated, and no
        Warrants shall issue, but upon probable cause, supported by
        Oath or affirmation, and particularly describing the place
        to be searched, and the persons or things to be seized.
    C:\USA\CONST                          Doc 1  Pg 11  Ln 23     Pos 10
```

Hanging indent

Figure 2-8.   Options for indenting text

numbered paragraphs that have the number at the left margin with the following text indented. If you try to indent each line manually using TAB and later add or delete text, you will have tabs in the middle of lines. Instead, use Indent at the first line and WordPerfect will wrap subsequent lines to the appropriate tab stop for you.

Pressing →Indent← (SHIFT-F4) indents each line from the left *and* right margins. This option is useful when displaying quotations and centering paragraphs. Pressing ENTER returns to the normal margins.

You can also create a *hanging indent* by pressing either Indent key, then releasing the first line back to the previous tab stop by pressing Left Margin Release (SHIFT-TAB).

Boldface

If you want a section of text to be printed in boldface (heavier print), press Bold (F6), type the text to be bolded, then press Bold again. If you want to boldface text that has

Keystrokes	Movement
↑	Move up one line
↓	Move down one line
→	Move right one character
←	Move left one character
CTRL →	Move to the beginning of the next word
CTRL ←	Move to the beginning of the previous word
−	Move to the top of the screen; continue pressing to move to the top of each previous screen
+	Move to the bottom of the screen. Continue pressing to move to the bottom of each following screen
HOME,↑	Same as − (screen up)
HOME,↓	Same as + (screen down)
HOME,→	Move to the end of the line
HOME,←	Move to the beginning of the line
END	Same as HOME,HOME, → (end of line)
PGUP	Move to the beginning of the previous page
PGDN	Move to the beginning of the next page
HOME,HOME,↑	Move to the beginning of the document
HOME,HOME,↓	Move to the end of the document
HOME,HOME,→	Move to the far right of the document (useful for documents wider than the screen)
HOME,HOME,←	Move to the far left of the document
CTRL-HOME	Go to .... Enter a number to go to that page or other character to go to the next occurrence of that character (you can also use ENTER or the SPACEBAR to go to the next hard return or space)

Table 2-4.   Cursor Movement Keys

already been typed, move the cursor to either the beginning or end of the text, press Block (ALT-F4), move the cursor to the opposite end of the text (the block of text will be highlighted), then press Bold.

Underlining

The steps for underlining text are similar to those for boldfacing text, except that F8 is used instead of F6. Press Underline (F8), type the text, then press Underline again. To underline existing text, Block (ALT-F4) the text, then press Underline.

Other attributes such as italics, strikeout, and double underlining are also available. See each item in Chapter 4, the alphabetical reference, for instructions.

Moving the Cursor

Table 2-4 summarizes the many options for moving the cursor discussed previously in this chapter and in Chapter 1. These cursor movement keys are found on the numeric keypad. If you press these keys and numbers appear, press NUM LOCK.

Other cursor movement keystrokes that are used less often are listed in Table 2-5.

The cursor will move only through text and codes. When you reach the end of a document, you can create blank space and move down by pressing ENTER.

Correcting Mistakes

Table 2-6 summarizes the keystrokes that can be used to delete text. Remember that you can delete codes, hard page breaks, and blank lines exactly as you would delete regular text. You can also use BACKSPACE and DEL in the Reveal Codes screen.

You can delete sentences, paragraphs, or any amount of text using Block (ALT-F4) to highlight the amount of text to

Keystrokes	Movement
CTRL-HOME,↑	Go to the top of the current page
CTRL-HOME,↓	Go to the bottom of the current page
CTRL-HOME,CTRL-HOME	Go to the previous cursor position
ESC,↑	Move up eight lines. ESC can also be combined with ↓, →, ←, PGUP, PGDN, −, and + to move in that direction eight times
ESC,#,↑	Move up specified number of lines. Can also be combined with ↓, →, ←, PGUP, PGDN, −, and + to move in that direction a specified number of times
CTRL-HOME,→	Used when working with text columns to move to the next column to the right (see *Columns* in Chapter 4 for more explanation)
CTRL-HOME,←	Used in text columns to move to the previous column to the left
CTRL-HOME,HOME,→	Moves to the far right text column
CTRL-HOME,HOME,←	Moves to the far left text column

Table 2-5.   Less Frequently Used Cursor Movement Keys

be deleted. After pressing Block, you can type a period (.) to highlight to the end of the sentence, ENTER to highlight to the end of the paragraph, or PGDN to highlight to the end of the page. After the block has been defined, press BACKSPACE or DEL and type **Y** to confirm the deletion. You are asked for a confirmation on a block delete and when deleting to the end of the page, as a precaution against accidentally deleting large amounts of text.

If you delete text accidentally, press Cancel (F1), then **1** to restore the deleted text or **2** to show the previous deletion. If you want to restore the deleted text in a different location,

Keystrokes	Deletion
BACKSPACE	Delete text to the left
DEL	Delete text at the cursor (appears to delete to the right)
CTRL-BACKSPACE	Delete the word at the cursor. Continue pressing to delete words to the right of the cursor
HOME,BACKSPACE	Delete from the cursor to the beginning of the current word. Continue pressing to delete words to the left of the cursor
HOME,DEL	Delete from the cursor to the end of the current word. Continue pressing to delete words to the right of the cursor
CTRL-END	Delete text from the cursor to the end of the line
CTRL-PGDN	Delete text from the cursor to the end of the page. You are asked to confirm this type of deletion

Table 2-6.   Keystrokes Used for Deletion

move the cursor to the appropriate location and press Cancel (F1). You can use this method as an alternative for moving text (see *Move* in this chapter and in Chapter 4). If you use the undelete feature to move text, remember that only the last three deletions can be restored.

Editing

One of the biggest advantages to using a word processor is being able to manipulate the text on the screen with little or no retyping.

You can edit text as you enter it, or make changes to a previously saved document on disk. When you retrieve a file from disk, you are only retrieving a "copy" of the original file. If you decide not to keep the changes made to the copy on the screen, you can clear the screen and the original on disk remains untouched. Or, after making changes, you can save the file and replace the original on disk.

The rest of this section provides short explanations of some of the more commonly used editing features in Word-Perfect.

Block

Block (ALT-F4) is one of the more powerful editing features. As you learned earlier, you can bold, underline, or delete a block of text. You can also change a block of text to upper- or lowercase, center it, print it, save it to a new file, or append it to another file. Many other options are discussed under *Block* in Chapter 4, "Commands and Features."

One of the most valuable uses of block is to *cut and paste* text. You can move as much text as you want without regard to page boundaries, and the remaining text automatically reformats. Use the following steps to cut or copy text from one location to another.

1. With the cursor at one end of the text to be moved, press Block (ALT-F4). "Block on" flashes in the lower left corner of the screen.

2. Move the cursor to the opposite end of the text. The block is highlighted.

3. Press Move (CTRL-F4).

4. Type **1** to cut the text or **2** to copy the text. Other options allow you to append the block to another file and to cut/copy columns and rectangles. See *Appending Text, Columns,* and *Move* in Chapter 4 for details.

5. Move the cursor to a new location.

6. Press Move (CTRL-F4), then type **5** to retrieve the text. You can also press Retrieve (SHIFT-F10), then ENTER to retrieve the unnamed block of text. Use whichever method you prefer.

The text that is cut or copied is saved in memory and can be retrieved repeatedly until another block of text is cut or copied. You even imagine the name of the block held in memory as being "enter" because you can press ENTER as the name of the document to be retrieved.

Move

When Block is not turned on and you press Move (CTRL-F4), you see the same menu you saw when retrieving the cut block of text.

```
Move 1 Sentence; 2 Paragraph; 3 Page; Retrieve 4 Column; 5 Text; 6 Rectangle: 0
```

You can use this menu to cut, copy, or delete the current sentence, paragraph, or page, and to retrieve a column, block of text, or rectangle.

After typing **1**, **2**, or **3** to highlight the sentence, paragraph, or page, type **1** to cut, **2** to copy, or **3** to delete the highlighted text.

Switching Between Documents

You can have two documents in memory at one time. Press Switch (SHIFT-F3) to move from one document to the other.

When you switch between documents, you will see a full screen for each document. If you want to split the screen and display both documents simultaneously, press Screen (CTRL-F3), type **1** for Window, then enter the number of lines you want to use for the current document. Enter **12** if you want to split the screen evenly. You can also press ↑ or ↓ rather than enter a number to divide the screen. A ruler indicating the current margin and tab settings is used to separate the two documents. When you want to see a full screen again, press Screen (CTRL-F3), type **1** for Window, then enter **24**.

When you press Switch to move between the two documents, the triangles indicating tab settings point to the doc-

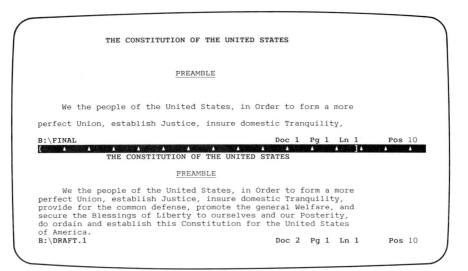

Figure 2-9. Tab setting indicators pointing to the document being edited

ument being edited as shown in Figure 2-9. To cut or copy text between the two documents, define the Block to be moved, press Move (select an option), press Switch, and press Move again (select an option) to retrieve the text. The only additional step is pressing Switch.

Search

When editing a document, you could spend a lot of time looking for a certain word, phrase, or code such as a margin change. →Search (F2) and ←Search (SHIFT-F2) can be used to search forward and backward, respectively, for both text and WordPerfect codes.

After pressing Search, enter the *string* of characters (note that uppercase finds only uppercase, while lowercase finds both upper and lowercase), then press Search again to start the search. If you press ENTER to start the search, it will display the Hard Return code [HRt]. Delete the code if it is not wanted, or it will try to find the search string and a hard return together.

You can search for a code by pressing the appropriate function key that usually inserts the code into regular text. For example, if you want to search for a bold code, press Bold (F6) to insert the Bold code. Typing [Bold] will find those exact characters—not the code.

When Search finds the search string, it places the cursor immediately after (to the right of) the word, phrase, or code. This is important to know because, when you search for a code and want to delete it, you can immediately press BACK-SPACE and confirm the deletion without first pressing Reveal Codes (ALT-F3).

Replace

This feature is like Search, except that you can replace the search string with something else. You can even use this feature to search without replacing it with anything, thus deleting all occurrences of the search string. This is extremely useful for removing all spacing changes, margin changes, and so on.

The following steps outline the search and replace procedure.

1. Press Replace (ALT-F2).

2. Type **Y** if you want to confirm each replacement or **N** for a global replacement.

3. Type the search string. Don't press ENTER unless you want to search for the [HRt] code.

4. Press Search (F2) to continue.

5. Type the replacement string. Skip this step if you want the search string to be deleted.

6. Press Search again to start the replacement. If you asked to confirm each replacement, the cursor will stop at each occurrence. Type **Y** or **N** to replace or not replace each occurrence.

Formatting

You can format a document at any time before, during, or after typing.

Format codes are inserted at the cursor's current location. When you insert a code into your text, WordPerfect uses the setting from that point forward until it finds another code telling it to change. For example, if you want double spacing from the beginning of the document, you would move the cursor to the beginning of the document and change the spacing. If you have a table that needs to be single-spaced, you would insert another spacing code for single spacing at the beginning of the table. If you want to return to double spacing after the table, insert a double-spacing code after the table.

When you want a certain format for the entire document, set the format at the beginning of the document. Go to the top of a page to change the format for that particular page.

There are three formatting menus in WordPerfect. Some options found on the menus display submenus, some ask for further information, and others make the change immediately.

The Line Format (SHIFT-F8) menu shown in Figure 2-10 controls the format from line to line. Options on this menu let you set tabs (regular, centered, right-aligned, and decimal-aligned), margins, and spacing. You can also control hyphenation and choose the alignment character from this menu. Tabs can be set by choosing either option 1 or 2. (In versions previous to 4.2, option 2 was used for setting extended tabs beyond position 160.)

The Page Format (ALT-F8) menu shown in Figure 2-11 gives you the choice of many page "extras" and is used to decide where a soft page break should occur. You can select page numbering, center a page from top to bottom, specify the top margin, set page length, and control headers and footers with this menu. You can also protect blocks of text from widows and orphans (lonely one-liners at the bottom or top of a page) with this menu.

```
1 2 Tabs; 3 Margins; 4 Spacing; 5 Hyphenation; 6 Align Char: 0
```

Figure 2-10. Line Format menu

```
Page Format

        1 - Page Number Position

        2 - New Page Number

        3 - Center Page Top to Bottom

        4 - Page Length

        5 - Top Margin

        6 - Headers or Footers

        7 - Page Number Column Positions

        8 - Suppress for Current page only

        9 - Conditional End of Page

        A - Widow/Orphan

Selection: 0
```

Figure 2-11. Page Format menu

The Print Format (CTRL-F8) menu shown in Figure 2-12 controls those features that are visible only at the printer. Pitch, font, lines per inch, right justification (text spaced evenly between the left and right margins, creating an even right margin), double underlining, and line numbering are some of the options on this menu. You can also use this menu to select a sheet feeder bin (if applicable) and insert a printer command in the text.

Detailed information for all of the options mentioned can be found in Chapter 4.

Checking the Spelling

WordPerfect's speller is extremely fast and efficient, so you should consider checking the spelling of your documents as a routine step in creating a document. The speller contains approximately 115,000 words, including medical and legal words.

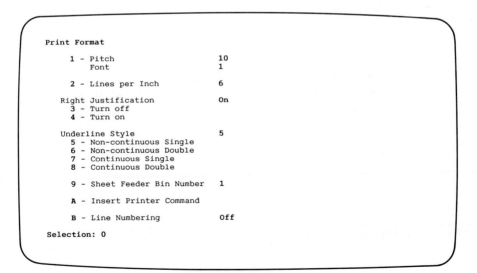

```
Print Format

     1 - Pitch                          10
         Font                           1

     2 - Lines per Inch                 6

   Right Justification                  On
     3 - Turn off
     4 - Turn on

   Underline Style                      5
     5 - Non-continuous Single
     6 - Non-continuous Double
     7 - Continuous Single
     8 - Continuous Double

     9 - Sheet Feeder Bin Number        1

     A - Insert Printer Command

     B - Line Numbering                 Off

 Selection: 0
```

Figure 2-12.   Print Format menu

If you have two disk drives, replace the data disk with the Speller diskette (usually in drive B). Press Spell (CTRL-F2) and the Speller menu will appear as shown in Figure 2-13. If you press Spell before inserting the Speller diskette, you will see the error message, "Main dictionary not found. Enter name:". Insert the Speller diskette in drive B and enter the full pathname B:LEX.WP. Do not replace the WordPerfect diskette with the Speller diskette.

If you have a hard disk, press Spell (CTRL-F2) and the Speller menu will appear as shown in Figure 2-13. If you see the error message telling you the dictionary file is not found, enter the full pathname where it can be found (for example, C:\DICT\LEX.WP). To avoid this error message in the future, follow the installation instructions found in Chapter 1 or see "Directories or Drives for Dictionary and Thesaurus files" in Chapter 3 for more information.

You will usually check the page or entire document. Other options listed are explained in detail under *Spell* in Chapter 4. Type **2** for Page or **3** for Document. The first word not found in the dictionary is highlighted and the menu shown in Figure 2-14 is displayed. Type the letter corresponding to the correct spelling and the misspelled word is replaced. If the correct spelling is not listed, type **1** to skip the word once, **2** to skip the word for the rest of the document, **3** to add the word to a supplementary dictionary, **4** to edit the word manually, **5** to look up the word using a word pattern, or **6** to display only phonetic possibilities.

The choices displayed are not always spelled correctly. The speller transposes characters, adds and deletes characters, and uses as much of a word pattern as possible to give you the choices. It also tries to find a phonetic match so that if you spell "schizophrenic" as "skitsofrenik," the correct spelling will be displayed.

When you type **5** to look up a word, you are asked for the word pattern. Type as many of the characters as you know, filling in the "blanks" with the wildcard characters (*, -, or ?). An asterisk (*) or hyphen (-) can be used in place of *any number* of characters and a question mark (?) can be used for

Section 1.   All legislative Powers herein granted shall be vested in a Congress of the United States, which shall consist of a Senate and House of Representatives.

Section 2.   The House of Representatives shall be composed of Members chosen every second Year be the People of the several States, and the Electors in each State shall have the Qualifications requisite for Electors of the most numerous Branch of the State Legislature.

No Person shall be a Representative who shall not have attained to the Age of twenty five Years, and been seven Years a Citizen of the United States, and who shall not, when elected, be an inhabitant of the State in which he shall be chosen.

Check: **1** Word; **2** Page; **3** Document; **4** Change Dictionary; **5** Look Up; **6** Count

Figure 2-13.   Speller menu

every thirty Thousand, but each State shall have at Least one Representative; and until such enumeration shall be made, the State of New Hampshire shall be entitled to chuse three, Massachusetts eight, Rhode-Island and Providence Plantations one, Connecticut five, New York six, New Jersey four, Pennsylvania eight, Delaware one, Maryland six, Virginia ten, North Carolina

==

A. chest	B. chewiest	C. chews
D. choice	E. choose	F. choosey
G. choosy	H. chose	I. coast
J. coos	K. cost	L. costa
M. coughs	N. cows	O. coyest
P. cozy	Q. cues	R. cuesta
S. cuss	T. cyst	U. kayos
V. kazoo	W. keys	X. kiowas

Not Found!   Select Word or Menu Option (0=Continue): 0
1 Skip Once; **2** Skip; **3** Add Word; **4** Edit; **5** Look Up; **6** Phonetic

Figure 2-14.   Menu displayed when a word is not found

a *single* character. (The hyphen is not documented in the WordPerfect manual.)

Follow the same basic procedure to use the thesaurus. Place the Thesaurus disk in drive B if you have two disk drives, press Thesaurus (ALT-F1), and follow the menu shown on the status line. If asked, the name of the thesaurus file is TH.WP. More detailed information is given under *Thesaurus* in Chapter 4.

Printing

WordPerfect allows you to print and edit at the same time. If you send several files to the printer, they are assigned a number and held in a print queue. The Printer Control menu found with Print (SHIFT-F7) allows you to control up to six printers and the print jobs held in the queue (see Figure 2-15). You can view the status of the job being printed, print a file, stop the printer, rush a print job, send the printer a "go" (for hand-fed paper), display print jobs, and cancel any or all jobs in the queue.

Option 1 on the Printer Control menu can be used to select the number of copies to be printed, the printer to be used, and the binding width. Type **2** to display the printers and fonts selected. Choose **3** to select a printer definition and fonts, port, and type of form (continuous, hand-fed, or sheet feeder). If you have not selected a printer definition, see Chapter 1.

There are three ways to print a document. One is to print directly from the screen without having to first save the document.

1. Press Print (SHIFT-F7).

2. Type **1** to print the full document or **2** to print the current page. The document is saved in a temporary print file so you can continue editing the same or another document.

The other two methods print documents already saved on the disk. You can print from the Printer Control menu or

```
 Printer Control
                                    C - Cancel Print Job(s)
 1 - Select Print Options           D - Display All Print Jobs
 2 - Display Printers and Fonts     G - "Go" (Resume Printing)
 3 - Select Printers                P - Print a Document
                                    R - Rush Print Job
 Selection: 0                       S - Stop Printing


 Current Job

 Job Number: 1                      Page Number:  1
 Job Status: Waiting for a "Go"     Current Copy: 1 of 1
 Message:    Place next sheet in printer--Press "G" to continue

 Job List

 Job  Document             Destination          Forms and Print Options
  1   (Screen)             Ptr  1               HandFed


 Additional jobs not shown: 0
```

Figure 2-15.   Printer Control menu

from List Files (F5). The advantage to using the Printer Control menu is that you can print selected pages of a document.

1. Press Print (SHIFT-F7).

2. Type **4** for Printer Control.

3. Type **P** to print a document.

4. Enter the name of the document.

5. Press ENTER to print all the pages of the document or enter the page numbers to be printed (such as **1-3,5-9,12**).

An option on the List Files menu also lets you send a file to the printer.

1. Press List Files (F5).

2. Press ENTER to view the displayed drive/directory or enter a different pathname.

3. Move the cursor to the file to be printed.

4. Type **4** to print the file.

If you are working on a document and want to print the latest draft of the document, you should print from the screen rather than from the disk unless you have just saved the document.

Filing

You can save a document at any time. Press Save (F10), then enter the filename (up to eight characters with an optional three-character extension). The file is automatically saved to the default drive/directory. If you want to save it to a different drive/directory, you should enter the full pathname. When using Save, the document is left on the screen.

If you want to save the document and clear the screen, press Exit (F7). Answer **Y** to save the document, enter the filename, and type **N** when asked if you want to exit WP.

When you make changes to a file and attempt to save it with the same filename used before, you are asked if you want to replace the former file. If you type N for no, you are given the opportunity to enter a new filename.

You might encounter an error message when trying to save a file. "File creation error" means that you have used illegal characters in a filename or you have exceeded the maximum number of files that can be saved to the root directory (the limit varies from computer to computer, but is usually 112). If you see "Disk full," replace the data disk with a disk which contains available space, or press List Files (F5) and delete unnecessary files.

The error message telling you that the "Drive door may be open" lets you close the door and retry or cancel and return to the document.

WordPerfect has a very complete method of managing your files. List Files (F5) can display all or selected files in each directory, change the default directory, and even create or delete directories. You can retrieve, delete, rename, print, look at, copy, or search through files.

After pressing List Files (F5), press ENTER to see a list of the files in the displayed (default) drive/directory, as shown in Figure 2-16. See *List Files* in Chapter 4, the alphabetical

```
11/25/87  09:46                  Directory C:\PERSONAL\*.*
Document Size:     0                               Free Disk Space:    9502

. <CURRENT>      <DIR>                   .. <PARENT>      <DIR>
ALTA    .MAC         8   04/26/86 23:18   ALTJ    .MAC        6   08/24/86 08:37
ALTK    .MAC        27   10/25/86 19:53   ALTL    .MAC       14   10/25/86 19:56
ALTZ    .MAC         4   10/25/86 23:08   APARTMNT.        4438   11/08/86 11:18
ARTICLE .         3734   01/01/80 03:02   BOOK    .         263   10/22/86 22:01
CLOSING .MAC        76   01/14/87 13:51   FORMAT  .MAC       35   01/14/87 13:50
HISTORY .1       33783   01/01/80 00:16   HISTORY .2      28953   10/19/84 01:29
HISTORY .3       51194   08/06/84 00:13   HISTORY .4      40244   08/07/84 00:41
HISTORY .5       20299   08/08/84 00:02   INVOICE .        2189   09/29/86 19:03
LESSON  .1        7185   10/01/86 23:28   LIST    .        5780   10/25/86 14:23
LIST    .3         322   01/14/87 13:52   NAVY    .       20033   04/24/86 16:41
NOTES   .           84   10/01/86 15:59   PICTURES.       14576   10/25/86 20:42
PROPOSAL.         7702   10/09/86 13:21   SORTED  .LST     5648   11/08/86 08:43
XMAS    .85       2182   12/26/85 23:31


 1 Retrieve; 2 Delete; 3 Rename; 4 Print; 5 Text In;
 6 Look; 7 Change Directory; 8 Copy; 9 Word Search; 0 Exit: 6
```

Figure 2-16.   List Files menu

reference, for information about looking into a different drive/directory.

The top of the menu shows the current date, time, and directory. If you have a document in memory, the document size (in bytes) is displayed as well as the amount of disk space available.

Any subdirectories and the parent directory are listed first. You can move the cursor to any of these directories, press ENTER to see the directory's pathname, then ENTER again to see the list of files in that directory. You can wander through directories without ever leaving List Files.

List Files has a Name Search feature so that if you know the name of a file, you can begin typing the name and the cursor will move in that direction. If you type M, the cursor moves to the files beginning with M. Continue typing the characters in the name to narrow the search to a specific file. Press ENTER, SPACEBAR, or an arrow key to leave Name Search and return to the normal List Files options. You can also use any of the cursor keys to move by file, screen, or to the beginning or end of the list.

Before you type 1 to retrieve a file, check the document size at the top of the screen to make sure there is not a document in memory. A common mistake that new users make is to go into List Files, highlight the file they were working on, and retrieve it again, not realizing that the document was already in memory. You might also have been working on a document, saved it but forgotten to clear the screen, and gone to List Files and retrieved another. If you do this, you can end up with several copies of the same document on the screen, or you could combine different documents. This feature is not meant to sabotage you, but is useful when you *want* to retrieve one document into another. Press Exit (F7) to leave List Files without retrieving a file.

When you type 2 to delete a file or directory, you are asked to confirm the deletion. A directory must be empty before you can delete it. To rename a document, type **3** and enter a new filename. Option 4 sends the file to the printer. If you type 5 to retrieve a text file, all codes that might "hang" WordPerfect are stripped from the file.

Option 6 lets you look at the contents of a file without retrieving it. While looking at the file, you can use ↓ or PGDN to move the cursor through the text. Any other key will return you to the list of files. Option 6 is the default answer, so pressing ENTER also lets you look at the highlighted file.

Type **7** to change the default directory. If you enter the name of a nonexistent directory, you are asked if you want to create a new directory. Option 8 lets you copy a file to another drive/directory.

You can search through all or selected files for a word or phrase by typing 9 and entering the string of characters. See *Word Search* in Chapter 4 for complete options.

You can mark files with an asterisk (type * while a file is highlighted), then delete, print, copy, or search through all marked files.

Press Exit (F7) or Cancel (F1) to leave the List Files menu.

Exiting WordPerfect

You should always use Exit (F7) when you want to leave WordPerfect. If you turn your computer off without exiting, you will see error messages the next time you try to enter WordPerfect, indicating the presence of overflow or backup files that were left open.

Lost clusters (a term used by DOS) can also eat up valuable disk space. To correct this problem, insert the DOS diskette into drive B and type **CHKDSK/F A:** at the B> DOS prompt. Answer **N** if asked if you want the lost clusters converted to files. If you are using a hard disk, enter **CHKDSK/F** at the DOS prompt.

When you press Exit (F7), you are always asked if you want to save the document whether you just saved it or not. If you didn't make changes to the file since the last time you saved it, a message is displayed on the right side of the status line indicating that the "text was not modified."

Save (F10) leaves the document on the screen, while Exit lets you clear the screen for another document or exit Word-Perfect. After you choose whether the file is to be saved, you are asked the question "Exit WP? (Y/N) N." Type **Y** to exit WordPerfect. Any other key will clear the screen so you can begin working on another document.

If you have two documents in memory and attempt to exit WordPerfect, you are placed in the second document. Repeat the exit procedure.

If there are print jobs remaining in the print queue, you are asked if you want to cancel them. If you answer N, you will remain in WordPerfect and can exit after they are printed.

Common Questions

What if I deleted text by mistake?

Restore deleted text by pressing Cancel (F1), then **1** to restore. If you made other deletions in the meantime, press **2** to see previous deletions until you find what you're looking for. Remember that you can only restore the last three deletions.

How do I find out how to do a footnote?

The basic steps for each feature can be found in the Help screens. Press Help (F3), then the function key that you have questions about. If you don't know which function key invokes that feature, press the first letter of the feature after pressing Help, and all features beginning with that letter are listed.

   In this case, press Help (F3), type F for footnote, note that the feature is found on Footnote (CTRL-F7), and press that key to read about using footnotes.

How do I go to page 25 without pressing PgDn 25 times?

You can go to any page by pressing Go To (CTRL-HOME) and entering the number of the page.

How do I know where my files are being saved?

Press List Files (F5) and the default drive/directory is displayed. Press ENTER to look at the files or Cancel (F1) to return to the document.

What do I do when I see an error message on the screen?

Check *Error Messages* in Chapter 4, "Commands and Features," or look under the specific error message for solutions.

How can I tell where I am in the document?

The status line in the lower right corner of the screen tells you the page, line, and position of the cursor.

Where is the "main menu"?

There is not a main menu in WordPerfect. Instead, you can immediately begin creating documents, or use Retrieve (SHIFT-F10) to retrieve a document from disk.

The List Files menu (press List Files (F5) and ENTER) is similar to the main menus of other programs.

Where do I find out what all these codes in Reveal Codes mean?

Most codes are self-explanatory. However, if you don't understand a particular code, check the *Codes* section in Chapter 4 for a description.

How do I delete codes?

The easiest way is to press Reveal Codes (ALT-F3), move the cursor to the code, and press BACKSPACE or DEL.

When do I press ENTER?

You should press ENTER at the end of a paragraph or single line. Let WordPerfect wrap multiple lines for you.

If you see an instruction that says, "Enter the page number," you should type the page number, then press ENTER.

Do I have to repaginate each time I make changes to a document to make sure the right number of lines are on each page?

No. WordPerfect breaks lines and pages automatically for you.

I prefer margins of 12 and 90. How do I change margins permanently so that I don't have to set them for every document?

See "Customizing WordPerfect" in Chapter 3 and *Setup Menu* in Chapter 4 for information on changing default settings.

I'm not sure which key to use to get out of a WordPerfect menu. Should I use Cancel (F1), Exit (F7), ENTER, or the SPACEBAR?

Use the key most natural for you. If you decide to use ENTER, keep in mind that in the List Files menu, ENTER lets you look at a file. Use one of the other options for exiting from the List Files menu.

I pressed Exit (F7) and typed N when asked if I wanted to save the document. However, it is still on my screen and I've decided to save it. How do I get rid of the question "Exit WP?" without losing the document?

Press Cancel (F1). You can then follow the steps for saving the document.

I don't see right justification on the screen, but when I enter the Print Format menu, it says it's "on." How can I tell when it is on or off?

WordPerfect comes with right justification on, but you cannot see it on the screen. If it displayed right justification on the normal editing screen, you would lose some of the famous WordPerfect speed.

You can press Print Format (CTRL-F8) anytime to confirm whether it is on or off. The Preview feature will display right justification on the screen, but no editing is allowed on the preview screen.

How large can my documents be?

A document is limited by the amount of disk space available. Smaller files (less than 75 pages) are easier to work with because the larger a document, the longer it takes to scroll through it.

How do I insert text into a paragraph?

Move your cursor to the place where the text is to be inserted and begin typing. You do not have to press the INS key first. Text is automatically reformatted as you insert the text.

I made changes to a document and have now decided I want to go back to the original. Can I go back?

Yes. When you retrieve a document, you are only retrieving a copy. To go back to the original, clear the screen by pressing Exit (F7) and answer **N** to the question "Save Document?" (or type **Y** and save it under a different filename) and **N** to "Exit WP?" You can then retrieve another copy of the original document.

There are so many options to choose from. For instance, you can move and retrieve text several different ways. Which is the best way?

There is no best way. You should use the method easiest for you. Some ways require fewer keystrokes, while others (even though they have the same number of keystrokes) may be easier for you to remember.

I want to take out all margin changes in my document. What is the easiest way?

Rather than searching for each margin change and manually deleting it, use the Replace feature. You can search for a margin change and replace it with nothing, thus deleting it.

Can I keep working while printing?

Yes. You can work on the same or a different document. If you send the document on the screen to the printer, it makes a temporary copy of the document and prints that copy. You can continue making changes, but the changes not included in the temporary copy are not printed.

I keep getting multiple copies of a document on the screen. What is happening and why?

The problem usually arises when you have a document on your screen and go into List Files and retrieve the same or another document. You might also have used Save (F10) and assumed that it would also clear the screen. Save saves the document, but remains on the screen for future editing. Use Exit (F7) to save the document and clear the screen.

What if my computer locks up and I can't exit from WordPerfect? In fact, none of the keys seem to work. Do I lose my work on the screen?

Although it is rare, the computer may lock up because it encounters something it doesn't understand. When this happens, you cannot exit properly from WordPerfect. You have to turn the computer off and back on (or reboot by pressing CTRL-ALT-DEL). The document on your screen is lost.

To avoid losing very much work, use Save (F10) often, or set a timed backup. The document on the screen is saved periodically to a backup file and can then be retrieved if such a disaster occurs. See *Backing Up Files* in Chapter 4.

When is it safe to turn off the computer?

After you press Exit (F7) and answer the "Save Document?" question, type **Y** to "Exit WP?" You should then see the DOS prompt (B> or C:\ >LEARNING are examples). You can then turn off the computer.

If you are running WordPerfect Library, you are returned to the Shell menu. If there are no programs in memory (indicated by an asterisk by the program name), you can turn off the computer. If there are programs in memory, press Exit (F7) again and answer the questions that follow.

The Next Step

In this chapter, you will learn about using macros. A macro is not a feature by itself, but is used to remember text and keystrokes that invoke other features. Macros can be used in almost any application and are referred to throughout this book.

Now that you have become familiar with some of the default settings used by WordPerfect, you will learn how to change them to best fit your needs. You will also learn how to customize the colors for your color monitor if you have one. This chapter also discusses various options for starting WordPerfect.

Using Macros

This book lets you know how you can use macros to increase your productivity. A macro can do common tasks automatically for you in a fraction of the time it would take you to do them. Because macros are such a powerful part of WordPerfect, you should become familiar with them right away.

A macro is like a tape recorder. You turn it on, press the keys to be recorded, then turn it off. You can then play back the recorded keystrokes at any time. The only difference in the process is that you give a macro a name.

Applications

In Appendix C, you will find a library of macros that will be useful in itself, and will give you ideas for creating some macros of your own. The *Macros* entry in Chapter 4, "Commands and Features," can also give you ideas for more applications.

If you find yourself typing the same series of commands again and again, you should consider putting the keystrokes in a macro. It takes only a few more steps to start the macro definition, name the macro, then end it after you enter the keystrokes to be recorded.

You can record often-typed text as well as WordPerfect commands in a macro. In fact, anything you can do in WordPerfect can be included in a macro. Macros can simplify your work by inserting text automatically, editing documents, or setting up the format for a document more quickly. As you become more familiar with WordPerfect, you will begin to see the possibilities for using macros.

Defining Macros

The steps for defining a macro are as follows.

1. Press Macro Def (CTRL-F10) to start the macro definition. "Define Macro:" appears in the lower left corner of the screen.

2. Enter the macro name at the prompt (as shown below). See "Naming Macros" for options.

```
Define Macro: format
```

3. While "Macro Def" is flashing in the lower left corner of the screen, enter the keystrokes to be recorded.

4. Press Macro Def (CTRL-F10) again to end the macro definition.

After you end the macro definition, the macro is saved to disk and the extension .MAC is added automatically to the name of the file. This extension lets you differentiate between macros and other files (see Figure 3-1).

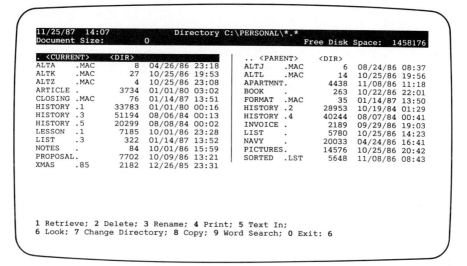

Figure 3-1.   List Files menu showing .MAC (macro) files

Naming Macros

There are three ways to name a macro:

ALT-key combination
Name using two to eight characters
Single-character name

The first two methods save the macro in a file on disk. The third method saves the macro in memory and is eliminated when you turn off the computer.

In Chapter 1, you learned that the ALT key can be used in conjunction with a key from A through Z to name macros. You should use this method if you want to recall the macro quickly (you only need to press the ALT-key combination again to recall the macro). An obvious disadvantage is that you can name only 26 macros with this method. Another disadvantage is that you might accidentally press the ALT key instead of the SHIFT key and invoke a macro rather than capitalize a letter.

A macro named with an ALT-key combination is saved to disk with a filename such as ALTA.MAC or ALTB.MAC. If you press an ALT-A-Z-key combination to name a macro, the name of the macro is not shown on the status line; instead, "Macro Def" will flash in the lower left corner of the screen, indicating that the macro has been named and you can start defining your macro.

Again, to invoke this type of macro, just press the ALT-key combination. You need to use Macro (ALT-F10) to start the other two types of macros.

The second method of naming macros uses two to eight characters and is also saved to disk using the .MAC extension. When you want to invoke this type of macro, press Macro (ALT-F10), then enter the name of the macro without the .MAC extension. Although it is not as fast or easy to invoke this type of macro as it is an ALT-key macro, the macro name can be more descriptive, such as FORMAT (sets up the standard format for letters), CLOSING (inserts the proper closing at the end of a letter, then sends it to the printer), or NASA (types "National Aeronautics and Space Administration" for you).

The third method is to name a macro with a single character, the ENTER key, or even the SPACEBAR. Because this type of macro is stored in memory, not on disk, it will be deleted when the computer is turned off. This type of macro could be used when you need a task repeated during a single editing session. These temporary macros will not only save disk space, but will also save time when you are cleaning up a disk by deleting unnecessary files.

To invoke this type of macro, press Macro (ALT-F10) and enter the single character or ENTER if you named the macro using the ENTER key.

A macro is automatically saved to the default drive unless another is specified when entering the macro name (\LET-TERS \FORMAT or \LETTERS \ALTF, for example). Note that you need to type out the word ALT and the character to be used if you want to use another directory for an ALT-key macro.

If you attempt to save a second macro with the same name as one that already exists on the disk (ALT-key name or two-through eight-character name), you are asked if you want to replace the previous macro with the new one, as shown below.

```
Replace FORMAT.MAC? (Y/N) N
```

Type **Y** to replace the macro, or **N** to use a different name. If you type N, you are prompted to enter a new name. If you use a single character which has already been used to name a macro, the previously defined macro is automatically replaced with the new macro.

Invoking Macros

As we have just seen, there are three ways of naming macros but only two ways to invoke them.

To invoke an ALT-key macro, hold down ALT and press the character used to name the macro. For instance, if you used ALT-G to name the macro, press ALT-G to invoke it.

If you used a single character or two through eight characters to name a macro, press Macro (ALT-F10) and enter the name of the macro. Although not as convenient, you can use this method to invoke an ALT-key macro by pressing Macro and typing the word ALT and the character used, as in ALTG.

If the macro is not found on the default drive or directory, the drive/directory where the WP.EXE file is found is then searched. Once a macro is recalled from the disk, it is kept in memory (until you turn the computer off) for faster execution the next time you need it. Of course, the number of macros you can keep in memory depends on how much RAM is available.

You can pause macros for input, make macros visible,

chain macros, and create conditional macros. See *Macros* in Chapter 4, "Commands and Features," for more detailed information.

Customizing WordPerfect

WordPerfect comes with certain default settings. The margins, tabs, and even the color on color monitors has been preset for you. While these are the most commonly used settings, they might not be suited to your needs.

When WordPerfect Corporation receives an overwhelming request for a feature, such as displaying the name of the current file on the screen, the program designer chooses the default setting when incorporating the feature. There are options on the Setup menu that let you turn off or change such features if you prefer not to have them.

Some users who have used other word processors that display a ruler line on the screen, have "typeover" rather than "insert" as the default, or automatically back up documents every few minutes may want these options included in WordPerfect. The Setup menu lets you include such features as part of the default settings for your copy of WordPerfect.

WordPerfect Setup

Instead of typing WP to enter WordPerfect, you can type WP/S to enter the Setup menu. This menu, shown in Figure 3-2, lets you change the initial settings; specify different directories for the dictionary and thesaurus files; set the screen size (for those who have a larger or smaller screen); decide whether or not the computer will beep at the end of a search, during hyphenation, or when there is an error; and create backup files for your documents.

After making the desired changes, press **0** to enter WordPerfect. The changes are saved in the WP.EXE file and become part of the WordPerfect program. If you decide you do not want

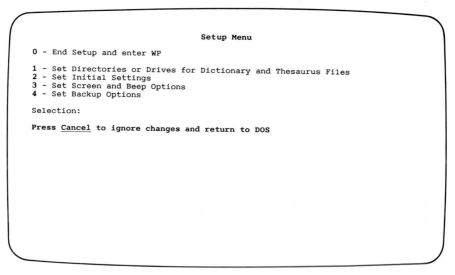

```
                           Setup Menu
0 - End Setup and enter WP

1 - Set Directories or Drives for Dictionary and Thesaurus Files
2 - Set Initial Settings
3 - Set Screen and Beep Options
4 - Set Backup Options

Selection:

Press Cancel to ignore changes and return to DOS
```

Figure 3-2.   Setup menu

to keep the changes, press Cancel (F1) to cancel the changes and return to DOS.

If you want to override the /S settings on a temporary basis, start WordPerfect by entering WP/X. If you want to return to the original defaults set by WordPerfect Corporation permanently, you can enter WP/X/S once rather than returning to the Setup menu and resetting each changed item.

Directories or Drives for Dictionary and Thesaurus Files

If you have a hard disk, you would usually copy all the WordPerfect diskettes, including the Speller and Thesaurus diskettes, into one directory. WordPerfect assumes you are using a directory called WP, but any name can be used. If you copied both diskettes into the same directory as the WordPerfect program file, WP.EXE, you will not have to change this option.

If you are using a system with two floppy disk drives, WordPerfect will check the default drive (usually drive B), but not the default directory, for the spelling dictionary (LEX.WP), supplemental dictionary ({WP}LEX.SUP), and thesaurus (TH.WP) files. If you are using a hard disk, the directory where the WordPerfect files are kept is searched. If they are not found in the default drive or in the WordPerfect directory, you will see a message asking you to enter the full pathname where they can be found.

If you find it necessary to keep the dictionary and thesaurus files in a directory other than where you keep the WordPerfect program files, you should choose option 1 on the Setup menu. There is no real advantage in keeping the dictionary and thesaurus files in a different directory unless you are using several different dictionaries. The following questions appear on the screen one at a time:

```
Where do you plan to keep the dictionary (LEX.WP)?
Enter full pathname: C:\LEX.WP
Where do you plan to keep the supplementary dictionary file?
Enter full pathname: C:\{WP}LEX.SUP
Where do you plan to keep the thesaurus (TH.WP)?
Enter full pathname: C:\TH.WP
```

Enter the full pathname for each question. If you have the files on the hard disk in a directory called SPELL, you would enter C:\SPELL\LEX.WP, C:\SPELL\{WP}LEX.SUP, and C:\SPELL\TH.WP. Remember that the full pathname includes the name of the file.

Initial Settings

WordPerfect offers great flexibility. As you learned in Chapter 2, you can change the format settings as many times in a document as you want. WordPerfect also lets you customize the settings so that whatever you use most often can be the default. For instance, you might want margins set at 12 and 90, printing in 12 pitch, and right justification turned off for most of your documents.

Be careful about changing default settings if you are sharing documents with someone else, if you plan to print your document using someone else's computer and printer, or if more than one person will be using your computer. In cases such as these, you might want to store the common format settings in a macro or file rather than change the WordPerfect defaults. Otherwise, the changes may confuse other users and documents created with another copy of WordPerfect may be formatted incorrectly when they are retrieved.

If you want to change the initial settings, type **2** at the Setup menu. The Change Initial Settings screen, shown in Figure 3-3, is displayed. Notice that the features in WordPerfect that can be changed are listed on the right and the keys to press are listed on the left. You will use the same function keys in this menu that you would while in WordPerfect to change a setting. For instance, if you want to change the left and right margins, you would press Line Format (SHIFT-F8) just as you would if you were changing the margins while in WordPerfect.

You can also use this menu to customize such things as the date format, paragraph numbering styles, footnote options, printer number, and binding width.

The changes you make are considered permanent until you

```
 _____
/                                                              \
|  Change Initial Settings                                     |
|                                                              |
|  Press any of the keys listed below to change initial settings |
|                                                              |
|  Key                 Initial Settings                        |
|                                                              |
|  Format              Tabs, Margins, Spacing, Hyphenation, Align Character |
|  Page Format         Page # Pos, Page Length, Top Margin, Page # Col Pos, W/O |
|  Print Format        Pitch, Font, Lines/Inch, Right Just, Underlining, SF Bin # |
|  Print               Printer, Copies, Binding Width          |
|  Date                Date Format                             |
|  Insert/Typeover     Insert/Typeover Mode                    |
|  Mark Text           Paragraph Number Definition, Table of Authorities Definition |
|  Footnote            Footnote/Endnote Options                |
|  Escape              Set N                                    |
|  Screen              Set Auto-rewrite                         |
|  Text In/Out         Set Insert Document Summary on Save/Exit |
|                                                              |
|  Selection:                                                  |
|                                                              |
|  Press Enter to return to the Setup Menu                     |
|                                                              |
_____/
```

Figure 3-3.   Change Initial Settings screen

enter the Setup menu and change them again or use the WP/X option.

Unlike most menus in WordPerfect, you cannot leave this menu with the Cancel or Exit keys. Press ENTER when you are finished.

Screen and Beep Options

When you choose option 3 on the Setup menu, the following questions are displayed.

```
Set Screen Options

  Number of rows: 25
  Number of columns: 80
  Hard return displayed as ascii value: 32
  Display filename on status line? (Y/N) Y

Set Beep Options

  Beep when search fails? (Y/N) N
  Beep on error? (Y/N) N
  Beep on hyphenation? (Y/N) Y
```

If your system can display more than the standard 80 columns and 25 rows, WordPerfect will support that capability. Some can show 132 columns across the screen and a legal-sized page of text.

The first two questions ask for the number of rows and columns supported by your system. Enter the new settings or press ENTER to use the defaults. You should enter only the same number of rows and columns that are supported by your system, or the text will not be displayed correctly.

The next option is "Hard return displayed as ASCII value: 32." Some WordPerfect users prefer to see a character displayed on the screen when they press the ENTER key. The default number "32" means that a space is used rather than a character. If you want to change this number, you might enter 17 for ◄, 27 for ←, 174 for <<, or press ENTER to use the default of 32. See Appendix A for a complete chart of ASCII values.

The last screen option asks if you want the filename displayed on the status line. The default is "yes." Type **N** if you do not want it displayed, or press ENTER to use the default.

WordPerfect displays messages at the end of a search, when there is an error, or when a word is displayed for hyphenation. If you look more at a hard copy rather than at the screen while typing, you can have WordPerfect beep to call your attention to the messages being displayed. You can also turn off the beep if you find it annoying. Type **Y** or **N** for each of the three options or press ENTER to accept the defaults.

After you answer the last question, you are returned to the Setup menu. If you want to leave this Screen and Beep menu before reaching the last question, press Exit (F7).

Backup Options

If nothing else, you should bring up the Setup menu and choose the option to back up your work. Granted, you can save a document to disk every few minutes while in WordPerfect, but if you have ever lost even 15 minutes of work, you will know how valuable it can be to have the backup feature set.

Type **4** at the Setup menu to Set Backup Options and you will see the Set Timed Backup screen, shown in Figure 3-4. There are two backup options available: a timed backup and an original backup. You do not have to choose between them; both can be used.

The Timed Backup will save the document on your screen to a *temporary* file on disk ({WP}BACK.1 for Document 1 and {WP}BACK.2 for Document 2). When you clear the screen and begin working on a new document or exit WordPerfect properly using the Exit key, the temporary file is cleared. If you want the document to be saved *permanently*, you need to save it to disk using the Save or Exit key.

There is no default time between backups. You should enter a number that is equal to the number of minutes of work you are willing to lose (such as 15 or 20 minutes). You are then asked where you want the timed backup files to be stored. Enter the drive and directory usually used as the default (for example, C: \LETTERS). If you regularly use more than one

```
Set Timed Backup

To safeguard against losing large amounts of text in the event of a power or
machine failure, WordPerfect can automatically back up the document on your
screen at a chosen time interval and to a chosen drive/directory (see Setup
in the WordPerfect Installation pamphlet).  REMEMBER--THIS IS ONLY IN CASE OF
POWER OR MACHINE FAILURE.  WORDPERFECT DELETES THE TIMED BACKUP FILES WHEN YOU
EXIT NORMALLY FROM WORDPERFECT.  If you want the document saved as a file you
need to say 'yes' when you exit WordPerfect normally.

Number of minutes between each backup: 15
Where should timed backup files be stored?
Enter full pathname: C:\WP

Set Original Backup

WordPerfect can rename the last copy of a document when a new version of the
document is saved.  The old copy has the same file name with an extension of
".BK!".  Take note that the files named "letter.1" and "letter.2" have the
same original backup file name of "letter.bk!".  In this case the latest
file saved will be backed up.

Back up the original document? (Y/N) N
```

Figure 3-4.   Set Timed Backup screen

directory, it might be best to keep the backup files in the same directory containing the WordPerfect program files (for example, C: \WP). If you do not enter a pathname, the temporary files are automatically saved in the same drive/directory where the WordPerfect program files are located.

When you reenter WordPerfect, "* Please Wait *" appears on the screen each time the document is backed up. You do not have to stop typing when this happens, but a few characters may be dropped, depending on how large the document is (the larger it is, the more time it takes to save), how large the keyboard buffer is (the number of characters that can be held), and how fast you type.

If the machine hangs and you have to reboot, or if there is a power failure, you can retrieve the backup files. Again, the names of these files are {WP}BACK.1 and {WP}BACK.2.

The Original Backup works as WordStar's backup does. Each time you save a document after the first time, you are asked if you want to replace the former file with that name. If you answer "yes," the new file is saved and the old file is deleted. If you type **Y** in answer to the Backup Screen question,

"Backup the original document?," the old file is not deleted, but is renamed using the extension .BK!

When you use this backup option, you will always have the previous copy to fall back on if you ruin the original. A disadvantage to using this backup option is that you will have many documents with the extension .BK! taking up space on your disk. Also, if you have more than one file using a similar name (the same name except for the extension) such as CONTRACT.12, CONTRACT.13, and CONTRACT.14, the same backup file (CONTRACT.BK!) will be used for those files, but only the last file saved will be backed up.

Once you enter the Backup menu, you can leave it only by pressing ENTER, EXIT, or CANCEL to move through the options.

Remember to press **0** to enter WordPerfect after making changes in the Setup menu. If you press Cancel (F1), the changes are forgotten. You can reenter the Setup menu and make changes whenever you feel it is necessary.

Colors

Those who have color monitors might see WordPerfect with a black or blue background and white letters. A different or more intense color is used for boldface and underlined text. Some single-color graphics monitors, such as those used by Compaq, might not display boldface and underlined text correctly when you first bring up WordPerfect. If boldface or underlined text is so light that you can barely see it, or if you just want to experiment with different colors, you should set the color options.

You can choose different colors for each of the two screens (documents) in WordPerfect.

1. Start WordPerfect.

2. Press Screen (CTRL-F3).

3. Type **4** for Colors. If you have a monochrome monitor, you will see the message, "Not a color monitor."

4. Type **1** if you have a color monitor or **2** if you have a single-color monitor.

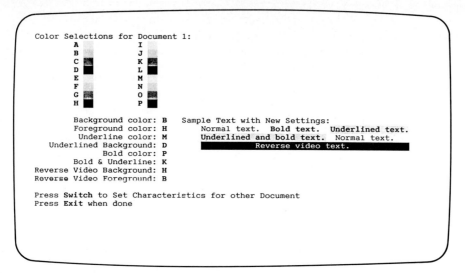

Figure 3-5.   Color Selection screen

5. Type **Y** for fast text display. If you see flickering or "snow" on your screen after answering this question, press Cancel (F1), reenter the color menu, and type **N**.

6. If you chose 1 for color monitor, you will see the screen shown in Figure 3-5. If you chose 2 for single-color monitor, you are asked to type 1 if you want underlined text displayed in reverse video or 2 if you want to use underlining. Some single-color monitors, such as the AT&T, can display the underline. Others, such as Compaq, will have to use reverse video unless you have special DOS software or other hardware. After making this selection, skip to step 8.

7. The menu displayed for color monitors labels the color choices with letters A through P. Below the color choices you see questions asking which color you want to use for the background, foreground, underlined text, boldface text, and text that is both underlined and boldface. A sample of the current selections is found to the right of the questions. As you make changes in the menu, the changes are reflected in this sample.

Type a letter from A through P to indicate which color is to be used after each question. Continue to make changes until you are satisfied with the sample.

8. If you want to change the screen colors for Document 2, press Switch (SHIFT-F3) and repeat the steps.

9. Press Exit (F7) when finished.

See *Colors* in Chapter 4, "Commands and Features," for more detailed information.

Special Characters

As mentioned in Chapter 1, you can use the CTRL and ALT keys to map special characters to the keyboard. The following characters are only a sample of those not regularly found on a computer keyboard that are used quite frequently.

$$\S \quad \P$$

$$\cent \quad \pounds \quad \yen$$

$$\tfrac{1}{4} \quad \tfrac{1}{2} \quad \div$$

$$\pi \quad \degree \quad \sqrt{}$$

$$\alpha \quad \beta \quad \Sigma$$

$$\iquest \quad \iexcl$$

Other characters used in foreign languages, such as ç, î, ö, ñ, è, and á, are also available. However, few uppercase characters are provided with accents.

Graphics characters such as

$$\| \quad + \quad ╓ \quad ▓ \quad \|$$

can be used to simulate a graph or create illustrations within text. Before you map a graphics character, you might want to experiment with WordPerfect's Line Draw feature (see *Line Draw* in Chapter 4, "Commands and Features"). It uses the arrow keys rather than mapped keys to draw lines, boxes, and other illustrations, using any of the ASCII characters.

Each character found in the computer's ROM (*read only memory*) is assigned a number. This number, called the decimal value, is referred to at various places in the WordPerfect program and this book. See Appendix B for a list of characters and their decimal values.

With most programs, including WordPerfect, you can hold down the ALT key and type the decimal value on the numeric keypad to display a character. For instance, 20 is the decimal value for the paragraph symbol ¶, so you could type 20 on the numeric keypad while holding down the ALT key to display the ¶ character. The disadvantage to using this method is that you have to remember the decimal value for the characters each time you need them. With WordPerfect, you can display these characters by mapping them to a CTRL- or ALT-key combination that might be easier for you to remember (such as CTRL-S for § ¶ or ALT-Q for ¿.

To map special characters, use the following procedure as a guide.

1. Press Screen (CTRL-F3).

2. Type **3** for CTRL or ALT key. The menu in Figure 3-6 is displayed. The characters you see at the bottom of the menu are what you get. If you have a different ROM in your computer, you may have more, less, or different characters displayed. Numbers 32 through 126 do not have characters displayed because these characters are already found on the keyboard (such as A through Z and 0 through 9). If you want other characters that are not found on this table (such as the Portuguese characters õ and ã), you can use the Overstrike feature to create them by overstriking an a or o with the tilde.

Your printer might have the ability to print other characters not found on this table. See Chapter 7 for more information on printing these types of characters.

3. Press the CTRL- or ALT-key combination that you want to map.

4. Find the character and the corresponding decimal value in the table.

```
Key     Value     Key     Value     Key     Value     Key     Value
Alt-A    0        Alt-N    0        Ctrl-A   0        Ctrl-N   0
Alt-B    0        Alt-O    0        Ctrl-B   0        Ctrl-O   0
Alt-C    0        Alt-P    0        Ctrl-C   0        Ctrl-P   0
Alt-D    0        Alt-Q    0        Ctrl-D   0        Ctrl-Q   0
Alt-E    0        Alt-R    0        Ctrl-E   0        Ctrl-R   0
Alt-F    0        Alt-S    0        Ctrl-F   0        Ctrl-S   0
Alt-G    0        Alt-T    0        Ctrl-G   0        Ctrl-T   0
Alt-H    0        Alt-U    0        Ctrl-H   0        Ctrl-U   0
Alt-I    0        Alt-V    0        Ctrl-I   0        Ctrl-V   0
Alt-J    0        Alt-W    0        Ctrl-J   0        Ctrl-W   0
Alt-K    0        Alt-X    0        Ctrl-K   0        Ctrl-X   0
Alt-L    0        Alt-Y    0        Ctrl-L   0        Ctrl-Y   0
Alt-M    0        Alt-Z    0        Ctrl-M   0        Ctrl-Z   0

        0123456789112345678921234567893123456789412345678 9
  0 -   ☺☻♥♦♣♠•◘○◙♂♀♪♫☼►◄↕‼¶§▬↨↑↓→←∟↔▲▼
100 -                            ÇüéâäàåçêëèïîìÄÅÉæÆôöò
150 -   ûùÿÖÜ¢£¥₧ƒáíóúñÑªº¿⌐¬½¼¡«»░▒▓│┤╡╢╖╕╣║╗╝╜╛┐└┴┬├─┼╞╟
200 -   ╚╔╩╦╠═╬╧╨╤╥╙╘╒╓╫╪┘┌█▄▌▐▀αßΓπΣσµτΦΘΩδ∞φε∩≡±≥≤⌠⌡÷≈°·
250 -   ·√ⁿ²■

Press key to be defined (Press Exit to return):
```

Figure 3-6.   Special Characters screen

5. Enter the decimal value.

6. Continue with steps 3-5 until all desired characters are mapped. Press Exit (F7) when finished. You can change the mapped characters any time you find it necessary.

Remember that you can use ALT-key combinations to name macros. Although it is best to avoid using the same ALT-key combination for both purposes, it can be done. The mapped character is not affected, but if there is a macro named with the same ALT-key combination, you must press Macro (ALT-F10), before you press the ALT-key combination to invoke the macro. When you see the special character after "Macro:;" press ENTER.

Options for Starting WordPerfect

The basic way to start WordPerfect is to type WP. There are other ways of starting the program; some of which are optional, but some may be necessary for your system.

As already mentioned in this chapter, you can type WP/S

to display the Setup menu to make changes before entering WordPerfect.

Some of the options that may be necessary for WordPerfect to run properly on your system are listed below.

/I (Install)   If you install WordPerfect on your system with a copy rather than the original, or if you started WordPerfect from drive A before copying it to your hard disk, it might not work properly. When it looks for WordPerfect overlay files, it may look to the wrong drive and display the message, "Insert WordPerfect disk and press any key to continue." If this happens, you need to enter WordPerfect with the option only once and the problem will be corrected.

/NF (Non-Flash)   At one time, there were two WordPerfect program disks sent with each package, a flash and a non-flash version. The difference between the two is that the flash version rewrites the screen much more quickly than the non-flash version. WordPerfect now comes with just one program disk to avoid confusion, but the option is still necessary at times. If you press Reveal Codes (ALT-F3) and the text on your screen disappears (or if text appears only when Reveal Codes is pressed), or if you are using Windows or another windowing program (excluding TopView), you should use the /NF option each time you enter WordPerfect.

/NS (Non-Sync)   If you have a Hyperion computer, you will need to use this option every time you start WordPerfect or it will hang and you will need to reboot. You can also use this option with color monitors to make them display the text faster, but it may cause "snow" on the screen.

Some options that are not necessary, but which can be quite useful, are the following:

/B-*number* (Backup)	You can use either this option or the Setup menu (WP/S) to create a timed backup. The number you enter after /B- is the number of minutes between each backup. If you plan to back up your files, you will most likely want to make the option permanent with the Setup menu. If you have chosen the timed backup option in the Setup menu and want to temporarily change the number of minutes between each backup, the /B-*number* option will override the permanent setting for the current editing session.
Filename (Retrieve a File)	If you want to start WordPerfect and have a file retrieved immediately, type WP, a space, file retrieved immediately, type WP, a space, then the name of the file. If the file is not on the default drive, you should enter the full pathname.
/M-*macroname* (Invoke a Macro)	You can have a macro invoked immediately after WordPerfect is started by typing WP/M- and the name of the macro.
/R (RAM Resident)	This option will load the entire WordPerfect program (except for overflow files) into memory. This makes the program run faster and accesses the disk only for the overflow files. You need at least 320Kb of memory to use this option. See the next option for advantages to combining /R and /D.
/D-*drive/ directory* (Divert)	Usually the overflow files and other temporary files are kept on the same drive and directory where the WordPerfect program file (WP.EXE) is located. If you want to keep these files elsewhere, enter the drive/directory after the /D-.
	If you have two floppy disk drives with WordPerfect in drive A and want to redirect the overflow files to drive B, you should not remove the disk from drive B at any time. If you have a RAM drive, you can redirect the

files to that drive. Depending on the document size, it could speed up the program because there would be no disk access for the text in the overflow files. If you combine the /R and /D options (WP/R/D-B:), you can remove the WordPerfect diskette and use drive A for the Speller or Thesaurus diskette and eliminate continuous disk switching.

/X (Cancel /S)   As already mentioned, use /X to temporarily override changes made in the Setup menu. Enter /X/S to return to the original Word-Perfect defaults permanently.

You can combine any of the above options except /S to further customize the way WordPerfect is started. For example,

WP/NF/R/D-D:/B-20

would start the non-flash version of WordPerfect in memory, redirect the overflow and temporary files to the RAM drive, and back up the current documents every 20 minutes.

If you plan to use the same command line each time, consider putting it in your AUTOEXEC.BAT file as a DOS SET command. This sets the *environment* so that you can type WP to start WordPerfect without having to type the other options each time. An example of a SET command you could include in the AUTOEXEC.BAT file would be

SET WP=/NF/R/D-D:/B-20

If you use WordPerfect Library, there is a space reserved for startup options. You can also have WordPerfect pause each time it is started so you can manually insert startup options.

Reference

This portion of the book is an exhaustive A through Z reference guide to all WordPerfect menus, keys, commands, and features. Each entry includes a short description, a list of keystrokes, helpful hints, and special applications, as well as a list of related entries for further reading.

While each topic is listed under its WordPerfect name, you can usually look up a feature's generic equivalent for a reference to the correct entry.

P
A
R
T

T
W
O

Commands & Features

Addition

WordPerfect's Math feature lets you add a column of numbers.

Keystrokes

To add a single column of numbers, you do not have to define math columns first; however, you do have to turn on Math.

1. Press Math/Columns (ALT-F7).

2. Type **1** to turn on Math.

3. Press Tab and type the first number. It is automatically aligned at the decimal point.

4. Press ENTER to move to the next line and repeat steps 3 and 4 until all numbers are entered.

5. On a blank line below the column of numbers, press TAB once again, type **+**, and press ENTER.

6. Press Math/Columns (ALT-F7) and type **2** to Calculate.

Your screen will be similar to the one shown in Figure 4-1.

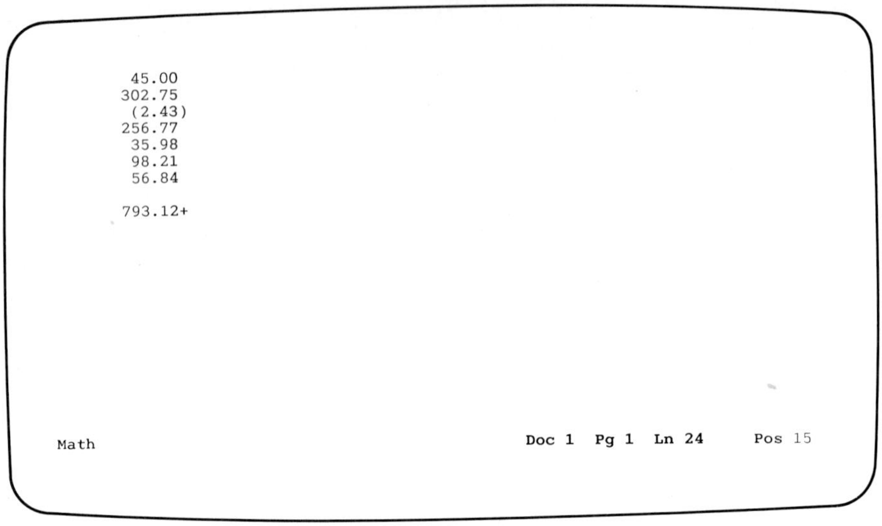

```
        45.00
       302.75
        (2.43)
       256.77
        35.98
        98.21
        56.84

       793.12+
```

Math   Doc 1 Pg 1 Ln 24   Pos 15

Figure 4-1.   Math/Columns screen

Hints

You must have at least one tab setting for the previous example to work. However, if you are using the defaults set by WordPerfect, you do not have to make changes.

If you want to enter a negative value in the column, enclose the number in parentheses, as shown in Figure 4-1.

The example given shows only how one column of numbers can be added. You can add several columns vertically by separating each column with a tab (Align codes are automatically inserted) and placing a + below each column. It is best to set tabs first when doing this.

WordPerfect's Math feature can also add across columns. This requires you to define the math columns first. See *Math* in this chapter for details.

If you have WordPerfect Library, you can use the calculator included with the program for simple addition. The calculations or final result can be saved to the shell's clipboard and retrieved into WordPerfect. You might even find it easier to switch between WordPerfect and the calculator rather than turn on Math for calculating.

Applications

You can use the Addition feature for a quick calculation, then delete the column or include it in the document. Because the + is considered a math code, it will not be printed with the document.

Use the + key at the top of the keyboard. If you have NUM LOCK on, you could also use the + on the numeric keypad. If NUM LOCK is not on, it will move down one screen.

You can also underline or double underline the last number in the column to set it off from the total. If you want the number underlined, either press Underline (F8) before and after typing the number or press Block (ALT-F4) and underline the number after it has been entered. See *Underline* for more information.

Related Entries

Math

Underline

See also Chapter 8, "Software Integration"

Advance the Printer to a Specific Line

The Advance feature can be used to advance the printer to a specific line on the page.

Keystrokes

1. Press Super/Subscript (SHIFT-F1).

2. Type **6**.

3. Enter the number of the line that the printer should advance to.

Hints

The cursor will not change position on the screen. For reassurance, check the "Ln" number on the status line to see if the number entered is the current line number or press Reveal Codes (ALT-F3) to see the code [AdvLn:#] inserted at the cursor's location.

You will most often use the Advance feature to move down the page. Not all printers support this feature. Some printers can only advance down, but not up. Laser printers are among those that can move to a previous line on the page.

There is also an Advance Up and Advance Down feature for advancing the printer up or down one-half of a line. The Superscript and Subscript feature moves the printer one-third of a line.

Applications

For those using a laser printer, Advance can be used to produce a document similar to the one shown in Figure 4-2.

WordPerfect Corporation uses this method to create professional looking newsletters. The following steps should be used to create such a document.

1. Calculate where the text will be inserted, and draw the lines and boxes using the Line Draw feature.

2. At the end of the page, use the Advance feature to advance back up to the first (or other appropriate) line.

3. Enter the text, noting where the lines and boxes were drawn. If you are using columns of text as shown, you can use the Columns feature.

To save time, create the form, save it to disk, and use it again when inserting new text. A sample of this document can be found on the supplemental disk.

You could use Advance to advance to the bottom line of the page and label illustrations or figures rather than pressing ENTER repeatedly or entering a footer.

Corporate Update

Volume II Number 12   *Internal Communication*   *November 25, 1987*

Inter-office Mail Reminder -- For those employees who use the numbering system when addressing inter-office mail, please be advised that the Accounting Department has now been changed to #11. For those of you who are not using the numbering system, please do the couriers a favor and write employees first and last names and departments legibly.

Vacation Schedule Correction -- In an employee vacation schedule distributed with the December 15, 1986 edition of the newsletter, the Thanksgiving holiday is marked as Thursday, November 19, 1987, which is incorrect. The correct date for the holiday is Thursday, November 26, 1987.

Insurance Update -- If you are admitted to a hospital for any reason, please specify your employer upon admittance. The billing departments of all hospitals have been advised of our insurance coverage and are aware of the information needed to process a claim.

Don't forget that, when filing you first claim each year, one fully completed claim form must be submitted for each family member. Subsequent claims may be submitted with only a receipt for services rendered (unless the claim is accident-related, in which case a fully completed claim form is required.

Business Card Orders -- All employees who will be attending the computer convention and need to reorder business cards are requested to do so before December 15. Please call Laurie with your order.

Third-Party Software Registration -- The Testing department is compiling a list of all third-party software products currently owned by the company. If you have such a product in your office, please send a memo to Gary in Testing. Briefly describe the product name, manufacturer, and version number. If you have no need for the program in your office, please forward the entire package to Gary.

Training Classes -- The next session of product training classes begins on December 8, but classes are beginning to fill up now. If you have questions regarding possible enrollment, please see the receptionist in your building for a list of registered participants.

Insurance Questions? -- All questions regarding company insurance policies--i.e., coverage, eligibility, and reimbursements--should now be directed to Mandy in Accounting at extension 304.

Printer Planner -- Melinda Riggs in Engineering is the one to call if you need to borrow a printer for another department for any reason. When you call with your request, she will need to know the length of time the printer is needed and the purpose for requesting the printer. Please be considerate of both Melinda and the individual(s) from whom you are borrowing the printer and give sufficient advance notice so that convenient scheduling can be arranged. Melinda can be reached at extension 423.

Travel Policies -- Due to recent changes in the company travel policies and procedures, an authorization number is needed before airline tickets can be issued. If you will be traveling for the company, please have your travel form filled out and signed by your supervisor prior to submitting it to May in Accounting. She will then give the authorization number to the travel agent.

Modular Office Space? -- We are currently reviewing plans for the utilization of office space in the new building and are considering both the

Figure 4-2.   Document created using the Advance command

Related Entries

Advance Up or Down One-Half Line

Superscript and Subscript

See also Chapter 5, "Laser Printers"

Advance Up or Down One-Half Line

Advance Up and Advance Down can be used to print text up or down one-half line.

Keystrokes

1. Press Super/Subscript (SHIFT-F1).

2. Type **4** to Advance Up or **5** to Advance Down a half-line. The cursor's position will not change. Check the "Ln" indicator on the status line to see the change.

3. Type the text.

4. If necessary, press Super/Subscript (SHIFT-F1), then type **4** or **5** to move back to the original line.

Hints

If you use Superscript and Subscript instead, the printer will print up or down one-third of a line.

Another difference between the two features is that Superscript and Subscript will advance the printer for a single character, then return to the original position automatically. With Advance Up and Advance Down, you have to choose the opposite feature (up or down) to return to the original line.

Applications

This feature can be used when typing equations and formulas. It can also be used in combination with the Overstrike feature to create phonetic words such as "nīt" (knight). In this situation, you would Advance Up, type the underscore character, Advance Down, and Overstrike it with an *i*.

Related Entries

Advance the Printer to a Specific Line

Overstrike a Character

Superscript and Subscript

Aligning Text

Text can be aligned at tab settings or at the right margin.

Options

For details on each of the following options, see the specific command indicated.

Decimal Tabs   Aligns characters at a decimal point (period).

```
   5.90          67.80            35.42
 150.34           2.30         3,456.00
  23.32            .54            20.00
    .03         324.18           836.51
```

Tab Align   (CTRL-F6) Aligns text at a decimal point or any designated character, such as a colon, as shown below. This key can be used without setting a decimal tab.

```
                      MEMO
    DATE:
      TO:
    FROM:
 SUBJECT:
```

Tabs   Set to center-, left-, or right-align text at any particular tab setting.

```
    The text          The text                     The text
       at                at                            at
      this             this                          this
  tab setting       tab setting                  tab setting
  is centered       is left-aligned         is right-aligned
```

Flush Right (ALT-F6)   Aligns text at the right margin.

```
                              Mr. Robert B. Jones
                              4532 Westwood Lane
                              Detroit, MI  78787
```

```
To Whom It May Concern:
```

```
Please send information about your product to the
address listed above.  Thank you in advance for your
assistance.
```

Right Justification   Creates a smooth left and right margin.

```
                  PREAMBLE
```

```
We the people of the United States, in Order to form a
more perfect Union, establish Justice, insure domestic
Tranquility, provide for the common defense, promote the
general Welfare, and secure the Blessings of Liberty to
ourselves and our posterity, do ordain and establish
this Constitution for the United States of America.
```

Math   Automatically aligns numbers at the decimal point in a numeric column.

```
                  INVOICE
```

```
    5      Flags               30.00          150.00
    5      Flag Poles         545.00        2,725.00
  250      Stars                1.89          472.50
   65      Stripes              5.95          386.75

           TOTAL                            3,734.25
```

ALT Key

The ALT key has no function when used alone. It is used in combination with the function keys to execute the features printed in blue on the template.

ALT (and CTRL) can be used with the letters A through Z to map special characters to the keyboard. ALT can also be used with the letters A through Z to name and execute macros.

Keystrokes

Macros

1. Press Macro Def (CTRL-F10).

2. Hold down the ALT key and press any letter from A to Z when prompted for the macro name.

3. Type the keystrokes to be recorded in the macro.

4. Press Macro Def (CTRL-F10) to finish the macro definition.

To invoke the macro, hold down the ALT key and press the letter.

Special Characters

1. Press Screen (CTRL-F3).

2. Type **3** for CTRL/ALT keys. Figure 4-3 shows how the screen will appear.

3. Hold down the ALT (or CTRL) key while pressing a letter A through Z.

4. Enter the decimal value for the character (found at the bottom of the screen).

5. Press Exit (F7) when finished.

In WordPerfect, hold down the ALT key and press the letter to display the character on the screen.

Hints

You can use the same ALT-key combination for a macro and a special character. However, when you press the ALT-key combination, the special character is displayed rather than starting the macro. To invoke the macro, press Macro (ALT-F10), press the ALT-key combination (the special character will appear), then press ENTER. To avoid these steps, you

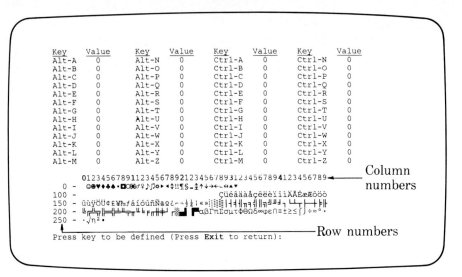

Figure 4-3.   CTRL and ALT Key Mapping menu

might want to use the CTRL key rather than ALT to display special characters.

Only the letters from A through Z can be used in an ALT-key combination. You cannot use punctuation or other keys such as ? or $.

No ALT Key

If your computer does not have an ALT key, try using the CTRL and SHIFT keys together.

Related Entries

CTRL Key

Macros

Special Characters

Appending Text

The Append feature is used to add a block of text to the end of an existing file.

Keystrokes

1. To define a block, move the cursor to one end of the text to be appended and press Block (ALT-F4).

2. Move the cursor to the opposite end of the block.

3. Press Move (CTRL-F4).

4. Type **3** for Append.

5. Enter the name of the file to which the block is to be appended.

Hints

Any formatting codes included in the block are also appended to the file. If there are no formatting codes included, the block uses the format of the file.

See *Move* for information about inserting a block of text within a document rather than at the end.

Related Entries

Block

Move

"Are Other Copies of WordPerfect Running?"

This message might be displayed when trying to start WordPerfect. The following is an explanation of why the error message occurs and what you can do to prevent it.

Reason

When WordPerfect is started, several temporary files are opened. Some files are used to save cut or copied text, deleted text, and backups. Other files, sometimes referred to as overflow files, hold parts of large documents that cannot fit in memory.

If you turn off the computer without first using Exit (F7), the temporary files are left open. The next time Word-Perfect is started, it finds these files open. It cannot distinguish between files left open after an improper exit, or those used by another copy of WordPerfect, so it asks if there are other copies of WordPerfect running.

As has been suggested, you could have WordPerfect loaded more than once. For example, if you use Shell (CTRL-F1) to go to DOS and enter **WP** at the DOS prompt, another copy would be loaded. You can also have more than one copy of WordPerfect loaded if you use DesqView or Microsoft Windows. Each copy of WordPerfect, however, must have its own set of temporary overflow files.

You might also get the error message if a network is not set up properly.

Solution

If you are sure that no other copies of WordPerfect are running, respond **N** to the question and WordPerfect is started. This lets WordPerfect overwrite the temporary files.

Always remember to use Exit (F7) to leave WordPerfect. When you see a DOS prompt (such as A>, B>, or C: \>) you can turn off the computer.

If you really want to have a second copy of WordPerfect running, respond **Y**. The following message is then displayed, telling you that a new directory must be specified.

Directory is in use. New WP Directory: C: \WP \

Notice that the current directory is shown. Do not press ENTER to accept that directory. It is shown only as a reminder that it is currently being used so that it won't be entered as the new directory. Remember that each copy of WordPerfect must have its own set of overflow files. If you specify the same directory, the overflow files will become corrupted. Also, if you use the same directory for more than one copy of WordPerfect and exit one copy, you might see the error message, "Insert WP disk back into drive and strike any key to continue." This is displayed because the overflow files were closed when the first copy was exited. Therefore, when the second copy of WordPerfect tried to access them, it could not find them and assumed you removed the WordPerfect disk. If this happens, you will have to reboot.

Each copy of WordPerfect requires at least 200Kb of memory to run.

Arrow Keys

See *Cursor Keys*

ASCII Files

All WordPerfect files are saved in an ASCII (American Standards Committee for Information Interchange) format. However, they are not readable by most other programs because WordPerfect uses the extended ASCII characters as program codes.

If you need to transfer files to and from other programs, you should use Text In/Out (CTRL-F5) to save and retrieve DOS text files (text without codes). Because codes such as headers, footers, footnotes, and endnotes, all of which contain text, would also be stripped, you could consider printing the document to a file on disk. All text normally included within a code is "printed" to the file as if it were regular text.

Related Entries

DOS Text Files

Print to Disk

Text In/Out

AUTOEXEC.BAT File

The AUTOEXEC.BAT file contains a batch of DOS commands that are automatically executed each time the computer is started.

Keystrokes

You can create or edit the AUTOEXEC.BAT file within WordPerfect.

1. Press Line Format (SHIFT-F8), type **3** for Margins, and enter **0** and **80** for the left and right margins. This step prevents words from wrapping when the AUTO-EXEC.BAT file is retrieved.

2. Press Text In/Out (CTRL-F5).

3. Type **2** to Retrieve a DOS text file (each carriage return or line feed becomes a hard return).

4. Enter **a:\autoexec.bat** if you are using two disk drives or **c:\autoexec.bat** if you are using a hard disk. If you see the message "ERROR: File not found," press ENTER to leave the Text In/Out menu.

5. If the file is found, it is displayed on the screen for editing. If it is not found, you can create the file.

6. Make necessary changes to the existing file, or, if you are creating a new AUTOEXEC.BAT file, enter the commands to be included. The following is a sample AUTOEXEC.BAT file.

```
echo off

prompt $p $g

path c: \;c: \library;c: \wp;c: \plan;c: \system

cl/i

cd \letters

wp/b-15/m-startup
```

7. Press Text In/Out (CTRL-F5) and type **1** to Save the DOS text file. It must be saved as a DOS text file rather than as a regular WordPerfect file.

8. Enter **a: \autoexec.bat** or **c: \autoexec.bat** depending on which system you are using. If the name is already displayed, press ENTER and type **Y** to replace the previous file.

9. Press Exit (F7) and type **N** twice. Do not save the document normally or it will be saved in WordPerfect format rather than DOS text format.

Hints

Chapter 1 gives more information about creating and editing an AUTOEXEC.BAT file from DOS. You can use the DOS TYPE command to type the AUTOEXEC.BAT file to the screen, copy the information, then reenter it with changes. You could also use DOS's line editor, EDLIN, to make changes.

Applications

The AUTOEXEC.BAT file lets you store commands so you don't have to enter them each time the computer is started. If you enter a DOS command repeatedly, consider placing it in a batch file.

Other batch files can be created using the same steps. Up to eight characters and the .BAT extension are used to name a batch file. See Chapter 1 for examples.

Related Entries

DOS Text Files

Text In/Out

See also Chapter 1, "Getting Started"

Backing Up Files

Timed Backup will periodically save the documents on the screen to a temporary backup file to guard against power or machine failure. Original Backup can be used to save the previous draft of a document. The Copy option in the List Files menu can be used to manually back up your files.

Keystrokes

Timed Backup and Original Backup

1. From the DOS prompt where WordPerfect resides, type WP/S to enter the Setup menu.

2. Type **4** to Set Backup Options. Figure 4-4 shows the screen that appears.

3. Enter the number of minutes between each backup. See "Hints" for suggestions.

4. Enter the drive/directory where the backup files are to be stored.

5. Type **Y** or **N** to back up the original document. See "Hints" for a definition of an original document.

Retrieve the Backup File(s)

1. Press List Files (F5).

2. Enter the drive/directory which contains the files to be copied.

```
Set Timed Backup

To safeguard against losing large amounts of text in the event of a power or
machine failure, WordPerfect can automatically backup the document on your
screen at a chosen time interval and to a chosen drive/directory (see Set-up
in the WordPerfect Installation pamphlet).  REMEMBER--THIS IS ONLY IN CASE OF
POWER OR MACHINE FAILURE.  WORDPERFECT DELETES THE TIMED BACKUP FILES WHEN YOU
EXIT NORMALLY FROM WORDPERFECT.  If you want the document saved as a file you
need to say 'yes' when you exit WordPerfect normally.

Number of minutes between each backup: 0


Set Original Backup

WordPerfect can rename the last copy of a document when a new version of the
document is saved.  The old copy has the same file name with an extension of
".BK!".  Take note that the files named "letter.1" and "letter.2" have the
same original backup file name of "letter.bk!".  In this case the latest
file saved will be backed up.

Backup the original document? (Y/N) N
```

Figure 4-4.   Backup options

3. Move the cursor to the backup file to be retrieved. ({WP}BACK.1 and {WP}BACK.2 are the names of the timed backup files. The .BK! extension marks an original file.)

4. Type **1** to Retrieve the file.

Manual Backup

1. Press List Files (F5).

2. Press ENTER to back up the files in the displayed drive/directory or enter the drive/directory containing the files to be backed up.

3. Move the cursor to each desired file and press * to mark the file.

4. Type **8** to Copy.

5. Type **Y** in answer to the question, "Copy Marked Files?" If you type **N**, WordPerfect assumes you want to copy only the file highlighted by the cursor.

6. "Copy All Marked Files To:" appears. Enter the drive/directory where the files are to be copied.

If you get a "Disk Full" error message, replace the backup disk with a disk that has more space and repeat the steps. You might want to check if some of the files were successfully copied before marking them to be copied again.

Hints

You can also use the DOS COPY command to back up files without using WordPerfect.

A suggested interval between timed backups is 15 minutes. If you are working with documents longer than 100 pages, you might want to consider increasing the time because the longer the document, the longer it takes to back it up.

At each timed backup, document 1 is saved to a file named {WP}BACK.1 and document 2 is saved to {WP}BACK.2 depending on the location of the cursor. If the cursor is in document 1, only that document is backed up.

When you clear the screen to begin working on a new document or exit WordPerfect properly using Exit (F7), the temporary backup file is deleted. Use Save (F10) to permanently save a document.

If you do not specify a drive/directory for storing the backup files, the directory containing WP.EXE is used.

The File Manager included with the Library utility program from WordPerfect Corporation also lets you mark and copy files. Instead of giving you a "disk full" message that makes it necessary to start again, it tells you when to insert the next diskette to continue backing up the files.

How Original Backup Works

When a file is saved and a file with the same name exists, you are asked if you want to replace the "original" document. If you type **Y**, the original is named with a .BK! extension, the new copy is saved, then the original with the .BK! extension is deleted. This process protects you in the case of a power failure during a save.

If you choose **Y** to back up the original document, the original with the .BK! extension is not deleted during the save process.

Files that do not have a unique first name (as in LET-TERS.JAN, LETTERS.FEB, and so on) use the same backup file (LETTERS.BK!). In this case, the most recent file is the one saved in the backup file.

Setting Timed Backup Temporarily

You can set the timed backup on a temporary basis by entering WordPerfect with the /B option. When entering WordPerfect, type **WP/B=20** (substitute any number for the 20) instead of WP. Enter **WP/B=0** to temporarily turn off the backup option.

Related Entries

Setup Menu

Timed Backup

BACKSPACE Key

The BACKSPACE key deletes characters to the left of the cursor.

Keystrokes

BACKSPACE is located in the same position as on a typewriter. However, unlike most typewriters, it deletes characters rather than moves over text. If you want to move the cursor to the left (a nondestructive backspace) use the left arrow key [←]. See Figure 4-5 for the location of the BACKSPACE key and left arrow key on the keyboard.

Press BACKSPACE once to delete the character to the left of the cursor. Continue pressing the key to delete more than one character to the left.

Options

BACKSPACE can be used in combination with other keys to delete a larger group of text.

Delete Word at the Cursor   Press CTRL-BACKSPACE (together) to delete the word at the cursor. Continue pressing to delete words at (to the right of) the cursor.

Delete Word to the Left of the Cursor   Press HOME, then BACKSPACE (one after the other) to delete from the cursor to the beginning of the word. Continue pressing to delete words to the left of the cursor.

Delete a Block of Text   After defining a Block (ALT-F4), press BACKSPACE (or DEL) and answer **Y** to delete the highlighted text. Type **N** to leave the block.

Hints

BACKSPACE can also be used to delete blank lines (hard returns), spaces, and codes.

If you are deleting in the regular screen (not in Reveal Codes) and a code is encountered, you might be asked to confirm the deletion depending on the code encountered. Answer **Y** to delete the code or press any other key (including BACKSPACE) to skip over the code. When using BACKSPACE in the Reveal Codes screen, you are not asked to confirm the deletion.

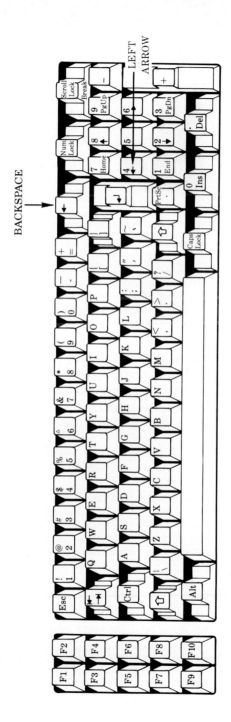

IBM keyboard

Figure 4-5.   BACKSPACE key and LEFT ARROW key

You are asked to confirm the deletion of most WordPerfect codes. However, codes such as [TAB] and [Indent] do not need a confirmation.

If Typeover is on, BACKSPACE replaces the character to the left of the cursor with a space.

Related Entries

DEL Key

Delete Codes

Typeover

Undelete

Beep

WordPerfect causes your computer to beep when it wants to make you aware of certain conditions. You can turn the beep on or off according to your personal preference.

Keystrokes

The following procedure allows you to choose whether the computer will signal you with a beep when it encounters an error, when a hyphenation choice must be made, or when it reaches the end of a Search procedure.

1. At the DOS prompt where WordPerfect is located, type **WP/S**.

2. Type **3** to Set Screen and Beep Options.

3. Press ENTER until you reach the beep options.

4. Type **Y** or **N** to answer the displayed questions.

```
Set Screen Options

  Number of rows: 25
  Number of columns: 80
  Hard return displayed as ascii value: 32
  Display filename on status line? (Y/N) Y

Set Beep Options

  Beep when search fails? (Y/N) N
  Beep on error? (Y/N) N
  Beep on hyphenation? (Y/N) Y
```

5. After answering the questions, you are returned to the Setup menu.

6. Type **0** to end the Setup and enter WordPerfect.

Hints

If you answer **Y** to "Beep when search fails," you will also hear a beep when Replace is finished.

Beep During Printing

WordPerfect sounds a beep to let you know when the printer needs to be sent a "Go" (when using hand-fed paper or changing print wheels). If you want a beep to sound for other printing situations, see Chapter 7 for information on inserting the <F> command in the printer definition.

Beep During a Macro

WordPerfect beeps when a macro pauses for more information. This cannot be turned off.

Related Entries

Error Messages

Hyphenation

Macros

Replace

Search

Setup Menu

See also Chapter 7, "Printer Program"

Bibliographies

See *Hanging Paragraphs and Indents*

Binding Width

When printing pages to be used for double-sided copies, you can use the Binding Width feature to shift the printing to the right on odd pages and to the left on even pages so that space is allowed for binding along the spine of the document.

Keystrokes

Change Binding Width for a Single Print Job

1. Press Print (SHIFT-F7).

2. Type **3** for Options.

3. Type **3** for Binding Width.

4. Enter the width in tenths of an inch. If you want the printing to be moved one-half inch, enter **5**. If you want it moved 2 inches, enter **20**, and so on.

5. Press ENTER to leave the Options menu.

6. Type **1** or **2** to print the full text or just the current page. You can also type **4** and print a file from disk.

The binding width is returned to 0 when the job has been printed.

Change Binding Width for Multiple Documents

1. Press Print (SHIFT-F7).

2. Type **4** for Printer Control.

3. Type **1** to Select Print Options.

4. Type **3** for Binding Width.

5. Enter the width in tenths of an inch.

6. Press ENTER to leave the Options menu.

7. Press ENTER again if you want to leave the Printer Control menu.

Hints

The Binding Width feature allows you to decide how much to add to or subtract from the left margin. It pertains only to the left margin, not to the edge of the paper.

Be sure to set wide enough margins so that the text will not print off the page after the binding width adjustment is made.

If you want to allow extra space for binding, but will not be making double-sided copies, change the left margin rather than use the Binding Width feature.

Related Entries

Print Options

Block

Block (ALT-F4) is used to identify a section of text that will be moved, copied, or deleted (among many other editing functions).

Keystrokes

To define a block:

1. Move the cursor to one end of the block (either the beginning or the end).

2. Press Block (ALT-F4). "Block on" flashes on the status line.

3. Move the cursor to the opposite end of the block. The text is highlighted in reverse video, as shown in Figure 4-6.

4. Perform a block operation (see "Options" for a complete list).

5. If Block is not automatically turned off, press Block (ALT-F4) or Cancel (F1).

With Block you can highlight by word, sentence, line, or paragraph. Turn on Block and use the following keys to highlight particular sections of text.

SPACEBAR	Highlight by word
Period (.)	Highlight from the cursor to the end of the sentence
↓	Highlight line by line

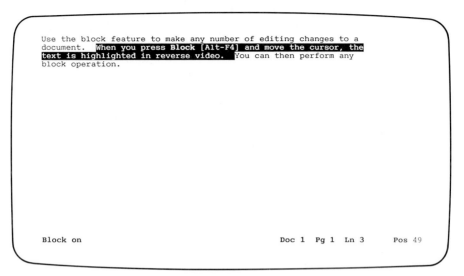

```
Use the block feature to make any number of editing changes to a
document.  When you press Block [Alt-F4] and move the cursor, the
text is highlighted in reverse video.  You can then perform any
block operation.
```

```
Block on                                    Doc 1  Pg 1  Ln 3      Pos 49
```

Figure 4-6.   Block of highlighted text

ENTER	Highlight from the cursor to the end of the paragraph (text is highlighted up to the next [HRt])
Search (F2)	Search for and highlight to the end of the search string

You can also type any character and the cursor moves to the next occurrence of that character.

Hints

Block is automatically turned off after most Block operations, with the exception of Print, Save, Replace, and Switch. You can either perform another Block function, or press Block (ALT-F4) or Cancel (F1) to turn off Block.

If you find yourself redefining the same block of text for more than one function (for example, you want the block both underlined and bolded), you can redefine the block more easily by pressing Block (ALT-F4); then press Go To (CTRL-HOME) and Block to return the cursor to the point where Block was originally turned on.

Be aware that WordPerfect codes can be included in a block. Therefore, you might want to press Reveal Codes (ALT-F3) if you are not sure of the cursor's location in relation to the codes. Block can be turned on after entering the Reveal Codes screen; the location is marked in Reveal Codes with [Block].

Options

Among the following Block options, the most commonly used applications are discussed first.

Bold or Underline a Block

Define a block, then press Bold (F6) or Underline (F8). A [B] or [U] is inserted at the beginning of the block and a [b] or [u] at the end. You can also assign other attributes to a block (see *Redline* and *Strikeout* for more information).

Delete a Block

Define a block, then press BACKSPACE or DEL. Confirm the deletion by typing **Y**.

Move a Block

Define a block, press Move (CTRL-F4), then type **1** to Cut. Move the cursor to a new location in any document, press Move (CTRL-F4), then **5** to Retrieve the text. (You could also press Retrieve (SHIFT-F10) and Enter instead, to retrieve the cut block.) See *Move* for more information.

Copy a Block

Follow the steps for moving a block, except type **2** to Copy instead of **1** to Cut. Retrieve the block as you would a cut block.

Protect a Block from Page Breaks

Define a block, press Page Format (ALT-F8), then type **Y** to keep a block from being split between two pages. See *Block Protect* for more information.

Save a Block

Define a block, press Save (F10), then enter the name of a file. If you enter the name of a file already on disk, you are asked if you want to replace the existing file with the block. This feature is useful for saving often-used paragraphs or text.

    Although undocumented, you can press just ENTER to save an"unnamed" block in memory. To retrieve the block, press Retrieve (SHIFT-F10) and press ENTER. You do not have to enter a name. Some prefer using this method to copy text.

    After saving a block, the text remains highlighted in case you want to delete it or perform some other Block operation. Press Block (ALT-F4) or Cancel (F1) to turn off Block.

Append a Block to an Existing File

To add a block of text to the end of a file on disk without first retrieving the file, define the block, press Move (CTRL-F4), type **3** for Append, then enter the name of the file. The block is appended to the file and the text remains on your screen. Block is automatically turned off.

Center or Flush Right a Block

Define a block, press Center (SHIFT-F6) or Flush Right (ALT-F6), then type **Y** to confirm the action. A Center On code [C] or Align On code [A] is inserted at the beginning of each line and a Center Off code [c] or Align Off code [a] and Hard Return code [HRt] is inserted at the end of each line.

Print a Block

Define a block, press Print (SHIFT-F7), then type **Y** to confirm the action. The block remains highlighted. Press Block (ALT-F4) or Cancel (F1) to turn off Block.

Change a Block to Uppercase or Lowercase

Define a block, press Switch (SHIFT-F2), then **1** to change to uppercase or **2** to change to lowercase. If you include the ending punctuation of the previous sentence and choose 2 for lowercase, the first character in the sentence will remain in uppercase. Block is not turned off automatically. You can either perform another Block operation or turn off Block by pressing Block (ALT-F4) or Cancel (F1).

Superscript or Subscript a Block

Define a block, press Super/Subscript (SHIFT-F1), then type **1** for Superscript or **2** for Subscript. A [SuprScrpt] or [SubScrpt] code is placed before each character in the block.

Mark Text for Table of Contents, Lists, Index, Redline, or Strikeout

Define a block, press Mark Text (ALT-F5), then **1** for TOC, **2** for Lists, or **5** for Index. (After choosing an option, follow the directions displayed on the screen.) You can also choose 3 to Redline or 4 to Strikeout the block.

Replace Text or Codes in a Block

The Replace feature usually works from the cursor to the end of the document. If you want to use the feature in a specific block of text, define a block and press Replace (ALT-F2). See *Replace* if you need further assistance in answering the prompts.

Check the Spelling in a Block

Define a block, then press Spell (CTRL-F2). See *Spell* for information on checking a word, page, or document.

Sort a Block

If you have a list of items within a document that you want sorted, or you don't want title headings to be included in a sort, block the items to be sorted, then press Merge/Sort (CTRL-F9). Choose the applicable options, then type **1** to Perform Action. The sorted list replaces the former block.

If the sort routine comes up with a blank screen, you probably used the Select feature in Sort and no records were found that satisfied the select criteria. Press Cancel (F1), then **1** to restore the original block.

Blocking a Column

WordPerfect has several different types of columns: newspaper, parallel, and tabbed. You can use Block in any type of column just as you would in regular text. The following are options for using Block to cut or copy tabbed columns or rectangular blocks.

Cut/Copy Columns Including Tabs   You must have at least one tab between each column. Place the cursor at the beginning of the first line of the column to be cut or copied. Press Block (ALT-F4). Move the cursor to the last line in the column (if you want to cut or copy more than one column, move the cursor to the right into the next column). A regular block rather than the column is highlighted until you press Move (CTRL-F4) and type **4** to Cut/Copy Column. The column(s), including the tabs preceding the columns, are highlighted. Type **1** to Cut, **2** to Copy, or **3** to Delete the block. At the new location (see *Columns*, for more information on positioning the cursor), press Move (CTRL-F4), then **4** to retrieve the column.

Rectangular Block   Although most often used in tabbed columns, the rectangular block can be used in regular text. A rectangular block is not dependent on tabs to define columns. Instead, it is defined from corner to corner. With the cursor at one corner (upper left or lower right), press Block (ALT-F4). Move the cursor to the opposite corner, press Move (CTRL-F4), then **5** to Cut/Copy Rectangle. Only the rectangle is highlighted. Figure 4-7 shows an example of a highlighted rectangle. Type **1** to Cut, **2** to Copy, or **3** to Delete the rectangle. If you choose to cut or delete, any remaining text is moved to the left. At the new location, move the cursor to the position where the text should be retrieved, press Move (CTRL-F4), then **6** to Retrieve the Rectangle. (Note: Be sure to have a hard return rather than a soft return at the end of each line of text in the block to prevent automatic reformatting.)

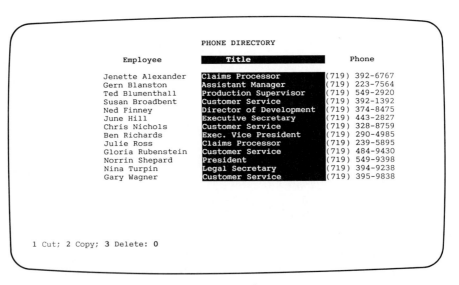

Figure 4-7.   Highlighted rectangle

Related Entries

Appending Text

Block Protect

Bold

Center Text

Columns

Copy Text and Columns

Cut Text and Columns

Delete

Flush Right

Index

Lists

Lowercase Text

Mark Text

Move

Print

Redline

Replace

Save

Spell

Strikeout Text

Superscript and Subscript

Table of Contents

Underline

Uppercase Text

Block Protect

Block Protect is used to prevent splitting a block of text between two pages.

Keystrokes

1. Move the cursor to one end of the text.

2. Press Block (ALT-F4).

3. Move to the opposite end.

4. Press Page Format (ALT-F8).

5. Type **Y** to confirm that you want the block protected. [BlockPro:On] and [BlockPro:Off] codes are inserted at the beginning and end of the block.

Hints

If the end of the page happens to fall within a protected block, WordPerfect will search for the last hard return preceding the [BlockPro:On] code and change it to a page break. However, if that hard return is also protected in another block, it will cause problems. Therefore, it is important when protecting consecutive blocks of text, to leave an unprotected hard return between the blocks. If you remember to define your block from the first character in the block to the last character in the block, you should not have a problem.

Widow/Orphan

If a block refuses to be protected (as with two- and three-line paragraphs), check to see if you have Widow/Orphan Protect on. It can be turned off temporarily if you prefer by moving the cursor just above the block, pressing Page Format (ALT-F8), and typing **A** for widow/orphan.

Block Protect and Parallel Columns

The Parallel Columns feature uses the Block Protect codes to protect a group of columns from being split across the page.

When columns are turned on, a [BlockPro:On] code is inserted just before the [Col on] code. When columns are turned off, a [BlockPro:Off] code is inserted just before the [Col off] code. The following shows how the codes are inserted to end the first group and begin a new one.

[BlockPro:Off][Col off]

[HRt]

[BlockPro:On][Col on]

See *Columns* for more information.

Protecting Footnotes

You cannot use Block Protect in footnotes or endnotes. However, the Footnote Options menu lets you specify how many lines should be kept together before breaking to the next page.

Applications

Use Block Protect for a block that must always stay together no matter how much text is added and deleted within the block. Conditional End of Page should be used to protect a specific number of lines, as in a title or heading and the first two lines of a paragraph immediately following.

You can use Block Protect to keep a page break from splitting a table or chart where the number of lines may increase or decrease later.

Related Entries

Conditional End of Page

Widows and Orphans

Bold

Bold (F6) is used to produce darker, heavier print at the printer and brighter text on the screen. When printed, it adds emphasis to titles and headings.

Keystrokes

Bold Text as You Type

1. Press Bold (F6) to turn on Bold. Note that the position number on the status line is shown in a higher intensity (or in a different color on a color monitor). See "Hints" if you don't see an indication for bold on screen.

2. Type the text.

3. Press Bold (F6) to turn off Bold.

Bold Text After Typing

1. Move the cursor to one end of the text to be bolded.

2. Press Block (ALT-F4) to turn on Block.

3. Move the cursor to the opposite end of the text to be bolded. The text is highlighted as you move the cursor through it.

4. Press Bold (F6).

Remove Bold

1. Move to the beginning or end of the bolded text.

2. Press Reveal Codes (ALT-F3) to view the text and codes.

3. Locate the Bold On code [B] or Bold Off code [b] and move the cursor next to either code (if not already there).

4. Press BACKSPACE if the code is to the left of the cursor or DEL if the code is to the right of the cursor. Deleting either the [B] or [b] will remove the bold.

After you become more familiar with WordPerfect codes, you can tell where the bold code is by watching the position number on the status line.

Hints

When you press Bold (F6) to turn on Bold, the Bold On and Bold Off are both actually inserted at the same time. The cursor remains between the two codes. When Bold (F6) is pressed again to turn off Bold, no code is inserted; instead, the cursor moves *over* the code. Therefore, you could use a cursor key such as →, END, or ↓ to move the cursor past the Bold Off code and accomplish the same purpose.

If you have a section of bolded text and decide you want only part of it to remain in bold, move the cursor to the end of the text you want to remain in bold and press Bold (F6). A Bold Off code [b] and Bold On code [B] is inserted with the cursor remaining between the two as shown in the illustration.

```
                    THIS IS THE TITLE IN BOLD

It is a common mistake to type the title and forget to turn off
bold.  To correct this, move the cursor to the end of the title
and press Bold (F6).  This illustration shows how the Bold Off
code [b] and Bold On code [B] are inserted.  Press DEL and type Y
to delete bold after the cursor.
                                         ↳  Doc 2  Pg 1  Ln 1      Pos 55
████████████████████████████████████████████████████████████████████████
[C][B]THIS IS THE TITLE IN BOLD[b]-[B][c][HRt]
[HRt]
It is a common mistake to type the title and forget to turn off[SRt]
bold.  To correct this, move the cursor to the end of the title[SRt]
```

WordPerfect automatically inserts the [B] code because it senses that the text to the right is in bold and assumes you want to keep it that way. Immediately press DEL to delete the [B] code to the right and type **Y** when asked to confirm the deletion. Bold is removed from the text to the right of the cursor.

Adjusting Bold on the Screen

Monochrome Monitor   Bolded text should appear in a higher intensity on a monochrome monitor. If you cannot see the difference, use the brightness and contrast controls to adjust intensity levels.

Single-Color/Graphics Monitor   If the bolded text is almost invisible, you probably have a single-color monitor. Press Screen (CTRL-F3), type **4** for Colors, type **2** for a single-color monitor, type **Y** for fast text display, then choose from the options for underlined text. (If you see flickering on the screen, repeat the steps, but type **N** when asked if you want fast text display.)

Color Monitor   Bolded text is displayed in a different color when using a color monitor. To change the color, press Screen (CTRL-F3), type **4** for Colors, type **1** for a color monitor, then type **Y** or **N** for fast text display. The available colors are displayed on the left and the same colors in a higher intensity on the right. Choose the colors for each option. If you choose a high-intensity color for the background, WordPerfect will use the lower-intensity color instead. Press Switch (SHIFT-F3) to choose the colors for document 2, then press Exit (F7) when finished.

If the bolded text blinks in reverse video, some other program has set it to a single-color monitor with a MODE BW80 command at DOS. You should exit WordPerfect, enter **mode co80** to return the "mode" to color, and then reenter WordPerfect. (For Tandy computers, the command is MODE COLOR.) If you have this problem often, especially after running Lotus 1-2-3, you should consider putting the MODE CO80 command in the batch file used to start WordPerfect.

If you are using a Compaq Portable III, bold is displayed as reverse video and there is no underline. However, by running three programs before starting WordPerfect, bold can be displayed as extra-wide characters and underline as underline. Two of the programs are on the Compaq Utility disk and are in files named CHARSET.COM and ADAPT.COM. The other program is the DOS MODE command. Copy the files to the boot disk (or root directory on a hard disk) and enter **charset thinus** to choose a thinner U.S. character set for the regular text. Enter **adapt** and choose the "Change the character appearance" option. Choose the option to "Use alternate character" and press ESC until you leave the ADAPT program and return to DOS. Next, enter **mode und on**. Unfortunately, these settings must be run each time you boot your computer. The CHARSET and MODE commands can be included in the AUTOEXEC.BAT file. See *AUTOEXEC.BAT File* for further information.

Moving Bolded Text

If text is moved from a bolded sentence or paragraph, Bold On and Off codes are inserted at the beginning and end of the block so the text will remain bolded when it is retrieved. However, if you retrieve the bolded block into another bolded section of text, bold will be turned off following the inserted block. This is because the Bold Off code at the end of the block supersedes the Bold Off code at the end of the original section.

If this happens you can block the text that was unbolded and then press Bold (F6).

Using Typeover and Line Draw with Bold

Typeover will not type over codes, nor are codes allowed to type over other characters. Therefore, if you want bolded text within a box (see *Line Draw*), it is best to type the bolded text first, then draw the box around it later. If you want to bold text that is already inside a box, use Block to highlight the text, then use Bold.

Some printers cannot do a second pass to get Bold when printing a special character on the same line (see the following illustration). If this is the case, note that it is a printer limitation and you probably will not be able to get bold or underlined text within a box.

```
This is how bold might look
                bold
```

Bolding at the Printer

Some printers print bold by doing a double (or more) pass with the printer, while some move the printhead slightly to the right and reprint the character (shadow printing). Others have a thicker font that is used for boldface type.

If you are not satisfied with the way boldface text is printed, check the printer manual for options and modify the printer driver (see Chapter 7). Chapter 6 lists specific printer limitations.

Printer Switch Settings

If the boldface text prints like the following illustration, check the internal switch settings (sometimes referred to as DIP switches) and make sure the switch for Auto LF (automatic line feed) is OFF. If it is on, both WordPerfect and the printer are sending line feeds.

```
If your bolded text looks like this when it prints, check the
            bolded
Auto LF switch and make sure it is off.
```

Related Entries

Block

Bottom Margin

The bottom margin is the space at the bottom of the page where text is not printed. The Page Length and Top Margin are used to determine what the bottom margin will be.

Keystrokes

WordPerfect has preset a 66-line page to allow for 54 lines of single-spaced text on a 66-line page. This setting provides 1-inch top and bottom margins. To change the bottom margin, you should increase or decrease the number of text lines that can be printed on the page.

1. Move the cursor to the page where the change is to take effect.

2. Press Page Format (ALT-F8).

3. Type **4** for Page Length.

4. Type **3** for Other.

5. Press ENTER to accept 66 lines for the form length. If you are using legal-sized paper, enter **84**.

6. Enter a number larger than 54 if you want a smaller bottom margin, or a number smaller than 54 if you want a larger bottom margin. For example, if you want a 2-inch bottom margin, enter 48. For a 1/2-inch bottom margin, enter 57.

Hints

Whether you are printing with eight lines per inch or six lines per inch, the form length is figured in six lines per inch. However, if you are printing at eight lines per inch, the number of text lines should be changed to 72 in order to retain a 1-inch bottom margin.

You should change the form length only if you have paper longer or shorter than the standard 11 inches. Do not change the form length even if you are printing with a landscape or rotated font on a laser printer.

Top Margin

Option 5 on the Page Format menu lets you change the top margin. You might want to consider changing the top margin when the bottom margin is changed so that the page will print evenly between the top and bottom of the page.

Footers in the Bottom Margin

If you have a footer longer than one line, it will print into the bottom margin. You can have multiple-line headers or footnotes without having this problem, but WordPerfect assumes that most users have one-line footers. If you have a multiple-line footer, you might want to adjust the number of text lines accordingly.

Applications

The bottom margin is most often changed because you have to "fit it all on one page." As with all formatting codes, the change is in effect until another code of its kind is encountered. Therefore, you can change the bottom margin for a crowded page, then change it back to the original setting for the remainder of the document.

Related Entries

Footers

Page Length

Top Margin

Bullets

The IBM character set has several characters that can be used as bullets. These include ASCII 7 (●), 9 (○), and 249 (·). You can get these characters by holding down ALT and typing the number on the numeric keypad or assigning them to an ALT or CTRL key. See *Special Characters* for other options.

Cancel

Use Cancel (F1) to back out of menus and prompts or to cancel a procedure. If a menu is not on the screen, or a macro, search, or other function is not in progress, Cancel is used to restore deleted text.

Keystrokes

Cancel Menus and Prompts

When in a WordPerfect menu or prompt, press Cancel (F1) to return to your document.

Cancel a Procedure

During execution of a Macro, Search, or Replace function, press Cancel (F1) to cancel the procedure. To cancel or end a Merge, press Merge E (SHIFT-F9).

If asked to hyphenate a word, you can press Cancel (F1) instead of ESC if you don't want the word hyphenated.

Restore Deleted Text

1. Position the cursor where you want the last deletion to be retrieved.

2. Press Cancel (F1). The last deletion is highlighted.

3. Type **1** to Restore or **2** to Show Previous Deletion.

Hints

A *deletion* is defined by WordPerfect as a group of consecutive deletions before any other key (including a cursor movement key) is pressed. Any combination of deletion keys can be used in one deletion.

When NUM LOCK is pressed, "Pos" on the status line blinks temporarily. Although it automatically stops blinking after a short time, you can press Cancel (F1) *twice* to stop it immediately. NUM LOCK remains on.

Related Entries

Cancel a Print Job

Macros

Merge

Replace

Search

Undelete

Cancel a Print Job

You can cancel a single print job or all print jobs in the queue.

```
Printer Control
                                C - Cancel Print Job(s)
1 - Select Print Options        D - Display All Print Jobs
2 - Display Printers and Fonts  G - "Go" (Resume Printing)
3 - Select Printers             P - Print a Document
                                R - Rush Print Job
Selection: C                    S - Stop Printing
Cancel which job? (*=All Jobs) 8

Current Job

Job Number: 8                   Page Number:  1
Job Status: Printing            Current Copy: 1 of 1
Message:    None

Job List

Job  Document          Destination          Forms and Print Options
 8   (Screen)          Ptr  3               Continuous


Additional jobs not shown: 0
```

Figure 4-8.   Cancel print job in Printer Control menu

Keystrokes

1. Press Print (SHIFT-F7).

2. Type **4** for Printer Control.

3. Type **C** to Cancel Print Job(s). Figure 4-8 shows how the screen will appear. Continue with one of the following options.

Cancel current print job.

The current print job number is displayed. Press ENTER.

Cancel other print job.

Type the job number for the print job to be cancelled, then press ENTER.

Cancel all print jobs.

Type * (rather than a number) for all print jobs. Type **Y** to confirm the cancellation.

Hints

The printer will not always stop printing immediately because it needs to empty its *buffer* first. You may see a message, "Press ENTER if printer does not respond." If you press ENTER, the print file is deleted so no additional data is sent to the printer. You can manually clear the buffer by turning the printer off and on after the print job has been cancelled.

If you wait long enough after cancelling a print job, the printer will clear the buffer and reset itself automatically. However, if you pressed ENTER in answer to the message "Press ENTER if printer does not respond," you may see a message telling you that printing has stopped and that you should press **G** to continue. It is then up to you to reset the printer if necessary.

Rather than cancelling print jobs so another can be printed first, use **R** to Rush a Print Job.

If you need to stop the printer because of jammed paper

or other temporary problems, use **S** to Stop Printing. The current print job remains in the queue and will start printing again when the printer is sent a "Go." You can restart printing on any page after stopping the printer. See *Print* for specifics.

Related Entries

Print

Rush a Print Job

Stop Printing

"Can't Find Correct Copy of WP"

If you see this error message, enter the full path and filename. If WordPerfect is found in a directory named WP, you should enter **c:\wp\wp.exe**. Note that the name of the program WP.EXE should also be included.

Reasons

If you see this error message you might have one of the following situations.

If you are using DOS version 2.x, it might appear once, but should never appear again after being answered the first time.

You might be using DOS version 2.x with an AT, Compaq DeskPro 286, or other AT compatible. You should run *only* DOS version 3.x on an AT or compatible.

If you are using DOS version 3.x, you might have mixed 2.x and 3.x files. To check, exit WordPerfect with Exit (F7)—not Shell (CTRL-F1). When at DOS, enter **VER**. The version of DOS is displayed. Next, run COMMAND.COM by entering command at the DOS prompt. The commands should both display the same version of DOS.

You might see this message when running a stand-alone version of WordPerfect on a network. Use the Network version of WordPerfect instead.

Solution

You should have to respond to this error message only once (if ever). If you are using an AT or compatible, verify that you are running only DOS version 3.x. If versions of DOS are mixed, recopy COMMAND.COM from the DOS master disk onto the boot disk and reboot.

Capitalization

You can capitalize text as you type or after the text has been entered.

Keystrokes

Capitalize While Typing

To capitalize a single character, hold down either SHIFT key and type the character.

To capitalize several characters, press CAPS LOCK, type the text, then press CAPS LOCK again to turn it off. While Caps Lock is on, "Pos" on the status line is shown in caps ("POS").

Capitalize Text After Typing

1. Move the cursor to one end of the text to be in uppercase.

2. Press Block (ALT-F4) to turn on Block.

3. Move the cursor to the opposite end of the block.

4. Press Switch (SHIFT-F3).

5. Type **1** to change the block to uppercase.

6. Press Block (ALT-F4) to turn off Block (or perform another block function).

Hints

If you press SHIFT when CAPS LOCK is on, any letter that is typed will be lowercase rather than uppercase. If you have the program *Repeat Performance* by WordPerfect Corporation, you can disable this "reverse CAPS LOCK" and always get uppercase characters even if the SHIFT key is pressed accidentally.

CAPS LOCK affects only the letters A through Z. If you want a character such as the ampersand (&) or quotation mark ("), typically obtained by pressing SHIFT and another key, you will still need to press the SHIFT key.

Related Entries

Block

Switch

Carriage Return

The carriage return on a typewriter is referred to as the ENTER or RETURN key on a computer. Refer to *ENTER Key* for more information.

When you print a document, a "carriage return" (ASCII 13) and "line feed" (ASCII 10) are sent at the end of each line. These codes return the printer carriage to the left side and move it down one line. Some printers that do not have an underline function might get underlining by performing a carriage return, then printing a solid line under the specified text. This method is also used by some printers to overprint a line for bolded text.

If you save a file as a DOS text (ASCII) file, each Hard Return code [HRt] is converted to a carriage return/line feed code.

Related Entries

DOS Text Files

ENTER Key

Center Page from Top to Bottom

The Center Page command centers a single page vertically between the top and bottom margins.

Keystrokes

1. Press Go To (CTRL-HOME), then ↑ to move the cursor to the very top of the page.

2. Press Page Format (ALT-F8).

3. Type **3** to Center Page Top to Bottom. The Page Format menu will flash, but other than that, there is no immediate indication that the command has taken effect.

4. Press ENTER to leave the menu and return to the document. (For reassurance, press Reveal Codes (ALT-F3) to see the [Center Pg] code.)

Hints

Before you choose the Center Page command, the cursor must be at the very beginning of the page before any text. If you need to select a sheet feeder bin, however, the [Bin#:] code should come first. A printer with a sheet feeder needs to receive the bin number selection *before* the Center Page command (see *Sheet Feeder Bin Number* for more information).

Pressing Go To (CTRL-HOME)], then ↑ will move the cursor to the top of the page before all codes and text. Pressing Reveal Codes (ALT-F3) will show the location of codes in relation to the cursor.

For the Center Page command to work correctly, you should have no hard returns before the first line or after the last line of text. If extra lines are included, they will be taken into consideration during the centering operation.

Use Center (SHIFT-F6) to center text between the left and right margins.

Center Page with Hand-Fed Paper

If you are printing with hand-fed paper, WordPerfect will assume that you are feeding the paper one inch. When printing a centered page, you should continue to allow for the standard top margin when feeding the paper into the printer. See *Top Margin* for more information.

Applications

The Center Page command could be placed in a format macro for single-page letters. You can also use it at the beginning of document title pages, as shown in Figure 4-9.

Related Entries

Center Text

Sheet Feeder Bin Number

Top Margin

Center Text

Center (SHIFT-F6) is used to center text between the left and right margins or to center text over a specific position.

```
                    Humanities 101
                    Professor Green
                     Section 21


                   THE RENAISSANCE



                  Ms. Sharon Brown
                November 25, 1987
```

Figure 4-9.   Title page created using the Center Page command

Keystrokes

Center Between Margins

1. Move the cursor to the left margin.

2. Press Center (SHIFT-F6). The cursor is centered between the current margins.

3. Type the text to be centered.

4. Press ENTER to turn off centering.

Center Existing Text

1. Move the cursor to the beginning of the line.

2. Press Center (SHIFT-F6).

3. Press ↓ and the line is centered. (If the cursor does not move down and the line is not centered, there is no hard return [HRt] at the end of the line. Press END to move to the end of the line, then press ENTER to center the line.)

A second option does not require a hard return at the end of the line.

1. Position the cursor anywhere in the line to be centered.

2. Press Block (ALT-F4). (You do not have to move the cursor to define the block.)

3. Immediately press Center (SHIFT-F6).

4. Type **Y** to center the line.

Center an Existing Block of Text

If you have several lines of text to be centered, you can center a block rather than one line at a time, as shown in Figure 4-10.

1. Move the cursor to one end of the block to be centered.

2. Press Block (ALT-F4) to turn on Block.

3. Move the cursor to the opposite end of the block.

4. Press Center (SHIFT-F6).

5. Type **Y** when asked "[Center]? (Y/N) N."

A Center On code [C] is placed at the beginning of each line and a Center Off code [c] is placed at the end of each line. Each soft return [SRt] in the block is changed to a hard return [HRt].

Center at a Specific Position

You can center text at a specific position rather than between the left and right margins, as in the following illustration.

a) Block highlighted

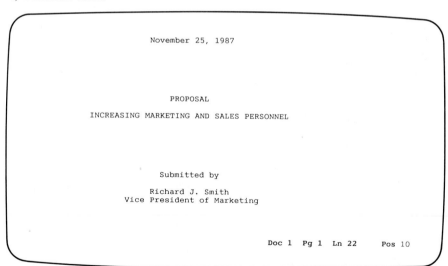

November 25, 1987

PROPOSAL
INCREASING MARKETING AND SALES PERSONNEL

Submitted by
Richard J. Smith
Vice President of Marketing

[Center]? (Y/N) N

b) Centered block

November 25, 1987

PROPOSAL
INCREASING MARKETING AND SALES PERSONNEL

Submitted by
Richard J. Smith
Vice President of Marketing

Doc 1 Pg 1 Ln 22   Pos 10

Figure 4-10.   Centering a block of text, using the Block and Center commands

PROJECTED REVENUES FOR
FIRST QUARTER 1988

	Sales	Expenses	Total
January	34,000.00	20,000.00	14,000.00
February	38,000.00	22,000.00	16,000.00
March	45,000.00	24,000.00	21,000.00
April	57,000.00	30,000.00	27,000.00

1. Use SPACEBAR or TAB to move the cursor to the position where the text is to be centered. The cursor must be at least three spaces or one tab away from the left margin.

2. Press Center (SHIFT-F6).

3. Type the text to be centered.

4. To continue centering at a specific position on the same line, press TAB (then SPACEBAR if necessary) to move to the next location and repeat steps 2 and 3.

Remove Centering

To remove centering, you must delete either the Center On code [C] or Center Off code [c]. Press Reveal Codes (ALT-F3) and delete either code, or follow the steps below to remove centering on the normal screen.

1. Move the cursor to the first character in the centered text.

2. Press BACKSPACE.

3. Type **Y** in answer to the question, "Delete [Center]? (Y/N) N."

Hints

When Center is pressed, a Center On code [C] is inserted. As soon as text is typed, the Center Off code [c] is inserted at the end of the text. Pressing ENTER moves past the [c] code, thus ending centering. Pressing →, TAB, or Flush Right (ALT-F6) will also move the cursor past the [c].

Text can be centered between the margins even if there is text at the left or right margin, as in the following illustration.

MONTHLY DEPARTMENT NEWSLETTER

| Volume I Number 11 | Confidential | November 25, 1987 |

Place the cursor at the end of the first line, then press Center (SHIFT-F6). If you are more than three spaces from the end of the line, the text will be centered at that position rather than between the margins.

See *Tabs, Clear and Set* for more information about centering text at a tab setting. WordPerfect also has an option to center a page vertically between the top and bottom margins; for more information, see *Center Page from Top to Bottom.*

Disappearing Text

The Center codes take precedence over other text. If you are in the middle of a line and press Center, or if you type text from the left margin that runs into a Center code, the text may disappear. If this happens, press Reveal Codes (ALT-F3) to make the editing changes (deleting either the [C] or the text that ran into the Center code).

Line Draw Around Centered Text

If you want to draw lines around centered text, move the cursor at least one space away from the left margin before starting to draw the box. Otherwise, the line will run into the Center code at the left or right margin and will not draw the box correctly.

Applications

You can use Center for titles and headings in regular documents or columns. Figure 4-11 shows how Center can be used before and within columns.

BILL OF RIGHTS

The first ten amendments form what is known as the "Bill of Rights" ratified on December 15, 1791.

ONE

Congress shall make no law respecting an establishment of religion, or prohibiting the free exercise thereof; or abridging the freedom of speech, or of the press; or the right of the people peaceably to assemble, and to petition the Government for a redress of grievances.

TWO

A well regulated Militia, being necessary to the security of a free State, the right of the people to keep and bear Arms, shall not be infringed.

THREE

No Soldier shall, in time of peace be quartered in any house, without the consent of the Owner, nor in time of war, but in a manner to be prescribed by law.

FOUR

The right of the people to be secure in their persons, houses, papers, and effects, against unreasonable searches and seizures, shall not be violated, and no Warrants shall issue, but upon probable cause, supported by Oath or affirmation, and

particularly describing the place to be searched, and the persons or things to be seized.

FIVE

No person shall be held to answer for a capital, or otherwise infamous crime, unless on a presentment or indictment of a Grand Jury, except in cases arising in the land or naval forces, or in the Militia, when in actual service in time of War or public danger; nor shall any person be subject for the same offense to be a witness against himself, nor be deprived of life, liberty, or property, without due process of law; nor shall private property be taken for public use, without just compensation.

SIX

In all Criminal prosecutions, the accused shall enjoy the right to a speedy and public trial, by an impartial jury of the State and district wherein the crime shall have been committed, which district shall have been previously ascertained by law, and to be informed of the nature and cause of the accusation; to be confronted with the

witnesses against him; to have compulsory process for obtaining witnesses in his favor, and to have the Assistance of Counsel for his defense.

SEVEN

In suits at common law, where the value in controversy shall exceed twenty dollars, the right of trial by jury shall be preserved,.and no fact tried by a jury, shall be otherwise reexamined in any Court of the United States, than according to the rules of the common law.

EIGHT

Excessive bail shall not be required, nor excessive fines imposed, nor cruel and unusual punishments inflicted.

NINE

The enumeration in the Constitution, of certain rights, shall not be construed to deny or disparage others retained by the people.

TEN

The Powers not delegated to the United States by the Constitution, nor prohibited by it to the States, are reserved to the States respectively, or to the people.

Figure 4-11.   Document created using the Center command before and within columns

Related Entries

Block

Center Page from Top to Bottom

Columns

Tabs, Clear and Set

Change Directory

You can change the default directory to be used for saving and retrieving files from within WordPerfect or from DOS.

Keystrokes

Change Directory Within WordPerfect

1. Press List Files (F5).

2. Type = to change the default directory.

3. Enter the pathname for the new directory (such as **b:**, **c:\wp**, or **c:\personal\letters**).

4. Press Cancel (F1) to set the new directory and return to the document or ENTER to see the list of files within that directory.

If you enter the List Files menu and decide to change the default directory, you can do it in the List Files menu there rather than leaving that menu and following the previous steps.

1. After pressing List Files (F5) and then ENTER to see the list of files, type **7** to Change Directory.

2. Enter the pathname for the new directory.

3. Press ENTER to see the list of files within the new directory.

4. Press Exit (F7) to return to the document.

You can also move the cursor to the directory listed in the List Files menu that is to be used as the new default, type 7, and press ENTER twice.

Change Directory from DOS

Hard Disk   Before entering WordPerfect, you can use the DOS CD command to change the default directory.

1. Type **CD**, then enter the name of the new directory.

2. Type **WP** from the new directory to start Word-Perfect.

If the message "Bad command or file name" is displayed, the directory containing the WordPerfect files is not in the path. The following is a sample PATH command that could be placed in the AUTOEXEC.BAT file.

    path c: \;c: \wp

If necessary, substitute for WP the name of the directory where WP.EXE is located.

If you are using DOS version 3.x, you don't need to enter a PATH command. Instead, you can specify the directory with the command as in \WP\WP. See Chapter 1 for more information about the PATH command and AUTO-EXEC.BAT file.

Two Disk Drives   For those using two disk drives rather than a hard disk, WordPerfect advises that you choose drive B as the default drive for saving and retrieving files.

After starting your computer, insert the WordPerfect disk in drive A and a data disk in drive B. Enter **B:** from DOS to display the B> DOS prompt, then type **A:WP** to start WordPerfect from drive A.

Hints

If you enter the name of a directory that does not exist, you are asked if you want to create a new directory. Type **Y** or **N**.

While in the List Files menu, you can move from one directory to another without changing the default directory. You can move up the tree structure by moving the cursor to ".. <PARENT> <DIR>" (as shown in Figure 4-12), and pressing ENTER twice.

If you are in a directory called C:\LEARN, the parent directory is the root directory (\ ). If you are in a directory called C:\PERSONAL\LETTERS, the parent directory is \PERSONAL.

You can also move down the tree structure to look into subdirectories. For instance, if you are in the root directory,

```
11/25/87  14:07                 Directory C:\PERSONAL\*.*
Document Size:          0                      Free Disk Space:    1458176

 . <CURRENT>     <DIR>                 .. <PARENT>     <DIR>
ALTA    .MAC          8  04/26/86 23:18   ALTJ    .MAC        6  08/24/86 08:37
ALTK    .MAC         27  10/25/86 19:53   ALTL    .MAC       14  10/25/86 19:56
ALTZ    .MAC          4  10/25/86 23:08   APARTMNT.        4438  11/08/86 11:18
ARTICLE .          3734  01/01/80 03:02   BOOK    .         263  10/22/86 22:01
CLOSING .MAC         76  01/14/87 13:51   FORMAT  .MAC       35  01/14/87 13:50
HISTORY .1        33783  01/01/80 00:16   HISTORY .2      28953  10/19/84 01:29
HISTORY .3        51194  08/06/84 00:13   HISTORY .4      40244  08/07/84 00:41
HISTORY .5        20299  08/08/84 00:02   INVOICE .        2189  09/29/86 19:03
LESSON  .1         7185  10/01/86 23:28   LIST    .        5780  10/25/86 14:23
LIST    .3          322  01/14/87 13:52   NAVY    .       20033  04/24/86 16:41
NOTES   .            84  10/01/86 15:59   PICTURES.       14576  10/25/86 20:42
PROPOSAL.          7702  10/09/86 13:21   SORTED  .LST     5648  11/08/86 08:43
XMAS    .85        2182  12/26/85 23:31   |

1 Retrieve; 2 Delete; 3 Rename; 4 Print; 5 Text In;
6 Look; 7 Change Directory; 8 Copy; 9 Word Search; 0 Exit: 6
```

Figure 4-12.   Moving up the tree structure by choosing <PARENT> <DIR>

```
11/25/87  10:42              Directory C:\*.*
Document Size:     2825                      Free Disk Space:  1892352

.  <CURRENT>    <DIR>                    ..  <PARENT>     <DIR>
BOOK      .     <DIR>    12/01/86 10:08   CLIENTS  .     <DIR>    09/22/85 20:36
COMM      .     <DIR>    09/22/85 20:20   DATA     .     <DIR>    09/21/85 22:23
JEFF      .     <DIR>    09/22/85 20:19   KAREN    .     <DIR>    09/22/85 20:19
LEARNING.       <DIR>    01/08/87 10:32   LIBRARY  .     <DIR>    03/05/86 20:52
MATH      .     <DIR>    09/22/85 21:20   NEWDATA  .     <DIR>    01/06/86 11:32
PERSONAL.       <DIR>    09/22/85 20:51   SYSTEM   .     <DIR>    01/01/80 00:05
TEMP      .     <DIR>    04/05/87 22:21   WP       .     <DIR>    09/21/85 22:30
WP50      .     <DIR>    04/04/87 22:17   401K      .MPW    6832  12/15/86 13:11
ANSI     .SYS    1664    10/20/83 12:00   APPOINT  .APP       0   02/16/87 17:34
AUTOEXEC.BAT      128    03/05/86 20:49   AUTOTIME.EXE    1314    08/05/80 16:33
BOOK     .MPW    3824    10/24/86 12:42   COMMAND  .COM   23210   03/07/85 13:43
CONFIG   .SYS     116    03/16/87 11:44   DB       .        650   04/07/86 23:18
MARKS    .WP       80    03/18/87 20:43   PROGRAM  .       3485   03/18/87 21:07
PRTCHG   .COM      80    01/01/86 15:43   PRTSCR   .COM    1587    03/21/86 08:16
PRTSCR   .DOC    1744    03/21/86 08:18   PRTTGL   .COM      23   01/01/86 14:52
RP       .EXE    9712    08/29/86 09:25   RP       .INS    9072    08/29/86 09:14
RP       .SYS    5136    07/01/86 21:15   RPINSTAL.EXE    32496   08/29/86 09:16
RPREMOVE.EXE     5872    08/29/86 06:23   SCREEN   .DAT   18459   01/14/87 14:12

1 Retrieve; 2 Delete; 3 Rename; 4 Print; 5 Text In;
6 Look; 7 Change Directory; 8 Copy; 9 Word Search; 0 Exit: 6
```

Figure 4-13.   List Files menu in root directory

you might see a List Files menu similar to the one shown in Figure 4-13. You can move the cursor to any directory listed and press ENTER twice to see the files in that subdirectory.

Related Entries

Directories

Characters per Inch

See *Pitch*

Clear Tabs

See *Tabs, Clear and Set*

Codes

WordPerfect codes control how a document is formatted and printed.

When a WordPerfect feature such as Bold, Underline, Indent, or Footnote is chosen, a code is placed in the document at the cursor's location. These codes are not visible within the text so the text on the screen can look more like the printed document. However, there is usually an indication on the screen that the function has been chosen (the text will be bolded, underlined, or indented, or a number for a footnote will be inserted).

If you want to see the text *with* the codes, press Reveal Codes (ALT-F3). The screen is split, showing a ruler line with the regular screen above and the text with codes below. The following illustration shows a Reveal Codes screen. Text is shown as regular text while codes are shown in boldface.

```
                    THE CONSTITUTION OF THE UNITED STATES

                              PREAMBLE

     We the people of the United States, in Order to form a more
perfect Union, establish Justice, insure domestic Tranquility,
provide for the common Defense, promote the general Welfare, and
B:\PREAMBLE                               Doc 1  Pg 1  Ln 1      Pos 10
[         ▲     ▲    ▲        ▲       ▲        ▲     ▲      ▲   ]▲     ▲     ▲
-[C][B]THE CONSTITUTION OF THE UNITED STATES[c][b][HRt]
[HRt]
[C][U]PREAMBLE[u][c][HRt]
[HRt]
```

For more information about editing text while in the Reveal Codes screen, see *Reveal Codes*.

List of Codes

Following is a list of all the WordPerfect codes as they appear on the Reveal Codes screen. In the code designations, *n* represents a number that may appear in the code.

Code	Meaning
▬ (blinking)	Cursor position
[ ]	Hard space
[-]	Hard hyphen
-	Soft hyphen
/	Cancel hyphenation
[A][a]	Tab Align or Flush Right (begin and end)
[Adv ▲]	Advance Up ½ line
[Adv ▼]	Advance Down ½ line
[AdvLn:n]	Advance to specific line number
[Align Char:n]	Alignment character (n = character)
[B][b]	Bold (begin and end)
[Bin#:n]	Sheet feeder bin number
[Block]	Beginning of block
[BlockPro:Off]	Block Protect off
[BlockPro:On]	Block Protect on
[C][c]	Centering (begin and end)
[Center Pg]	Center page top to bottom
[Cmnd:]	Embedded printer command
[CndlEOP:n]	Conditional End of Page (n = number of lines)
[Col Def:]	Column definition
[Col Off]	End of text columns
[Col On]	Beginning of text columns
[Date:n]	Date/Time function (n = format)
[DefMark:Index,n]	Index definition (n = format)
[DefMark:List,n]	List definition (n = list number)

Code	Meaning
[DefMark:ToC,n]	Table of Contents definition (n = ToC level)
[EndDef]	End of index, list, or Table of Contents
[EndMark:List,n]	End marked text (n = list number)
[EndMark:ToC,n]	End marked text (n = ToC level)
[Font Change:n,n]	Specify new font or print wheel (n = pitch, font)
[FtnOpt]	Footnote/Endnote options
[Hdr/Ftr:n,n;text]	Header or Footer definition (n = type, occurrence)
[HPg]	Hard page
[HRt]	Hard return
[Hyph off]	Hyphenation off
[Hyph on]	Hyphenation on
[HZone Set:n,n]	Reset size of hyphenation zone (n = left, right)
[→Indent]	Beginning of indent
[→Indent←]	Beginning of left/right indent
[Index:heading;subheading]	Index mark
[LnNum:Off]	End of line numbering
[LnNum:On]	Beginning of line numbering
[LPI:n]	Lines per inch
[←Mar Rel:n]	Left margin release (n = positions moved)
[Margin Set:n,n]	Left and right margin reset
[Mark:List,n]	Begin marked text for list (n = list number)

Code	Meaning
[Mark:ToC,n]	Begin marked text for ToC (*n* = ToC level)
[Math Def]	Definition of math columns
[Math Off]	End of math
[Math On]	Beginning of math
!	Formula calculation
t	Subtotal entry
+	Do subtotal
T	Total entry
=	Do total
*	Do grand total
[Note:End,n;[note#]text]	Endnote (*n* = endnote number)
[Note:Foot,n;[note#]text]	Footnote (*n* = footnote number)
[Overstk]	Overstrike preceding character
[Par#:Auto]	Automatic paragraph/outline number
[Par#:n]	Fixed paragraph number (*n* = level number)
[Par#Def]	Paragraph numbering definition
[Pg#:n]	New page number
[Pg# Col:n,n,n]	Column position for page numbers (*n* = left, center, right)
[Pg Lnth:n,n]	Set page length (*n* = form lines, text lines)
[Pos Pg#:n]	Set position for page numbers
[RedLn][r]]	Redline (begin and end)
[Rt Just Off]	Right justification off

Code	Meaning
[Rt Just On]	Right justification on
[Set Ftn #:n]	New footnote number
[Smry/Cmnt:n]	Document summary/comment (n = first 100 characters of summary or comment)
[Spacing Set:n]	Spacing set
[SPg]	Soft new page
[SRt]	Soft return
[StrkOut][s]	Strikeout (begin and end)
[SubScrpt]	Subscript
[Suppress:n]	Suppress page format options (n = format(s))
[SuprScrpt]	Superscript
[TAB]	Move to next Tab stop
[Tab Set:]	Tab reset
[ToA:n;[short form];]	Mark Table of Authorities with short form
[ToA:n;[short form];<Full Form>]	Mark Table of Authorities with full form (n = section number)
[Top Mar:n]	Set top margin in half-lines
[U][u]	Underlining (begin and end)
[Undrl Style:n]	Underline style
[W/O Off]	Widow/Orphan off
[W/O On]	Widow/Orphan on

Related Entries

Reveal Codes

Colors

You can customize the colors used by WordPerfect for color monitors. The Color Selection menu is also used to choose attributes for single-color graphics monitors.

Keystrokes

1. Press Screen (CTRL-F3).

2. Type **4** for Colors. (If you have a monochrome monitor without a graphics card, you will see the message "Not a color monitor.")

3. Type **1** if you have a color monitor or **2** if you have a single-color monitor.

4. Type **Y** for fast text display. (If you see flickering or "snow" on your screen after answering this question, press Cancel (F1), then repeat the above steps and type **N**.)

5. If you have a color monitor, type **1**. If you have a single-color monitor, type **2**. Then type **1** if you want underlined text displayed in reverse video or **2** if you want to use underlining and go to step 8.

6. Figure 4-14 shows a facsimile of the Color Selection menu. Using the color bar as a guide, type a letter from A through P to indicate which color is to be used for the background, foreground, underline, bold, and other elements to be colored. A sample of current selections is found to the right of the menu choices. As you make changes in the menu, the new colors are shown in this sample.

7. Press Switch (SHIFT-F3) to select the colors for document 2.

8. Press Exit (F7) when finished.

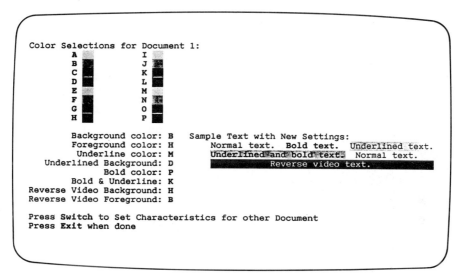

Figure 4-14.   Color Selection menu

Hints

You can choose different colors for each of the two screens (documents) in WordPerfect. If you split the screen using the Window feature, each document retains its colors.

Some single-color monitors, such as the AT&T, can display the underline as underline. Others, such as Compaq, might need to use reverse video. (You might try entering the command MODE UND ON from DOS to see if it will allow underlining on your Compaq monitor. You need the MODE.COM file on the disk to run this command.)

Colors Not Holding

Upon exiting WordPerfect, the screen is restored to the original mode that existed before running WordPerfect. This is necessary because other programs might not be able to run in color. Some programs, such as Lotus, change the screen from color to single-color mode, but do not return to the original mode.

If you find that the colors you selected are not returning when you reenter WordPerfect, another program might have reset the Mode. Enter **MODE CO80** (or **MODE COLOR** for a Tandy computer) to return to color. Remember that you need the MODE.COM file on the appropriate disk to run this command.

If you need to reset the mode often, consider putting it in a batch file used to start WordPerfect. See Chapter 1 for more information on batch files.

If the colors refuse to hold, define a startup macro that sets the colors. To avoid executing the macro each time you start WordPerfect, edit the AUTOEXEC.BAT file to include the command SET WP=/M-COLORS. The SET command tells DOS that whenever the command WP is entered, it should also execute the named macro.

Paradise Color Card

If you try to select colors and have a Paradise color card, you might see the message "Error: not a color monitor." Check the switch settings on the computer system board and switches on the Paradise board. They should both be set at 80×25.

Black and White or Single-Color Graphics Monitors

If underlined text does not show up clearly on the screen, change colors, select single-color monitor, and try the underline option. If there is still a problem, select reverse video to display the underlined text.

Colors at the Printer

Some printers, such as the IBM Color Jetprinter, can print in different colors. In these situations, WordPerfect has defined some or all of the eight fonts to print in a different color. Print the files PRINTER.TST and PRINTER2.TST found on the Learning diskette to see which color is assigned to each font.

Related Entries

AUTOEXEC.BAT File

MODE Command

Columns

Three types of columns are available in WordPerfect: tabbed columns, newspaper-style columns, and parallel columns.

Tabbed columns are useful for creating tables and charts. Newspaper columns should be used for text that flows from one column to the next, even when editing changes are made. Parallel columns can be used when you do not want added or deleted text in one column to affect another.

Keystrokes

Tabbed Columns

1. Press Line Format (SHIFT-F8).

2. Type **1** or **2** for Tabs.

3. Press HOME, HOME, ← to move to position 0.

4. Press Del to End of Line (CTRL-END) to clear all tabs.

5. Set tabs for each column. You can use the formula found in "Hints" for setting evenly spaced tabs. Or you can estimate the tab settings and adjust them later for

proper spacing after the table has been entered. See Tabs for options and more help if necessary.

6. Press Exit (F7) to return to your document.

7. Enter the columns.

8. If you need to adjust the tab settings, move to the right of the [Tab Set:] code, reenter the Tab menu, and change the settings. When you Exit from the menu, the columns are readjusted automatically. The previous [Tab Set:] code does not need to be deleted.

See "Parallel Columns" if you want text to wrap within a column, but want the look of tabbed columns.

Parallel Columns

When creating parallel (or scriptwriter's) columns, remember the following basic steps: define columns, turn on columns, and type the text. Separate each column using CTRL-ENTER.

1. If necessary, first change the left and right margins: press Line Format (SHIFT-F8), type **3**, and enter the new left and right margins. When you define columns, these settings are used to calculate evenly spaced columns.

2. Press Math/Columns (ALT-F7).

3. Type **4** for Column Def (define columns). Figure 4-15 shows the menu that appears.

4. Type **Y** or **N** in answer to the question "Do you wish to have evenly spaced columns?"

5. If you chose **N**, skip to the next step. If you typed **Y**, enter the number of spaces that will be used to separate each column.

6. Type **2** for Parallel with Block Protect.

7. Enter the number of text columns (as many as 24).

```
Text Column Definition

        Do you wish to have evenly spaced columns? (Y/N) N
        If yes, number of spaces between columns:
        Type of columns: 1
             1 - Newspaper
             2 - Parallel with Block Protect

        Number of text columns (2-24): 0

        Column    Left       Right      Column    Left       Right
          1:                              13:
          2:                              14:
          3:                              15:
          4:                              16:
          5:                              17:
          6:                              18:
          7:                              19:
          8:                              20:
          9:                              21:
         10:                              22:
         11:                              23:
         12:                              24:
```

Figure 4-15.   Text Column Definition menu

8. If you typed **Y** for evenly spaced columns, the margins are set for you. If you typed **N**, the margins are estimated and you are automatically given five spaces between columns. In either situation, you can press ENTER to move through the settings or enter new margins if necessary.

9. When the margins are set correctly, press Exit (F7) or press ENTER until you leave the menu.

10. The one-line Math/Columns menu is again displayed on the screen. Type **3** to turn on columns (or you can wait and turn them on later in the document). "Col 1" appears on the status line to indicate that the cursor is in the first column.

11. After entering the text for the first column, press CTRL-ENTER and begin entering text for the second column. After completing the last column, CTRL-ENTER returns the cursor to the left margin, where you can repeat the process.

A Hard Page (CTRL-ENTER) is used to separate columns. If

you want to move the cursor from column to column, press Go To (CTRL-HOME), then → or ←, depending on the direction you want to move. See "Hints" for complete details on moving between columns.

Newspaper Columns

For text that should wrap from column to column, follow the steps listed for defining parallel columns, but in step 6 instead of typing 2 for Parallel, type **1** for Newspaper columns.

Instead of pressing CTRL-ENTER to go to the next column as you do in parallel columns, you will most likely wait until the end of the page. (You do, of course, have the option of using CTRL-ENTER to force a column to end.) When a page break is encountered at the bottom of the column you are filling, you are automatically placed at the top of the next column. After all the columns have been filled, the cursor moves to the next page and continues in columns.

You can use the same keystrokes that are used in parallel columns to move from column to column. Press Go To (CTRL-HOME) and → or ←, depending upon the direction you want to move. See "Hints" for more options.

Hints

Tabbed Columns

Moving Tabbed Columns   You can cut (move), copy, or delete a tabbed column or a rectangular section of text.

1. Move to the first character in the column to be cut, copied, or deleted.

2. Press Block (ALT-F4) to turn on Block.

3. Move straight down the column if only that column is to be affected. If you want to cut, copy, or delete more than one column, move the cursor to the right into the applicable column(s). At this point it does not appear

that the proper text is being highlighted as shown in Figure 4-16a; be patient until the next step.

4. Press Move (CTRL-F4) and type **4** to Cut/Copy the column. The column is now highlighted (see Figure 4-16b). If you moved the cursor into columns to the right, then they also will be highlighted. Note that the [TAB] preceding the column is also highlighted as part of the column.

5. Type **1** to Cut, **2** to Copy, or **3** to Delete the column. Columns to the right will be readjusted automatically, as shown in Figure 4-16c.

6. When you are ready to retrieve the cut or copied column, position the cursor just after the last character in the column to the left, at the left margin, or after the last column.

7. Press Move (CTRL-F4) and type **4** to Retrieve the column. Remember that a [TAB] was included as part of the column, so if you retrieve a column at the left margin, it will be sent to the first tab setting. Delete each [TAB] code at the beginning of each line if necessary to move it to the left margin.

Moving a Rectangle   The Move Rectangle option lets you define a block of text from the top left corner to the bottom right corner, while the Column option assumes columns are separated by tabs, Tab Align codes, or Indent codes. Figure 4-17 shows a highlighted rectangle. The following steps will cut or copy a rectangle.

1. Place the cursor at one corner (upper left or bottom right) and press Block (ALT-F4).

2. Move to the opposite corner. A regular block is highlighted until the next step.

3. Press Move (CTRL-F4) and type **5** to Cut/Copy a Rectangle. The rectangle is highlighted.

4. Type **1** to Cut, **2** to Copy, or **3** to Delete.

a) Highlighted text

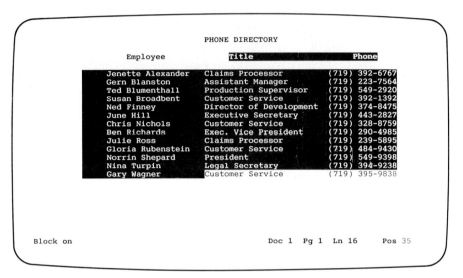

b) Highlighted column

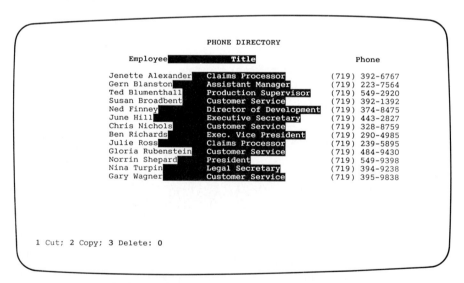

Figure 4-16.   Highlighted text (a); the column to be cut, copied, or deleted (b); and the screen showing the result of deleting the center column (c)

c) Column deleted

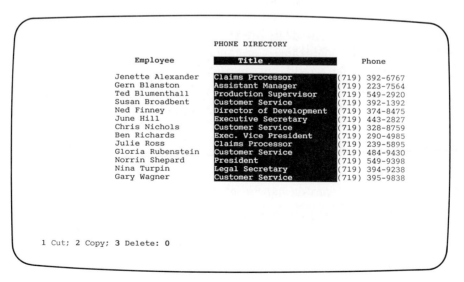

```
                        PHONE DIRECTORY

            Employee              Phone

            Jenette Alexander    (719) 392-6767
            Gern Blanston        (719) 223-7564
            Ted Blumenthall      (719) 549-2920
            Susan Broadbent      (719) 392-1392
            Ned Finney           (719) 374-8475
            June Hill            (719) 443-2827
            Chris Nichols        (719) 328-8759
            Ben Richards         (719) 290-4985
            Julie Ross           (719) 239-5895
            Gloria Rubenstein    (719) 484-9430
            Norrin Shepard       (719) 549-9398
            Nina Turpin          (719) 394-9238
            Gary Wagner          (719) 395-9838




C:\WP\PHONE.LST                   Doc 1  Pg 1  Ln 16      Pos 10
```

Figure 4-16.   Highlighted text (a); the column to be cut, copied, or deleted (b); and the screen showing the result of deleting the center column (c) (*continued*)

```
                        PHONE DIRECTORY

            Employee           Title              Phone

            Jenette Alexander  Claims Processor   (719) 392-6767
            Gern Blanston      Assistant Manager  (719) 223-7564
            Ted Blumenthall    Production Supervisor (719) 549-2920
            Susan Broadbent    Customer Service   (719) 392-1392
            Ned Finney         Director of Development (719) 374-8475
            June Hill          Executive Secretary (719) 443-2827
            Chris Nichols      Customer Service   (719) 328-8759
            Ben Richards       Exec. Vice President (719) 290-4985
            Julie Ross         Claims Processor   (719) 239-5895
            Gloria Rubenstein  Customer Service   (719) 484-9430
            Norrin Shepard     President          (719) 549-9398
            Nina Turpin        Legal Secretary    (719) 394-9238
            Gary Wagner        Customer Service   (719) 395-9838




1 Cut; 2 Copy; 3 Delete: 0
```

Figure 4-17.   Highlighted rectangle

5. Position the cursor anywhere on the screen.

6. Press Move (CTRL-F4) and type **6** to Retrieve the rectangle. The complete rectangle will be retrieved at that point. If it is not retrieved at the left margin, spaces are inserted so the format of the rectangle is retained.

If [TAB] codes are included in a cut rectangle, remaining columns are automatically moved to the left. If you don't want the remaining columns to move to the left, do not include a [TAB] code. In this case, the last line has to be at least as long as the longest line in that column. If it isn't, add spaces to the end of the line for the rectangle to include all characters in all lines. See *Cut Text and Columns* for clarification.

To adjust the amount of space between columns, adjust the tab settings.

The text involved when you cut or copy a block, column, or rectangle is kept in separate temporary files. You must choose the correct option (text, column, or rectangle) when retrieving the block or you will get the wrong block. The option of retrieving a normal cut/copied block of text (pressing Retrieve (SHIFT-F10) and ENTER) cannot be used to retrieve a column or rectangle.

Moving the Cursor in Tabbed Columns   Unlike parallel or newspaper columns, you can move through tabbed columns just as you would normal text. However, if you prefer to jump over the text to the next tab setting, press INS to toggle on Typeover. Pressing TAB in this instance will move to the next tab setting rather than inserting a [TAB] code and will help you move across columns more quickly.

Formula for Setting Evenly Spaced Tabbed Columns   The following formula can be used to set evenly spaced tabs.

1. First, determine the total line width.

$$\text{(Right margin)} \quad - \quad \text{(Left margin)} \quad = \quad \begin{array}{l}\text{(Total number of}\\ \text{spaces available)}\end{array}$$

2. Next, find the longest line in each column and add them together. You should also note how many columns you have.

$$\frac{\text{(Total number of spaces available)} - \text{(Combined total of longest lines of all columns)}}{\text{(Number of columns} - 1)} = \text{(Number of spaces between columns)}$$

3. The left margin could be used for the first column.

$$\text{(Length of the first column)} + \text{(Number of spaces between columns, from step 2)} = \text{(First tab setting)}$$

Continue adding the numbers to the last tab setting until all tabs have been set.

Parallel and Newspaper Columns

When columns are defined, the following code is placed in the document:

[Col Def:2,10,39,45,74,0,0,0,0, ...]

The first number in the definition is the number of columns. The remaining numbers indicate the left and right margin for each column. A total of 48 numbers for the left and right margins are displayed, even if the numbers are zero.

A [Col On] code is displayed in Reveal Codes where columns are turned on and a [Col Off] code is inserted where columns are turned off.

Moving from Column to Column   Most cursor keys function the same as they do when not working in columns. The following options are available for moving the cursor among columns.

Arrow keys   Work within columns just as they do in normal text. When at the end of a newspaper column, ↓ and →

	move into the next column. At the beginning of a column, ↑ and ← move to the previous column. When in parallel columns, ↑ and ↓ move up and down within the same column, while → and ← follow the text as it was entered.
Go To → or ←	Pressing Go To (CTRL-HOME) displays "Go To" at the bottom of the screen. Press ← to go to the previous column or → to move to the next column.
Go To, HOME, → or ←	After pressing Go To (CTRL-HOME), which displays "Go To" on the screen, you can press HOME, then ← or → to move to the far left or far right column.

Turning Columns On and Off   You cannot turn on Columns if the columns have not yet been defined. If you attempt to do so, you will see the following message: "ERROR: No text columns defined."

You can turn Columns on and off throughout a document as many times as you would like. This enables you to have standard text and multiple columns within the same document. To turn off Columns within a document, press Math/ Columns (ALT-F7) and type **3**. You do not have to turn Columns on and off at the end of the document if the entire document is in columns. Parallel columns turn off and on automatically to achieve the parallel effect. See "Parallel Columns Only" for more information.

Different column definitions can exist on the same page. However, you cannot define columns while in Columns mode. You should first turn off Columns, create the new column definition, turn on Columns, then continue.

Columns can be turned on before or after text has been entered. In fact, you might find it easier (and much faster) to create and edit a document first, move to the beginning of the text, and turn on Columns.

If a document is in columns and you want to change it back to the standard left and right margins, move the cursor to the [Col On] code and delete it.

Increasing the Speed of Columns   In versions prior to 4.1, WordPerfect did not display columns side by side. Instead, a page break was used to separate columns and "Col #" was included on the status line to show which column the cursor was in. Text in columns was reformatted as quickly as text not in columns.

When WordPerfect Corporation decided to display columns side by side on the screen, there was a noticeable delay when text was added, deleted, or when automatic reformatting took place. To help with the problem, a feature was added to the Screen (CTRL-F3) key to allow Auto Rewrite (option 5) to be turned off. If Auto Rewrite is off, the screen will only reformat as the cursor is moved down through the text; if turned on, reformatting is done when a single cursor key is pressed.

With the release of version 4.2, WordPerfect added a feature that lets you decide how columns are to be displayed; you press Math/Columns (ALT-F5) and type **5** for Column Display. The alternative to displaying columns side by side is to separate them with a page break. They will appear in the appropriate position on the screen instead of being "stacked" as they were in version 4.1. If you type **N** to not display columns side by side, reformatting takes place at the normal speed of noncolumnar text.

Changing the Number of Columns   If you need to change the number of newspaper columns, place the cursor just after the previous [Col Def] code and redefine columns. The columns will automatically readjust. Changing the number of parallel columns is a little more tricky. See "Parallel Columns Only" for details.

Moving Columns   You should not use the Cut/Copy Column option in newspaper or parallel columns. If you want to move sections of text, use the regular Block-Move procedure. See *Move* for complete information.

Column Limitations   Currently, you cannot create footnotes while in columns, but you can create endnotes. You can sort items within columns, but you might get unpredictable results, so save the document first!

Although you have access to the Line Draw feature, it is impossible to draw lines around newspaper or parallel columns. See "Applications" for information about using Advance to get around this limitation. If you want to advance the printer, you must do so before turning on Columns.

While in Columns, you cannot change the spacing or margins. This will adversely affect those who want one parallel column single-spaced and the other double-spaced.

Parallel Columns Only

When you choose parallel columns, a Block Protect code is placed at the beginning of the first column and at the end of the last column. The Block Protect codes keep the columns together across the page without letting a soft page break split the group. One limitation of parallel groups appears if a column is longer than one page. In this case, the soft page break will act as a hard page break and will split an individual column into two columns rather than leaving the cursor in the same column and continuing onto the next page.

When you turn on parallel columns, the codes [Block Pro:On][Col On] are inserted together at the beginning of the first column. When CTRL-ENTER is pressed between columns, a [HPg] code is inserted into the text, but a page break is not visible on the screen. At the end of the last column, CTRL-ENTER does not insert a [HPg]. Instead, the following codes are inserted to end the first group of parallel columns, insert a blank line, and begin the second group.

[BlockPro:Off][Col Off]

[HRt]

[BlockPro:On][Col On]

If you want to add text to the last column in a group, be sure that you do not place the cursor between the [Block Pro:Off] and [Col Off] codes or you might see the error message "Divide Overflow" near the end of a page. It is caused by too many characters trying to fit within a set boundary, in this case [BlockPro:Off] and [Col Off].

If you are in parallel columns and want to convert to normal text, you must delete the [Col On] code at the beginning of each parallel section. You should also delete the [BlockPro:On] code. Instead of manually searching for the codes, use the Replace feature to search for them and replace them with nothing. When parallel columns are returned to normal text, a Hard Page code [HPg] appears between each "column." You could then use the Search feature to search for a hard page and replace it with something else, such as a hard return.

Changing the Number of Parallel Columns   Because it is easy to make a mistake during this process, Save (F10) the document before attempting any changes. The following should give you at least an idea as to the procedure.

If you redefine parallel columns and add a column, the new column is added at the end of the group by inserting a Hard Page code [HPg]. If you want the column within the group rather than at the end, use Block (ALT-F4) to move text from one column to another.

If you want to remove a column, you should first remove the text from that column, then redefine the columns. Extra [HPg] codes are automatically deleted, leaving the correct number of columns.

If you need more than 24 text columns, determine which columns do not require word wrap and set tabs for additional columns within columns.

Applications

Tables and Charts

If you want to draw lines around columns, as shown in Figure 4-18, it is easiest to use tabbed columns. If you use the Advance feature, you can print lines and boxes with any type of columns.

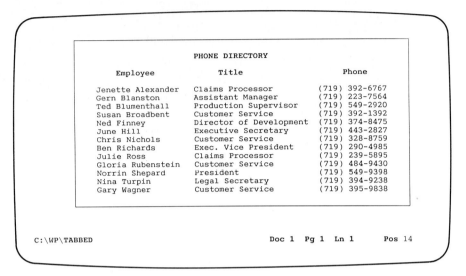

```
                          PHONE DIRECTORY

          Employee              Title                     Phone

     Jenette Alexander    Claims Processor          (719) 392-6767
     Gern Blanston        Assistant Manager         (719) 223-7564
     Ted Blumenthall      Production Supervisor     (719) 549-2920
     Susan Broadbent      Customer Service          (719) 392-1392
     Ned Finney           Director of Development    (719) 374-8475
     June Hill            Executive Secretary       (719) 443-2827
     Chris Nichols        Customer Service          (719) 328-8759
     Ben Richards         Exec. Vice President      (719) 290-4985
     Julie Ross           Claims Processor          (719) 239-5895
     Gloria Rubenstein    Customer Service          (719) 484-9430
     Norrin Shepard       President                 (719) 549-9398
     Nina Turpin          Legal Secretary           (719) 394-9238
     Gary Wagner          Customer Service          (719) 395-9838


C:\WP\TABBED                         Doc 1  Pg 1  Ln 1      Pos 14
```

Figure 4-18.   Line drawn around columns

If you use Line Draw with any kind of columns, you will not be able to print in proportional spacing. If you must print in proportional spacing, draw the lines first, use the Advance feature to advance the printer back up the page (after making sure that your printer can move both up and down the page), turn on proportional spacing, and enter the columns of text. If your printer has a special line draw font, it should be selected before drawing the lines and will probably need to be changed to the proportionally spaced font after the lines have been drawn.

Scriptwriting

Use parallel columns for writing scripts. One column could be "action" and the other column could be "dialog." You could have additional columns for lighting, sound, and so on. When you make changes to one of the columns, you can be sure that the group of columns will stay together.

Invoices

Parallel columns function well for invoices because invoices normally have one or two text columns that may vary in length. If an item description is changed, for example, it will not adversely affect the other columns. See the following example.

```
              INVOICE FOR OFFICE SUPPLIES

                  November 25, 1987


Quantity        Description        Price      Total

   5            5¼" Floppy         45.00     $225.00
                diskette holders

   3            Horizontal          5.00       15.00
                stacking trays
                (smoke)

  12            Boxes small paper   2.00       24.00
                clips

   5            Desk organizers    18.00       90.00
                (12" x 9" smoke)

  20            Boxes (12 each)     3.25       65.00
                ball point pens
                (black ink)
```

Newsletters

Most owners of WordPerfect use newspaper columns to create newsletters. Remember that if you need to draw lines and boxes around columns, you should draw the lines first, use Advance to move to the correct line, define and turn on columns, then enter the text. Figure 4-19 shows a newsletter created with WordPerfect using Line Draw, Advance, and newspaper columns.

Related Entries

Advance the Printer to a Specific Line

Cut Text and Columns

Line Draw

Move

```
┌─────────────────────────────────────────────────────────────┐
│  ┌─────────────────────────────────────────────────────────┐ │
│  │                                                         │ │
│  │                 Corporate  Update                       │ │
│  │                                                         │ │
│  └─────────────────────────────────────────────────────────┘ │
│                                                               │
│  Volume II Number 12        Internal Communication      November 25, 1987 │
```

Inter-office Mail Reminder -- For those employees who use the numbering system when addressing inter-office mail, please be advised that the Accounting Department has now been changed to #11. For those of you who are not using the numbering system, please do the couriers a favor and write employees first and last names and departments legibly.

Vacation Schedule Correction -- In an employee vacation schedule distributed with the December 15, 1986 edition of the newsletter, the Thanksgiving holiday is marked as Thursday, November 19, 1987, which is incorrect. The correct date for the holiday is Thursday, November 26, 1987.

Insurance Update -- If you are admitted to a hospital for any reason, please specify your employer upon admittance. The billing departments of all hospitals have been advised of our insurance coverage and are aware of the information needed to process a claim.

Don't forget that, when filing you first claim each year, one fully completed claim form must be submitted for each family member. Subsequent claims may be submitted with only a receipt for services rendered (unless the claim is accident-related, in which case a fully completed claim form is required.

Business Card Orders -- All employees who will be attending the computer convention and need to reorder business cards are requested to do so before December 15. Please call Laurie with your order.

Third-Party Software Registration -- The Testing department is compiling a list of all third-party software products currently owned by the company. If you have such a product in your office, please send a memo to Gary in Testing. Briefly describe

the product name, manufacturer, and version number. If you have no need for the program in your office, please forward the entire package to Gary.

Training Classes -- The next session of product training classes begins on December 8, but classes are beginning to fill up now. If you have questions regarding possible enrollment, please see the receptionist in your building for a list of registered participants.

Insurance Questions? -- All questions regarding company insurance policies-- i.e., coverage, eligibility, and reimbursements--should now be directed to Mandy in Accounting at extension 304.

Printer Planner -- Melinda Riggs in Engineering is the one to call if you need to borrow a printer for another department for any reason. When you call with your request, she will need to know the length of time the printer is needed and the purpose for requesting the printer. Please be considerate of both Melinda and the individual(s) from whom you are borrowing the printer and give sufficient advance notice so that convenient scheduling can be arranged. Melinda can be reached at extension 423.

Travel Policies -- Due to recent changes in the company travel policies and procedures, an authorization number is needed before airline tickets can be issued. If you will be traveling for the company, please have your travel form filled out and signed by your supervisor prior to submitting it to May in Accounting. She will then give the authorization number to the travel agent.

Modular Office Space? -- We are currently reviewing plans for the utilization of office space in the new building and are considering both the

---

Figure 4-19.   Newsletter created using Line Draw, Advance, and newspaper columns

Comments

Sometimes referred to as "hidden text," comments can be placed throughout your document without being printed.

Keystrokes

1. Press Text In/Out (CTRL-F5).

2. Type **B** to Create a Comment. A double-lined box appears.

3. Type the text for the comment.

4. Press Exit (F7) when finished.

The comment is displayed on the screen where the cursor was located and is enclosed in a box, as shown in Figure 4-20.

Hints

When a comment is inserted into the document, the following code is visible when Reveal Codes (ALT-F3) is pressed.

[Smry/Cmnt: Text]

Although a comment can contain and display up to 1,024

```
on the Journal of each House respectively.  If any Bill shall not

be returned by the President within ten Days (Sundays excepted)

after it shall have been presented to him, the Same shall be a

Law, in like Manner as if he had signed it, unless the Congress

by their Adjournment prevent its Return, in which Case it shall

be a Law.
  ┌─────────────────────────────────────────────────────────────┐
  │ Question for Final Exam:                                      │
  │ How many days does the President have to veto a bill?         │
  └─────────────────────────────────────────────────────────────┘

     Every Order, Resolution, or Vote to which the Concurrence of

the Senate and House Representatives may be necessary (except on

a question of Adjournment) shall be presented to the President of

                                 Doc 1  Pg 6  Ln 17     Pos 10
```

Figure 4-20.   Boxed comment

characters (including spaces) or approximately 14 lines, only the first 100 characters are displayed in the Reveal Codes screen.

If you need to change the text in a comment and it is the only comment in the document, press Text In/Out (CTRL-F5), then **C** to Edit a Comment. It will find the comment regardless of its location. If there is more than one comment, position the cursor just after the comment to be edited, then press Text In/Out (CTRL-F5) and **C** to Edit a Comment. After editing, press Exit (F7).

By default, WordPerfect has been set to display a comment on the screen. You can choose not to display the comment (or document summary) by pressing Text In/Out (CTRL-F5) and typing **D** for Display Summary and Comments. Type **Y** or **N** for the document summary (see *Document Summary* for more information), then **Y** or **N** for comments.

If you want to delete a comment permanently, move the cursor above the comment and press DEL, or move just below the comment and press BACKSPACE. You are asked to confirm the deletion. Type **Y** to the question "Delete [Smry/Cmnt]? (Y/N) N" or **N** if you change your mind.

If you want to search for a summary or comment, press Search (F2) and Text In/Out (CTRL-F5). The code [Smry/Cmnt] is automatically inserted as the search string.

A document summary uses the same principles and codes as a comment. However, no matter where the cursor is located, the summary is always placed at the beginning of the document and, unlike comments, there can be only one summary.

If you are looking at a file from the List Files menu, a document summary will appear at the beginning of the document, but comments are not displayed in the Look screen.

Applications

When editing a document for someone else, you can use the Comment feature to make comments directly within a file. During further editing, these comments can be manually incorporated into the document and then deleted as comments. If more than one person is editing a document, each person can insert his or her name and the date in the comment so that multiple suggestions and responses can be tracked by the author.

See Chapter 8, "Software Integration," for more information about a program called ForComment that has the same type of function and works well with WordPerfect. Among many other features, it allows you to swap the text in the comment with text in the document to see what the final draft might look like.

Comments are also quite useful when creating macros and merge documents. For instance, if you have a macro or merge that pauses for user input, a comment can be displayed to give instructions. As a final step in the macro, you could choose to not display the comments so they will be removed from the screen. Even if you don't include the step, you have the reassurance that they will not print. See *Macros* and *Merge* for more information and examples.

Related Entries

Document Summary

Macros

Merge

Concordance

A concordance is a list of words and phrases that are to be included in an index. Instead of marking each phrase individually in a document, a concordance can be used to save time and keystrokes.

Keystrokes

1. Clear the screen and type each word or phrase on a separate line. Each phrase can be one line in length, as shown in the following illustration.

```
Congress
Senate
President of the United States
Senator
Representative
Legislator
Vice President
Chief Justice
```

2. Sort the concordance file if you want the index to be generated more quickly. See "Hints" for the exact steps.

3. Mark each phrase in the file as a major index heading or subheading. (If you want all phrases listed to be major headings, marking the entries is unnecessary.) See "Hints" for more information.

4. Save the file as you normally would.

5. Retrieve the document to be indexed and position the cursor at the end of it. (An index can be successfully generated only when it is at the end of a document.)

6. If you want the index to begin on a separate page, insert a hard page break and label the page if desired.

7. Press Mark Text (ALT-F5).

8. Type **6** for Other Options.

9. Type **5** to Define the Index.

10. "Concordance Filename (Enter=none):" appears. Enter the name of the file which contains the words and phrases to be indexed.

11. Type the number indicating how the page numbers are to appear in the index.

12. To generate the index, press Mark Text (ALT-F5), type **6** for Other Options, **8** to Generate Tables and Index, and **Y** if you want to continue.

Hints

When you define an index and specify a concordance file, the following code is inserted in the document.

[DefMark:Index,n;filename]

The information tells you that it is an index definition mark, the page numbering option that was selected, and the name of the file that is to be used for the concordance.

A WordPerfect index can contain headings and sub-headings. Each phrase found in the concordance file is used automatically as a major heading. If you want a different heading or subheading, or if you want each phrase to be listed in the index several different ways, mark each entry to indicate the heading or subheading to be used.

1. Use Block (ALT-F4) to block the phrase. If the phrase consists of just one word, move the cursor to the word; blocking the word is not necessary.

2. Press Mark Text (ALT-F5).

3. Type **5** for Index.

4. "Index Heading:" appears with the blocked phrase (or word). Press ENTER to accept the displayed heading or enter a new one. (You can edit the displayed heading rather than enter a new one, and then press ENTER to accept it.)

5. "Subheading:" appears. If you edited the blocked phrase or entered a new heading, the block is again displayed as the subheading. Press ENTER to accept it as the subheading (remember, you can edit the subheading listed), enter a new one, or press Cancel (F1) if you don't want a subheading.

An Index Mark code is inserted at the cursor's location.

[Index:Heading;Subheading]

If you mark a phrase in the concordance, it will no longer be used automatically as a major heading by itself. The index markings will be used instead to determine the level of the heading.

Each phrase can be marked as many times as you want using different headings or subheadings. For example, you could mark the phrase "U.S. Constitution" several times so the entries in the index could appear as follows.

```
Constitution
       U.S.  . . . . . . . . . . . . . . . . . . . . . . . 1-5
U.S.
       Constitution  . . . . . . . . . . . . . . . . . . 1-5
United States of America . . . . . . . . . . . . . . . . 1-5
```

If you have endnotes in the same document, they are printed after the index. If you want the endnotes printed on a separate page, press hard page (CTRL-ENTER) at the very end of the document.

Sorting the Concordance

Sorting the concordance (from A to Z) makes generating the index faster. Retrieve the concordance file to the screen if it is not already there.

1. Press Merge/Sort (CTRL-F10).

2. Type **2** to Sort.

3. You are asked for the input file and the output to be sorted. Press ENTER twice to accept the default of sorting what is displayed on the screen to the screen.

4. Type **1** to Perform Action.

These steps assume that no changes were made to the Sort menu. WordPerfect is already set to do a Line Sort using the first word as the key. If you have made changes to this setup, you will need to change it back to the original settings before typing 1 to Perform the Action.

Not Enough Memory

If you see the error message "Not enough memory to use entire concordance file. Continue? (Y/N)," there are a few things you can do. First, type **N** to stop the process and check to see if you have another document in memory (such as document 2). Exit the document. Also, if you are in the habit of previewing a document and press Switch (SHIFT-F3) instead of Exit (F7) to leave the screen, the preview document is still in memory. Reenter the preview screen using Switch (SHIFT-F3), then press Exit (F7). You could also remove all other programs from memory (such as SideKick, Prokey, or Library), then try to generate the index again.

Second, you could type **Y** to continue and let as much of the concordance file be used as possible. You can then save as a separate file the part of the index that was successfully generated, edit the concordance file so that it contains only words that were not yet indexed, and regenerate the index. After it has been regenerated, combine the two documents.

Related Entries

Index

Sort and Select

Conditional End of Page

The Conditional End of Page feature keeps a specified number of lines together.

Keystrokes

You should count the number of lines to be protected *before* completing the following steps because when you enter the number of lines to be protected, you are in a menu and cannot see the text. Figure 4-21 shows the Page Format menu which obscures the view of the text.

1. Position the cursor on the line just above the section of lines to be kept together. It does not have to be a blank line.

2. Press Page Format (ALT-F8).

3. Type **9** for Conditional End of Page. The message "Number of lines to keep together = " appears.

4. Enter the number of lines.

5. Press ENTER to leave the Page Format menu.

Hints

The Conditional End of Page code [CndlEOP:n] is placed in the document and will not allow a soft page break to fall within the specified number of lines. If the protected lines fall near the end of a page, the page break will occur just after the [CndlEOP:n] code and right before the protected lines.

The section of text is protected from soft page breaks but a Hard Page (CTRL-ENTER) can be inserted at any location.

Conditional End of Page protects a specific number of lines, whereas Block Protect protects a block of text. When trying to decide which feature is better for a particular

```
Page Format

      1 - Page Number Position

      2 - New Page Number

      3 - Center Page Top to Bottom

      4 - Page Length

      5 - Top Margin

      6 - Headers or Footers

      7 - Page Number Column Positions

      8 - Suppress for Current page only

      9 - Conditional End of Page

      A - Widow/Orphan

Number of lines to keep together =
```

Figure 4-21.   Page Format menu

situation, first determine whether it is important to keep certain lines together (as with a heading and the first two lines of a paragraph), or if the block of text must be kept together regardless of the amount of text added or deleted from the block.

If you have double-spaced or even triple-spaced text, the Conditional End of Page feature takes any blank lines into consideration. For example, if you are using double-spacing and you want to protect the heading and first two lines in a paragraph, enter **6** (not **3**) as the number of lines to keep together.

Applications

Conditional End of Page is most often used to keep a title or heading with the first two lines of a paragraph, or to keep three-line paragraphs together (the Widow/Orphan feature will not protect in these types of situations).

Depending on how often you would use such a feature, you might consider placing the steps in a macro. The macro could then be executed before each paragraph heading. Be sure to take the spacing (as noted in "Hints") into consideration.

Related Entries

Widows and Orphans

Block Protect

Continuous Paper

See *Forms*

Convert Program

The Convert program, included on the Learning disk, is used to convert documents to and from WordPerfect format.

Keystrokes

1. Place the Learning disk in drive A. If you have a hard disk and have not already done so, you should copy the CONVERT.EXE file to the hard disk. The following command would copy the file from drive A to the WP directory on the hard disk.

>copy a:convert.exe c:\wp

If you have two disk drives, leave the Learning disk in drive A and place the disk containing the documents to be converted in drive B.

2. If you have two disk drives, enter the following commands.

>b:

B>a:convert

If you have a hard disk, change to the directory where the documents to be converted are stored and enter **CONVERT**. If the path includes the WP directory, you should be able to type CONVERT at any DOS prompt. If you see "Bad command or file name," see Chapter 1 for information about entering a PATH command.

3. Enter the name of the file to be converted (input file). Include the full pathname (where the file is located) if it is not on the default drive.

4. Enter the name of the file that will be used to save the converted document (output file). The input and output filenames must be different. If you enter the name of a file already saved to the disk, you are asked if you want to overwrite the existing file. The menu in Figure 4-22 appears.

5. Type the number indicating the format for the input file. If you type **1** for WordPerfect, the menu in Figure 4-23 appears. Type the number corresponding to the type of conversion desired.

```
Name of Input File? C:\BOOK\CHAPTER.1
Name of Output File? A:CHAPTER.1WS

1 WordPerfect to another format
2 Revisable-Form-Text (IBM DCA Format) to WordPerfect
3 Navy DIF Standard to WordPerfect
4 WordStar 3.3 to WordPerfect
5 MultiMate 3.22 to WordPerfect
6 Seven-bit transfer format to WordPerfect
7 Mail Merge to WordPerfect Secondary Merge
8 WordPerfect Secondary Merge to Spreadsheet DIF
9 Spreadsheet DIF to WordPerfect Secondary Merge

Enter number of Conversion desired
```

Figure 4-22.   Convert menu

```
Name of Input File? C:\BOOK\CHAPTER.1
Name of Output File? A:CHAPTER.1WS


1 WordPerfect to another format
2 Revisable-Form-Text (IBM DCA Format) to WordPerfect
3 Navy DIF Standard to WordPerfect
4 WordStar 3.3 to WordPerfect
5 MultiMate 3.22 to WordPerfect
6 Seven-bit transfer format to WordPerfect
7 Mail Merge to WordPerfect Secondary Merge
8 WordPerfect Secondary Merge to Spreadsheet DIF
9 Spreadsheet DIF to WordPerfect Secondary Merge

Enter number of Conversion desired 1

1 Revisable-Form-Text (IBM DCA Format)
2 Final-Form-Text (IBM DCA Format)
3 Navy DIF Standard
4 WordStar 3.3
5 MultiMate 3.22
6 Seven-bit transfer format

Enter number of output file format desired
```

Figure 4-23.   Additional choices when option 1 is selected from the
Convert menu

If you choose the Mail Merge option (format used by
WordStar, dBASE II/III, and other programs), you are
asked to supply the field delimiter, the record delimiter, and
characters to be stripped. If you do not know what to
answer, type a comma (,) for the field delimiter, {13}{10} as
the record delimiter, and a quotation mark (") as the character to be stripped.

Options

See Chapter 8 for information about converting documents
created with specific products such as PlanPerfect (formerly MathPlan), dBASE II/III, and Lotus 1-2-3.

The following discussion is included to help you decide
which format is best suited to your document. If you are
still unsure, see *DOS Text Files* for details on import-
ing/exporting DOS text files (sometimes referred to as
ASCII Files).

Revisable-Form-Text/Final-Form-Text (DCA)

DCA (Document Content Architecture) is IBM's standard format for storing documents. Programs not listed as options on the Convert menu, such as Microsoft Word, might have the option of converting their documents to DCA. They can then be converted into WordPerfect format.

WordStar and MultiMate

Documents can be transferred to and from WordStar 3.3 and MultiMate 3.22. If you have WordStar 2000, transfer the WordStar 2000 document to WordStar 3.3 format first, then use Convert. All possible formatting is retained.

Seven-Bit Transfer Format

WordPerfect documents can usually be transmitted electronically without any conversion. However, because some modems and communications lines can accept only seven bits, the eighth bit will be stripped during the transfer. This can affect the format of the transferred file because Word-Perfect uses the eighth bit for program codes. If you want to keep all formatting, use this option to convert a regular WordPerfect document to seven-bit format. After it has been transferred, the person receiving the file can convert it back to WordPerfect format.

If you want to send a text file with no WordPerfect codes, save the document as a DOS text (ASCII) file with Text In/Out (CTRL-F5).

Mail Merge

Choose this option to transfer data from a data base into a secondary WordPerfect file. The data base file must first be converted in a delimited format where fields and records are separated with specific characters. This option can also be used for WordStar Mail Merge data files.

DIF

DIF (Data Interchange Format) is a standard format used by some spreadsheets to help transfer documents between programs. A spreadsheet file should be converted to DIF first. It can then be converted to a WordPerfect secondary merge file. A WordPerfect secondary merge file can also be used to return a file to DIF.

Navy DIF

Navy DIF is a format used by the Navy to aid in the transfer of documents. These are considered word processing-type documents rather than spreadsheet files.

Applications

The Convert program allows you to share documents with others who are using various types of software.

If you are a writer, your publisher might accept only text in either ASCII or WordStar format. If you convert a document to WordStar, many WordPerfect codes will be converted rather than removed (as is the case with an ASCII file).

Rather than creating a report in a data base, you can export the file to a delimited (Mail Merge) format, convert it to a WordPerfect secondary merge file, and use WordPerfect's advanced formatting features to create form letters, envelopes, and labels.

Related Entries

> dBASE II/III
>
> DCA Format
>
> DIF
>
> DOS Text Files
>
> WordStar
>
> *See also* Chapter 8, "Software Integration"

Copy Files

You can copy files from one disk to another while in Word-Perfect's List Files menu.

Keystrokes

1. Press List Files (F5).

2. The current default drive/directory is displayed. Press ENTER if the file(s) to be copied are in that drive/directory. If not, enter the appropriate drive/directory.

3. Move the cursor to the file to be copied. If you need to copy more than one file to the same destination, type * to mark each file. Press Mark Text (ALT-F5) to mark all files in the directory.

4. Type **8** for Copy. If you have marked files with *, you are asked, "Copy Marked Files? (Y/N) N." Type **Y** or **N**. If you type **N**, "Copy This File To:" appears, letting you copy the file highlighted by the cursor.

5. Enter the drive/directory where the file(s) is to be copied.

If a file with the same name appears on the destination drive/directory, you are asked if you want to replace the existing file. Type **Y** or **N**.

Hints

You can also copy files while in DOS. See Chapter 1 for more information.

Related Entries

List Files

See also Chapter 1, "Getting Started"

Copy Text and Columns

Text, columns, or a rectangular block of text can be copied within a document or between documents. Figure 4-24 shows highlighted text, columns, and rectangular block, respectively.

Keystrokes

Copy a Block

1. Move the cursor to the beginning or end of the block to be moved and press Block (ALT-F4).

2. Move to the opposite end. As the cursor moves through the text, the text is highlighted.

a) Regular text block

```
              THE CONSTITUTION OF THE UNITED STATES

                            PREAMBLE

        We the people of the United States, in Order to form a more
   perfect Union, establish Justice, insure domestic Tranquility,
   provide for the common Defense, promote the general Welfare, and
   secure the Blessings of Liberty to ourselves and our Posterity,
   do ordain and establish this Constitution for the United States
   of America.

   ARTICLE I.
        Section 1.  All legislative Powers herein granted shall be
   vested in a Congress of the United States, which shall consist of
   a Senate and House of Representatives.
        Section 2.   The House of Representatives shall be composed
   of Members chosen every second Year by the People of the several
   States, and the Electors in each State shall have the
   Qualifications requisite for Electors of the most numerous Branch
   of the State Legislature.
        No Person shall be a Representative who shall not have
   attained to the Age of twenty five Years, and been Years a
   Citizen of the United States, and who shall not, when elected, be
   an inhabitant of the State in which he shall be chosen.
Block on                                Doc 1  Pg 1  Ln 15      Pos 48
```

b) Column block

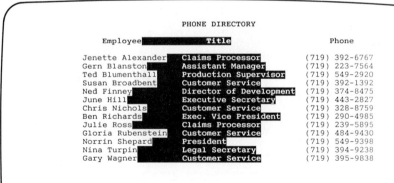

```
                       PHONE DIRECTORY

         Employee          Title                     Phone

   Jenette Alexander   Claims Processor         (719) 392-6767
   Gern Blanston       Assistant Manager        (719) 223-7564
   Ted Blumenthall     Production Supervisor     (719) 549-2920
   Susan Broadbent     Customer Service         (719) 392-1392
   Ned Finney          Director of Development   (719) 374-8475
   June Hill           Executive Secretary      (719) 443-2827
   Chris Nichols       Customer Service         (719) 328-8759
   Ben Richards        Exec. Vice President     (719) 290-4985
   Julie Ross          Claims Processor         (719) 239-5895
   Gloria Rubenstein   Customer Service         (719) 484-9430
   Norrin Shepard      President                (719) 549-9398
   Nina Turpin         Legal Secretary          (719) 394-9238
   Gary Wagner         Customer Service         (719) 395-9838




1 Cut; 2 Copy; 3 Delete: 0
```

Figure 4-24.   Highlighted block of text (a), column block (b), and
rectangular block of text (c)

c) Rectangular block

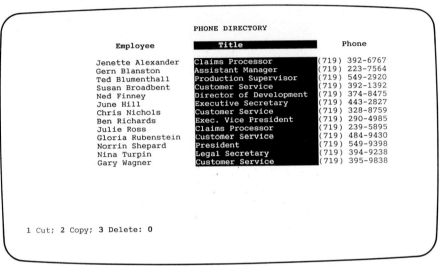

PHONE DIRECTORY

Employee	Title	Phone
Jenette Alexander	Claims Processor	(719) 392-6767
Gern Blanston	Assistant Manager	(719) 223-7564
Ted Blumenthall	Production Supervisor	(719) 549-2920
Susan Broadbent	Customer Service	(719) 392-1392
Ned Finney	Director of Development	(719) 374-8475
June Hill	Executive Secretary	(719) 443-2827
Chris Nichols	Customer Service	(719) 328-8759
Ben Richards	Exec. Vice President	(719) 290-4985
Julie Ross	Claims Processor	(719) 239-5895
Gloria Rubenstein	Customer Service	(719) 484-9430
Norrin Shepard	President	(719) 549-9398
Nina Turpin	Legal Secretary	(719) 394-9238
Gary Wagner	Customer Service	(719) 395-9838

1 Cut; 2 Copy; 3 Delete: 0

Figure 4-24. Highlighted block of text (a), column block (b), and rectangular block of text (c) (*continued*)

3. Press Move (CTRL-F4).

4. Type **2** to Copy the block.

5. Position the cursor at the point where the text should be retrieved, whether it is in the current document or another document (use Switch (SHIFT-F3) to move between two documents).

6. Press Move (CTRL-F4) and type **5** to Retrieve the text.

Another way to copy a block of text is to highlight the block, press Save (F10), and press ENTER. This saves the block in the same temporary file that is used to hold text that was cut or copied with Move. You can retrieve this temporary, unnamed file by pressing Retrieve (SHIFT-F10) and pressing ENTER when prompted for the name.

Copy a Sentence, Paragraph, or Page

The steps for copying a block will work to copy a sentence, paragraph, or page, but WordPerfect gives you an additional way to do it.

1. Position the cursor anywhere in the sentence, paragraph, or page to be copied.

2. Press Move (CTRL-F4).

3. Type **1** for Sentence, **2** for Paragraph, or **3** for Page. The appropriate text is highlighted.

4. Type **2** to Copy the text.

5. Position the cursor where the text is to be retrieved.

6. Press Move (CTRL-F4) and type **5** to Retrieve the text.

Copy a Column

The following steps are to be used only for tabbed columns (columns separated with Tabs, Tab Aligns, or Indents). If you want to copy text from parallel or newspaper columns, use the steps to Copy a Block.

1. Move to the first character in the column to be copied.

2. Press Block (ALT-F4) to turn on Block.

3. Move straight down the column if only that column is to be affected. If you want to copy more than one column, move the cursor to the right into the applicable column(s). At this point it does not appear that the proper text is being highlighted; be patient until the next step.

4. Press Move (CTRL-F4) and type **4** to Cut/Copy the column. The column is now highlighted. Note that the [TAB] preceding the column is also highlighted as part

of the column. If you move the cursor into columns to the right, they will also be highlighted.

5. Type **2** to Copy the column.

6. When you are ready to retrieve the copied column, position the cursor just after the last character in the column to the left, at the left margin, or after the last column.

7. Press Move (CTRL-F4) and type **4** to Retrieve the column. Remember that a [TAB] was included as part of the column, so if you retrieve a column at the left margin, it will be sent to the first tab setting. Delete each [TAB] code at the beginning of each line if necessary to return it to the left margin.

Copy a Rectangle

You can copy a rectangle, which is a block of text from the top left corner to the bottom right corner, to a different location.

1. Place the cursor at one corner (upper left or bottom right) and press Block (ALT-F4).

2. Move to the opposite corner. As the cursor moves, a regular block is highlighted until the next step.

3. Press Move (CTRL-F4) and type **5** to Cut/Copy a Rectangle. The rectangle is highlighted.

4. Type **2** to Copy.

5. Position the cursor anywhere on the screen.

6. Press Move (CTRL-F4) and type **6** to Retrieve the rectangle. The complete rectangle will be retrieved at that point. If it is not retrieved at the left margin, spaces are inserted so the format of the rectangle is retained.

Hints

Cut/copied text is saved in a temporary "move" file. It will remain there and can be retrieved again and again until another cut/copy is performed or until you turn off the computer.

If you don't want to remember two ways of copying text (Block and Move), use the Block method because you can easily define a sentence, paragraph, or page. If the cursor is at the beginning of a sentence, paragraph, or page, press Block (ALT-F4) and type a period (.) to highlight the sentence, ENTER to highlight a paragraph, or PGDN to highlight the page.

The Cut option on the Move menu removes the text instead of making a copy. Cut text is saved in the same temporary file as copied text. The Delete option lets you delete a sentence, paragraph, or page. The deleted text is saved in a temporary "undelete" file and can be retrieved by pressing Cancel (F1) and typing **1** to Restore. Remember that only the last three deletions can be restored with this method.

The text involved when you copy a block, column, or rectangle is kept in separate temporary files. You should choose the correct option when retrieving the block (text, column, or rectangle) or you will retrieve the wrong block. The option of retrieving a normal block of text (press Retrieve (SHIFT-F10) and ENTER) cannot be used to retrieve a column or rectangle.

Copying a Document

See *Print Options* for details on printing more than one copy. See *Copy Files* for information about copying documents from one disk to another.

If you want more than one copy of a document on the

screen, you can retrieve the document from disk again and again. See *Merge* for creating duplicate copies where only certain information changes from copy to copy (form letters, for example).

If you find that you have more than one copy of your document on the screen and you wanted only one, you have accidentally retrieved the file again without first clearing the screen. If this happens often, check to see if you are doing one of the following. With Save (F10), a document is saved, but not removed from the screen. If you want to clear the screen *and* save the file, use Exit (F7) instead. Another reason this could happen is that you might have entered the List Files menu while working on a document, moved the cursor to the current document filename, and pressed **1** to Retrieve the document, not realizing that instead of returning you to your work, it actually retrieves another copy of the document. To see if you have a document in memory before you retrieve a file, check the upper left corner of the List Files menu. "Document Size:" is displayed as part of the List Files heading. If shown as 0, there is no document already in memory.

Applications

The Copy feature can copy the name and address in a letter and place it on an envelope. See Appendix C for an envelope macro that uses Copy.

If you have typed text in one document and need it duplicated in another, copy the text rather than retype it.

Related Entries

Cut Text and Columns

Merge

Move

Number of Copies

Print Options

Rectangular Cut, Copy, and Move

Undelete

See also Appendix C, "Macro Library"

Count Lines

See *Line Numbering*

Count Words

See *Word Count*

Create a Directory

A hard disk can be divided into several directories for better organization. You can create a new directory on your disk from within WordPerfect.

Keystrokes

1. Press List Files (F5). The name of the current default directory is displayed.

2. Press = to change the default directory. "New directory =" and the name of the current directory are displayed.

3. Enter the name for the new directory.

4. When asked if you really want to create the new directory, type **Y** or **N**.

5. The directory is created and the default directory remains as it was.

Hints

You can also create a new directory while in the List Files menu. If you type **7** to Change Directory and enter the name of a nonexistent directory, it will ask if you want to create the directory you have named.

Like filenames, a directory name can consist of up to eight characters and an optional three-character extension.

When dividing your directory, be aware that WordPerfect allows only 39 characters in the full pathname. The pathname includes the drive, directory, subdirectories, and filename. This limitation exists because there just isn't room for a longer pathname in the List Files menu or on the status line.

You can use the DOS MD command to make a new directory from DOS. See Chapter 1 for more information.

Related Entries

Directories

List Files

See also Chapter 1, "Getting Started"

Critical Disk Error Occurred

A disk error message may appear when you are trying to save or print a file.

Reasons

When you save a file or print from the screen (which creates a temporary print file), WordPerfect and DOS create a new file on the disk. If that particular location on the disk is damaged, the error message will be displayed.

Solutions

You should run the Diagnostics test or try the DOS CHKDSK command to determine if the problem lies with the disk. If you are saving a file, you should save it to another disk or directory.

You might also check to see if you have more than one copy of WordPerfect on a hard disk in different directories. If this is the case, delete the older versions of the program.

If you have a memory resident print spooler, this might also be the cause of the problem. Remove the spooler from memory and see if the problem corrects itself.

CTRL **Key**

Like the ALT key, CTRL has no function when used alone. It is used in combination with the function keys to execute the features printed in red on the template.

There are two other ways to use CTRL in WordPerfect. Both the CTRL and ALT keys can be used with a key from A through Z to map special characters to the keyboard. The CTRL key can also be used to create control codes that determine the type of information to be merged into a document.

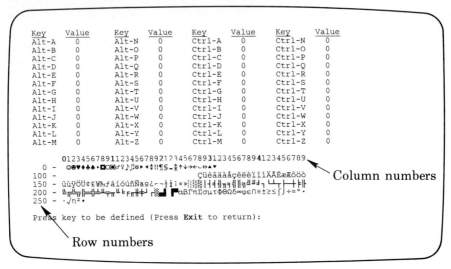

Figure 4-25.   Screen display for mapping special characters, with decimal values shown at bottom

Keystrokes

Special Characters

1. Press Screen (CTRL-F3).

2. Type **3** for CTRL/ALT keys.

3. Hold down the CTRL key while pressing a letter from A through Z.

4. Enter the decimal value for the character. Find the decimal values at the bottom of the screen, as shown in Figure 4-25. (Add the corresponding column and row numbers to determine the decimal value for the character you want displayed.)

5. Press Exit (F7) when finished.

In WordPerfect, hold down the CTRL key and press the letter to display the character on the screen.

Control Codes

If a CTRL-key combination is not mapped to a special character, it can be used to perform another function. The following lists each CTRL-key combination and its corresponding feature.

^A Displayed but not used.

^B Inserts the current page number at print time. Not a merge code.

^C Merge code. Pauses a Merge so text can be entered from the *console* (keyboard).

^D Merge code. Inserts current *date* and time.

^E Merge code. ^E[HRt] marks the *end* of a record. If ^E is found in a primary file or if Merge E (SHIFT-F9) is pressed during a Merge, the Merge will end at that point.

^F Merge code. Inserts a specific *field* from the secondary merge file (should appear as ^F1^).

^G Merge code. Starts a macro (*go*).

^H Not displayed and not used.

^I Inserts a [TAB] code into the document. Former Word-Star users can use this key combination instead of Tab if they want to feel more at home.

^J Inserts a Hard Return code [HRt].

^K Deletes to the end of the line. CTRL-END accomplishes the same task. If a line of text disappears because you have accidentally pressed these keys, you can press Cancel (F1) and **1** to restore the deleted text; there is no confirmation message for this type of deletion.

^L Deletes to the end of the page. A message asks you to confirm the deletion. CTRL-PGDN is the documented Word-Perfect feature to delete to the end of the page.

^M Inserts a space. Can be used to search for a [SRt] (useful in some macros).

^N Merge code. Tells WordPerfect to merge with the *next* record. If ^N is included in a header or footer, it prints the current page number. ^B was added to WordPerfect so the current page number could be included within the document—not just within a header or footer.

^O Merge code. Used with ^C to display (*output*) a message (usually instructions to the user) when the Merge pauses for entry from the keyboard.

^P Merge code. Retrieves other *primary* files during a Merge.

^Q Merge code. Used to *quit* the merge operation.

^R Merge code. ^R[HRt] is used as a "merge Return" to separate fields in a secondary Merge (data) file. If a merge pauses for input from the console at a ^C, you must press Merge R to continue.

^S Merge code. Used to call another *secondary* (data) file during a merge.

^T Merge code. Everything merged to the ^T is sent to the printer.

^U Merge code. *Updates* the display to that point during a Merge.

^V Merge code or an alternate way of displaying special characters. See *Merge Codes* and *Special Characters* for more information.

^W Moves the cursor up a line.

^X Moves the cursor right one character.

^Y Moves the cursor left one character.

^Z Moves the cursor down one line.

Note that most of the control codes are used as merge codes. If you map a special character to a CTRL-key combination, you can still display the merge code by pressing Merge Codes (ALT-F9) and pressing the character. In fact, it is the only documented way to enter a merge code. To learn more about the control characters used in a Merge, see *Merge Codes*.

Hints

Only the letters A through Z can be used in a CTRL-key combination. You cannot use punctuation or other keys such as ? or $.

Because ALT-key combinations can be used to name and start macros, it is suggested that you use CTRL-key combinations for special characters where possible, thus freeing up more ALT-key combinations for single-key macros.

Related Entries

ALT Key

Merge Codes

Special Characters

Cursor Keys

WordPerfect has several options for moving the cursor through text. The major keys used to control the cursor (arrow keys, END, PGUP, PGDN, −, and +) are found on the numeric keypad. They can also be combined with HOME, CTRL, and ESC to move through larger sections of text.

Figure 4-26 shows the numeric keypad with each cursor key labeled.

Keystrokes

Arrow Keys

↑	Move up one line
↓	Move down one line
→	Move right one character
←	Move left one character

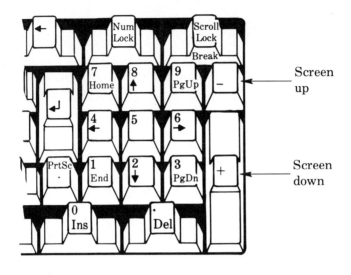

Screen up

Screen down

Figure 4-26.   Cursor keys on numeric keypad

HOME, CTRL, and ESC

Pressing HOME once before pressing an arrow key moves the cursor to the edges of the screen. Pressing HOME twice before an arrow key moves the cursor to the extreme edges of the document.

CTRL is used with the arrow keys to move through words, or can be combined with HOME and the arrow keys to move to the top/bottom of a page or from column to column.

ESC is a counter key and can be used to repeat any number of keystrokes. ESC can be used with the arrow keys, PGUP, and PGDN to move in a specific direction n times.

By Word

CTRL→   Move to the beginning of the next word

CTRL←   Move to the beginning of the preceding word

To the Edges of the Screen

HOME,↑	Move to the top of the screen, then scroll backward one screen at a time
HOME,↓	Move to the bottom of the screen, then scroll forward one screen at a time
HOME,→	Move to the right side of the screen (or end of the line)
HOME,←	Move to the left side of the screen

By Screen

− or HOME-↑	Move to the top of the screen, then backward one screen at a time
+ or HOME-↓	Move to the bottom of the screen, then forward one screen at a time

By Page

PGUP	Move to the top of the preceding page
PGDN	Move to the top of the next page
CTRL-HOME,n	Go to a specific page
CTRL-HOME,↑	Go to the top of the current page
CTRL-HOME,↓	Go to the bottom of the current page

To the Edges of the Document

HOME,HOME,↑	Move to the beginning of the document
HOME,HOME,↓	Move to the end of the document
HOME,HOME,→	Move to the far right of the document (end of the line—useful for documents which are wider than the screen)
END	Same as HOME,HOME,→
HOME,HOME,←	Move to the far left of the document

HOME,HOME,HOME,← Move to the extreme left *before* any WordPerfect codes

In Columns

CTRL-HOME,→ Use when in text columns to move to the column to the right (see *Columns* for more explanation)

CTRL-HOME,← Use in text columns to move to the column to the left

CTRL-HOME,HOME,→ Move to the far right text column

CTRL-HOME,HOME,← Move to the far left text column

Move "n" Times

ESC,↓ Move down eight lines (can also be combined with ↑, ←, or → to move in that direction eight times)

ESC,n,↓, Move down a specified number of lines (can also be combined with ↑,←, or → to move in that direction a specified number of times)

Back to the Original Position

CTRL-HOME, CTRL-HOME Go To the original cursor after a "major" cursor key is pressed, or after a feature involving the cursor (such as Search or Replace) is started (see *Go To* for more information)

To a Specific Character or Phrase

CTRL-HOME, character Go To the first occurrence of the character

Search (SHIFT-F2) or Search (F2) Searches for a string of characters or WordPerfect codes

Hints

Rather than pressing an arrow key several times in succession to move through several lines or characters, you can hold it down to move more quickly.

If you press ← or → and the cursor doesn't appear to move, it is most likely moving over a WordPerfect code. The arrow keys work in Reveal Codes just as they do on the normal screen.

You can press ↑ after retrieving a document to move past any WordPerfect codes to the first character in the document.

Programs such as Repeat Performance (produced by WordPerfect Corporation) help accelerate cursor speed and eliminate extra movement after you release a cursor key.

Related Entries

CTRL Key

ESC Key

Go To

HOME Key

Search

Cut Text and Columns

You can cut a block of text, a column, or a rectangular block from one location and move it to another. Refer to Figure 4-24 in *Copy Text and Columns* to see the difference between the three forms of text.

Keystrokes

Cut a Block

1. Move the cursor to the beginning or end of the block to be moved and press Block (ALT-F4).

2. Move to the opposite end. As the cursor moves through the text, the text is highlighted.

3. Press Move (CTRL-F4).

4. Type **1** to Cut the block.

5. Position the cursor at the point where the text should be retrieved, whether it is in the current document or another document (use Switch (SHIFT-F3) to move between two documents).

6. Press Move (CTRL-F4) and type **5** to Retrieve the text.

Cut and Paste Using Delete and Undelete

After deleting any amount of text, you can move the cursor to a new location (or leave it in the same location), press Cancel (F1) and type **1** to Restore the deletion. You can restore any or all of the last three deletions by typing **2** to show the previous deletion(s). As long as you continue to delete (even if you use any number of delete keys) without typing or moving the cursor, it is considered one deletion.

If you plan to use this feature to move text, be sure to restore it as soon as possible because only the last three deletions are saved. In other words, don't stop along the way to make editing changes if you have an important "undelete" to do.

Cut a Sentence, Paragraph, or Page

Although you can cut a sentence, paragraph, or page using Block, WordPerfect provides yet another alternative.

1. Position the cursor anywhere in the sentence, paragraph, or page to be cut.

2. Press Move (CTRL-F4).

3. Type **1** for Sentence, **2** for Paragraph, or **3** for Page. The appropriate text is highlighted.

4. Type **1** to Cut the text. You can also type **3** to Delete the text. If you choose to delete the text, you can retrieve it by pressing Cancel (F1) and **1** to Restore.

5. Position the cursor where the text is to be retrieved.

6. Press Move (CTRL-F4) and type **5** to Retrieve the text.

Cut a Column

The following steps are to be used only for tabbed columns (columns separated with Tabs, Tab Aligns, or Indents). If you want to cut text from parallel or newspaper columns, use the steps to Cut a Block.

1. Move to the first character in the column to be cut.

2. Press Block (ALT-F4) to turn on Block.

3. Move straight down the column if only that column is to be affected. If you want to cut more than one column, move the cursor to the right into the applicable column(s). At this point it does not appear that the proper text is being highlighted; be patient until the next step.

4. Press Move (CTRL-F4) and type **4** to Cut/Copy the column. The column is now highlighted. Note that the [TAB] preceding the column is also highlighted as part of the column. If you move the cursor into columns to the right when defining the block, then those columns are also highlighted.

5. Type **1** to Cut the column. Type **3** if you have no intention of retrieving the column again. Remaining columns are moved to the left.

6. When you are ready to retrieve the cut column, position the cursor just after the last character in the column to the left, at the left margin, or after the last column.

7. Press Move (CTRL-F4) and type **4** to Retrieve the column. Remember that a [TAB] was included as part of

the column, so if you retrieve a column at the left margin, it will be retrieved at the first tab setting. Delete the [TAB] code at the beginning of each line if necessary to move the column to the left margin.

Cut a Rectangle

You can cut a rectangle, which is a block of text from the top left corner to the bottom right corner, and move or delete the block.

1. Place the cursor at one corner (upper left or bottom right) and press Block (ALT-F4).

2. Move to the opposite corner. A regular block is highlighted until the next step.

3. Press Move (CTRL-F4) and type **5** to Cut/Copy a Rectangle. The rectangle is highlighted.

4. Type **1** to Cut. If you don't plan to retrieve the column again, you can type **3** to Delete the rectangle. If you included a [TAB] in the rectangle, all remaining columns are moved to the left. If not, the space remains vacant.

5. Position the cursor anywhere on the screen.

6. Press Move (CTRL-F4) and type **6** to Retrieve the rectangle. The complete rectangle will be retrieved at that point. If necessary, spaces are inserted so the format of the rectangle is retained.

Hints

Cut/copied text is saved in a temporary "move" file. It will remain there and can be retrieved again and again until another cut/copy is performed or until you turn off the computer.

An alternate way of retrieving cut text is to press Retrieve (SHIFT-F10), then ENTER. You could think of the name of the temporary file as ENTER, which means you only have to press ENTER instead of typing the name of the file to be retrieved.

If you want to remember only one method of cutting/copying text, use the Block method. If the cursor is at the beginning of a sentence, paragraph, or page, you can press Block (ALT-F4) and type a period (.) to highlight the sentence, ENTER to highlight a paragraph, or PGDN to highlight the page.

The Copy option on the Move menu makes a copy rather than removing the text. Copied text is saved to the same temporary file as cut text. The Delete option lets you delete a sentence, paragraph, or page. Even though the deleted text is not saved in the temporary "move" file, it is saved in a temporary "undelete" file and can be retrieved by pressing Cancel (F1) and typing **1** to Restore. Remember that only the last three deletions can be restored if you use this method.

The text involved when you cut a block, column, or rectangle is kept in separate temporary files. You should choose the correct option when retrieving the block (text, column, or rectangle) or you will retrieve the wrong block. The option of retrieving a normal block of text (press Retrieve (SHIFT-F10) and ENTER) cannot be used to retrieve a column or rectangle.

If you accidentally chose **3** to delete a column or rectangle, you can restore it with the Cancel key at the left margin (preferably on a blank screen), then cut it as a column or rectangle rather than deleting it.

Applications

The most common application for Cut in any word processor is to move text. Some examples are explained below.

Cut a Column Without Readjusting Remaining Columns

Use the rectangle cut without including the [TAB] codes to cut a column and leave the space empty. Remaining columns will not move to the left. Figure 4-27 illustrates the

a) Cut column

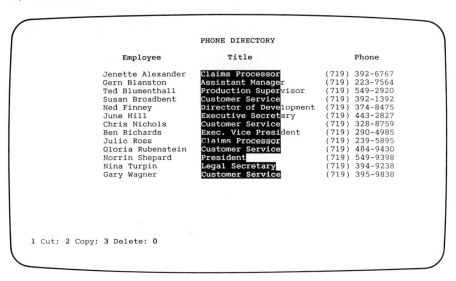

b) Spaces added to last line

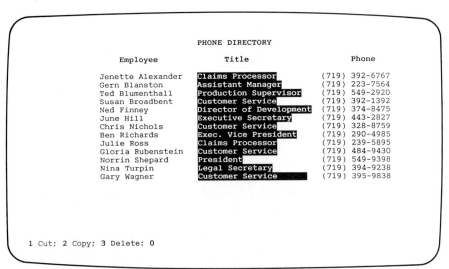

Figure 4-27. Highlighted text indicating cut column (a), and spaces added to last line of highlighted column (b)

```
                          PHONE DIRECTORY

              Employee                          Phone

         Jenette Alexander                 (719) 392-6767
         Gern Blanston                     (719) 223-7564
         Ted Blumenthall                   (719) 549-2920
         Susan Broadbent                   (719) 392-1392
         Ned Finney                        (719) 374-8475
         June Hill                         (719) 443-2827
         Chris Nichols                     (719) 328-8759
         Ben Richards                      (719) 290-4985
         Julie Ross                        (719) 239-5895
         Gloria Rubenstein                 (719) 484-9430
         Norrin Shepard                    (719) 549-9398
         Nina Turpin                       (719) 394-9238
         Gary Wagner                       (719) 395-9838




  A:\SCREENS.RF1                    Doc 1  Pg 49  Ln 24    Pos 3
```

Figure 4-28.   Column cut without readjustment of remaining columns

highlighted column and adjustment to it before cutting. If you do not plan to include the [TAB] codes, the last line in the rectangle must be the longest line (or at least as long as the longest line) in the rectangle. To avoid including the [TAB] code in the column, add spaces to the last line to make it the longest. Figure 4-28 shows the result of cutting a column without readjusting the remaining columns.

Cutting a Column with the Column Heading

Usually if you are going to cut a column, you will want the heading to go with it. In previous versions of WordPerfect, you had to fill the blank line separating the heading and column with [TAB] codes in order for this to work. With version 4.2, you can use either the column or rectangle option to accomplish this without filling the line with [TAB] codes.

Equations, Graphs, and Statistical Typing

When you create an equation or draw a box or graph with Line Draw, you can create it at the left margin first, then use the rectangle cut option to move it anywhere on the screen.

If you have a rectangular piece of a formula that must be removed, you can cut or delete the rectangle and the rest of the formula will readjust to fill the vacant space.

Related Entries

Copy Text and Columns

Move

Rectangular Cut, Copy, and Move

Undelete

Dashes

There is a particular way you should enter single (-) and double dashes (--) in WordPerfect.

Keystrokes

Single Dash

If you press the hyphen/underscore key, you will get a hyphen instead of a dash. This is fine if you want a hyphen, but when a hyphen is found at the end of a line, the word will be broken. When you don't want a word broken, you should use a dash.

To use the dash, press HOME, then the hyphen key to

insert a single dash. The - character is inserted rather than the hard hyphen code [-].

Double Dash

If you press the hyphen key twice to enter a double dash, the dashes could be separated if located at the end of a line. To avoid this, make the first one a regular dash.

1. Press HOME, then the hyphen key.
2. Press the hyphen key.

If you use two regular dashes to make the double dash, the double dash could end up at the beginning of a line rather than always at the end of a line.

Applications

Use a single dash (minus sign) in equations to prevent the equation from being separated between two lines.

In the case of compound names (such as a woman's use of her family name and married name together), the names may be separated with a single dash. The dash prevents breaking the compound name between lines.

An *M dash* is a longer dash used by typographers instead of the double dash that is familiar in typewritten text or computer hard copy. The M dash is not available on most computers and printers. If you have a laser printer, you can create the M dash by sending a printer command that will print a dash, back up a little, print another, back up a little, and print another for a total of three run-together dashes. To insert a printer command, press Print Format (CTRL-F8), type **A**, and enter the command.

You could place these steps in a macro, but you cannot see the character on the screen. You may want to edit the character table with the Printer program to include this command as one of the characters that can be displayed on the screen.

See Chapter 7 for more information about editing printer definitions and character tables.

Related Entries

Hyphenation

Printer Commands

See also Chapter 7, "Printer Program"

Date and Time

Date (SHIFT-F5) can be used to insert the current date/time, provide for updating the current date/time each time a document is retrieved or printed, or change the way the date/time is displayed.

Keystrokes

Insert Date/Time

1. Press Date (CTRL-F5). The following menu appears.

```
Date: 1 Insert Text; 2 Format; 3 Insert Function: 0
```

2. Type **1** to Insert Text or **3** to Insert Function.

The first option "types" the current date/time as text. The third option displays the current date/time, but actually inserts a function code. The function code inserts the current date/time each time a document is retrieved or printed.

Change the Date/Time Format

WordPerfect has chosen to display the date/time in the form "Month Date, Year" (as in November 25, 1987). Use the following steps if you want to change the way it is displayed.

1. Press Date (SHIFT-F5).

2. Type **2** for Format. Figure 4-29 shows the Date Format menu.

3. Type the string of numbers that will determine the format, including other desired characters such as a comma, slash, dash (hyphen), colon, or period.

4. Press ENTER to set the format. The Date menu is displayed again, letting you insert the date/time.

5. Type **1** or **3** to insert the date/time or press ENTER to leave the menu.

```
Date Format

     Character    Meaning
         1        Day of the month
         2        Month (number)
         3        Month (word)
         4        Year (all four digits)
         5        Year (last two digits)
         6        Day of the week (word)
         7        Hour (24-hour clock)
         8        Hour (12-hour clock)
         9        Minute
         0        am / pm
         %        Include leading zero for numbers less than 10
                     (must directly precede number)

     Examples:  3 1, 4      = December 25, 1984
                %2/%1/5 (6) = 01/01/85 (Tuesday)
Date Format: 3 1, 4
```

Figure 4-29.   Date Format menu

Hints

When the date format is changed, a code is not inserted in the document. The only code inserted is when you choose to "Insert Function," which will result in showing the current date format, such as [Date:13 1, 4], in Reveal Codes.

You can have several Date functions within a document and each can have its own format. To do this, change the format each time before inserting a function. You can enter up to 29 characters for the date format.

If you press Cancel (F1) while changing the date format, changes are ignored and the format returns to its original setting.

Use the WordPerfect Setup menu to change the date format permanently. Type **WP/S** at the DOS prompt rather than WP and type **2** to change the initial settings.

Wrong Date and Time?

WordPerfect uses whatever date and time have been entered at the DOS level. Therefore, it is important that the correct date and time be entered when the computer is started. If the wrong date and time appear when you use the Date key, exit from WordPerfect and enter **DATE** at the DOS prompt. Enter the correct date when prompted. Next, enter **TIME**, then the correct time. You could use Shell (CTRL-F1) to go to DOS and make the change without exiting WordPerfect *unless* you are using WordPerfect Library. If Library is also running, it will create problems with the Calendar program.

Inserting the Date During a Merge

If you include the ^D merge code in a primary merge document, the current date/time will be inserted during the merge. A ^D is exactly like inserting a Date function into a merge document. However, rather than assigning a specific format to the ^D code, as is done with the Date function, the current date format is used.

Viewing the Current Time

The Date function does not work like a clock. The time is updated only when a file is retrieved or printed. If you want to see the current date or time, press List Files (F5) and ENTER. The date and time are displayed in the upper left corner of the screen.

Applications

You can include the date (text or function) as part of a letter or memorandum macro.

If including the date in a primary merge document, use ^D or the Date function. If you insert the date as text, you will have to change the date manually in the document each time you merge.

Related Entries

List Files

Merge

Setup Menu

dBASE II/III

You can convert the data created with dBASE to a Word-Perfect secondary merge file where the fields are separated by ^R[HRt] and records are separated with ^E[HRt].

Keystrokes

1. While in dBASE, enter the following command.

Use (*name*)

2. After this process is finished, enter

COPY TO (*filename*) DELIMITED

The new filename should be different from the original filename, and can include the drive and directory where the new file is to be stored. The extension .DBF is automatically added to the filename. See "Hints" for other options.

3. Exit dBASE.

4. Start the Convert program at DOS. If you are not sure of the exact steps, see *Convert Program*.

5. Enter the input filename (file to be converted) and the output filename (file which will hold the converted data). Remember to enter the full pathname if necessary (for example, B:MAILING.DBF or C:\DBASE \MAILING.DBF).

6. Type **7** or **8** (depending on your version of Convert Program) to convert a Mail Merge file to WordPerfect Secondary Merge format.

7. Enter a comma (,) as the field delimiter. If you specified a different character as the delimiter, enter that character.

8. Enter {**13**} {**10**} as the record delimiter.

9. Enter a quotation mark (") as the character to be stripped from the file.

Using a dBASE Report in WordPerfect

You can print a report to disk and retrieve it into WordPerfect for advanced formatting before printing.

1. Open the data base file with the dBASE USE command.

Use (name)

2. Next, give dBASE the following command.

REPORT FORM (*report name*) TO FILE (*filename*)

The extension .TXT is assigned unless you specify a different one.

3. Exit dBASE and enter WordPerfect.

4. Change the margins if necessary with Line Format (SHIFT-F8), option **3**.

5. Press Text In/Out (CTRL-F5) and type **2** or **3** to retrieve the file. (See *DOS Text Files* or *Text In/Out* for options.)

Hints

If you want to have the files sorted in dBASE before converting them, enter the following command instead of USE (*name*).

USE (*name*) index (*INDEX files to be used*)

This command opens a data base file and sorts the records according to the specified index.

If you use the COPY TO (*filename*) DELIMITED command, fields are delimited with commas (character fields are further delimited with quotation marks), and records are delimited with a carriage return/line feed. If you want to specify a different field delimiter, you can enter the following command.

COPY TO (*filename*) DELIMITED WITH (*delimiter*)

If you want to specify which fields are to be included, you can enter a command like the following.

COPY TO (*filename*) FIELDS (*field list*) DELIMITED

There are also options for selecting the records to be included in the copy. See "COPY" in your dBASE manual for further information.

Related Entries

Convert Program

Text In/Out

See also Chapter 8, "Software Integration"

DCA FORMAT

DCA (Document Content Architecture) is the standard text format used by IBM. The Convert program can convert documents to and from DCA format.

Keystrokes

There are actually two DCA formats: Revisable-Form-Text and Final-Form-Text. As its name implies, Revisable-Form-Text can be edited. Therefore, a document in this format can be transferred to WordPerfect format, but one in Final-Form-Text cannot. A WordPerfect document can be converted to either DCA format.

1. Start the Convert program from DOS. If you are unsure of the exact steps, see *Convert Program* for details.

2. Enter the input filename (file to be converted) and the output filename (file which will hold the converted data). Remember to enter the full pathname if necessary (for example, b:contract.* or c: \dca \contract.12).

3. If converting a WordPerfect document to DCA, type **1**. If converting from DCA Revisable-Form-Text, type **2**. If you choose option 2, the conversion takes place.

4. If you type **1** from step 3, another menu is presented. Type **1** to convert the WP document to Revisable-Form-Text or **2** to convert it to Final-Form-Text.

Hints

The following functions are retained during the Word-Perfect-DCA conversion.

Hard/soft returns

Hard/soft page breaks

Tab/Indent/Tab Align

Bold

Underline

Center

Flush right

Right justification on/off

Hard space

Hard/soft hyphens

Superscript/subscript

Tab set

Margin set

Spacing set

Left margin release

Hyphenation zone reset

Pitch

Lines per inch

Underline style

Page number set

Page number inserted

Top margin

Form length

Header/footer

Footnotes

Set footnote number

Auto outline

Strikeout on/off

Extended characters

If a feature is not converted, it is most likely because DCA does not have a code for the function. Sometimes there are multiple codes in DCA for a particular function. For example, IBM 5520 uses one format for centering text while Displaywrite uses another. WordPerfect can successfully convert all types of formats into WordPerfect, but must choose one type when converting back to DCA. In WordPerfect version 4.1, the center code was converted to the IBM 5520 method. Because of a high demand, centering is now converted to the code used by Displaywrite.

Related Entries

Convert Program

See also Chapter 8, "Software Integration"

DEC Computers

WordPerfect is available on the DEC Rainbow microcomputer and the DEC VAX minicomputer.

The same WordPerfect function codes are used for the DEC Rainbow, DEC VAX, and IBM versions. This means that files created with WordPerfect on one system can be transferred to another without converting the documents. The data must be transferred serially, however, because the disks are incompatible. Digital Equipment Corporation will be able to assist with the hardware needed to transfer documents.

In May 1987, a new VAX version of WordPerfect 4.08 was released, increasing the speed by 800 percent. The current version for the DEC Rainbow is WordPerfect 4.2, which has been updated to provide faster screen display and an alternate keyboard mapping. As of this writing, WordPerfect version 4.2 is scheduled for release in the third quarter of 1987. WordPerfect Corporation will continue to support the DEC Rainbow, especially since WordPerfect has entered the VAX marketplace.

DEC Rainbow users can use the standard keyboard layout or the mapping and template that match the VAX/VMS format. Separate disks for each version are provided with the WordPerfect package. The alternate mapping was provided to make it easier for the DEC Rainbow to be used as a VAX/VMS terminal and to provide a more seamless connection between the two.

Because the DEC Rainbow does not have an ALT key, you can use SHIFT and CTRL together when the use of an ALT key is suggested. The CTRL-SHIFT combination can be used for ALT-macros and ALT-key mapping for special characters.

Related Entries

See Chapter 6, "Printer Specifics"

Decimal Tabs

Tab Align (CTRL-F6) can be used to align numbers at a decimal point. You can also set decimal tabs and use the TAB key to align numbers.

Keystrokes

Choose the method you prefer. If you have a large table of numeric columns, setting decimal tabs is probably preferable.

Tab Align

1. Press Tab Align (CTRL-F6). The cursor moves to the first tab setting and "Align Char = ." appears at the bottom of the screen.

2. Type the number. Characters are pushed to the left until the decimal point is typed. Remaining numbers are inserted to the right.

3. Press Tab Align (CTRL-F6) to enter another number at the next tab setting or press ENTER to return to the left margin.

Set Decimal Tabs

1. Press Line Format (SHIFT-F8) and type **1** or **2** for Tabs.

2. Delete all tabs if necessary by pressing HOME, HOME, ←, then Delete to End of Line (CTRL-END).

3. Enter the number where the tab is to be set and type **D**, or change normal tab settings to a D. Continue until all tabs have been set.

4. Press Exit (F7) to return to the document.

When you press TAB to go to a decimal tab setting, "Align Char = ." appears at the bottom of the screen and numbers are aligned at the decimal point.

Hints

Both methods insert an Align On [A] and Align Off [a] code. If you are editing numbers that are aligned, you will probably see "Delete [Aln/FlshR]? (Y/N) N" on the screen. This question is telling you that you have tried to delete the [A] or [a] code and is asking for confirmation. Type **Y** to delete it or **N** to leave it. Don't be discouraged; it takes time to get used to working with the Align codes.

When setting decimal tabs, remember that the decimal point will be placed at the tab setting. Keep this in mind when trying to set evenly spaced tabs.

If you get into the practice of always setting correct tabs for tables, it will save a lot of time and trouble later when editing the table. If you have numeric columns, set decimal tabs for those columns. Of course, you can use Tab Align (CTRL-F6) to align numbers at a normal tab setting, but pressing the TAB key is easier.

If you don't like working with the Align codes and prefer to enter a table using normal tabs, you can create a macro to align numbers after they have been entered. The following illustration shows a table entered with regular tabs.

```
$115.87      $2,556.00     $445.34       $1,212.45
198.87       817.00        282.11        392.89
74.00        98.74         34.00         1,980.00
```

The next illustration shows the same table after the macro has been executed.

```
$115.87      $2,556.00     $445.34       $1,212.45
 198.87         817.00       282.11         392.89
  74.00          98.74        34.00       1,980.00
```

A macro is necessary because you cannot change normal tabs to decimal tabs and have the table automatically realign. Also, you cannot use Replace to substitute Align codes for [TAB] codes.

To set up the macro:

1. Move just to the right of the [Tab Set:] code being used for the table. Press Line Format (SHIFT-F8) and type **1** or **2** to change regular tab settings to decimal tab settings for columns containing numbers.

2. Press Macro Def (CTRL-F10) and enter a name for the macro (ALIGN is a suggestion).

3. Press Search (F2), press TAB, then Search again to search for the first [TAB] code.

4. Press Block (ALT-F4).

5. Press Search (F2) twice to search for the next [TAB] code.

6. Press ← once to position the cursor just before the [TAB] code. The text in the first line, first column, should be highlighted.

7. Press Move (CTRL-F4) and type **1** to Cut Block.

8. Press BACKSPACE to delete the previous [TAB] code, then TAB to insert a new [TAB] code. In the case of a decimal tab, Align codes [A] and [a] are inserted.

9. Press Move (CTRL-F5) and type **5** to Retrieve Text. The number will be aligned correctly.

10. Press Macro (ALT-F10) and enter the name of this macro (enter **ALIGN** if you gave that name to the macro). This step chains the macro so it repeats until it can no longer find [TAB] codes.

11. Press Macro Def (CTRL-F10) to end the macro definition.

Keep in mind that when you execute this macro, it will search for each tab from the cursor forward and complete the steps. Therefore, if the table is found within a document, you should Save (F10) the document, then use Block (ALT-F4) and Move (CTRL-F4) to cut the table and retrieve it into document Doc 2 (press Switch (SHIFT-F3) to switch between documents). After the table is changed, you can block and move the table back into document 1.

When you are ready to execute the macro, place the cursor at the beginning of the table, press Macro (ALT-F10), and enter the name of the macro. When it is finished, you might see "Block On" flashing on the screen and the last number not aligned properly. If so, it could not find another [TAB] code to finish the process. If this happens, press Block (ALT-F4) to turn off Block, press BACKSPACE to delete the previous [TAB] code, then press TAB to insert the new [TAB] or Align code manually.

Related Entries

Tab Align

Tabs, Clear and Set

Default Directory

The default directory is used to save and retrieve files unless another directory is specified. This means that when you save or retrieve a file, you have to enter only the filename instead of the full pathname.

You can change the default directory from DOS before or after entering WordPerfect. From DOS, use the CD command to change directories. From within WordPerfect, press List Files (F5), type =, then enter the name of the new default directory.

See *Change Directory* for complete information.

Default Settings

WordPerfect has chosen common default settings for margins, tabs, spacing, page size, pitch, and so on. The WordPerfect Setup menu lets you change the defaults to better fit your needs.

Keystrokes

1. Enter **WP/S** instead of WP at the DOS prompt to enter the Setup menu.

2. Type **2** to Set Initial Settings. Figure 4-30 shows the resulting menu that allows you to change the listed options.

3. As a rule, press the same keys used in WordPerfect to change options. The same menus and prompts appear. Make the desired changes.

4. Press **0** to set the changes and enter WordPerfect. Or press Cancel (F1) to leave the settings as they were and return to DOS.

Hints

You can reenter the Setup menu and make changes any time.

Remember that changing the default settings could adversely affect others who might be using your computer. If you share documents with others who prefer different defaults, the documents will not appear to be formatted correctly.

To temporarily set the defaults back to the standard WordPerfect settings, enter **WP/X** intead of WP to start WordPerfect. To permanently return to the standard defaults, enter **WP/X/S**.

If you prefer to print in a pitch other than 10, it is best

```
Change Initial Settings

Press any of the keys listed below to change initial settings

Key                     Initial Settings

Format          Tabs, Margins, Spacing, Hyphenation, Align Character
Page Format     Page # Pos, Page Length, Top Margin, Page # Col Pos, W/O
Print Format    Pitch, Font, Lines/Inch, Right Just, Underlining, SF Bin #
Print           Printer, Copies, Binding Width
Date            Date Format
Insert/Typeover Insert/Typeover Mode
Mark Text       Paragraph Number Definition, Table of Authorities Definition
Footnote        Footnote/Endnote Options
Escape          Set N
Screen          Set Auto-rewrite
Text In/Out     Set Insert Document Summary on Save/Exit

Selection:

Press Enter to return to the Set-up Menu
```

Figure 4-30.   Change Initial Settings menu

to change the pitch, margins, and tabs, as they all work
together.

If you decide not to change the defaults, but would have
to change the settings in each document, consider placing
the settings in a macro instead.

Related Entries

Macros

Setup Menu

See also Chapter 3, "The Next Step"

DEL Key

The DEL key is used to delete text at the cursor.

Keystrokes

Press DEL once to delete the character at the cursor. Continue pressing to delete characters to the right.

Hints

Press BACKSPACE to delete characters to the left of the cursor.

After highlighting a block of text, you can press DEL or BACKSPACE to delete the block. You are asked to confirm the deletion.

If you "run into" a code while deleting text, you might be asked to confirm the deletion. Type **Y** to delete the code or press any other key (including DEL) to move past the code.

Text accidentally deleted can be restored by pressing Cancel (F1) and typing **1**. You can restore the last three deletions.

Related Entries

BACKSPACE Key

Cancel

Delete Codes

Delete

Any of the following keystrokes can be used to delete text and codes.

Keystrokes

BACKSPACE	Delete text to the left.
DEL	Delete text at the cursor. Continue pressing to delete text to the right.
CTRL-BACKSPACE	Delete the word at the cursor. Continue pressing to delete words to the right of the cursor.
HOME,BACKSPACE	Delete from the cursor to the beginning of the current word. Press both again to delete words to the left of the cursor.
HOME,DEL	Delete from the cursor to the end of the current word. Press both again to delete words to the right of the cursor.
CTRL-END	Delete text from the cursor to the end of the line.
CTRL-PGDN	Delete text from the cursor to the end of the page. You are asked to confirm this type of deletion.

Hints

Press Block (ALT-F4) to highlight a larger section of text, then press DEL or BACKSPACE to delete the block. You are asked, "Delete Block? (Y/N) N." Type **Y** to delete it or press any other key to leave the block. If you decide to leave the block, it remains highlighted.

Move (CTRL-F4) can be used to delete a sentence, paragraph, or page.

1. Place the cursor in the text to be deleted and press Move (CTRL-F4).

2. Type **1** for the current Sentence, **2** for the Paragraph, or **3** for the entire Page. The text will be highlighted.

3. Type **3** to Delete the highlighted section.

Move can also be used to delete a tabbed column or rectangle. See *Columns, Rectangular Cut, Copy, and Move,* or *Move* for more information.

If you accidentally delete text, you can restore it by pressing Cancel (F1) and typing **1**. Type **2** to display the previous two deletions.

Applications

Deleting and restoring operations can be used to move text. Instead of the usual five or more keystrokes, you can delete the text, move the cursor to the new location, press Cancel (F1), and type **1** to Restore. Remember that only the last three deletions can be restored.

Related Entries

BACKSPACE Key

Block

Cancel

Columns

DEL Key

Move

Rectangular Cut, Copy, and Move

Delete a Directory

You can delete a directory from the hard disk while in DOS or WordPerfect.

Keystrokes

A directory must be empty before it can be deleted. You also must be in the parent directory to delete a directory. See *Directories* in this chapter for an explanation of parent directory.

1. Press List Files (F5).

2. Enter the name of the parent directory of the directory to be deleted.

3. When the list of directories and files appears, move the cursor to the directory to be deleted. Directories are marked with <DIR>. See Figure 4-31 for clarification.

4. Type **2** to Delete.

5. Type **Y** or **N** to confirm the deletion.

Hints

Instead of typing the entire name of a directory after pressing List Files (F5), you can edit the displayed name or

```
11/25/87  10:42              Directory C:\*.*
Document Size:      2825                          Free Disk Space:   1892352

. <CURRENT>      <DIR>                    .. <PARENT>     <DIR>
BOOK     .       <DIR>   12/01/86 10:08   CLIENTS .       <DIR>   09/22/85 20:36
COMM     .       <DIR>   09/22/85 20:20   DATA    .       <DIR>   09/21/85 22:23
JEFF     .       <DIR>   09/22/85 20:19   KAREN   .       <DIR>   09/22/85 20:19
LEARNING.        <DIR>   01/08/87 10:32   LIBRARY .       <DIR>   03/05/86 20:52
MATH     .       <DIR>   09/22/85 21:20   NEWDATA .       <DIR>   01/06/86 11:32
PERSONAL.        <DIR>   09/22/85 20:51   SYSTEM  .       <DIR>   01/01/80 00:05
TEMP     .       <DIR>   04/05/87 22:21   WP      .       <DIR>   09/21/85 22:30
WP50     .       <DIR>   04/04/87 22:17   401K    .MPW      6832   12/15/86 13:11
ANSI     .SYS     1664   10/20/83 12:00   APPOINT .APP         0   02/16/87 17:34
AUTOEXEC.BAT       128   03/05/86 20:49   AUTOTIME.EXE      1314   08/05/80 16:33
BOOK     .MPW     3824   10/24/86 12:42   COMMAND .COM     23210   03/07/85 13:43
CONFIG   .SYS      116   03/16/87 11:44   DB      .          650   04/07/86 23:18
MARKS    .WP        80   03/18/87 20:43   PROGRAM .         3485   03/18/87 21:07
PRTCHG   .COM       80   01/01/86 15:43   PRTSCR  .COM      1587   03/21/86 08:16
PRTSCR   .DOC     1744   03/21/86 08:18   PRTTGL  .COM        23   01/01/86 14:52
RP       .EXE     9712   08/29/86 09:31   RP      .INS      9072   08/29/86 10:23
RP       .SYS     5136   07/01/86 21:15   RPINSTAL.EXE     32496   08/29/86 09:45
RPREMOVE.EXE      5872   08/29/86 04:32   SCREEN  .DAT     18459   01/14/87 14:12

1 Retrieve; 2 Delete; 3 Rename; 4 Print; 5 Text In;
6 Look; 7 Change Directory; 8 Copy; 9 Word Search; 0 Exit: 6
```

Figure 4-31.   List of files and directories in parent directory

press ENTER to see the default directory. You can then move to the parent directory and press ENTER twice to move into it.

Because a directory has to be empty before it can be deleted, you can list the files in that directory, press Mark Text (ALT-F5) to mark all files, then type **2** and confirm the deletion of all files. After the files are deleted, move the cursor to ". . <PARENT> <DIR>," press ENTER twice, move to the <DIR> to be deleted, type **2**, and confirm the deletion.

You can remove a directory from DOS with the RD (remove directory) command. First, change to the parent directory of the directory to be deleted, then enter the command **RD DIRECTORY**, where "directory" is the name of the directory to be deleted. Remember that the directory must be empty before it can be deleted.

Related Entries

Directories

See also Chapter 1, "Getting Started"

Delete Codes

WordPerfect codes can be deleted in the same manner as regular text.

Keystrokes

1. Press Reveal Codes (ALT-F3). The screen is split, showing the regular screen above and the text with codes below.

2. Move the cursor to the code to be deleted. Any of the cursor keys can be used.

3. Press BACKSPACE if the code is to the left of the cursor, or DEL if the code is to the right of the cursor.

Hints

Delete Codes in the Normal Screen

After you have spent some time with WordPerfect, you can usually tell the approximate location of a code by the appearance of the text on the screen. For example, if the margins change on the screen, there is probably a Margin Set code or at least an Indent code at that location. Text that is bolded, underlined, or centered will also have codes close by.

Sometimes when using ← and →, the cursor does not appear to move and the position number in the lower corner of the screen does not change. When this happens, you are moving over a code. If you are deleting text using BACKSPACE or DEL and run into a code, you are usually asked for a confirmation similar to the following.

Delete [Code]? (Y/N) N

Type **Y** to delete the code or press any other key (including the DEL key) to move past the code. Some codes that are easy to insert, such as [TAB], [Indent], and a hard space [ ], do not ask for confirmation.

If you delete with keys other than BACKSPACE or DEL, codes are automatically deleted with the text. This includes a word delete, block delete, Delete to End of Line, Delete to End of Page, and so on.

Search for a Code

The Search feature can be used in the normal screen or in Reveal Codes to locate a code quickly.

1. Press Search (F2) or ← Search (SHIFT-F2), depending on whether you want to search forward or backward. It

might be advisable to move to the top of the document (HOME,HOME,↑), then use Search (F2).

2. Press the appropriate function key to insert the code. For example, if you are searching for Bold codes, press Bold (F6). If you need to search for margin settings, press Line Format (SHIFT-F8) and type **3** to insert [Margin Set] as the search string.

3. Press Search (F2) to start the search.

Of course you can combine text and codes together in the search string. Codes are bolded in the string. You cannot search for a code just by typing the characters. You must press the function key and choose options if applicable.

When the search string is found, the cursor is always placed to the right of the code. Therefore, you can always press BACKSPACE to delete the code and confirm the deletion without having to enter the Reveal Codes screen to check its location.

Delete Codes with the Replace Feature

Replace (ALT-F2) can be used to search for codes and replace them with nothing, thus deleting them. You can also selectively delete codes by asking to confirm each "replacement."

1. Press Replace (ALT-F2).

2. If you want to confirm the deletion of each code, type **Y** in answer to the question "w/Confirm? (Y/N)." If you want each code to be deleted automatically, type **N**.

3. Press the appropriate function key (and choose an option from a menu if necessary) to insert the code.

4. Press Search (F2) twice—once to enter the search string and once to enter nothing as the replacement string.

If you asked to confirm each replacement, the cursor will stop at each code found. Type **Y** to delete the code or **N** to leave the code.

With the exception of a few single-byte functions (such as [TAB], [B]/[b], [U]/[u], or [Center Pg]), you cannot replace one code with another. To get around this limitation, you can create a macro that searches for a code, deletes it, and inserts a new code. You could then execute this macro *n* times using the ESC key, or chain the macro to itself so that it will continue until no other codes are found.

Applications

If you are having problems with a document, you should be able to find the code causing the problem with Search or Replace and delete it. These features are also helpful when editing another person's documents.

If you have single and double spacing or various margin settings throughout a document and wish to return to the default settings, use Replace to search for the codes and delete them.

Related Entries

Codes

DEL Key

Macros

Replace

Reveal Codes

Search

Delete Files

Files can be deleted from the List Files menu in WordPerfect or while in DOS.

Keystrokes

1. Press List Files (F5).

2. Press ENTER to see the list of files in the displayed directory or enter the name of a different directory. If you know the name of the file to be deleted, enter the name of the file.

3. When in the List Files menu, move the cursor to the file to be deleted. If you want to delete more than one file, type * to mark each file.

4. Type 2 to Delete the file(s).

5. If you marked files, you are asked, "Delete Marked Files? (Y/N) N." Type **Y** or **N**. If you type **N** or if no files were marked, you are asked to confirm the deletion of the highlighted file. Type **Y** or **N**.

Hints

Files can also be deleted while in DOS. From the DOS prompt, enter **DEL** or **ERASE** (depending on your preference) and the name of the file to be deleted. To delete more than one file, you can use wildcard characters. For example, if you want to delete all files ending with the extension .DOC, enter **DEL *.DOC**, using the * wildcard character to indicate any filename. To delete all files, enter **DEL *.*.** You are asked by DOS to confirm this type of deletion.

You can also use wildcard characters in WordPerfect to specify all documents or particular documents to be deleted. After pressing List Files (F5) the current directory is displayed, followed by *.*. All files will be displayed. If you want to delete all the files, press ALT-F5 and all files are marked. Type 2 and confirm the deletion. If you want only the files having the .DOC extension deleted, press List Files

(F5) and enter ***.DOC** as the "listing." Mark all the displayed files and delete them as described above.

Related Entries

Delete a Directory

List Files

Dictionary

See *Spell*

DIF

Some spreadsheet programs (including Lotus 1-2-3) can save their files as DIF (Data Interchange Format) files. These files can be converted to a WordPerfect secondary merge file and back again.

Keystrokes

The following steps assume that you have converted a spreadsheet file to DIF first.

1. Start the Convert program at the DOS prompt. (See *Convert Program* for the exact steps.)

2. Enter the name of the input file (file to be converted) and the name of the output file (file which will contain the converted data).

3. Type **8** to convert the file from a WordPerfect secondary merge file to DIF, or type **9** to convert a DIF file to secondary merge format.

Hints

If you are using Lotus, you should first run the Translate utility (from the Access menu) to convert a 1-2-3 worksheet to DIF. If converting a file from a WordPerfect secondary merge file to DIF, you will need to run the Translate utility (after Convert) to translate it to a 1-2-3 file. See Chapter 8 for step-by-step instructions on converting Lotus 1-2-3 worksheets.

Each row in the DIF file is considered a record, while each column in the row is considered a field. In a WordPerfect merge file, records are separated with a ^E and a hard return, while fields are separated with a ^R and a hard return.

Navy DIF Standard (Option 3) is used by the Navy as an intermediate file transfer format. This format is used to transfer files between word processors, not spreadsheets. If you choose option 3, the file is converted to a normal WordPerfect document instead of a secondary merge file.

PlanPerfect (a spreadsheet produced at WordPerfect Corporation) can import and export files in WordPerfect, WordPerfect secondary merge, Lotus, DIF, dBASE, and other formats. If you have PlanPerfect, you can use it to retrieve a file in one format and save it in another.

Related Entries

See also Chapter 8, "Software Integration"

Directories

A disk can be divided into several directories for better organization.

When a disk is formatted, it contains only one directory, the root directory. There is a limit on the number of
files that can be saved in the root directory, so you would
usually divide it into several directories. These directories
act as large files that can hold several other files. They are
named as you would name any other file, but appear in a
list of files with the label <DIR> indicating that each is a
directory.

The root directory is named with a single backslash
(\ ). The DOS prompt naming the drive and directory would
appear as C: \ . The names of directories are separated with
a backslash. For example, if you have a directory named
WP, the pathname would appear as C: \WP. C: \WP \LET-
TERS would be the name of a directory called LETTERS
created within the WP directory.

The term *parent directory* is used to identify the directory just above a directory. In the previous examples, WP is
the parent directory for LETTERS, and the root directory is
the parent directory for WP. There is no parent directory for
the root directory. Figure 4-32 shows one possible organization of directories on a hard disk.

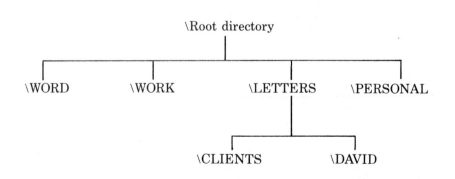

Figure 4-32.   Organization of a hard disk

Although you can divide the disk into as many subdirectories as you want, you should be aware that WordPerfect can support only up to 39 characters in a pathname. It also slows down DOS a little longer to search through longer pathnames for a file or command.

See Chapter 1 for complete information about organizing your disk into directories from DOS.

WordPerfect's List files menu can be used to manage the directories. It lets you move "up" into the parent directory or "down" into subdirectories. Figure 4-31 shows the directory information available in the List Files menu. You can use List Files (F5) to create (make) directories, change directories, delete directories, and, of course, list the files in each directory.

When in the List Files menu, you can press Print (SHIFT-F7), and a listing of the directory will print.

Related Entries

Change Directory

Create a Directory

Default Directory

Delete a Directory

List Files

See also Chapter 1, "Getting Started"

"Disk Full" Error Message

When saving a file or printing from the screen, you may encounter the error message "Disk full--strike any key to continue," indicating that there is no available space on the disk.

Reasons

If you retrieve a large file from disk and attempt to replace the original file, you might get this error message even when it appears that there should be plenty of disk space available. What actually happens is that the original file is renamed with the extension .BK!, the current file is saved, then the original is deleted. (If you have chosen to back up the original document, the .BK! file is not deleted.) If you want the file to be saved on the same disk, you can enter the List Files menu, delete the original copy, and then save the file from the disk. However, if there is a power failure during this process, you could lose your document. It is safest to use a new disk.

When you print from the screen, a copy of the document is saved to the disk with a temporary filename, then printed. However, if there is not enough room on the disk, you will get the "disk full" error message. If this happens, save the file to a disk first, then print from disk using the Printer Control or List Files menu.

Solutions

If you see this error message, press any key to return to the document.

You have two options. Either replace the data disk with one containing more space and save the file again, or press List Files (F5), ENTER, then use option **2** to delete unnecessary files. Press Exit (F7) to return to the document and save the file again.

As shown in Figure 4-31, the heading on the List Files menu tells you how much disk space is available and how much is needed for the current document. Also see *Disk Space* for more information.

A file {WP}.SPC is created each time WordPerfect is started. This temporary file occupies 4K of space on the disk so that if a "disk full" error message occurs, WordPerfect lets you fix the situation and try again.

Related Entries

Backing Up Files

Disk Space

"File Creation Error"

Disk Space

WordPerfect's List Files menu tells you how much disk space is available, how much disk space is being used by each file, and the size of the document in memory.

Keystrokes

1. Press List Files (F5).

2. Press ENTER to look into the displayed directory or enter the name of the drive/directory in question.

The screen in Figure 4-33 appears.

Each file in the directory is displayed with the file size and the date/time it was last edited. In the heading you can find "Document Size:", which indicates the size of the document currently in memory, and "Free Disk Space:", which displays the amount of space available on the disk.

Hints

The numbers displayed are the number of *bytes*. A two-sided, double-density disk usually contains 360K, which is actually 368,640 bytes (1K = 1,024 bytes). As a rule, each character equals one byte. In a WordPerfect file, each code takes at least one byte, but usually consists of several bytes.

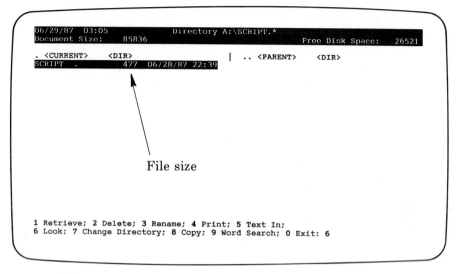

Figure 4-33.   File size indicated to the right of filename

You can fit approximately 2800 to 2900 characters on a single-spaced page. This would allow for about 130 single-spaced pages per disk. This figure does not take WordPerfect codes into account. A [HRt] is equal to one byte, whereas a Tab Align code equals five bytes. Should you want to estimate the amount of space taken by a code, you can clear the screen, enter the code, then look in the List Files menu to see how many bytes are in the current document.

See *"Disk Full" Error Message* for options when the disk is full.

Related Entries

"Disk Full" Error Message

List Files

Display Print Jobs

The first three jobs waiting to be printed are automatically displayed in the Printer Control menu. However, all print jobs can be displayed.

Keystrokes

1. Press Print (SHIFT-F7).

2. Type **4** for Printer Control.

3. Type **D** to Display All Print Jobs. The screen displays a list of the print jobs waiting (including the three automatically displayed in Printer Control).

4. Press any key to return to the Printer Control menu.

5. Press ENTER to return to the document.

Hints

Although you can queue up to 255 documents for printing, only 24 can be displayed at one time. If you have more, the screen will scroll to show you the last 24 jobs in the queue.

Print jobs are assigned a number. The jobs start numbering at 1 each time WordPerfect is started. If some print jobs are printed or canceled, the remaining jobs are not renumbered.

Applications

Display All Print Jobs is useful when you need to know how many documents (and which documents) are waiting to be printed.

If you need to cancel or rush a print job, you can use this feature to see the number assigned to the job.

Related Entries

Cancel a Print Job

Rush a Print Job

Display Printers and Fonts

You can display the six printers and assigned fonts with the Display Printers and Fonts option in Printer Control.

Keystrokes

1. Press Print (SHIFT-F7).

2. Type **4** for Printer Control.

3. Type **2** to Display Printers and Fonts. The first three printers and their fonts are displayed.

4. Press any key to see the next three printers and fonts.

5. Press any key to return to Printer Control.

6. Press ENTER to return to the document.

Hints

Only the six printer definitions that have been selected are displayed. To select different printers, choose option **3** in Printer Control.

The fonts displayed are actually the character tables being used for each font. The fonts may have different attributes (such as italics, expanded, or condensed type) that are not indicated on the screen. If you want to see the attribute assigned to each font, print the files PRINTER.TST and PRINTER2.TST found on the Learning disk.

A program included on the Printer 2 disk called PRHELP can be started by entering **PRHELP** at the applicable DOS prompt. You should also refer to Chapter 6 for the fonts, attibutes, suggested pitch settings, and other information.

Applications

Use this feature to remind you of the printer/font selections. This information is important when you want to print to a different printer or select fonts in the Print Format menu.

Related Entries

Fonts

Print

Print Format

Printer Control

Printer Number

Select Printers

Chapter 6, "Printer Specifics"

"Divide Overflow" Error Message

The message "Divide overflow--strike any key to continue" can be caused by too many characters trying to fit within set boundaries.

Reasons

This message should almost never occur. It could happen when attempting to set spacing in a footnote (not possible with later 4.2 versions) or when characters are entered between the left margin and a margin setting (also not currently possible).

Earlier 4.2 versions sometimes displayed this error message when working with parallel columns. If characters are entered between the [BlockPro:Off] and [Col off] codes, the message was displayed because characters were trying to fit within set boundaries. It could also happen when characters are entered between the [BlockPro:On] and [Col on] codes.

Solutions

When a situation creates a problem, WordPerfect makes every attempt to correct the situation. In the case of footnotes and margin settings, WordPerfect has changed the program so that a situation is not allowed; therefore, the problem cannot occur.

If you see this error message, you should check the version and date of WordPerfect. Confirm that it is version 4.2 dated later than July 10, 1987.

WordPerfect tries to let you return to your document after the message is displayed. If you encounter this error message, contact WordPerfect Corporation. If your computer locks up, the document will be lost. Thus, it is important to always set the timed backup. See *Backing Up Files* for more information.

Document Size

WordPerfect displays the size of a document in the List Files menu.

Keystrokes

1. Press List Files (F5).

2. Press ENTER to see the displayed directory or enter another directory name. If you know the name of the file in question, enter the name of the file.

3. The size of the file is indicated just after the file-name, as shown in Figure 4-33.

Hints

To find the size of the document in memory, press List Files (F5) and ENTER. "Document Size:" in the heading indicates the size of the current document. Note that the document size is for either document 1 or document 2; not both. The document size is shown for the document the cursor was in when List Files was pressed. Document size is indicated in bytes.

If you are in the List Files menu and decide to retrieve a file, check the document size at the top of the menu first. By making sure it is shown as 0, you will ensure that you are not retrieving a copy of one document into another already in memory.

You can have approximately 100 to 130 single-spaced pages on a double-sided, double-density disk. See *Disk Space* for more information.

Related Entries

Disk Space

List Files

Document Summary

A document summary, which contains the date the file was created, the author's and typist's names, and notes about the document, can be inserted into any document.

Keystrokes

1. From anywhere in the document, press Text In/Out (CTRL-F5).

2. Type **A** to Create/Edit Summary. The filename and date are automatically inserted.

3. Type the author's name, the typist's name, and any comments about the document. Figure 4-34 shows the Document Summary menu with sample entries.

4. Press Exit (F7) to leave the menu and return to your position in the document.

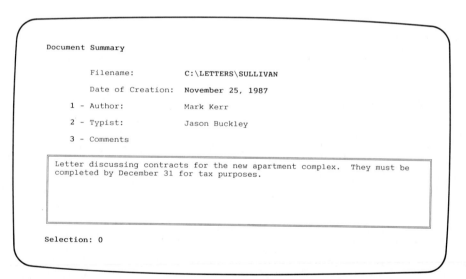

```
Document Summary


        Filename:            C:\LETTERS\SULLIVAN

        Date of Creation:    November 25, 1987

   1 - Author:              Mark Kerr

   2 - Typist:              Jason Buckley

   3 - Comments

   ┌──────────────────────────────────────────────────────────────────────┐
   │ Letter discussing contracts for the new apartment complex.  They must be │
   │ completed by December 31 for tax purposes.                             │
   │                                                                        │
   │                                                                        │
   │                                                                        │
   └──────────────────────────────────────────────────────────────────────┘

Selection: 0
```

Figure 4-34.   Document Summary menu and sample entries, as displayed at beginning of document

Hints

Despite the location of the cursor, the Document Summary code [Smry/Cmnt:] is always placed at the beginning of the document and the cursor is returned to its original location. If you press Reveal Codes (ALT-F3) at the beginning of the document, the first 100 characters of the summary are shown along with the [Smry/Cmnt:] code.

Forty characters each are allowed for the author's and typist's names and 880 characters can be used for the summary comment. Only Bold (F6) and Underline (F8) can be used in the comment section.

Displaying the Summary

The document summary is not automatically displayed on the screen; only the code is inserted. Follow the steps below to display the summary.

1. Press Text In/Out (CTRL-F5).

2. Type **D** to Display Summary and Comments.

3. Type **Y** to Display Summary. Type **Y** or **N** to Display Comments. The document summary is displayed at the beginning of the document.

The Look feature in List Files also displays the document summary, even if it was not displayed on the normal editing screen.

Editing the Summary

Use the same procedure as outlined in "Keystrokes," making appropriate selections and changes from the menu where needed. After all changes are made, press Exit (F7) until you return to the document.

In contrast to the document summary, which appears only once at the beginning of a document, you can have more than one comment in a document. Thus, the operations of creating and editing comments are covered by separate menu options. See *Comments* for more detail.

Automatic Document Summary

The Setup menu has an option to prompt you for the document summary information when a document is saved the first time. This feature, which uses either Save (F10) or Exit (F7) is useful if you want to make a practice of creating a document summary for every document.

1. Type **WP/S** at the DOS prompt (instead of WP) to enter the Setup menu.

2. Type **2** to Set Initial Settings.

3. Press Text In/Out (CTRL-F5). Type **Y** or **N** in answer to the question "Enter Document Summary on Save/Exit? (Y/N) N."

4. Press ENTER to leave the Initial Settings menu.

5. Type **0** to enter WordPerfect.

If you choose this option, WordPerfect checks for a document summary when you press Exit (F7) and type **Y** to save the document or when you press Save (F10). If it is not found, you are automatically placed in the Document Summary screen. Enter the information and press Exit (F7) twice when finished. If you do not want to create a summary for that particular document, press Cancel (F1) twice and continue saving the document.

Applications

The Word Search feature in the List Files menu searches through the document *and* summary for key words and phrases. If you want to list all the files by a certain date of creation, by a specific author or typist, or by a key word found in the comment section of the summary, type **7** for Word Search and enter the date, author, typist, or key word. Only those files satisfying the search will be displayed. See *Word Search* for more information.

Disk maintenance is a little easier when you can Look at a file from the List Files menu and see the document summary at the beginning of the file.

Related Entries

Comments

Text In/Out

Word Search

DOS

WordPerfect works closely with DOS (Disk Operating System) to print and manage files.

Chapter 1 covers DOS and specific DOS commands. Only the DOS features necessary to install and use WordPerfect are explained. Information about more advanced DOS commands can be found in the DOS manual.

Related Entries

Go To DOS

See also Chapter 1, "Getting Started"

DOS Text Files

WordPerfect can save and retrieve DOS text files (text without codes) for use with other software programs.

Keystrokes

Save a DOS Text File

1. Retrieve the file that is to be converted to a DOS (ASCII) text file.

2. Press Text In/Out (CTRL-F5).

3. Type **1** for Save.

4. Enter the name of the file or press ENTER to use the

displayed name. To save both versions (regular and DOS text), use a different filename. If you use the same filename, you are asked if you want to replace the original file.

WordPerfect codes are stripped from the file and soft returns are converted to hard returns. Tabs, indents, and centering are maintained with spaces, and paragraph numbers are inserted as text.

Retrieve a DOS Text File

There are two options for retrieving a DOS text file.

Using Text In/Out:

1. Set the margins to match the line length in the file being retrieved (usually 0 and 80 will do).

2. Press Text In/Out (CTRL-F5).

3. Type **2** to retrieve a file with all CR/LFs (carriage returns/line feeds) converted to hard returns or **3** to retrieve a file and convert CR/LFs falling within the hyphenation zone to soft returns.

Using List Files:

1. Set the margins to match the line length in the file to be retrieved.

2. Press List Files (F5).

3. Move the cursor to the file to be retrieved.

4. Type **5** for Text In.

If this option is used, all CR/LFs are converted to hard returns.

Hints

If the computer locks up or goes into an endless hyphenation loop when you retrieve a file using Retrieve (SHIFT-F10), exit the document if possible or reboot if necessary. After reentering WordPerfect, try to retrieve the file using Text In/Out. You might still encounter problems if the file is not strictly text.

After saving a file as a DOS text file, it remains on the screen. Use caution when saving the file again, because you could replace the file previously saved with the WordPerfect file on the screen.

Codes that contain text (such as headers, footers, footnotes, and line numbering) are stripped when saving a file as a DOS text file. If you want to keep the text included as codes with the file, print the file to disk. See *Print to Disk* for more information.

If you want tab settings to convert to DOS tabs rather than spaces, use option **6** on the Text In/Out menu to save the file in a generic word processor format. See *Text In/Out* for more information.

See Chapter 8 about integration with other software programs.

Applications

You can use this feature to edit DOS text files (batch files, CONFIG.SYS, and so on) or program source files. When you retrieve this type of file, the ^Z marking the end of the file is removed. When saved as an ASCII file, the ^Z is added to the end of the file (you should not reenter it). If you do not want word wrap, it may be necessary to set the right margin to position 250.

If you use the Program Editor included with WordPerfect Library (a utility program produced by WordPerfect Corporation), you do not have to go through a separate procedure for saving and retrieving text files and words will not wrap.

Related Entries

Convert Program

List Files

Print to Disk

Text In/Out

See also Chapter 8, "Software Integration"

Dot Leader

A dot leader can precede any type of tab, except a center tab. The following sample shows a typical use of dot leaders.

Name	Phone Number
Bob Jones	555-2121
Suzanne Parker	555-9898
Sandra J. Fallows	555-7309

The Table of Contents, Tables of Authorities, Lists, and Index features all have options for inserting a dot leader preceding the page number.

Double Spacing

See *Spacing*

Double Underlining

WordPerfect can print a double (or single) underline. However, double underlining appears as a single underline on the screen.

Keystrokes

1. Press Print Format (CTRL-F8).

2. Type **6** or **8**, depending on whether you want noncontinuous or continuous double underlining. Continuous underlines extend between tabs; noncontinuous underlines break between columns. Both underline spaces.

3. Press ENTER to leave the menu.

4. Press Underline (F8), type the text, then press Underline again to turn off underlining.

5. Press Print Format (CTRL-F8).

6. Type **5** or **7** to return to noncontinuous or continuous single underlining.

7. Press ENTER to leave the menu.

Hints

The underline style can be changed *after* text has been underlined. A code such as [Undrl Style:6] is placed in the document, indicating that underlining from that point forward will be changed until another underline style code is encountered.

If you often use double and single underlining together, consider putting the steps into two different macros.

1. Press Macro Def (CTRL-F10) and enter the name of the macro (DBLON or DBLOFF are suggestions).

2. Press Print Format (CTRL-F8).

3. Type **6** or **8** for the "on" macro, and **5** or **7** for the "off" macro.

4. Press ENTER to leave the menu.

5. Press Underline (F8) to turn underlining on or off.

6. Press Macro Def (CTRL-F10) when finished.

When you want double underlining, press Macro (F10) and enter the name of the "on" macro. After you have finished typing the text, press Macro (F10) and enter the name of the "off" macro.

Related Entries

Underline

Downloading Fonts

See *Fonts*. If you are using a laser printer, see Chapter 5, "Laser Printers."

Drawing Lines and Boxes

See *Line Draw*

Editing Documents

WordPerfect has several features that can be used to edit and revise text.

Keystrokes

See *Delete* for options to delete and restore text. Following is a list of other features that can be used for editing.

Block (ALT-F4)	Used to move, delete, and give attributes to text that has already been entered (bold, underline, uppercase, center, superscript, and so on).
←Search (SHIFT-F2) and Replace (ALT-F2)	You can search for text and WordPerfect codes with the Search feature. To replace or delete them, use the Replace feature.
Switch (SHIFT-F3)	When working with more than one document, you can switch documents to facilitate moving text between the two.
Mark Text (ALT-F5)	Redline and Strikeout are useful for marking text to be added to or deleted from a document. Remove can then be used to remove redline markings and text that was struck out.

See Chapter 2 for general information on editing documents.

Related Entries

Block

Move

Redline

Replace

Search

Strikeout Text

Switch

See also Chapter 2, "WordPerfect Basics"

Encrypting a File

See *Lock and Unlock Documents*

END Key

The END key found on the numeric keypad is used to go to the end of a line.

Keystrokes

Pressing END is the same as pressing HOME,HOME,→. It will move the cursor to the very end of a line—even when the text goes beyond the edge of the screen.

To delete to the end of the line, hold down the CTRL key and press END. All text and codes from the cursor to the very end of the line are deleted. To restore the deleted text, press Cancel (F1), then **1** to Restore.

Related Entries

Cursor Keys

Endnotes

See *Footnotes and Endnotes*

ENTER Key

WordPerfect refers to the return key or carriage return as the ENTER key. It is used to end short lines, create blank lines, execute commands, and leave menus.

Keystrokes

To end a line before the right margin or add blank lines, press ENTER. A hard return is inserted. In Reveal Codes, a Hard Return code is shown as [HRt].

Before a command can be executed, you may be prompted for information such as the name of a file, macro, or directory. After you type the information, press ENTER to indicate the end of the name and execute the command. If you find yourself waiting for the computer to do something, you may have forgotten to press the ENTER key after entering a command or information.

You can leave any menu (except List Files) by pressing ENTER. Exit (F7) or SPACEBAR lets you exit the List Files menu.

Hints

Because of automatic word wrap, you do not have to press ENTER at the end of each line. If you type more text than will fit within the margins, WordPerfect automatically wraps the text to the next line, inserting a soft return, shown in Reveal codes as [SRt].

Unlike a typewriter, if you press ENTER to move downward through text, blank lines are added. Instead, use the down arrow key to move downward through text. If you accidentally press ENTER, you can use BACKSPACE to delete the blank lines above the cursor.

Displaying a Character for a Hard Return

Those who have used a different word processor might be used to seeing a character displayed on the screen when they press ENTER. WordPerfect can also show a nonprinting character.

1. Instead of typing WP, type **WP/S** to start WordPerfect and enter the Setup menu.

2. Type **3** for Screen and Beep Options. The following menu appears.

```
Set Screen Options

   Number of rows: 25
   Number of columns: 80
   Hard return displayed as ascii value: 32
   Display filename on status line? (Y/N) Y

Set Beep Options

   Beep when search fails? (Y/N) N
   Beep on error? (Y/N) N
   Beep on hyphenation? (Y/N) Y
```

3. Press ENTER twice to move to the option for changing the hard return character. (The default number 32 means that a space is used rather than a character.)

4. Enter **17** for ◀ , **27** for ← , **174** for « , or any other value. You could also use **249** for • or **250** for · . See Appendix A for a complete chart of ASCII values. Press ENTER to use the default 32.

5. Press Exit (F7) to leave the Screen and Beep Options.

6. Type **0** to leave the Setup menu and enter WordPerfect.

Figure 4-35 shows a sample screen with « as the enter character.

Related Entries

Carriage Return

Setup Menu

```
                          November 25, 1987«
 «
 «
 «
 Mr. Robert J. Smith«
 4567 Westview Drive«
 Los Angeles, CA  94949«
 «
 Dear Mr. Smith«
 «
 Thank you for your letter of October 15.  We were pleased to find
 that our proposal was accepted by your firm.«
 «
 We will be in touch by phone within the next few days to make
 further plans.«
 «
                          Sincerely,«
 «
 «
 «
                          Ms. Sue Sullivan«


                             Doc 1   Pg 1   Ln 22      Pos 10
```

Figure 4-35.   Sample screen with « chosen as the ENTER character

Envelope

See *Type-thru* or *Merge* to the Printer. If you are using a laser printer, see Chapter 5, "Laser Printers."

Erase

See *Delete*

Error Messages

From time to time you will see error messages at the bottom of the screen. Most error messages are related to the feature being used. If this seems to be the case, check the feature entry in this chapter for possible solutions.

If you see a specific error message such as "Disk full--strike any key to continue," you should refer to the entry with that message.

Hints

DOS and WordPerfect Error Messages

If you see a number preceding an error message while in WordPerfect, it is most likely coming from DOS. These numbered messages are usually referred to by DOS as extended error codes. See the DOS manual index to locate a description of a specific error message.

To help distinguish further between DOS and WordPerfect, WordPerfect displays "ERROR:" before all error messages. For example:

ERROR: File not found

If DOS sends an error message, it is usually associated with the inability to read the drive that was specified. This could be due to a bad disk, a write-protect tab, or an open drive door. For example, if you were in DOS and tried to copy a file from one disk to another and the drive door was not closed, you would see a message similar to the following.

Not ready error reading drive A

Abort, Retry, Ignore?

If you received a message such as this while saving a document in WordPerfect and typed A to abort, you would lose the current document and be returned unceremoniously to DOS. However, since version 4.1, WordPerfect captures the "critical errors" sent from DOS and gives you an opportunity to correct the situation and retry, or return to the document. WordPerfect displays the following message instead of the DOS error message.

Drive door may be open - Drive not ready reading drive A

1 Retry 2 Cancel and return to document 1

Network WordPerfect

Some error messages are unique to the network version of WordPerfect. See your network documentation for information.

Related Entries

"Are Other Copies of WordPerfect Running?"

"Can't Find Correct Copy of WP"

"Critical Disk Error Occurred"

"Disk Full" Error Message

"Divide Overflow" Error Message

"File Creation Error"

"Insufficient Memory" Error Message

"Nonsystem Disk or Disk Error"

"Put WP Disk Back in Drive"

"Unable to Save Printer Selections on WP Disk"

ESC Key

ESC acts as a counter key to determine how many times a keystroke is to be repeated. It can also be used to "escape" from a WordPerfect prompt or menu.

Keystrokes

When ESC is pressed, "n = 8" appears on the status line, indicating that a keystroke will be repeated eight times.

You can change the default for a single procedure, one editing session, or permanently.

Change "n" for a Single Procedure

1. Press ESC.

2. Type the new number (do not press ENTER).

3. Press the keystroke to be repeated.

Change "n" for One Editing Session

1. Press ESC.

2. Type the new number.

3. Press ENTER.

The number is changed until you exit WordPerfect or change the number again.

Change "n" Permanently

Use the Setup menu to change the value of n permanently.

1. Enter **WP/S** instead of WP to enter the Setup menu.

2. Type **2** to Set Initial Settings.

3. Press ESC.

4. Enter the new number.

5. Press ENTER to return to the Setup menu.

6. Type **0** to enter WordPerfect.

Keys That Will Repeat

Any character	Types the character n times
SPACEBAR	Inserts n spaces
↑ or ↓	Moves the cursor up or down n lines

← or →	Moves the cursor left or right n spaces
PGUP or PGDN	Moves the cursor backward or forward n pages
Macro (ALT-F10)	Repeats the named macro n times
Delete EOL (CTRL-END)	Deletes n lines from the cursor down
DEL	Deletes n characters to the right of the cursor

Hints

If you press ESC accidentally or decide not to repeat a keystroke, press ESC again or Cancel (F1).

Esc can also be used to escape from any WordPerfect menu except Help. Use ENTER or SPACEBAR to leave Help.

Some users prefer to use ESC,↑ or ESC,↓ to move through a document rather than "screen up" or "screen down." If you want the first or last line of a screen to appear in the preceding or next screen, change the value of n to 21 or 22 for single spacing and 10 or 11 for double spacing. Pressing ESC,↑ or ESC,↓ will then move partial screens, giving you the desired overlap.

Repeat Macros

ESC is commonly used to repeat macros. If you want a macro to repeat a certain number of times, press ESC, type the desired number (do not press ENTER), and start the macro. If you want the macro to repeat until it reaches the end of the file, you should estimate the number of times it should repeat and type the number after pressing ESC. It is best to overestimate the number because as soon as it reaches the end of the file, it will stop repeating if it contains a search. This feature is similar to chaining a macro to itself. See *Macros* for more information.

Make Space

Some word processors have a feature that allows you to create an open space in which the cursor can be moved to any location without pressing ENTER or the SPACEBAR.

To do this in WordPerfect, press ESC, type a large number, then press SPACEBAR. If you want to make a full screen of space, type the number 1500. If you are using double spacing, type 750 to make one screen.

This feature is useful when creating formulas and equations. Make the space first, then use the cursor keys to move anywhere and type the necessary symbols. Be sure to turn off right justification first, so that the soft returns at the end of each line do not create spacing problems. If you leave right justification on, the text will appear correct on the screen, but not when printed.

Related Entries

Cancel

Macros

Exit

Exit (F7) can be used to exit a document and the WordPerfect program.

Keystrokes

1. Press Exit (F7). You are always asked if you want to save the current document.

2. Type **Y** or **N** in answer to the question. If you type **N**, skip to step 3. If you type **Y**, "Document to be Saved:" is displayed. If the file has been saved before, the name of the document is shown. Press ENTER to accept the name or enter a new name. If you use the name of a file already on the disk, type **Y** or **N** to replace the former file.

3. "Exit WP? (Y/N) N" or "Exit Doc 1 (or 2)? (Y/N) N" appears on the status line, depending on whether you

have one or two documents in memory. Type **N** to exit the document and remain in WordPerfect, type **Y** to exit WordPerfect, or press Cancel (F1) to cancel the exit procedure and remain in the document. If you have two documents in memory, the cursor goes to the second document. Repeat the steps to exit WordPerfect.

Hints

Although it might seem time-consuming and keystroke-intensive to exit a document or WordPerfect, there are many built-in safety features to protect you from losing your documents.

Remember that you can press Cancel (F1) to cancel the procedure and keep the document on the screen up to the very last step.

If you press Save (F10) to save the document, then use Exit (F7), you are still asked if you want to save the document. If there were no changes made to the document, the message "(Text was not modified)" is displayed on the status line with the message "Save Document? (Y/N) Y." You can then type **N** because the document has already been saved.

Exit (F7) can also be used to exit from any WordPerfect menu except Help. Use ENTER or SPACEBAR to leave Help.

Related Entries

Save

Extended Search/Replace

Headers, footers, footnotes, and endnotes are not searched during a normal Search, Reverse Search, or Replace. If you want to include them, press HOME before pressing Search (F2), ← Search (SHIFT-F2), or Replace (ALT-F2).

See *Search* for more information.

"File Creation Error"

"File creation error" is a DOS error message sometimes displayed when trying to save or print a file.

If you attempted to use "illegal" characters in a filename, the new file cannot be created. The following characters are acceptable for use in filenames.

A-Z 0-9 ! @ # $ % ' ' ( ) - { } — ^ & ~ .

You cannot use the following:

* + = [ ] " < > ? | , : ; / \

Be extra cautious about not using the characters *, ?, or ,. Even if they seem to be allowed, they should never be used.

Most operating systems have a limit on the number of files the root directory can contain even though there is ample disk space available. If you have reached this limit, you have two options: (1) delete or move files from the root directory, or (2) create a new directory. (Floppy diskettes can be divided into directories with the same commands used for a hard disk.) See Chapter 1 for more information about creating directories and copying files.

If you get the error message while trying to replace a file on a network, check to see if the file is marked "read only" and cannot be replaced.

When you press Print (SHIFT-F7) and type **1** to print the full text or **2** to print the current page, a copy of the document or page is saved to a temporary file in memory and then printed. After available memory is filled, print jobs are kept on the drive/directory where WP.EXE resides. It is unlikely that you will get this error message during this procedure. If you do, it is possible that the temporary print file exceeded the limit of the number of files in the root directory (you either have a floppy disk system, or have WordPerfect stored in the root directory on the hard disk). If this happens, delete or move files from the WordPerfect diskette, or install WordPerfect in a subdirectory where there is no limit to the number of files that can be created.

Filing Documents

WordPerfect has several features to help in filing documents. Among those are List Files, Save, and Retrieve. Directories on a hard disk can also be organized to facilitate filing different types of documents.

Related Entries

Directories

List Files

Retrieve

Save

Flush Right

Flush Right (ALT-F6) lets you align text at the right margin.

Keystrokes

Flush Right a Single Line of Text

1. Press Flush Right (ALT-F6). The cursor moves to the right margin.

2. Type the text.

3. Press ENTER when finished.

Flush Right Existing Text

1. Position the cursor at the beginning of the line.

2. Press Flush Right (ALT-F6).

3. Press ↓ and the line should be aligned at the right margin. If the cursor does not move down and the line is not moved to flush right, there is no hard return code [HRt] at the end of the line. Press END to move to the end of the line and press ENTER to insert the [HRt] code.

A second option does not require a hard return at the end of the line.

1. Move the cursor to the beginning of the line.

2. Press Block (ALT-F4). (You do not have to move the cursor to define the block.)

3. Press Flush Right (ALT-F4).

4. Type **Y** to align the text. The block of text should be aligned as shown in the following illustration.

```
                              Mrs. Suzanne Marshall
                               9832 Bay View Drive
                           San Francisco, CA  98789
```

Flush Right a Block of Text

A block of text consisting of several lines can be aligned at the margin at once instead of pressing Flush Right (ALT-F6) at the beginning of each line.

1. Press Block (ALT-F4) at one end (top or bottom) of the block.

2. Move the cursor to the opposite end to highlight the block of text.

3. Press Flush Right (ALT-F6).

4. Type **Y** in answer to the question "[Aln/FlshR]? (Y/N) N." The block will be aligned.

An Align On code [A] is placed at the first of each line and an Align Off code [a] is placed at the end of each line.

Each soft return code [SRt] in the block is changed to a hard return code [HRt].

Hints

When Flush Right is pressed, an Align On code [A] is inserted. As soon as a single character is typed, the Align Off code is inserted at the end of the text. Pressing Flush Right again will not turn off Flush Right. Instead, you should use ENTER to turn off Flush Right and move past the [a] code. Pressing ↓ or → will also move the cursor past the [a].

Text can be aligned at both the left margin and right margin, as shown in the following illustration.

MONTHLY DEPARTMENT NEWSLETTER

Volume I Number 11   Confidential   November 25, 1987

Place the cursor at the end of the line found at the left margin, press Flush Right (ALT-F6), and enter the line to be aligned at the right margin.

If a line or block of text contains an [Indent] code, it will be removed during the process.

Align (and Center) codes take precedence over other text. If text disappears, press Reveal Codes (ALT-F3) and delete the [A] code if necessary.

Use the Decimal Tab feature or Tab Align to align numbers at a decimal point or any other character.

See *Right Justification* to create even left and right margins.

Related Entries

Aligning Text

Decimal Tabs

Right Justification

Tab Align

Fonts

A font is a set of characters that have similar attributes. WordPerfect usually refers to a font as the type of characters that are available in that font, rather than the size or style of characters.

See Chapter 6, "Printer Specifics," for a list of fonts available with your printer. You can also run the PRHELP program included on the Printer 2 disk for more printer and font information. See "Hints" for details.

Keystrokes

Display Fonts

When you select a printer definition, the eight fonts assigned to that printer are also selected during the process. Follow the steps below to display the list of assigned fonts (see Figure 4-36 for an example).

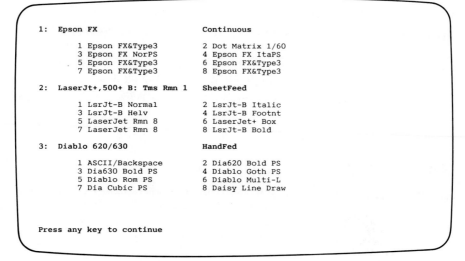

```
1:  Epson FX                      Continuous

        1 Epson FX&Type3          2 Dot Matrix 1/60
        3 Epson FX NorPS          4 Epson FX ItaPS
        5 Epson FX&Type3          6 Epson FX&Type3
        7 Epson FX&Type3          8 Epson FX&Type3

2:  LaserJt+,500+ B: Tms Rmn 1    SheetFeed

        1 LsrJt-B Normal          2 LsrJt-B Italic
        3 LsrJt-B Helv            4 LsrJt-B Footnt
        5 LaserJet Rmn 8          6 LaserJet+ Box
        7 LaserJet Rmn 8          8 LsrJt-B Bold

3:  Diablo 620/630                HandFed

        1 ASCII/Backspace         2 Dia620 Bold PS
        3 Dia630 Bold PS          4 Diablo Goth PS
        5 Diablo Rom PS           6 Diablo Multi-L
        7 Dia Cubic PS            8 Daisy Line Draw




Press any key to continue
```

Figure 4-36.   List of assigned printer fonts

1. Press Print (SHIFT-F7).

2. Type **4** for Printer Control.

3. Type **2** to Display Printers and Fonts.

Select a Font

Because the character set is usually all that is used to label a font, you cannot always tell the attributes just by looking at the list. The "Hints" section tells you how to test the fonts that are available with your printer.

1. After you have determined which font is desired, press Print Format (CTRL-F8).

2. Type **1** for Pitch/Font.

3. Enter a new pitch or press ENTER to accept the displayed pitch. If printing with a proportionally spaced font, add an asterisk to the pitch number. See "Hints" for more information on pitch.

4. Enter the number of the font.

5. Press ENTER to leave the Print Format menu.

Hints

When the pitch or font is changed, a code similar to [Font Change:12*,3] is inserted at the cursor's location and takes effect until another font code is encountered.

Font Assignments

Check Chapter 6 for details on fonts assigned to your printer. Some printers have a different color assigned to each font, while others (such as IBM Quietwriter, HP LaserJet, and TI 855) use cartridges to produce various fonts.

A program called PRHELP (Printer Help) can be found on the Printer 2 disk. Place the disk in one of the disk drives and enter **PRHELP** at the appropriate DOS prompt.

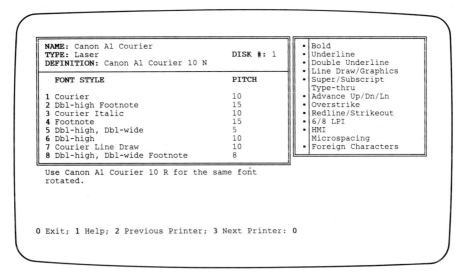

```
NAME: Canon A1 Courier                          · Bold
TYPE: Laser                         DISK #: 1    · Underline
DEFINITION: Canon A1 Courier 10 N               · Double Underline
                                                 · Line Draw/Graphics
   FONT STYLE                   PITCH            · Super/Subscript
                                                   Type-thru
1 Courier                        10              · Advance Up/Dn/Ln
2 Dbl-high Footnote              15              · Overstrike
3 Courier Italic                 10              · Redline/Strikeout
4 Footnote                       15              · 6/8 LPI
5 Dbl-high, Dbl-wide              5              · HMI
6 Dbl-high                       10                Microspacing
7 Courier Line Draw              10              · Foreign Characters
8 Dbl-high, Dbl-wide Footnote     8

Use Canon A1 Courier 10 R for the same font
rotated.




0 Exit; 1 Help; 2 Previous Printer; 3 Next Printer: 0
```

Figure 4-37.   Sample screen from PRHELP

It lists the fonts and pitch settings as well as the features supported by the printer (see Figure 4-37).

WordPerfect has included several other options for testing the font characteristics and the characters included in each font. Three files are included on the Learning disk that can be printed from WordPerfect: PRINTER.TST, PRINTER2.TST, and FONT.TST.

Figure 4-38 shows a sample printing of PRINTER.TST. Several WordPerfect features are printed with the individual capabilities of the printer. PRINTER2.TST (as shown in Figure 4-39) is used to test fonts and pitch and shows the options for printing text containing lines and boxes. If you have a daisy-wheel printer, you will have to enter the Printer Control menu and type G to send the printer a "Go" when it stops at a font change. You should decide whether or not you want to change print wheels during the process.

If you want to see the actual characters that are included in a font, print the FONT.TST file. If you are using a daisy-wheel printer, print the document with all

<u>WordPerfect Printer Test Document</u>

In this document each word associated with a feature is printed with that feature (e.g., **bold**, ^{super}script, _{sub}script, and strikeout). Oversŧŗɏɪ̷ƙé is sometimes used to build new characters like ≠ ā ≑. This paragraph is redlined. Redline will print a vertical bar or a plus symbol in the left margin.

Text can be centered or flushed right.

If a feature described does not appear on your printout, your printer may not have that capability.

Continuous	Double underlining	Continuous
Non-Continuous	Double underlining	style
Continuous	Single underlining	underlines
Non-Continuous	Single underlining	tabs.

WordPerfect has left, center, right, and decimal aligned tabs. Centered tabs center on the tab stop, not between the margins. Several types will be demonstrated with dot leaders included.

Left Aligned   Centered. . . . . Decimal.aligned
Left   Center $4.50

1   At this point, each line will   within columns. There are two
2   be numbered in the left margin. types of columns, parallel and
3   The column feature allows text   newspaper. This is an example
4   to be right and left justified   of newspaper columns.
5
6   This document has been printed in 10 pitch with font 1. In the
7   next few lines, pitches and fonts will be changed as specified.
8   If your printer changes pitch when only a font change was
9   specified, your printer may be pitch/font specific, meaning the
10 pitch can only be changed with the font.

This is 12 pitch in font 1. You may notice that the margins are a little different for this block of text. For one-inch margins 12 pitch, the margins should be set at 12 and 89.

This is 15 pitch in font 1. For one inch-margins 15 pitch, use 15 and 112. This paragraph is also printed in eight lines per inch. Unless your printer prints 15 pitch in condensed print, the lines may look too close with this character size.

This is 10 pitch in font 2.

This is 13* pitch in font 3. Font three is usually a proportionally spaced font in WordPerfect. Notice the asterisk after the pitch which specifies PS.

This is 10 pitch in font 4.

This is 10 pitch in font 5.

This is 10 pitch in font 6.

This is 10 pitch in font 7.

This is 10 pitch in font 8.

Advance up and down move text up or down 1/2 line.
                                          Advance up
Advance down   Text on a regular line   Normal

For More Available Features, Refer To Printer2.tst

1

Auto page number is centered above.   This is a footer.

Figure 4-38.   Sample printout of PRINTER.TST

print wheels available. Figure 4-40 shows the FONT.TST document printed on an IBM Quietwriter.

A macro on the Learning disk will also help you print FONT.TST in the fonts you desire. The files used are FONTTEST.MAC, FONT.TST, and FNTTEST2.MAC. Follow the steps below to run the macro.

```
                    WordPerfect Auxiliary Printer Test

        Pitch/Font   Capabilities       This  section  shows  the  printer
        capability of pitch and font.  If pitch changes do not print as
        specified, your printer may be pitch/font specific.

          font 1, 10 pitch
         font 1, 12 pitch
     font 1, 15 pitch
       font 1, 13* pitch

          font 2, 10 pitch
         font 2, 12 pitch
          font 2, 15 pitch
          font 2, 13* pitch

          font 3, 10 pitch
         font 3, 12 pitch
     font 3, 15 pitch
       font 3, 13* pitch

          font 4, 10 pitch
         font 4, 12 pitch
          font 4, 15 pitch
        font 4, 13* pitch

              font 5, 10 pitch
             font 5, 12 pitch
          font 5, 15 pitch
        font 5, 13* pitch

              font 6, 10 pitch
            font 6, 12 pitch
             font 6, 15 pitch
        font 6, 13* pitch

          font 7, 10 pitch
         font 7, 12 pitch
     font 7, 15 pitch
       font 7, 13* pitch

          font 8, 10 pitch
         font 8, 12 pitch
     font 8, 15 pitch
       font 8, 13* pitch
```

Figure 4-39.   Sample printout of PRINTER2.TST

1. Place the Learning disk in drive B if you have two disk drives, or drive A if you have a hard disk.

2. Press List Files (F5), type =, then enter the name of the drive (**A** or **B**).

3. Press Cancel (F1) to avoid entering the List Files menu.

4. Press Macro (ALT-F10) and enter **FONTTEST**. Follow the instructions on the screen, then print the document when the macro is finished.

```
This prints all characters:

        0                   1
        0 1 2 3 4 5 6 7 8 9 0 1 2 3 4 5 6 7 8 9

000     ☺ ☻ ♥ ♦ ♣ ♠ • ▪ □ ○ ◙ ♂ ♀ ♪ ♫ ☼ ► ◄ ↕ ‼

020     ¶ § ▬ ↨ ↑ ↓ → ← └ ↔ ▲ ▼   ! " # $ % & '

040     ( ) * + , - . / 0 1 2 3 4 5 6 7 8 9 : ;

060     < = > ? @ A B C D E F G H I J K L M N O

080     P Q R S T U V W X Y Z [ \ ] ˆ _ ` a b c

100     d e f g h i j k l m n o p q r s t u v w

120     x y z { ¦ } ˜   Ç ü é â ä à å ç ê ë è ï

140     î ì Ä Å É æ Æ ô ö ò û ù ÿ Ö Ü ¢ £ ¥ ₧ ƒ

160     á í ó ú ñ Ñ ª º ¿ ⌐ ¬ ½ ¼ ¡ « »  ▒ ▓ │

180     ┤ ╡ ╢ ╖ ╕ ╣ ║ ╗ ╝ ╜ ╛ ┐ └ ┴ ┬ ├ ─ ┼ ╞ ╟

200     ╚ ╔ ╩ ╦ ╠ ═ ╬ ╧ ╨ ╤ ╥ ╙ ╘ ╒ ╓ ╫ ╪ ┘ ┌ █ ▓

220     ▄ ▌ ▐ ▀ α β Γ π Σ σ µ τ Φ Θ Ω δ ∞ φ ε ∩

240     ≡ ± ≥ ≤ ⌠ ⌡ ÷ ≈ ° ∙ · √ ⁿ ² ■ (end)

        0 1 2 3 4 5 6 7 8 9 0 1 2 3 4 5 6 7 8 9
        0                   1

This is a test of footnote numbers[234].
```

---

[234]This is footnote 234!

Figure 4-40.   Sample printout of FONT.TST

Assigning Fonts to Printers

Where possible, WordPerfect has tried to adhere to a system for assigning fonts. Keep in mind that these are generalities and there are many exceptions to the rule. For example, to get Line Draw with an HP LaserJet, use font 8 instead of font 7.

Font 1   Letter-quality

Font 2   Draft or italics

Font 3   Proportionally spaced

Font 4   Italics

Font 5   Expanded

Font 6   Compressed

Font 7   Line Draw

Font 8   Draft

If you want a different font selection, consult your printer manual and find the printer commands used to change to the specific font. You can either insert these codes as a Printer Command (press Print Format (CTRL-F8) and type **A** to Insert a Printer Command) or you can change the printer definition (see Chapter 7).

WordPerfect usually assigns letter-quality to font 1 and draft to font 8. However, your printer may default to draft. Print PRINTER2.TST to verify the font assignments. If you prefer to have draft (or letter-quality) as the default, consider changing the default in the Setup menu to font 8. You could also change the printer definition (again, see Chapter 7).

Pitch and Font

Daisy-Wheel Printers   Each print wheel usually has a specific pitch assigned. For example, Courier 10 should be printed in 10 pitch and Elite 12 should be printed in 12 pitch.

If printing with a proportionally spaced print wheel, you should almost always use 13 pitch (13*). Remember that if you are printing in proportional spacing, an asterisk must be placed after the pitch number.

Changing fonts with a daisy-wheel printer is done by changing the print wheel. When WordPerfect encounters a font change for a daisy-wheel printer, it stops the printer and sends a beep to the computer. To continue printing after changing the print wheel, press Print (SHIFT-F7), type **4** to enter Printer Control, then type **G** to send the printer a "Go."

If you want to use a specific print wheel, check the

fonts assigned to the printer to determine which font selection should be used. If none are suitable, see Chapter 7 about changing the font selections.

Dot-Matrix Printers   Some dot-matrix printers do not change pitch when the font is changed. Others have the flexibility to print a font in several different pitches. Usually, the fonts of dot-matrix printers are specified as regular, expanded, or compressed and will appear that way whether the pitch is changed or not. Print the PRINT-ER2.TST document to see if changing pitch with your dot-matrix printer will make a difference.

If your dot-matrix printer has the capability to print proportionally spaced fonts, 11* is most commonly used but 12* or 13* can also be tried.

Remember that when changing the pitch or font, you will probably also need to change the margins. More characters will fit on a line with compressed printing; less will fit when printing in expanded type.

Laser Printers   Since laser printers have more flexibility, you can specify practically any pitch when working with PS (proportionally spaced) fonts. Suggested PS fonts include 11*, 12*, or 13* (note the asterisk used to indicate proportional spacing).

Some cartridges and soft fonts have their own pitch. While you can usually specify any pitch, you should use the suggested setting to get the best quality of print.

Downloading Soft Fonts

Soft fonts are those kept on disk rather than within the printer or in a cartridge. They must be *downloaded* to the printer's memory before they can be used. Most printers have a specific command that is used to send the soft font to the printer. Others just require that a file be "printed" to the printer. If you are working with a laser printer, refer to

Chapter 5 for detailed information. The following is a general guide to downloading fonts.

1. Press Print Format (CTRL-F8).

2. Type **A** to Insert a Printer Command.

3. Press Retrieve (SHIFT-F10).

4. Enter the name of the file containing the soft font or other printer commands.

5. Press ENTER to leave the Print Format menu.

Nothing will appear on the screen. A code similar to the following is placed in the document; the code <126> tells WordPerfect to retrieve that file into the printer.

[Cmnd:<126>a:download.fnt]

Follow the same steps for additional fonts. If you always use the same soft fonts, consider putting all the commands into one file, then save the file and reuse it when necessary because the soft font commands are stored in the printer until it is turned off and must be downloaded again when you need the fonts. Because there is no indication on screen of the type of soft fonts being downloaded, consider using the Document Summary or Comment feature to "label" the file. The summary or comment will not print.

When your work session on a document is complete, you can print the document as you would print any other WordPerfect document.

If you are downloading fonts to an HP LaserJet+ or HP Series II, send two commands with each font downloaded. The first assigns an I.D. number required by the printer.

After pressing Print Format (CTRL-F8) and typing **A** to Insert a Printer Command, enter

<27>*C#D

where # is the I.D. number. Insert the second command, to retrieve the font file to the printer. If you press Reveal Codes (ALT-F3), you will see something similar to

[Cmnd:<27>*c1D][Cmnd:<126>b:TR12I#US.SFP]

You can usually download as many as 32 fonts to the printer. The actual number, though, is entirely dependent on the printer's available memory.

Because it is very easy to make a mistake when downloading several fonts, WordPerfect provides an HP Utility Disk that always has the latest soft font information and helps automate the downloading process.

Reassigning Fonts

You can reassign fonts by using the Printer Program (discussed in Chapter 7), or by entering the Setup menu (typing **WP/S** instead of WP when entering WordPerfect) and changing the default. For example, if you want draft rather than letter-quality for font 1, select that font as the default.

Included on the Printer 2 disk is a printer program that lets you customize your printer definition. Use the Printer program to reassign the fonts to be used. See Chapter 7 for complete details.

Miscellaneous

Headers, footers, footnotes, and endnotes will print in the same font as the document unless a font change is specified within the header, footer, footnote, or endnote. If you change the font for a document after the headers, footers, footnotes, and endnotes have been created, and you want them to be in the same font as the document, enter each header, footer, and so on, then exit. No changes have to be made; just enter, then exit, and that header, footer, footnote, or endnote will be updated automatically.

If a page length code follows a pitch/font change, the page length code may be ignored.

See Chapter 7 to customize your printer definition. You can assign different fonts and control the codes sent to the printer for each character.

Other powerful options in dealing with fonts in the Printer program are the <U>, <V>, and <W> options. These can be used to combine characters from different fonts. Also see Chapter 7 for more details.

Related Entries

Display Printers and Fonts

Pitch

See also Chapter 7, "Printer Program"

Footers

WordPerfect allows two headers and two footers per page. For details and options, see *Headers and Footers;* the information here pertains only to footers.

Keystrokes

1. Press Page Format (ALT-F8).

2. Type **6** for Headers or Footers.

3. Type **3** or **4** for Footer A or B. Either one can be used.

4. Type a number to select the Occurrence. Note that there are options to discontinue or edit the footer, as shown in Figure 4-41.

5. Type the text for the footer. If you want to include the current page number in a footer, press CTRL-B to insert ^**B**.

6. Press Exit (F7) when finished.

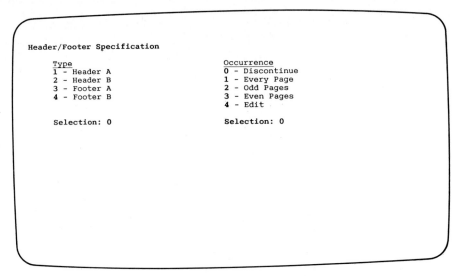

```
Header/Footer Specification

    Type                            Occurrence
    1 - Header A                    0 - Discontinue
    2 - Header B                    1 - Every Page
    3 - Footer A                    2 - Odd Pages
    4 - Footer B                    3 - Even Pages
                                    4 - Edit

    Selection: 0                    Selection: 0
```

Figure 4-41.   Header/Footer Specification menu

Hints

WordPerfect automatically subtracts the number of lines in a header and *one line for a footer* from the total number of lines on a page. Even though you can have several lines in a footer, WordPerfect assumes you will have only one and compensates only for a single line. Therefore, if you have a footer that is several lines long, the first line will be printed on line 54, but the remaining lines will print into the bottom margin. If this is unacceptable, decrease the number of text lines per page. See *Page Length* for more information.

See *Page Numbering* for more page numbering options.

Related Entries

Headers and Footers

Page Length

Page Numbering

Footnotes and Endnotes

Footnotes are printed on the page where they are referenced. Endnotes are placed at the end of a document.

Keystrokes

Create a Footnote or Endnote

1. Press Footnote (CTRL-F7).

2. Type **1** to Create a Footnote or **5** to Create an Endnote. The footnote/endnote screen appears and the appropriate note number is inserted.

3. Type the footnote or endnote text.

4. Press Exit (F7) when finished.

After creating a footnote or endnote, the number is placed in the document at the cursor's position. It is not superscripted on the screen, but will be when printed.

Edit a Note

1. Press Footnote (CTRL-F7).

2. Type **2** to Edit a Footnote or **6** to Edit an Endnote. "Ftn #?" or "Endn #?" is displayed with the number of the next available footnote or endnote.

3. Press ENTER to edit the displayed footnote or endnote, or enter the number of the note to be edited.

4. Press Exit (F7) when finished editing.

Delete a Note

1. Position the cursor at the number of the footnote or endnote to be deleted.

2. Press DEL. If the footnote is to the left of the cursor, press BACKSPACE.

3. Type **Y** or **N** in answer to the question "Delete [Note]? (Y/N) N."

Search (F2) can be used to search for a footnote or endnote by code, but not by number. See "Hints" for more information about searching for footnote/endnote codes.

Hints

When a footnote or an endnote is created, a code similar to the following is inserted.

[Note:End,1;[Note #]Text]

The code tells whether it is a footnote or endnote ("Foot" or "End"), the number of the note, then the text of the note. Up to 50 characters of text are shown with the code.

There is no practical limit to the amount of text that can be included in a footnote or endnote. Up to 16,000 lines each are available.

Assign a New Footnote or Endnote Number

WordPerfect automatically numbers footnotes and endnotes and renumbers them when others are added or deleted. However, if a footnote or endnote must have a specific number, as in the case of continuing the numbering from one chapter to another, press Footnote (CTRL-F7), type **3** for New #, and enter the number for the next note. A code such as [Set Note #:25] is inserted into the document and the following footnotes and endnotes are numbered according to the specified number. The new number affects both footnotes and endnotes. Be aware that if you have both footnotes and endnotes in a document, both will start with the new number.

```
Footnote Options

     1 - Spacing within notes                      1
     2 - Spacing between notes                      1
     3 - Lines to keep together                     3
     4 - Start footnote numbers each page           N
     5 - Footnote numbering mode                    0
     6 - Endnote numbering mode                      0
     7 - Line separating text and footnotes         1
     8 - Footnotes at bottom of page                N
     9 - Characters for notes                        *
     A - String for footnotes in text        [SuprScrpt][Note]
     B - String for endnotes in text         [SuprScrpt][Note]
     C - String for footnotes in note              [SuprScrpt][Note]
     D - String for endnotes in note         [Note].

  For options 5 & 6:              For option 7:
      0 - Numbers                     0 - No line
      1 - Characters                  1 - 2 inch line
      2 - Letters                     2 - Line across entire page
                                      3 - 2 in. line w/continued strings


  Selection: 0
```

Figure 4-42.   Footnote Options menu

Options

WordPerfect has chosen a specific format for footnotes and endnotes. To view or change the current settings, press Footnote (CTRL-F7) and type **4** for Options. The menu shown in Figure 4-42 appears.

If changes are made, a code [FtnOpt] is inserted at the cursor's location and footnotes/endnotes from that point forward are affected. To make changes that will affect all footnotes/endnotes, move to the beginning of the document before entering the menu.

Because you will probably want the footnote/endnote format options to be changed for all documents, consider making the changes in the Setup menu. Enter **WP/S** instead of WP when entering WordPerfect and change the defaults permanently.

Spacing   Notes will automatically be single-spaced with one blank line between notes. You cannot change the spacing while in the note. Instead, use option 1 in the Footnote

Options menu to change the spacing within notes or 2 to change the spacing between notes.

If you want WordPerfect to control the spacing between notes, do not press ENTER after typing the text. Pressing ENTER will insert extra blank lines.

Lines to Keep Together   If a footnote or endnote is longer than the space available on a page, it will continue to the next page. Because the Widow/Orphan feature does not apply to footnotes and endnotes, option 3 lets you specify how many lines should be kept together if the note continues to other pages.

Option 7 can be used to attach a "(continued...)" string at the end of the footnote on its first page and the beginning of its continuation on the next page. To select the "(continued...)" string, type **3** after choosing option 7. This item does not apply to endnotes.

Start Footnote Numbers Each Page   Option 4 has been set with a default "No" so that footnotes will number continuously in a document. However, some publishers and universities require that the footnotes on each page begin with number 1. If this is the case, select this option and type **Y**.

Numbering Mode (Style)   A number (rather than a letter or character) is used by default to number footnotes and endnotes. Choose option **5** to change the numbering style for footnotes, or **6** to change the style for endnotes. As indicated in the lower section of the menu, 0 (the default) indicates numbers, 1 indicates characters, and 2 indicates letters. (See "Characters for Notes" for details on using Option 9 to specify which characters are to be used for notes.)

Line Separating Text and Footnotes   WordPerfect is preset to separate the document text and footnotes with a 2-inch horizontal line. The selections for option 7 are listed on the lower portion of the Footnote options menu. Selection 1 is the default 2-inch line, type **0** for no line, **2** for a line across the entire page, or **3** for a 2-inch line with "(con-tinued . . .)" strings as needed. This feature affects footnotes only.

Footnotes at the Bottom of the Page   In the past, Word-Perfect was set to print footnotes just below the text—no matter where the text ended on the page. Currently the default is set to print the footnotes at the very bottom of the page. Y or N could be the default, depending on your version of 4.2. If you want to make a change, choose option **8**, and type **Y** to print them at the bottom of the page, or **N** to leave them just below the text.

Characters for Notes   When you select characters as the numbering style for options 5 or 6, you can use option 9 to choose the characters that will be used. An asterisk is the default. Each footnote or endnote will be "numbered" with n number of asterisks. For example, the third footnote will have three asterisks (***).

You can choose up to five characters. The most com-monly used characters are asterisks and daggers (ALT-197 for † is the closest thing on the IBM PC to a dagger), but any character can be used. After all the characters have been used, they are doubled and used again.

Strings in Text/Note (Number Display)   Options A, B, C, and D determine how a footnote or endnote number will appear in the text of a document and in the note itself. WordPerfect has been set to display the text reference number for both footnotes and endnotes as a superscripted number. The number within a footnote is indented five spaces and superscripted. The number within an endnote is followed by a period and is not superscripted.

To change this preset format, select the option that applies. "Replace with:" appears on the status line with the current string. Delete unnecessary codes and add others. To insert the [Note] code, press Footnote (CTRL-F7) and type **1**. You are quite limited in your choice of codes to add. Some codes, such as [SubScrpt], appear possible, but are deleted

Once ENTER is pressed to insert the string. See "Specify Alternatives to String" for suggestions.

Although you cannot leave a string blank, you can manually delete the number that appears in the note. If you attempt to delete the number, "Delete [Note #]? (Y/N) N" appears. Type **N** to leave the number, or **Y** to delete it.

Specify Alternatives to String

Before superscripting was readily available, typists would indicate a footnote in the following manner: 1 /. Even though superscripting is now standard with most word processors, some users want to keep the underline and slash and combine it with superscripting. To get this type of format, enter the Footnote Options menu and press the listed keystrokes to enter the following string for option A.

[SuprScrpt][Undrline][Note][u]/

1. Press Super/Subscript (SHIFT-F2).

2. Press Underline (F8).

3. Press Footnote (CTRL-F7) and type **1**.

4. Press Underline (F8).

5. Type the slash character (/).

6. Press ENTER when finished.

Insert the same string for option C, but precede the string with five spaces if desired.

Some printers may not be able to superscript an underscore character. If you have one of these printers, leave out the [SuprScrpt] code.

Another change that could be made is to add a space to the strings in options C and D, thus avoiding having to manually add the space each time you create a note. Remember that Tab and Indent codes cannot be used as part of the string.

Consider making such changes in the Setup menu so that they do not have to be made for every document.

Margin Settings for Notes

Margins can be set within footnotes or endnotes. If a margin setting is not found, the notes take on the margins of the original document. If multiple margin settings are found within a document, the notes falling between those margin changes will also vary. However, if you change margins *after* the notes have been created, the margins within the notes do not change.

If you are using footnotes, you probably want the notes to be updated with the current margin changes. If you are using endnotes, you would most likely not want them to change because they should all have the same margins.

There are three ways of updating margins. First, you can enter each affected note, then exit, and the margins are updated. You can do a Word Count (press Spell (CTRL-F3) and type **6**) to update the margins automatically. The fastest method would be to use the Extended Search (HOME-F2) feature to search for a nonexistent code (such as [Math On]).

If you use footnote (CTRL-F7) to edit a note, the margins will be updated even if you don't want them to be.

To return to the previous margin setting, move to the beginning of the note and reset the margins.

Columns and Notes

You can create an endnote while in columns. However, because a footnote would usually span all columns at the bottom of a page rather than being formatted into a column, and because it would affect the wrapping of one column to another, it is not possible to create a footnote while in columns.

If you reformat text containing footnotes into columns, the footnotes are automatically converted to endnotes.

Search for Notes

Footnotes and their associated codes are sometimes hard to find. Usually you would set footnote options at the beginning of the document. If you are assigning a new number to a footnote, you would most likely specify the new number right before the footnote. However, if you can't find the right code, go to the top of the document, press Search (F2), then Footnote (CTRL-F7). The following options appear.

```
1 Footnote/Endnote; 2 Set Footnote #; 3 Footnote Options; 4 Footnote #: 0
```

Type **1** to search for the first [Note] (specific notes cannot be chosen), **2** to search for a [Set Note #] code (used when reassigning a number to a footnote), **3** for (FtnOpt) (Footnote options menu changes), or **4** for [Note #]. This last feature not only finds the first note, but places you within the note itself. The first option just finds the note in the document.

If you want to search for or replace text that might be found within a footnote or endnote, you should use the Extended Search or Extended Replace feature. Press HOME before pressing Search (F2) or Replace (ALT-F2). The document, notes, and headers/footers will be searched during an extended search.

Preview Notes

The Preview feature lets you see exactly how the footnotes and endnotes will appear on the printed page. You can preview either the entire document or a single page. If you just want to see how the endnotes will appear, go to the end of the document and preview the last page. If you want the endnotes to start printing on a separate page, insert a Hard Page (CTRL-END) at the end of the document.

To do a Preview, press Print (SHIFT-F7), type **6** for Preview, then type **1** for Document or **2** for Page.

Any cursor keys can be used while in Preview. Although editing cannot be done in this screen, you can press Exit (F7) and make necessary adjustments before printing the document.

If you want to print only the endnotes, position the cursor on the last page (or blank page at the end of the document) and print (press Print (SHIFT-F7) and type **2**).

Change Footnotes to Endnotes

If you format text into columns, all footnotes are automatically converted to endnotes. You can then delete the column definition and Columns On codes to return the text to normal. The endnotes remain as endnotes. See *Columns* for more information about defining columns.

The WordPerfect manual suggests that you create a macro to convert footnotes to endnotes (or vice versa). The macro calls up each footnote for editing, blocks the text for the footnote, cuts the block with Move, exits the footnote, deletes the footnote, creates an endnote, and retrieves the text in the endnote. The same could be done to convert endnotes into footnotes. (Note that the step that deletes the actual footnote is missing from the current documentation.) If you prefer to use this method, see Appendix C for the complete macro.

Related Entries

Preview a Document

Search

Thesaurus

Foreign Languages

WordPerfect is presently available in 14 languages. Spelling dictionaries are also available for all versions except Finnish.

Because of WordPerfect's special-character key mapping, you have access to foreign characters when typing in any language. If you are using the English version of WordPerfect and type a document in another language, you can use the applicable dictionary to check the spelling. Each additional dictionary can be obtained separately from WordPerfect Corporation. Table 4-1 shows the WordPerfect languages and spelling dictionaries available and the number of entries in each dictionary.

When using a foreign-language version of WordPerfect, consider installing the appropriate ROM so that all the characters in that language are available. For example, the õ and ã are not available in the IBM U.S. ROM, but are in the Portuguese ROM.

Related Entries

Special Characters

Spell

Formatting

The format of a document refers to how it will look when printed. Margins, spacing, tabs, page numbering, and right justification are only a few available formatting options. See each individual option entry in this chapter for details.

Options

WordPerfect has three format keys: Line Format (SHIFT-F8), Page Format (ALT-F8), and Print Format (CTRL-F8).

The Line Format menu shown in the following illustration controls formatting such as tabs, margins, and spac-

Language	Words in Dictionary
English	115,621
English with U.K. Dictionary	102,765
Danish*	116,985
Dutch	75,657
Spanish	82,093
Portuguese	70,000 (approximately)
French	128,368
German	85,337
German with Swiss German Dictionary	85,276
Icelandic**	108,648
Swedish	75,011
Norwegian	60,874
Finnish without Dictionary	N/A

*Besides English, Dutch is the only version that has a thesaurus.
**To use the Icelandic speller, you must have the Icelandic ROM installed.

Table 4-1.   WordPerfect Languages and Dictionary Entries

ing that affect individual lines. Hyphenation and alignment character options are also included on this menu because Line Format is the most appropriate location for such choices.

```
1 2 Tabs; 3 Margins; 4 Spacing; 5 Hyphenation; 6 Align Char: 0
```

Figure 4-43 shows the Page Format menu. These items deal with the total number of lines on a page and determine

```
Page Format

      1 - Page Number Position

      2 - New Page Number

      3 - Center Page Top to Bottom

      4 - Page Length

      5 - Top Margin

      6 - Headers or Footers

      7 - Page Number Column Positions

      8 - Suppress for Current page only

      9 - Conditional End of Page

      A - Widow/Orphan


Selection: 0
```

Figure 4-43.   Page Format menu

where the page "extras" will appear. You can control page numbering, center a page from top to bottom, choose the length of a page, change the top margin, include headers and footers, and go an additional step in determining where the page should break, with the Conditional End of Page and Widow/Orphan options.

The Print Format menu shown in Figure 4-44 contains options that control the printer. Pitch, font, lines per inch, right justification, double underlining, and line numbering are controlled with this menu. You can also specify the sheet feeder bin number and send specific printer commands to the printer.

All options selected from the menus insert a code in the document which can be seen by pressing Reveal Codes (ALT-F3). A code affects the document from that point forward until the cursor reaches another code that changes the setting.

All the features in the Line Format menu have some way of making their presence known. Margins, spacing, and so on show immediately on the screen. However, not all the options in the Page Format and Print Format menus

```
Print Format

        1 - Pitch                     10
            Font                      1

        2 - Lines per Inch            6

      Right Justification             On
        3 - Turn off
        4 - Turn on

      Underline Style                 5
        5 - Non-continuous Single
        6 - Non-continuous Double
        7 - Continuous Single
        8 - Continuous Double

        9 - Sheet Feeder Bin Number   1

        A - Insert Printer Command

        B - Line Numbering            Off

   Selection: 0
```

Figure 4-44.   Print Format menu

appear on the screen.

If you want to see page numbering, headers, footers, right justification, line numbering, and other such options on the screen, press Print (SHIFT-F7) and type **6** for Preview. Type **1** to preview the entire document or **2** to see the current page. The page will appear on the screen as closely as possible to the printed page. Press Exit (F7) to leave the preview screen.

Other items, such as columns or outlining, could be considered formatting features. Refer to a specific feature for step-by-step instructions on its use.

Related Entries

Line Format

Page Format

Preview a Document

Print Format

Form Letters and Forms Fill-In

See *Merge*

Forms

WordPerfect defines forms as being hand-fed, continuous, or sheet-fed paper.

Because WordPerfect can have up to six printers, you can use some of those definitions for the same printer, and change only the type of form. Then, when printing, you can send a print job to a specific printer (Printer 1 = hand-fed, Printer 2 = continuous, etc.).

Keystrokes

Assigning the Type of Forms to a Printer Selection

The type of forms are selected when printers are selected. These settings can be changed any time.

1. Press Print (SHIFT-F7).

2. Type **4** for Printer Control.

3. Type **3** to Select Printers. A list of currently selected printers is displayed.

4. Note the number of the printer (Printer 1-6) and the printer definition assigned. Press ENTER to use the same definition. If you want to select a different printer, insert one of the Printer disks in drive A or B, press PGDN, type the letter of the drive, and select the new printer definition. See *Select Printers* for more detail.

5. Type the number corresponding to the type of port. Parallel printers use an LPT port and serial printers use a COM port.

6. You are then asked for the type of forms. Type **1** for Continuous, **2** for Hand-Fed, or **3** if you have a Sheet Feeder. If you type 3 for a sheet feeder, you will be asked several additional questions. If you are not sure of the correct answers, use the default settings. Choose the type of sheet feeder. See *Sheet feeder Bin Number* for details on these settings.

Continuous-Forms   A continuous form is defined as any type of form that is automatically fed into the printer without an electronic cut-sheet feeder. This includes tractor feeders for perforated paper and laser printers with a paper tray. When printing with perforated paper, the print head should be positioned at the perforation.

Hand-Fed Forms   When hand feeding paper into the printer, WordPerfect assumes that you are feeding it in at least 1 inch. If you have set the top margin for less than 1 inch, feed it in accordingly. If the top margin is set at more than 1 inch, feed it in 1 inch. WordPerfect will add the extra number of half-lines for anything over 1 inch.

Hand-fed paper also requires a "Go" from the Printer Control menu before it will begin printing. This feature lets you feed the paper into the printer and start printing it when you are ready. However, most users don't like having to enter the Printer Control menu each time a page is fed into the printer. Instead, you can define a single-key macro that sends a "Go" to the printer so you can continue working without stopping to enter the menu.

1. Press Macro Def (CTRL-F10).

2. Press ALT-G to name the macro. Use a different name if desired.

3. Press Print (SHIFT-F7).

4. Type **4** for Printer Control.

5. Type **G** to send the printer a "Go."

6. Press ENTER to leave the menu.

7. Press Macro Def (CTRL-F10) to end the macro definition.

Each time the printer needs a "Go," press ALT-G to start the macro.

Displaying the Type of Forms Selected

You can display the type of form selected without going into the printer selection procedure.

1. Press Print (SHIFT-F7).

2. Type **4** for Printer Control.

3. Type **2** to Display Printers and Fonts.

Each printer is listed with the type of form selected and the assigned fonts. See Figure 4-45.

Printing to a Specific Type of Form

To change the printer (and type of form) for a single job, retrieve the document on the screen if it is not already there. Press Print (SHIFT-F7), type **3** for Options, and change option 1 to the desired printer number. When you leave the Print Options menu, you will again see the Print menu. Type **1** to print the full text or **2** to print the page.

To change the printer for several documents, press Print (SHIFT-F7), type **4** for Printer Control, and choose **1** to Select Print Options. Change the printer number. The setting remains until you exit WordPerfect.

Related Entries

Select Printers

```
1:   Panasonic KX-P1091/1093        Continuous

         1 IBM Graphics              2 IBM Graphics
         3 IBM Graphics              4 IBM Graphics
         5 IBM Graphics              6 IBM Graphics
         7 IBM Graphics              8 IBM Graphics

2:   Star PowerType                 HandFed

         1 ASCII/Backspace           2 ASCII/Backspace
         3 ASCII/Backspace           4 ASCII/Backspace
         5 ASCII/Backspace           6 ASCII/Backspace
         7 ASCII/Backspace           8 ASCII/Backspace

3:   Canon A1 Garland PS N          SheetFeed

         1 A1 Garland PS             2 A1 Garland Ftn
         3 A1 Garland PS             4 A1 Garland Ftn
         5 A1 Gar PS DW              6 A1 Garland PS
         7 A1 LineDraw               8 A1 Gar Ftn DW



Press any key to continue
```

Figure 4-45.   Printer name with type of form selected and assigned printer fonts

Function Keys

A template provided by WordPerfect Corporation is used to label ten functions keys that WordPerfect applies to various commands. If you misplace the template, press Help (F3) twice and see the screen shown in Figure 4-46. Press ENTER or SPACEBAR to leave Help.

If you have a keyboard, such as the IBM Enhanced Keyboard or Centronics, on which the function keys are arranged in two rows across the top, an alternate template is provided. See Figure 4-47.

There are four "levels" of commands listed on each template. In general, the features used most often are assigned so that a function key can be pressed by itself to obtain that feature. On keyboards with function keys arranged down the left side, related features are placed together. For example, the →Indent and →Indent← functions are on key

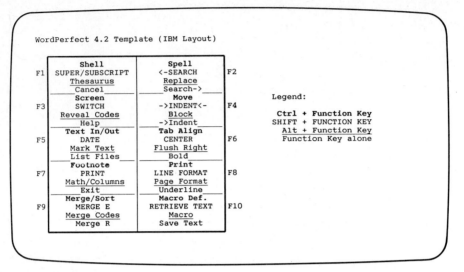

Figure 4-46. On-screen template with function key commands

F4, which is adjacent to the TAB key. With the introduction of the function keys across the top of the keyboard, some key assignments make less sense (such as Bold being two away from Underline instead of being next to it).

If a feature is printed in black on the template, press the function key by itself to obtain the feature. If printed in green, press SHIFT with the function key. For blue features, use the ALT key. For features printed in red, use the CTRL key. Refer to the template for the color code, or place the colored "stick-on" labels provided with WordPerfect on the SHIFT, ALT, and CTRL keys.

Note the extra features listed on the template. These features are assigned to other keystrokes, such as Delete to End of Line (CTRL-END).

Global Search and Replace

See *Replace*

F1	F2	F3	F4	F5
Shell	Spell	Screen	Move	Text In/Out
SUPER/SUBSCRIPT	<-SEARCH	SWITCH	->INDENT<-	DATE
Thesaurus	Replace	Reveal Codes	Block	Mark Text
Cancel	Search->	Help	->Indent	List Files

F6	F7	F8	F9	F10
Tab Align	Footnote	Print Format	Merge/Sort	Macro Def
CENTER	PRINT	LINE FORMAT	MERGE E	RETRIEVE TEXT
Flush Right	Math/Columns	Page Format	Merge Codes	Macro
Bold	Exit	Underline	Merge R	Save Text

Ctrl + Function Key
SHIFT + FUNCTION KEY
Alt + Function Key
Function Key alone

Figure 4-47. Alternate on-screen template with function key commands (courtesy WordPerfect Corporation)

Go To

WordPerfect's Go To feature lets you go to a specified page or character. When working in text columns, Go To can be used to move from one column to the next.

Keystrokes

Go To a Specific Page

1. Press Go To (CTRL-HOME).

2. Type the number of the page. The cursor will move to the top of that page.

Go To Top or Bottom of Page

1. Press Go To (CTRL-HOME).

2. Press ↑ to go to the top of the current page or ↓ to go to the bottom of the current page.

Go To a Column

When working in text columns (newspaper or parallel), Go To can be used to move to the next or preceding column, or to the far left or right column.

1. Press Go To (CTRL-HOME).

2. Press → to move to the column to the right or ← to move to the column to the left.

HOME,→ cannot be used to move to the far right column as in regular text. Instead, it moves to the "right margin" of the current column. To move to the far right column, press Go To (CTRL-HOME), then press HOME,→. Press Go To (CTRL-HOME),HOME,← to move to the far left column.

Go To a Character, End of Sentence, or End of Paragraph

1. Press Go To (CTRL-HOME).

2. Type the character and the cursor will go to the next occurrence of that character.

Instead of typing a character, type a period (.) to go to the end of a sentence or press ENTER to go to the end of the paragraph (it actually finds the next occurrence of a hard return).

Go To Original Position

After pressing any cursor key other than ↑, ↓, →, or ←, or CTRL ← or CTRL → or doing a Search or Replace, you can press Go To (CTRL-HOME) twice to return the cursor to its original position.

Go To Beginning of Block

If you turn on Block and begin highlighting text, then decide you have defined the block incorrectly, you can press Go To (CTRL-HOME) and Block (ALT-F4) to return to the point where Block was turned on. Block stays on so you can start again.

As noted in the *Block* entry, Block stays on after some operations and is automatically turned off after others. If you want to do more than one Block operation on a block of text and Block is turned off automatically, you can immediately press Block (ALT-F4), then Go To (CTRL-HOME), and Block (ALT-F4) to redefine the original section of text.

Hints

Use Search (F2) when you want to go to the next occurrence of a string of characters rather than a single character.

If you press a cursor key by mistake, press Go To twice to return to the original position. Go To, Go To can also be used in macros to remember the last location.

Related Entries

Block

Columns

Cursor Keys

Search

Go To DOS

You can use Shell (CTRL-F1) to temporarily go to DOS. Word-Perfect is not exited, but is kept in memory.

Keystrokes

1. Press Shell (CTRL-F1).

2. Type **1** to Go To DOS.

3. After completing the DOS functions, type **EXIT** and press ENTER (F7) to return to WordPerfect.

Hints

When you go to DOS while in WordPerfect, another copy of DOS (COMMAND.COM) is loaded. WordPerfect adds the message "Enter 'EXIT' to return to WordPerfect" to the DOS prompt.

You must have enough memory (RAM) available to load the additional copy of DOS. When in DOS, you can use most commands, such as DIR, COPY, or DEL. If you want to use another program while in DOS, you must have sufficient memory available. Although most programs can be run when you go to DOS, you should not try to load memory-resident (TSR) programs while WordPerfect is still running. If you plan to load memory-resident programs, use Exit (F7) to leave WordPerfect first. Although it is not always harmful, this should be done to avoid any problems.

If you have WordPerfect Library running and you press Shell (CTRL-F1), you will be asked if you want to type **1** to Go To Shell or **2** to Retrieve the Clipboard. If you choose option 1, you will be placed in the shell. Type **1** from there to Go To DOS.

To return to WordPerfect, remember to enter **EXIT** at the DOS prompt. If you go to DOS from WordPerfect Library, you can press Exit (F7) to return to WordPerfect. Do not enter WP, or another copy of WordPerfect will be loaded into memory. If this happens, you are asked if other copies of WordPerfect are running. Press Cancel (F1) to return to DOS if you don't want another copy of WordPerfect loaded.

One advantage to using the Go To DOS feature is that any documents in memory remain in memory. When you return to WordPerfect, your cursor is returned to the same point in the document as it was when you left.

Related Entries

DOS

Exit

Shell

Hand-Fed Paper

If your printer does not have a paper tray, tractor feeder, or sheet feeder, you are most likely feeding paper into the printer by hand. WordPerfect lets you specify that you have hand-fed forms when selecting the printer definition. If hand-fed forms are selected, the printer will wait for a "Go" so that the paper can be inserted first.

Sending the Printer a "Go"

When printing with hand-fed paper, the printer stops for you to insert each page (even if you are printing only one page) and sends a beep to the computer telling you to give the printer a "Go." Press Print (SHIFT-F7), type **4** for Printer Control, and type **G**. If you print with hand-fed paper often, consider putting the steps into a macro (ALT-G is a suggestion) so you don't have to leave the document when sending a "Go" to the printer. See Appendix C for exact steps.

Top Margin

WordPerfect assumes that you will feed a piece of paper 1 inch into the printer. If you set the top margin in WordPerfect at anything less than 1 inch, you should feed the paper in that much. If the top margin is set to more than 1 inch, do not feed it in more than 1 inch; WordPerfect will add the additional number of half-lines over 1 inch. For example, if you set the top margin at 16 half-lines (12 half-lines = 1 inch) WordPerfect assumes you have fed the paper in 1 inch and will move down two additional lines (four half-lines).

Hand Feeding
with Laser Printers

Laser printers usually have the apparatus for hand feeding a piece of paper or envelope. You do not have to create a special printer definition to do this. Before you queue the print job, place the piece of paper against the paper guide facing up.

If you use this method, you will actually get two sheets of paper fed through the printer. However, the hand-fed page is the one that will be printed. If you don't want the additional piece of paper, you must define the laser printer as having a sheet feeder. The paper tray is then considered bin 1 and the hand-fed method is considered bin 2.

Related Entries

Forms

Select Printers

Hanging Paragraphs or Hanging Indents

A hanging paragraph or hanging indent is a paragraph or group of lines which indents all lines after the first one at a common setting.

Keystrokes

1. Press →Indent (F4) to indent all lines.

2. Press Left Margin Release (SHIFT-TAB) to return the first line to the margin.

Hints

The keystrokes depend upon the current tab settings. The paragraph will be indented five spaces if you leave the tab settings as WordPerfect has set them. Remember that the Left Margin Release (SHIFT-TAB) returns to the previous tab. If you don't have a tab setting at the left margin, this feature will not work.

There are a variety of ways this feature may be accomplished. One way is to set the left margin farther to the right (where the paragraph should be indented). You would then only need to press Left Margin Release (SHIFT-TAB) to go to a previous tab setting to the left of the left margin. If you use this option, remember that there must be a tab setting in the margin area for this to work.

Press →Indent← (SHIFT-F4) instead of →Indent (F4) to

indent from both right and left margins.

If you want the paragraph indented more on the left, press Indent (F4) until you reach the desired location, then press Left Margin Release (SHIFT-TAB) an equivalent number of times.

Applications

Hanging paragraphs are commonly used when typing bibliography entries, as shown in the following example.

```
Smith, Robert J., and Kathryn Morris.  "Raising the
     Two-Year Old."  The Joy of Children, November 25,
     1987, 40-43.
```

You should not use a hanging indent for numbered items. Instead, type the number (or use the Paragraph Numbering feature) and press Indent (F4).

Related Entries

Indent

Left Margin Release

Hard Hyphen

A Hard Hyphen can be used as a minus sign or dash. Unlike a regular hyphen, it can also be used to keep hyphenated words (such as Carolyn Smith-McBride) from being separated at the end of a line.

Keystrokes

Press HOME and the hyphen key.

When HOME,- is pressed, the dash character - is inserted into the document. WordPerfect considers the dash a regular character and will not use it as a hyphen during hyphenation.

Pressing the hyphen key alone inserts a required hyphen that will be used to break hyphenated words if necessary. Pressing CTRL and the hyphen together inserts a soft hyphen — the same type of hyphen used by WordPerfect during automatic or assisted hyphenation. This type of hyphen is not displayed on the screen if the word no longer needs to be hyphenated (for example, after editing changes have been made). A required hyphen appears as [-] in Reveal Codes and a soft hyphen appears as a bolded hyphen -.

Applications

Use a hard hyphen between two last names used together or between cumulative page numbers in a bibliographical entry. The hard hyphen will prevent breaking the hyphenated text between lines.

You can also use a hard hyphen as part of a dash. Pressing two regular hyphens will not guarantee that they will always be kept together. Instead, press HOME,-,- to insert --. See *Dashes* for more information.

A hard hyphen can also be used in an equation as a minus sign. If used in an equation, the equation will not be broken between two lines.

Related Entries

Dashes

Hyphenation

Hard Page

Sometimes called a "new page" by other word processors, the Hard Page is used to insert a page break and start a new page. When working in columns, the Hard Page is used to divide columns and pages.

Keystrokes

Simply press Hard Page (CTRL-ENTER).

Hints

A dashed double line is used to indicate the presence of a Hard Page code [HPg]. WordPerfect uses a single dashed line to indicate soft page breaks entered automatically.

WordPerfect will adjust soft page breaks, but will not adjust a hard page break. If you want to remove the page break, position the cursor just below the page break at the left margin and press BACKSPACE, or position the cursor just above the line and press DEL.

Applications

Use a hard page break to end short pages and to manually decide where the page break will occur. For example, if you want a table within a document to be on a page by itself, you could precede and follow it with a Hard Page. However, remember that other text will not flow *over* that page, so it might be best to insert the table at the beginning or end of a document. You could also put it into a separate document.

Related Entries

Page Breaks

Hard Space

A Hard Space is sometimes called a "required space" and is used to keep separate words together as one word.

Keystrokes

Instead of pressing SPACEBAR to insert a regular space, press HOME, then SPACEBAR.

In Reveal Codes, a space appears as a space. A Hard Space appears as a space in brackets, indicating that it is the WordPerfect Hard Space code [ ].

Applications

Use a Hard Space to prevent separation of words or other text entries that you wish to stay together on the same line. For example, if you don't want the phrases "Robert L. Smith," "November 25, 1987," or "x + y = z" to break at the end of a line, use Hard Spaces instead of regular spaces.

A Hard Space can be inserted as you type or after the text has been typed.

Headers and Footers

Headers are printed at the top of the page and footers are printed at the bottom of the page. They can be used to print such items as a running title, company name, date, or page number. See Figure 4-48 for a sample header and footer.

Keystrokes

1. Move to the top of the document (or to the top of the page where the header or footer is to appear first).

2. Press Page Format (ALT-F8).

3. Type **6** for Headers and Footers. The following menu appears.

```
Header/Footer Specification

    Type                          Occurrence
    1 - Header A                  0 - Discontinue
    2 - Header B                  1 - Every Page
    3 - Footer A                  2 - Odd Pages
    4 - Footer B                  3 - Even Pages
                                  4 - Edit

    Selection: 0                  Selection: 0
```

4. Type the number that applies to the desired header or footer.

5. Choose the occurrence. Note that option 4 lets you edit the selected header or footer.

6. Type the text for the header or footer.

7. Press Exit (F7) when finished to return to the Page Format menu.

8. Continue creating headers and footers or press ENTER to leave the menu.

Hints

When a header or footer is created, a code similar to the following is placed in the document at the cursor's location.

[Hdr/Ftr:1,1;Text.]

The first number indicates the type of header or footer selected; the second number indicates the occurrence. Up to 50 characters of the header or footer are displayed. If there are more characters in the header or footer, "..." is displayed at the end of the 50 characters.

WordPerfect automatically inserts a blank line between a header or footer and the regular text. If you want additional lines inserted, press ENTER at the end of a header or at the beginning of a footer. The extra lines are considered part of the header or footer and will be adjusted automatically within the document.

```
U.S. Constitution                              September 17, 1787
Citizen of the United States, and who shall not, when elected, be

an inhabitant of the State in which he shall be chosen.

     Representatives and direct Taxes shall be apportioned among

the several States which may be included within this Union,

according to their respective Numbers, (which shall be determined

by adding to the whole Number of free Persons, including those

bound to Service for a Term of Years, and excluding Indians not

taxed, three fifths of all other Persons.)  The actual

Enumeration shall be made within three Years after the first

Meeting of the Congress of the United States, and within every

subsequent Term of ten Years, in such Manner as they shall by Law

direct.  The Number of Representatives shall not exceed one for

every thirty Thousand, but each State shall have at Least one

Representative; and until such enumeration shall be made, the

State of New Hampshire shall be entitled to choose three,

Massachusetts eight, Rhode-Island and Providence Plantations one,

Connecticut five, New York six, New Jersey four, Pennsylvania

eight, Delaware one, Maryland six, Virginia ten, North Carolina

dive, South Carolina five, and Georgia three.

     When vacancies happen in the Representation from any State,

the Executive Authority thereof shall issue Writs of Election to

fill such Vacancies.

     The House of Representatives shall chose their speaker and

other Officers; and shall have the sole Power of Impeachment.




                         Page 2
```

Figure 4-48.   Sample header and footer

WordPerfect automatically accounts for the total number of lines in a header plus the blank line separating it from the rest of the text when making page breaks. If a footer is more than one line, however, extra lines will print in the bottom margin. See *Footers* for more information about footers only.

If you want a header to start on a specific page, define it at the top of that page. A footer can be created at any location on the page and will take effect from that point forward. Unfortunately, if text is added or deleted, the code moves with the text. Therefore, you might consider placing a Hard Page (CTRL-ENTER) before the header definition.

Editing Headers and Footers

1. Press Page Format (ALT-F8).

2. Type **6** for Headers and Footers.

3. Type the number applying to the header or footer to be edited.

4. Type **4** to Edit.

5. When finished, press Exit (F7).

When you ask to edit a header or footer, WordPerfect searches *backward* for the last or most current header or footer. If you move to the top of the document, the first header or footer definition is displayed for editing.

A header or footer can contain most format settings, including margin, font, and spacing changes. The Date function (SHIFT-F5) can be used to insert the date and time. Merge codes cannot be included in a header or footer. If you press TAB while in a header or footer, the appropriate number of spaces are inserted at that point in text; this may create problems in proportionally spaced documents, or where you desire a hanging indent for lines in the header or footer. Therefore, use Indent (F4) where possible.

If you change margins, pitch/font, or other settings for the rest of the document *after* the headers and footers have been created, the headers and footers are not updated with the rest of the document. Follow the steps above to enter the header or footer and press Exit (F7). Just entering the header or footer will update the margins and other settings.

A better way of updating margins and other settings is to press Spell (CTRL-F2) and type **6** to do a Word Count. Even faster is an Extended Search (HOME,F2) for an unused code (such as Table of Authorities).

You can use the Speller and Thesaurus while creating or editing a header or footer. Words in a header or footer are automatically checked when you check the rest of the document.

Deleting, Discontinuing, or Suppressing a Header or Footer

There are several options for deleting, discontinuing, or suppressing a header or footer.

First, if you want to have several different headers and footers within the same document, you can redefine them at the applicable locations. You do not have to discontinue the original one first. For example, if you want to have a header for the introduction of a book, define header A at the beginning of the document. Then, when you reach the first chapter, define header A again to include different header information. This new definition does not affect the previous header; it only changes header A from that point forward.

If you want a header or footer to be printed on several pages, then discontinued for the rest of the document, go to the point of the document where it is to be discontinued and do the following.

1. Press Page Format (ALT-F8) and type **6** for Headers and Footers.

2. Select the header or footer to be discontinued.

3. Type **0** to discontinue the header or footer from that point forward.

If you have defined a header or footer for the entire document but don't want it to print on selected pages, such as the title page and pages containing only tables and charts, you can suppress the printing for the current page. The following steps will accomplish this task.

1. Press Page Format (ALT-F8).

2. Type 8 to Suppress Page Format for <u>Current</u> Page Only. The menu shown in Figure 4-49 appears.

3. Select the option (or options, typing + between selections) that should be suppressed for that page.

4. Press ENTER to leave the Page Format menu.

To delete a header or footer from a document, delete the code. Use the Search feature (see "Searching for Headers and Footers"), press BACKSPACE, and type **Y** or **N** when you see the message "Delete [Hdr/Ftr]? (Y or N) N."

```
Suppress Page Format for Current Page Only

    To temporarily turn off multiple items, include a "+" between menu entries.
    For example 5+6+2 will turn off Header A, Header B, and Page Numbering
    for the current page.

        1 - Turn off all page numbering, headers and footers

        2 - Turn page numbering off

        3 - Print page number at bottom center (this page only)

        4 - Turn off all headers and footers

        5 - Turn off Header A

        6 - Turn off Header B

        7 - Turn off Footer A

        8 - Turn off Footer B

    Selection(s): 0
```

Figure 4-49.   Menu to suppress printing of a header or footer on a current page

Searching for Headers and Footers

As previously mentioned, if you ask to edit a header or footer, WordPerfect searches backward to find the most current definition. To search for header/footer codes, press Search (F2) or Reverse Search (SHIFT-F2), press Page Format (ALT-F8), then type **6** to insert [Hdr/Ftr]. Press Search (F2) again to begin the search.

When you do a Search, Reverse Search, or Replace in WordPerfect, the text in headers, footers, footnotes, and endnotes is not searched. If you want the text in these features to also be searched, use the Extended Search feature. To start an extended search, press HOME before pressing Search (F2), Reverse Search (SHIFT-F2), or Replace (ALT-F2). Note that you press HOME, then the search key. Do not hold HOME down or you will start a regular search.

Too Many Lines

A header or footer can contain up to a page of text. If you forget to press Exit (F7) after the header or footer and continue typing the document, you might exceed the page limit. If this happens, the message "ERROR: Too many lines" is displayed and the cursor is placed at the end of the header or footer.

To correct the problem, turn on Block (ALT-F4), highlight the text that doesn't belong in the header or footer, press Move (CTRL-F4), and type **1** to Cut the text. Exit the header or footer and retrieve the text in the document. See *Cut Text and Columns* for additional help on cutting text from one place to another.

Alternating Headers or Footers

The option of two headers and two footers makes it possible for them to appear on alternating sides of the page. For example, one header could be placed flush right on odd-numbered pages and the other could be placed at the left margin on even-numbered pages. If both headers or footers contain the same text, you can copy the text from one header to the other to avoid retyping.

Previewing and Printing with Headers and Footers

Headers and footers do not appear on the regular editing screen. If you want to see how they will appear, you can preview a page or the entire document before printing.

1. Press Print (SHIFT-F7).

2. Type **6** for Preview.

3. Type **1** to preview the document or **2** to preview just one page. Naturally, it takes longer to preview a document, so if you are interested only in the placement of a header or footer, type **2** to preview the page.

4. Use the cursor keys to move through the Preview screen and press Exit (F7) when finished.

Remember, too, that the header or footer code displays the first 50 characters in the Reveal Codes screen.

If a page number and a header or footer is selected in the same location (for example, a header on line 1 and page number at top left of the page), they will overlap each other when displayed during the Preview and when printed. To obtain both a page number and text in a header or footer, insert a ^B in the header or footer to print current page numbers.

If you choose both headers or both footers for the same page, avoid overprinting them by inserting blank lines or placing one at the left and the other at the right of the page.

Applications

Printing a header on alternating pages is useful for bound documents. See *Binding Width*.

Using Headers or Footers
to Number Pages

If you want to include text with a page number, as shown in the footer in Figure 4-48, use the header/footer code instead of the Page Numbering option on the Page Format menu. To print the current page number within a header or footer, press CTRL-B; this inserts a $^\wedge$B, which inserts the current page number during printing.

The current page number in a header or footer can also be printed by using $^\wedge$N, but this keystroke is used as a merge code instruction to "get the next record" when found in the regular text of a document. $^\wedge$B can be used to print the current page number anywhere in the document (header, footer, or regular text).

If you want a header or footer to read "Page *n* of *n*," create a macro that goes to the end of the document, pauses so you can take note of the total number of pages, then creates the header or footer, pausing for you to enter the total number of pages. See *Page Numbering* or Appendix C for the exact steps.

Headers for Letters and Memos

When creating letters or memos longer than one page, you might want to place a header on subsequent pages to identify the recipient of the letter, recipient's address, page number, or date. This process can be totally automatic if you always start a letter in a specific place and follow the same format from letter to letter. A macro could be defined to Block and Copy the name or address, retrieve it into a header, use the Date key (SHIFT-F5) to insert the date, and ^B to insert the current page number. The last step in the macro should suppress the header on the first page. See Appendix C for the exact steps.

Related Entries

Footers

Page Numbering

Suppress

Help

Help (F3) can display a description of each feature, tell you what keystrokes activate a feature, and display an on-screen WordPerfect template.

```
┌─────────────────────────────────────────────────────────────┐
│                                                               │
│  Help                                         WP 4.2  07/02/87│
│                                                               │
│      Press any letter to get an alphabetical list of features.│
│                                                               │
│          The list will include the features that start with that letter, along │
│          with the name of the key where the feature is found.  You can then     │
│          press that key to get a description of how the feature works.          │
│                                                               │
│      Press any function key to get information about the use of the key.        │
│                                                               │
│          Some keys may let you choose from a menu to get more information        │
│          about various options.  Press HELP again to display the template.      │
│                                                               │
│      Press the Enter key or Space bar to exit Help.           │
│                                                               │
│                                                               │
│                                                               │
└─────────────────────────────────────────────────────────────┘
```

Figure 4-50.   Help options menu

Keystrokes

1. Press Help (F3). A menu appears describing the Help options. See Figure 4-50. If the help files are not found, you will see, "WPHELP.FIL not found. Insert Learning Diskette and press drive letter:." If you are using two floppy disk drives, insert the Learning disk in drive B and type **B**.

2. Choose one of the following options.

• Type a letter to see an alphabetical listing of WordPerfect features and their keystrokes. See Figure 4-51.

• Press a function key to see a description of the features that are assigned to that key. Instructions for using the feature are included with this Help option. See Figure 4-52.

• Press Help (F3) again to display the template on the screen. This option is useful if you misplace the template included in the WordPerfect package.

```
Function Key      Feature                       Key Name

       F5         File Management               List Files
Alt -F6           Flush Right                   Flush Right
Ctrl-F8           Font/Print Wheel              Print Format - 1
Alt -F8           Footers                       Page Format - 6
Ctrl-F7           Footnotes                     Footnote
       F2         Forward Search                -> Search
Shft-F7           Full Text Print               Print - 1

Alt -F5           Generate                      Mark Text - 6
Shft-F7           "GO" - Start Printer          Print - 4 Printer Control
Ctrl-Home         Go To                         GoTo
Ctrl-F1           Go to DOS                     Shell

Shft-F7           Hand-Fed Paper                Print - 4 then 3 Select Printers
Home-Space        Hard Space                    Home-Space
Alt -F8           Headers                       Page Format - 6
       F3         Help                          Help
Shft-F8           H-Zone Size                   Line Format - 5
Home "-"          Hyphen Character (minus)      Home "-"
     "-"          Hyphen Code                   "-"
Shft-F8           Hyphenation On/Off            Line Format - 5
```

Figure 4-51.   Help screen showing partial alphabetical list of WordPerfect features and their keyboard locations

```
 Block On/Off

      Defines a block of text on which various editing operations may be
      performed.  The block will be █highlighted█ as it is defined.

 To define a block:

   1.  Position the cursor at the beginning or end of the block of text.
   2.  Press the Block key.
   3.  Move the cursor to the opposite end of the block.

 You may then
      Bold, Underline, Superscript, Subscript, Center, Flush Right, Print, Save,
      Append      - Use the Move key to append the block to the end of a file.
      Delete      - Use Del or <- to delete the block.
      Mark Text - Mark the block for Table of Contents, Lists, Index, Redline,
                    Strikeout, or Table of Authorities.
      Move        - Press the Move key and select an option to Cut or Copy a block
                    of text or columns and move it to another location.
      Protect     - Prevent page breaks within the block (Page Format key)
      Replace     - Characters, words or certain functions.
      Spell       - Check the spelling against the words in the dictionary.
      Upper/Lower Case Conversion   - Use the Switch key to change case.
```

Figure 4-52.   Help screen showing the features of a function key

3. Press ENTER or SPACEBAR to leave the Help screens.
Exit (F7) and Cancel (F1) display information about their
particular functions rather than letting you cancel or
exit from the Help screens.

Hints

If you are using WordPerfect on a two-disk-drive system,
insert the Learning disk into drive B each time you need
Help. To avoid seeing the error message and typing **B** each
time, insert the disk before pressing Help (F3). If you are
using a hard disk and see the message telling you that the
help files cannot be found, consider copying the two help files
WPHELP.FIL and WPHELP2.FIL to the directory on the
hard disk where WP.EXE is kept. (WPHELP.FIL contains
help for each function key. WPHELP2.FIL lists the features
alphabetically.)

When you press Help (F3), the first screen displays the

version of WordPerfect running and the date of its release in the upper right corner of the screen.

Many features are "hidden" in submenus. If you can't find a feature listed on the template, press Help (F3) and type the first letter of the feature. A display lists the function keys to be used and the corresponding numbers of the options on the menu. The IBM version of WordPerfect also lists the keystrokes, as shown in Figure 4-51.

If you encounter an error message, refer to the entry in this chapter on the feature, the specific error message, or *Error Messages.*

Applications

Help (F3) can also be used to help you learn the program. You can press Help and any function key. After reading the instructions, press ENTER to return to the screen and experiment. You could also stay in Help and continue pressing function keys to learn about each WordPerfect feature.

Related Entries

Error Messages

Hidden Codes

See *Codes*

Hidden Text

See *Comments*

Highlighting Text

Block (ALT-F4) is used to highlight a section of text in reverse video. Among many other options, you can cut, copy, or delete the block.

Bold (F6) will display text in a higher intensity on the screen and in darker print at the printer.

Related Entries

Block

Bold

HOME Key

The HOME key has no feature of its own, but is used with other features to extend their functions.

Keystrokes

Move to the Edges of the Screen

HOME can be combined with any arrow key to move the cursor to the edges of the screen. HOME,↑ moves the cursor to the top of the screen, HOME,← moves the cursor to the left edge of the screen, and so on.

Move to the Extreme Edges of the Document

Pressing HOME twice before an arrow key will move the cursor to the extreme edges of the document. HOME,HOME,↑ moves the cursor to the top of the document, HOME,HOME,→ moves the cursor to the far right margin (useful for text wider than the screen), and so on.

Go To

Pressing CTRL-HOME displays "Go To" at the bottom of the screen. Enter a number to go to a specific page or type a character to go to the next occurrence of that character. See *Go To* for a list of options.

Move Within Columns

Combining Go To (CTRL-HOME) and an arrow key lets you move from column to column. Pressing Go To (CTRL-HOME), HOME, then ← or → moves the cursor to the far left or right column.

Extended Search, Reverse Search, and Replace

Search (F2), Reverse Search (SHIFT-F2), and Replace (ALT-F2) do not search through headers, footers, footnotes, or endnotes. Pressing HOME before starting a Search or Replace extends the selected feature into these areas. If the Search stops in a header, footer, footnote, or endnote, you can press HOME and the Search key to continue the extended search or press Exit (F7) to leave the header, footer, footnote, or endnote and return to the document.

Hard Space

A Hard Space is used to combine two or more words as one so that they will not be broken at the end of a line. Press HOME,SPACEBAR to insert a Hard Space.

Hard Hyphen

If you want a dash or minus sign, press HOME with the hyphen key (HOME ,-). Its function, like that of a Hard Space, is to prevent a word or equation from breaking at the end of a line.

Related Entries

Cursor Keys

Go To

Hard Hyphen

Hard Space

Search

Hyphenation

WordPerfect provides the options of automatic and assisted hyphenation.

Keystrokes

Turning On Hyphenation

WordPerfect comes with hyphenation off. You can either turn on hyphenation and make hyphenation decisions while typing, or wait until the document has been entered, then go to the top of the document and turn on hyphenation. Hyphenation decisions can then be made all at once.

1. Go to the beginning of the document or to the location where hyphenation is to be turned on.

2. Press Line Format (SHIFT-F8).

3. Type **5** for Hyphenation. The following menu is displayed on the status line.

```
[HZone Set] 7,0  Off Aided  1 On; 2 Off; 3 Set H-Zone; 4 Aided; 5 Auto: 0
```

Note the default settings listed for the "HZone," or hyphenation zone. These are explained in detail in "Hints."

4. Type **1** to turn on hyphenation.

5. If you want WordPerfect to hyphenate words automatically, type **5** for Auto. Otherwise, it will suggest the location for the hyphen, but leave the decision up to you.

6. Press ENTER to return to the document.

Making a Hyphenation Decision

If you choose Aided hyphenation, words needing hyphenation are displayed on the status line with a suggested hyphen.

You have one of three choices when a word is presented for a hyphenation decision.

1. Press ESC to accept the position of the hyphen.

2. Use ← and → to move the hyphen. When finished, press ESC.

3. Press Cancel (F1) if you don't want the word to be hyphenated. The word will wrap to the next line.

Hints

When hyphenation is turned on or off, a [Hyph on] or [Hyph off] code is inserted into the document. Therefore, it is important to move the cursor to the location where you want hyphenation to begin (or end) before choosing the option.

When you press Cancel (F1), a code is placed in front of the word indicating that it should not be hyphenated or even presented for hyphenation again. The code used to indicate this type of decision appears as a bolded slash "/" in the Reveal Codes screen. If you want the word to be hyphenated, you will need to delete the "/" first.

If you want to turn off hyphenation temporarily while scrolling or searching, press Exit (F7) when asked for a hyphenation decision. As soon as you are finished scrolling or searching, hyphenation will be turned on again.

If words have a Hard Space or Hard Hyphen between them, they are presented as a single word. Because the Hard Space or Hard Hyphen has been inserted to prevent a line break at that point, press Cancel (F1) and the word will not be hyphenated.

If, when in the Setup menu, you are asked where you want to keep the hyphenation module, press ENTER without entering an answer. The hyphenation module is used in the Spanish version of WordPerfect and is not applicable to the English version.

Hyphenation Zone

The hyphenation zone surrounds the right margin. Both the hyphenation zone and the right margin are used to determine where a line should break.

If hyphenation is on, the hyphenation zone is used to determine whether a word should be hyphenated or wrapped to the next line. If a word starts before the left side of the hyphenation zone and extends past the right side, it will be hyphenated or presented for a hyphenation decision. If hyphenation is off, a word fitting this description would be wrapped to the next line instead of being hyphenated. Figure 4-53 shows the area where hyphenation decisions are made.

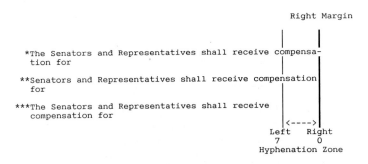

Figure 4-53. Hyphenation zone

The size of the hyphenation zone also determines exactly where the hyphen can occur. For example, with the default hyphenation zone set at 7 and 0, you can position the hyphen seven spaces to the left of the right margin or zero positions to the right of the right margin. If you decrease the size of the H-Zone, there will be less space for a possible hyphen, and, therefore, less accurate decisions. If you increase the H-Zone, you broaden the possibilities for correct placement.

The following steps should be followed to change the hyphenation zone.

1. Press Line Format (SHIFT-F8).

2. Type **5** for Hyphenation.

3. Type **3** to Set the H-Zone.

4. Enter the number for the left hyphenation zone (number of spaces to the left of the right margin).

5. Enter the number for the right hyphenation zone (number of spaces to the right of the right margin). If you have a dot-matrix printer, this number should be 0 or characters will "hang" over the right margin.

Laser, daisy-wheel, and some dot-matrix printers can squeeze extra characters into a line. Most dot-matrix printers, however, can only spread out characters.

Automatic Versus Aided

WordPerfect uses an algorithm to determine where the hyphen should be placed. The same algorithm is used to determine the position of the hyphen whether automatic or aided hyphenation is chosen.

The decision is not always correct, so you may prefer to use aided hyphenation, in which a hyphen can be suggested only within the hyphenation zone. With the default of 7 and 0, there are only seven possible positions for the hyphen. Even if the hyphen placement would be more logical outside the hyphenation zone, the next best place within the hyphenation zone will be suggested.

With automatic hyphenation, WordPerfect does not ask for a hyphenation decision unless the word is unique and the algorithm cannot find a rule which applies to the situation. This could happen if you have a long acronym that is not really a word.

If you choose automatic hyphenation, it might be best to turn it on so that words are hyphenated as you type. Then, if there is an inaccuracy, you can correct it immediately. To correct an incorrect hyphenation decision, go to the position in the word where the hyphen should be placed and press Soft Hyphen (CTRL-hyphen). Then delete the incorrect hyphen so it will not be used again. The easiest way is to press Reveal Codes (ALT-F3) and delete the code, indicated by a bold hyphen.

Getting a Smoother Right Margin

If you want a more even right margin without right justification on, turn on hyphenation. Decreasing the hyphenation zone will create an even smoother right margin, but keep in mind that the hyphen must be placed within that zone, so the zone should not be too small. Remember that you can always press Cancel (F1) if a hyphen cannot be placed accurately.

Less Space During Justification

Because some printers can provide right justification only by inserting more space between words, you might want to turn off justification for these types of printers. If you don't want to give up justification, try turning on hyphenation and possibly decreasing the hyphenation zone.

Related Entries

Right Justification

Indent

The Indent feature can be used to indent any line or group of lines in a paragraph without changing the margins or pressing TAB for each line.

Keystrokes

Indents are dependent on the current tab settings.

1. Set tabs if necessary. Press Line Format (SHIFT-F8), type **1** or **2** for Tabs, set tabs, and press Exit (F7) when finished.

2. Press Indent (F4) to indent the left side of the paragraph only. Press →Indent← (SHIFT-F4) to indent equally from the left and right margins.

3. Press ENTER to end the indent and return to the left margin.

Hints

When you press Indent (F4), an Indent code [→Indent] is inserted. When →Indent← (SHIFT-F4) is pressed, the code [→Indent←] is inserted. Text will wrap within the temporary margins set by the Indent codes until ENTER is pressed or an [HRt] code is encountered.

Use TAB to indent a single line or just the first line in a paragraph. If all lines are to be indented, use one of the Indent keys. If TAB is used for multiple lines and editing changes are made, the text will not be formatted correctly.

When →Indent← (SHIFT-F4) is used, an equal number of spaces is subtracted from the right side, regardless of the tab settings. Therefore, you need to be concerned only with the tab settings for the left indented margin.

Applications

Use Indent for numbered paragraphs. As shown in the following illustration, the number is at the left margin. After typing the number, press Indent (F4) to indent to the first tab setting.

```
1.     In which city and state was the U.S. Constitution
       signed?

2.     Name at least five people who signed the U.S.
       Consitution.
```

For bulleted items, press TAB, type the chosen bullet character (see *Bullets* for suggestions), then press Indent (F4) to indent the text.

Indented, single-spaced quotations can be created with →Indent← (SHIFT-F4), as shown in the following illustration.

```
ARTICLE II.

       Section 1.  The Executive Power shall be vested in a
       President of the United States of America.  He shall
       hold his Office during the Term of four Years, and,
       together with the Vice President, chosen for the same
       term, be elected, as follows.

Each State shall appoint, in such Manner as the Legislature

thereof may direct, a number of Electors, equal to the Whole

Number of Senators and Representatives to which the State may be
```

When followed by Left Margin Release (SHIFT-TAB), Indent (F4) can be used to create hanging indents or paragraphs. See the following illustration for a sample bibliography entry.

```
Schuler, Robert B.  Our American Heritage.  Boston, MA:  Harvard
       University Press, 1976.
```

Related Entries

Hanging Paragraphs and Indents

TAB Key

Tabs, Clear and Set

Index

WordPerfect can generate an index with headings and sub-headings. The index is sorted alphabetically and the page number for each entry marked in the document is listed.

Keystrokes

There are three basic steps to building an index: creating a concordance (or manually marking each item in the document), defining the page number listing style, and generating the index.

Marking Entries

In versions prior to 4.2, you had to search for a word or phrase that was going to be included in the index and mark *each* occurrence so when the index was generated, it would find the mark and reference that page. With version 4.2, WordPerfect lets you create a concordance in which an entry needs to be marked only once. You could write a macro to help automate the procedure for marking each item within a document, but the fastest, easiest way is to use a concordance. Because the Concordance feature was designed to eliminate much of the manual labor, this book documents that feature.

If you decide to mark each item individually within the document rather than create a concordance, use steps 2-6 below.

1. Type a list of the entries as you want them to appear in the index. An entry can be one line in length and must end with a hard return [HRt].

If each entry is to be used as a heading and there are to be no subheadings in the index, skip to step 8. The next six steps concern marking each entry for a heading *and* subheading.

2. If the entry consists of one word, place the cursor anywhere in the word. If the entry should include an entire phrase, move to one end, press Block (ALT-F4), and move to the opposite end.

3. Press Mark Text (ALT-F5).

4. Type **5** for Index.

5. The current word or blocked phrase appears following "Index Heading:". Press ENTER to accept it as the heading, edit the displayed heading, or enter a new one.

6. If you edited the heading or entered a new one, the original is displayed as a possible subheading. Press ENTER to accept it as the subheading, edit the displayed subheading, enter a new one, or press Cancel (F1) if no subheading is desired.

7. Each entry can be marked more than once using different headings and subheadings. Continue until all entries have been marked. Remember that if an entry is to be a heading with no subheading, it is not necessary to mark it.

8. Press Merge/Sort (CTRL-F9), type **2** to Sort, press ENTER twice, and type **1** to sort the concordance file. If you complete this step, the index will be generated more quickly.

9. Press Exit (F7) and type **Y** to save the file. Enter the name of the file and type **N** to remain in WordPerfect.

Defining the Page Number
Listing Style

1. Retrieve the document to be indexed and go to the end of the document (HOME,HOME,↓).

2. If you want the index to be generated on a separate page, press Hard Page (CTRL-ENTER). Type a heading for the index if desired.

3. Press Mark Text (ALT-F5).

4. Type **6** for Other Options.

5. Type **5** to Define the Index.

6. Enter the name of the concordance file. If you marked each entry in the document and are not using a concordance, press ENTER. The Index Definition menu shown in Figure 4-54 is displayed.

7. Select the style of page number listings.

Generating the Index

1. Press Mark Text (ALT-F5).

2. Type **6** for Other Options.

3. Type **8** to Generate Tables and Index.

4. Type **Y** or **N** in answer to the question "Existing tables, lists, and indexes will be replaced. Continue? (Y or N) Y."

```
Index Definition

    1 - No Page Numbers
    2 - Page Numbers Follow Entries
    3 - (Page Numbers) Follow Entries
    4 - Flush Right Page Numbers
    5 - Flush Right Page Numbers with Leaders




    Selection: 0
```

Figure 4-54.   Index Definition menu

If you find mistakes while generating an index, you can make corrections to the index markings in the concordance (or document) and regenerate the index. By typing **Y**, you will not get duplicate indexes. However, if you want more than one index, type **N** and delete the [EndDef] code from the end of the first index. When you generate the index again, both will remain.

Hints

When an entry is marked for an index, an Index code

[Index:heading;subheading]

is inserted. When an index is defined (concordance and page number listing style selected), a definition code

[DefMark:Index,5;Concordance]

appears. The code indicates the type of definition mark "Index," the page number style option selected (5), and, if any, the name of the concordance file being used.

When an index is generated, an [EndDef] code is placed at the end of the index. If you generate the index again, the [DefMark] and [EndDef] codes are used to decide the index to be replaced. If the [EndDef] mark is not found, the previously generated index is considered as text and will not be deleted. You could use this to your advantage if you wanted more than one index generated for the document.

If you have more than one [DefMark] code for an index, you will get unpredictable results. If you decide to change the page number listing style or the name of the concordance file, delete the previous [DefMark] code and redefine the index.

Related Entries

Concordance

Mark Text

INS Key

The INS key is used to toggle between inserting or replacing text (Typeover).

Keystrokes

WordPerfect is designed to insert text as it is typed. If you want to type over existing text, press INS. "Typeover" is displayed on the status line, indicating that characters at the cursor will be replaced.

Hints

Typeover will not allow you to type over codes. Likewise, codes cannot replace characters.

Some keys, such as TAB and BACKSPACE, work differently when in Typeover. When you press TAB, the cursor moves over text to the next tab setting rather than inserting a [TAB] code. BACKSPACE deletes the character at the left of the cursor, but inserts a blank space in its place.

Applications

When you use Line Draw, spaces are inserted between lines and boxes. If you want to include text in a chart or box, you can use Typeover so that the spaces will be replaced. If you insert text rather than use Typeover, you will need to delete the same number of spaces so the lines and boxes will line up properly.

When typing equations, you can "make space" and use Typeover to replace the space with the equation. When using this method, you can move the cursor freely and do not need to key in spaces as you go with ENTER and SPACEBAR. To make space, press ESC, type a number (300 will make four or five lines of space), then press SPACEBAR to insert that many spaces.

Related Entries

Typeover

Insert a Printer Command

See *Printer Commands*

Installing WordPerfect

Chapter 1 has detailed information on how to install Word-Perfect. The following is a summary of the procedure.

1. Copy all WordPerfect disks and use the copies. Keep the originals in case the backups become damaged.

If you have a hard disk, make a directory for the WordPerfect program files (WP is a suggestion). Copy the WordPerfect, Speller, and Thesaurus disks to that directory. Insert the Learning disk and copy WPHELP. FIL and WPHELP2.FIL from the Learning disk to that directory. Copy CONVERT.EXE from the Learning disk and PRINTER.EXE from the Printer 2 disk to the same directory if you think you will need to use the Convert and Printer programs.

If you plan to use the Tutorial or go through the lessons in the manual, create another directory and copy the Learning disk to that directory. If you don't want to duplicate files on the hard disk, delete CONVERT.EXE, HELP2.FIL, and HELP2.FIL from the Learning directory.

2. Select a printer definition (see *Select Printers* for steps). Do not copy the printer files from the Printer 1 and Printer 2 diskettes to the hard disk. When you select

printers, the applicable printer definitions are copied for you. If you copy the files to the hard disk, you will waste valuable disk space.

3. Customize WordPerfect to fit your needs (see Chapter 3 for details on changing colors, changing defaults, mapping special characters to the keyboard, and so on).

If you have a hard disk with DOS version 2.x, you will want to create or edit the path that lists the WordPerfect directory and perhaps create a batch file for starting Word-Perfect. See Chapter 1 for more information.

Related Entries

AUTOEXEC.BAT File

Colors

Select Printers

Setup Menu

Special Characters

Start WordPerfect

WordPerfect Files

See also Chapter 1, "Getting Started"

See also Chapter 3, "The Next Step"

"Insufficient Memory" Error Message

The error message "Insufficient Memory" might be displayed if you attempt to retrieve two documents in memory at once (document 1 and document 2). It can also be displayed when you try to use the Thesaurus, Sort, Table of Contents, Lists, Index, or Speller features.

Reasons

WordPerfect requires that you have at least 256Kb of RAM to run WordPerfect. You can actually have less and still run WordPerfect, but some features that require additional memory may not work.

When WordPerfect is loaded, half of the available memory is reserved for editing document 1 and document 2. The other half is allocated as a memory cache, which is used during a cut or copy operation, for undelete buffers, virtual files, macros, and other operations that normally require disk access. The cache enables WordPerfect to run much faster because the text used in these operations is kept in memory.

If you have loaded other memory-resident (TSR) programs, and you have a total of 256Kb, they may be taking some of the necessary RAM to run WordPerfect.

If you press Switch (SHIFT-F3) or try to split the screen with Screen (CTRL-F3) and see this error message, WordPerfect cannot find the minimum of 11Kb of RAM needed for document 2.

Sorting, previewing, and generating (for tables, lists, and the index) operations all need to have a second document available. If the two document screens are occupied, Word-Perfect creates a document 3 to perform these functions. It is possible for you to have enough memory space for two documents in memory, but to be unable to complete chosen operations because there is not enough memory left for the third document.

The Thesaurus does not use the third document but still takes a considerable amount of memory from the cache.

Solutions

There are a few things you can try if you get this message. First, remove all other memory-resident programs (such as SideKick, Turbo Lightning, or any other program that comes up with a "hot key") by rebooting with a regular DOS diskette (without an AUTOEXEC.BAT file).

Second, if you can load two documents, but cannot run a Sort, Preview, or Generate operation, load only one document into memory. The memory normally used for document 2 can then be used for the chosen operation.

Third, you could load the document in document 2 and leave document 1 empty. (Document 1 allotted twice as much memory as document 2. Up to 64Kb can be given to document 1 while a maximum of 32Kb can be given to document 2.)

Last, you can increase the amount of memory in your computer, usually at a minimal cost.

If running under the shell in WordPerfect Library, use the /W switch to increase the amount of memory that can be used.

Italics

Many prefer to use italics instead of underlining to add emphasis. WordPerfect uses a font change to print italicized type.

Keystrokes

Finding the Italics Font

A daisy-wheel printer uses a different print wheel to print in italics, whereas dot-matrix and laser printers generally have one of the eight fonts assigned as an italics font.

If you have a daisy-wheel printer, press Print (SHIFT-F7), type **4** for Printer Control, then **2** to Display Printers and Fonts. Even though only the character tables are usually listed, an italics font might also be identified.

Because any font change will send a signal to the printer to pause and wait for a "Go" (letting you change the print wheel), you can change to any other font listed. However, if you are printing with a proportionally spaced font and want to change to italics, be sure to change to another proportionally spaced font. If you are printing in nonproportional spacing, select another nonproportionally spaced font.

To find which font is assigned as an italics font on a dot-matrix or laser printer, print the document PRINTER2.TST found on the Learning diskette. As a rule, italics type is usually assigned to font 2 or 4, but there are exceptions, as shown in Figure 4-55.

WordPerfect Auxiliary Printer Test

Pitch/Font Capabilities   This section shows the printer
capability of pitch and font. If pitch changes do not print as
specified, your printer may be pitch/font specific.

font 1, 10 pitch
font 1, 12 pitch
font 1, 15 pitch
font 1, 13* pitch

font 2, 10 pitch
font 2, 12 pitch
font 2, 15 pitch
font 2, 13 pitch*

font 3, 10 pitch
font 3, 12 pitch
font 3, 15 pitch
font 3, 13 pitch*

font 4, 10 pitch
font 4, 12 pitch
font 4, 15 pitch
font 4, 13* pitch

font 5, 10 pitch
font 5, 12 pitch
font 5, 15 pitch
font 5, 13* pitch

font 6, 10 pitch
font 6, 12 pitch
font 6, 15 pitch
font 6, 13* pitch

font 7, 10 pitch
font 7, 12 pitch
font 7, 15 pitch
font 7, 13* pitch

font 8, 10 pitch
font 8, 12 pitch
font 8, 15 pitch
font 8, 13* pitch

Figure 4-55.   PRINTER2.TST on the Canon laser printer

Selecting Italics

1. Press Print Format (CTRL-F8).

2. Type **1** for Pitch or Font.

3. Enter the desired pitch or press ENTER to accept the current setting. If using a PS font, type an * after the pitch.

4. Enter the number of the font that is used for italics. If using a daisy-wheel printer, changing to any other font will send a signal to the printer to stop and wait for a "Go."

5. Press ENTER to leave the Print Format menu.

After typing the text to be printed in italics, follow the steps above to change back to the original font. If you use a daisy-wheel printer, the printer will stop at the proper location and wait for you to change print wheels. After you have finished, press Print (SHIFT-F7), type **4** for Printer Control, then type **G** to send the printer a "Go." See Appendix C for an ALT-G macro that can be used to send the printer a "Go."

Hints

Italics type does not show as being italicized on the screen. Instead, a font change code similar to [Font Change:10,2] is inserted, indicating the pitch and font selected.

Selecting italics requires more keystrokes and time than pressing Bold (F6) or Underline (F8). If you will be using italics often, you might want to define two ALT-key macros to turn Italics on and off. To define each macro, press Macro Def (CTRL-F10), name the macro (ALT-I for "italics on" and ALT-O for "italics off" are suggestions) and follow the above steps for selecting italics. When finished with the steps, press Macro Def (CTRL-F10) to end the macro. Thereafter, when you need italics, press ALT-I, type the text, then press ALT-O.

Related Entries

Fonts

Justification

See *Right Justification*

Keep Text Together

There are three options for preventing a section of text from being split between pages.

Options

Widow or Orphan Protection

WordPerfect can be set to protect one-liners from appearing at the top or bottom of the page. However, the Widow or Orphan Protect feature does not protect titles or three-line paragraphs.

1. Go to the top of the document and press Page Format (ALT-F8).

2. Type **A** for Widow and Orphan.

3. Type **Y** or **N** to turn Widow and Orphan Protect on or off.

If you prefer to always have the widows and orphans protected, consider changing the option permanently in the Setup menu.

Block Protect

Block Protect is used to protect a block of text from being split between pages. It is best used for text that needs to be protected when the number of lines in the block might increase or decrease during editing.

1. Press Block (ALT-F4) to turn on Block.

2. Move to the opposite end of the block.

3. Press Page Format (ALT-F8).

4. Type **Y** to protect the block or **N** if you change your mind

If Widow and Orphan is on, Block Protect does not always work.

Conditional End of Page

Conditional End of Page should be used to protect a specific number of lines.

1. Count the number of lines to be protected. Include the blank spaces between the lines if the text is double- or triple-spaced.

2. Move the cursor to the line above the text to be protected. It does not have to be a blank line.

3. Press Page Format (ALT-F8).

4. Type **9** for Conditional End of Page.

5. Enter the number of lines to be kept together.

Applications

Block Protect can be used to protect a table or chart from breaking between pages. Though Conditional End of Page could be used, Block Protect is more appropriate if the number of lines in the table might change after editing.

Conditional End of Page can be used to keep a title with the first couple of text lines so it will never appear on a page by itself.

If you want to protect a paragraph from breaking across pages, use Block Protect.

Related Entries

Block Protect

Conditional End of Page

Widows and Orphans

Keyboard Mapping

WordPerfect does not allow you to completely reconfigure the keyboard. However, you can map special characters to ALT- and CTRL-key combinations, or reassign up to 26 features as ALT-key macros. The keys must be the letters A through Z.

See *Macros, Special Characters, ALT Key,* and *CTRL Key* for complete information.

Keypad

See *Keypad*

Labels

WordPerfect can be used to print either a strip of mailing labels or multiple columns of labels. You can create a macro to set up the format, save the format in a file that can be used again and again, or set up a primary label file that can be used in a merge.

Keystrokes

Use the Merge feature or set up a format for the label and type each by hand. If the secondary merge file has already been created or if you will be using the same names and addresses again, consider using the Merge feature.

If you have a printer setup that prints only labels or if you print only a few labels as you need them, you could define a macro to set up the format and print them all at once.

Single Width, Continuous Labels

Because a laser page printer cannot usually print single-width labels, these instructions are specifically for daisy-wheel or dot-matrix printers set for continuous forms. If you have selected hand-fed forms for your printer, change to continuous whether you have a tractor feeder or not. (You can control the feeding manually.)

Label Macro   To create a label macro, press Macro Def (CTRL-F10) and name the macro (LABELS is a suggestion). Complete the following steps for setting up the labels, then press Macro Def (CTRL-F10) again to turn off macro definition.

1. Measure the label. Figure the number of lines (vertical length × 6) and spaces (width × pitch). The following shows a sample 2-inch by 4-inch label.

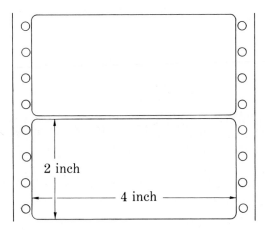

2. Press Page Format (ALT-F8) and type **3** to Center Page Top to Bottom (each label will be considered a page).

3. While in the Page Format menu, type **4** to Set the Page Length.

4. Type **3** for Other and enter the number of lines (figured in step 1) for both "Form Length in Lines" and "Number of Single-Spaced Text Lines."

5. Type **5** from the Page Format menu to Set the Top Margin. Enter **0** as the number of half-lines.

6. Press ENTER to leave the Page Format menu.

7. Press Line Format (SHIFT-F8) and type **3** for Margins. Enter the left and right margins (5 and 35 are suggested settings for a 4-inch-wide label if printing in 10 pitch).

When you want to use the label macro, press Macro (ALT-F10), enter the name of the macro, and begin entering names and addresses. Separate each label with a Hard Page (CTRL-ENTER).

Label Format File　If you are not creating a macro, save the steps in a file (name it LABELS). When you want to create a label, retrieve the file, press (HOME,HOME,↓) to move past the format codes, and begin entering names and addresses. Each name and address should be separated with a Hard Page (CTRL-ENTER).

After entering the names and addresses into the format file, print and clear the screen. If you must save the file after entering the names and addresses, save it with a name other than LABELS. You can then use the original LABELS file again and again.

Because the file contains only codes which cannot be seen on the screen, you might want to add a document summary to identify its contents. See *Document Summary* for more information.

Merge File　You can use the label format file to create a primary merge file. The following steps explain how to insert merge codes into the LABELS file. If you do not understand merges, refer to the various Merge entries.

First, if the secondary file has already been created, retrieve it and find the name, company (if applicable), and address fields. Make a note of the field numbers. If you are using a secondary merge file created with WordPerfect Library's Notebook utility, you can use the names of the fields instead of the numbers.

You can either insert the format codes as the first step, or wait until the entire merge is complete, then insert the format codes at the beginning of the document. If you place them in the primary merge file, the format codes are duplicated with each record.

1. On a clear screen (or one where the format codes have been inserted), press Merge Codes (ALT-F9) and type **F** for Field.

2. Enter the number of the "name" field.

3. Press ENTER to move down to the next line.

4. Press Merge Codes (ALT-F9), type **F** for Field, and type the number of the "company" field if you want to include the company name on the label. If not all records have information in the "company" field, type ? after the field number. The question mark will prevent a blank line in the label if the "company" field is empty. In this case, the status line would look like

   Field Number? 2?

After you press ENTER, the code ^F2?^ is displayed on the screen.

5. Press ENTER to move to the next line, press Merge Codes (ALT-F9), type **F** for Field, and enter the number of the "address" field. If the address requires more than one field, continue until all the fields that make up the address are on the label. List the fields in the format that you want them printed. In the following example, the city, state, and zip code are all separate fields in the secondary file.

```
^F1^
^F2?^
^F3^, ^F4^  ^F5^
```

6. Save the file (LABELS.PF is a suggestion, with PF meaning primary file).

This file can then be used with any secondary merge file that has the fields accordingly. If they aren't numbered the same way, edit the LABELS.PF file to change just the field numbers. See *Merge* for the exact steps on setting up a data (secondary merge) file and merging. "Hints" also gives the steps for merging.

Multiple-Width Labels

The Columns feature is used to create multiple-width labels. Either parallel or newspaper-style columns can be selected. Because it is not practical to do one label or even a few labels at a time on this type of form, the following steps create a primary merge file. Remember that although there seem to be many steps, you have to create the file only once. It can then be used again and again with the Merge feature.

This example will work with a laser printer *only* if there are the same number of text lines on each label. If you want to include a "company" field on the label, all records must have information in that field. You cannot use the "?" designation shown in the previous example.

1. Press Page Format (ALT-F8) and type **4** for Page Length.

2. Type **3** for Other and enter **66** as the "Form Length in Lines" and **60** as the "Number of Single-Spaced Text Lines."

3. Type **5** in the Page Format menu to Set the Top Margin. Enter **4** as the number of half-lines.

4. Press ENTER to leave the Page Format menu.

5. Press Line Format (SHIFT-F8) and type **3** for Margins. Enter the left and right margins. If printing in 10 pitch, enter **3** and **85**. In 12 pitch, try **4** and **102**.

6. Press Math/Columns (ALT-F7) and type **4** to define the columns.

7. Type **Y** for evenly spaced columns, enter **3** as the number of spaces between columns (enter **4** if printing in 12 pitch), type **1** or **2** for Newspaper or Parallel columns, and enter **3** as the number of columns. Your screen should appear as shown in Figure 4-56. (If printing in 12 pitch, the margins will be different.)

8. Press Exit (F7) to leave the Text Column Definition menu and type **3** to turn on Columns.

```
Text Column Definition

     Do you wish to have evenly spaced columns? (Y/N) Y
     If yes, number of spaces between columns: 3
     Type of columns: 1
          1 - Newspaper
          2 - Parallel with Block Protect

     Number of text columns (2-24): 3

     Column      Left      Right      Column      Left      Right
       1:         3         28         13:
       2:        32         57         14:
       3:        61         85         15:
       4:                              16:
       5:                              17:
       6:                              18:
       7:                              19:
       8:                              20:
       9:                              21:
      10:                              22:
      11:                              23:
      12:                              24:

Press EXIT when done
```

Figure 4-56.   Text Column Definition menu

9. Press Merge Codes (ALT-F9), type **F**, and enter the number of the "name" field. Press ENTER to go to the next line.

10. Press Merge Codes (ALT-F9), type **F**, and enter the number of the "address" field. If the address is kept in more than one field, continue until all fields are included for that label.

11. Press Hard Page (CTRL-ENTER) to go to the next column.

12. Press Merge Codes (ALT-F9) and type **N** (or press CTRL-N) to insert ^N. This code tells WordPerfect to merge with the next record.

13. Repeat steps 9-12 for column 2. ^N will appear at the beginning of column 3 in the last step.

14. Repeat steps 9 and 10 to finish column 3.

15. When finished with column 3, press Math/Columns (ALT-F7) and type **3** to turn off Columns. The cursor is returned to the left margin.

16. Press ENTER three times to move to the next set of labels. If you will have four lines on the label, press ENTER only twice.

17. Hold down CTRL and type **N,P,P**, to insert ^N^P^P. These codes allow the merge to continue with the next record without inserting page breaks. Do not press any other keys (including ENTER) after the second ^P. The screen should appear as follows.

```
^F1^                          ^N^F1^                       ^N^F1^
^F2^                          ^F2^                         ^F2^
^F3^                          ^F3^                         ^F3^


^N^P^P
```

18. Save the file. This file will be considered a primary merge file during a merge. See "Hints" for more information or *Merge* for complete details.

Hints

As with any of the examples in this book, you can adjust the settings to fit your situation.

Merging

The following steps assume you have placed the names and addresses in a secondary merge file. If you haven't, see *Merge* for complete information.

1. With a clear screen, press Merge/Sort (CTRL-F9).

2. Type **1** for Merge.

3. Enter the name of the primary file. This would be the LABELS file just created.

4. Enter the name of the secondary file. This file contains the names and addresses that are to be merged into the labels form.

5. "* Merging *" appears on the screen. When finished, print the file.

If you will be using labels with the same names and addresses again and again, you might consider saving them in a separate file. For example, you might send a newsletter to the same people weekly. If the list of people does not change constantly, you could use that file each week. Otherwise, merging each time you need labels saves disk space and is not that time-consuming once you set up the primary labels form.

Merge Codes ^N and ^P

In the multiple-width example, you are asked to insert a ^N so that WordPerfect will merge with the next record. If you leave the code out, it will continue to merge with the first record until it reaches the end of the "page" because Word-Perfect's Merge feature is designed to merge with a record any number of times on a page. This lets you customize a mailing by inserting someone's name as many times as you want in a form letter. However, when you want different records on the same page, you must insert the ^N, forcing WordPerfect to merge with the next record.

The ^P codes tell WordPerfect to repeat this file (because no other filename is found between the ^Ps) until all records in the secondary file are gone. If you didn't enter these codes, you would have to create the entire primary file with the ^F merge codes. In other words, the ^Ps save you a lot of work.

Printing Problems

Remember that laser printers have an unprintable zone of approximately 1/4 inch on all sides. The multiple-width example can be used with laser printers only if each label will have the same number of lines.

Some printers, such as the Toshiba P1240, might insist on ejecting the page after printing one label. When all else fails, enter the Printer program and create a new printer driver which uses the original as a model. When asked to enter a name, enter the name of the printer and specify that it be used for labels. Enter the Printer Initialization screen and remove the page eject code <12> from option 5, Reset Printer at End of Page. Insert a carriage return/line feed <13><10> and exit the program. Assign that printer definition to one of the six available printers and use that printer when printing labels. See Chapter 7 for complete details on the Printer program.

Applications

If you have a printer dedicated to printing labels, you could create a macro that would copy the address, set up the format, and print it to that specific printer. See Appendix C for a macro to print addresses on envelopes. The same concept could be used for labels.

Related Entries

Columns

Merge

See also Chapter 7, "Printer Program"

Leaving WordPerfect

Use Exit (F7) to leave WordPerfect. You are always asked if you want to save the document before exiting. Never turn off the computer before exiting properly. As soon as you see a DOS prompt (or the Shell menu if you are using WordPerfect Library), you can turn off the computer.

See *Exit* for complete details.

Left Indent

To indent text from the left margin, use →Indent (F4). To indent text from both the left and right margins, use →Indent← (SHIFT-F4).

Press TAB if you want only the first line of a paragraph indented.

See *Indent* and *TAB Key* for more information.

Left Margin Release

Pressing Left Margin Release (SHIFT-TAB) will move the cursor backward to the previous tab setting. If the cursor is at the left margin, Left Margin Release moves into the left margin *if* there is a tab setting in the left margin area.

Keystrokes

Press Left Margin Release (SHIFT-TAB) to move back to the previous tab setting.

Hints

After you have pressed Left Margin Release, the code [← Mar Rel:5] appears. The number in the code indicates the number of spaces the cursor moved to the left. For example, if you press (SHIFT-TAB) at position 50 and the previous tab setting is at position 30, the code [←Mar Rel:20] will be inserted.

If you delete a Left Margin Release code, the cursor will move forward rather than backward, as it does when deleting any other code. If you are confused when deleting these codes, enter Reveal Codes (ALT-F3) and delete the codes from there.

As previously mentioned, this feature is dependent on tab settings. If you want to release the left margin, you must have tabs set in the margin. For example, if the left margin is set at position 10, and you want to release the margin seven spaces, a tab must be set at position 3. If there is no tab setting the code [←Mar Rel:0] is inserted, indicating that the cursor moved zero spaces to the left. You should have no problem releasing the margin five or ten spaces if you are using WordPerfect's default tab settings, as they begin at position 0 and are set every five spaces.

To create a hanging indent (used in bibliographies), either press Left Margin Release (SHIFT-TAB) while at the left margin to move the first line to the left, or press Indent

(F4), then (SHIFT-TAB). The first method places the first line outside the left margin. Use the second method if you want the first line of the entry to stay within the margins. Both methods are shown in the following illustration.

```
Himstreet, William C., and Wayne Murlin Baty.  Business
    Communications:  Principles and Methods.  Belmont, CA:
    Wadsworth, 1977, pp. 305-396.

    Himstreet, William C., and Wayne Murlin Baty.  Business
        Communications: Principles and Methods.  Belmont, CA:
        Wadsworth, 1977, pp. 305-396.
```

Related Entries

Bibliographies

Indent

TAB Key

Line Draw

Line Draw can be used to draw single or double lines. You can also use any other character with Line Draw to create boxes, diagrams, simulated graphs, borders, and so on.

Keystrokes

Drawing Single Lines

1. Press Screen (CTRL-F3).

2. Type 2 for Line Draw. The following menu appears at the bottom of the screen.

```
1 |; 2 ||; 3 *; 4 Change; 5 Erase; 6 Move: 1          Ln 1      Pos 10
```

3. Type 1 for single lines and use the arrow keys to draw the lines.

4. Press Exit (F7) to leave the Line Draw menu.

WordPerfect inserts spaces to preserve the space between lines and [HRt]s are inserted at the end of each line.

Changing the Line Draw Character

If you want double lines, type **2** at the Line Draw menu. If your printer does not have line drawing capabilities, you can use option 3 to print an asterisk as the line character. You can find specific line drawing information about your printer in Chapter 6.

The following steps will enable you to use any other character.

1. Press Screen (CTRL-F3).

2. Type **2** for Line Draw.

3. Type **4** to Change the character. The following menu is presented.

```
1   ; 2   ; 3 ▓; 4 ▮; 5 ▄; 6 ▌; 7 ▐; 8 ▀; 9 Other: 0
```

4. Type the number of the desired option. If you want to use a character that is not displayed, type **9** for Other.

If you type **9** for Other, you are asked for the "Solid Character." Type any character found on the keyboard. If you want to use a special character not on the keyboard, hold down the ALT key and type the ASCII decimal value on the numeric keypad. See Appendix A for possible characters and their ASCII decimal values.

5. The original Line Draw menu reappears, with option 3 displaying the newly selected line drawing character. Option 3 is also automatically selected as the default so you can use the arrow keys immediately to begin drawing with that character.

Erasing Line Drawing

Option 5 on the Line Draw menu can be used to erase line drawing (or any other character encountered). Instead of just erasing a character, a space is inserted to replace the character so that the format of the remaining text and lines is preserved.

Moving the Cursor

Choose option 6 if you want to use the arrow keys as regular cursor keys. Only ↑, ↓, ←, and → can be used. All other cursor keys (such as HOME , →) are disabled.

When in WordPerfect, the arrow keys will not move beyond text unless there are [HRt] codes or spaces in which to move. With option 6 on the Line Draw menu, you can move the cursor anywhere and it creates its own spaces and new lines where needed.

Hints

To combine text and line drawing, it is usually easier to type the text, then use Line Draw when finished. If you want to draw the lines and boxes first and insert the text later, press INS to turn on Typeover. Characters will not be inserted, but will type over the existing spaces. If you insert rather than type over, the lines will be misaligned and you will have to delete as many spaces as characters were inserted.

If you turn on Bold or Underline (or insert any other code) when typing in a box, characters will be inserted even if you have Typeover on (codes will not type over characters). If you want to insert bolded or underlined text, you should type the text first using Typeover, then bold or underline the text using Block (ALT-F4). See *Bold* or *Underline* for details.

Unfortunately, you cannot use keystrokes such as HOME, → or HOME , ↓ to quickly draw lines. Rather than holding down the arrow keys to draw the lines, however, you can press ESC, enter a number, then press the arrow key when in Line Draw mode. Lines will not be drawn past the right margin, so entering a larger number than necessary to draw a line across the screen is not a problem.

Using ESC also helps you create accurately spaced lines and boxes. For example, if you need to create an organizational chart where each box is 20 spaces wide and 4 lines high, you could press ESC, type **20**, and press → to insert 20 line characters. Then press ESC, type **4**, and press ↓ to draw four lines down. Continue with the other sides.

Creating Duplicate Boxes

If you need several boxes that are the same size (as in the organization chart example), create a single box and copy it with the Rectangular Copy feature found on the Move (CTRL-F4) menu.

1. Go To the top left corner of the box and press Block (ALT-F4).

2. Move to the bottom right corner of the box. The box might not appear to be highlighted correctly at this point. It will be highlighted correctly when you reach step 4.

3. Press Move (CTRL-F4).

4. Type **5** to Cut/Copy a Rectangle. The box is highlighted.

5. Type **2** to Copy (or **1** to Cut if you don't want the original box in that location).

6. Move the cursor to the position where the box will be copied.

7. Press Move (CTRL-F4) and type **6** to retrieve the rectangle.

8. Since the box is kept in the cut/copy buffer until you cut or copy another rectangle, continue retrieving the rectangle anywhere on the screen until finished.

If you retrieve a copy of the box in an incorrect position,

you can cut the rectangle using the steps listed above and move it elsewhere.

Changing the Size of a Box

If a box is too large, you can remove a cross-section (using Rectangular Cut) to make it smaller instead of redrawing and erasing portions. If a box is too small, you can define a cross-section as a rectangle, copy it, then retrieve it into the box to make it larger.

Use the steps listed above or see *Rectangular Cut, Copy, and Move* for more details.

Line Drawing Around Centered Text

If you want to draw lines around centered text, you will most likely encounter problems when the Line Draw character hits the [C] or [c] code. To "fix" this problem, start Line Draw at least one space away from the left margin. Also, you cannot draw lines right next to a centered line of text. Draw the lines at least one space away from the beginning or end of the centered text.

Line Draw Limitations

It is not possible to draw lines normally around indented, justified, or aligned text. If text is flush against the left and/or right margin, and you try to draw lines around the text, the characters at the margins will be replaced. However, you can draw the lines and boxes first, then use the Advance feature to advance text up into the drawing. Advance Up will not work with all printers, but works well for laser printers.

Printer Limitations

Most printers have some type of line drawing capabilities. Many do not contain all the characters necessary to draw double lines or insert the proper corner and intersecting characters. Some can draw lines if set at 8 lines per inch (instead of the standard 6) so that the lines are printed closer together. If this is still not acceptable, try half-line spacing. You can even have 8 lines per inch *and* half-line spacing. Remember that your screen will not display 8 lines per inch or half-line spacing. Therefore, you should double (or otherwise compensate for) the number of lines in an illustration.

Font 7 is usually defined as a Line Draw font. To see what line drawing capabilities exist in your printer, print PRINTER2.TST on the Learning disk. Boxes are drawn with single and double lines in each font. The first part of the file is printed at 6 lines per inch and the second part at 8 lines per inch. Figure 4-57 is a partial sample printout of this file on the IBM Quietwriter. Notice that the lower example (at 8 lines per inch) has better resolution for vertical lines. If you print this document with a daisy-wheel printer, be prepared to send the printer a "Go" from the Printer Control menu after each font change.

You cannot print Line Draw in proportional spacing. However, you can draw the line in a regular font, use Advance to advance back up the page, change into a proportionally spaced font, then enter the text.

Newsletters with Line Draw

You can create a newsletter with Line Draw by advancing the columns up the page after the lines are drawn. Refer to *Columns* for more detailed explanation of the newspaper-style column format.

Graphs and Charts

The following graph was created with the graphics characters in Line Draw. PlanPerfect, a spreadsheet program produced by WordPerfect Corporation, can also create these types of graphs. You can save the graph in PlanPerfect, then retrieve it into WordPerfect without conversion.

Line Drawing   On most printers single line draw will print well. On others 1/2 line spacing or eight lines per inch produces a better printout. **If the line drawing results shown below do not look good, your printer may not have line drawing capability.**

This is line draw at six lines per inch showing single, double, mixed:

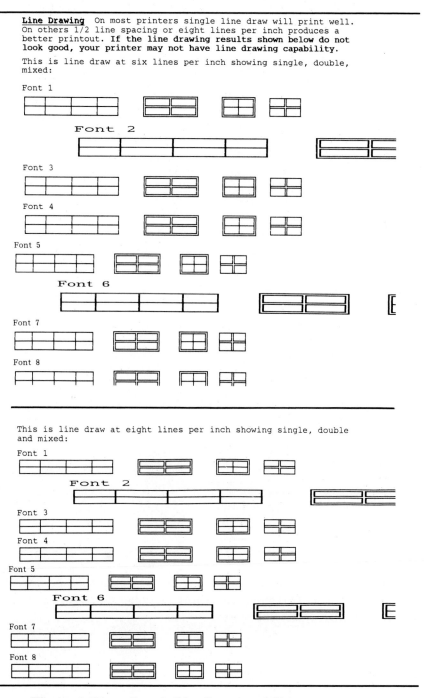

Figure 4-57.   Sample Line Draw capabilities

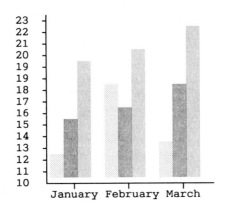

```
23
22
21
20
19
19
18
17
16
15
14
13
12
11
10
    January  February  March
```

Related Entries

Advance the Printer to a Specific Line

Columns

Rectangular Cut, Copy, and Move

Typeover

See also Chapter 5, "Laser Printers"

See also Chapter 6, "Printer Specifics"

See also Chapter 7, "Printer Program"

Line Format

Line Format (SHIFT-F8) has options for setting tabs, changing mrgins and spacing, controlling hyphenation, and specifying the alignment character.

Options

When you press Line Format (SHIFT-F8), the following menu appears.

```
1 2 Tabs; 3 Margins; 4 Spacing; 5 Hyphenation; 6 Align Char: 0
```

Tabs can be set with option 1 or 2. In versions prior to 4.2, option 2 was used to set "extended tabs" beyond position 160. With version 4.2, tabs can now be set to position 250 without a separate menu. However, because most users were accustomed to using 3 for margins, 4 for spacing, and so on, WordPerfect Corporation chose not to renumber the menu.

There are actually three format menus: the Line Format menu, Page Format (ALT-F8), and Print Format (CTRL-F8). Note that all three are called up by the F8 function key. Line Format controls options that can change from line to line and controls where lines will break. Page Format contains many options and features that determine where page breaks will occur. Included are items such as page numbering, headers and footers, top margin, and page length. Print Format controls the options that are seen only at the printer: pitch, font, right justification, lines per inch, and so on (these can also be viewed in Preview).

If you are used to seeing a "format line" showing margins and tabs, consider displaying the ruler on the screen. Press Screen (CTRL-F3), type **1** for Window, and enter **23** for the number of lines in the window. Current margins and tab settings are displayed with brackets [and triangles ▲. If a tab and margin are in the same location, a brace { is shown.

Usually when changing pitch or font, you will also change the margins and tabs. Consider placing all changes in a macro to eliminate extra keystrokes.

Related Entries

Aligning Text

Hyphenation

Margins

Spacing

Tabs, Clear and Set

Line Numbering

The Line Numbering feature is used to number the lines of a document upon printing. The line numbers are not visible on the screen, unless you use the Preview feature.

Keystrokes

1. Move the cursor to the point in the document where line numbering is to begin.

2. Press Print Format (CTRL-F8).

3. Type **B** for Line Numbering. The Line Numbering menu appears, as shown in Figure 4-58.

4. Type **2** to turn on Line Numbering.

5. Select other options if applicable.

6. Press ENTER twice to leave the Line Numbering and Print Format menus.

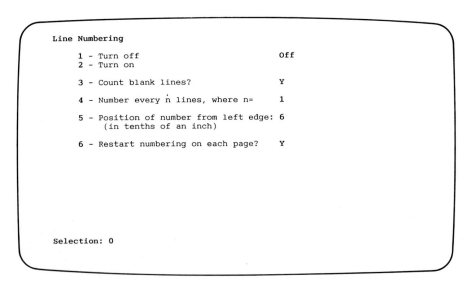

Figure 4-58.   Line Numbering menu

Hints

Line Numbering will number the lines in footnotes, but will not number headers or footers.

Options

Turn Off/On   You can turn Line Numbering on and off at any location in a document. Line numbering begins with number 1 regardless of the location of the code on the page. If you turn it off, then turn it back on later in the document, the numbering will start over with 1.

Count Blank Lines   The default is set to count blank lines. If you want to count the exact number of lines actually typed, choose **N** for this option. For a macro that will do the counting, see Appendix C.

Number Every n Lines   Every line will be numbered unless you change this option. To number every other line, enter **2**. Any number can be entered.

Position of Number   This option decides how far from the left edge of the page (not the left margin) the line number will be printed. The default setting is at 6/10 inch. This measurement is in inches and does not depend on the current pitch setting.

Restart Numbering on Each Page   Leave the option at Y to restart numbering on each page. Changing this option to N would put successive numbers through the document.

Preview Line Numbering

Line numbering occurs at the printer, not on the screen. You can use the Preview feature, however, to see a copy of the document (or page) as it will appear when printed. Press Print (SHIFT-F7), type **6** for Preview, then **1** for Document or **2** for Page. Remember that it takes longer to preview the document. If you choose to preview a page, be aware that the Preview feature requires progressively more time to call up pages that are farther toward the end of the document. If you choose to preview the last page, for example, it takes just as long as it would if you opted to preview the entire document.

Single or Double Space Limitation

Line numbering does not have a spacing option. Therefore, it works together with the spacing that is set in the document. For example, if you want every other line numbered and have both single and double spacing in the document, every other single-spaced line is numbered and every double-spaced line is numbered.

The line numbers cannot be printed *either* single spaced or double spaced if the document itself is not consistent in its spacing. For example, if you have created a legal pleading paper with single spacing for the heading information (Attorney, Plaintiff, Case number, and so on) and double spacing for the text below, numbering cannot be double-spaced down the left side of the page.

A way of getting around this limitation is to print the line numbers (and line drawing if desired) first, then print the document on the same piece of paper. The form then only needs to be created and saved once, and it avoids the use of preprinted forms that have an obvious mismatch of typeface style with that of the document. Use the following steps to create a form such as the one shown in Figure 4-59 that can be used to print pleading papers.

1. On a clear screen, press Page Format (ALT-F8).

2. Type **4** for Page Length and **3** for Other.

3. Press ENTER once to leave the form length at 66.

4. Enter **56** as the number of text lines. Press ENTER again to leave the Page Format menu.

5. Press Print Format (CTRL-F8) and type **B** for Line Numbering.

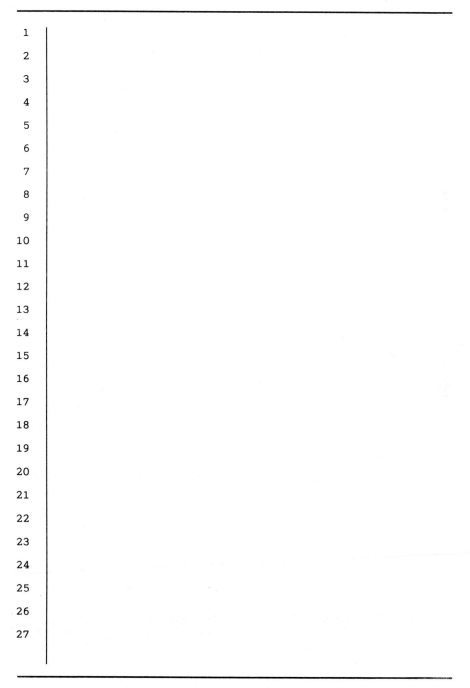

Figure 4-59.   Printout of line numbers and vertical line drawn on the left edge of numbered sheet form

6. Type **2** to turn on Line Numbering and press ENTER twice to return to the document.

7. Press Line Format (SHIFT-F8) and type **4** for Spacing.

8. Enter **2** for double spacing.

9. Press ENTER until you reach the end of the page (27 times). If you go past the page break, press BACKSPACE to delete the page break.

Print the page if you just want the line numbering. If you want the line drawn down the left margin and you have a printer that will advance backward to a previous line (this includes laser printers), continue with the following steps.

10. Press Print Format (CTRL-F8), type **B** for Line Numbering, then **1** to turn off Line Numbering. Press ENTER twice to return to the document.

11. Press Superscript/Subscript (SHIFT-F1), type **6** for Advance Line, and enter **1** to return to line 1.

12. Press Line Format (SHIFT-F8) and type **3** for Margins. If printing the pleading paper in 10 pitch with margins at 10 and 74, enter **9** and **74**. In 12 pitch, try **11** and **90** for 1-inch margins. Adjust if necessary.

13. Press Line Format (SHIFT-F8) and type **4** for Spacing. Enter **1** for single spacing.

14. Press Screen (CTRL-F3) and type **2** for Line Draw.

15. Select **1** or **2**, depending on the type of line desired.

16. Press ↓ to draw the line to the end of the page. Save this form (PLEADING.FRM is a suggested filename). You can print several copies at once, and then print the regular document on the form.

"Count Lines with Line Numbering"

Those who do production typing often charge per line. The Line Numbering feature can be used to help count the lines in a document. Remember that headers and footers are not included, but the lines in footnotes are. If you will use this feature often, consider putting the steps in a macro. The following procedure will set up such a macro.

1. To define a macro, press Macro Def (CTRL-F10) and enter the name of the macro (LINCOUNT is a suggestion). When finished with the keystrokes below, press Macro Def to end the macro definition.

2. Press HOME,HOME,↑ to move to the beginning of the document.

3. Press Print Format (CTRL-F8) and type **B** for Line Numbering.

4. Type **2** to turn on Line Numbering.

5. Type **3** and answer **N** to not "Count blank lines."

6. Type **6** and answer **N** to not "Restart numbering on each page."

7. Press HOME,HOME,↓ to go to the end of the document.

8. Press Print (SHIFT-F7), type **6** to Preview, then **2** to Preview the Page. If it is a long document, it will take quite some time. When you do a Preview, it actually prints the entire page to disk, then displays the page. When you are previewing the last page, the program must first go through the entire document to format the last page properly.

9. Press CTRL-PGUP and then ENTER twice to create a pause. You can then press ↓ until you reach the last line on the page. The number assigned to the last line is the total number of lines typed.

10. Press Exit (F7) to return to the document.

11. Press HOME,HOME,↑ to go to the top of the document and delete the line numbering code.

12. Press Macro Def (CTRL-F10) again to end the macro definition.

Related Entries

Paragraph Numbering

Word Count

Lines per Inch

Currently, WordPerfect allows eight or six lines per vertical inch.

Keystrokes

1. Press Print Format (CTRL-F8).

2. Type **2** for Lines per Inch.

3. Enter **6** or **8** as the number of lines per inch. (The default is six lines per inch.)

4. Press ENTER to leave the Print Format menu.

If you choose eight lines per inch and want to fill an entire 8 1/2″ × 11″ page, you should also change the number of lines which can be printed on the page.

1. Press Page Format (ALT-F8).

2. Type **4** for Page Length.

3. Type **3** for Other.

4. Press ENTER to accept 66 as the Form Length (note that this is always figured in six lines per inch, not eight).

5. Enter **72** as the number of text lines. (For an 11 inch page with 2 inches total for top and bottom margins, 9 inches $\times$ 8 lines per inch = 72 lines.) If printing on legal-sized paper, enter **96**.

6. Press ENTER to leave the Page Format menu.

Hints

It is mentioned in the WordPerfect manual that combining eight and six lines per inch on a page may create problems when feeding the next page into the printer. This applies only to continuous forms. You may want to place a <12> (form feed) as the code to "Reset Printer at End of Page" in the Printer Initialization screen. Also check to see that the top of form and form length switches at the printer are set correctly. See Chapter 7 for more information on the Printer program.

Printing eight lines per inch will enable you to squeeze more lines on a page. It can also be used alone or with half-line spacing to create more solid vertical lines on some printers. See *Line Draw* for more information.

Related Entries

Line Draw

Page Length

List Files

List Files (F5) helps organize and manage your files.

Keystrokes

1. Press List Files (F5).

2. The name of the current default directory is displayed. You have several options.

Press ENTER to see the files in that directory.

Enter a different drive/directory. Be sure to precede the name of a directory with a backslash (\ ). This option only looks into a directory; it does not change the default directory.

Type the name of a single file or use the wildcard characters * and ? to display a group of files. For example, if you want to display a file named SMITH.LTR, enter that as the file to be displayed. If you want to list all the files ending with .NOV, enter *.**NOV**.

Type = and enter the name of a different drive/directory. This option changes the default directory.

3. Select an option from the menu.

4. Press Exit (F7), Cancel (F1), or SPACEBAR to leave the List Files menu. ENTER will not return to the document as it normally does. Instead, it is set as the default to Look at a file.

Hints

The List Files menu displays general information such as the current date and time, the full pathname of the directory and files being displayed, the size of the current document in memory, and the amount of space available on the disk.

The last two items are especially helpful if you are wondering whether you have enough room on the disk to save the current document.

The full pathname of the current directory at the top of the menu tells you the name of the drive, directory, and group of files that are displayed. "*.*" indicates that all files in the directory are being shown. If you entered *.LTR after pressing List Files (F5), you would see the default drive and directory with all the .LTR files.

Directory Organization

If you are using a hard disk, List Files can be especially helpful in organizing directories. You can also print the listing of a directory by pressing Print (SHIFT-F7) while in the List Files menu.

As explained in Chapter 1, the root directory is indicated by a single backslash. If you have directories created under the root directory, they are listed by name on the menu with <DIR> added to indicate a directory. If you divide one of these directories, it would be considered a parent directory and would list its own directories on the List Files menu.

You can move the cursor to the PARENT <DIR> and press ENTER twice to move up to that directory. You can then move the cursor to any <DIR> and press ENTER twice to move down into that directory. (If you use option 7 after highlighting a <DIR>, instead of just pressing ENTER, the default directory will be changed.) See *Directories, Change Directory,* and *Create a Directory* for complete information.

File Information

Each file in the List Files menu is listed alphabetically from left to right. To the right of each filename is the number of bytes in the file. Each character is equal to one byte (with the exception of special characters, which are three bytes); WordPerfect function codes vary in the amount of bytes used. Also displayed with each filename is the date and time it was last edited.

Searching for a File

Use any cursor movement key to move the cursor to a filename listed in the menu. To quickly scroll through the files, press −, +, HOME,↑ or HOME,↓, HOME,HOME,↑ or HOME,HOME,↓, PGUP or PGDN.

If you know the first letter of a filename, type the letter and the cursor will move to the listed files beginning with that letter. Continue typing to narrow the selection. To reset the Name Search, press SPACEBAR, ENTER, or any arrow key and the List Files menu will reappear.

If you delete characters from the Name Search string, the cursor will jump to the appropriate location.

Mark Files

If you want to Delete, Print, Copy, or do a Word Search on selected files, press * to mark each file. If you mark a file by mistake, press * again to unmark the file.

To mark all the files in a directory, press Mark Text (ALT-F5) or HOME,*. Pressing those same keys again will unmark the files. Files are also unmarked when you exit the List Files menu.

If there are files that have been marked and you type **2** to Delete, 4 to Print, or 8 to Copy, you are asked if you want to delete, print, or copy the marked files.

Options

Nine options are listed on the List Files menu. A short description of each follows.

Retrieve   Option 1 lets you retrieve the highlighted file to the screen. Before retrieving a file, take note of the current document size (shown at the top left of the List Files menu). If a number other than 0 is displayed, there is another document in memory. Be aware that if you retrieve a file, it will be inserted into the other document at the cursor's location. If you do not want this to happen, exit the List Files menu and clear the screen before retrieving the other file.

Delete   If you choose option 2, you are asked to confirm the deletion of the file. Type **N** to leave the file or **Y** to delete it. If you delete it, you can restore it with the aid of a program such as Norton's Utilities.

Remember that you can mark more than one file with an * for deletion. If you select option 2, and files have been marked, you are first asked if you want to delete all the marked files. Typing **Y** will delete them all. If you type **N**, you are asked to confirm the deletion of the file currently highlighted.

Rename   Option 3 lets you rename the highlighted file. If you enter a name that already exists in that directory, you will see the message "ERROR: Can't rename file." If this happens, choose another filename.

Print   If you type 4 to print a file, it is immediately sent to the queue. If you are editing the same file on the screen and want to print the most recent copy, print from the screen or save the document to disk first. You cannot print selected pages of a document from List Files. Instead, use the Printer Control menu to print selected pages.

You can mark more than one file for printing. If marked files are found, you are asked if you want to print all the marked files. If you type **Y**, they are all queued. If you type **N**, the highlighted document is immediately sent to the printer. No confirmation is necessary.

Text In   Option 5 is used to retrieve a DOS text (ASCII) file. It is exactly the same as option 2 on the Text In/Out menu.

Look   Choose option **6** (or press ENTER) to look at the contents of a file or look into another directory.

If you look into a document which contains a document summary, it is also displayed in the Look screen. Press ↓, Screen Down (+), or PGDN to scroll through the file. Any other key will return you to the List Files menu.

You can look into a directory without changing the default directory using this option. Position the cursor on a directory name (labeled with <DIR>), and type **6** or press ENTER. The full pathname of the directory is displayed and can be edited. Press ENTER to go into that directory.

This option is set as the default. In other words, if you press ENTER, the highlighted file is displayed. The Look feature is useful when cleaning up your disk if you are not sure of the contents of a file.

Change Directory   Choosing option 7 lets you change the default drive within the List Files menu. As mentioned before, you can change the default drive without entering the List Files menu; press List Files (F5), type =, then enter the name for the default drive.

This option is also used to create new directories. If you enter the name of a nonexistent directory, you are asked if you want to create the new directory.

Copy   If you choose option 8, you are prompted with "Copy This File To:". Enter the drive, directory, and a different filename if desired. If the filename exists on the other drive/directory, you are asked to confirm the replacement of the existing file.

If you want to copy more than one file, mark all applicable files with an asterisk and type 8. You are asked if you want to copy all the marked files. If you type **Y**, enter the destination for the files. If you type **N**, you can copy the highlighted file.

You can also create a directory with this option. If you enter the name of a nonexistent directory as the destination for a file, you are asked if you want to create the new directory.

Word Search   If you are having trouble locating a specific file, option 9 lets you search the files in the directory for a specific phrase or word pattern. You can narrow the search further by marking specific files to be searched.

You can enter a maximum of 20 characters in the Word Search string. Any of the following can be combined, but be aware that the more conditions you include, the longer it will take to search the files.

Use * as a wildcard character to match any number of characters (until a [HRt] is encountered).

Use ? as a wildcard character to match a single character.

Use " " around any text that includes a comma, space, semicolon, or single quotation mark.

Use ; or a space to indicate an *and* situation. For example, if you entered JOHN BROWN, all files containing both John and Brown are displayed.

Use , to indicate an *or* situation. If you entered JOHN,BROWN all files containing John or Brown are displayed.

Related Entries

Change Directory

Copy Files

Create a Directory

Delete a Directory

Delete a File

Directories

Document Size

Look at a File

Print

Rename a File

Retrieve

Word Search

Lists

Up to five lists for illustrations, figures, tables, and charts can be generated for each document.

Keystrokes

There are three basic steps to creating a List. First, mark the text to be referenced in the list. Then define the type of page number style in the list and location of the list. Finally, generate the list.

Mark the Text for the List

1. Move the cursor to the text to be referenced and press Block (ALT-F4). Remember that any code included in the block (such as bold, underlining, or centering) will also appear in the list when it is generated.

2. Move the cursor to the opposite end of the text to be referenced.

3. Press Mark Text (ALT-F5).

4. Type **2** for List.

5. Type the number of the appropriate list. Remember that you can have up to five lists and you decide which entries go into each list.

The code [Mark:List,1] is inserted at the beginning of the block and [EndMark:List,1] is inserted at the end. These codes are visible when Reveal Codes (ALT-F3) is pressed. The number included in the code could be any number 1 through 5 and indicates the list in which the entry is to be included.

Define the Page Numbering and Location

A list can appear anywhere in the document. Usually, however, it is included at the beginning of the document just after the Table of Contents. If you want it to appear at the beginning of the document, it is important to include a New Page Number code at the beginning of the regular text, following the Table of Contents and lists definitions. Otherwise, a reference on page 1 might appear on page 3 because the Table of Contents and List are occupying pages 1 and 2.

1. Move to the location where the list is to appear.

2. If you want a heading for the list, enter the heading.

3. Press Mark Text (ALT-F5).

4. Type **6** for Other Options.

5. Type **3** to Define List.

6. Enter the number of the list being defined. When the list is generated, all references with corresponding marks will appear in that list.

7. Select the page number listing option from the List Definition menu.

```
List 1 Definition

   1 - No Page Numbers
   2 - Page Numbers Follow Entries
   3 - (Page Numbers) Follow Entries
   4 - Flush Right Page Numbers
   5 - Flush Right Page Numbers with Leaders
```

8. If you want the list to be generated on a separate page, insert a Hard Page (CTRL-ENTER).

9. Move the cursor to the first regular text page of the document. Press Page Format (ALT-F8), type **2** for New Page Number, and enter **1**. Type **1** for Arabic.

The code [DefMark:List,1] appears in Reveal Codes at the cursor's location. The number indicates the list number.

To number the pages of the lists (and other introductory pages) with roman numerals, go to the beginning of the document and repeat step 9 except for the last option. Type **2** for Roman instead of **1** for Arabic.

Generate the List(s)

A Table of Contents, the Tables of Authorities, lists, and index are all generated at once.

1. From anywhere in the document, press Mark Text (ALT-F5).

2. Type **6** for Other Options.

3. Type **8** to Generate Tables (Lists) and Index. The following message is displayed.

```
Existing tables, lists, and indexes will be replaced.  Continue? (Y/N): Y
```

4. This message is a warning that other tables, lists, and index previously generated will be replaced. Type **Y** to continue or **N** to cancel the procedure.

A counter is displayed on the status line to let you know the progress. A sample of a finished list with option 5 (Flush Right Page Numbers with Leaders) is shown in Figure 4-60.

```
                              ARTICLES

        Article I. . . . . . . . . . . . . . . . . . . 1

        Article II . . . . . . . . . . . . . . . . . . 5

        Article III. . . . . . . . . . . . . . . . . . 7

        Article IV . . . . . . . . . . . . . . . . . . 8

        Article V. . . . . . . . . . . . . . . . . . . 8

        Article VI . . . . . . . . . . . . . . . . . . 9
```

Figure 4-60.   List with dot leaders

Hints

If you want to delete a mark, press Reveal Codes (ALT-F3), move to the [Mark:List,1] or [EndMark:List,1] code and delete either one. If you make changes to marks or text included in a marked entry, you should generate the list again.

Entries are entered into the list in the order that they appear in the document. This is similar to the Table of Contents feature.

If you have more than one list, you do not have to define the lists in any particular order. The numbers 1 through 5 are used only to group entries into the various lists.

You can redefine the page number listing style after a list has been generated. Choose the new option and generate the list again.

If you choose option 1 or 2 as the page number listing style, the number is placed two spaces after the entry, with or without parentheses, depending on the option selected. Options 4 and 5 place the number flush against the right margin. The dot leader included with option 5 will adjust automatically if text is added or deleted from the list after it is generated.

Related Entries

Index

Mark Text

Table of Authorities

Table of Contents

Load a Document

See *Retrieve*

Lock and Unlock Documents

Sensitive documents can be protected, or *locked*, with a password. If you transfer files electronically, you can lock them before sending them. The person receiving the file can then retrieve the file using the same password. Even if a file is intercepted by an unauthorized person, it cannot be unlocked without the password.

Keystrokes

Lock a Document

1. With the document on the screen, press Text In/Out (CTRL-F5).

2. Type **4** to save the document as a locked document.

3. Enter the password. Up to 75 characters (including spaces) can be used.

4. Reenter the password. This precaution guards against mistakes. If the two passwords do not match, the error message "Incorrect password" is displayed. You are then allowed to try again. Be aware, though, that if you enter the password incorrectly both times (if your hands are not positioned correctly), you will lock the file under an unknown password.

5. Name the document. If a file with that name already exists, you are asked to confirm the replacement of the original file. Type **Y** or **N**. If you type **N**, you are given the opportunity to enter another name.

6. You are returned to the document on your screen. If you ask to save the document again when clearing the screen, you must enter the password again.

Retrieve a Locked File

There are three options for retrieving a locked file. The first two are the recommended methods because they will retrieve both locked and unlocked documents. The only difference is that you must enter the password for a locked document.

Press Retrieve (SHIFT-F10), enter the name of the file, and enter the password when prompted.

Press List Files (F5), then ENTER to see a list of files. Move the cursor to the filename to be retrieved. Type **1** to retrieve the highlighted file. Enter the password when prompted.

Press Text In/Out (CTRL-F5), type **5** to retrieve the file, and enter the password.

Unlock a Document

If you want to unlock a document (not just retrieve it), use the following steps.

1. With the locked file on the screen, press Save (F10).

2. Press ENTER to use the same filename or enter a different filename. If you use the same name, type **Y** or **N** to replace the previous file.

3. When prompted for the password, press ENTER instead of entering the password.

Hints

A file remains locked until it is unlocked. Retrieving a file does not unlock it. After editing a locked document and pressing Save (F10) or Exit (F7), you are again asked to enter the password twice. Remember that if you decide to unlock the file, press ENTER when asked for the password.

A locked file is actually encrypted. If you try to retrieve the file with any other editor, or try to TYPE the file from DOS, you will see only a jumble of special characters and control characters.

Passwords

If you use a different password from document to document, you could easily forget the password and lose the document. Instead, consider using the same password for all your locked files.

The longer the password, the harder it is to "break." It is even harder when you put spaces in unexpected places. If you forget the password, the document is lost. Even the programmers at WordPerfect Corporation cannot retrieve the file.

If you enter an incorrect password, you will see the error message "File is locked."

Look at or Print a Locked Document

If you want to look at a file in the List Files menu, you are required to enter the password.

To print a locked document, you must retrieve it to the screen first, then print from the screen. If you accidentally send a locked document from the disk to the printer, it will remain in the queue, but will not be printed. The error message "File is locked" is displayed in the message section and you are asked to send the printer a "Go." Pressing "Go" will not print the document but will attempt to reset the printer. You will have to cancel the print job to clear it from the queue.

Related Entries

Retrieve

Save

Look at a File

When maintaining your files (deleting, copying, and so on), you can quickly check the contents of a file without retrieving it with the Look option in List files. You can also use the Look feature to look at the list of files in other directories without changing the default directory.

Keystrokes

Look at a File

1. Press List Files (F5).

2. Press ENTER to enter the displayed drive/directory or enter a different directory.

3. Move the cursor to any filename.

4. Type **6** or press ENTER to look at the file. The screen would appear as shown in Figure 4-61.

```
Filename C:\CONST\DRAFT                          File Size:     30194

   ┌──────────────────────────────────────────────────────────────┐
   │ September 10, 1787                                              │
   │ American Statesmen                                             │
   │                                                               │
   │ To be signed on September 17, 1787.                           │
   └──────────────────────────────────────────────────────────────┘
               THE CONSTITUTION OF THE UNITED STATES

                          PREAMBLE

       We the people of the United States, in Order to form a more
   perfect Union, establish Justice, insure domestic Tranquility,
   provide for the common Defense, promote the general Welfare, and
   secure the Blessings of Liberty to ourselves and our Posterity,
   do ordain and establish this Constitution for the United States
   of America.

   ARTICLE I.
       Section 1.  All legislative Powers herein granted shall be
   vested in a Congress of the United States, which shall consist of
   a Senate and House of Representatives.
   NOTE: This text is not displayed in WordPerfect format.
   Press any key to continue
```

Figure 4-61.   The screen after choosing to look at a file

5. Use ↓, Screen Down (+), or PGDN to scroll through the text.

6. Press any other key to return to the List Files menu.

Look Into a Directory

If you press List Files and enter the name of a different drive/directory, you can look at the files without changing the default drive. You can also use the Look feature within the List Files menu to look at the files in a directory.

1. Move to any directory name in List Files. (Each directory is labeled with <DIR>.)

2. Type **6** or press ENTER to look into the directory.

3. The name of the highlighted directory is displayed, allowing you to edit the pathname if desired. For example, you could press HOME, →, BACKSPACE, then type NOV to look at the files ending with the .NOV extension in that directory.

4. Press ENTER again to look at the files.

Hints

When looking at a file, the full pathname of the file/directory/filename is displayed along with the size of the file in bytes. Pressing ↓ moves down one line at a time. Both Screen Down (+) and PGDN move down through the file one screen at a time. When moving one screen at a time, one line from the previous screen overlaps so you will not easily lose your place in the document. You cannot scroll up. If you try, you will be returned to the List Files menu.

If a file contains a document summary, it is displayed at the beginning of the file during a Look.

The note at the bottom of Figure 4-61 that says, "This text is not displayed in WordPerfect format" means that any WordPerfect commands will not be displayed. For example, if the document is formatted into columns, it will not be formatted in columns in the Look screen.

You can better understand the structure of your hard disk by wandering through the directories with the Look feature. For example, in List Files if you place the cursor on the <PARENT><DIR> and press ENTER once, the name of the parent directory is displayed. Pressing ENTER again lists the files in that directory.

Any subdirectories are also listed in the List Files menu. You can move down through the levels as well by using Look.

Related Entries

Change Directory

Default Directory

Directories

Retrieve

Lotus 1-2-3

See *DIF* and Chapter 8, "Software Integration"

Lowercase Text

See *Switch*

Macros

Macros are used to record a series of keystrokes, thus eliminating the time and repeated keystrokes necessary to perform a certain function more than once.

If you have never worked with macros before, read the first part of Chapter 3. It provides a good basic introduction to macros, how they are named, and their usefulness. The discussion here includes exact keystrokes, options, and hints.

Keystrokes

There are two types of macros: those saved to disk with a .MAC extension and those saved in memory until the computer is turned off.

Define a Macro

1. Press Macro Def (CTRL-F10). "Define Macro:" appears on the screen.

2. Name the macro, using one of the following methods.

Press ALT and a letter A-Z for an ALT-key combination macro. This type is saved to disk with a .MAC extension (for example, ALTA.MAC).

Enter two to eight characters. This type is also saved to disk with a .MAC extension.

Enter a single character or press ENTER to create a temporary macro that is kept in memory only until the computer is turned off. If you press ENTER , WordPerfect saves it as an "unnamed" macro. SPACEBAR can also be used instead of ENTER. Use one or the other, because both are saved as the same unnamed macro.

3. "Macro Def" flashes on the screen. Enter the keystrokes to be recorded. Don't worry about making mistakes; the corrections are also recorded.

4. Press Macro Def (CTRL-F10) in order to end the macro definition.

Invoke a Macro

If you defined an ALT-key macro, press the ALT-key combination (hold down the ALT key and press the letter) to start the macro.

Use the following steps to start a named macro (either temporary or one saved to disk).

1. Press Macro (ALT-F10).

2. Enter the name of the macro. If you named the macro with ENTER or SPACEBAR , press either as the name for the unnamed macro.

Options

The additional macro features discussed here often have little meaning until you actually have an application in mind. Several macros are listed in Appendix C that should help you better understand how these options can be applied.

Pausing a Macro

During the definition process, you can insert a pause so that during the operation of a macro, it will pause for you to provide variable information. For example, instead of defining eight separate macros that each change to a different font, you could have one macro that pauses in the Print Format menu for you to manually specify the font. After typing the number for the desired font and pressing ENTER , the macro would continue.

You could create a memorandum macro that pauses for you to insert the variable heading information (TO:, FROM:, SUBJECT:, and so on). When you run the macro, it will allow you to enter any amount of text as long as you don't press ENTER. For example, the SUBJECT: entry could be several lines long. You can press any key (except ENTER) to insert, delete, and correct the text. When finished, press ENTER and the macro will continue.

1. During the macro definition, press CTRL-PGUP to start the macro pause.

2. Press ENTER twice. If you must enter information during this step, do so between the two presses of ENTER. You would normally insert the variable information only when the macro is actually run.

3. Continue with the remaining keystrokes and end the macro definition.

As mentioned in step 2, you will sometimes have to enter information while defining a pause in a macro. For example, if you pause at a prompt (such as Search, Save, or Retrieve), you usually have to enter some type of information or you will get an error message and you might not be able to continue the macro. If this happens, press (CTRL-PGUP), then press ENTER, type the information, and press ENTER again. The information entered will be ignored when the macro is run because it was typed between the two ENTER keystrokes. Do not type numbers between the two ENTER keystrokes or you will cause the macro to delay that many tenths of a second. If a menu calls for a number, enter a letter instead.

When you run a macro that contains a pause, the computer will beep when it reaches the pause, alerting you to the fact that it has paused. As soon as ENTER is pressed, the macro will continue. If you are selecting a menu option during a pause, remember that you still have to press ENTER to make the macro continue.

A macro is usually "invisible" when it is run, meaning that menus and prompts are not displayed on the screen. However, when you pause a macro, it becomes visible so that the necessary menu or prompt is displayed. If you decide to make the macro invisible again after the pause, it will remain so even if you insert a second pause. Therefore, either leave the macro visible so you can see future menus and prompts, or be sure to make the macro visible again just *before* the next pause. If you need to make it visible again, do so on the regular WordPerfect editing screen before entering the menu. "Invisible, Visible, and Delayed Macros" outlines the steps for making a macro visible or invisible.

Invisible, Visible, and Delayed Macros

To make a macro invisible after a pause, to make it visible before a pause, or to delay a macro in increments of tenths of a second, use the following steps.

1. From the regular WordPerfect editing screen, press CTRL-PGUP.

2. Enter any number from 0 to 255 (the number is not displayed on the screen). The values 0-255 have the following meanings.

0   Full speed, visible

1   Delay 1/10 second

2   Delay 2/10 second

.

.

.

254   Delay 254/10 seconds (25.4 sec.)

255   Full speed, invisible

3. Continue with the remaining keystrokes and end the macro definition.

Remember that if a macro is not pausing in a menu or at a prompt as it should, you need to insert a step making the macro visible *before* the pause.

If you have a printer that uses hand-fed paper and you only want to print a single page, you could write a macro that sends that page to the printer, delays 5 seconds so it has a chance to be placed in the queue, then sends the printer a "Go." The delay value might have to be adjusted for your situation. The paper should be fed into the printer before executing this macro. See Appendix C for the exact steps.

Chaining and Repeating Macros

If you want a macro to repeat a specific number of times, press ESC, type the desired number (do not press ENTER after the number), then start the macro. It will execute that many times or until a search condition is no longer found.

You can also chain (link) a macro to itself to create a repeating macro. If the macro contains a Search and the search condition is not found, the macro automatically stops. If the macro does not include a Search, the macro will continue until you press Cancel (F1). A macro does not stop at the end of a Replace, so you can include as many Replaces as you want in a macro.

1. Press Macro Def (CTRL-F10) and name the macro.

2. During the definition process, press Macro (ALT-F10) and enter the name of the macro to be chained. If it is an ALT-key macro, press the ALT-key combination.

3. Continue with the remaining keystrokes and end the macro.

You can use the same steps to chain different macros together. In fact, you can ask to start macros that haven't been defined yet. Of course, they must be defined before the macro can be run successfully.

When you press Macro (ALT-F10) during macro definition and enter the name of another macro, only the keystrokes are stored. The macro is not started during the definition procedure.

If you want to chain several macros together, it is best to store the keystrokes that start one macro while defining another. In other words:

>   Macro A calls Macro B
>
>   Macro B calls Macro C
>
>   Macro C calls Macro D, and so on.

Continue until all are chained with only one being started in each macro. If you start several macros during the definition of a macro, it could become a conditional macro.

   A chained macro does not begin until the first macro is completely finished. Even if you put the chained macro first in the sequence of steps, it is placed in a buffer and will be started after the first macro finishes. Therefore, unless you are creating a conditional macro, it is not important where the second macro appears in the first macro.

Conditional Macro

A conditional macro can execute one of two macros, depending on whether or not a search condition exists. If the search is successful, a specific macro is started. If the condition does not exist, a different macro is started.

   1. Start the macro definition.

   2. Press Macro (ALT-F10) and enter the name of the macro that should be started if the condition *is not* found. The following text discusses why this step must be placed before the search.

   3. Search for the condition.

   4. Press Macro (CTRL-F10) and enter the name of the macro that should be started if the condition *is* found.

   5. End the macro definition.

   Remember that a macro does not start a chained macro until it is finished. For example, if you start one macro and it finds another macro in the sequence of steps, it stores it in a buffer until it is finished. When the first macro is finished, the second macro is started.

Therefore, when you define the conditional macro, you should always put the "not found" macro before the Search. When the original macro is run and it finds the "not found" macro, it stores it and continues with the first macro.

If the condition is found, the macro found at the end of the macro is started and given control. The "not found" macro stored in the buffer is never executed because control was passed to the "found" macro.

However, if the condition is not found, the macro is ended before it reaches the "found" macro. (A macro automatically ends if a search condition is not found.) Because the macro is finished, it looks in the buffer, finds the "not found" macro, and starts it. Figure 4-62 shows how a conditional macro and a repeating conditional macro are organized and run.

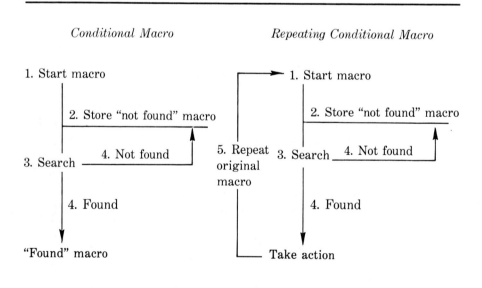

Figure 4-62. Organization of a conditional macro and a repeating conditional macro

Repeating Conditional Macro

The conditional macro is based on a single decision. If you want to continue a macro until all occurrences are found and the condition is acted upon (usually the steps in a "found" macro), you should define a repeating conditional macro. Instead of doing a Search, then passing control to a "found" macro, place both steps (the Search and "found" macro) into a macro that is chained to itself. The "not found" macro would still be inserted just before the Search. Thus, you only have two macros involved instead of three.

1. Start the macro definition.

2. Press Macro (ALT-F10) and enter the name of the macro that is to be started if the condition is not found.

3. Search for the condition.

4. Enter the keystrokes that are to be run if the condition is found.

5. Press Macro (ALT-F10) and enter the name of this macro (name entered in step 2) to chain it to itself.

6. End the macro definition.

Hints

If you are defining a macro that is to do certain things under certain conditions, you need to define the macro when those conditions exist. For example, you cannot create a "transpose word" macro unless you have at least two words on the screen. You cannot define a macro that searches for a [Bold] code if there is no bolded text in the current document.

As mentioned previously, an unsuccessful Search will end a macro, but an unsuccessful Replace will not.

If you start a merge in a macro, the macro is automatically ended. You do not have to press Macro Def (CTRL-F10) to end the definition.

You can end the macro definition while in a WordPerfect menu or prompt by pressing Macro Def (CTRL-F10) while there.

Saving Macros on Disk

When you define a macro, it is automatically saved to the default drive/directory unless a different path is specified. If you want to define an ALT-key macro and have it saved elsewhere, type the full pathname, type **ALT**, then the letter of the macro. For example, if you want to save an ALT-F macro to the drive/directory where WordPerfect is kept, enter **C:\WP\ALTF** if WP.EXE is kept in a directory named "WP."

When you start a macro, either with an ALT-key combination or Macro (ALT-F10), and the drive/directory is not specified, the following places are searched in the order listed.

1. RAM memory

2. Default drive/directory

3. Drive/directory where WP.EXE is kept

4. Where the temporary overflow files are kept (if they were redirected to a different drive/directory with the /D option)

If you want all macros saved in one directory, you can either store them where the WP.EXE file is kept or save them in a separate directory just for macros. If you store the macro files with WP.EXE, WordPerfect will find them automatically. If you want to store them in a macro directory by themselves, you should use the /D option and redirect the overflow files to that directory (named MACRO, as a suggestion) so WordPerfect will eventually find them. To use the /D option, enter **WP/D-C:\MACRO** to start WordPerfect instead of **WP**.

All macros (except the temporary macros that are kept in memory) are saved to disk with an extension .MAC. WordPerfect does not allow you to retrieve a .MAC file. Therefore, you should not use the .MAC extension for regular WordPerfect files, because you will not be able to retrieve them. If this happens, enter the List Files menu and rename the affected file, deleting the .MAC extension.

Starting Macros

When a macro is run for the first time, it is loaded into memory. The next time it is needed, it is immediately available without having to access the disk.

Therefore, if you use an ALT-F macro that sets up a letter format in a directory named LETTERS, then change the default directory to LEGAL and try to use an ALT-F macro from that directory that contains the format for pleading papers, the original ALT-F macro used for LETTERS will be started because it was found in memory.

To start the pleading paper macro, you would need to press Macro (ALT-F10) and enter C:\LEGAL\ALTF so that it would look in that directory first before searching RAM.

Editing Macros

You cannot edit a macro while in WordPerfect. You either have to redefine the macro from the beginning or use the Macro Editor included with WordPerfect Library.

The following illustration shows a macro in the Macro Editor that prints a single page, delays 5 seconds, then sends a "Go" to the printer.

```
<Delay 050><Print>2<Print>4g


MAC C:\WP\ALTG.MAC                              Mac 1   Ln 1      Pos 1
```

All function keys are shown in bold with < and > around them, while regular keystrokes are shown normally.

The Macro Editor lets you add, delete, and move sections of a macro. For example, if you decided to change the macro above so it would send the entire document (rather than just one page) to the printer, you would change the 2 to 1.

While in the Macro Editor, you can change to the Word-Perfect keyboard so that WordPerfect keystrokes can be recorded and inserted into the macro. For example, if you toggle to the WordPerfect keyboard and press F6, a <Bold> keystroke is inserted. If you press BACKSPACE, a <Back-space> keystroke is entered. To delete codes, switch back to the Macro Editor keyboard and use DEL and BACKSPACE. The Macro Editor also has Block (ALT-F4) and Move (CTRL-F4) that can be used to move sections of a macro.

If you want Exit (F7) to be placed at the end of a macro, it must be inserted with the Macro Editor.

Some keys are not recorded when you define a macro. For example, pressing CAPS LOCK is not recorded. SHIFT, ALT, and CTRL when pressed alone are also in this category, but functions and keystrokes used with SHIFT, ALT, and CTRL are recorded.

Applications

Macros are extremely powerful. If WordPerfect does not have a function to do a specific task (such as transpose characters or words), you can write a macro. If you change the pitch/ font in WordPerfect, it is often necessary to change the margins and tabs, too. You could write a macro that changes all the settings at once with a keystroke or two. A macro could set up the format for a letterhead, an envelope, or any other type of document. If you find yourself doing a specific chore again and again, consider defining a macro that will do it for you automatically.

For those who have difficulty remembering the key-strokes that perform a certain function, create a macro and give it a name which you can easily remember. For example, a macro called KEEP could use the Conditional End of Page feature to always keep a title with the first two lines of the following paragraph. The macro could be started when the cursor is on the title instead of placing the cursor above the title, counting the lines, pressing Page Format (ALT-F8), typing 9 for Conditional End of Page, entering the count, then pressing ENTER to return to the document.

All of the macros mentioned in this book can be found in Appendix C. Additional applications follow, including information on how to set up a Macro Library.

Macros to Replace Codes with Codes

While you can search for any WordPerfect code, you cannot always replace it with another code. For example, if you decided to change all [->Indent] codes to [->Indent<-] codes, you could not use Replace to search and replace for you. However, you could write a repeating macro to accomplish this task. Remember that you must have at least one occurrence of the code in the document before defining the macro.

1. Press Macro Def (CTRL-F10) and name the macro.

2. Press Search (F2).

3. Press the function key and select any necessary options to insert the code as the search string (in the example, you would press Indent (F4)).

4. Press BACKSPACE and type **Y** to confirm the deletion of the code (if necessary).

5. Press the appropriate function key to insert the replacement code into the document (press Indent (SHIFT-F4) for the example above).

6. Press Macro (ALT-F10) and enter the name of this macro to chain the macro to itself.

7. Press Macro Def (CTRL-F10) to end the macro.

When you start this macro, it will repeat until the search fails and it cannot find any more [->Indent] codes.

Unfortunately you cannot search for parameters within a code. For example, you can search for a [Font Change] code, but not a specific font change (such as italics).

Macros That Edit Documents

If you have a file that needs extensive editing because it was brought in from another program, you could use a macro because the editing changes are usually consistent from one line or record to the next. For example, if you imported text from a data base and a person's first and last name were in separate fields but you wanted them listed in the same field, you could write a macro to find the first name field, insert it before the second name, then remove the extra ^R[HRt].

You could use macros and Switch (SHIFT-F3) to help create a second document. For example, if you have a legal document that consists of standard paragraphs that could be used in a specific type of brief, you could define a macro (such as ALT-P for Paragraph) that copies the current paragraph, switches documents, retrieves the paragraph, goes to the bottom of the document with HOME,HOME,↓, then returns to the first document. While scrolling through the first document, you could press ALT-P (or another macro name) when you want a paragraph to be copied to document 2 and the steps would be done for you. After scrolling through the first document, switch documents and see the finished product.

If the macro is to be created for editing purposes, you might consider making it a temporary macro, as it might only be used under unique circumstances.

Creating a Macro Library with Merge

WordPerfect's Merge uses a ^G to start a macro after a merge is complete. The format for the command is

    ^Gmacroname^G

These codes can be placed anywhere in the document, but are started only when the merge is finished.

These merge codes can be used to create a Macro Library. Figure 4-63 shows a sample Macro Library where the name and description of each macro is listed.

```
                        MACRO LIBRARY

GO          Send printer a "Go."

LETTER      Format for a business letter.

ENV         Print an envelope from the current document.

LEGAL       Format for printing on legal sized paper with the HP+.

PLEADING    Format for a pleading paper.

NUMBER      Number pages in "Page n of n" format.


        *** Press (SHIFT-F9) to Cancel the Macro Library ***



Macro:
```

Figure 4-63.   Sample Macro Library

The following steps can be used to create your own Macro Library. It should look something like Figure 4-64 when finished.

1. On a clear screen, make a list of your macros and a description for each one. Limit the list to one screenful. Label the list "Macro Library" if you wish. You cannot use functions such as Center, Margin Set, or Indent in this list.

2. Press (HOME,HOME,↑) to go to the top of the screen.

3. Press Merge Codes and O to insert a ^O. If you don't have a special character mapped to CTRL-O, you can press this key combination instead.

4. Press (HOME,HOME,↓) to go to the bottom of the screen. Remember that the list should not be longer than one screen or it will scroll off the screen.

5. Type a message similar to:

    Press (SHIFT-F9) to Cancel the Macro Library.

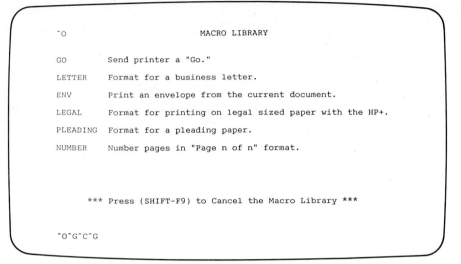

```
^O                        MACRO LIBRARY

GO          Send printer a "Go."
LETTER      Format for a business letter.
ENV         Print an envelope from the current document.
LEGAL       Format for printing on legal sized paper with the HP+.
PLEADING    Format for a pleading paper.
NUMBER      Number pages in "Page n of n" format.



        *** Press (SHIFT-F9) to Cancel the Macro Library ***


^O^G^C^G
```

Figure 4-64.   The screen after creating a Macro Library

6. Press Merge Codes (ALT-F9) and type an **O**. Continue with a **G**, **C**, and another **G**. You should see ^O^G^C^G on the screen. Do not press ENTER or any other key after entering these keystrokes.

7. Press Exit (F7) and save the file (LIBRARY is a suggested name). Do not exit WordPerfect.

The ^O codes output the message (the Macro Library) on the screen during a merge. The ^G codes are used to start a macro. The ^C between the ^Gs forces the merge to pause so that the name of a macro can be entered. When the name of a macro is entered (you could even enter one not displayed on the screen), the menu disappears and the macro is started.

The following steps help you display the Macro Library with a minimum of keystrokes. If you don't use these steps, you would have to start a merge each time you wanted to use the macro library.

1. Press Macro Def (CTRL-F10).

2. Name the macro (ALT-L for Library is a suggestion).

3. Press Merge/Sort (CTRL-F9).

4. Type **1** for Merge.

5. Enter **LIBRARY** as the name of the primary file. (If you used a different name, enter that name instead.)

6. There is no secondary file to merge, so press ENTER when asked for the name of the secondary file.

7. The macro definition is automatically ended when the merge takes place. Press Merge E (SHIFT-F9) to cancel the procedure.

Running the Macro Library

If you followed the steps for creating a Macro Library, you could press ALT-L and the menu would be displayed. Enter the name of a macro on the menu or any other macro. The merge ends and the macro is started.

When you want to change the menu, retrieve the LIBRARY file and edit it. As long as you do not disturb the merge codes, you can add and delete macros or change the entire look of the screen. The ALT-L macro does not have to be adjusted, it will always use the most recent LIBRARY file.

If you prefer, you can assign a number to each macro as shown in Figure 4-65 so that you would enter only a number instead of the entire macro name. Macros named with one character are considered temporary macros. Therefore, you would have to name each macro with at least two characters. In order to show just the number on the screen, you would have to put the rest of the macro name in the ^G prompt. For example, you could include other characters with the number such as #1, 1M (to show that it is a macro found on a menu), or ⎯1. If you use this system, place all of the name except the number in the ^G^C^G string. The ^C would take the place

```
                         MACRO LIBRARY


    1.   Send printer a "Go."

    2.   Format for a business letter.

    3.   Print an envelope from the current document.

    4.   Format for printing on legal sized paper with the HP+.

    5.   Format for a pleading paper.

    6.   Number pages in "Page n of n" format.



    *** Press (SHIFT-F9) to Cancel the Macro Library ***




Macro:
```

Figure 4-65.   Numbering each item can save entire macro names

of the number in the name, as shown in the following examples.

$$\^G\#\^C\^G \text{ or } \^G\^Cm\^G \text{ or } \^G\_\^C\^G$$

Any characters appearing before the number will be displayed on the prompt line. Characters after the number are not displayed.

See *Merge* if you have further questions about the merge codes used in this example.

Start a Macro When WordPerfect Is Started

If you want a macro started each time you start WordPerfect, enter **WP/M-MACRONAME** instead of WP. "Macroname" is the name of the macro to be started (without the .MAC extension). Place the command in a batch file, or enter the following SET command in the AUTOEXEC.BAT file.

> SET WP=/M-MACRONAME

This command sets the DOS environment so that when you type WP, it starts the macro without having to enter the /M option.

Related Entries

> ALT Key
>
> AUTOEXEC.BAT File
>
> Merge
>
> Replace
>
> Search
>
> *See also* Appendix C, "Macro Library"
>
> *See also* Chapter 3, "The Next Step"

Mail Merge

See *Merge* for details on doing a WordPerfect merge.

Mail Merge is a format used by WordStar to store data files. Data base programs can usually convert their files to a delimited Mail Merge format. Fields are separated with a comma (some programs can specify a different character) and records are separated with a carriage return and line feed. Fields that normally include commas (city, state) have quotation marks around them, as shown in the following illustration:

```
"Robert Smith, Jr.",765 N. Locust Lane,"Chicago, IL",45678
"Susan Jones",P.O. Box 2011,"Santa Monica, CA",76765
"Jonathan Fallows",2121 Ridge Way #30,"San Francisco, CA",55005
```

WordPerfect's Convert program can convert these types of files so that they can be used as secondary merge files.

Keystrokes

1. Start the Convert program (found on the Learning disk) from DOS. If you are not sure of the exact steps, see *Convert Program.*

2. Enter the input filename (file to be converted) and the output filename (file which will hold the converted data). Remember to enter the full pathname if necessary (for example, B:MAILING.DBF or C:\DBASE\MAILING.DBF).

3. Type 7 to convert a Mail Merge file to a WordPerfect secondary merge file.

4. Enter a comma (,) if it is the field delimiter. If another character is used, enter that character.

5. If the record delimiter is carriage return/line feed (CR/LF), it should be entered as {13}{10}. (The decimal equivalent for a carriage return is 13 and a line feed is 10).

6. Enter " as the character to be stripped from the file if fields containing commas are enclosed in quotation marks.

When the conversion is finished, you can enter WordPerfect and retrieve the file. All fields are separated with a ^R[HRt] and each record is separated with a ^E[HRt].

Related Entries

Convert Program

dBASE II/III

See also Chapter 8, "Integrated Software"

Mailing Labels

See *Labels*

Mapping the Keyboard

See *Keyboard Mapping*

Margins

Line Format (SHIFT-F8) is used to change the left and right margins. They can be changed as many times as you want in a document.

Keystrokes

1. Press Line Format (SHIFT-F8).

2. Type **3** for Margins. The following statement, showing the current margins, is displayed.

```
[Margin Set] 10 74 to Left =
```

3. Enter the left margin, then press ENTER to set the left margin. You are now asked to enter the right margin.

```
[Margin Set] 10 74 to Left = 12 Right =
```

4. Enter the right margin. The right margin can be set up to position 250.

Hints

A [Margin Set:n,n] code is inserted at the cursor position. The first number in the code is the left margin and the second number is the right margin. If the cursor is not at the left margin, a Hard Return [HRt] is inserted just before the [Margin Set] code and the cursor is returned to the left margin on the next line. The new margin remains in effect until it encounters another Margin Set code.

To change the margin setting permanently, use the Setup menu (enter **WP/S** instead of WP to start WordPerfect). Option 2 lets you change all defaults for the program.

When you press Reveal Codes (ALT-F3), the ruler separating the regular text above from the text and codes below shows the current margin (and tab) settings in relation to the screen. Margin settings appear as [and] on the ruler line. If a tab is set in the same position as a margin, that margin setting appears as { or }. Tab settings appear as triangles.

If you want to see the ruler on the screen for an entire editing session, press Screen (CTRL-F3), type **1** for Window, and enter **23** as the number of lines in the window. You could enter a number less than 23 to see more than one document on the screen. Use the Setup menu if you want the ruler to show on the screen permanently. See *Ruler* and *Setup Menu* for more information.

Margin Release

When at the left margin, press Left Margin Release (SHIFT-TAB) to release the left margin for the current line only. You cannot release the right margin temporarily. You must change the margin instead.

Using Indent for Temporary Margins

→Indent (F4) or →Indent← (SHIFT-F4) can be used to set temporary left, or left and right margins. The amount of space the margins move inward depends on the current tab settings. The temporary margins stay in effect until a [HRt] is encountered.

Pitch/Font and Margins

If you change pitch or font, you will usually change the margins to match. For example, if you want 1-inch left and right margins and you change to the expanded font for the Epson, you would use margins of 5 and 37.

You can figure 1-inch margins with this simple formula.

Left Margin = Pitch
Right Margin = Pitch × Page width − Left margin

For example, if you are using 12 pitch, the left margin would be set at 12. The right margin would be

12 × 8.5 inches = 102 − 12 = 90

In general, 1-inch margins require the following settings for the listed pitch.

Pitch	Margin Settings
10	10 and 74
12	12 and 90
15	15 and 112

If you change the margins and still want tabs set every five spaces, you might need to change the tab settings also.

If you change the pitch/font often, consider putting the pitch/font change, margins, and tab settings in a macro so that all three will change at once.

Change to 4.1 Display

In version 4.2, the screen shows the left margin at the far left side of the screen so you can see more of the text at once. If you want to see the space at the left margin as in version 4.1, go to the left margin, press Left Margin Release (SHIFT-TAB) twice, then BACKSPACE twice to delete the [<-Mar Rel] codes. A macro could be defined to do these steps for you.

If you want to create a macro, you must make it "visible" because it needs the automatic screen rewrite to work. To make the macro visible, press (CTRL-PGUP), type **0**, then press ENTER as the first steps in the macro. The macro will only be in effect until you clear the screen. It will have to be run for each document. See appendix C for exact instructions.

Change Margins for DOS File Retrieval

Change the margins to match the line length of a DOS text (ASCII) file before you retrieve it with Text In/Out (CTRL-F5) or option 5 in the List Files menu. This is especially important if you want to use option 3 on the Text In/Out menu to convert all hard retu]rns that fall within the hyphenation zone to soft returns. Typically, margins of 0 and 80 are sufficient.

Related Entries

Indent

Left Margin Release

Ruler

Setup Menu

Text In/Out

Margin Release

See *Left Margin Release* (SHIFT-TAB). You cannot release the right margin without resetting the margins.

Mark Text

Mark Text (ALT-F5) is used to create outlines, number paragraphs, strikeout or redline text, or create a Table of Contents, Tables of Authorities, up to five lists, or an index.

Keystrokes

There are actually two Mark Text menus; the one you use depends on whether you have Block (ALT-F4) on or off.

If Block is off, the Mark Text menu is used to turn some features on and off or select options for other features. The following is the Mark Text menu with Block off.

```
1 Outline; 2 Para #; 3 Redline; 4 Short Form; 5 Index; 6 Other Options: 0
```

If Block is on, the Mark Text menu lets you mark the blocked text for use with a specific feature. The following is the Mark Text menu with Block on.

```
Mark for: 1 ToC; 2 List; 3 Redline; 4 Strikeout; 5 Index; 6 ToA: 0
```

Some of the options listed on the first menu have several submenus. For example, if you choose option 6 for Other Options, you will see the menu shown in Figure 4-66. See *Options* for general information about each feature. For detailed instructions, see the entries in this chapter.

Options

Mark Text Menu with Block Off

The following discussion summarizes the features listed on the Mark Text menu when Block is off.

Outline   The Outline option lets you create an outline without having to think about the numbering for levels or within each level. Each time ENTER is pressed, a first-level number is inserted. Press TAB to move to the next level. Up to seven levels of numbering are available. SHIFT-TAB will return you to the previous level.

```
Other Mark Text Options

     1 - Define Paragraph/Outline Numbering

     2 - Define Table of Contents

     3 - Define List

     4 - Define Table of Authorities

     5 - Define Index

     6 - Remove all Redline Markings and all Strikeout text from document

     7 - Edit Table of Authorities Full Form

     8 - Generate Tables and Index




Selection: 0
```

Figure 4-66.   Other Mark Text Options menu

```
                              SPEECH OUTLINE


 I.    Introduction

       A.    Company's Background
             1.    Incorporated in 1979
             2.    Officers of the Company
                   a.    Thomas B. Mandel, Chairman of the Board
                   b.    Richard M. Nelson, President

       B.    Position in the Market
             1.    Past performance
             2.    Number one this year
                   a.    Quote marketing research
             3.    Future predictions


 II.   Plans for 1988

       A.    Marketing Strategy
             1.    New advertising campaign
             2.    Open new offices in New York and California

 Outline                                Doc 1  Pg 1  Ln 1      Pos 10
```

Figure 4-67.   Sample outline with automatic numbering

If entries are added or deleted, the outline is automatically renumbered. See the outlining example in Figure 4-67.

Outlining is actually automatic paragraph numbering (see the next option). The same [Par#] code is used for both features.

To change the style of numbering, choose option **6** for Other Options, then type **1** to Define Paragraph/Outline Numbering.

Para #   The paragraph numbering option is used to manually insert a paragraph number. In versions prior to 4.2, the paragraph number was inserted as soon as option 2 was selected and the level was decided according to the location of the cursor (levels are decided by tab settings). An option was added in version 4.2 to let you specify the paragraph level at any location, but pressing ENTER still inserts the appropriate paragraph number automatically.

Redline   If you have text that is being considered for addition to a document, choose the Redlining option and enter the text. A vertical bar will appear in the left margin when the document is printed (or previewed). Your printer may be defined to show redlining differently.

When you turn on Redlining, a "+" is added to the position number on the status line. When you select the option again to turn it off, the "+" is removed. The [RedLn] code is inserted at the beginning of the redlined text and a [r] code is inserted at the end.

See *Other Options* to see how to remove the redline markings and delete the text marked with strikeout.

Short Form   A Short Form is a feature of Table of Authorities. When text is blocked and marked for a Table of Authorities entry, it is treated as the Full Form that will actually appear in the Table of Authorities. At that time you also assign a shortened form that can be used as a nickname for that entry. Thereafter, when you come to a citation that should be included in the Table of Authorities, you would choose this option and mark the entry with the Short Form option. A [ToA:;shortform;] code is inserted in the document and is used when the table is generated.

Index   This option is used to mark an individual word as an index entry. The code [Index:Heading;subheading] is inserted at that point, indicating the heading and subheading to be used.

   If you want to mark a phrase, first define it as a Block (ALT-F4). Then press Mark Text (ALT-F5) and choose the Index option.

   You can also create a concordance so that you only have to mark each entry once instead of each time it occurs in the document. See *Concordance* for more information.

Other Options   If you choose 6 for Other Options, you will see the menu shown in Figure 4-66. This menu lets you choose the paragraph/outline numbering style, define the location and format in which tables, lists, and the index will appear, remove redline markings and strikeout text, edit the nearest Table of Authorities full form to the left of the cursor, and generate the tables, lists, and index.

Mark Text Menu with Block On

After you block (highlight) text, the following Mark Text options can be applied to the block.

ToC   Each entry for the Table of Contents needs to be marked using this method. After this option is selected, you are asked to indicate the level (1 through 5) for the entry. Major headings would be classified as level 1 entries, subheadings as level 2 entries, and so on. A [Mark:ToC,n] code is inserted at the beginning of the block and a [EndMark: ToC,n] code is inserted at the end, with *n* being the level number.

List   Each entry for up to five lists (such as lists of figures or tables) should be blocked and marked with this option.

[Mark:List,n] and [EndMark:List,n] codes are inserted at the beginning and end of each block, with *n* representing the number of the list.

Redline   As previously mentioned, Redlining is used to mark text being considered for addition to a document. You can use this option from the Block On menu to mark the text after it has been entered. Or you can press Mark Text (ALT-F5) (without Block on) and choose the Redlining option to redline text as it is typed.

The codes [RedLn] and [r] are inserted at the beginning and end of the block and a "+" is added to the position number to indicate that Redlining is on. A vertical bar appears in the left margin when the document is printed or previewed to indicate Redlining.

Strikeout   The Strikeout option can be used to mark text for possible deletion from a document. When printed, a "-" strikes through each character in the block. The codes [StrkOut] and [s] are inserted at the beginning and end of the block, and a "-" is added to the position number on the status line to indicate that Strikeout is on.

Index   This option is identical to the one found on the "Block off" Mark Text menu, but is used to mark a block of text rather than a single word.

ToA   Each entry to appear in a Table of Authorities needs to be blocked and marked with this option. After entering the section number (as many as 16) for the table, the blocked text is placed in a separate editing screen and is considered the full form. After editing the full form and pressing Exit (F7), you are asked to enter a short form for the entry. The short form can then be used to mark future occurrences of the citation.

A [ToA:n;shortform;<Full Form>] code is inserted at the cursor location. The <Full Form> in the code is used to indicate the blocked entry. The *n* indicates the section of the Table of Authorities to be used.

Hints

Remember that any codes included in a block that has been marked for a Table of Contents, Table of Authorities, or list will appear with the entry when the tables and lists are generated.

The steps for creating tables, lists, and the index are the same. Mark each entry, define the location and format, then generate. Remember that the last two steps are found as options on the Other Mark Text Options menu (See Figure 4-66).

Related Entries

Concordance

Index

Lists

Outline

Paragraph Numbering

Remove Redline and Strikeout

Strikeout Text

Table of Authorities

Table of Contents

Math

The Math feature can be used to calculate subtotals, totals, and grand totals for columns. You can also combine addition, subtraction, multiplication, and division for calculations across columns. For simple addition, see *Addition*.

Note: If you want to use advanced spreadsheet applications, consider using PlanPerfect or another spreadsheet program. You can, however, use the Math feature to accomplish many calculations without ever having to buy another program.

If you have PlanPerfect and WordPerfect Library, you can save a block of figures in PlanPerfect and retrieve it into WordPerfect with just a few keystrokes. Appropriate margins and tabs are set and columns are automatically separated with Tab Align codes. For quick calculations, you could use the calculator provided with the WordPerfect Library.

Keystrokes

The basic steps for using the Math feature are as follows. Each step is covered in detail following the list.

1. Set tabs for each column.

2. Enter titles for the columns if applicable.

3. Define the Math columns.

4. Turn on Math.

5. Enter text, numbers, and math operators. (An operator is the symbol that indicates the type of calculation performed.)

6. Calculate.

7. Turn off Math.

Set Tabs for Each Column

1. Press Line Format (SHIFT-F8).

2. Type **1** or **2** to set tabs. See *Tabs, Clear and Set* for further details.

3. When finished, press Exit (F7).

The first tab setting is considered the first column. Text can be entered at the left margin, but any numbers entered there will not be considered during calculation.

You do not need to set decimal tabs for numeric columns, as the Math definition can be used to decide which columns should be aligned at the decimal point.

Be aware that when setting tabs for numeric columns, the decimal point will be placed at the tab setting. You should be careful to set tabs so that text or numbers will not overlap from one column to another. When setting the tab closest to the right margin setting, allow enough room at the right margin for any calculations so they will not wrap to the next line.

You can display a ruler line on the screen to indicate where tabs have been set. Press Screen (CTRL-F3), type **1** for Window, then enter **23**. See *Ruler* for more information.

Headings for the Columns

Type headings for each column if desired. It is important to enter the headings *before* turning on Math or any *T*s, *t*s, or *N*s will not print. (As explained later, these characters are considered as math operators if found in a numeric column.) Of course, you can wait and enter the headings after the columns are typed so that you can better estimate placement. Just be sure to place the cursor before (to the left of) the [Math On] code.

Define Math

1. Press Math/Columns (ALT-F7). The following one-line menu is shown.

```
1 Math On; 2 Math Def; 3 Column On/Off; 4 Column Def; 5 Column Display: 0
```

2. Type **2** for Math Definition. The menu shown in Figure 4-68 is displayed.

```
Math Definition               Use arrow keys to position cursor

Columns                       A B C D E F G H I J K L M N O P Q R S T U V W X

Type                          2 2 2 2 2 2 2 2 2 2 2 2 2 2 2 2 2 2 2 2 2 2 2 2

Negative Numbers              ( ( ( ( ( ( ( ( ( ( ( ( ( ( ( ( ( ( ( ( ( ( ( (

# of digits to                2 2 2 2 2 2 2 2 2 2 2 2 2 2 2 2 2 2 2 2 2 2 2 2
the right (0-4)

Calculation     1
Formulas        2
                3
                4

Type of Column:
      0 = Calculation    1 = Text      2 = Numeric     3 = Total

Negative Numbers
      ( = Parenthesis (50.00)          - = Minus Sign  -50.00

Press EXIT when done
```

Figure 4-68.   Math Definition menu

3. Use the arrow keys to move to only those items that need to be changed and enter the new values. The following discussion contains detailed information on each option. Step 4 follows the discussion.

Each tab setting is considered a column. The left margin (even though it might have a tab setting in the same position) is not considered a column. You can have up to 24 columns. As you can see in the menu shown in Figure 4-68, each column is "numbered" from A through X. The attributes (type of column, how negative numbers are to be displayed, and the number of digits to be displayed to the right of the decimal point) are listed below each column.

Types of Columns   Columns may be one of four types: text, numeric, calculation, or total. Up to 4 of the 24 columns can be used for calculation. Numeric is selected as the default for all columns.

A text column can contain text or numbers and is not considered when calculating. If you have a "date" column or a "numbered" column (1, 2, 3, and so on), you should define it as a text column. You cannot combine WordPerfect's text Columns feature with Math, so if there is more than one line in a column, you will have to wrap each line manually.

If you choose to have a calculation column, the cursor is placed at "Calculation Formulas." You can then enter a formula using letters to indicate specific columns, numbers, and the following operators. The operators are used to perform the calculation.

+   Add (such as A+B)

−   Subtract (such as A−B−C)

*   Multiply (such as B*1.06)

/   Divide (such as C/3)

You can combine as many operators as you want. Calculations will be made from left to right unless you enclose part of the formula in parentheses. If parentheses are found, the calculations within the parentheses are performed first from left to right.

You can also use the following operators alone in a calculation column. They cannot be used with any other letters, numbers, or operators. The first two deal with numeric columns and the last two with total columns.

+   Total of all numeric columns

+/   Average of all numeric columns

=   Total of all total columns

=/   Average of all total columns

A total column uses the numbers from the column to the left and those above in the same column to calculate subtotals, totals, and grand totals. Column 3 in Figure 4-69 is a total column.

```
         Revenues
            January        $356,478
            February        498,212
            March           555,389

                                      $1,410,079+
         Liabilities
            January        $187,098
            February        190,744
            March          210,503

                                      N$588,345+

         Profit                       $821,734=
```

Figure 4-69.   Example of a total column in column 3

Notice that there is more than one math operator found in the total column. If you type a *t* or *T* at the beginning of a number, it identifies the number as a subtotal or total that has been entered manually and that is used in the final calculation.

Numbers in numeric, total, and calculation columns are automatically aligned at the decimal point just by pressing TAB. If you enter a +, =, or * for a subtotal, total, or grand total, they are placed just to the right of the align codes so the numbers can be inserted between the codes instead.

Negative Numbers   You can *manually* enter a negative number with a minus sign (−), enclose it in parentheses ( ), or type *N* before the number. However, WordPerfect needs to know how to display any negative numbers that are calculated. You can either use the default (enclosing a negative number in parentheses) or type a −.

This option is included so the results in calculations can match up with your style of entering negative numbers. The *N* cannot be used as an option in this menu.

 # Digits You can manually enter any number with as few or as many digits to the right of the decimal point as you want, but only the first four are considered in any given calculation.

This option is used to determine how many digits will be displayed for a calculated result. Numbers can be rounded to the fourth digit. The following illustration shows how the number 30.45678 is rounded when 0, 1, 2, 3, and 4 are selected respectively for the columns.

30.45678 Rounded to:

0 digit	1 digit	2 digits	3 digits	4 digits
30+	30.5+	30.46+	30.457+	30.4567+

4. After making changes to the menu, press Exit (F7). A [Math Def] code is inserted at that point and the original one-line menu is displayed again.

5. Type **1** to turn on Math. "Math" is displayed in the lower left corner of the screen and a [Math On] code is inserted.

Enter Text, Numbers, and Math Operators

1. Press TAB to enter the text or numbers in each column. Notice that numbers are automatically aligned at the decimal point and text is aligned at the left. If you make a mistake, press Delete Word (CTRL-BACKSPACE) and reenter the value. It will still be aligned correctly.

If you have a calculation column, pressing TAB will insert an exclamation mark (!). This mark indicates that WordPerfect will perform the calculation for you. The ! is considered a code and will not be printed.

2. Enter additional math operators if you want subtotals, totals, or grand totals calculated down the columns.

The following is a list of "total" operators.

+	Subtotal	Add numbers listed above not previously summed. If found in a total column, a + will add the numbers from above and to the left.
=	Total	Add all subtotals above not previously totaled. If found in a total column, an = will add the subtotals from above and to the left.
*	Grand Total	Add all totals above not previously totaled. If placed in a total column, an * will add the totals from above and to the left.

If more than one +, =, or * is found in the same column, the totaling will not overlap. Instead, it will only total the numbers from that code to the next.

The following operators should be used if you want to manually insert an additional subtotal or total in a column:

t	Subtotal	t$45.00
T	Total	T$1,299.76

For example, if you have a calculation that includes the revenues for the second quarter, you can manually insert the first quarter total as a subtotal or a total. These numbers will be included in total calculations as described above.

If you want to force a number to be a negative number without typing a − or () around it, you can type N before the number, as in N$52.10.

A minus sign and parentheses will print, whereas an N is considered a math operator and will not print. The N is especially useful if you need to force a number to be negative when it is a positive result of a WordPerfect calculation. The example in Figure 4-69 shows how a positive total can be used as a negative in further calculations.

If you make a mistake when entering an operator, delete the operator *and* align codes, then reenter the operator for that column. If you delete the first operator and type the second, it is considered only a character. There is one exception, however. As mentioned in step 1, when you tab to a calculation column, a "!" is automatically inserted. The "!" is inserted between the alignment [A] and [a] codes, not after them as the other operators are. You can delete the "!" if necessary and insert a different operator in its place without also having to delete the alignment codes.

If you press Reveal Codes (ALT-F3), all operators should appear in bold, indicating that they are codes.

Calculate

1. Press Math/Columns (ALT-F7).

2. Type **2** to Calculate.

Note on the following menu illustration that when Math is on, option 1 is changed to "Math Off" and option 2 is changed from "Math Def" to "Calculate."

```
1 Math Off; 2 Calculate; 3 Column On/Off; 4 Column Def; 5 Column Display: 0
```

If you need to change any of the numbers in the math section, press Math/Columns (ALT-F7) and type **2** to Calculate. All calculations will be updated.

If calculations are not performed properly, check the operators in Reveal Codes (ALT-F3) and make sure they are shown in bold. If not, they are considered as characters only and need to be reentered.

The placement of the operators is also important. The calculation mark (!) should be between the align codes, as in [A]![a]. After the calculation is performed, the operator is moved outside the codes to the right of the calculated number. An *N*, *T*, or *t* should be entered with the number, thus appearing within the [A][a] codes. All other operators will appear just to the right of the [A][a] codes.

Turn Off Math

1. Press Math/Columns (ALT-F7).

2. Type **1** to turn off Math.

This step is not necessary if the entire document is a math document. However, if you intend to continue with a regular document, be sure to turn off Math where appropriate.

Math can be turned on and off as many times in a document as you want. You can use the previous [Math Def] code for future calculations or define Math columns again.

Hints

It is not necessary to define columns if you only have numeric columns and are calculating totals down those columns. If no changes are made to the menu, all calculations will be rounded to two digits to the right of the decimal and negative numbers will be shown in parentheses.

If you enter a wrong value in a column and don't want to delete both text and align codes, press Delete Word (CTRL-BACKSPACE). Only the text will be deleted and you can re-enter the correct value without worrying about incorrect alignment.

Aligning on a Different Character

All the previous examples show how numbers are aligned at the decimal point. You can change the alignment character at the beginning of the math document. For example, if you want to align numbers on a comma (European format), define that character (or any other character) as the alignment character.

1. With the cursor above the math portion of the document, press Line Format (SHIFT-F8).

2. Type **6** for Align Char.

3. Type a comma (,).

The code [Align Char:,] is inserted into the document and is used to align all numbers in numeric, total, or calculation columns.

Applications

Math is best used to do simple calculations for invoices and statements or when you find it necessary to insert a calculated table of figures into a document.

It was not intended to do complicated spreadsheet applications. See Chapter 8 for more information about WordPerfect Corporation's spreadsheet program, PlanPerfect, and the WordPerfect Library. Other programs can also be used, but you will give up the ease of integration and the familiarity included with PlanPerfect and WordPerfect Library.

Related Entries

Addition

Tab Align

See Also Chapter 8, "Software Integration"

Menus and Messages

Most WordPerfect commands are chosen by pressing a function key. Some function keys show one-line or full-screen menus, while others prompt you with a message for more information.

Prompts and Messages

If you press Save (F10), Search (F2), Macro (ALT-F10), List Files (F5), and others, you are prompted for further information. "Document to be Saved," "->Search," "Macro," and "C:\WORK" are among those prompts.

Some prompts display an "answer" that can be used, edited, or changed completely. For example, if you have done a search and then press Search (F2) again, the last search string is displayed. If you have previously saved a document and you press Save (F10), the name of the document is displayed.

You can press ENTER to accept the displayed characters or you can enter something completely different. With version 4.2, a feature was added to let you edit the displayed characters. If you begin typing, the previous string is cleared and the new one is entered. If you press a cursor key first, you can edit the string of characters by adding and deleting text where necessary. For example, if you press List Files (F5) and you see "Dir C:\LETTERS*.*" you could press the right arrow key or END to go to the end of the string, delete the last *, and add "DEC" to enter the C:\LETTERS directory and display all files ending with the extension .DEC.

Yes/No Questions

WordPerfect displays the safest answer as the default to any yes/no questions. For example, if you press Exit (F7), you will see the following.

Save Document? (Y/N) Y

Pressing any other key but N would save the document. This includes ENTER, SPACEBAR, or even Exit (F7). You would have to specifically type N to not save the document.

Menu Options

Each option on a menu is assigned a number. Letters are used when more than nine options are on a menu so that a single keystroke can be used to select an option. The Print Format menu in Figure 4-70 shows an example where eleven options are numbered 1 through 9 and A through B.

```
Print Format

     1 - Pitch                      10
         Font                        1

     2 - Lines per Inch              6

     Right Justification            On
     3 - Turn off
     4 - Turn on

     Underline Style                 5
     5 - Non-continuous Single
     6 - Non-continuous Double
     7 - Continuous Single
     8 - Continuous Double

     9 - Sheet Feeder Bin Number     1

     A - Insert Printer Command

     B - Line Numbering             Off

   Selection: 0
```

Figure 4-70.   Print Format menu

Exiting a Menu

All menus have a default answer for most options. Most show a 0 as the default option which means you can exit by pressing ENTER, SPACEBAR, ESC, Exit (F7), Cancel (F1), or any other key that is not listed as an option on the menu. For example, you could even type an *M* to leave a menu because it is not listed as an option.

Some menus, such as Column Definition and Math Definition, require that you press Exit (F7) because ENTER is used to enter values into the menu. You can also press Cancel (F1) to leave this type of menu without making changes or inserting codes in the document. You cannot use ENTER to leave the List Files menu because the Look option is the default selected.

Inserting Codes and Changing Modes

Most menu options insert a code into the document. Some insert an "on" code and change the mode of operation, as with Columns, Math, and Hyphenation. Another option can be chosen to insert an "off" code and return to the standard settings. Some keys only change the mode, as with INS/TYPEOVER or CAPS LOCK.

If codes are inserted, those codes will affect text from that point in the document forward. Therefore, it is important to note the location of the cursor *before* entering a menu and making a change.

See Chapter 2 for more basic information about how WordPerfect menus are designed.

Merge

WordPerfect's Merge feature can be used to merge two or more documents together. You can merge a list of data (referred to as a secondary merge file) with form letters, mailing labels, or envelopes (referred to as a primary merge file). Merge can assist you in filling out pre-printed forms or compile a document containing standard paragraphs that have already been saved to disk.

How Merge Works

There are three elements to a merge: the primary file(s), the secondary file(s), and the merged file that results.

The primary file is the "form" which contains merge codes that signal the type of information to be merged into the document at that point. The secondary file contains the data to be merged. You do not always need a secondary file because the merge can pause for information from the keyboard.

When you choose to merge, you are asked to enter the name of the primary file (form) and secondary file (data). WordPerfect retrieves the primary file to the screen, opens the secondary file, and positions the cursor at the first record. WordPerfect scans the form (primary file) for merge codes and upon finding one, inserts the appropriate data.

When WordPerfect reaches the end of the primary file and all merge codes have been processed, a Hard Page is inserted, the pointer goes to the second record in the secondary file, and the same primary file is retrieved. The process is repeated until the end of the secondary file is reached or until another secondary file is specified.

Merge Codes

Merge Codes (ALT-F9) is used to insert the merge codes into the primary file. When you press Merge Codes (ALT-F9), you see the following menu.

^C; ^D; ^F; ^G; ^N; ^O; ^P; ^Q; ^S; ^T; ^U; ^V:

A description of each merge code is included in Table 4-2.

If there are no special characters mapped to the same CTRL-key combinations, they could be used to insert the merge codes. For example, pressing CTRL-C could insert the ^C merge code. This method does not work, however for ^V; it must be entered with Merge Codes (ALT-F9) and **V**. Typing the caret symbol "^" followed by the letter is not an alternative. They would be considered characters rather than a merge code.

The codes ^R and ^E are applicable only to secondary files. The other merge codes relate mainly to primary files. A description of how each can be used follows.

^R and ^E   In the secondary file, each field is separated with a ^R and a Hard Return code [HRt]. These codes are inserted by pressing Merge R (F9), sometimes called "merge return." A ^E and a [HRt] mark the end of each record. This is inserted by pressing Merge E (SHIFT-F9) and is sometimes

Code	Function
	Primary File Codes
^C	Pause so text can be entered from the Console (keyboard). Merge R (F9) must be pressed to continue.
^D	Insert the current Date and/or time.
^Fn^	Insert the specified Field at that point. If the field name or number is followed by a question mark and the field is empty, the resulting blank line is removed. This code could appear as **^F1^**, **^Faddress^**, or **^F1?^**.
^G	Go to a macro when the merge is finished. The code must be entered in pairs: **^Gmacroname^G**.
^N	Point to the Next record in the secondary file.
^O	Output the message found between the two ^O codes: **^Omessage^O**. Should always be followed by a ^C so the merge will pause and display the message.
^P	Retrieve a Primary file at that point in the document. The filename must be included between two ^P codes: **^Pfilename^P**.
^Q	Quit the merge operation.
^S	Open a new Secondary (data) file and point to the first record. The secondary filename must be included between a pair of ^S codes: **^Sfilename^S**.
^T	Print (Type) everything merged up to that point. Must be followed by ^N^P^P to avoid an extra page break between records.
^U	Update the display to that point during a merge. Useful when a ^C pauses inside a ^Omessage^O.
^V	Pass other merge codes through into the finished product without processing or interpreting them. The merge code must appear between ^V codes: **^V^R^V**.
	Secondary Files Codes
^E	Marks the End of a record. If ^E is found in a primary file or if Merge E (SHIFT-F9) is pressed during a merge, the merge will end at that point.
^R	Separates fields within each record (Return at the end of a field). Merge R (F9) must be pressed to continue after a merge pauses at a ^C merge code.

Table 4-2.   Merge Codes for Primary and Secondary Files

```
     Mr. Bob Richards^R
     Bob^R
     375 N. Crestview Drive^R
     Raleigh^R
     NC^R
     45678^R
     (919) 555-3434^R
     Charlotte^R
     Bob sent his membership fee in on August 30, 1987.  He also
     donated an additional $50 for the annual children's parade.^R
     ^E
     Ms. Kathryn B. Johnson^R
     Kathy^R
     Valley Bank
     Accounts Payable
     3rd Floor
     964 W. Main Street^R
     Raleigh^R
     NC^R
     45678^R
     (919) 555-8791^R
     ^R
     Kathy is our current Treasurer.^R
     ^E
C:\LISTS\ASSOC                              Doc 1   Pg 12   Ln 24      Pos 10
```

Figure 4-71.   Example of secondary file with empty fields and variable length fields

referred to as "end of record" or "merge end." See Figure 4-71 for an example of a secondary file that has empty fields and variable length fields.

When the merge starts, it opens the secondary file and positions the cursor at the first record. When the end of the primary file is reached or when a ^N is encountered, Word-Perfect searches for the ^E code to find the next record and points to the record just after that ^E.

^Fn^   When WordPerfect finds a ^F*n*^ merge code in a primary file, it looks in the current record for that specific field and retrieves the information at that point. Each field in the secondary file is given a number according to the number of ^R merge codes found. If you are using the Notebook program included with WordPerfect Library to manage your data lists, you can insert the name of a field instead of the number (for example, ^FADDRESS^).

Fields in each record can be used as many times and in any order as needed. If a field is empty, WordPerfect inserts a hard return and goes on. You can prevent the hard return by typing a question mark after the field number (as in

^F3?^). If that specific field is empty, the hard return will not be inserted. Named fields can also include a question mark (?). However, a field with a question mark must be alone on a line because the entire line will be deleted.

^G   When a ^G is found, the macro named between two ^Gs is stored and started after the merge is finished, regardless of its location in the file.

Only one macro can be started after the merge is finished. If you have more than one macro specified in the primary file, the last one listed is used.

^P and ^S   If, during the process, a ^P is encountered, WordPerfect retrieves the named primary file at that point. If a ^S is encountered, a new secondary file is opened and data from that file is used. If no name is found between the ^P^P and ^S^S codes, the current file is used again.

^N   As mentioned earlier, once the end of primary file is finished, a Hard Page code is inserted, the merge points to the next record, and the primary file is retrieved so the process can be repeated.

If you do not want a page break to be inserted, you can manually insert the ^N code before it reaches the end of the file and has an opportunity to insert the page break. It is then followed by ^P^P codes to retrieve the same primary file (or another primary file) and continues the process until the end of the secondary file is reached (without inserting a page break). The entire code usually appears as ^N^P^P at the end of the file.

You could also use the ^N in the secondary file to skip a record.

^O, ^C, and ^U   When a ^C is reached, WordPerfect pauses for keyboard entry at that point. You must press Merge R (F9) to continue. WordPerfect can also display a message with the ^O code. Because the merge stops at each ^C, the ^Omessage^O should precede the ^C code. If there is no keyboard entry, the merge is "invisible."

If you want the ^C to pause in the message on the status line, not in the document, include the ^C code within the ^O codes. For example, you could have a menu of choices and have the merge pause there to make a choice instead of pausing in the document.

Remember that when the ^C is found in the prompt or message, the document will not be updated to that point because it is pausing in the message, not in the document. If you want to update the screen to the point of the message, insert a ^U just before the first ^O code. Otherwise, it is not needed.

^T   If you use the ^T merge code to send all text merged up to that point to the printer, an extra page will be inserted after each document is sent (remember the automatic page break), thus creating a blank page between each record. To prevent this, you should insert ^N^P^P after the ^T so the end of the document is never reached and the Hard Page code is not inserted.

^V   When any merge code is encountered, it is immediately processed. If you don't want a code to be processed, enter ^V before and after the code (^V^R^V). The merge code will then be placed into the finished document just as regular text would.

^Q   If a ^Q is encountered in a primary or secondary file, the merge is ended. To stop a merge that is in progress, you can press Merge Codes (ALT-F9) and type **Q**, or press Merge E (SHIFT-F9) to end the merge. The ^Q could also be placed within a secondary file so that only the records up to that point would be merged.

Keystrokes

Note that all Merge functions are assigned to F9, whether pressed alone or with SHIFT, ALT, or CTRL.

1. Create and save the primary file with the applicable Merge Codes (ALT-F9). Figure 4-72 shows a sample primary file.

```
          ^D


          ^F1^
          ^F2^
          ^F3^,  ^F4^   ^F5

          Dear ^F1^:

          The Freedom Association is planning to celebrate the 200th year
          anniversary of the signing of the United States Constitution on
          Thursday, September 17.  We would like to invite you and a
          partner to join us in the celebration.

          Dinner will be served at 6:30 with a program to follow at 7:30.
          We hope to see you there.

          Sincerely,



          George A. Smith
          President
C:\LETTERS\INVITE                        Doc 1   Pg 3   Ln 25      Pos 10
```

Figure 4-72.   Merge letter

2. Create and save the secondary file with a ^R (F9) at the end of each field and a ^E (SHIFT-F9) at the end of each record.

Each record must have the same number of fields. If a field is empty, you must still press Merge R (F9) to insert the necessary ^R. If a field has more than one line, let it wrap or press ENTER to end the lines normally.

3. Clear the screen and start the merge. First, press Merge/Sort (CTRL-F9), then type **1** for Merge. Enter the name of the primary file. Then enter the name of the secondary file if applicable. If you are only entering text from the keyboard during the merge, press ENTER.

Hints

When a merge is run, the finished document is displayed on the screen. You can then either send the document to the printer or save it to disk. Think twice, however, before saving it to disk, as the primary file is duplicated for each record in the secondary merge file, creating a large document. Instead, merge the files again when the document is needed.

When creating the secondary file, you should decide if an address field should be broken up into city, state, and zip code fields and even whether the first and last name should be together in a field. The choice is up to you, but if you plan to sort or select records with Sort, you should make sure the information is consistent not only from field to field, but from line to line and word to word. You might also give yourself more flexibility if the data is separated into more fields. For example, you might want to use a person's first name in a letter more often than the full name.

You should not include extra spaces, lines, or hard page breaks in the secondary merge file. Merge and Sort will not perform properly when they encounter such items.

When creating the primary document, it is easy to forget the number of a field from the secondary file. You can retrieve the secondary file into document 2 so that you can switch between the two documents, or you could split the screen with Screen (CTRL-F3) and option 1 for Window. The fields in the secondary file could then be viewed on the same screen while you are creating the primary file.

You cannot place merge codes in a header or footer.

Eliminating Blank Lines

When specifying the field to be merged, enter a ? after the field name or number so that if that field is empty, a blank line will not be included.

Remember, however, that a ? was designed to be placed in a field that is on a line by itself. If you follow it with other fields or text, they will be deleted.

Selective Merging

Sorting and selecting specific records to be included in a merge is not part of the Merge function. Refer to *Sort and Select* for detailed information about sorting and selecting records before doing a merge.

The Notebook included with WordPerfect Library can do a simple sort and will let you select the records to be merged either manually or with a selection criteria.

Using the Notebook to Create the Secondary Merge File

You can create and manage the secondary merge files in Notebook, which is included with WordPerfect Library. You can set up the fields and enter the data just as you would in a data base program. Each field is labeled and you press ENTER to move from field to field. For those fields with more than one line, press TAB to move from field to field.

The most convincing reason to use the Notebook, however, is that it automatically stores the records and fields in the ^R and ^E format. You can then use the file without converting it.

Figure 4-73 shows a sample screen from the Notebook. From WordPerfect you can merge with any of the Notebook files (you can have as many as you want), or you can mark

```
 FREEDOM   ASSOCIATION   MEMBERS
┌──────────────────────────────────┬─────────────────────────────┐
│ Name: Arthur Schofield           │ Salutation: Art             │
├──────────────────────────────────┼─────────────────────────────┤
│ Address: 3214 Mojave             │ Home Phone: 222-9878        │
│          Albuquerque, NM  87404  │                             │
│                                  │ Work Phone: 375-3849        │
├──────────────────────────────────┼─────────────────────────────┤
│ Birthday: 4/1/39                 │ Spouse: Janet               │
├──────────────────────────────────┴─────────────────────────────┤
│ Notes:    Has offered to get the guest speaker for our          │
│           meeting in February.                                  │
└─────────────────────────────────────────────────────────────────┘

|<-- Previous field;   -->| Next field;    F7 Exit;        RECORD 7
```

Figure 4-73.   Sample screen from the Notebook

specific files with an * and save them to a separate file that can then be used in the merge.

A shell macro could be used to start a merge, enter the Notebook, pause so you can mark a name, and merge with that record. (Shell macros are like WordPerfect macros, but are provided with WordPerfect Library and can be used to help with integration between programs.) See Appendix C for exact details.

Using Data from Other Software Programs

If you have already created lists of records with another program, use the Convert program to convert the file to a secondary merge file. The only requirement is that it have field and record delimiters that can be converted to the ^R and ^E format.

WordStar's Mail Merge uses a comma to separate fields (further delimited with quotation marks for those fields containing commas), and a carriage return/line feed at the end of each record. A data base program such as dBASE II/III can also save a file in this format. See *Convert Program*, *dBASE II/III*, or *Mail Merge* for more information.

Merge Pause vs. Macro Pause

Many of the same applications can be done using either a merge or a macro. Both can be used to set up formats and pause for information. A macro records keystrokes, whereas a merge uses a primary file to store keystrokes. If the information needs to be edited often, you might consider putting it into a primary file because it is much easier to change.

The only differences between the different types of pauses are that after a merge pause, you press Merge R (F9) to continue and after a macro pause, you use the ENTER key to continue. A message can be placed between two ^O codes to prompt the user for the type of information needed in a merge, and a comment could be used with both.

A macro can be used to start a merge, and a merge can be used to call a macro. You should decide which combination would be best for you to use. Appendix C contains several macro examples that use pauses.

Error Messages

If you get an error message such as "Not enough room on WP disk to retrieve text" or "WP disk full—Strike any key to continue," the merged document is too large to fit into memory and into the extra space on the WP disk reserved for virtual files. If this happens, you can try several things.

> Use Block (ALT-F4) and Save (F10) to save sections of the secondary merge file into separate files. Each of these smaller files can then be merged separately with the primary file.
>
> Use the ^T merge code at the end of the primary file. As each record is merged, it is sent directly to the printer, the screen is cleared, and the process begins again. (Add a ^N^P^P after the ^T to avoid inserting an extra page between copies.) The only drawback to using a ^T is that the computer and printer are both tied up and no other operation is possible until it is finished. If you need to interrupt the merge, you can press CTRL-Q or Merge Codes (ALT-F9), then **Q**.
>
> Increase the amount of memory or disk space. WordPerfect will use up to 64K for document 1 and 32K for document 2, so make sure you use document 1 when merging so you can have the maximum amount of memory available.

When merging, you might see the error message "Invalid nesting of ^O, ^P, ^S, or ^G's." If this happens, check the primary file and make sure all of the applicable codes are found in pairs.

Another error message, "Functions not allowed between ^O, ^P, ^S, or ^G's," could appear if you have tried to insert codes such as [Center] and [Indent] between the named codes.

Unfortunately, the error messages appear during the

merge, not when you actually enter the codes. This is because the codes are not interpreted until the merge takes place. In either situation, return to the original primary file and correct any problems.

Applications

The applications for the Merge feature could fill an entire book. Combining merges and macros would make the book much larger. The following discussion of suggested applications provides typical examples that help reinforce the explanations provided earlier.

Mass Mailings and Form Letters

Probably the most common use of Merge is to create personalized form letters. You can place ^F codes anywhere in the document. The codes do not have to be in any particular order and they can appear more than once in the primary document, as shown in Figure 4-72.

Remember that only the information in the field itself will be merged. Therefore, should you want extra spacing (such as two spaces between the state field and zip code field) or extra characters (such as a comma after the city and a colon after the salutation), these must be placed in the primary document.

Envelopes, Labels, and Lists

Many users just want to use the secondary merge file as it is, but without the ^R and ^E codes. Instead of searching and replacing the codes, create a form and use the Merge feature. The following illustration is a primary file that will merge names and addresses and remove the ^R and ^E codes.

```
^F1^
^F2?^
^F3^
^F4^, ^F5^  ^F6^
```

A page break will separate each record. After the merge, the file can be formatted for envelopes or mailing labels. If you are doing envelopes, change the top and left margins to fit the envelope. If you are hand feeding envelopes into the printer, you won't need the top margin setting because you can feed the envelope to exactly the right position. See *Labels* for more information about mailing labels.

The next two sample primary files could be used to create lists. The first would list the fields down the page and the second would list the fields across the page. The placement of the fields is up to you.

```
^F1^
^F2^
^F3^,  ^F4   ^F5
^F6

^N^P^P
```

```
^F1^                         ^F2^                              ^F6^
                             ^F3^,  ^F4^   ^F5^

^N^P^P
```

Notice that because fields 2, 3, 4, and 5 are divided, you can place them anywhere on the screen. If all the information were placed in one field, additional lines would wrap to the left margin instead of remaining at that position. In fact, if a field has more than one line, the additional lines will end up at the left margin. To avoid this situation, define parallel columns and turn on Columns at the beginning of the file.

If you don't want each record to be broken by page breaks, use Block Protect around the merge codes. See *Block Protect* for the exact steps.

In the first example, there were no ^N^P^P codes, so each record was separated with a page break. In the last two examples, the records should not be separated with page breaks. Remember that by inserting the ^N, you will force WordPerfect to go to the next record without inserting a page break, then merge with the original primary file.

The name of a different primary file can be placed between the two ^P codes. If a name isn't included, the same primary file is used. Of course you could fill the entire page with ^Ns (followed by the fields to be merged), but the ^Ps save you the trouble.

If you want the records to be listed one after another, place the ^N^P^P immediately below the field codes. If you want to add space between each record, place the ^N^P^P a line or two below the field codes.

If you want to label a list with a title or heading, do the merge, then add the heading. Otherwise, the heading will be repeated for every record.

Pausing a Merge for Forms Fill-In

Other than ^F, probably the most used merge code is ^C. It can be used in a form, memo, or even an envelope to pause a merge so information can be inserted from the keyboard. The ^C can be used alone or in combination with ^O codes so that a message can be displayed which prompts the user for the necessary information.

If you have a form or memo, set up the format and insert ^C codes where you want it to pause for information to be entered. If the type of information to be inserted is not obvious, enter a message between the ^O codes to prompt or remind the user.

When creating the form, you should be aware of the following items.

Positioning the Entries   When you insert codes such as ^Omessage^O^C in the primary file, the cursor will actually stop where the first ^O appears.

If you are inserting a pause in a memo, letter, or other type of document that contains regular text, it is easy to place the ^Cs in the right location. However, if you are working with a pre-printed form, it can be very frustrating when trying to place the prompts in the proper location. The WordPerfect manual suggests you create a grid that can be printed over the form. An alternate way of creating the grid could be to create one line and "copy" it down the page. Turn line numbering on at the beginning of the page, then print the page over the form.

Set Tabs Where Necessary   Usually the information on a form changes in position from line to line. If this is the case, as shown in Figure 4-74, set tabs where applicable. If you just press TAB *n* times to get to the position, or even space to the position, the final document might not be aligned properly.

This often requires you to change tabs for every line. Remember, though, that you only need to create the primary document once.

Overlapping ^O Messages   When placing messages within the ^O codes, there might not be enough room on the line for every prompt. You can either shorten the prompts or use the following procedures if your printer supports Advance Up.

Press Superscript/Subscript (SHIFT-F1) and type **4** for Advance Up. The cursor moves up one-half line (indicated by the status line). Press ENTER to move down a full line, then Advance Up again to move back to the original line. Press

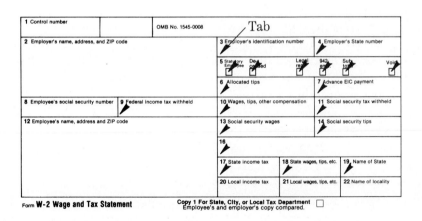

Figure 4-74.   Form in which information changes in position from line to line

TAB to reach the appropriate position and enter the remaining merge codes. It will appear that you are on a different line, but the status line shows that both lines have the same line number. They will be printed on the same line if your printer supports Advance Up.

Using Merge to Set Up a Format or Boilerplate

A primary file can contain any type of formatting commands so that you can merge information into the form without having to figure out the format each time. Some refer to boilerplating as the ability to create a document from several previously saved standard paragraphs.

Anytime you are creating a document, you can always press Retrieve (SHIFT-F9) and enter the name of the document to be retrieved at that point. You can merge several different documents together using this method. If you want to automate the process, use ^P merge codes in a primary document.

Either place the name of a file between two ^P merge codes, as in ^Pfilename^P, or make the merge more flexible by using the ^C and ^O codes to pause within the ^P codes so that you are asked for the name of the primary file when it is merged.

If you want the paragraphs to be automatically numbered as they are brought in, place a [Par#] code with each paragraph saved to disk. The same number will be displayed in each file, but when they are retrieved into the completed document they will be numbered appropriately. See *Paragraph Numbering* to learn how to change the numbering style and other options.

Using a New Secondary File

If you want to keep several mailing lists separate, but need to send a single mailing to everyone on all lists, you can insert ^Sfilename^S at the end of each secondary file to chain them together. When the end of one file is reached, a new secondary file is opened and used.

Related Entries

Block Protect

Convert Program

dBase II/III

Labels

Macros

Mail Merge

Paragraph Numbering

Sort and Select

Merge Codes

Codes to be used in a merge document are entered with Merge Codes (ALT-F9). You can also use this key to enter any other control character (such as ^B) that might be mapped to a special character.

See *Merge* for complete information. Table 4-2 and the command card have a complete description of each merge code.

Merge E and Merge R

Merge E (SHIFT-F9) and Merge R (F9) have two specific functions in Merge. See *Merge* for complete information.

Merge R (F9)

Merge R is sometimes referred to as a merge return because you press it instead of ENTER to end a field. A ^R[HRt] code is inserted between each field as shown in Figure 4-71 in the Merge entry.

Merge R is also used instead of ENTER to continue a merge after a pause.

Merge E (SHIFT-F9)

Merge E is often called a merge end because it is used to end each record in the secondary merge file. When pressed, a ^E[HRt] code is inserted.

It can also be used to end a merge that is in progress.

Merge/Sort

Merge/Sort (CTRL-F9) is used to start a merge or use the Sort feature. The features are associated because you can use Sort first to sort and select the records to be merged. See *Merge* and *Sort and Select* for complete details.

Minus Key

The minus key on the keyboard is used as a required hyphen in WordPerfect. To insert a minus (negative) sign or a dash, press HOME,- instead.

See *Dashes* and *Hyphenation* for complete information.

MODE Command

MODE is a DOS command that can be used if you are having difficulty with colors not holding in WordPerfect.

Some programs change the mode from CO80 (color, 80

columns) to BW80 (black and white) because they can't run in color. These programs might not return to the original mode and thus would not allow WordPerfect to display colors.

Keystrokes

From DOS, enter **MODE CO80**. If you see the message "File not found," you need to copy the MODE.COM file from the original DOS diskette to the hard disk or boot disk. If colors are displayed upon entering WordPerfect, you have corrected the problem.

If this does not work, check the switches on the Color/Graphics Monitor Adapter card. The system board might also have switches that need to be set for color.

Hints

Consider placing the MODE CO80 command in a batch file that starts WordPerfect. You could also place it at the end of the batch file used to start the other program that changed the MODE. See Chapter 1 for more information about creating and editing batch files.

Related Entries

Colors

See Also Chapter 1, "Getting Started"

Modems

WordPerfect files can be sent through communication lines via a modem.

Keystrokes

You can send a WordPerfect file in binary format or use the Save option on Text In/Out (CTRL-F5) to save the file in ASCII format. If you use the latter option, all WordPerfect codes will be stripped from the file.

Convert Program

If you want to send a file that contains WordPerfect codes over a seven-bit modem or communications line, all codes will be stripped because they use eight bits. If you want to keep the codes, use the Convert program to convert the file to seven-bit format before sending it. The recipient of the file must then convert it back to WordPerfect format through the Convert program.

1. Start the Convert program found on the Learning disk. If you are not sure of the exact steps, see *Convert Program*.

2. Enter the name of the file to be converted.

3. Enter the name of the file which will hold the converted data. If the file exists, you will be asked if you want to replace the original file. Type **Y** or **N**.

4. If you are converting from WordPerfect to seven-bit, type **1** for WordPerfect, then **7** for seven-bit transfer. To convert a file back to WordPerfect format, choose option **7**. No other information is needed for the conversion.

DOS Text (ASCII) File

You can also save the file as a DOS text file. This option strips out all WordPerfect codes.

1. Press Text In/Out (CTRL-F5).

2. Type **1** to Save the file.

3. Enter the name of the file. Be careful not to overwrite the original WordPerfect file if you don't want it replaced.

Print to Disk

Some codes that are stripped contain text, such as headers, footers, and footnotes. If you want to retain all the text, print the file to disk.

The following procedure assumes that you have left Printer 6 as a DOS text printer that will print to a file on disk called DOS.TXT. If you have reassigned another printer definition to Printer 6 (choose option 2 in Printer Control to see the list of printer assignments), you will need to select printers again before completing the following steps.

1. With the document to be printed to disk on the screen, press Print (SHIFT-F7).

2. Type **3** for Options.

3. Type **1** for Printer Number.

4. Type **6** for printer number 6 if that is the DOS text printer.

5. Press ENTER to return to the document and the one-line print menu.

6. Type **1** to print the full text.

By default, the DOS.TXT file will normally be saved to the root directory because there is no pathname included with the filename. The pathname and filename can both be specified when selecting printers.

Related Entries

DOS Text Files

Print to Disk

Select Printers

Move

There are several ways in which text can be moved. Move (CTRL-F4) can be used to cut or copy a sentence, paragraph, or page; Block (ALT-F4) can highlight a variable amount of text, a column, or a rectangle that can then be cut or copied with Move (CTRL-F4); or you can delete any amount of text, then restore it in any location with Cancel (F1).

Keystrokes

Move (CTRL-F4)

Use Move (CTRL-F4) to cut or copy a sentence, paragraph, or page.

1. Position the cursor in the sentence, paragraph, or page to be moved. Press Move (CTRL-F4).

2. Type **1** for Sentence, **2** for Paragraph, or **3** for Page.

3. The appropriate section of text is highlighted.

4. Type **1** to Cut or **2** to Copy the section.

5. Move the cursor to the new location and press Move (CTRL-F4).

6. Type **5** to Retrieve the text.

If you prefer, you can retrieve the cut/copied text by pressing Retrieve (SHIFT-F10), then ENTER. This retrieves the "unnamed" block used to store the cut/copied text.

Block (ALT-F4)

You can highlight any amount of text with Block (ALT-F4) and then cut or copy the text with Move (CTRL-F4).

1. Position the cursor at one end of the text to be cut or copied.

2. Press Block (ALT-F4).

3. Move the cursor to highlight the block. You can also press any character key to highlight text to the next occurrence of that character, SPACEBAR to highlight to the next space, ENTER to highlight to the next [HRt], or PGDN to highlight to the next page.

4. Press Move (CTRL-F4).

5. Type **1** to Cut or **2** to Copy.

6. Position the cursor in the location where the cut/copied text is to be retrieved.

7. Press Move (CTRL-F4), then **5** to Retrieve the cut/copied text.

If you prefer, you could press Retrieve (SHIFT-F10) and ENTER to retrieve the cut/copied text.

Columns

Block (ALT-F4) and Move (CTRL-F4) can be used to highlight and cut/copy a column (tabbed column) or rectangle. If you want to move text within a text column (newspaper or parallel), use the regular Block move. See *Copy Text and Columns* and *Cut Text and Columns*, for specific details.

Restore Deleted Text with Cancel (F1)

A simple way of moving text added in version 4.2 follows.

1. Delete any amount of text.

2. Move the cursor to a new location.

3. Press Cancel (F1). The last deletion is displayed and highlighted.

4. Type **1** to Restore the text.

If necessary, type **2** to see the previous deletions. Up to three can be restored.

If you use this option, it is best to restore the deleted text immediately or you might lose it. Remember that only the last three deletions can be restored.

Hints

The amount of text that can be moved or deleted and re-stored is limited only by the amount of disk space available.

If you press Switch (SHIFT-F3), you can retrieve a second document into memory. After cutting or copying text, you can press Switch (SHIFT-F3) again and retrieve the text into the other document.

Cut and copied text is saved to the same unnamed file. The section of text remains there until another section of text is cut or copied, letting you retrieve it in several places. This would be useful if you accidentally typed 1 to Cut instead of 2 to Copy. You could immediately retrieve the text back into the original location, then move to the new location and retrieve it again. This feature is also useful if you need to retrieve several copies of a certain block of text onto the screen.

Move (CTRL-F4)

When using Move (CTRL-F4) alone, a sentence is defined as a block of text from the first capitalized letter in a sentence up to and including at least three spaces after a period (.), question mark (?), or exclamation mark (!). (However, there are usually only one or two spaces at the end of a sentence.)

A paragraph is defined as a block from one [HRt] up to and including the next [HRt]. A single line or sentence preceded and followed by a [HRt] could be considered a paragraph. Note that only the ending [HRt] is included with the paragraph.

A page is defined as a block of text from one hard page [HPg] or soft page [SPg] break up to and including the next hard or soft page break. Only the ending page break is included with the page.

See the entries for columns for more information about cutting/copying columns.

Block

If you highlight a block, press Save (F10), then ENTER, you will save the block of text to the same unnamed block used for cut/copied text. As mentioned, an alternate way of retrieving the unnamed block is to press Retrieve (SHIFT-F10), then ENTER.

To move a block of text to the end of an existing file, define the Block (ALT-F4), press Move (CTRL-F4), and type **3** to Append. Enter the name of the file to which the block should be appended.

Restore Deleted Text

Any group of consecutive deletions is considered to be a single deletion. Therefore, you could press Delete Word (CTRL-BACKSPACE), DEL, Delete to End of Line (CTRL-END), and BACKSPACE, and they would all be considered one deletion. The single deletion is stored in memory as soon as you press any other nondeleting key.

If you press BACKSPACE or DEL and encounter a code that needs confirmation before it can be deleted, you can type **Y** and the deletion continues. If you skip over the code without typing Y, the consecutive deletion is ended at that code.

Related Entries

Cancel

Columns

Copy Text and Columns

Cut Text and Columns

Switch

Undelete

Moving the Cursor

See *Cursor Keys*

Multiple Copies

The number of copies to be printed can be specified by pressing Print (SHIFT-F7) and choosing **3** for Options to change the number of copies for the current print job, or by choosing option **4** for Printer Control, then **1** under Select Print Options to change the number of copies for each document printed until you exit WordPerfect.

See *Number of Copies* for complete details.

New Page

You can force a page break by pressing Hard Page (CTRL-ENTER). Otherwise, WordPerfect will break the page automatically when the maximum number of lines is reached.

When working with columns, a Hard Page is also used to end one column and begin another.

See *Hard Page* for more information.

New Page Number

WordPerfect can be set to number pages automatically. However, if you must assign a specific number to a page, you can choose the New Page Number option on the Page Format (ALT-F8) menu.

This feature is also used to choose between Arabic or Roman numerals as the style of numbering to be used.

Keystrokes

1. Move the cursor to the beginning of the page that is to be renumbered. If it is the current page, press Go To (CTRL-HOME, ↑), to move to the top of the page.

2. Press Page Format (ALT-F8). "New Page #:" is displayed on the screen.

3. Type **2** for New Page Number.

4. Enter the new page number.

5. Type **1** for Arabic numbering (1, 2, 3, and so on) or **2** for Roman numerals (i, ii, iii, iv, and so on).

Hints

A code [Pg#:n] is inserted into the document. The *n* displays the selected page number. If you assigned 4 as the new page number in Roman numerals, the code would appear as [Pg#:iv]. The new page number is reflected on the status line (shown in Arabic style only).

The code takes effect until a new code is encountered. The code is also used to determine the number and style to be used for automatic page numbering. This includes the ^B code (which inserts the page number at print time anywhere on a page or in a header or footer) or a ^N (which inserts the page number in a header or footer at print time).

Printing with Renumbered Pages

When you print from Printer Control, you can specify which pages are to be printed. Before version 4.2, each physical page was considered to be numbered consecutively from page 1 regardless of new page number assignments. If you had a new page 1 five pages into the document, it was considered as page 5 instead of the second page 1.

With the introduction of 4.2, you can more logically specify the exact page numbers to be printed. Each time a new page number is assigned, WordPerfect considers it a "section." The sections are divided into Arabic sections and Roman sections, so if you change the page numbering four times in a document (two Arabic and two Roman), WordPerfect sees two sections of each. When entering the number of a specific page or pages to be printed, you can include the section, a colon, then the physical page found within that section. The numbering style option (Roman or Arabic) chosen with Page format determines which type of section it will search for.

You can combine entries by separating them with a space or comma. You can also specify ranges within or across sections. See *Print* for more details.

Page Numbers in Tables, Lists, and the Index

When you generate a Table of Contents, Table of Authorities, lists, or an index, the page number where the entry is located is noted. These features take new page numbers into account and will display both Arabic and Roman numerals when applicable.

If you insert several hard page breaks so tables and lists will be generated on separate pages, those pages are also taken into consideration during the process. If a New Page code is not found immediately after these extra pages, the numbers that are generated will not be accurate (unless, of course, you want the front matter to be included in the consecutive numbering).

Applications

Introduction or front matter pages can be numbered with lowercase Roman numerals. At the beginning of the first "real" page, you can insert another [Pg#:] code specifying that it should be considered as a new page 1 in the document and should be printed using Arabic numbers.

This feature can also be used to continue consecutive page numbering from one document to another. For example, if you have two very large documents and the first one ends with page 130, you could insert a new page number at the beginning of the second document to start with page 131.

Related Entries

Footers

Headers and Footers

Index

Lists

Page Numbering

Print

Table of Authorities

Table of Contents

Newspaper-Style Columns

The Columns feature can be used to create either newspaper-style or parallel columns. See *Columns* for complete details and steps.

"Non-system Disk or Disk Error"

This error message will be displayed if you try to start the computer with a diskette that does not contain the DOS system files.

Reasons

You must start the computer with the DOS disk or a disk formatted with the /S option (meaning "formatted with the system").

You might get this message if you have a hard disk and a non-system disk is in drive A (and, in certain cases, drive B) and the drive door is closed.

Solutions

If you have two disk drives, replace the disk with the DOS disk or one that has been formatted with the /S option. The file COMMAND.COM must be on the disk.

If you have a hard disk, remove the disks from drive A and B or open the disk drive doors. The computer will then look for COMMAND.COM and other system files on the hard disk.

NUM LOCK Key

Num Lock is used to toggle between using the numeric keypad to enter numbers or to move the cursor. The numeric keypad is useful when entering numbers into a table of numbers or when using the Math feature.

Keystrokes

Some computers have both a numeric keypad and a middle section that can be used to move the cursor. In this type of situation, Num Lock is usually turned on automatically when the computer is started.

To turn Num Lock on or off, press NUM LOCK. If Num Lock is on, "Pos" will temporarily flash to remind you of the status. If you want to immediately stop "Pos" from flashing, press ENTER. Num Lock remains on even if "Pos" stops flashing. Press NUM LOCK , again to turn off Num Lock.

If numbers appear on the screen when you are trying to

move the cursor, you might have accidentally pressed NUM LOCK. Press it again to turn it off.

Number of Copies

You can change the number of copies for a single print job or for several jobs.

Keystrokes

Change the Number of Copies for a Single Job

1. Press Print (SHIFT-F7).

2. Type **3** for Options.

3. Type **2** for Number of Copies.

4. Enter the number of copies for that job.

5. Press ENTER to return to the document and the one-line print menu.

6. Type **1** to print the full text, **2** to print the page, or type **4** for Printer Control and use the P option to print a document.

Change the Number of Copies for Several Print Jobs

1. Press Print (SHIFT-F7).

2. Type **4** for Printer Control.

3. Type **1** to Select Print Options.

4. Type **2** for Number of Copies.

5. Enter the number of copies.

6. Press ENTER twice to return to the document.

Hints

When changing the number of print jobs for one document, you must immediately send the print job to the printer when presented with the one-line print menu or the temporary options will be reset.

When selecting the option through the Printer Control menu, all print jobs queued from that point will be affected until the number of copies is changed again or until you exit WordPerfect and reenter.

Related Entries

Print

Outline

WordPerfect can help create outlines by automatically numbering each entry (up to seven levels). When items are added or deleted, the outline is automatically renumbered. The following illustration shows the numbering style assigned to each level.

```
I.   Level 1
     A.   Level 2
          1.   Level 3
               a.   Level 4
                    (1)  Level 5
                         (a)  Level 6
                              i)   Level 7
```

Keystrokes

Create an Outline

1. Press Mark Text (ALT-F5).

2. Type **1** for Outline. "Outline" appears in the lower left corner of the screen.

3. Press ENTER to insert the first number. A [Par#:Auto] code is inserted and the appropriate number is displayed.

You can then do one of the following:

Press →Indent (F4), →Indent← (SHIFT-F4), or SPACEBAR and type the outline entry.

Press TAB to move the number to the next tab setting, changing the level number.

Press ENTER as many times as you want to add space between each item. (The first time ENTER is pressed, the number is inserted. If the cursor is just to the right of the number, ENTER inserts [HRt] codes as it normally does.)

To move back a level, press Left Margin Release (SHIFT-TAB).

Change the Outline Style

1. Move the cursor to the beginning of the outline (either before or after it is created).

2. Press Mark Text (ALT-F5).

3. Type **6** for Other Options.

4. Type **1** to Define Paragraph/Outline Numbering. The menu shown in Figure 4-75 appears.

```
Paragraph Numbering Definition

    1 - Paragraph Numbering, e.g. 1. a. i. (1) (a) (i) 1)
    2 - Outline Numbering, e.g. I. A. 1. a. (1) (a) i)
    3 - Legal Numbering, e.g. 1. 1.1. 2.2.1 etc.
    4 - Other

Selection: 0

Levels:               1    2    3    4    5    6    7
  Number Style:       0    2    4    3    4    3    1
  Punctuation:        1    1    1    1    3    3    2

Number Style                              Punctuation
0 - Upper Case Roman                      0 - #
1 - Lower Case Roman                      1 - #.
2 - Upper Case Letters                    2 - #)
3 - Lower Case Letters                    3 - (#)
4 - Numbers
5 - Numbers with previous levels separated by a period

Starting Paragraph Number (in Legal Style): 1
```

Figure 4-75.   Paragraph Numbering Definition menu

5. Type **1** for Paragraph Numbering, **2** if you want the same Outline Numbering style but want to begin with a new number, or **3** for Legal Numbering.

The following shows the numbering style assigned to Paragraph Numbering.

```
1.
      a.
           i.
               (1)
                   (a)
                       (i)
                           1)
```

The next illustration demonstrates how each level is numbered when Legal Numbering is chosen.

```
1.
    1.1.
        1.1.1.
            1.1.1.1.
                1.1.1.1.1.
                    1.1.1.1.1.1.
```

You can also type **4** to create a style of your own. If you choose this option, you are placed at the Number Style option for level number 1. Press ENTER to accept the current setting or type a number from the menu. Choose the punctuation for the number. Continue until all the levels have been entered.

6. The last menu question, "Starting Paragraph Number (in Legal Style):" lets you decide which number will be first in the outline. For example, if you enter 10, the first number in level 1 will be 10, XX, xx, J, or j, depending on the style chosen.

Hints

When you turn Outline on and off, codes are not inserted. Instead, you will see "Outline" in the lower left corner of the screen. The message indicates that whenever ENTER is pressed, a new paragraph number code [Par#] is inserted.

When the Paragraph/Outline Numbering style is changed, a [Par#Def] code is inserted into the document which affects the [Par#] codes from that point forward.

Next or Previous Level

Besides ENTER, the other two keystrokes that differ slightly when Outline is on are TAB and Left Margin Release (SHIFT-TAB). When the cursor is to the right of a [Par#] code and TAB is pressed, the cursor pulls the paragraph number to the next tab setting and changes it to the next level. When Left Margin Release (SHIFT-TAB) is pressed, the number is pushed back to the previous tab setting and changes to the previous level.

If TAB is used, a [Tab] code is inserted just before the [Par#] code and the level of the number changes. If Left Margin Release (SHIFT-TAB) is pressed and the cursor is just to the right of the [Par#] code, a [<-Mar Rel:] code is not inserted; only the outline number is changed. However, if the cursor is just to the left of the code, the number is changed *and* a [<-Mar Rel:] code is inserted.

Deleting a Paragraph Number

You can either delete the paragraph number on the regular editing screen or in the Reveal Codes (ALT-F3) screen with any of the deleting keys.

Because the "number" is really a code, you would only need to press BACKSPACE or DEL once instead of several times to delete the number. Remaining numbers are automatically updated.

Multiple Outlines

If you want to have more than one outline in a document and you want each to begin with 1, redefine the Paragraph/Outline Numbering style, choose the same style again, and enter **1** as the answer to the "Starting Paragraph Number" question.

In versions previous to 4.2, you could start another outline with number 1 just by selecting the same or a different numbering style. With 4.2, the "Starting Paragraph Number" option was added so an outline could start with any number.

Outline Number Positions

The level of a paragraph number is decided by tab settings. If the physical position of the levels needs to be changed, change the tab settings with Line Format (SHIFT-F8), option 1 or 2.

Outlining Versus Paragraph Numbering

The Outline and Paragraph Numbering features use the same codes: [Par#] and [Par#Def]. When Outline is on, the [Par#] codes (numbers) are inserted automatically when the ENTER key is pressed—thus the [Par#:Auto] code.

If you want to manually choose the placement of the number and the level to be assigned, use Paragraph Numbering. This feature is helpful in situations where you need to choose the exact position and level of the number. The following illustration shows where Paragraph Numbering would be used to number a centered title with the first level.

ARTICLE III

AMENDMENT, REVOCATION, AND ADDITIONS TO TRUST

    3.1 <u>Rights of the Undersigned</u>. As long as the Undersigned is alive, the Undersigned reserves the right to amend, modify or revoke this Trust in whole or in part, including the principal, and the present or past undisbursed income from such principal.

If you had used Outline to insert the number in this example, it would have been numbered as the seventh level because the code fell after the seventh tab setting.

You can actually use both features together. Just remember that Paragraph Numbering is used to manually assign an automatic number, while Outline inserts the number and decides the level according to tab settings.

Aligning Outline or Paragraph Numbers

The WordPerfect manual describes how to align each number on the right as it is typed. An easier way is to create the outline, then run a repeating macro that searches for all paragraph numbers and aligns them. Then you do not have to start the macro before each entry. Running the macro after the outline is created takes all levels into account, not just the first one. If you find a better way, you could put those steps into the macro instead.

1. Press Macro Def (CTRL-F10) and enter a name for the macro (ALIGN is a suggestion).

2. Press HOME,HOME, ↑ to move to the beginning of the document.

3. Press Search (F2).

4. Press Mark Text (ALT-F5) and type **2** to search for a [Par#] code.

5. Press Search (F2) again to begin the search.

6. Press ← once to move to the left of the number.

7. Press Tab Align (.08CTRL-F6) to align the number.

8. Press → once to move the cursor just to the right of the number.

9. Press SPACEBAR twice and type a period (.) to force the number back to its original position and stop the alignment.

10. Press BACKSPACE once to delete the period. The alignment codes remain.

11. Press Super/Subscript (SHIFT-F1) and type **3** for Overstrike. The cursor will back up one space so the existing Indent codes will go to the appropriate tab setting.

12. Press Macro (ALT-F10) and enter the name of this macro so it will repeat. Press Macro Def (CTRL-F10) to end the macro definition.

This macro would affect all paragraph numbering codes and is dependent on having Indent codes between a paragraph number and the entry.

Related Entries

Paragraph Numbering

Tabs, Clear and Set

Overstrike a Character

The Overstrike feature allows more than one character to be printed in the same position.

Keystrokes

1. Type the first character.

2. Press Super/Subscript (SHIFT-F1).

3. Type **3** for Overstrike.

4. Type the second character. The first character is replaced with the second character on the screen. Both will be printed, but only the last character typed appears on the screen.

Hints

When Overstrike is selected, an [Ovrstk] code is inserted. Remember that only the last character typed will appear on the screen, so you should type the character that you want to be "visible" last. If you created the characters ã and õ, and typed the tilde last, you would not be able to tell the difference between the two on the screen. They would both appear as "~" on the screen. You would have to press Reveal Codes (ALT-F3) to see the character "underneath."

To delete the overstrike, you cannot just delete the second character typed because the [Ovrstk] code remains and will assume that the character will be used as the overstrike character. Instead, delete the code in Reveal Codes (ALT-F3) or confirm the deletion when asked, "Delete [Ovrstk]? (Y/N) N."

You can actually overstrike as many characters as you want. Overstrike is simply a code that tells WordPerfect to back up one space and print another character in the same position (or with some printers, do a second, third, or even fourth pass to print each character in the same position).

In addition to Overstrike, WordPerfect has a feature that will strike through several characters with a dash (-). See *Strikeout Text* for details.

Applications

Use Overstrike to create special characters not included with the computer. While many characters such as Ä and Û are available for mapping to ALT- or CTRL-key combinations (see *Special Characters*), other characters like the Portuguese ã and õ are not, but can be created with Overstrike.

You could map these special characters to an ALT-key

combination by writing an ALT-key macro that types the first character and overstrikes it with the second. It would not be mapped in a true sense, but would be created when the ALT-key combination was pressed.

Strikeout is another WordPerfect feature that is similar to Overstrike. It uses a dash to strike out text that is being considered for deletion. If you want to use a different character such as a slash, you should consider changing the strikeout character to a slash in the Printer program instead of using Overstrike on each character. See Chapter 7 for specifics.

Related Entries

Special Characters

Strikeout Text

Page Breaks

WordPerfect automatically inserts a page break when the end of a page is reached. This type of page break is called a Soft Page. A hard page break can be entered manually at any location by pressing Hard Page (CTRL-ENTER).

Keystrokes

A soft page break is displayed as a single dashed line across the screen. To insert a hard page break, press CTRL-ENTER. A double dashed line appears. See the following illustration for an example of soft and hard page breaks.

```
    A Soft Page break [SPg] is displayed as a single dashed line.
    ------------------------------------------------------------------

    A Hard Page break [HPg] is displayed as a double dashed line.
    ==================================================================
```

Hints

WordPerfect comes with the form length set at 66 lines with 54 single-spaced lines on each page. If the page contains a header, one-line footer, page number, or footnotes, the appropriate number of lines is subtracted from the 54 lines. WordPerfect also subtracts an extra line for spacing between a page number, header, footer, footnotes, and the text.

If you want to increase or decrease the number of text lines that can be printed on the page, press Page Format (ALT-F8) and type **4** for Page Length. You can choose letter size paper (the standard default setting), legal size paper (72 lines of text on an 84-line page), or you can specify your own length (up to 108 lines).

You can move freely across page breaks with any cursor keys and can see the text from one page to the next. There are no limitations on the amount of text that can be cut or copied between pages.

Move to a Specific Page

Press PGUP or PGDN to move the cursor to the top of the previous or next page. To go to a specific page, press Go To (CTRL-HOME) and enter the page number. The cursor moves to the top of that page.

If you want to go to the top or bottom of the current page, press Go To (CTRL-HOME) and ↑ or ↓. The following is a summary of these keystrokes:

Previous page	PGUP
Next page	PGDN
Go to page n	Go To (CTRL-HOME),n
Go to the top of the page	Go To (CTRL-HOME),↑
Go to the bottom of the page	Go To (CTRL-HOME),↓

Applications

Insert a Hard Page manually if you want the text that immediately follows to always begin on a new page. You can also use a Hard Page to end a short page.

If you are generating a Table of Contents, Table of Authorities, lists, or an index, you can create a separate page for those features before they are generated. Place the [Def Mark] codes in that new page so the table, list, or index will be generated there.

Related Entries

Footers

Footnotes and Endnotes

Go To

Headers and Footers

Page Length

Page Numbering

Table of Contents

Page Format

Page Format (ALT-F8) gives you several page options that appear only when a document is previewed or printed. Among those are page numbers, headers, footers, top margin, and center page. Other options make their presence known as you type, such as page length, widow/orphan protection, and conditional end of page. All the options on the menu help decide where a page break will occur.

Keystrokes

1. Move the cursor to the position where the change is to take place (usually at the beginning of a document or page).

2. Press Page Format (ALT-F8). You will see the menu shown in Figure 4-76.

```
Page Format

     1 - Page Number Position

     2 - New Page Number

     3 - Center Page Top to Bottom

     4 - Page Length

     5 - Top Margin

     6 - Headers or Footers

     7 - Page Number Column Positions

     8 - Suppress for Current page only

     9 - Conditional End of Page

     A - Widow/Orphan

Selection: 0
```

Figure 4-76.   Page Format menu

3. After selecting an option, you are placed in a sub-menu or see a message prompting you for more information. If you select option 3 to Center a Page from Top to Bottom, the screen rewrites quickly as the only indication that the code has been inserted.

4. After selecting an item, you will remain in the Page Format menu so you can continue making selections.

5. When finished, press ENTER or Exit (F7) to return to the document.

Options

Page Number Position and Page Number Column Positions

WordPerfect is set to *not* number pages. However, you can choose automatic page numbering at any time with the first option on the Page Format menu. If you type **1** for Page

Number Position, you will see a list of eight options for the page number position: top left, center, or right; bottom left, center, or right; or alternating left and right on the top or bottom of each page. At any point in the document, you can enter the Page Number Position submenu and type 0 to discontinue page numbering from that point forward.

Option 7, Page Number Column Positions, is closely tied to this first option because it determines the exact position of the left corner, center, or right corner. The default settings (in tenths of an inch) are 10, 42, and 74. This option could be used if you have a 2-inch right margin and have chosen to print a page number in the upper right corner. You would most likely want to change the page number position setting for the right corner from 74 to 64 so that the number and text will align correctly. Remember that in this menu, 1 inch = 10 spaces even if you are printing in 12 pitch or any other pitch.

The page number column position code [Pg# Col:10,42,64], should appear before the page number position code [Pos Pg#:1] so it will be in effect for all page numbers. See *Page Numbering* for details.

Assigning a New Page Number and Choosing Roman or Arabic Style

Page numbering can be set to start with a specific page number with this option. After entering the new page number, you can choose between Arabic numbering (1, 2, 3, and so on) or Roman numerals (i, ii, iii, and so on).

Center Page from Top to Bottom

This code must be placed at the top of a page before any text. It should, however, follow other codes such as a page length setting or bin number selection. If you are not sure where it should be placed, look at the codes and decide in which order the printer would need to receive them in order to print the page correctly.

When you choose this option, the screen quickly rewrites, but you have no other indication that the [Center Pg] code has been inserted. When you return to the document, you can press Reveal Codes (ALT-F3) for reassurance.

Page Length

This option lets you choose between letter or legal size paper. You can create your own page length ranging from 1 to 108 lines. This is useful for odd size paper, envelopes, or mailing labels.

Two different settings must be chosen: the actual length of the page (in six lines per inch), and the number of actual text lines that will be printed (taking both six and eight lines per inch into account).

The page length setting is also used in conjunction with the top margin (see the following) to determine the bottom margin. If you want to make the bottom margin smaller, increase the number of text lines to be printed. To make it larger, decrease the number of text lines.

Top Margin

The top margin is preset for 12 half-lines, which is one full inch. The top margin reacts differently depending on the type of forms you have selected. If you have continuous paper, this setting is used to determine the amount of space to move down on the page.

If you have hand-fed paper, WordPerfect assumes you will feed the paper in 1 inch. If the top margin is set at less than 1 inch, the paper should be rolled in to that point. If the setting is more than 1 inch, the paper should still be fed in 1 inch and WordPerfect will add the appropriate number of lines needed to move beyond 1 inch.

Headers or Footers

This option lets you print a header or footer on every page, odd pages, or even pages. Two headers and two footers are available for a document, so that alternating headers and footers are possible. Instead of using the page number position option, you can include a page number in a header or footer. In fact, you have more flexibility if you put the page number code (^B) in a header or footer because you can decide the exact placement, how much space to put between the number and the text, and include text with the page number.

WordPerfect automatically adjusts the page length for the number of lines in a header, but only for one line of a footer. A blank line is automatically inserted between the header or footer and the rest of the text on the page. If you want more space, insert extra lines at the end of a header or at the beginning of a footer. In the case of a footer, also change the page length option and decrease the number of text lines that can be printed on the page accordingly.

Suppress for Current Page Only

This code should appear at the beginning of the page before header, footer, or page numbering codes. You can turn off any combination of features, or you can choose to print the page number at the bottom center of the current page even if another position was previously chosen.

Conditional End of Page

This option is used to protect a specific number of lines from being split between pages. Before choosing the option, move to the line just above the text to be protected and count the number of lines including blank lines.

Widow/Orphan

If you type **Y** in answer to the question "Widow/Orphan Protect?," WordPerfect will not allow the first or last line of a paragraph to appear at the top or bottom of a page. Titles and headings are not automatically protected. Use Conditional End of Page to keep a title and the first few lines of a paragraph together.

Block Protect

After Block is on, pressing Page Format (ALT-F8) will not display the normal menu. Instead, you will see the message "Protect Block? (Y/N) N." This option is used to protect a block of text rather than a specific number of lines. This option can be used to keep a section of text together in spite of editing changes that could affect the number of lines.

Hints

Page Format codes usually belong at the beginning of a page. For example, if you define a header in the middle of a page, it cannot appear at the top of that page because the printer will not have received the code in time. However, if you define a footer in the middle of the page, or make the page length longer near the end of the page, the change will take place on the current page because the code will have reached the printer in time.

Most of the options found on the Page Format menu can be changed permanently in the Setup menu. Enter **WP/S** instead of **WP** to start WordPerfect and type **2** to change the initial settings.

Related Entries

Block Protect

Center Page from Top to Bottom

Conditional End of Page

Footers

Headers and Footers

New Page Number

Page Length

Page Numbering

Setup Menu

Suppress

Top Margin

Widows and Orphans

Page Length

Two common page length settings have been predefined for letter and legal size paper. You can also customize the page length setting to include anywhere from 1 to 108 lines on a page.

Keystrokes

1. Press Page Format (ALT-F8).

2. Type **4** for Page Length. The menu shown in Figure 4-77 appears.

3. Type **1** for Letter, **2** for Legal, or **3** for Other. If you choose "other," enter the form length (page length x 6), then enter the number of single-spaced text lines that should be printed on the page.

4. After you change the page length, the cursor remains in the Page Format menu. When finished entering changes, press ENTER to return to the document.

Hints

When you change the page length, a code such as [Pg Lnth:66,54] is inserted and will affect the document from that point forward. It should usually be one of the first codes

```
Page Length

    1 - Letter Size Paper: Form Length = 66 lines (11 inches)
        Single Spaced Text lines = 54 (This includes lines
        used for Headers, Footers and/or page numbers.)

    2 - Legal Size Paper: Form Length = 84 lines (14 inches)
        Single Spaced Text Lines = 72 (This includes lines
        used for Headers, Footers and/or page numbers.)

    3 - Other (Maximum page length = 108 lines.)

Current Settings

    Form Length in Lines (6 per inch):  66

    Number of Single Spaced Text Lines: 54




Selection: 0
```

Figure 4-77.   Page Length menu

on the page. If you are using a laser printer, it should even be
inserted before a [Bin#] code.

The page length and top margin work closely together to
determine the bottom margin. If you increase the number of
lines on a page, you will make the bottom margin smaller. If
you want to split the space between the top and bottom margins, decrease the top margin accordingly.

Page Length and Printing Eight Lines per Inch

If you have chosen to print in eight lines per inch, you should
also increase the number of text lines that can be printed on
the page. For example, if you are printing eight lines per
inch, you can fit 72 lines in the space normally taken by 54
lines of text in six lines per inch. However, the form length
should always be figured at six lines per inch.

If you use legal size paper most of the time, consider changing the page length setting in the Setup menu (enter **WP/S** instead of **WP** and choose option 2).

Landscape Printing and Page Length

Most laser printers have the ability to print in *landscape,* or rotated mode; this means that they can print vertically instead of horizontally on a page.

When printing landscape, do not change the number of lines in the form length. The number of single-spaced text lines can be adjusted to any applicable length. With laser printers, the page length code should precede all other codes and text on the page.

Applications

If you need to fit just a line or two more on a page, you can increase the page length. Remember that the form length will remain the same; only the number of text lines will change.

You can set up a format for envelopes and mailing labels that require a smaller page length. Instead of having to figure a bottom margin, set the top margin at 0 and make the form length and the number of text lines the same. Then choose to center a page from top to bottom with Page Format (ALT-F8) option 3. The few lines for the label or envelope would then be centered on the length of the "page."

Related Entries

Bottom Margin

Center Page from Top to Bottom

Labels

Lines per Inch

Top Margin

Page Numbering

Page numbering can be done by selecting a page number position or by including a ^B in a header, footer, or anywhere else on a page.

Keystrokes

1. Go to the top of the document or page to be numbered.

2. Press Page Format (ALT-F8).

3. Type ́1 for Page Numbering. The menu shown in Figure 4-78 is displayed.

4. Type any of options **1** through **8** to set the position for the page number. If you are discontinuing page numbering from that point forward, type **0**.

```
Position of Page Number on Page

    0 - No page numbers

    1 - Top left of every page

    2 - Top center of every page

    3 - Top right of every page

    4 - Top alternating left & right

    5 - Bottom left of every page

    6 - Bottom center of every page

    7 - Bottom right of every page

    8 - Bottom alternating left & right


Selection: 0
```

Figure 4-78.   Position of Page Number on Page menu

5. Press ENTER to leave the Page Format menu and return to the document.

A code [Pos Pg#:1] is inserted to indicate that page numbering has been selected. The number in the code indicates the selected menu option.

Page numbers will be printed with one blank line between the number and the text.

Hints

Page Number in a Header or Footer

To include a page number in a header or footer (or anywhere else on the page), press CTRL-B to insert a ^B. If a special character has been "mapped" to CTRL-B, you will see the special character instead. If this happens, you can use ^N or redefine your keyboard mapping to remove the special character from the B combination.

The current page number will be inserted at the location of ^B when the document is printed. This feature is useful when you want to include text (such as a chapter title or the word "Page") with the page number. See "Creating 'Page n of n' Page Numbers" for a macro that will create a header or footer that prints the total number of pages.

Among the choices for page number positions are top or bottom alternating left and right. You can do something similar with headers and footers, but it takes a few more steps. For example, for the pages in an Appendix I, you could define Header A to print "Page I-^B" at the left margin of even-numbered pages, then define Header B to print "Page I-^B" at the right margin of odd-numbered pages.

If you want more than one blank line between the page number and the text, consider placing ^B in a header or footer. To add the extra space, press ENTER at the end of the header or beginning of the footer. If you add extra space to the footer, remember that WordPerfect only adjusts for one line; the remaining text in the footer will be printed in the bottom margin. If this is unacceptable, decrease the number of text lines that will be printed on the page with the Page Length option.

Do not request both a header or footer *and* a page number, because they will most likely print on the same line. To avoid this, insert a blank line in the header or footer so the page number can print in that space, or place a ^B in the header or footer.

In previous versions of WordPerfect, only a ^N was documented as the method to insert a page number in a header or footer. It can still be used; however, ^B is now the suggested method because it can be placed anywhere in a document, not just in a header or footer. A ^N outside a header or footer would act as a merge code to go to the next record in a secondary merge file.

Changing the Page Number Column Positions

If you place the page number in a header or footer, you can decide the exact position for the number. Features such as Center (SHIFT-F6) and Flush Right (ALT-F6) can be used in a header or footer to help place the ^B in the center or at the right margin.

If you choose the Position of Page Number feature, as directed in "Keystrokes," the left corner is considered to be 1 inch from the left edge of the paper, center is 4 1/4 inches from the left edge of the paper, and the right corner is 7 1/2 inches from the left edge of the paper (1 inch from the right margin on a standard 8 1/2-inch wide page).

If you have selected a page number for the upper right corner, but have a 2-inch right margin, the page number will not line up with the text at the right margin. The same could happen with the left corner and the center position. To solve this problem, you can use the Page Number Column Positions option on the Page Format menu.

Change the page number column position before the page number code so that all page numbers will be affected by the change.

1. Press Page Format (ALT-F8).

2. Type **7** for Page Number Column Positions. The following menu is displayed.

```
Reset Column Position for Page Numbers

  (L = Left Corner, C = Center, R = Right Corner)

     1 - Set to Initial Settings (In tenths of an inch)
              L=10 C=42 R=74

     2 - Set to Specified Settings
Current Settings

        L=10 C=42 R=74
```

3. Type **2** to change the settings listed or **1** if you are returning to the initial settings.

4. If you choose option 2, enter the new column positions for the left, center, and right positions.

5. Press ENTER to return to the document.

Remember to always figure the column positions in tenths of an inch (1 inch = 10 spaces) regardless of the current pitch setting.

Assigning New Page Number and Choosing Arabic or Roman Style

The second option on the Page Format menu lets you assign a new page number to the current page and lets you choose between Arabic (1, 2, 3, and so on) or Roman (i, ii, iii, and so on) as the style of numbering to be used. This code should be placed at the top of the page so it can affect the number and style for all page numbers. See *New Page Number* for more information.

Creating "Page n of n" Page Numbers

Although WordPerfect doesn't have the ability to include the last page number as part of a header or footer, as in "Page *n* of *n*," you can go to the end of the document, note the page number, and return to the beginning of the document to define a header or footer that includes that number. The following steps create a macro that makes the process easier than doing it yourself.

1. Press Macro Def (CTRL-F10) and enter the name for the macro (PAGE# is a suggestion).

2. Press (HOME,HOME,↓) to go to the end of the document.

3. Press (CTRL-PGUP,ENTER,ENTER) to insert a pause. When the macro is run, it would pause here to let you make a note of the last page number. You could even insert a comment into the document before the pause to prompt the user to take note of the page number.

4. Press (HOME,HOME,↑) to move to the beginning of the document.

5. Press Page Format (ALT-F8) and type **6** for Headers or Footers. Choose the type of header or footer and the occurrence.

6. Type **Page ^B of**, remembering to press CTRL-B to insert the ^B code. If you have a special character mapped to CTRL-B, that character will be displayed instead. If this happens, use ^N. If ^N is also mapped, you will have to go to the CTRL and ALT Key Mapping menu and remove the special character from the CTRL-B combination.

7. Press (CTRL-PGUP,ENTER,ENTER) to insert a second pause immediately after "Page ^B of" so that during the macro you can insert the last page number.

8. Press Exit (F7) to leave the Header/Footer menu and ENTER to return to the document.

9. Press Macro Def (CTRL-F10) in order to end the macro definition.

The macro should be run after the document is completely finished. If you run the macro more than once in a document, the previous header or footer should be deleted or you will get the wrong last page number.

Related Entries

Footers

Headers and Footers

New Page Number

Page Up/Down

Press PGUP to move to the beginning of the previous page in the document or PGDN to move to the beginning of the next page.

If you want to move up or down screen by screen instead of page by page, press the gray minus or plus keys on the numeric keypad.

Go To (CTRL-HOME) can be used to go to a specific page by entering the page number. You can also move quickly to the top or bottom of the current page by pressing Go To (CTRL-HOME) and ↑ or ↓.

See *Cursor Keys* for complete information.

Pagination

Repagination is not necessary in WordPerfect because the document is automatically reformatted when text is added or deleted. See *Page Numbering* if you need instructions on numbering a document.

Paragraph Numbering

You can assign numbers to paragraphs that will be automatically updated when a paragraph is added or deleted.

Keystrokes

1. Move the cursor to the position where the paragraph number is to appear.

2. Press Mark Text (ALT-F5).

3. Type **2** for Para #. You will see the following prompt.

```
Paragraph Level (ENTER for automatic):
```

4. Press ENTER if you want WordPerfect to assign the paragraph number at the appropriate level (levels are decided by tab settings) or enter the level number (from 1 through 7) if it should be assigned a specific level.

Hints

A [Par#:] code is inserted at the cursor's location. It can either be an automatic paragraph number (meaning that WordPerfect assigns the level number according to the existing tab settings) or a fixed paragraph number (when you have assigned a specific level to the number). The two codes differ slightly in appearance when Reveal Codes (ALT-F3) is pressed: [Par#:Auto] is the code used when WordPerfect assigns the level and is the same code that appears when you use the Outline feature. When you specify a level, a paragraph number code is inserted in the form of [Par#:1]. The number indicates the level to be used.

The Outline and Paragraph Numbering features use the same codes and the same style of numbering. Outline inserts the numbers automatically when ENTER is pressed and numbers each one according to the current tab settings. Paragraph numbers are automatic numbers that can be inserted manually and can be assigned a specific level of numbering. Both are automatically renumbered when other [Par#] codes are added or deleted.

The level number is determined by tab settings. If a paragraph number is placed between tabs, the preceding level will be used. If you insert a [TAB] that pushes the code to the next tab setting, the number will change to that level (unless you have assigned a specific level to the number).

If the position of the levels needs to be changed, change the tab settings in Line Format (SHIFT-F8), option 1 or 2.

Change the Numbering Style

WordPerfect has been preset to number each level in an Outline format.

```
I.    Level 1
      A.    Level 2
            1.    Level 3
                  a.    Level 4
                        (1)  Level 5
                             (a)  Level 6
                                  i)   Level 7
```

You can use this style, change to paragraph or legal numbering, or choose a format of your own. The style can be changed before or after paragraph numbers have been entered.

1. Move the cursor to the beginning of the document or the beginning of the section of text to be numbered.

2. Press Mark Text (ALT-F5).

3. Type **6** for Other Options.

4. Type **1** to Define Paragraph/Outline Numbering. The menu shown in Figure 4-79 appears.

5. Type **1** for Paragraph Numbering, **2** if you want the same Outline Numbering style but want to begin with a new number, or **3** for Legal Numbering.

```
Paragraph Numbering Definition

    1 - Paragraph Numbering, e.g. 1. a. i. (1) (a) (i) 1)
    2 - Outline Numbering, e.g. I. A. 1. a. (1) (a) i)
    3 - Legal Numbering, e.g. 1. 1.1. 2.2.1 etc.
    4 - Other

Selection: 0

Levels:              1   2   3   4   5   6   7
   Number Style:     0   2   4   3   4   3   1
   Punctuation:      1   1   1   1   3   3   2

Number Style                          Punctuation
0 - Upper Case Roman                  0 - #
1 - Lower Case Roman                  1 - #.
2 - Upper Case Letters                2 - #)
3 - Lower Case Letters                3 - (#)
4 - Numbers
5 - Numbers with previous levels separated by a period

Starting Paragraph Number (in Legal Style): 1
```

Figure 4-79.   Paragraph Numbering Definition menu

The following shows the numbering style assigned to Paragraph Numbering.

```
1.
     a.
          i.
               (1)
                    (a)
                         (i)
                              1)
```

The next illustration demonstrates how each level is numbered when Legal Numbering is chosen.

```
1.
     1.1.
          1.1.1.
               1.1.1.1.
                    1.1.1.1.1.
                         1.1.1.1.1.1.
```

You can also type **4** to create a style of your own. If you choose this option, you are placed at the Number Style option for level number 1. Press ENTER to accept the current setting or type a number from the menu. Choose the punctuation for the number. Continue until all the levels have been entered.

6. The last menu question, "Starting Paragraph Number (in Legal Style):" lets you decide which number will be used first. For example, if you enter 10, the first number in level 1 will be 10, XX, xx, J, or j, depending on the style chosen.

Hints

If you use paragraph numbering often, and don't want to repeat the four or five steps it takes to insert a paragraph number, define a macro to do the same thing (ALT-P is a suggested name).

The following illustration shows a sample legal document in which three different numbering styles are used.

ARTICLE IV

OFFICERS

    Section 4.1 The Chairman of the Board. The Chairman of the Board, if there be such an officer, shall have the following powers and duties:

    (a) He shall preside at all stockholders' meetings.

    (b) He shall preside at all meetings of the Board of Directors.

    (c) He shall be a member of the Executive Committee, if any.

Notice that only the third level of numbering, using (a), (b), and so on, can be automatic. The rest must be assigned a particular level when the paragraph number is inserted. If WordPerfect would have assigned the level, "ARTICLE #" would have been numbered as the seventh level because the code fell after the seventh tab setting. The "Section #" would have been given a third level number because it falls between the third and fourth tab settings.

Adding Entries in an Outline

If you have created an outline with the Outline feature and need to go back and add an entry, you can do so with a Paragraph Number. This might be easier than turning on the Outline feature and trying to place the entry in the right location.

Automatically Numbering Lines

WordPerfect has a feature to number lines in the left margin. However, these numbers do not appear until printed and there is no choice of numbering style.

If you have a list of items that you decide need to be numbered, you can create the following macro to insert paragraph numbers for you. Go to the beginning of a list before defining this macro.

1. Press Macro Def (CTRL-F10) and enter the name for the macro (PARA# is a suggestion).

2. Press Search (F2), ENTER (to insert a [HRt]), and Search (F2) again to start the search. If you have paragraphs to be numbered instead of lines, press ENTER twice to insert two [HRt] codes as the search string.

3. Press Mark Text (ALT-F5) and type **2** to insert a paragraph number.

4. Press ENTER to choose the automatic paragraph level.

5. Press Indent (F4).

6. Press Macro Def (CTRL-F10) to end the macro.

To run the macro *n* times to number *n* lines, press ESC, type the number of lines to be numbered (do not press ENTER), press Macro (ALT-F10), and enter the name of the macro. These steps are mentioned because it is the safest method (if text followed the list of lines or paragraphs, it would also be numbered each time a [HRt] was found).

If the document comprises only the lines or paragraphs

to be numbered, you could insert an extra step between steps 4 and 5 to create a repeating macro (press Macro (ALT-F10) and enter the name of the original macro). This step would allow the macro to run until it can find no more [HRt] codes and would save you the step of pressing ESC and specifying the number of lines or paragraphs to be numbered.

Related Entries

Outline

Table of Contents

Tabs, Clear and Set

Parallel Columns

WordPerfect's parallel columns can be used in situations where text must wrap within a column, but must always be kept parallel on a page with other related columns.

Parallel columns could be used by scriptwriters to show several related activities such as action, words, and lighting. When text is added to or deleted from a column, the group of columns below will not be reformatted. They will move as a group to accommodate the text changes in the preceding group. Newspaper-style columns do just the opposite; text flows down the page, then into the next column, and additions or deletions of text result in reformatting of the text that follows.

See *Columns* for information on all options: tabbed columns, newspaper-style columns, and parallel columns.

Password Protection

Files can be locked with a password so that only the author of the file can retrieve, print, or look at the document. See *Lock and Unlock Documents* for complete details.

Pitch

Pitch refers to the number of characters that will be printed per horizontal inch.

Keystrokes

WordPerfect is preset to print in 10 pitch. To change the pitch, use the following procedure.

1. Press Print Format (CTRL-F8).

2. Type **1** for Pitch/Font.

3. Enter the pitch. If printing in a proportionally spaced font, enter an asterisk after the pitch (as in 13*).

4. Enter a number from 1 through 8 to select a new font or press ENTER to use the displayed font.

5. Press ENTER to leave the Print Format menu and return to your document.

Hints

A pitch/font code similar to [Font Change:13*,3] is inserted and will affect the number of characters printed per inch from that point forward. The first number indicates the selected pitch, the asterisk indicates proportional spacing, and the last number indicates the font selected.

Pitch and Font Combinations

If you are using a daisy-wheel printer, the print wheel decides the pitch to be used. Print wheels come in 10 pitch, 12 pitch, or even 15 pitch. If a wheel is marked "PS" for proportionally spaced, try 13* when specifying pitch.

A dot-matrix printer has several fonts that may or may not be affected by a pitch setting. For example, with some printers, you can change to an expanded or compressed font without also having to change the pitch. Some fonts, however, can take advantage of the pitch setting. Refer to Chapter 6 for the suggested pitch settings for each font, or print the files PRINTER.TST and PRINTER2.TST on the Learning disk to see the options available.

A proportionally spaced font is usually printed in 11* pitch on a dot-matrix printer, but can be adjusted to 12* or to 13*.

Laser printers often refer to point sizes (height of a character) instead of pitch. As a general rule, a 12-point font is usually printed in 10 pitch and a 10-point font is usually printed in 12 pitch. Again, Chapter 6 gives pitch settings for various point sizes.

Pitch, Font, Margins, and Tab Settings

If you change the pitch/font setting, you must usually change the margins and tabs to match. For example, if you want 1-inch margins, tabs set every five spaces, and the pitch changed from 10 to 12, you would need to change the left margin to 12 and the right margin to 90. Tabs could then be set every five spaces beginning with position 12.

The following simple formula can be used to figure 1-inch margins according to the pitch being used.

Pitch $\times$ Page width (in inches) = Total number of spaces

1-inch left margin = pitch

1-inch right margin = total number of spaces − left margin

If you want to avoid making all the changes for each document, consider making the changes once in the Setup menu. (Enter **WP/S** instead of **WP** to start WordPerfect and choose option **2** to change the initial settings.) The new settings will then be considered the default.

You can also write macros for each type of situation. For example, if you have one set of format settings for letters and another for legal documents, you can record the keystrokes for each in a macro. The next time you start to enter the format changes, press Macro Def (CTRL-F10) and name the macro first. When finished, press Macro Def (CTRL-F10) again. When you want to recall the settings later, press Macro (ALT-F10) and enter the name of the macro.

Related Entries

Fonts

Margins

See also Chapter 6, "Printer Specifics"

Preview a Document

A document can be previewed before printing so you can see the exact location and appearance of headers, footers, footnotes, line numbering, page numbering, and right justification.

Keystrokes

1. With the document on the screen, press Print (SHIFT-F7).

2. Type **6** for Preview.

3. Type **1** to preview the Document or **2** to preview the Page.

4. Move through the page or document with any of the cursor keys.

5. Press Exit (F7) when finished.

Hints

When you preview a document or page, it is actually printed to a temporary file on disk, then displayed in "Doc 3" (note the status line). It will take less time to preview a page than if you preview an entire document. However, if you preview a page at or toward the end of the document, it will take almost as much time as if you had previewed the entire document. This is because WordPerfect checks the entire document for formatting codes so it can correctly format a page.

Preview Limitations

Editing cannot be done in the Preview screen. However, Switch (SHIFT-F3) can be used to switch between the Preview screen and the document in the normal editing screen.

If you have set the right side of the hyphenation zone so that it extends past the right margin (any number except 0), or if you have chosen a proportionally spaced font, the text may not be perfectly justified.

Features such as superscript, subscript, advance, overstrike, strikeout, pitch, and font will not appear in the Preview screen. It is just not possible to display more than one character in the same location, or show a super/subscript or advance in the text mode (not graphics) that is used by WordPerfect on an IBM personal computer.

If a header or footer and a page number are set to appear on the same line, they will not be displayed properly. This is not a flaw; when printed, they would most likely overlap each other. To avoid this, consider placing the page number in the header or footer.

Applications

Preview can be used to quickly check that a top margin or page length has been set correctly. You can verify that a page will be centered from top to bottom, or that headers, footers, and page numbers are correctly positioned.

Previewing a page is much quicker (and wastes less paper) than printing a page to check for possible formatting problems.

Related Entries

Print

Print to Disk

Print

You can print a block of text, a page, or the entire document from the screen. There are also options for printing all or only selected pages of a file already saved to disk.

Keystrokes

Print a Page or Document from the Screen

1. With the document to be printed on the screen, press Print (SHIFT-F7). The following one-line menu appears:

```
1 Full Text; 2 Page; 3 Options; 4 Printer Control; 5 Type-thru; 6 Preview: 0
```

2. Type **1** to print the Full Text or **2** to print the Current Page. See *Preview a Document, Print Options, Printer Control,* and *Type-thru* for information about the other items listed on the menu.

If you are using hand-fed paper, you will need to give the printer a "Go" before each page can be printed.

1. Press Print (SHIFT-F7).

2. Type **4** for Printer Control.

3. Type **G** to send the printer a "Go" (that is, resume printing).

Consider putting these keystrokes in a macro (ALT-G is a suggested name). See Appendix C for the exact keystrokes.

Print a Block

A block of text can consist of a word, a few lines, or several pages of text.

1. At the beginning (or end) of the block to be printed, press Block (ALT-F4).

2. Move the cursor to the opposite end of the block.

3. Press Print (SHIFT-F7) to print the block.

4. Type **Y** or **N** in answer to the question, "Print Block? (Y/N) N."

Print a File or Selected Pages from Disk

You can use the Printer Control menu to print an entire document or selected pages from a file on disk. If you are not sure of the filename or need to print more than one file, enter the List Files menu and print from there. The List Files menu does not have an option to print selected pages.

To print from the Printer Control menu:

1. Press Print (SHIFT-F7).

2. Type **4** for Printer Control. The menu shown in Figure 4-80 appears.

3. Type **P** to Print a Document.

4. Enter the filename of the document to be printed. Include the drive/directory if the file is not found on the default drive.

```
 Printer Control
                                   C - Cancel Print Job(s)
  1 - Select Print Options         D - Display All Print Jobs
  2 - Display Printers and Fonts   G - "Go" (Resume Printing)
  3 - Select Printers              P - Print a Document
                                   R - Rush Print Job
  Selection: 0                     S - Stop Printing


  Current Job

  Job Number: n/a                  Page Number:  n/a
  Job Status: n/a                  Current Copy: n/a
  Message:    The print queue is empty

  Job List

  Job  Document           Destination        Forms and Print Options



  Additional jobs not shown: 0
```

Figure 4-80.   Printer Control menu

5. The following prompt appears.

```
 Printer Control
                                   C - Cancel Print Job(s)
  1 - Select Print Options         D - Display All Print Jobs
  2 - Display Printers and Fonts   G - "Go" (Resume Printing)
  3 - Select Printers              P - Print a Document
                                   R - Rush Print Job
  Selection: P                     S - Stop Printing
  Page(s): (All)
```

Press ENTER to print all the pages in the document or enter the numbers of the pages to be printed. Individual pages should be separated with commas or spaces (3,5,10) while a range of pages is indicated with a dash (10-13). You can combine these options to print selected pages and ranges (for example, 3,5,7-9,12). See "Hints" for complete details.

To print from the List Files menu:

1. Press List Files (F5).

2. Press ENTER to see a list of files from the displayed drive/directory or enter a new drive/directory name.

3. Move the cursor to the file to be printed. If you want to queue several files at once, move to each filename and type * to mark the files.

4. Type **4** to Print.

5. If you marked a single file, it is immediately placed in the queue. If you marked more than one file, "Print Marked Files? (Y/N) N" appears. If you type Y, they are all placed in the queue. If you type N, only the file that is currently highlighted is sent.

6. Press Exit (F7) when finished.

The marked files are placed in the queue in the order in which they appear in the List Files menu (in alphanumeric order). If you want to print all files, press Mark Text (ALT-F5) or HOME,* to mark all the files. Then type **4** to print. If you want a printout of the list of the files, enter the List Files menu (F5) and press Print (SHIFT-F7). A list of all the files in that drive/directory will be printed.

Hints

When printing a page or block, WordPerfect scrolls through the document up to the point of the block or page, searching for formatting commands so the text will be formatted correctly. Therefore, if you are queuing a single page near the end of a large document, it will not begin printing immediately. In fact, you can go into the Printer Control menu and watch the "Page Number:" option change as it moves through each page.

If you are editing a document and want to print the latest copy, print from the screen because the version on the disk will not be the most recent. If you want to print from disk, save the document on the screen first.

You might want to Preview a document before printing to avoid wasting paper. You will be able to see the location and content of headers, footers, footnotes, page and line numbering, and right justification. See *Preview a Document* for more information.

The Print Queue

When you give the command to print a document, the document you've specified is assigned a number and placed in the queue. The list of documents, their location, destination, type of form (such as continuous or hand-fed), and print options are all listed in the queue file {WP}.Q. WordPerfect displays the contents of this file in the lower section of the Printer Control menu in the form of a Job List. Only the first three print jobs are listed. If you want to see all the jobs that have been queued, type **D** to Display All Print Jobs on a separate screen.

See *Printer Control* for information about managing the print jobs in the queue.

Printing from the Screen

When you print from the screen, a copy of the document is saved in a temporary file that is then used for printing. This feature (often called background printing) lets you edit that document or a different document while printing. If you have sufficient memory, the temporary print file is held in memory. Once you fill memory, the temporary print files are saved to disk in the default drive/directory.

The temporary print files are named as {WP}1, {WP}2, and so forth, on disk. If you look in the Printer Control menu, you will see "(Screen)" as the document to be printed instead of a filename. Because it is not required that you give a document a name before it can be printed, you can type a document, print it, and clear the screen without ever saving and naming the document.

The temporary print files are automatically deleted when the job is printed. If you want to delete a print job, do so from the Printer Control menu instead of deleting the {WP}# files. See *Cancel a Print Job* for details.

If you try to exit WordPerfect before it has sent the print files, you are asked the question, "Cancel all print jobs? (Y/N) N." If you type Y, the print jobs are deleted. If you type N, you will remain in WordPerfect until they are printed.

If you try to print from the screen and get a disk error message, such as "Disk full," it means that the temporary print file cannot be saved on the disk. This is most likely to happen if you are moving through the document and queue several separate pages to the printer. A copy of the document up to that point is saved in the temporary file, so if you are working with a large file and are queuing several pages near the end of the document, the file will be duplicated again and again, taking up disk space. Instead, save the file to disk and specify the pages to be printed from the Printer Control menu.

Printing Specific Pages or a Range of Pages

If you use the Printer Control menu to print a document from the disk, you can specify certain pages or a range of pages. After typing **P** to Print a Document and entering the filename, you are asked for the "Page(s):"; "(All)" is displayed as the default. You can press ENTER to print all the pages in the document, or enter single page numbers separated with a comma or space. A range of pages is indicated with a dash. The following list illustrates the options that can be used to indicate which pages are to be printed. The options can be used in combination with each other.

1-10	Print pages 1 through 10
-4	Print pages 1 through 4
4-	Start with page 4 and print to the end of the document
1 3 5	Print pages 1, 3, and 5
1,3,5	Print pages 1, 3, and 5

1-3,5-7   Print pages 1 through 3 and 5 through 7

1-3,7,9   Print pages 1 through 3, page 7, and page 9

2,13-   Print page 2 and page 13 to the end of the document

If you have assigned new page numbers, you have chosen between roman numerals or arabic numbering. If a section is numbered with roman numerals, you can specify the page numbers in that format (i, iv, xx, and so on) when listing pages to be printed.

If several different sections have been renumbered, you can specify pages to be printed from those sections by using a colon (:) to separate the section and page number. The following list includes several examples of how pages can be specified when new page numbers are assigned.

1   Prints the first page (whether arabic or roman).

i   Searches for the first occurrence of a roman page change and prints the first page.

1:1   Similar to the first example in that it prints the first page unless it finds a roman page change at the beginning of that page. It then searches for the first arabic page change and prints the first page.

1:i   Same as the second example in that it prints the first page of a roman page change.

2:1   Searches for the second occurrence of an arabic page change and prints the first page.

2:i   Searches for the second occurrence of a roman page change and prints the first page.

You can combine sections and page numbers. For example, 2:3-5,3:1 means print pages 3-5 of the second section and page 1 of the third section.

Type of Forms

If you have continuous paper, you should start printing with the print head at the perforation. WordPerfect will feed in the appropriate amount of paper for the top margin.

If you are using hand-fed paper, WordPerfect assumes that you will feed the paper in at least 1 inch past the print head. If the top margin in WordPerfect is set to less than 1 inch, feed in the paper accordingly. If more than 1 inch, only feed in the paper 1 inch. WordPerfect will move down the additional space.

Printing Problems

If you have a question about what your printer can do, what fonts have been assigned, how to support a non-supported or limited support printer, or how to print special characters, you can refer to the following entries and chapters in this book.

See *Select Printers* in this chapter if you need help in setting up your printer.

The introduction to Chapter 6 will help you work through some possible problems. The introduction is followed by a summary of each supported printer, including capabilities, limitations, and solutions to possible problems. Printing the files PRINTER.TST and PRINTER2.TST from the Learning disk will also give you valuable information about your printer.

If your printer is a non-supported or limited support printer, refer to Chapter 7 for ways to customize or create a printer definition.

To see what special characters have been defined for your printer, print the file FONT.TST on the Learning disk in each font. The FONTTEST macro will help automate this procedure. Also see *Special Characters* in this chapter for more details on how to display and print special characters.

If you have a laser printer, refer to Chapter 5 for general

information and specific tips on getting the most out of your laser printer.

Using Your Printer as a Typewriter

WordPerfect has a feature called Type-thru that lets you use your printer as a typewriter. This feature is especially useful for filling out a quick form or printing an envelope.

Most daisy-wheel printers can Type-thru either by line or by character (printing the line when ENTER is pressed, or printing each character as it is typed), while most dot-matrix printers can only Type-thru by line. Laser printers cannot support Type-thru. See *Type-thru* for complete details.

Related Entries

Cancel a Print Job

Display Print Jobs

Preview a Document

Print Options

Print to Disk

Printer Commands

Printer Control

Printer Number

Restart the Printer

Type-thru

See also Chapter 5, "Laser Printers"

See also Chapter 6, "Printer Specifics"

See also Chapter 7, "Printer Program"

Print Format

Print Format (CTRL-F8) controls those items affected at or by the printer. Pitch, font, lines per inch, right justification, underlining style, sheet feeder bin, printer commands, and line numbering are the options listed on the Print Format menu.

Keystrokes

1. Press Print Format (CTRL-F8). The menu shown in Figure 4-81 appears.

2. The cursor remains in the Print Format menu after each selection so that all applicable options can be selected.

3. When finished selecting all applicable items, press ENTER to return to the document.

```
Print Format

    1 - Pitch                      10
        Font                       1

    2 - Lines per Inch             6

  Right Justification              On
    3 - Turn off
    4 - Turn on

  Underline Style                  5
    5 - Non-continuous Single
    6 - Non-continuous Double
    7 - Continuous Single
    8 - Continuous Double

    9 - Sheet Feeder Bin Number    1

    A - Insert Printer Command

    B - Line Numbering             Off

Selection: 0
```

Figure 4-81.   Print Format menu

Options

Pitch and Font

Pitch refers to the number of characters that will be printed per horizontal inch. A font is a set of characters with common attributes such as size, weight, or slant. Depending on your printer, the pitch and font can be set independent of each other or they might need to be set together because the font requires a particular pitch.

If choosing proportional spacing, an asterisk (*) must follow the pitch setting.

Lines per Inch

You can choose to print six or eight lines per inch. If you choose eight lines per inch, you might want to increase the number of text lines that can be printed on a page. See *Lines per Inch* and *Page Length* for more details.

Right Justification

Right justification creates a smooth right margin by inserting small amounts of space between words. Right justification is preset to be on, but can be turned on and off many times throughout the document. If you prefer to have right justification off at all times, it can be changed through the Setup menu.

Underline Style

Continuous underlining includes the space between tabs. Both continuous and noncontinuous underlining include spaces between words and sentences. WordPerfect is preset to use a single, noncontinuous underline. There are options for single, double, continuous, and noncontinuous underlining.

Not all printers have the ability to print double underlining. Print PRINTER.TST on the Learning disk to see how your printer prints all options of continuous, noncontinuous, single, and double underlines.

Sheet Feeder Bin

This option only affects those with multiple sheet feeder bins. When used, the option selection should precede any text on the page.

Insert Printer Command

When you select features like bold, underline, centering, pitch, or font, you are inserting printer commands through WordPerfect. If WordPerfect does not have a feature to control a certain aspect of your printer, you can insert a printer command. For example, WordPerfect lets you assign eight fonts. Of course, it is easier to choose a font (1-8) than to enter a printer command, but if you want to change to a font that is not listed, you can insert a printer command for that font.

Printer commands can be used to download files (such as soft fonts) to the printer, or retrieve graphics files via programs such as Inset. See *Printer Commands* in this chapter, Chapter 5, and Chapter 8 for complete details.

Line Numbering

Line numbers can be set to print in the left margin. If line numbering is chosen, you can see how the pages will appear by previewing the document.

Hints

The Print Format options do not appear on the normal editing screen, but right justification and line numbering can be viewed when a document is Previewed.

All of the options listed can be changed permanently in the Setup menu. (Enter **WP/S** instead of **WP** to start WordPerfect and choose option **2** to Change Initial Settings.)

Related Entries

Fonts

Line Numbering

Lines per Inch

Pitch

Preview a Document

Printer Commands

Right Justification

Setup Menu

Sheet Feeder Bin Number

Underline

See also Chapter 5, "Laser Printers"

See also Chapter 8, "Software Integration"

Print Options

You can change the print options to affect a single print job or all the print jobs until you leave WordPerfect. Print options consist of changing the printer number (1 through 6), number of copies, and binding width.

Keystrokes

Change Print Options for a Single Print Job

The options can be changed for a document on the screen or on disk.

1. Press Print (SHIFT-F7).

```
Change Print Options Temporarily

     1 - Printer Number           1

     2 - Number of Copies         1

     3 - Binding Width (1/10 in.)  0




Selection: 0
```

Figure 4-82.   Change Print Options Temporarily menu

2. Type **3** for Options. The menu shown in Figure 4-82 appears.

3. Make the applicable selections for printer number, number of copies, or binding width.

4. Press ENTER when finished to return to the one-line Print menu.

5. Type **1** to print the Full Text, **2** to print the current page, or type **4** and use the P command to print a file from disk.

Change Options to Affect Multiple Print Jobs

1. Press Print (SHIFT-F7).

2. Type **4** for Printer Control.

3. Type **1** to Select Print Options. The same screen that is displayed in Figure 4-82 is shown with the heading "Select Print Options" instead of "Change Print Options Temporarily."

4. Make the applicable selections for printer number, number of copies, and binding width.

5. Press ENTER when finished to return to the Printer Control menu.

6. Press ENTER to return to the document.

The changes will be in effect until they are changed again or until you exit WordPerfect.

Hints

If you use the temporary print options, you need to immediately queue the print job. If you neglect to do this, the print options will be set back to the default and you will have to change them again.

Use the Setup menu if you want to change the default settings for all documents.

Related Entries

Binding Width

Number of Copies

Print

Printer Number

Setup Menu

Print to Disk

WordPerfect lets you print a document to a file on disk. Although similar to saving a DOS text (ASCII) file, this method retains all text that is normally included in codes such as headers, footers, and footnotes. It also right-justifies text if applicable and includes features like page numbering, line numbering, and redline markings.

Keystrokes

WordPerfect has initially defined printer 6 as a DOS text printer. These steps assume that you have kept printer 6 defined as the DOS text printer. See "Hints" for more information.

1. With the document on the screen, press Print (SHIFT-F7).

2. Type **3** for Options.

3. Type **1** for Printer Number.

4. Enter **6** as the new printer number.

5. Press ENTER to return to the document.

6. Type **1** for Full Text.

Hints

The printed file is automatically kept in a file named DOS.TXT in the root directory on the default drive. You have the option of changing the name of the file or including a drive and directory during the printer selection.

When selecting printers, you might have assigned a different printer definition to printer 6. The following sections will help you determine how printer 6 has been defined and how to change the definition if necessary.

Display Printer Assignments

If you are not sure if a DOS text printer definition is assigned to one of the printers, press Print (SHIFT-F7), type **4** for Printer Control, then **2** to Display Printers and Fonts. The first three printers and their definitions are displayed. Press any key to see the next three printer assignments.

If the DOS text printer definition is assigned, make a note of the printer number and use that number in step 4 above when specifying the printer number.

Changing the Printer Assignments and Filename

If the DOS text printer definition has not been assigned, or if you want to change the drive, directory, or filename for the resulting print file, use the following steps.

1. Press Print (SHIFT-F7).

2. Type **4** for Printer Control.

3. Type **3** to Select Printers. The menu shown in Figure 4-83 appears. You will most likely have other printers listed in addition to "Standard Printer" and "DOS Text Printer." These steps assume you will use the DOS text printer, but any printer can be selected.

4. While looking at the printer number in the lower left corner, press any arrow key until you see printer 6 appear.

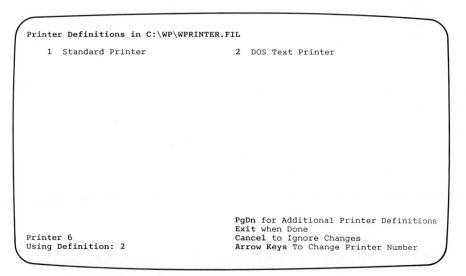

```
Printer Definitions in C:\WP\WPRINTER.FIL

    1  Standard Printer              2  DOS Text Printer
```
```




                                    PgDn for Additional Printer Definitions
                                    Exit when Done
Printer 6                           Cancel to Ignore Changes
Using Definition: 2                 Arrow Keys To Change Printer Number
```

Figure 4-83.   Printer Definitions screen

5. Enter **2** (DOS Text Printer) as the definition to be used for printer 6. (If the DOS text printer is not listed for some reason, insert the Printer 1 disk into a disk drive and press PGDN. Indicate the letter of the disk drive and continue pressing PGDN until you see the DOS text printer definition. Enter the number assigned to that definition.)

6. When prompted for the printer port, type **8** for Device or File Pathname.

7. When prompted for the device or file pathname, enter the full pathname (drive, directory, and filename), which will be used for the printed file, as shown in the following illustration.

```
Printer Port
     0 - LPT 1     1 - LPT 2     2 - LPT 3
     4 - COM 1     5 - COM 2     6 - COM 3     7 - COM 4
     8 - Device or File Pathname = C:\BOOK\DOS.TXT
Selection: 8
```

8. You are then asked for the type of forms. Type **1** for Continuous or **3** for Sheet Feeder. If you type 3, you will need to select a sheet feeder definition. In this case, the "insert page" and "eject page" codes will also be included in the file when it is printed.

9. Press Exit (F7) when finished.

Other Options

You can actually use any printer definition for printing to disk. The exact printer codes would then be included in the file along with the text. For example, if you have a section of bolded text, the printer codes for Bold On and Bold Off would be included.

To use a different printer definition, select that printer instead of the DOS text printer in the preceding set of steps. If the appropriate printer definition is not listed on the screen, press PGDN. If the printer files are not found, insert the Printer 1 or Printer 2 disk in a disk drive and type the letter for that drive. Continue as outlined in the steps.

Applications

One reason to print to disk with a different printer definition is that it allows you to print a document later with that particular printer without having WordPerfect on the computer. For example, if someone in your office (who doesn't use WordPerfect) has a different printer with a specific font that you need, you can type and format a document for that printer, then print the document to disk using that printer definition. After the file is printed to disk, you can take the disk to that computer and, from DOS, copy the file to the appropriate port.

If the file were saved on the disk in drive A, and the printer was attached to LPT1, the exact command would be

>COPY A:FILENAME LPT1

If the printer is attached to a different port, use that port instead of LPT1.

Related Entries

DOS Text Files

Print

Printer Number

Select Printers

Printer Commands

Each time you select a WordPerfect feature, whether it be Page Length, Bold, Right Justification, or Center, you are inserting a printer command through WordPerfect. During printing, the current printer definition is used to translate the WordPerfect codes into printer commands.

The Printer Command option on the Print Format menu lets you insert a printer command directly into the document. It can also be used to download a file to the printer.

Keystrokes

1. Move the cursor to the point where the printer command is to be inserted.

2. Press Print Format (CTRL-F8).

3. Type **A** to Insert a Printer Command.

4. Enter the command found in the printer manual in decimal form. See "Hints" for the exact format.

If you are downloading a file to the printer, press Retrieve (SHIFT-F10) and enter the name of the file.

5. Press ENTER to return to the document.

Hints

If you press Reveal Codes (ALT-F3) after inserting a printer command, you will see a code similar to [Cmnd:<126> HV12BPN.USP]. The <126> indicates that you pressed Retrieve (SHIFT-F10) to send the named file to the printer.

You will usually find printer commands listed as Escape sequences (ESC Q or ESC 1A are examples) or in a BASIC format, such as CHR\$(27);"E";CHR\$(15). These should be translated and inserted in decimal format.

Escape Sequences

As a rule, any number less than 32 or greater than 126 should be entered between angle brackets < and >. All other characters can be entered as themselves or can be translated to a decimal value and entered between angle brackets. For example, ESC Q could be entered as <27>Q or <27><81> because 81 is the decimal value for Q and <27> is the decimal value for ESC.

Commonly used commands, their abbreviations, and

decimal values include the following:

Backspace	BS	<8>
Line feed	LF	<10>
Form feed	FF	<12>
Carriage return	CR	<13>
Escape	ESC	<27>

You cannot press the ESC key to enter the <27> in the printer command or you will "escape" from the menu. See Appendix A for all characters and their decimal values.

Converting BASIC to Decimal

You may have a BASIC file to be downloaded, or find the printer command listed in a BASIC format, such as the one illustrated here.

    10 LPRINT CHR$(15);CHR$(24);CHR$(34);

    20 LPRINT CHR$(27);"E";CHR$(15);

You can use the following rules to convert the file to the decimal format used by WordPerfect.

Replace all parentheses with angle brackets.

Delete any quotation marks, but do not change the text found between the quotation marks.

Any other text, such as the line number, LPRINT, CHR$, and semi-colons (;), should be deleted.

The illustrated example would then appear as

    <15><24><34>

    <27>E<15>

Printer Program

If you often find yourself inserting printer commands to change to a particular font, you might consider redefining the printer so it will assign that printer command to one of the font changes. For example, if you seldom use font 6, you could enter the Printer program, delete the printer commands that shift into font 6, and enter the new printer command.

If you don't like the way a feature is defined for your printer, you can change it by inserting new printer commands in the Printer program. For example, if you would prefer to have underlined text print as italics, you could enter the printer commands necessary to turn italics on and off in the place of "Auto Underline On" and "Auto Underline Off." If you don't want to give up underlining, you might want to insert the codes for the double underlining on and off options.

Other Options

As mentioned before, you can download a file to the printer by pressing Retrieve (SHIFT-F10) and entering the filename as the printer command. If you have several commands to be sent, you can type the commands on a blank screen and save them in a text file (use Text In/Out (CTRL-F5)). That file can then be downloaded to the printer at once instead of entering each command separately.

You can include a command that inserts a graphics image into the document with programs such as Inset and Hotshot.

Related Entries

Fonts

See also Chapter 7, "Printer Program"

See also Appendix A, "ASCII Chart"

Printer Control

The Printer Control menu is used to select printers, display a list of the selected printers and fonts, and select print options (printer number, number of copies, and binding width) for multiple print jobs. It is also used to manage the print jobs that have been sent to the printer. You can cancel, display, and rush print jobs or stop and restart the printer from this menu.

Keystrokes

1. Press Print (SHIFT-F7).

2. Type **4** for Printer Control. The Printer Control menu shown in Figure 4-84 appears.

3. After making the desired changes, press ENTER to return to the document.

```
Printer Control
                                     C - Cancel Print Job(s)
1 - Select Print Options             D - Display All Print Jobs
2 - Display Printers and Fonts       G - "Go" (Resume Printing)
3 - Select Printers                  P - Print a Document
                                     R - Rush Print Job
Selection: 0                         S - Stop Printing


Current Job

Job Number: n/a                      Page Number:  n/a
Job Status: n/a                      Current Copy: n/a
Message:    The print queue is empty

Job List

Job  Document              Destination            Forms and Print Options



Additional jobs not shown: 0
```

Figure 4-84.   Printer Control menu

Options

The upper portion of the Printer Control menu contains the actual commands. The middle and lower sections give information about the current print job and those jobs waiting in the queue.

In the options on the upper left, the most commonly used option is listed first. The options at the right are listed in alphabetical order. A short description of each option follows; each is covered in detail in an entry in this chapter.

Select Print Options

The first option on the menu lets you specify the printer number, number of copies, and binding width. Your selections remain in effect until changed again or until you leave WordPerfect.

Display Printers and Fonts

Up to six printers can be selected using option 3, Select Printers. After selecting printers, you can use the second option to display the printer choices, the character tables (fonts) that are defined for each printer, and the type of forms selected for each.

Select Printers

Option 3 lets you select the printer, printer port, and type of forms (continuous, hand-fed, or sheet feeder) for each of the six available printers. Although printer 1 has already been set to print using the standard printer definition, you will most likely want to select the printer definition that was created for your printer.

While you can assign different printer definitions to each of the six printers, you can also assign the same definition to each printer, but choose a different type of form for each. This would let you print with hand-fed paper, continuous paper, or with a sheet feeder on the same printer.

The printer definitions are kept on the Printer 1 and Printer 2 disks. See *Select Printers* for complete information on selecting printers.

Cancel Print Job(s)

You can cancel any print job or all the print jobs with this option. If you choose this option by typing C, the current print job number is automatically displayed. Press ENTER to cancel that job, enter a different job number, or enter an asterisk (*) and type **Y** to cancel all print jobs.

If the printer does not respond immediately, press ENTER and the temporary print file(s) are deleted from the disk. Turn the printer off and on to empty the printer's buffer. Follow any instructions telling you to reset the top of the form at the printer and send the printer a "Go" if necessary.

Display All Print Jobs

Information about the current print job is displayed in the middle section of the Printer Control menu. The next three jobs in the job list (queue) are listed in the lower section of the screen. The job number, document to be printed, destination, forms, and print options are listed for each job, as shown in the following screen.

```
Job List

Job  Document         Destination    Forms and Print Options
 1   (Screen)         Ptr  1         Copies=3,Continuous
 2   C:\CONTRACT\AMEND Ptr  2        HandFed
 3   C:\BOOK\CHAPTER.9 Ptr  2        HandFed

Additional jobs not shown: 4
```

Note that "Additional jobs not shown:" (at the bottom of the screen) shows four jobs. To display all print jobs in the queue, type **D**. A separate screen appears, which is similar to the following illustration. Press any key to return to the Printer Control menu.

```
                          Job List

Job   Document          Destination      Forms and Print Options
  1   (Screen)          Ptr  1           Copies=3,Continuous
  2   C:\CONTRACT\AMEND  Ptr  2           HandFed
  3   C:\BOOK\CHAPTER.9  Ptr  2           HandFed
  4   (Screen)          Ptr  1           Continuous
  5   B:NOTES           Ptr  1           BindWid=10,Continuous
  6   C:\BOOK\OUTLINE    Ptr  1           Continuous
  7   C:\LETTERS\JONES   Ptr  2           HandFed
```

"Go" (Resume Printing)

If you are using hand-fed paper or are changing fonts on a daisy-wheel printer, the printer will pause at the beginning of each page and at each font change so that you can feed the paper into the printer or change the print wheel. Type **G** to send a "Go" to the printer and resume printing.

If you stop the printer (with the S option on the menu), type **G** to restart the print job. If more than one page has been printed, you are asked to enter the page number from which to restart the printing.

If the printer is not printing when you think it should, check the "Job Status" and "Message" lines in the center of the Printer Control menu to see if it is waiting for a "Go."

Print a Document

You can use this option to print a file from disk and specify the exact pages to be printed.

Rush Print Job

When you choose this option, the last print job number is automatically displayed as the job to be rushed. Press ENTER to rush that job or enter a different job number. You can either interrupt the printing of the current document or place it next in the queue. "RUSH" is added to the "Forms and Print Options" column to indicate that the job was rushed.

Stop Printing

If you choose this option, the printer may not stop right away. No further information will be sent from the computer to the printer, but information already sent to the printer will continue printing until finished.

If you want to stop printing immediately, switch the printer off, then back on to clear the printer's buffer. Type **G** to restart the job from a specific page.

Hints

Each print job is given a number corresponding to the order in which it was queued. If all print jobs are canceled or printed, the order does not begin again with 1; it will start over at 1 only after you exit and reenter WordPerfect.

If you see "(Screen)" listed among the print jobs, it means that the print job was queued from the screen.

The print queue can contain up to 255 documents. The number of print jobs that can be queued depends on the amount of disk space available.

Related Entries

Cancel a Print Job

Display Print Jobs

Display Printers and Fonts

Print

Print Options

Restart the Printer

Rush a Print Job

Select Printers

Stop Printing

Printer Number

Use the Printer Number option in the Print Options menu to send a document to a specific printer.

Keystrokes

You can either send the current document to a different printer or change the print options to affect more than one print job.

Change the Printer Number for a Single Document

1. Press Print (SHIFT-F7).

2. Type **3** for Options.

3. Type **1** for Printer Number.

4. Type the printer number (1 to 6).

5. Press ENTER to return to the one-line Print menu and type **1** to print the Full Text, **2** to print the Current Page, or type **4** and use the P command to print a document from the disk.

Select a New Printer Number for Multiple Print Jobs

This change will remain in effect until changed again or until you exit WordPerfect.

1. Press Print (SHIFT-F7).

2. Type **4** for Printer Control.

3. Type **1** to Select Print Options.

4. Type **1** for Printer Number.

5. Type the printer number (1 to 6).

6. Press ENTER to return to the Printer Control menu.

7. Press ENTER again if you want to return to the document.

Hints

If you do not know which printer definitions have been assigned to each of the six printers, choose option 2 in the Printer Control menu to Display Printers and Fonts. The printer definitions, character tables (fonts), and the type of form selected are displayed for each printer.

If you want to reassign the printer definitions, choose option 3 in the Printer Control menu to Select Printers. The printer number and the definition being used are displayed in the lower left corner of the screen. For complete steps, see *Select Printers*.

You could also change the default printer number permanently in the Setup menu.

When you choose option 3, Select Printers, you can select the same printer definition for each printer, but select a different type of forms for each one. You can then change the printer number instead of reselecting the forms for printer 1 when changing the type of forms (continuous, hand-fed, or sheet feeder).

Related Entries

Display Printers and Fonts

Print Options

Select Printers

Setup Menu

Proportional Spacing

WordPerfect offers an option to print proportionally spaced characters. Narrow characters, such as *l* or *i*, and punctuation take up less space than characters like *w* or *m* and capital letters.

Keystrokes

1. Move the cursor to the beginning of the document or to the point where proportional spacing is to begin.

2. Press Print Format (CTRL-F8).

3. Type **1** for Pitch and Font.

4. Enter the pitch to be used, followed by an asterisk.

5. Enter the font number.

6. Press ENTER to return to the document.

Hints

If you have a daisy-wheel printer, you would usually enter 13* as the pitch. Dot-matrix printers usually work best when using 11* for a PS font. Laser printers can use practically any pitch. The pitch will depend on the point size of the selected font.

WordPerfect usually defines font 3 as the proportionally spaced font, although others may also be defined. If you have any question as to the best pitch and font to be used for proportional spacing, or which fonts are defined as PS fonts, refer to your printer listed in Chapter 6. You can also run the PRHELP program found on the Printer 2 disk to find similar information.

Information about PS fonts is also available when choosing the option to Display Printers and Fonts (option 2) in the Printer Control menu.

When you select proportional spacing, WordPerfect uses a general-purpose character width table to determine where line breaks should occur on the screen and, thus, at the printer. Therefore, if you have a line with all capital letters, it will break before appearing to reach the right margin. If you have a line containing smaller characters, more characters will be allowed to fit on the line.

Proportional Spacing Problems

If you have difficulty printing in proportional spacing, check the following items.

Make sure your printer has PS capability.

Choose the correct font. Most proportionally spaced character tables have been assigned to font 3.

Choose the correct pitch.

Remember to type an asterisk (*) after the pitch number to indicate that it is a proportionally spaced font.

Check the switch settings on the printer. The general rule is to turn off any PS switches and let WordPerfect control the printer. If the printer has a switch asking for the type of print wheel installed, it can be switched to PS.

Adjust the Amount of Space Between Words

If there is an unacceptable amount of space between words, you can do one or more of the following.

Turn on hyphenation.

Decrease the hyphenation zone to create a more even right margin.

Decrease the pitch. If using 13*, try 12*.

Turn off right justification.

Change the "Maximum Width of Space Character" and "Minimum Width of Space Character" in the Pitch/Miscellaneous screen of the Printer program. See Chapter 7 for full details.

Printers either adjust for proportional spacing and right justification by using HMI (horizontal motion index) or microspacing a specific number of units at a time. Therefore, PS and/or right justification will be slower and sometimes more "jumpy" than when printing nonjustified, nonproportionally spaced text.

Printing and Preview Limitations

If you choose proportional spacing and Preview the document or page, the line breaks will not always appear to be within the right margin, and will usually not be right justified if right justification has been selected.

Lines containing all capital letters may not be printed correctly when using proportional spacing. Again, the character width table that is used to decide where the line should end on the screen will probably be slightly different than the character widths used in the printer's PS character table.

Kerning, the ability to fit characters in words such as "We" or "to" closer together by squeezing one character into the width allowed for the other character, is not currently supported.

Related Entries

Fonts

Pitch

See also Chapter 6, "Printer Specifics"

See also Chapter 7, "Printer Program"

Protect a Block of Text

You can prevent a block of text from being split between pages with the Block Protect and Conditional End of Page features. Block Protect can be used to protect a block of text where the number of lines may change after editing. Use Conditional End of Page to protect a specific number of lines. See *Block Protect* and *Conditional End of Page* for complete details.

Protect a Document

See *Lock and Unlock Documents*

PRTSC Key

Most computers have a PRTSC key that is used to print the contents of the screen. It is usually used with the SHIFT key so you don't do a "screen dump" by mistake.

If you use this feature, it will print all text on the screen, including the status line. If you have a laser printer, you must send a form feed to eject that page after a Print Screen.

WordPerfect lets you print a block of text or a single page without the status line. See *Print* for more information.

"Put WP Disk Back in Drive"

You might see this error message if you have removed the WordPerfect disk from the drive and it is trying to access the program files.

Reasons

The overflow files are usually kept where the WP.EXE file is located. If you redirected the overflow files to another disk drive with the /D option, then removed the disk from that drive, you could get the error message.

If you press Shell (CTRL-F1) and go to DOS, then try to start WordPerfect again (instead of typing EXIT to return), you are asked if other copies of WordPerfect are running. If you type N, but there is another copy running, WordPerfect will overwrite the overflow files for the first copy. If you then exit the second copy of WordPerfect and return to the first copy, it will not find the temporary files when it tries to access the disk and will display the error message. You will have to turn the computer off in this case.

This error message could also occur if you go to DOS and delete the temporary WordPerfect files (marked with {WP} as part of the filename), then reenter WordPerfect.

If you have mixed different versions of DOS on your computer, you might also see this message.

Solutions

Place the WordPerfect disk back into the appropriate disk drive and press any key to continue. If you have redirected the overflow files to another disk drive, insert that disk into the appropriate drive.

If you want to load the WordPerfect program into memory and redirect the overflow files to a RAM drive, you can remove the WordPerfect disk and use the drive for the Speller or Thesaurus diskette to eliminate disk switching.

If you go to DOS with Shell (CTRL-F1), return to Word-Perfect by typing the word **EXIT** at the DOS prompt. Do not start another copy of WordPerfect and overwrite the overflow files or delete the temporary files from DOS.

Related Entries

RAM Drives

WordPerfect Startup Options

Quit Printing

See *Stop Printing*

RAM Drives

If you have a large amount of memory, you can create a drive in random access memory (RAM). However, because Word-Perfect takes advantage of all available memory, there are very few advantages to creating a RAM drive.

Hints

WordPerfect uses all available memory for memory caching. This means that temporary files ordinarily kept on disk will be kept in memory until memory is filled.

If you create a RAM drive, you will be stealing memory from WordPerfect, and the temporary files will go to disk much sooner.

When WordPerfect is started, it loads as much of the program into memory as possible without going over the 256Kb limit. If you have at least 384Kb of RAM available, you can load the entire WordPerfect program file into memory without creating a RAM drive. Use the /R option to start WordPerfect (enter **WP/R** instead of **WP** at the DOS prompt). If you choose this option, there is no disk access for the overlay files.

However, because WP.EXE was started from the disk, the temporary overflow files are created there. You can redirect the overflow files to another disk drive or to the RAM drive if you have one available, then remove the WP disk so the disk drive can be used for the Speller or Thesaurus disks.

If you keep the Speller and Thesaurus files in a drive other than the default drive (including a RAM drive), use the Setup menu to tell WordPerfect where to look for the LEX.WP, {WP}LEX.SUP, and TH.WP files.

Applications

You can create a RAM drive to load the Speller or Thesaurus files (LEX.WP and TH.WP) so that they will run faster and eliminate switching disks.

Related Entries

Speller Utility

WordPerfect Startup Options

Rectangular Cut, Copy, and Move

WordPerfect lets you define a rectangular block of text from one corner to the opposite corner. The rectangle can be cut or copied to another location or deleted entirely.

Keystrokes

1. With the cursor in the upper left or lower right corner of the rectangle, press Block (ALT-F4).

2. Move the cursor to the opposite corner. A regular block is highlighted until step 4.

3. Press Move (CTRL-F4).

4. Type **5** to Cut/Copy Rectangle. The rectangle is then highlighted.

5. Type **1** to Cut, **2** to Copy, or **3** to Delete the rectangle.

If you cut or copied the rectangle, you can retrieve it anywhere in a document.

6. Move the cursor to the location where the rectangle is to be retrieved and press Move (CTRL-F5).

7. Type **6** to Retrieve the rectangle.

If the cursor is not at the left margin when the rectangle is retrieved, spaces are inserted between the left margin and the rectangle.

Hints

If you included a [TAB] code in the rectangle, all remaining columns are moved to the left. If not, the space remains vacant. You can use the Columns option instead of Rectangle if you want the [TAB] code preceding the column to be cut or copied with the column. See *Columns* for more information.

If you accidentally typed 3 to Delete a column or rectangle instead of 1 to Cut, you can restore it with Cancel (F1) at the left margin (preferably on a blank screen), then cut it as a column or rectangle.

Applications

Cut a Column Without Readjusting Remaining Columns

Use the rectangular cut without including the [TAB] codes to cut a column and leave the space empty, as shown in Figure 4-85. Remaining columns will not move to the left. If you do not plan to include the [TAB] codes, the last line in the rectangle must be the longest line (or at least as long as the longest line) in the rectangle. To avoid including the [TAB] code in the column, add spaces to the last line to make it the longest. See Figure 4-86 for clarification.

Cutting a Column with the Column Heading

Usually if you are going to cut a column, you will want the heading to go with it. In previous versions of WordPerfect, you had to fill the blank line separating the heading and

```
                      PHONE DIRECTORY

     Employee               Title                  Phone

Jenette Alexander    Claims Processor          (719) 392-6767
Gern Blanston        Assistant Manager         (719) 223-7564
Ted Blumenthall      Production Supervisor     (719) 549-2920
Susan Broadbent      Customer Service          (719) 392-1392
Ned Finney           Director of Development   (719) 374-8475
June Hill            Executive Secretary       (719) 443-2827
Chris Nichols        Customer Service          (719) 328-8759
Ben Richards         Exec. Vice President      (719) 290-4985
Julie Ross           Claims Processor          (719) 239-5895
Gloria Rubenstein    Customer Service          (719) 484-9430
Norrin Shepard       President                 (719) 549-9398
Nina Turpin          Legal Secretary           (719) 394-9238
Gary Wagner          Customer Service          (719) 395-9838


 1 Cut; 2 Copy; 3 Delete: 0
```

Figure 4-85.   Rectangular cut without including [TAB] codes

column with [TAB] codes in order for this to work. With version 4.2, you can use either the column or rectangle option to accomplish this without filling the line with [TAB] codes.

Equations, Graphs, and Organizational Charts

When you create an equation, or draw a box or graph with Line Draw, you can create it at the left margin first if that is easiest, then use the Rectangle Cut option to move it anywhere in the document. This is useful for organizational charts where each box is the same size and can be moved to any location on the screen. See *Line Draw* for more tips about using Rectangular Cut, Copy, and Move to help change the size of a box.

a) Rectangular cut

```
                        PHONE DIRECTORY

          Employee              Title                    Phone

     Jenette Alexander    Claims Processor          (719) 392-6767
     Gern Blanston        Assistant Manager         (719) 223-7564
     Ted Blumenthall      Production Supervisor     (719) 549-2920
     Susan Broadbent      Customer Service          (719) 392-1392
     Ned Finney           Director of Development   (719) 374-8475
     June Hill            Executive Secretary       (719) 443-2827
     Chris Nichols        Customer Service          (719) 328-8759
     Ben Richards         Exec. Vice President      (719) 290-4985
     Julie Ross           Claims Processor          (719) 239-5895
     Gloria Rubenstein    Customer Service          (719) 484-9430
     Norrin Shepard       President                 (719) 549-9398
     Nina Turpin          Legal Secretary           (719) 394-9238
     Gary Wagner          Customer Service          (719) 395-9838


     1 Cut; 2 Copy; 3 Delete: 0
```

b) Column is now empty

```
                        PHONE DIRECTORY

          Employee                               Phone

     Jenette Alexander                       (719) 392-6767
     Gern Blanston                           (719) 223-7564
     Ted Blumenthall                         (719) 549-2920
     Susan Broadbent                         (719) 392-1392
     Ned Finney                              (719) 374-8475
     June Hill                               (719) 443-2827
     Chris Nichols                           (719) 328-8759
     Ben Richards                            (719) 290-4985
     Julie Ross                              (719) 239-5895
     Gloria Rubenstein                       (719) 484-9430
     Norrin Shepard                          (719) 549-9398
     Nina Turpin                             (719) 394-9238
     Gary Wagner                             (719) 395-9838

                      Doc 1   Pg 1   Ln 24      Pos 10
```

Figure 4-86.   Rectangular cut with last line the longest (a), and result of rectangular cut with column empty (b)

If you have a rectangular piece of a formula that needs to be removed, you can cut or delete the rectangle and the rest of the formula will readjust to fill the vacant space.

Related Entries

Columns

Copy Text and Columns

Cut Text and Columns

Line Draw

Redline

The Redline feature marks text that is being considered for addition to a document. Usually a vertical bar prints in the left margin, as shown below.

```
        The  townhouse  located  at  3982  E.  Oak  Street  will  be
available as of November 25, 1987.  Monthly rent is $640 with a
│$150 deposit.   There will be an additional $50 deposit if the
│person renting has pets.
```

Keystrokes

You can Redline text as you type or after the text has been entered.

Redline as You Type

1. Press Mark Text (ALT-F5).

2. Type **3** for Redline. A "+" is added to the "Pos" number on the status line to indicate that Redline is on.

3. Type the text to be Redlined.

4. Press Mark Text (ALT-F5).

5. Type **3** for Redline again. The "+" is removed from the "Pos" number to indicate that Redline is off.

Redline Text After It Has Been Typed

1. Move the cursor to one end of the text to be redlined and press Block (ALT-F4) to turn on Block.

2. Move the cursor to the opposite end to highlight the text.

3. Press Mark Text (ALT-F5).

4. Type **3** to Redline the block.

Hints

When you turn on Redline, the [RedLn] code is inserted. The Redline Off code appears as [r]. The only indication on screen that Redline is on is the "+" that appears next to the position number on the status line, as shown in the following illustration.

Doc 1   Pg 13   Ln 21   Pos 34+

Although Redline does not show on the normal editing screen, you can see the vertical lines in the left margin if you Preview the document. Press Print (SHIFT-F7), type **6** to Preview, then **1** or **2** to preview the Document or Page. Press Exit (F7) when finished with the preview.

While most printers are defined to print redlined text with the vertical bar in the left margin, some print the text shaded or in a different color. For example, the Canon laser printer prints redlined text with a shaded background. Print the file PRINTER.TST, included on the Learning disk, to see how your printer is defined for Redline. If the method defined for redlining is not acceptable, you can change the codes in the Printer program. See Chapter 7 for more information.

See *Strikeout Text* for a similar feature that strikes through text being considered for deletion.

If you decide to add the redlined text to the document and remove the redline marks, you can use the Remove or Replace feature. The Remove feature is used to remove all redline marks (and delete the strikeout text). If you only want to remove the redline marks, use the Replace feature to search for the [RedLn] codes and replace them with nothing, thus deleting them. You can also select which marks to remove by confirming each replacement. See *Replace* and *Remove Redline and Strikout* for complete details.

Instead of using Redline in the conventional method, you can change the codes for Redline On and Redline Off and use the feature to access an additional nonproportionally spaced font. See Chapter 7 for complete details.

Related Entries

Block

Remove Redline and Strikeout

Replace

Strikeout Text

See also Chapter 7, "Printer Program"

Reformatting

If a change is made to a document, the text automatically reformats when any cursor key is pressed. Therefore, there is no repagination command necessary with WordPerfect. See *Rewrite the Screen* for more information.

Remove Redline and Strikeout

The Remove feature is used to delete all Redline marks and all text marked for Strikeout.

Keystrokes

1. Press Mark Text (ALT-F5).

2. Type **6** for Other Options.

3. Type **6** to Remove all redline markings and all strike-out text from the document.

4. Type **Y** or **N** in answer to the question, "Delete Red-line markings and Strikeout text? (Y/N) N."

5. You will remain in the Other Options menu of Mark Text until the removals are completed, then the cursor is placed at the end of the document.

Hints

You can selectively remove only the redline marks, delete only the text marked for strikeout, or remove selected redline marks and selected sections of strikeout text.

Remove All or Selected Redline Markings

The following steps can be used to delete all redline markings or just selected markings.

1. Move the cursor to the beginning of the document (HOME,HOME,↑) and press Replace (ALT-F2).

2. Type **Y** to confirm each replacement if you want to delete only selected redline marks or **N** if you want all redline marks removed.

3. When "-> Srch:" appears, press Mark Text (ALT-F5) and type **4** for Redline to insert the [RedLn] code as the search string.

4. Press Search (F2) twice to start the Replace feature. No replacement string should be used so that the code will be deleted.

5. If you type **Y** to confirm each replacement, the cursor will pause at each [RedLn] code and ask if it should be replaced. Type **Y** to delete the code or **N** to leave it.

Delete All or Selected Strikeout Text

If you want to delete only selected sections of strikeout text, you can use Replace just as it was shown for use with redline marks. Type **Y** in answer to the question "w/Confirm? (Y/N) N" and, instead of searching for [RedLn] codes, specify a search for [StrkOut] codes. Although it may seem confusing, type **Y** to replace (delete) the [StrkOut] code and thus leave the text in place. If the text should be removed with the Remove feature, type **N** to leave the [StrkOut] code.

When finished, follow the steps for Remove to delete the text that remains and is marked with the [StrkOut] codes.

If you want to delete all the strikeout text, but leave the redline marks intact, you will need to define a macro. Replace can delete the [StrkOut] codes, but not the text between the codes.

The macro should search for the Strikeout On [StrkOut] code, turn Block on, search for the Strikeout Off [s] code, and delete the block. The macro could then be chained to itself so it would repeat until no further occurrences of [StrkOut] were found.

Related Entries

Redline

Replace

Strikeout Text

Rename a File

The List Files menu in WordPerfect lets you rename a file without having to leave WordPerfect and use the DOS RENAME command.

Keystrokes

1. Press List Files (F5). The default drive/directory is displayed.

2. Press ENTER to see a list of the files in that directory, edit the displayed drive/directory and press ENTER, or enter the name of a different directory.

3. Move the cursor to the file to be renamed.

4. Type **3** to Rename the file.

5. Enter the new filename.

6. Press SPACEBAR to leave the List Files menu.

Hints

If you enter the name of a file that already exists, or use illegal characters, you will see the error message, "Can't rename file."

You can use option 8 on the menu to copy a file to another drive/directory and give it a new name at that time. After moving the cursor to the file to be copied, type **8** for Copy, and enter the full pathname (including the new filename).

If you want to rename a file at DOS, enter the following command at the DOS prompt.

>RENAME OLDFILENAME NEWFILENAME

Related Entries

List Files

Repeat a Command or Character

The ESC key can be used to repeat the next key pressed *n* times. It can also be used to repeat macros *n* times. See *ESC Key* for complete details.

Replace

Replace can be used to search for text or WordPerfect codes and replace them with something else or delete them entirely. You can confirm each replacement (or deletion) if desired.

Keystrokes

Move the cursor to the point where the Replace is to begin. Replace works in a forward direction.

1. Press Replace (ALT-F2).

2. Type **Y** or **N** in answer to the question, "w/Confirm? (Y/N) N."

3. "-> Srch:" appears. Type the characters for the search string. If you want to include a WordPerfect code, press the function key normally used to start the feature. See "Hints" for more information about searching for Word-Perfect codes.

4. Press Search (F2) to continue. Do not press ENTER to enter the search string because a [HRt] code will be inserted instead.

5. "Replace with:" appears. Type the characters to be used as the replacement string. A limited number of codes can also be used. See "Hints" for more information about using WordPerfect codes with Replace.

   If you want to delete the search string without replacing it with anything, leave the replacement string blank.

6. Press Search (F2) to start the process. (Again, avoid pressing ENTER or a [HRt] will be inserted.) If you decide against the replacement, press Cancel (F1) to cancel the procedure.

Hints

In earlier versions of WordPerfect, ESC was used to insert the search string or replacement string and begin the procedure. This key can still be used as well as any of the Search or Replace keys.

   After a Replace is finished, the cursor remains at the last successful replacement. To return the cursor to its original location before Replace (SHIFT-F2) was used, press Go To (CTRL-HOME) twice.

Replace Within a Block

Replace works in a forward direction only. If you have a section within the document to be affected, define a Block first, then follow the keystroke steps listed.

Case-Sensitive Replace

WordPerfect will search for both upper and lowercase characters if the search string is entered in lowercase. If you enter the search string in uppercase, however, only uppercase occurrences will be found.

The replacement string will be inserted exactly as you type it, with one exception. If the search string is found in uppercase, the first character of the replacement string will automatically be capitalized.

Whole-Word Search and Replace

WordPerfect does not have an option for whole-word searches. Instead, you must place a space before and after a word to indicate that it should be searched for as a whole word and not as part of another word. For example, if you wanted to search for "and" but did not include spaces, you would find occurrences of "band," "demands," "landmark," and so on.

When you include spaces before and after, be aware that the search string will not be found if the word is found at the beginning or end of a sentence.

Wildcard Characters in a Search String

You can include the wildcard character ^X as part of the search string which can be used to match any character. However, it cannot be used as the first character in the string.

Earlier versions of WordPerfect let you press CTRL-X to insert the ^X code. With version 4.2, you need to press CTRL-V first, then CTRL-X. It will appear bolded because it is considered a code rather than text.

Using WordPerfect Codes in Replace

You can search for any WordPerfect code, but it must be entered correctly. You cannot type a facsimile of the code; it must be entered with the appropriate function key. For example, if you want to search for the Bold On [B] code, you would press Bold (F6) when prompted for the search string.

Some codes will appear differently in the search string than in Reveal Codes. In the previous example, if you press Bold (F6), you will see [Bold] instead of [B]. Both are considered the same code. Codes are shown in boldface, while characters are displayed normally.

To search for an "off" code, press the applicable function key twice; once to insert the "on" code and again to insert the "off" code. If only the "off" code is needed, move the cursor to the "on" code and delete it.

Often, when pressing a function key to insert a code, you will see a menu of choices. Type the number for the desired code to insert it into the search string.

If you want to search for a hard return [HRt], press ENTER. To search for a soft return [SRt], press CTRL-V ("n =" appears), then CTRL-M. To search for a hard page break, press CTRL-ENTER. To search for a soft page break [SPg], press CTRL-V ("n =" appears), then CTRL-K.

You cannot search for specific parameters within codes. You can search for margin changes or font changes, but you cannot search for specific margins (such as 12 and 90) or specific font changes (such as only those where you changed to font 5). However, if you use the Program Editor provided with WordPerfect Library, you can identify the codes used for each function, then search for and replace the codes. If you cannot determine the exact function code that should be used, contact WordPerfect Corporation. The list of function codes is available if you are willing to sign a nondisclosure form.

While all codes can be searched for, only certain codes can be used in the replacement string. In general, codes that take one byte, as opposed to several, can be used. A [TAB] code is a single-byte code, while an [->Indent] code takes five bytes. Rather than listing each code that can be used, try inserting the code as the need arises. If the code is not accepted, it cannot be used in Replace. However, it can be done with a macro. See "Using Macros to Replace a Code with Any Other Code."

Using Macros to Replace a Code with Any Other Code

While you cannot always use Replace to replace one code with another, you can define a macro to Search (F2) for a code, delete it, then insert the new code. The macro could then be chained to itself so it would repeat until no further occurrences of the search string are found. See *Macros* for complete details.

Using Replace in a Macro

If you include a Search in a macro and the search string is not found, the macro is automatically ended. A macro will not end when a Replace is finished so more than one can be included in a macro.

Applications

If you have created a letter or document and later find that the same letter needs to be sent to a few other people, you can use Replace to search for all occurrences of one name and replace it with another rather than set the letter up for a merge.

One of the most powerful features of Replace is to "search and delete" by leaving the replacement string empty. This feature is useful for deleting all margin changes in a document, various page length settings, or for stripping out bold or underline codes. If you are having some type of problem with a document, you can use Replace to search for a possible offending code and delete all occurrences of that code.

Related Entries

Macros

Search

Restart the Printer

Typing G while in the Printer Control menu will send a "Go" and restart the printer if it has stopped for you to feed in a piece of paper or change the print wheel. It can also be used if you stopped the printing of a document from the Printer Control menu.

Keystrokes

1. Press Print (SHIFT-F7)

2. Type **4** for Printer Control.

3. Type **G** to send a "Go" and restart the printer.

4. Press ENTER to return to the document.

Hints

If you are using hand-fed paper or are changing print wheels often, you might consider defining a macro that will send the printer a "Go" without leaving the current document. To define the macro, press Macro Def (CTRL-F10) and name the macro (ALT-G is a suggestion), then enter the keystrokes listed above. When finished, press Macro Def (CTRL-F10) again to end the macro definition.

If you stop the printer on the first page, then restart it by sending a "Go," it will resume printing at the beginning of the document. If more than one page was printed, you will see "Restart on page:" with the last page number sent to the printer displayed as the default answer. Enter the page number to start with, indicating the number of the physical page (disregard page numbering).

Related Entries

Printer Control

Stop Printing

Restore Deleted Text

Any amount of text can be deleted, then restored with Cancel (F1). In fact, the last three deletions can all be restored. See *Undelete* for details.

Retrieve

Retrieve (SHIFT-F10) can be used to retrieve a file to the screen or to retrieve cut or copied text. Files can also be retrieved from the List Files menu.

Retrieve (SHIFT-10) and move (CTRL-F4) can both be used to retrieve cut or copied text.

Keystrokes

Retrieve a File with Retrieve (SHIFT-F10)

1. Press Retrieve (SHIFT-F10).

2. Enter the name of the file. If it is not saved in the default drive/directory, you should also enter the drive and directory where the file can be found.

If the file is not found, you will see an error message, "File not found," and you are prompted to try again. If the file is found, it will be retrieved at the cursor's position.

Retrieve a File from the List Files Menu

If you don't want to retrieve a file into the document currently on the screen, clear the screen first using Exit (F7).

1. Press List Files (F5).

2. Press ENTER to see a list of the files in the displayed directory, edit the directory name and press ENTER, or enter the name of a different directory. If you know some of the characters in the filename, you can enter a "template" with wildcard characters. For example, if you know the file contains the name "Smith," but you are not sure of the exact extension, enter **SMITH.***.

3. Position the cursor at the file to be retrieved.

4. Check the "Document Size" in the upper left corner of the menu before typing 1 to Retrieve the file. If the number is "0," there is not a document on the screen, and the files will not be combined. If there is any other number for the current document size, typing 1 to Retrieve the file will insert it where the cursor was positioned in the document.

If the file to be retrieved is a DOS text (ASCII) file, type 5 for Text In instead of 1 for Retrieve.

Retrieve Cut or Copied Text

You can retrieve text that was cut or copied with Retrieve (SHIFT-F10) instead of Move (CTRL-F4). Although the same number of keystrokes is involved, pressing Retrieve might feel more natural, and you do not have to look at a menu to make a selection. Remember, however, that Retrieve works only for regular text, not for columns or rectangular blocks.

1. After the options to cut or copy are chosen, the text is placed in a temporary, unnamed file.

2. Move the cursor to the new location and press Retrieve (SHIFT-F10).

3. When asked for the document to be retrieved, press ENTER or SPACEBAR instead of entering a name.

Hints

When you retrieve a file, only a copy of the file is actually retrieved. The original remains on the disk so you can return to it if necessary. When you save the copy on the screen with Save (F10) or Exit (F7), you are asked if you want to replace the original on disk with the copy on the screen. If you type **Y**, the original is renamed with a .BK! extension, the copy is saved, then the original is deleted. If you have Original Backup on, the .BK! file is kept on disk instead of being deleted. If you do not have Original Backup on and want to save both the original and the copy, type **N** and enter a different name for the copy.

While in the List Files menu, you can check the contents of a file before retrieving it. Press ENTER or type **6** to Look at the file. If the document includes a document summary, it is displayed at the beginning of the file. If you know a unique term used in the file, but cannot remember the filename, you can use the Word Search feature (option 9 on the List Files menu).

If you press Retrieve (SHIFT-F10) and cannot remember the filename, you can press List Files (F5) and see a list. However, if you entered characters for the "Document to be Retrieved:" prompt, or if you entered an invalid filename and got the error message "File not found," pressing List Files will not bring up the list of files. In such a case, press Cancel (F1), then use the List Files method to retrieve the file.

You can also use Retrieve (SHIFT-F10) or the Retrieve option in the List Files menu to retrieve a locked document. If the file is locked, you are asked for the password. After it is entered, the file is retrieved at the cursor's position.

Cut and copied text is saved to the same unnamed file until another cut or copy is performed. When you retrieve the cut/copied text, it only retrieves a copy. This feature allows the same text to be retrieved several times in different locations.

Retrieve is also used when downloading files to the printer. When inserting a Printer Command with Print Format option A, you can press Retrieve (SHIFT-F10) and enter the name of a file. When the document is printed, the file is sent directly to the printer.

Related Entries

Backing Up Files

Block

Columns

Lock and Unlock Documents

Move

Retrieve Text from the Clipboard

If you have WordPerfect Library running and press Shell (CTRL-F1), you will see the following menu.

```
1 Go to Shell; 2 Retrieve Clipboard: 0
```

The second option lets you retrieve text that was saved to the Clipboard by WordPerfect and other products. See *Shell* for more information.

RETURN Key

See *ENTER Key*

Reveal Codes

WordPerfect displays text on the screen with an appearance as close as possible to that of the printed document. Codes are not shown on the regular screen. Reveal Codes (ALT-F3), however, lets you look "behind the scenes" at the codes that have been inserted into the text.

Keystrokes

1. Press Reveal Codes (ALT-F3).

2. The screen is divided into upper and lower halves by a ruler line that shows margin and tab settings. The top of the screen displays approximately six lines of text, while text *and* codes are displayed below. Figure 4-87 shows a sample Reveal Codes screen.

3. The cursor is marked with a small, heavy bar ▬ . You can use any of the cursor keys to move the cursor, including Search (F2) and Reverse Search (SHIFT-F2). When you move the cursor, it changes positions on screen both above and below the ruler line.

4. Press ENTER, SPACEBAR, or Exit (F7) to leave the Reveal Codes screen.

Hints

You can use DEL and BACKSPACE to delete text or codes while in Reveal Codes. You can also use a cursor key, Search, or Block (ALT-F4). Any other editing keystrokes will exit the Reveal Codes screen.

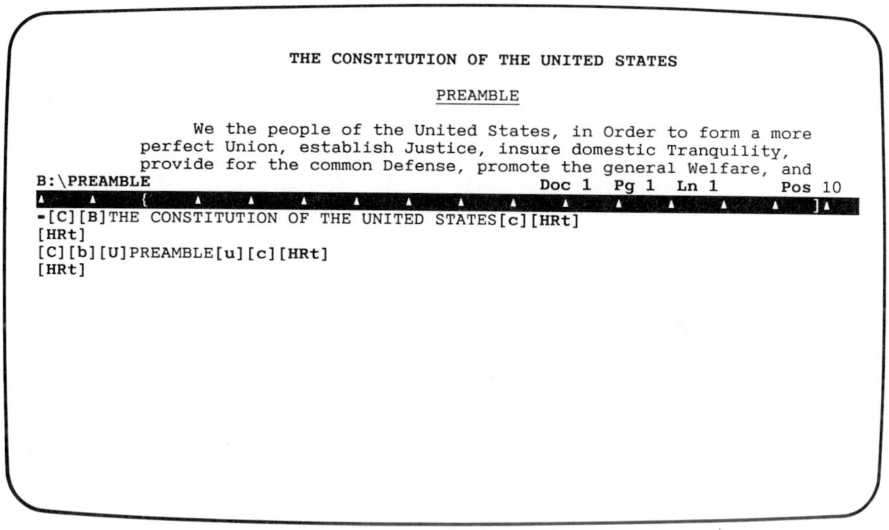

```
                  THE CONSTITUTION OF THE UNITED STATES

                                 PREAMBLE

               We the people of the United States, in Order to form a more
         perfect Union, establish Justice, insure domestic Tranquility,
         provide for the common Defense, promote the general Welfare, and
B:\PREAMBLE                           Doc 1   Pg 1   Ln 1        Pos 10
▲    ▲     {    ▲      ▲      ▲      ▲      ▲      ▲      ▲      ▲      ]▲
■-[C][B]THE CONSTITUTION OF THE UNITED STATES[c][HRt]
[HRt]
[C][b][U]PREAMBLE[u][c][HRt]
[HRt]
```

Figure 4-87.   Sample Reveal Codes screen

While in the Reveal Codes screen, you can press Block (ALT-F4) so you can see which codes to include or exclude when defining the block.

See *Codes* for an explanation of each code.

You can display the ruler line on the screen with Screen (CTRL-F3) and option 1 for Windows (see *Ruler*). However, if you want to briefly check the margin and tab settings, pressing Reveal Codes (ALT-F3) is more convenient.

Related Entries

Block

Codes

Cursor Keys

Ruler

Search

Reverse Search

Reverse Search (SHIFT-F2) can be used to search backward from your present location in a document for text or Word-Perfect codes. To search in a forward direction, use Search (F2). See *Search* for complete details.

Rewrite the Screen

When you use any cursor key, WordPerfect rewrites the screen from the cursor down.

Keystrokes

If the screen does not appear to reformat correctly, or if you want to rewrite the entire screen (not just from the cursor down), use the following steps.

1. Press Screen (CTRL-F3). The following menu appears.

```
0 Rewrite; 1 Window; 2 Line Draw; 3 Ctrl/Alt keys; 4 Colors; 5 Auto Rewrite: 0
```

2. Press ENTER or SPACEBAR, or type **0** to Rewrite the screen.

Hints

If you want to turn Auto Rewrite on or off (it is preset to be on), press Screen (CTRL-F3), type **5** for Auto Rewrite, then type **Y** or **N** in answer to the question, "Auto Rewrite? (Y/N) Y."

If you turn off Auto Rewrite, text will still be reformatted automatically, but you will be required to move the cursor through the text with ↓ , Screen Down (+ on the numeric keypad or HOME, ↓), or PGDN. You could also use the steps listed to rewrite the entire screen.

Applications

Turning off Auto Rewrite helps to slightly speed up the text display. It is particularly useful when working in side-by-side newspaper columns where there is constant reformatting when text is added or deleted.

Related Entries

Columns

Right-Aligned Text

Text can be aligned at the right margin with Flush Right (ALT-F6). You can also right-align text at a tab setting by setting a Right Align Tab. See *Flush Right* and *Tabs, Clear and Set* for more information.

Right Indent

Indent (SHIFT-F4) can be used to indent text equally from the left and right margins. See *Indent* for complete details and options.

Right Justification

Right justification creates a smooth right margin by inserting small increments of space between characters and words.

Keystrokes

WordPerfect is preset to print with right justification on.

1. Press Print Format (CTRL-F8).

2. Type **3** to Turn Off Right Justification or **4** to Turn On Right Justification.

3. Press ENTER when finished.

Hints

The codes [Rt Just Off] and [Rt Just On] are inserted into the document at the cursor location. Text is affected from that point forward until another right justification code is encountered.

If you prefer to have right justification off for most of the documents you create, use the Setup menu to change the default to off (enter **WP/S** instead of WP to start WordPerfect and choose option 2 to change the initial settings).

How Right Justification Is Accomplished

Some printers use HMI (horizontal motion index) to adjust for extra space, while others use microspace units. HMI lets the printer adjust each character to the left and right while microspacing can only adjust in a forward direction.

With HMI, WordPerfect counts the number of characters on the line and calculates how much space is needed to spread or squeeze characters in order to meet the right margin. The space is divided equally between characters. If you are printing with a proportionally spaced font, the width of each character is taken into account and the extra spacing is divided accordingly.

If your printer supports microspacing, the printer inserts the extra space between words instead of spreading or squeezing characters.

Printing is usually slower and more "jumpy" when using right justification or proportional spacing because of all the necessary calculations and adjustments.

Adjusting the Amount of Space

If your printer uses HMI, you can squeeze characters tighter together as well as spread them out to create a smooth right margin. Currently, WordPerfect presets the hyphenation zone at 7 and 0. This means that words can end up to seven spaces before the right margin, but characters cannot extend past the right margin. You can set the hyphenation zone (H-Zone) so you have less "space" to fill in and can even possibly squeeze in characters from the right.

If you find that there is an unacceptable amount of "white space" between words, try any or all of the following.

Turn on hyphenation at the beginning of the document, or where you want hyphenation to begin. When hyphenation is off, longer words that would have required hyphenation wrap to the next line, creating more space that must be taken into account during right justification. If you plan to use hyphenation often, change the default setting in the Setup menu. (Most writers, however, prefer to write uninterrupted and make the hyphenation decisions later.)

Decrease the hyphenation zone. This can also be done permanently through the Setup menu. Keep in mind, though, that if you make the total hyphenation zone smaller, you will have fewer locations in which to place the hyphen.

Adjust the "Maximum Amount of Space for Space" and "Minimum Amount of Space for Space" in the Printer program. If you decrease the maximum amount of space that can be used between words, WordPerfect will adjust by inserting small amounts of space between letters. See Chapter 7 for more details.

Applications

Use right justification and proportional spacing in news-paper style columns to create a typeset look.

Most letters and memos are written without using right justification. Many feel that right justification creates a less personal, more computerized look, especially when proportional spacing is not available.

Related Entries

Proportional Spacing

See also Chapter 7, "Printer Program"

Ruler

A ruler showing the current margins and tab settings can be displayed temporarily with Reveal Codes (ALT-F3), for a single editing session with Screen (CTRL-F3), or on a permanent basis through the Setup menu.

Keystrokes

Display the Ruler Temporarily

1. Press Reveal Codes (ALT-F3). The screen is divided by the ruler line, as shown in Figure 4-88.

2. Press SPACEBAR or ENTER to remove the ruler from the screen and return to the normal editing screen.

Display the Ruler for a Single Editing Session

1. Press Screen (CTRL-F3).

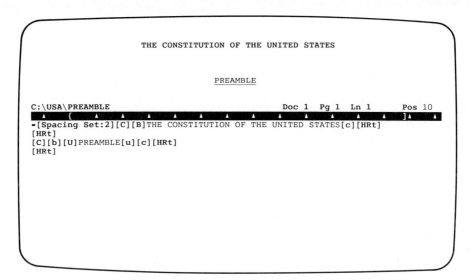

Figure 4-88.   Ruler line shown in Reveal Codes screen

2. Type **1** for Windows. The following appears at the bottom of the screen.

 # Lines in this Window: 24

3. Enter **23** to place the ruler at the bottom of the screen, or press ↑ once to move the ruler line to the bottom of the screen, and press ENTER.

4. The ruler is displayed just below the status line.

Margins are shown as square brackets [and], and tab settings are displayed as triangles. If a margin and tab occur in the same location, the margin is displayed as a brace { or }.

Removing the Ruler

1. Press Screen (CTRL-F3).

2. Type **1** for Window.

3. Enter **0**, **24**, or press ↓ until the ruler disappears from the screen.

Hints

When you display the ruler, it appears at the bottom of both document 1 and document 2.

If the ruler is not displayed at the bottom of the screen, it is used to split the screen and display both documents at once. They are shown in two separate "windows" divided by the ruler.

Applications

The ruler helps ease the adjustment period for those who are accustomed to seeing a ruler or format line in another word processing program.

The ruler is helpful when working with tables of tabbed columns, math columns, or newspaper or parallel columns. If you are working with newspaper or parallel columns and display the ruler on the screen, it will display the left and right margins for each column, as shown in the following illustration.

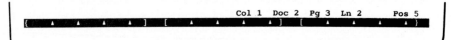

Related Entries

Windows

Rush a Print Job

You can move a job to the beginning of the print queue or interrupt the current job being printed.

Keystrokes

1. Press Print (SHIFT-F7).

2. Type **R** to Rush Print Job. The following message appears in the Printer Control menu with the number of the last print job in the queue.

```
Printer Control
                               C - Cancel Print Job(s)
1 - Select Print Options       D - Display All Print Jobs
2 - Display Printers and Fonts G - "Go" (Resume Printing)
3 - Select Printers            P - Print a Document
                               R - Rush Print Job
Selection: R                   S - Stop Printing
Rush which job? 3
```

3. Press ENTER to rush the displayed print job or enter the number of another job to be rushed.

4. If a job is already printing, you are asked, "Interrupt current job? (Y/N) N." If you type N, the job is placed next in the queue. If you type **Y**, you will see the message, "Completing page, press ENTER to interrupt job immediately."

Related Entries

Printer Control

Save

Save (F10) is used to save a document and leave it on the screen for further editing. Save can also be used to save a block of text to a separate file.

Keystrokes

Save a Document

1. Press Save (F10) to save the current document. "Document to be Saved:" appears on the status line, prompting you for the name of the file. If the file has been saved before, that filename is displayed.

```
Document to be Saved: C:\CONTRACT\LEASE.AGR
```

2. Enter the name of the file or press ENTER to use the displayed filename. Include the drive and directory if necessary.

3. If you press ENTER to use the same filename or if you enter the name of a file already saved on the disk, you are asked "Replace *filename?* (Y/N) N." Type **Y** to replace the file or **N** to save the file under a different name.

Save a Block of Text

1. Move the cursor to one end of the block to be saved and press Block (ALT-F4).

2. Move to the opposite end and press Save (F10). "Block Name:" appears.

3. Enter the filename for the block.

4. The block remains highlighted. Press Block (ALT-F4) to turn off block.

Instead of entering a name for the block, you can press
ENTER to save it as an "unnamed" block. An unnamed block
can be retrieved by pressing Retrieve (SHIFT-F10), then
ENTER without first typing a filename.

Hints

When you save a file and do not specify a drive or directory,
it will be saved to the default drive. If you are not sure which
drive/directory is the default, press List Files (F5) to display
the name at the bottom of the screen. To change the default
drive/directory, press = and enter the name of the new drive/
directory to be used. See *Default Directory* for more details.

When you save a file and type **Y** to replace the previous
version, the original file on disk is renamed with a .BK!
extension, the copy on the screen is saved, then the .BK! file is
deleted. If you choose to have Original Backup on, the .BK!
file will be kept on the disk instead of being deleted. See
Backing Up Files for more information.

If you have retrieved more than one document onto the
screen, the filename of the first file retrieved is displayed as
the filename to be used. Enter a different filename if
necessary.

Keep in mind that you do not have to save a document
when using WordPerfect. You can edit and print without giving a file a name. If it is a quick, temporary document, you
can create, edit, and print it, then clear the screen without
taking up space on the disk.

Using Exit (F7) to Save

Save (F10) saves the file and leaves it on the screen for further
editing. Use Exit (F7) to save the document and clear the
screen. If you have just saved a document with Save (F10),
then press Exit (F7), you are again asked if you want to save
the document as a precaution. If you have not made any
changes to the document since pressing Save (F10), the message "(Text was not modified)" is displayed in the lower right
corner of the screen.

Error Messages

If you see the "Disk Full" error message, strike any key until you return to the document. Replace the disk with one that has more disk space, or enter the List Files menu and delete unwanted files.

If you are replacing a file on disk with one on the screen, you might get the error message even when it appears that there is sufficient room for the file. Remember that when replacing a file on disk, the original file is renamed, the new one is saved, then the original is deleted. Thus, space is needed for both copies of the document. If you are not sure of the amount of disk space available and the amount needed, enter the List Files menu and find the information at the top of the screen under "Free Disk Space" and "Document Size."

Other error messages, such as "Sector not found," could mean you have a damaged disk. The "Drive door may be open" message and others will also let you recover and correct the situation.

Save in Other Formats

Text In/Out (CTRL-F5) lets you save a WordPerfect 4.2 document in several different formats. Options 1, 6, and 7 from the Text In/Out menu (shown in Figure 4-89) can be used to save a file as a DOS text file, in a generic word processor format, or in WordPerfect 4.1 format.

DOS Text File   If you choose option 1, only text is saved to the file on disk. While all WordPerfect codes are removed, some, such as Indent, Center, Align, and Paragraph Numbering, are converted to ASCII text. Soft returns [SRt] and hard returns [HRt] are converted to carriage return/line feeds and tabs are converted to spaces.

Generic Word Processor Format   Option 6 is similar to saving the file as a DOS text file where all codes are removed and only text remains. In generic format, however, tabs are kept as tabs, and soft returns [SRt] are converted to spaces to aid with word wrap in the other word processor.

```
Document Conversion, Summary and Comments

        DOS Text File Format
            1 - Save
            2 - Retrieve   (CR/LF becomes [HRt])
            3 - Retrieve   (CR/LF in H-Zone becomes [SRt])

        Locked Document Format
            4 - Save
            5 - Retrieve

        Other Word Processor Formats
            6 - Save in a generic word processor format
            7 - Save in WordPerfect 4.1 format

        Document Summary and Comments
            A - Create/Edit Summary
            B - Create Comment
            C - Edit Comment
            D - Display Summary and Comments


Selection: 0
```

Figure 4-89.   Text In/Out menu

WordPerfect 4.1 Format   While you can retrieve a file created with WordPerfect 4.1 into 4.2, you cannot do the reverse because there are codes in 4.2 that are not recognized by WordPerfect 4.1. Use option 7 to format a 4.2 document for use in 4.1.

Locking a Document

The Text In/Out menu also has an option to lock and save a document with a password. After you have locked a document, you are asked to enter the password twice during subsequent saves. See *Lock and Unlock Documents* for details.

Document Summary

A non-printing document summary can be inserted at the beginning of a document to identify the author, typist, and date of creation, and include notes about the file. Text In/Out (CTRL-F5), option A, is used to create a summary. If you want it displayed on the screen, use option D on the same menu.

The Setup menu has an option that automatically displays the document summary whenever a file is saved. See *Document Summary* or *Setup Menu* for more information.

Related Entries

Block

Document Summary

DOS Text Files

Lock and Unlock Documents

Setup Menu

Screen

Screen (CTRL-F3) presents options that affect the look of the screen. These features include Rewrite, Windows, Line Draw, CTRL- and ALT-key mapping, Colors, and Auto Rewrite.

Keystrokes

1. Press Screen (CTRL-F3).

2. Select an option from the menu shown in the following illustration.

```
0 Rewrite; 1 Window; 2 Line Draw; 3 Ctrl/Alt keys; 4 Colors; 5 Auto Rewrite: 0
```

Options

Rewrite

WordPerfect automatically reformats the document from the point of the cursor down when any cursor key is pressed. To rewrite the entire screen, or if the screen does not appear to be formatted correctly, press Screen (CTRL-F3) and press ENTER, SPACEBAR, or type **0** to rewrite the entire screen.

Windows

The Windows option can be used to place a ruler showing the current margin and tab settings at the bottom of the screen or split the screen so you can see both document 1 and document 2 at once.

Line Draw

Choose option 2 to draw single lines or double lines, or to create lines, boxes, diagrams, or graphs with any character.

CTRL- and ALT-Key Mapping

Option 3 lets you map special characters to the ALT and CTRL keys. For example, you can map the Alpha sign to CTRL-A so that when CTRL-A is pressed, the Alpha symbol appears on the screen. Up to 52 special characters can be mapped with this option.

Colors

If you have a color monitor, you can customize the background and foreground (text) colors as well as the colors to be used for bolded and underlined text. You can also set a different set of colors for each document (documents 1 and 2).

Auto Rewrite

WordPerfect is set to automatically rewrite the screen from the cursor down when any cursor key is pressed. You can speed up the reformatting slightly by turning off this option. The screen would then reformat only as you moved the cursor down through the text. You could also reformat quickly by choosing the Rewrite option on this menu.

Related Entries

Colors

Line Draw

Rewrite the Screen

Special Characters

Windows

Search

Search (F2) and Reverse Search (SHIFT-F2) can be used to search for text or WordPerfect codes. You can also do an Extended Search that would include headers, footers, footnotes, and endnotes in the search.

Keystrokes

A search can be done from the regular editing screen or while in the Reveal Codes screen.

1. Press Search (F2) to search from the cursor forward or Reverse Search (SHIFT-F2) to search from the cursor backward. "-> Srch:" or "<-Srch:" will appear on the status line with the last search string displayed.

2. Type up to 59 characters or WordPerfect codes or move the cursor and edit the displayed string, if desired. If you are searching for WordPerfect codes, they must be entered with the appropriate function keys and are limited in number by the available room on the status line. See "Hints" for more details.

3. Press Search (F2) to start the search in either direction. Do not press ENTER to start the search or you will enter a hard return [HRt] into the search string. If you press ENTER, you can delete it with BACKSPACE.

Hints

In the earliest versions of WordPerfect, ESC was used to start a search or replace. Currently you can press ESC or any search key, Search (F2), Reverse Search (SHIFT-F2), or Replace (ALT-F2) to begin a search.

If you want to cancel the search, press Cancel (F1) at any time and the cursor will return to the original position. You can return the cursor to its original position after a search is finished by pressing Go To (CTRL-HOME) twice.

Search does not include headers, footers, footnotes, or endnotes. If you want to include these features, you need to do an extended search. Press HOME, then any Search key to see "-> Extended Srch:" or "<-Extended Srch:" on the status line. Extended search can also be used for the Replace feature by pressing HOME, then Replace (ALT-F2).

Case-Sensitive Search

If you enter the search string in lowercase letters, all upper-case and lowercase occurrences of the string will be found. If you enter the search string in uppercase letters, it will find only uppercase occurrences. The search string "Constitution" would find any occurrence of the word "constitution" as long as the first character was capitalized. All other letters in this example could be in upper- or lowercase.

Whole-Word Searches

WordPerfect does not have an option for whole word searches. Instead, you must place a space before and after a word that should be considered a whole word and not part of another word. For example, if you wanted to search for "and" but did not include spaces, you would find occurrences of "band," "demands," "landmark," and so on.

If you include spaces before and after the word, however, be aware that the search string will not be found if the word is found at the beginning or end of a sentence because it would be preceded by [HRt] or [TAB], or followed by some type of punctuation.

Wildcard Characters in a Search String

You can include the wildcard character ^X as part of the search string to match any character. However, it cannot be the first character in the string.

Earlier versions of WordPerfect let you press CTRL-X to insert the ^X code. With version 4.2, you need to press CTRL-V first, then CTRL-X. It will appear bolded because it is considered a code rather than text.

Using WordPerfect Codes in a Search String

You can search for any WordPerfect code, but it must be entered correctly. You cannot type a facsimile of the code; it must be entered with the appropriate function key. For example, if you want to search for the Bold On [B] code, press Bold (F6) when prompted for the search string.

Some codes will appear different in the search string from their appearance in Reveal Codes. In the previous example, if you press Bold (F6), you will see [Bold] instead of [B]. Both are considered the same code. Codes are shown in boldface, while characters are displayed normally.

To search for an "off" code, press the applicable function key twice—once to insert the "on" code and again to insert the "off" code. If only the "off" code is needed, move the cursor to the "on" code and delete it.

Often, when pressing a function key to insert a code, you will see a menu of choices. Type the number for the desired code to insert that code into the search string.

To search for a hard return [HRt], press ENTER. To search for a soft return [SRt], press CTRL-V ("n =" appears), then CTRL-M. To search for a hard page break [HPg], press CTRL-ENTER. To search for a soft page break [SPg], press CTRL-V ("n =" appears), then CTRL-K.

You cannot search for specific parameters within codes. You can search for margin changes or font changes, but not for specific margins (such as 12 and 90) or specific font changes (such as only those where you changed to font 5).

Using Search to Define a Block

When defining a Block, you can press either search key to search for the previous or next occurrence of text or code. If the search string is found, the block will be highlighted to that point.

Search in Macros

If you include a search in a macro, the macro will end if the search string is not found. This feature is useful in creating macros that will repeat until no further occurrences of the search string are found. It can also be used to create conditional macros. A macro will not end when a Replace is finished, so you can do several without ending a macro. See *Macros* for complete details.

Applications

When editing a document from a hard copy, you can search for a specific word or phrase to quickly find that section of the text. This virtually eliminates scrolling manually through the document to make editing changes.

If a document is not formatted as it should be, search for the codes that might be affecting the format. You can search in the Reveal Codes screen so you can see the parameters of the code without having to press Reveal Codes (ALT-F3) each time. For example, it is much easier to find a tab setting by searching for it because there is no immediate indication on the screen that the tabs have been changed.

Related Entries

Block

Macros

Replace

Reveal Codes

Search and Replace

See *Replace*

Search for a File

List Files (F5) has a Word Search feature that lets you search through multiple files for a unique word or phrase. See *Word Search* for more information.

Select Printers

WordPerfect can support up to six printers. A standard printer definition has been preselected, but you should select a printer definition specifically for your printer.

During the procedure, keep in mind that you are selecting printer definitions for the six printers. The same printer definition can be used for all six printers (each with different forms selected) or each can have a different printer definition assigned.

Keystrokes

You can press Cancel (F1) at any time during the following procedure to back out of menus and cancel any selections.

1. Press Print (SHIFT-F7).

2. Type **4** for Printer Control.

3. Type **3** to Select Printers. Figure 4-90 shows the initial printer selection screen. At the top of the screen is the filename WPRINTER.FIL. This file comes on the WordPerfect program disk with the Standard Printer and DOS Text Printer definitions. In the bottom left

```
Printer Definitions in C:\WP\WPRINTER.FIL

    1  Standard Printer              2  DOS Text Printer










                                    PgDn for Additional Printer Definitions
                                    Exit when Done
Printer 1                           Cancel to Ignore Changes
Using Definition: 1                 Arrow Keys To Change Printer Number
```

Figure 4-90.   Initial printer selection screen

corner are the printer number (1-6) and the number of the printer definition that is being used for that printer.

4. Note that Printer 1 is shown. Press any arrow key if you need to choose a printer definition for one of the other six printers.

5. Press PGDN to select a new printer definition for that printer number. If you are using two disk drives or have not copied the files from the Printer 1 and Printer 2 disks to the hard drive, you will see the following message.

```
Can't Find Printer Files...

    Place a WordPerfect Printer Diskette
    in any floppy disk drive other than drive C:

    (If you don't have another floppy disk drive, you must
    install WordPerfect properly on your system before you
    can select printers.  See the "Getting Started" section
    of your WordPerfect manual for help with this.)

Press Drive Letter When Ready:
```

It is not advisable that you copy the files from the Printer 1 and Printer 2 disks to your hard disk because they take up a lot of space. You only need to select your printer definitions.

6. If the name of your printer begins with a letter from A thorugh M, insert the Printer 1 disk into a floppy disk drive. If it is identified with a letter N through Z, insert the Printer 2 disk. Releases of 4.2 before July 1987 had the definitions A through N on the Printer 1 disk and O through Z on Printer 2. An additional Printer 3 disk is now available from WordPerfect at no charge within one month of purchase; it contains all limited-support printers.

If you have a two-disk-drive system, leave WordPerfect in drive A and insert the printer disk in drive B.

7. Type the letter of the disk drive to see a list of printers, like that shown in Figure 4-91. Notice that the file containing the printer definitions is identified at the top of the menu (WPRINT1.ALL, WPRINT2.ALL, or WPRINT3.ALL, depending on whether the Printer 1, Printer 2, or Printer 3 disk is being used).

```
Printer Definitions in WPRINT1.ALL

     1   AMT Office Printer (Diablo)      2   AMT Office Ptr (IBM Color)
     3   AST TurboLaser Dutch PS          4   AST TurboLaser Landscape
     5   AST TurboLaser Portrait          6   AST TurboLaser Swiss PS
     7   Alps P2000                       8   Apple Imagewriter / DMP
     9   Apple Imagewriter II            10   Brother HR-1
    11   Brother HR-35/Dynax DX-25       12   Brother HR15XL/20/Dynax DX-15
    13   C.Itoh 8510 Prowriter           14   C.Itoh C310EP
    15   C.Itoh D10-40                   16   C.Itoh Starwriter/Printmaster
    17   Canon A1 Courier 10 N           18   Canon A1 Courier 10 N/R
    19   Canon A1 Courier 10 R           20   Canon A1 Elite 12 N
    21   Canon A1 Elite 12 N/R           22   Canon A1 Elite 12 R
    23   Canon A1 Garland PS N           24   Canon A1 Garland PS R
    25   Canon A1 Line Printer N/R       26   Canon A1 Pica 10 N
    27   Canon A1 Pica 10 N/R            28   Canon A1 Pica 10 R
    29   Centronics 351                  30   Centronics GLP II
    31   Cordata LP300X Bookman PS       32   Cordata LP300X Courier


                                     PgDn for Additional Printer Definitions
                                     Exit when Done
Printer 1                            Cancel to Ignore Changes
Using Definition:                    Arrow Keys to Change Printer Number
```

Figure 4-91.   Printer selections in WPRINT1.ALL

8. Each printer is assigned a number. Press PGDN until you see your printer on the list, then enter the number of the printer definition. If you need to look at the list on the other printer disk, replace the original printer disk and press PGDN. If you have a daisy-wheel printer and do not see your printer on the list, try the Diablo 620/630 definition. If you have a dot-matrix printer that is not listed, try selecting the Epson FX or IBM Proprinter definition.

After you select the printer definition, it is copied from the printer disk to the WPRINTER.FIL. At the same time, all fonts assigned to that printer are copied to a file named WPFONT.FIL.

9. You are then asked to select the port where the printer cable is attached.

```
Printer Port
     0 - LPT 1     1 - LPT 2     2 - LPT 3
     4 - COM 1     5 - COM 2     6 - COM 3     7 - COM 4
     8 - Device or File Pathname
Selection: 0
```

Type **0** for LPT1 if you have a parallel printer or **4** for COM1 if you have a serial printer. If you have more than one parallel or serial port, you may need to select a different port.

If you want to print a file to disk with the DOS Text Printer definition (or any other printer definition), choose option **8**, then enter the name of the file that will be used to store the printed file. See *Print to Disk* for more information.

10. If you chose a parallel port or option 8, go to the next step. Those with serial printers must answer some additional questions, as shown in Figure 4-92. You can find the answers to these questions in your printer manual. If they are set incorrectly, your printer might print random characters, stop after printing a few lines, or not print at all.

"Baud Select" requires you to specify the *baud*, or

```
Printer Port
      0 - LPT 1     1 - LPT 2     2 - LPT 3
      4 - COM 1     5 - COM 2     6 - COM 3     7 - COM 4
      8 - Device or File Pathname
Selection: 4

Baud Select
      0 -   110     1 -   150     2 -   300     3 -   600
      4 -  1200     5 -  2400     6 -  4800     7 -  9600
Selection: 4

Parity
      0 - None     1 - Odd       3 - Even
Selection: 3

Stop Bits (1 or 2): 1
Character Length (7 or 8): 7
```

Figure 4-92.   Serial printer specification screen

rate at which data is sent from the computer to the printer. One of the most common settings, 1200, is the default. Laser printers usually use 9600 baud. Type the number indicating the correct baud and move to the next question.

"Parity" is an error checking system where None, Odd, or Even are the choices. In general, if you have eight as the character length (data bits), you will have no parity. Other settings depend on how your printer is set up. Enter the number for the parity of your printer.

"Stop Bits" are the number of bits used to separate each byte (a character is considered one byte and is made up of seven or eight bits). Type **2** if the baud is set to 110. Other baud settings use **1** stop bit.

"Character Length" (sometimes known as data bits) can either be set at **7** or **8**, depending on what your printer will accept.

11. WordPerfect needs to know what type of forms you will be using. The choices are shown in the following illustration.

```
Type of Forms
    1 - Continuous
    2 - Hand Fed
    3 - Sheet Feeder
Selection: 2
```

If you choose option 8 at "Printer Port" for Device or File Pathname, only continuous forms and sheet feeder are listed as choices for the type of form.

Type **1** if you are using continuous (perforated) paper or if you have a laser printer that uses a paper tray similar to a copy machine.

Type **2** to use hand-fed paper. When printing with hand-fed paper, the printer pauses for you to insert each page and press **G** from the Printer Control menu to send it a "Go."

If you have a sheet feeder, type **3** and the following appears.

```
Sheet Feeder Information
    Number of Extra Lines Between Pages (12 LPI):   24
    Column Position of Left Edge of Paper (10 Pitch):   26
    Number of Sheet Feeder Bins (1-3):   1
```

12. This step is applicable only to those with a sheet feeder. If you do not have a sheet feeder, go to step 13. Check the printer or sheet feeder manual or see *Sheet Feeder Bin Number* for specifics.

The first question asks how many extra lines should be inserted between pages. Some mechanical sheet feeders require extra lines to eject the first page and insert the second. The default is set to 24, figuring 12 lines per inch. If you have an electronic sheet feeder, you would usually enter 0 because it uses Escape codes for inserting and ejecting pages.

Because a sheet feeder is not usually at the far left of the printer at position 0, 26 has been preset as the position where the left edge of the paper will most likely begin. If you are using a sheet feeder with a laser printer, this position should be set at 0. Keep in mind that this setting is figured in tenths of an inch (26 = 2.6 inches).

Enter the number of sheet feeder bins available with your sheet feeder. Include envelope bins in the count if you have any.

A menu appears with a list of supported sheet feeders, as shown in Figure 4-93. Enter the number that best fits your sheet feeder. If there is a "(continued)" option for your sheet feeder, it is automatically selected when you make a choice and should not be selected separately.

```
Sheet Feeder Information
      Number of Extra Lines Between Pages (12 LPI):   24
      Column Position of Left Edge of Paper (10 Pitch):   26
      Number of Sheet Feeder Bins (1-3):  1

Sheet Feeder Type

    1 Apple LaserWriter                   2 BDT LetterMate I,II,III
    3 BDT MF-830 6 bin Laser Feeder       4 BDT MF-830 6 bin La (continued)
    5 BDT MF-850 3 bin Laser Feeder       6 BDT MF-850 3 bin La (continued)
    7 Brother HR-15/HR-25/HR-35           8 Canon A1
    9 Diablo Single/Dual/Envl            10 Epson LQ-1500 Single/Dual
   11 HP LaserJet 500+                   12 HP LaserJet 500+    (continued)
   13 IBM 5218 Dual Bin/Envl Feed        14 IBM Pageprinter 3812
   15 NEC 3515/5515/7715 Single/Dual     16 NEC 3550 Single/Dual
   17 Qume Single Bin                    18 Rutishauser Dual Bin
   19 Texas Instruments 2015             20 Xerox 2700 Laser
   21 Ziyad PaperJet 400                 22 Ziyad PaperJet 400  (continued)




Selection: 1          (Use the PRINTER program to define a new sheet feeder)
```

Figure 4-93.   Sheet Feeder Information menu

13. After specifying the type of forms, you are placed again in the initial printer selection menu with Printer 2 (or the next printer) displayed on the status line. The printer definitions will have been given a new number because they have been copied from the file on the Printer disk to the "master" printer file, WPRINTER.FIL.

Start the printer selection process again to continue selecting printer definitions for all six printers, or press Exit (F7) to return to the Printer Control menu.

Hints

Even though you are limited to six printers, you can actually store as many as 32 printer definitions in WPRINTER.FIL. Then, when you need to change a printer assignment, you would have all the printer definitions listed without having to insert the printer disks again.

For example, if you have an HP LaserJet+ printer, you will see numerous printer definitions listed. If you have more than six cartridges or soft fonts, you would probably want to select all applicable choices and reassign printers when necessary. Follow the steps listed above without regard to printer number. After all the printer definitions have been copied, you can repeat the process to assign only six of the definitions for each of the six printers.

After the printer definitions have been selected, they are copied to WPRINTER.FIL. The actual printer assignments (printer definition, port, and type of forms) are saved along with color selections in a file named {WP}SYS.FIL.

When you first receive WordPerfect, the DOS text printer is automatically assigned to Printer 6 so it can be used to print a file on the screen to a file on disk. It has been preset to save the printed file on disk in a file named DOS.TXT. Option 8 of the "Printer Port" selections lets you send the file to a device or file, and specify the filename. If you are running a network version of WordPerfect, the device is used to identify the printer device as required by the network.

Display Printers and Fonts

Option 2 in the Printer Control menu lets you display printers and fonts that have been selected. The printer definition, character tables (fonts), and the type of forms for each of the six printers are shown.

Limited-Support Printers

Printer definitions marked with an asterisk (*) are limited-support printers; this means that WordPerfect Corporation does not have the printer in-house and cannot test any problems for a customer. Most of these definitions have been created from printer manuals or have been sent from customers who wanted to provide the definition for others who have the same printer.

Before July 1987, limited-support printers were listed on the Printer 2 disk. With the July release of 4.2, these printers had to be moved to a third printer disk which is not shipped with the WordPerfect package. It is available, however, from WordPerfect Corporation at no additional charge within one month of purchase.

Nonsupported Printers and Sheet Feeders

If you cannot find a printer definition that will fit your printer, you can use the Printer program (PRINTER.EXE) included on the Learning disk to create a printer or sheet feeder definition. See Chapter 7 for details.

Updating WordPerfect

If you order a 4.2 update to WordPerfect, do not copy the WPRINTER.FIL or WPFONT.FIL from the original WordPerfect program disk or you will copy over all the printer selections. You should only copy WP.EXE if you want to keep all the previous printer definitions.

Deleting Printers from WPRINTER.FIL

You need to use the Printer program if you want to delete printers from the list after they have been selected. See Chapter 7 for details.

Related Entries

Display Printers and Fonts

Print

Sheet Feeder Bin Number

See also Chapter 6, "Printer Specifics"

See also Chapter 7, "Printer Program"

Select Records from a Merge File

See *Sort and Select*

Set Tabs

Line Format (SHIFT-F8) is used to set and clear tabs. See *Tabs, Clear and Set* for details.

Setup Menu

WordPerfect comes with certain defaults already set. You can use the Setup menu to customize the defaults to fit your situation. The options include specifying the drive/directory for the Dictionary and Thesaurus files, changing the initial settings, setting the screen size and beep options, and choosing any backup options. Chapter 3 discusses each option in detail.

Keystrokes

1. From DOS, enter **WP/S** instead of WP to enter the Setup menu, as shown in the following illustration.

```
                              Set-up Menu

      0 - End Set-up and enter WP

      1 - Set Directories or Drives for Dictionary and Thesaurus Files
      2 - Set Initial Settings
      3 - Set Screen and Beep Options
      4 - Set Backup Options

      Selection:

      Press Cancel to ignore changes and return to DOS
```

2. Type **1** to Set Directories or Drives for Dictionary and Thesaurus Files, **2** to Set Initial Settings, **3** to Set Screen and Beep Options, or **4** to Set Backup Options.

Option 1 only needs to be changed if you have copied LEX.WP and TH.WP into a directory where WordPer-

```
Change Initial Settings

Press any of the keys listed below to change initial settings

Key                Initial Settings

Line Format        Tabs, Margins, Spacing, Hyphenation, Align Character
Page Format        Page # Pos, Page Length, Top Margin, Page # Col Pos, W/O
Print Format       Pitch, Font, Lines/Inch, Right Just, Underlining, SF Bin #
Print              Printer, Copies, Binding Width
Date               Date Format
Insert/Typeover    Insert/Typeover Mode
Mark Text          Paragraph Number Definition, Table of Authorities Definition
Footnote           Footnote/Endnote Options
Escape             Set N
Screen             Set Auto-rewrite
Text In/Out        Set Insert Document Summary on Save/Exit

Selection:

Press Enter to return to the Set-up Menu
```

Figure 4-94.   Change Initial Settings menu

fect is *not* located, or if you are not using the Speller or Thesaurus disks in the default drive on a two disk-drive system.

Option 2 displays the menu shown in Figure 4-94, which is used to change any of the defaults set by Word-Perfect. To change initial settings, press the function key listed at the left to change an option listed at the right. The settings are changed with the same menus and prompts as in WordPerfect.

Option 3 lets you change the screen options, as shown in the following.

```
Set Screen Options

   Number of rows: 25
   Number of columns: 80
   Hard return displayed as ascii value: 170
   Display filename on status line? (Y/N) Y

Set Beep Options

   Beep when search fails? (Y/N) Y
   Beep on error? (Y/N) Y
   Beep on hyphenation? (Y/N) N
```

Option 4 lets you select timed backup or original backup. See *Backing Up Files* for complete information.

3. When finished with all options, press ENTER to return to the Setup menu.

4. Type **0** to End Setup and enter WP.

Hints

The defaults that have been set in WordPerfect are shown in Table 4-3. These settings can be changed until they fit your needs.

When changes are made to the Setup menu, the WP.EXE file is altered. Colors, key mappings and printer

Feature		Default Setting
Line Format	Tabs	Every 5 spaces (1/2 inch in 10 pitch)
	Margins	Left = 10, right = 74 (1 inch in 10 pitch)
	Spacing	1 (single)
	Hyphenation	Off, aided, hyphenation zone = 7,0
	Align character	Decimal point (.)
Page Format	Page # Pos	None
	Page length	Form length = 66 lines, text lines = 54
	Top margin	12 half-lines (1 inch)
	Page # Col Pos	Left = 10, center = 42, right = 74
	Widow/Orphan	Off
Print Format	Pitch	10
	Font	1
	Lines per inch	6
	Right justification	On
	Underlining	Single, noncontinuous
	SF Bin #	1
Print	Printer #	1
	Copies	1
	Binding width	0
Date	Date format	Month day, year

Table 4-3.   Default Settings for WordPerfect

Feature		Default Setting
Insert/ Typeover		Insert
Footnote	Options	Spacing within notes = 1
		Spacing between notes = 1
		Lines to keep together = 3
		Start footnote numbers each page = N
		Footnote numbering mode = Numbers
		Endnote numbering mode = Numbers
		Line separating text and footnotes = 2 inches
		Footnotes at bottom of page = Y
		Characters for notes = *
		Footnotes in text = Superscripted #
		Endnotes in text = Superscripted #
		Footnotes in note = (five spaces) Superscripted
		Endnotes in note = Number followed by period
Escape	Set N	8
Screen	Auto-rewrite	On
Text In/Out	Doc. summary	Off (does not insert automatically on Save/Exit

Table 4-3.   Default Settings for WordPerfect (*continued*)

selections (not found on this menu) are stored in a file named {WP}SYS.FIL.

Returning to the Original Defaults

If you need to return to the original default settings for a single editing session (until you leave WordPerfect), enter **WP/X** instead of WP. If you want to return to the original defaults permanently, enter **WP/X/S** instead of WP.

Precautions

If you are sharing computers, printers, or files with others, be aware that changing your defaults might create problems for others. For example, if someone is using the standard default margins of 10 and 74 and the standard tab settings, while you have changed yours to 15 and 70, with tabs set every 10 spaces, a document created with his or her copy of WordPerfect would be formatted incorrectly if retrieved under your copy of WordPerfect. One of the items most affected are tables of tabbed columns.

Alternatives to changing items in the Setup menu include creating macros for different formats or placing format codes within the document, even when they are not necessary. For example, if you have set the default margins to 15 and 70 and take your file to be printed on a system where WordPerfect remains set at 10 and 74, your document would be reformatted for those settings. You would need to place a [Margin Set:15,70] code at the beginning of the document so it would remain in its original format.

Applications

If you are using another person's computer and a document does not appear to be formatted correctly, try entering Word-Perfect by typing **WP/X** to reset the defaults temporarily.

If you are accustomed to a Typeover mode instead of inserting characters, you can change the default setting by pressing INS while in the Setup menu.

The date format can be permanently changed if you prefer a different style (for example, "25 November 1987" instead of "November 25, 1987") or if you want to include the current time.

If your footnotes and endnotes must follow a specific style that is different from the default, you can change it in the Setup menu.

Quite often, you will need to change several settings because they are dependent upon each other. For example, if you use 12 pitch most often and you want to keep 1-inch margins as the default, you should change the margins to 12 and 90, and set tabs every five spaces beginning with position 2.

Related Entries

Backing Up Files

Beep

Speller Utility

Thesaurus

See also Chapter 3, "The Next Step"

Sheet Feeder Bin Number

WordPerfect supports sheet feeders that have from one to seven bins. See *Select Printers* for details on selecting a sheet feeder at the time of printer selection.

Keystrokes

1. Go to the beginning of the page which is to be fed from a different sheet feeder bin. (Go To (CTRL-HOME),↑ will move to the beginning of the current page.)

2. Press Print Format (CTRL-F8).

3. Type **9** to select a Sheet Feeder Bin Number.

4. Type the number (1 through 7) for the sheet feeder bin.

5. Press ENTER to leave the Print Format menu and return to the document.

Hints

When you change sheet feeder bins, a code such as [Bin:#2] is inserted into the document. All pages following that code are fed from the specified bin until another bin change is encountered.

A sheet feeder bin code should always be at the beginning of the page, preceding any text.

If you do not have a sheet feeder, but selected a sheet feeder definition, or if you selected the wrong sheet feeder, you might see extra characters printing at the top or bottom of the page. These characters are usually the result of incorrectly interpreted Escape codes.

Sheet Feeder Definitions

The definitions for all sheet feeders are found in a file named WPFEED.FIL on the WordPerfect program disk. After selecting a printer, you are asked about the type of forms that will be used. If you have a sheet feeder listed on the menu shown in Figure 4-95, you should answer yes.

If yours is not shown, the chances are that it is a single-bin mechanical sheet feeder that does not accept Escape codes for inserting and ejecting pages. This type of sheet feeder should usually be defined as continuous forms. If it does not eject the page correctly, use the Qume Single Bin definition, which contains no codes for inserting pages but uses a form feed (ASCII 12) to eject the page.

As you can see from the menu shown in Figure 4-95, three questions are asked in addition to the sheet feeder type. In fact, the list of sheet feeders is not displayed until you answer these questions. If you have a laser printer sheet feeder, enter **0** in answer to the first two questions, "Number

```
Sheet Feeder Information
      Number of Extra Lines Between Pages (12 LPI):  24
      Column Position of Left Edge of Paper (10 Pitch):  26
      Number of Sheet Feeder Bins (1-7):  1

Sheet Feeder Type

   1 Apple LaserWriter                2 BDT LetterMate I,II,III
   3 BDT MF-830 6 bin Laser Feeder    4 BDT MF-830 6 bin La (continued)
   5 BDT MF-850 3 bin Laser Feeder    6 BDT MF-850 3 bin La (continued)
   7 Brother HR-15/HR-25/HR-35        8 Canon A1
   9 Diablo Single/Dual/Envl         10 Epson LQ-1500/NEC P5
  11 HP LaserJet 500+                12 HP LaserJet 500+    (continued)
  13 IBM 5218 Dual Bin/Envl Feed     14 IBM Pageprinter 3812
  15 NEC 3515/5515/7715 Single/Dual  16 NEC 3550 Single/Dual
  17 Qume Single Bin                 18 Rutishauser Dual Bin
  19 Texas Instruments 2015          20 Texas Instruments 2115
  21 Xerox 2700 Laser                22 Ziyad PaperJet 400
  23 Ziyad PaperJet 400  (continued)


Selection: 1          (Use the PRINTER program to define a new sheet feeder)
```

Figure 4-95.   Sheet feeder selections

of Extra Lines Between Pages" and "Column Position of Left Edge of Paper." If you have any other type of sheet feeder and are not sure of the answers to these questions, leave them at the default settings and change them later if necessary.

Some of the sheet feeder definitions occupy two options with the second labeled "(continued)." The first option is used to store the codes for the first three bins and the second is used for the last four bins.

Creating a New Sheet Feeder Definition

The Printer program can be used to create, delete, rename, or edit a sheet feeder definition. As you can see in Figure 4-96, a typical sheet feeder definition is very simple. The Escape codes for inserting and ejecting pages can be found in the sheet feeder documentation. See Chapter 7, "Printer Program," for information about starting and working with the program.

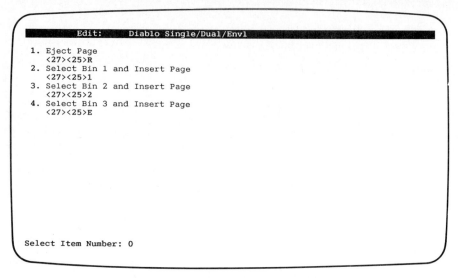

```
      Edit:        Diablo Single/Dual/Envl
1. Eject Page
   <27><25>R
2. Select Bin 1 and Insert Page
   <27><25>1
3. Select Bin 2 and Insert Page
   <27><25>2
4. Select Bin 3 and Insert Page
   <27><25>E




Select Item Number: 0
```

Figure 4-96.   Typical sheet feeder definition

Applications

If you have two sheet feeder bins, you could have letterhead stationery in one bin and white bond paper in the other. Since bin 1 is selected as the default, you would probably put the type of paper that is used most often in that bin.

If you have white bond paper in bin 1 and letterhead stationery in bin 2, you could create a print macro especially for letters that could be run *after* the document is finished. The macro could go to the beginning of the document and insert a bin change code to feed the first sheet of paper from bin 2. As the next step in the macro, press PGDN to go to the second page and insert another bin change to feed the remaining pages from bin 1.

If you have a third bin that is used as an envelope feeder, the macro could include steps to copy the address from the letter to an "envelope" form, then print it from that bin. See Appendix C for details.

Related Entries

Select Printers

See also Chapter 5, "Laser Printers"

See also Chapter 7, "Printer Program"

See also Appendix C, "Macro Library"

Shell

Shell (CTRL-F1) is used to suspend WordPerfect in memory and go to DOS. If you have WordPerfect Library running, Shell (CTRL-F1) goes to the Shell menu.

Keystrokes

1. Press Shell (CTRL-F1). The following menu appears.

```
1 Go to DOS: 0
```

If you have WordPerfect Library running, you will see the following prompt.

```
1 Go to Shell; 2 Retrieve Clipboard: 0
```

2. Type **1** to Go to DOS (or Go to Shell). If you go to DOS, the DOS prompt is altered to let you know Word-Perfect is still running.

```
Enter the DOS command 'EXIT' to return to the shell.

The IBM Personal Computer DOS
Version 3.20 (C)Copyright International Business Machines Corp 1981, 1986
          (C)Copyright Microsoft Corp 1981, 1986

(shell) C:\ ->
```

If Shell is running, you are placed in the Shell menu, as shown in Figure 4-97. The WordPerfect entry is marked with an asterisk to indicate that it is still running.

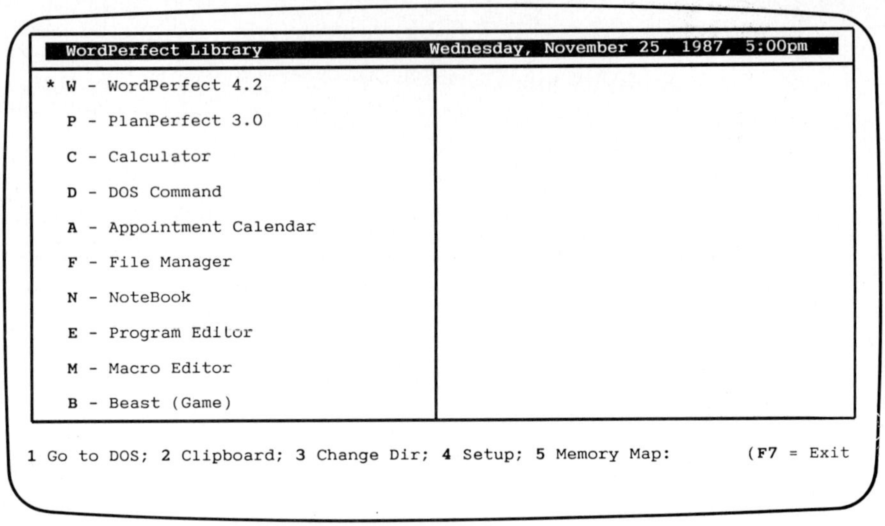

```
┌─────────────────────────────────────────────────────────────────────┐
│ ▐ WordPerfect Library           Wednesday, November 25, 1987, 5:00pm▌ │
│ * W - WordPerfect 4.2                │                                │
│                                      │                                │
│   P - PlanPerfect 3.0                │                                │
│                                      │                                │
│   C - Calculator                     │                                │
│                                      │                                │
│   D - DOS Command                    │                                │
│                                      │                                │
│   A - Appointment Calendar           │                                │
│                                      │                                │
│   F - File Manager                   │                                │
│                                      │                                │
│   N - NoteBook                       │                                │
│                                      │                                │
│   E - Program Editor                 │                                │
│                                      │                                │
│   M - Macro Editor                   │                                │
│                                      │                                │
│   B - Beast (Game)                   │                                │
│                                      │                                │
│ 1 Go to DOS; 2 Clipboard; 3 Change Dir; 4 Setup; 5 Memory Map:   (F7 = Exit │
└─────────────────────────────────────────────────────────────────────┘
```

Figure 4-97.   Shell menu

3. When finished at DOS, enter **EXIT** at the DOS
prompt to return to WordPerfect. To return to WordPerfect from the Shell menu, type the letter assigned to the
WordPerfect entry.

Hints

If you have WordPerfect Library running, option 1 on the
Shell menu also lets you go to DOS. You would then enter
EXIT to return to the Shell menu.

When you go to DOS, another copy of COMMAND.COM
is loaded into memory. If you do not have enough memory
available, you may get the message, "Not enough memory to
load COMMAND.COM."

Do not run the CHKDSK/F command while in DOS
because it will interfere with the open files that WordPerfect
creates while it is running. You should also be careful not to
delete any WordPerfect files while at DOS.

You should load any TSR (terminate stay resident) programs before starting WordPerfect. They should not be
loaded when you go to DOS temporarily.

Applications

If you have a document to be saved and you run out of disk space, you can go to DOS with Shell (CTRL-F1) and format a disk.

If you are running WordPerfect Library, you can go to the Shell menu and run other programs. More than one WordPerfect Corporation program can be kept in memory at once and text can be moved between programs via the Clipboard.

Related Entries

Go To DOS

Short Form

The Short Form option is found on the Mark Text (ALT-F5) menu and is used in conjunction with the Table of Authorities feature. Each entry in a Table of Authorities has a full form that will be the actual text printed in the table. The short form is a type of nickname that can be used to mark each subsequent occurrence of the full form. See *Table of Authorities* for details.

Single-Sheet Feeding

See *Forms*

Soft Page

When the maximum number of lines fill a page, a soft page break (a single dashed line) is automatically inserted by

WordPerfect. The number of lines allowed on a page is automatically calculated by WordPerfect, taking into account the page length setting, headers, footers, page numbers, and footnotes that appear on the page.

If text is added or deleted, the soft page break will automatically be updated (there is no repagination necessary with WordPerfect). You can see across both soft and hard page breaks and can move to specific pages with PGUP, PGDN, or Go To (CTRL-HOME).

A hard page break is displayed as a double dashed line and is manually inserted by pressing Hard Page (CTRL-ENTER).

Related Entries

Page Breaks

Sort and Select

Three types of sorts are available: line, paragraph, or merge. WordPerfect uses a data base concept for sorting and selecting records by viewing each line, paragraph, or merge record as a record. Each record is further divided into fields, lines, and words. For example, if you have a list of clients, each client would be considered a record. Each bit of information about that client (such as address, phone number, or birthdate) is considered a field.

You can use Sort to sort the records by one or more of the bits of information (sort by last name or ZIP code, for example) or select records that fit into the same category (such as all those who attended last year's benefit and have donated more than $50 during the year).

When reading the following sections, keep in mind that while there are many options available in the Sort feature, few changes (if any) need to be made to the Sort menu when doing a simple line sort.

Keystrokes

Sort a File

If you want to sort a file that appears on the screen, retrieve the file first.

> 1. Press Merge/Sort (CTRL-F9). The following prompt appears.

```
1 Merge; 2 Sort; 3 Sorting Sequences: 0
```

> 2. Type 2 to Sort. You are asked for the name of the input file.
>
> 3. Press ENTER to sort the contents of the screen, or enter the name of a file to be sorted. Include the drive and directory if necessary.
>
> 4. When prompted for the name of the output file, press ENTER to display the results on the screen or enter the name of the file which will be used to hold the sorted data. If you enter the name of a file that already exists, you are asked if you want to replace the original file. Type **Y** to replace the file or **N** and enter a different filename.
>
> 5. The Sort menu shown in Figure 4-98 appears. It has already been set to sort lines by the first word in each line. Make changes to the menu if necessary. See "Options" in this entry for information about all options on the menu.
>
> 6. Type **1** to Perform Action.

The number of records involved are counted at the bottom corner of the screen during the sort. When finished, the Sort menu disappears from the screen.

Sort a Block

You should use the block sort if you want to sort part of a document, or if you have a list of items but do not want to include any headings in the sort.

1. Retrieve the file containing the block to be sorted.

2. Move the cursor to one end of the block and press Block (ALT-F4).

3. Move the cursor to the opposite end to highlight the block.

4. Press Merge/Sort (CTRL-F9). The menu shown in Figure 4-98 appears.

5. Change options on the Sort menu if necessary. See "Options" for details.

6. Type **1** to Perform Action.

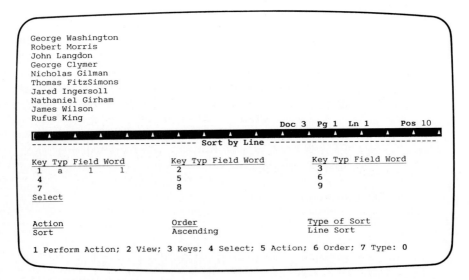

Figure 4-98.   Sort menu

Options

The Sort menu shown in Figure 4-98 displays a one-line menu with numbered options at the bottom of the screen. These numbered options are used to enter or change the information that is displayed in the menu.

The beginning of the menu displays the *keys*. A key is the item (word) by which the lines, paragraphs, or records are sorted. WordPerfect asks you to identify whether the "word" is alphanumeric or numeric, and where it is located. Up to nine keys can be defined for subsorting. The keys are also used to help determine the "select" criteria.

The rest of the menu displays the current selections. Each option is explained in detail in the following discussion.

Perform Action

After all selections have been made, type **1** to Perform Action. The term *Action* refers to sort, select, or select and sort. The current selection is displayed on the menu and can be changed with option 5 (Action) if a select criteria has been entered.

View

Option 2 lets you view the text to be sorted. You can use any of the cursor keys to move through the text. After viewing the text, press Exit (F7) to return to the Sort menu. If you are sorting a merge file and each record is larger than the amount of space at the top of the screen, this option can be used to check the field, line, or word number when defining the keys.

Keys

Before specifying the keys, you should verify that the type of sort is correct. Option 7 is used to choose between a line, paragraph, or merge sort.

Each type of sort has its own key selection. A line sort asks for the field and word (if you have tabbed columns on a line, each column is considered a field). A paragraph sort asks you to identify the line, field, and word. The merge sort asks for the field number first, the line number, then the word to be used. Figure 4-99 shows how the "keys" part of the menu is changed when you select a different type of sort.

In a merge record, each field is separated from the next one by a ^R. In lines and paragraphs, the fields are divided with a Tab or Indent code.

Dealing with Variable Lines and Words   In each record (line, paragraph, or individual merge record), there should always be the same number of fields. However, there are not always the same number of lines or words from record to record. For example, some records could have names that have a first name and a surname, while others have a first name, middle name, and a surname. Some fields and paragraphs have a different number of lines (a line is defined as any line ending with a hard or soft return).

```
------------------------------ Sort by Line ------------------------------

Key Typ Field Word          Key Typ Field Word          Key Typ Field Word
 1   a    1    1              2                           3
 4                           5                           6
 7                           8                           9


------------------------------ Sort by Paragraph ------------------------------

Key Typ Line Field Word     Key Typ Line Field Word     Key Typ Line Field Word
 1   a    1    1    1         2                           3
 4                           5                           6
 7                           8                           9


------------------------------ Sort Secondary Merge File ------------------------------

Key Typ Field Line Word     Key Typ Field Line Word     Key Typ Field Line Word
 1   a    1    1    1         2                           3
 4                           5                           6
 7                           8                           9
```

Figure 4-99.   Different types of sorts change the "key" column in the Sort menu

In these types of situations, use a negative number to identify the word or line from the opposite direction. For example, if the ZIP code is in the same field as the city and state, it could be the third word in "Topeka, Kansas 89898," the fourth word in "Bismarck, North Dakota 23232," or the fifth word in "Salt Lake City, Utah 56565." However, it will always be the last field in any of these situations. Therefore, you would use a negative 1 (−1) to identify the word number.

Figure 4-100 shows the Sort menu when three keys have been defined for a merge file having an inconsistent number of lines and words per field. Note that the negative number has been used in all three situations to sort by ZIP code, state, then surname.

Entering the Keys   When you select option 3 for keys, you see a one-line message at the bottom of the screen. This message prompts you to type **A** for an alphanumeric sort or **N** for a numeric sort. If the numbers to be sorted all have the same number of digits (as in a ZIP code or telephone number), either A or N could be used. If there is an unequal number of digits, you should use the numeric sort. If you

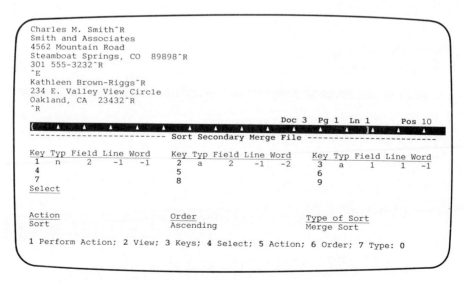

Figure 4-100.   Negative numbers identify words or lines from the opposite direction

were to use the alphanumeric sort, unequal numbers could be sorted incorrectly (1000 would be sorted before 7 because 1 comes before 7). A numeric sort compares the numbers from the right instead of the left.

When defining the keys, use the arrow keys to move to each item. When → is pressed, the information (a 1 1 1) is automatically inserted. You can move freely through the keys with any of the arrow keys and type a new letter or number to replace the existing option. To delete all the information in the last key, move to any previous key and press DEL.

When finished entering the keys, press Exit (F7) to return to the menu.

Select

The Select option can be used to select all records that have a particular item in common. For example, you could select all the records for those people age 25 to 30 who are living in St. Louis.

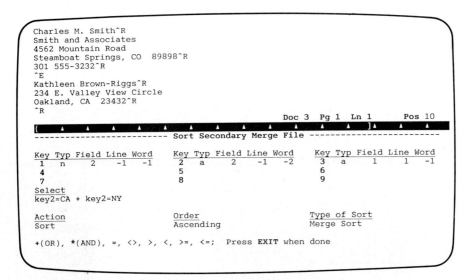

Figure 4-101.   Sort menu after choosing Select

In all but a global select (discussed later), you should define the keys before entering the select statement.

When you choose option 4, you see the Sort menu shown in Figure 4-101. When entering the select statement, you will identify the key to be used, the operator, and the condition to be met. You can combine keys with * and + to select all records that satisfy either condition or both conditions, respectively. Parentheses can be placed around entries to identify groups and change the order of the selection (usually done from left to right). Spaces should be used between keys, but not within keys. Table 4-4 describes each operator that can be used in a select statement.

As shown in Figure 4-101, you must identify a key for each option (key2=CA + key2=NY). You could not have used the select statement "key2=CA+NY." The + and * should only be used between keys, not within keys.

Symbol	Function
+ (or)	Place between keys to select records that meet one condition *or* the other
* (and)	Place between keys to select records where *both* conditions exist
=	Equal to
<>	Not equal to
>	Greater than
<	Less than
>=	Greater than or equal to
<=	Less than or equal to
( )	Place parentheses around keys that should be considered as one group; when parentheses are not used, selection is done from left to right

Table 4-4.   Operators Used in Select Statements

Select Statement	Explanation
key1=Johnson	Select all records for the Johnson family reunion mailing
key2>54700 * key2<75600	Select all records having a ZIP code greater than 54700 and less than 75600
key1>=a * key1<=n	Select records where the last name starts with a letter A through M (or a last name consisting *only* of N)
key6>=$75,000	Select all records that list a salary greater than or equal to $75,000
key4<>CA	Select all records except those from California
(key3=Toledo + key3=Columbus) * (key5>=25 * key5<=30)	Select records for all people between the ages of 25 and 35 living in Columbus or Toledo

Table 4-5. Select Statements Showing Use of Operations and Parentheses

Table 4-5 includes samples of select statements that should clarify how operators and parentheses are used. In the second, third, and sixth examples, * is used instead of +. To better understand why, look at the second example. If you used + in this situation, all the records greater than 54700 or those less than 75600 would be included. In essence, all records would be included because either condition could be met. If you use *, both conditions must be met, limiting the number of records accordingly.

Global Select   WordPerfect can select all records that contain a specific word *anywhere* in the record. For this reason, you do not have to identify the exact key.

Only one word can be used in a global select. You can enter the condition in either uppercase or lowercase. Unlike Search, uppercase will find both uppercase and lowercase occurrences (lowercase will also find both uppercase and lowercase).

An example of a global select statement could be KEYG=ESQ. to select all records that contain "Esq." after a person's name or company name. The statement KEYG> =ESQ would select all records that mention Esq, Esq., or Esquire because those phrases are greater than or equal to "Esq".

Action

If a select statement has not been entered, the Action is considered as a Sort. Option 5 (to change the Action) is disabled. If a select statement has been entered, the Action automatically changes to "Select and Sort." You can choose option 5 for Action and make a choice between "Select and Sort" or "Select Only."

Order

Option 6 on the Sort menu lets you determine whether records will be sorted in an ascending or descending order.

Type

Three types of sorting are available. If you choose option 7 for Type, the following choices appear.

```
Sorting Type: 1 Merge; 2 Line; 3 Paragraph: 0
```

A line sort is set as the default and is discussed first.

Line Sort   Use this option to sort lines ending with a hard or soft return. If there are blank lines between any of the lines, they are extracted and placed at the very beginning of the list after it is sorted. If you have used tabs or indents in the line, each tab or indent code separates a field.

Both of the following examples could be sorted by line. In the first example, each entire line is considered field 1 because there are no Tab or Indent codes. If you wanted to sort by the last name, you would specify a −1 because of the inconsistent number of words in each record.

```
Charles Grover
Kathleen Brown
Wallace M. Cleveland
Richard Washington
Jane S. Fremont
```

The second line sort example contains three fields in each record.

```
Charles Grover          301 555-7878    Consultant
Kathleen Brown          212 555-9893    Training Manager
Wallace M. Cleveland    415 555-3212    Distributor
Richard Washington      213 555-4567    Consultant
Jane S. Fremont         301 555-7654    Distributor
```

Paragraph Sort   Any group of text separated by two or more hard returns or a hard or soft page break is considered a paragraph. Thus, a paragraph can be up to one page in length. When specifying a key for a paragraph sort, you need to identify the line, the field (items separated with a Tab or Indent Code), and the word.

Merge Sort   If sorting a secondary merge file with fields separated by ^R and records separated by ^E, use the merge sort option. There should be no extra lines or hard page breaks in this type of file or it will not be sorted correctly. When defining a key for this type of sort, the field number should be specified, then the line within that field, and finally the word.

Hints

If the document to be sorted is in Document 1, Document 2 is used to sort the information. If both documents are filled, Document 3 is used. Document 3 is only used for features such as Sort, Preview, and generation of tables, lists, and an index.

If you get an error message indicating that there is not enough memory available for the Sort feature, you may need to clear the other document. Because there is twice as much memory allotted to document 1 as to document 2, you can leave document 1 empty and use document 2 for the document to be sorted. WordPerfect will then perform the sort in document 1 and can use the extra memory available there.

You should also check the amount of disk space you have available if you see the message "Not enough memory." You should have available at least 2.5 times the amount of disk space as the file to be sorted.

The last set of sort and select criteria is kept in the Sort menu until changed or until you exit WordPerfect.

If you have two or more words that should be considered as one word during a sort, insert a Hard Space (CTRL-SPACEBAR) between each word instead of a regular space. This is useful in cases where you need to sort by a last name, but have an abbreviation or title such as "M.D.," "Ph.D.," or "Jr." after the last name. If you did not use a hard space between the last name and the abbreviation, and entered -1 as the word to be used for the sort, the abbreviation would be considered as the last name in those situations.

After pressing Merge/Sort (CTRL-F9), you can choose option 3 to select the Sorting Sequences. The choices are US/European or Scandinavian. The US/European option is set as the default and sorts accented characters with the unaccented characters (for example, $\ddot{e}$ and $\grave{e}$ with the standard e) while the Scandinavian style places accented characters *after* the unaccented A thorough Z characters (for example, $\hat{a}$ would follow the z entries).

If you select records from a block or file and the result is a blank screen, there were no records found. Press Cancel (F1) and type **1** if you want to restore the original text.

Applications

Sort is considered by many to be as powerful as a data base when it comes to sorting and selecting records. It is especially useful when you keep all your merge records in one file, then select records to target specific groups and markets.

To take advantage of bulk mailing rates, you must presort envelopes or newsletters according to ZIP code. Use Sort to accomplish this instead of doing it by hand.

You can easily sort bibliographies using the paragraph sort. Enter each reference at random, then do the sort later. If items are added, do the sort again.

When you send copies of a letter to others, you usually put the abbreviation "cc:" at the bottom of the letter with the names of those to receive copies after it. You can block and sort the list to place them in alphabetical order.

If you sort a list that has been numbered with WordPerfect's paragraph numbering, the list will be renumbered correctly.

Related Entries

Block

Merge

Paragraph Numbering

Spacing

WordPerfect lets you specify the line spacing in half-line increments with no upward limit.

Keystrokes

1. Press Line Format (SHIFT-F8).

2. Type 4 for Spacing.

3. Enter the number for the new spacing.

Hints

When you change the line spacing, a code similar to [Spacing Set:2] is inserted into the document at that point. Text from that point forward is affected until another spacing change is encountered.

Half-line spacing is indicated in decimal form (.5 for a half-line, 1.5 for line-and-a-half spacing, and so on) rather than in fractions. Line spacing is displayed on the screen to the nearest full line. For example, if you have set spacing at 2, you will see it as such on the screen, while .5 spacing would appear as single spacing on the screen and 1.5 spacing would appear as double spacing on the screen. Check the status line if you need to know the exact line number. For example, if you have set spacing at 1.5, the "Ln" number on the status line would show 1, 2.5, 4, 5.5, 7, and so on as you move from line to line.

If you get double spacing at the printer when single spacing was specified, make sure the Auto Line Feed (LF) switch is off at the printer. Check the printer manual to find the location of the switch.

You can vary the "look" of line spacing from a loose to a tight appearance by combining half-line spacing with the Lines Per Inch feature, as shown in Table 4-6.

Spacing for Headers, Footers, Footnotes, and Endnotes

Changing the spacing in a document does not affect the spacing in a header, footer, footnote, or endnote. The spacing can be changed individually within a header or footer. Spacing for footnotes and endnotes must be changed through the Footnote Options menu (press Footnote (CTRL-F7) and type **4** for Options). You can change the spacing of the notes and the amount of space between each note. Currently, .5 spacing is not available in notes.

You can increase the amount of space between a header or footer and the text by inserting more space at the end of a header or the beginning of a footer. If you add more space to a footer, only the first line is printed above the bottom margin. Additional lines will print within the bottom margin.

Spacing	Lines per Inch	Total Number of Lines per Inch
2	6	3
2	8	4
1	6	6
1	8	8
.5	6	12
.5	8	16

Table 4-6.   Variations in Line Spacing

Changing Line Spacing for Special Elements

Usually, the same line spacing is used throughout a document. However, if you type double-spaced documents containing indented, single-spaced quotations, you can easily change the spacing before and after the quotation. If this is a common application for you, consider placing the steps in a macro. The macro could change to single spacing and indent the paragraph, then pause for you to enter the text. After entering the text and pressing ENTER to continue the macro, it would create the necessary space between the quotation and the text and return to double spacing. See Appendix C for the exact steps.

It is sometimes easier to set .5 line spacing when creating equations than to use Advance Up/Down or Superscript/Subscript.

If vertical lines in Line Draw do not match up exactly when printed, use .5 spacing and possibly even 8 lines per inch to create more solid lines.

Related Entries

Line Draw

Lines per Inch

Special Characters

WordPerfect can display special characters that are available in the computer's ROM (read only memory) and print those characters that are available with your printer.

Keystrokes

Display Special Characters

There are three ways to display special characters on the screen. You can map the special characters to a CTRL- or ALT-key combination, hold down the ALT key and type the decimal value for the character on the numeric keypad, or press CTRL-V ("n =" appears) and then enter the decimal value of the character with the numbers at the top of the keyboard. You should choose the one that best suits your needs.

The following steps are used for CTRL- and ALT-key mapping.

1. Press Screen (CTRL-F3).

2. Type **3** for CTRL/ALT keys. The screen shown in Figure 4-102 appears showing ALT-A through Z combinations on the left and CTRL-A through Z combinations on the right.

3. Find the character and its decimal value in the table at the bottom of the screen. To determine the value, read the numbers downward at the left then add the numbers along the top. Each multiple of ten is indicated by a bold number. For example, the character ç corresponds to the number 100 at the left and is at position 35 according to the numbers along the top. Therefore, the decimal value for ç is 135.

4. Choose which CTRL- or ALT-key combination should be used for the special character and press that combination.

5. Enter the decimal value for the desired character.

6. When finished, press Exit (F7).

Key	Value	Key	Value	Key	Value	Key	Value
Alt-A	0	Alt-N	0	Ctrl-A	0	Ctrl-N	0
Alt-B	0	Alt-O	0	Ctrl-B	0	Ctrl-O	0
Alt-C	0	Alt-P	0	Ctrl-C	0	Ctrl-P	0
Alt-D	0	Alt-Q	0	Ctrl-D	0	Ctrl-Q	0
Alt-E	0	Alt-R	0	Ctrl-E	0	Ctrl-R	0
Alt-F	0	Alt-S	0	Ctrl-F	0	Ctrl-S	0
Alt-G	0	Alt-T	0	Ctrl-G	0	Ctrl-T	0
Alt-H	0	Alt-U	0	Ctrl-H	0	Ctrl-U	0
Alt-I	0	Alt-V	0	Ctrl-I	0	Ctrl-V	0
Alt-J	0	Alt-W	0	Ctrl-J	0	Ctrl-W	0
Alt-K	0	Alt-X	0	Ctrl-K	0	Ctrl-X	0
Alt-L	0	Alt-Y	0	Ctrl-L	0	Ctrl-Y	0
Alt-M	0	Alt-Z	0	Ctrl-M	0	Ctrl-Z	0

```
        01234567891123456789212345678931234567894123456789
  0 -    ☺☻♥♦♣♠•◘○◙♂♀♪♫☼►◄↕‼¶§▬↨↑↓→←∟↔▲▼
100 -                               Çüéâäàåçêëèïîì ÄÅÉæÆôöò
150 -   ûùÿÖÜ¢£¥₧ƒáíóúñÑªº¿⌐¬½¼¡«»░▒▓│┤╡╢╖╕╣║╗╝╜╛┐└┴┬├─┼╞╟
200 -   ╚╔╩╦╠═╬╧╨╤╥╙╘╒╓╫╪┘┌█▄▌▐▀αßΓπΣσµτΦΘΩδ∞φε∩≡±≥≤⌠⌡÷≈°∙
250 -   ·√ⁿ²■

Press key to be defined (Press Exit to return):
```

Figure 4-102. Screen displaying special characters

7. Press the CTRL- or ALT-key combination in WordPerfect to display the character when it is needed.

Print Special Characters

WordPerfect has tried to define your printer so that it will print all the available special characters. A few printers will print all the characters you see on the screen, while others print different characters in their place. See Chapter 7, "Printer Program," to understand more about the character tables used by each printer.

To find out what special characters have been defined for your printer, use the following steps or try the FONTTEST macro described in "Hints."

1. Press Print (SHIFT-F7).

2. Type **4** for Printer Control.

3. Type **2** to Display Printers and Fonts. Sometimes the same font (actually a character table) is listed more than once. Make a note of each *different* font.

4. Press ENTER until you return to the regular screen.

5. Retrieve the file FONT.TST from the Learning disk.

6. Print the file to see the characters defined for font 1.

7. Using the list of different fonts go to the beginning of the FONT.TST document, press Print Format (CTRL-F8), type **1** for Pitch and Font, and change the font to the next font to be tested.

8. Repeat steps 5 through 7 until all fonts (character tables) have been tested.

If you have a laser printer, you will more than likely want to try all the fonts for all the cartridges you have.

Hints

Choosing ALT- and CTRL-Key Combinations

You can map up to 52 special characters with the ALT- and CTRL-key combinations. Most people try to assign the characters to a combination that is easy to remember. For example, CTRL-H could be used for 1/2 (one-half) and CTRL-F could be used for 1/4 (one-fourth). However, take note of the following considerations before assigning all the characters randomly.

If you want to reserve the ALT-key combinations for single-key macros, use the CTRL-key combinations for special characters.

If you do assign a special character to an ALT-key combination, you can define a macro for that combination, but it would not be as easy to recall. Instead of starting the macro by pressing the ALT-key combination, you would press Macro (ALT-F10), then press the ALT-key combination. The special character would appear. Press ENTER to accept the special character as the "name" of the macro and the macro will be started. You could also press Macro (ALT-F10), enter the ALT-key combination without the hyphen (ALTA if the macro were named ALT-A), then press ENTER.

If you plan to use C7TRL-key combinations to enter any of the merge codes ^C, ^D, ^F, ^G, ^N, ^O, ^P, ^Q, ^S, ^T, ^U, and ^V, do not map special characters to those combinations.

To avoid limiting yourself, choose only those merge codes that you use often. Even if you decide to assign special characters to those combinations, you can still enter the codes with Merge Codes (ALT-F9).

If you use ^B to insert the current page number in a header or footer at print time, do not map a special character to that combination. While a ^B can be entered on the regular screen by pressing Merge Codes (ALT-F9), then **B** (even though it is not on the list of codes), you cannot use this method in a header or footer because merge codes are not allowed there.

Using the FONTTEST Macro

Two macro files on the Learning disk, FONTTEST.MAC and FNTTEST2.MAC, can be used to automate the printing of the FONT.TST file in all fonts. Before using the macro, make sure all three files are in the default directory and that the screens in both documents are empty. The screen is cleared during the macro, removing anything in memory at the time.

Press Macro (ALT-F10) and enter **FONTTEST** when asked for the macro name to start the macro. Follow the instructions and print the result when finished.

See the section on character tables in Chapter 7 for information about creating or changing a character table.

Related Entries

ALT Key

CTRL Key

Macros

Merge Codes

Page Numbering

See also Chapter 7, "Printer Program"

Spell

WordPerfect can help check the spelling for a word, page, document, or any size block of text with its 115,000-word dictionary. This dictionary includes approximately 25,000 legal and medical terms.

Keystrokes

Check a Word, Page, or Document

WordPerfect checks the spelling of a document while it is on the screen.

1. If checking a word or page, move the cursor to that word or page.

2. If you are using WordPerfect on a two disk-drive system, remove the data disk from drive B and insert the Speller disk.

3. Press Spell (CTRL-F2). The following menu appears.

```
Check: 1 Word; 2 Page; 3 Document; 4 Change Dictionary; 5 Look Up; 6 Count
```

4. Type **1** to check the current word, **2** to check the current page, or **3** to check the entire document. See "Options" for details on the other options listed.

5. The appropriate selection is checked. If a word is not found in the spelling dictionary, the word is highlighted and possible correct spellings are displayed, as shown in Figure 4-103.

6. If the correct spelling is on the list, type the letter assigned to the word. The correctly spelled word will automatically replace the highlighted word. If the correct word is not displayed, press ENTER or SPACEBAR to

```
  Law and Equity, arising under this Constitution, the Laws of the

  United States, and Treaties made, or which shall be made, under

  thier Authority; to all Cases affecting Ambassadors, other public

  Ministers and Consuls; to all Cases of admiralty and maritime

  jurisdiction; to Controversies to which the United States shall

  be a Party; to Controversies between two or more States; (between

=================================================================================

  A. their              B. thief              C. tier
  D. trier              E. their              F. there
  G. they're            H. thor               I. thur




Not Found!  Select Word or Menu Option (0=Continue): 0
1 Skip Once; 2 Skip; 3 Add Word; 4 Edit; 5 Look Up; 6 Phonetic
```

Figure 4-103.   Possible correct spellings displayed when a word is not found in the spelling dictionary

display other choices. If more choices are not available, the current list of words is displayed again.

If the word is not listed, but is correctly spelled (your name, for example), type **1** to Skip the word Once, **2** to Skip further occurrences of the "misspelled" word in that document, or **3** to Add the Word to the supplementary dictionary.

Option 4 lets you correct the misspelling yourself and option 5 lets you look up the word in the dictionary according to the phonetic spelling or word pattern. Option 6 displays *only* phonetic choices, but is not very useful because it does not show any additional phonetic choices that are not already displayed in the list on the screen. More information about these choices can be found in "Options."

7. The next misspelling is highlighted and the process continues.

8. When finished, a Word Count or the one-line Speller menu is displayed (depending on what was checked). Press any key to leave the Word Count and ENTER to leave the one-line Speller menu.

9. If you have a two disk-drive system, be sure to replace the Speller disk with the data disk so you won't save the file on the Speller disk.

To stop spell checking at any time, press Cancel (F1) until you return to the document.

Check a Block of Text

1. Move the cursor to one end of the block to be checked and press Block (ALT-F4).

2. Move the cursor to the opposite end of the block (no limit in size) to highlight the block.

3. Press Spell (CTRL-F2). The spelling dictionary automatically starts checking the block of text.

4. Make corrections as previously indicated.

5. When finished, the total word count of the block is displayed. After pressing any key, you are returned to the document.

Options

Initial One-Line Speller Menu

As mentioned, when you first press Spell (CTRL-F2), the Speller menu appears. Each menu option is discussed in detail in the following paragraphs.

Word   Type 1 to check the current word. The cursor must be in the word or at the space just after the word to be checked. If the word is correct, the cursor moves to the next word and displays the Speller menu again so that you can make another choice. Press ENTER if you want to leave the menu and return to the document.

Page   To check the spelling for the current page, type 2. When finished, the total number of words on the page is displayed. After pressing any key to erase the word count, the one-line menu is displayed again. Make another choice from the menu or press ENTER to return to the document.

Document After checking the entire document, a final word count is displayed. Press any key to remove the word count, then press ENTER to leave the Speller menu and return to the document.

Change Dictionary WordPerfect uses two dictionaries to check a document. The main dictionary, LEX.WP, is included on the Speller disk. The supplementary dictionary, {WP}LEX.SUP, is automatically created when the Speller is first used. It is a regular WordPerfect file that is used to store the words added to the dictionary.

This option lets you change the names of the dictionaries to be used. For example, if you are writing in French, you can use the WordPerfect French dictionary to check the document even though it was created on an English version of WordPerfect. See *Dictionary* for a list of spelling dictionaries available.

If you are working on a special project that involves a particular set of technical terms, you can enter those words in a regular WordPerfect file and use that file as the supplementary dictionary.

When option 4 is chosen, you are asked to specify the name and location of the main dictionary.

```
Enter new main dictionary name: C:\WP\LEX.WP
```

You are then asked for the name and location of the supplementary dictionary.

```
Enter new supplementary dictionary name: C:\WP\{WP}LEX.SUP
```

The names of the dictionaries currently being used or searched for are displayed as the default. Press ENTER if you decide to use the displayed dictionary. The new dictionaries are used until changed again or until you exit WordPerfect.

After choosing a new dictionary, the Speller menu is again displayed so you can check the appropriate section of text.

Look Up   Option 5 lets you look up a word in the dictionary without first typing the word on the screen. Upon choosing this option, "Word or Word Pattern:" is displayed. You can type a phonetic spelling (type it like it sounds) or enter a word pattern using wildcard characters for "missing" characters.

For example, entering "sikadelik" would display the correct spelling "psychedelic." When entering a word pattern, enter the characters that you are sure of, filling in the blanks with the wildcard characters ?, *, or -.

?   Represents any single character

* or -   Represents any number of characters

If you did not know how many *c*s and *r*s were in the word *occurrence* and whether it ended with *ance* or *ence*, you could enter "oc-r-nce" to display the correctly spelled word.

You are then given the opportunity to enter another word or word pattern. Press ENTER to leave the prompt if you do not want to look up another word. The Speller menu is again displayed. Make a choice or press ENTER to exit the Speller.

Count   After a block, page, or document is checked, the number of words is displayed at the bottom of the screen.

```
Word Count: 1024          Press any key to continue
```

Option 6 counts all the words in the document without checking the spelling first.

Not Found! Menu

When a word is not found in the dictionary, possible choices are displayed and labeled with the letters A through X. Type the letter assigned to the correct spelling and the misspelled word is automatically replaced. The options listed in the Not Found! menu are described in the following paragraphs.

Skip Once   Type **1** to skip the misspelled word once. This option is useful if a word is misspelled within a quote and needs to remain misspelled. However, the next occurrence of that misspelling would be highlighted.

Skip   Type **2** to skip the word for the rest of the document. This option should be used when a word is spelled correctly but is not found in the dictionary. This option is useful if you don't want to stop on the word again in that document, but do not want to add the word to the dictionary.

Add Word   Choosing option **3** adds the highlighted word to the supplementary dictionary. {WP}LEX.SUP is used as the name of the supplementary dictionary unless another was specified with option 4 from the Speller menu to Change Dictionary.

Edit   You can edit a word manually by typing **4**. You can also edit the word by pressing ← or →, then typing the correct spelling. When finished, press ENTER. The word is checked again before the Speller continues.

Look Up   WordPerfect uses as much of a word pattern as possible to display the choices on the screen. If you want to enter a specific word pattern using the wildcard characters ?, *, or -, choose this option. Phonetic spellings are not accepted for this option. Words that match the word pattern are displayed. You can choose one of the choices from the menu or press ENTER to return to the Not Found! menu and make another selection.

Phonetic   This option has little use unless you only want to see the phonetic choices. You will not see any additional phonetic choices that are not already displayed.

Other Options

The Speller will also check words containing numbers and will find occurrences of double words.

Numbers in Words   The Speller does not check words containing only numbers. However, if a word contains a number (such as H_2O), it is checked and highlighted as a possible misspelling. The menu at the bottom of the screen changes slightly.

```
Not Found!   Select Word or Menu Option (0=Continue): 0
1 2 Skip; 3 Ignore words containing numbers; 4 Edit
```

Choose a correct spelling from the list of possible choices or type **1** or **2** to Skip the word containing number(s), **3** to skip future occurrences of words that contain numbers, or **4** to Edit the word and remove the numbers.

Double Words   If you have two identical words next to each other, both are highlighted and the following message is displayed.

```
Double Word!   1 2 Skip; 3 Delete 2nd; 4 Edit; 5 Disable double word checking
```

Make the appropriate selection and spell checking continues.

Hints

The list of possible choices is not always spelled correctly. WordPerfect offers phonetic choices, words that match some type of word pattern, and adds, deletes, and transposes characters to display possible choices.

In earlier releases of WordPerfect 4.2, some words were listed twice because both the phonetic and word pattern choices were displayed. Versions released later than February 1987 display the word only once per screen.

When you replace a misspelled word that was capitalized, the first letter of the replacement word will also be capitalized. However, only the first letter remains capitalized, even if every letter of the misspelled word was capitalized.

When you make a choice from the menu to replace a misspelled word, all subsequent misspellings of the same word are automatically replaced.

The Speller will skip over the following characters when they appear in a word because they are considered word delimiters.

$$( ) , . / \ ` [ ] \{ \} \text{ “ } < > ; : \sim - \_ = + \ \backslash \ | \ ! \ @ \ \# \ \$ \ \% \ \wedge \ \& \ *$$

Therefore, if you have pressed one of these keys accidentally, the Speller will not stop at the word unless the section of the word before or after the character is not spelled correctly.

If asked for hyphenation decisions during the spell checking of a document, you can press Exit (F7) to leave the hyphenation decisions until later.

How Spell Works

There are actually two word lists in the LEX.WP file: the common word list containing some 2,500 of the most commonly used words, and a main word list of approximately 113,000 words. A list of the common words can be viewed with the Speller Utility (SPELL.EXE). See *Speller Utility* for details. When you check the spelling of a document, the following occurs.

1. The "common word" list from LEX.WP and the words from the supplementary dictionary {WP}LEX.SUP (unless another is specified) are loaded into memory.

2. Each word in the document is checked against the words in memory (common word list and supplementary dictionary), then against the words in the main word list. "Please wait" is displayed on the screen while words are checked.

3. If you choose option 2 or 3 to Skip or Add the Word, the word is given a special "tag" identifying it as a skipped or added word and is placed into memory along with the common word list and the supplementary dictionary.

When skipping or adding words, you could eventually fill the amount of memory allotted. If this happens, skipped words will no longer be stored in memory. Because added words take priority, you can continue to add words (skipped words are deleted to make room as you add words) until memory is filled. When this finally happens, you will see the message "Dictionary Full." (See "Error Messages" for solutions.)

4. When you have finished checking the spelling of a document, the supplementary dictionary is completely re-written. All the words tagged as added words and those belonging to the supplementary dictionary are sorted alphabetically and saved in the file {WP}LEX.SUP (unless another was specified).

Error Messages

"Main Dictionary Not Found"   If you press Spell (CTRL-F2) and the main dictionary LEX.WP is not found on the default drive or where WP.EXE is located, you will see the following error message.

```
Main dictionary not found.   Enter name: C:\WP\LEX.WP
```

If you have a two disk-drive system, insert the Speller disk in drive B and enter **B:LEX.WP**. If you have a hard disk, enter the full pathname (drive, directory, and filename) where the main dictionary can be found.

If you have a hard disk and have not copied the LEX.WP file into the same directory that is used for WP.EXE, you will get this message continually. Either copy the file to the WP.EXE directory or use the Setup menu to specify where the dictionary files will be kept. (Enter **WP/S** instead of WP and choose option **1** to Set Directories or Drives for Dictionary and Thesaurus Files.)

If you are using a foreign dictionary, enter the name of that dictionary when you see the error message. If you are using it consistently, change the Setup menu so it looks for the foreign dictionary.

If you have problems with the computer locking up during a spelling check, you most likely have memory that is incorrectly installed. Check the installation and try checking the memory with a utility program (WordPerfect has a memory checker called TESTMEM that can be purchased for $15.00). The diagnostics test will usually not find the problem. If the problems persist, contact WordPerfect Support and let them know the exact details of your system to find a possible solution.

"Dictionary Full"   LEX.WP is limited in size only by the available disk space. A supplementary dictionary is limited only by the amount of memory available. If you see the message "Dictionary Full" when trying to add words during a spelling check, it means that there is not enough memory to hold the additional words. First make sure that only one document is loaded into memory, thereby freeing up the additional memory ordinarily used by the second document. If you still get the error message, edit the supplementary dictionary or consider adding some or all of the words to the main dictionary.

Adding and Deleting Words in the Dictionary

Adding and deleting words in the supplementary dictionary is relatively simple. Retrieve the {WP}LEX.SUP file just as you would any other WordPerfect file and add or delete words as needed. You can add words containing numbers to the supplementary dictionary, but they are not taken into consideration during the spelling check.

To add or delete words in the main dictionary, use the Speller Utility (SPELL.EXE). See *Speller Utility* (next entry) for more information about this and other dictionary options.

Applications

In addition to correcting spelling errors, Spell (CTRL-F2) can be used by authors to get an accurate word count for articles.

Although certainly not the primary function, you can use the Look Up feature to help solve crossword puzzles! Just enter the letters you know and a question mark (?) in the place of each letter you don't know. A six-letter word for "smart" would be "cl?ve?" (clever).

Related Entries

Dictionary

Setup Menu

Speller Utility

Word Count

Speller Utility

The Speller Utility program (SPELL.EXE) can be used to add or delete words in the main dictionary, create a new dictionary, or look up words.

Keystrokes

If WordPerfect is running, use Exit (F7) to exit and go to the DOS prompt.

Two Disk Drives

1. Insert the Speller disk (containing LEX.WP and SPELL.EXE) in drive A and a data disk in drive B.

2. Enter **A:** to display A> as the DOS prompt.

3. Enter **SPELL** to start the Speller Utility from drive A. The disk in drive B will be used during the process of adding and deleting words in the dictionary. The menu shown in Figure 4-104 is displayed.

4. Select options from the menu. See "Options" for a full explanation of those listed.

5. When finished, type **0** to leave the Speller Utility.

Hard Disk

1. Change to the directory where SPELL.EXE is located. If you copied the disks as directed in Chapter 1, both SPELL.EXE and LEX.WP are kept in the same directory as WP.EXE (WP was the suggested name of the directory).

2. Enter **SPELL** at the DOS prompt.

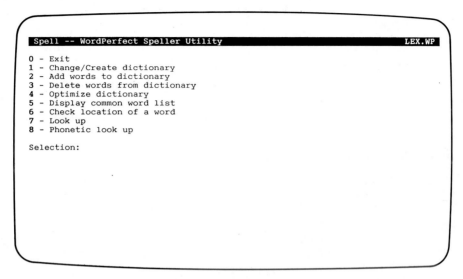

```
Spell -- WordPerfect Speller Utility                          LEX.WP

0 - Exit
1 - Change/Create dictionary
2 - Add words to dictionary
3 - Delete words from dictionary
4 - Optimize dictionary
5 - Display common word list
6 - Check location of a word
7 - Look up
8 - Phonetic look up

Selection:
```

Figure 4-104.   Speller Utility menu

3. Select any options from the menu shown in Figure 4-104. These are explained in "Options."

4. When finished, type **0** to leave the Speller Utility.

Options

Change/Create Dictionary

LEX.WP, displayed in the upper right corner of the Speller Utility menu, is the file used for all options. If you want to use a different dictionary, choose option 1 and enter a new filename. A message is displayed telling you that it is permissible to switch disks at this time. If the dictionary file is not found on the disk, you are asked if you want to create a new dictionary with that name.

Add Words to Dictionary

When you type 2 to add words to the dictionary, the following menu appears.

```
Spell -- Add Words                                                    LEX.WP
0 - Cancel - do not add words
1 - Add to common word list (from keyboard)
2 - Add to common word list (from a file)
3 - Add to main word list (from keyboard)
4 - Add to main word list (from a file)
5 - Exit

Selection:
```

You can choose any or all of the options to add words to the common word list and main word list from the keyboard or a file. If there is more than one file to be added, choose options 2 and 4 more than once. When you enter words from the keyboard, separate them by spaces.

After you are finished entering all the words or filenames, type **5** to Exit (update the dictionary). Type **0** if you want to Cancel the operation. The entire dictionary will be recopied, inserting each new word where it belongs and creating the phonetic information for that word.

If you are using two disk drives, or if your hard disk is full, you will see the following message after typing 5 to Exit.

```
Updating dictionary
* Please Wait *
Insufficient room on drive A: for temporary files.
Do not remove diskette in drive A:
Enter drive letter for temporary files:
```

If you have two disk drives, make sure you have a disk in drive B with sufficient space and type **B** (note that you should not remove the disk in drive A). If there is not enough room on the disk in drive B, you will see the message again. The situation must be corrected before it can continue. A file

LEX.BAK is created on the new disk to aid in the process.

When words are added (or deleted), messages are displayed notifying you of the progress. It takes approximately 20 minutes or less to add words, depending on whether you have a hard disk or floppy disk drives. If you have a RAM drive, consider copying the SPELL.EXE and LEX.WP files there to greatly increase the speed.

Delete Words from Dictionary

When you choose option 3 to Delete words from the dictionary, the following menu appears.

```
Spell -- Delete Words                                    LEX.WP

0 - Cancel - do not delete words
1 - Delete from common word list (from keyboard)
2 - Delete from common word list (from a file)
3 - Delete from main word list (from keyboard)
4 - Delete from main word list (from a file)
5 - Exit

Selection:
```

Choose any or all of the options to delete words from the common word list or main word list. The words to be deleted can be entered from the keyboard (separate each word with a space), or a file can be used.

After all applicable options have been chosen, type **5** to Exit (and update the dictionary) or type **0** to Cancel the procedure. If you have two disk drives, you will see a message telling you there is not enough room on drive A to create the temporary files. Confirm that there is a disk in drive B and type **B** as the drive to be used.

Messages are displayed keeping you informed of the status. It takes the same amount of time to delete words from the dictionary as it does to add them. Unfortunately, they cannot both be done at the same time.

Optimize Dictionary

After creating a new dictionary (with options 1 and 2) you should optimize it with this option. The dictionary is rewritten in a format that makes it smaller and faster. After optimizing, you can press ENTER to see lists of the words in the dictionary or Cancel (F1) to return to the main menu.

Display Common Word List

Choose this option if you are interested in viewing the words in the common word list. You will see the beginning of the common word list, as shown in Figure 4-105. Press ENTER (or any other key) to continue viewing each screen or press Cancel (F1) to return to the main menu.

Check Location of a Word

After choosing option 6 to Check the location of a word, you are asked to enter a word. A message is displayed telling you

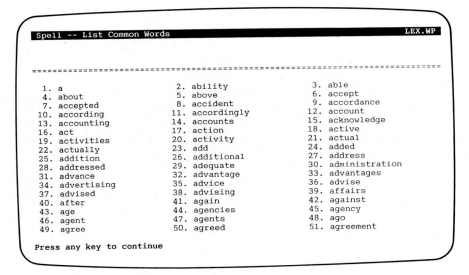

Figure 4-105.   Portion of common word list in Speller Utility

whether the word was found in the common word list or main word list. Continue checking words until finished, then press Cancel (F1) to return to the main menu. The next option will also help you determine if a word is in the common word list or main word list.

Look Up

The Speller Utility can be used to look up words according to parts of a word or a word pattern. You can use the wildcard characters ?, *, or - in the place of unknown characters.

> ?   Represents any single character

> * or - Represents any number of characters

Phonetic Look Up

Enter a phonetic spelling (spell the word the way it sounds) to find other words in the dictionary that sound similar to that word.

Hints

If you have a RAM drive, copy the files SPELL.EXE and LEX.WP to greatly increase the speed of updating the Speller.

You can add and delete words in the supplementary dictionary {WP}LEX.SUP or any other file by retrieving it into WordPerfect and editing the file as you would any other.

When the supplementary dictionary becomes too large for memory, you can add the words to the main dictionary until the available disk space is filled.

Related Entries

Dictionary

Spell

Split the Screen

See *Windows*

Start a New Page

See *Hard Page*

Start WordPerfect

The following procedures will start WordPerfect. Choose the one that applies to your system, depending on whether you have two disk drives or a hard disk.

Keystrokes

Two Disk Drives

1. Insert the WordPerfect disk in drive A. (You should always use a backup of the original disk.)

2. Insert a data disk into drive B.

3. Enter **B:** to change the default drive to B. (When you save or retrieve files, drive B will be used unless another is specified.)

4. Enter **A:WP** to start WordPerfect from drive A.

Hard Disk

1. Enter **CD \DIRECTORY** at the DOS prompt to change the default directory. Substitute the name of the directory where files are to be saved and retrieved in the place of DIRECTORY.

2. Enter **WP** to start WordPerfect.

If you have not set up WordPerfect correctly on the hard disk, the error message "Bad command or file name" might appear. Chapter 1 gives complete instructions for installation.

Options

When you start WordPerfect, you can add "switches" which perform certain functions when WordPerfect is started. Three important switches are

/s to start WordPerfect with the Setup menu

/m to start a macro when WordPerfect is started

/r to load WordPerfect into memory

The following paragraphs discuss each option that can be used.

WP Filename

This option can be used to retrieve the indicated file when WordPerfect is started.

WP/B-Number of Minutes for Timed Backup

You can set the number of minutes between each backup with this option. The backup is only effective for that editing session, but can be set permanently through the Setup menu.

WP/D-Drive/Directory

Overflow files are automatically kept where WP.EXE is located. If you want to keep them elsewhere, use the /d option and specify the name of the drive and directory to be used.

Although the use of a RAM drive is not strongly recommended, you can redirect the overflow files to a RAM drive. If the files are redirected elsewhere, and the wp/r option is used to load WordPerfect into memory, you can remove the WordPerfect disk.

WP/I (Install)

If you are using DOS version 2.x, WordPerfect may look to the wrong drive for the program files. Use the wp/i option (only once is necessary) to install WordPerfect in its present location. This is usually necessary if WordPerfect was initially run from the floppy disk before loading it onto the hard disk or if you are installing WordPerfect from a copy.

WP/M-Macroname

This option will start the named macro when WordPerfect is started. (Do not include .MAC in the macroname.)

WP/NF (Non-Flash)

When you run WordPerfect, it checks the system to see if it can handle the "flash" version, which rewrites the screen all at once instead of a line at a time.

If the screen goes blank when you press Reveal Codes (ALT-F3) or if you are using a windowing program, you may need to specify the non-flash version with this option when starting WordPerfect.

WP/NS (Non-Sync)

Again, when WordPerfect is loaded, it checks the system to see if the computer can handle the "sync" version of the program and uses it if possible. If you are using a color monitor and see "snow," or if you are using a Hyperion, you should use this option to load the non-sync version.

WP/R (Resident in Memory)

The /r option loads WordPerfect into memory. Since the overlay files, menus, messages, and other parts of the program are in memory, there is no disk access, which greatly increases the speed of WordPerfect. If you use the /d option to redirect the overflow files to another drive/directory, you can remove the WordPerfect disk.

WP/S (Setup Menu)

This option starts WordPerfect and displays the Setup menu. You can set the backup options, specify where the dictionary and thesaurus files are to be kept, and change the initial default settings, among other options.

WP/X

This option returns WordPerfect to the defaults set by WordPerfect Corporation for that editing session only.

WP/X/S

To return WordPerfect to the original defaults permanently, specify this option.

Hints

You can combine any of the options except /s. For example:

> WP/NS/M-FORMAT/B-20

However, /x/s can be combined with other options. If you use the same keystrokes to start WordPerfect each time, consider storing them in a batch file (a file containing a batch of commands). You would then need to enter only the name of the batch file instead of having to type all the keystrokes each time. Do not use WP as the name of the batch file, however, or it could cause the computer to hang, depending on your setup. See Chapter 1 for more information about creating batch files

If you do not want to use a batch file, you can change the DOS environment with the SET command so that each time you enter WP, the other commands will be recognized as part of the command. For example:

SET WP=WP/NS/M-FORMAT/B-20

If you have WordPerfect Library, you can install WordPerfect on the Shell menu so you only have to choose an item from the menu and never have to deal with DOS. In the Shell's Setup menu, you can specify the startup options (switches) to be used.

Related Entries

Setup Menu

Shell

See also Chapter 1, "Getting Started"

See also Chapter 3, "The Next Step"

Stop Printing

An option on the Printer Control menu lets you stop the printing of a document.

Keystrokes

1. Press Print (SHIFT-F7).

2. Type **4** for Printer Control.

3. Type **S** to Stop Printing. The message shown in Figure 4-106 is displayed, requesting that you fix the printer, set the top of the form, and send the printer a "Go"

```
Printer Control
                                    C - Cancel Print Job(s)
1 - Select Print Options            D - Display All Print Jobs
2 - Display Printers and Fonts      G - "Go" (Resume Printing)
3 - Select Printers                 P - Print a Document
                                    R - Rush Print Job
Selection: 0                        S - Stop Printing


Current Job

Job Number: 1                       Page Number:  3
Job Status: Waiting for a "Go"      Current Copy: 1 of 1
Message:    Fix printer--Reset top of form--Press "G" to continue

Job List

Job  Document            Destination         Forms and Print Options
 1   (Screen)            Ptr  1              SheetFeed


Additional jobs not shown: 0
```

Figure 4-106.   Printer Control menu after activating Stop Printing

when ready to continue. The printer will not stop printing immediately, but will continue to print until it empties the data in the printer's buffer. To stop it immediately, turn the printer off, then back on again to clear the buffer.

4. Type **G** to send the printer a "Go." If only the data for the first page was sent to the printer, printing will start again with the first page automatically. If the data for more than one page was sent, you are asked to specify the page on which to resume printing. The last page sent is displayed as the default as shown here:

```
Printer Control
                                    C - Cancel Print Job(s)
1 - Select Print Options            D - Display All Print Jobs
2 - Display Printers and Fonts      G - "Go" (Resume Printing)
3 - Select Printers                 P - Print a Document
                                    R - Rush Print Job
Selection: G                        S - Stop Printing
Restart on page: 10
```

Hints

If you want to pause printing without using WordPerfect commands, press the "On-Line" or "Ready" button on the printer to take the printer off-line. Press it again to return it to on-line status and resume printing.

If you want to cancel one or more print jobs instead of stopping the printer temporarily, choose the Cancel Print Job(s) option on the Printer Control menu. Again, you can turn the printer off and back on to clear the buffer if it does not stop printing immediately.

Related Entries

Cancel a Print Job

Strikeout Text

The Strikeout feature can be used to print a dash through text being considered for deletion.

Keystrokes

1. Move the cursor to one end of the text being considered for deletion and press Block (ALT-F4).

2. Move the cursor to the opposite end of the block to highlight the text.

3. Press Mark Text (ALT-F5).

4. Type **4** for Strikeout.

Hints

When you mark text for Strikeout, the codes [StrkOut] and [s] are inserted at the beginning and end of the block, respectively.

When you move the cursor through text marked for strikeout, a "-" is displayed next to the "Pos" (position) number on the status line.

Doc 1   Pg 28   Ln 10   Pos 12-

Redline, a feature used to mark text being considered for addition to a document, displays a "+" next to the "Pos" number.

Most printers are defined to print text marked for strike-out with a dash through the text. Others such as the Canon laser printer, print strikeout text with white lettering on a black background. If you want to change the character to be used or assign a different font to that feature, use the Printer program (explained in Chapter 7).

Overstrike, found with Superscript/Subscript (SHIFT-F1), is used to overstrike a single character with one or more characters.

Related Entries

Overstrike a Character

Redline

See also Chapter 7, "Printer Program"

Summary

See *Document Summary*

Superscript and Subscript

Superscript/Subscript (SHIFT-F1) can be used to elevate or lower a single character for use as a superscript or subscript. Other options on the menu include Overstrike, Advance Up, Advance Down, and Advance to a particular Line.

Keystrokes

1. Press Superscript/Subscript (SHIFT-F1). The following menu appears.

```
1 Superscript; 2 Subscript; 3 Overstrike; 4 Adv Up; 5 Adv Dn; 6 Adv Ln: 0
```

2. Type **1** to Superscript the next character or **2** to Subscript the next character. An "S" appears for superscript and an "s" appears for subscript in the lower left corner of the screen.

3. Type the character. It will not appear as a super-scripted/subscripted character on the screen.

Hints

When superscript is chosen, the code [SuprScrpt] is inserted into the document; [SubScrpt] indicates a subscript.

Superscript and subscript characters usually print up or down one-third of a line. Some dot-matrix printers print a compressed character on the upper or lower half of the line.

If you want to print the character up or down a full half-line, use Advance Up and Advance Down. Remember, however, that instead of only affecting a single character, Advance Up stays in effect until you choose to Advance Down again.

A shortcut to using the menu is to press CTRL-2 for superscript or ALT-2 for subscript. These keys were the designated superscript and subscript keys in versions previous to 4.0 and have been retained for early users of WordPerfect.

If you have a NEC 3550 printer and the text prints in the left margin after printing a superscripted or subscripted character (footnote numbers included), check the SW2-5 switch. It must be on.

Applications

Superscripts are often used for footnote numbers. However, WordPerfect has a footnote feature that will automatically insert a superscripted number, let you create the footnote, then keep track of the number of lines allowed per page. You could use Superscript if you need to reference a footnote more than once on a page. For example, the first reference for the first footnote could be the regular footnote number inserted by WordPerfect (footnote number[1]). The second time it is referenced, you could insert a superscripted 1 manually (second reference[1]).

Superscript and Subscript can be used in formulas or equations such as H_2O and 10^5.

Related Entries

Advance the Printer to a Specific Line

Advance Up or Down One-Half Line

Footnotes and Endnotes

Overstrike a Character

Suppress

An option on the Page Format menu lets you suppress the printing of a header, footer, or page number for the current page or print the page number at the bottom of the page.

The Suppress option is extremely useful for title pages (allowing the page number to be printed at the bottom of that page) or for a page containing a table or chart.

Keystrokes

Before choosing this feature, move the cursor to the top of the page to be affected. It must precede any text on the page.

1. Press Page Format (ALT-F8).

2. Type **8** to Suppress for <u>Current</u> Page Only. The menu shown in Figure 4-107 appears.

3. Choose an item from the menu. If you want more than one option suppressed, type the number of each option with a plus sign (+) between options.

4. Press ENTER to return to the Page Format menu, then ENTER again to return to the document.

Hints

When you ask to suppress page format options, a code similar to [Suppress:2+5] is inserted into the document.

If you want a header, footer, or page number to begin printing on the second page, it is better to define those items on the first page, then immediately suppress them. If you place the header, footer, or page number code at the top of the second page, the code could change location after editing changes, yielding unpredictable results.

If you type two-page letters or memos often, consider creating a format macro that can be run before or after the letter or memo is finished. In addition to the standard format

```
 Suppress Page Format for Current Page Only

    To temporarily turn off multiple items, include a "+" between menu entries.
    For example 5+6+2 will turn off Header A, Header B, and Page Numbering
    for the current page.

       1 - Turn off all page numbering, headers and footers

       2 - Turn page numbering off

       3 - Print page number at bottom center (this page only)

       4 - Turn off all headers and footers

       5 - Turn off Header A

       6 - Turn off Header B

       7 - Turn off Footer A

       8 - Turn off Footer B

 Selection(s): 0
```

Figure 4-107.   Suppress Page Format for Current Page menu

commands, the macro could create a header that includes a page number, the current date, and the name of the person to whom the letter is addressed. The next step in the macro would suppress the header on the first page.

Related Entries

Headers and Footers

Page Numbering

Switch

Switch (SHIFT-F3) is used to switch between documents (Document 1 and Document 2). If Block is on, Switch (SHIFT-F3) gives you the option of switching the block to uppercase or lowercase.

Keystrokes

Switch Documents

Press Switch (SHIFT-F3) to switch between the two document screens.

Switch to Uppercase or Lowercase

1. Move the cursor to one end of the text to be changed and press Block (ALT-F4).

2. Move the cursor to the opposite end to highlight the text.

3. Press Switch (SHIFT-F3). The following options appear.

```
Block:  1 Uppercase;  2 Lowercase:  0
```

4. Type **1** to change the block to Uppercase or **2** for Lowercase.

5. Press Block (ALT-F4) to turn off Block.

Hints

When you switch documents, the cursor remains in its original position in the document. For example, if you were in document 1 and the status line read "Doc 1 Pg 10 Ln 3 Pos 50," then you switched to document 2 and back again, the status line would still read "Doc 1 Pg 10 Ln 3 Pos 50."

If you split the screen with the Windows option on Screen (CTRL-F3), you can see both documents on the screen at once. Pressing Switch (SHIFT-F3) moves the cursor between the two.

When switching to lowercase, the first word of the sentence remains capitalized if any end-of-sentence punctuation just before that word is included as part of the block. For example, if the block is highlighted as shown below, then switched to lowercase, the first letter of the sentence will remain capitalized.

```
of the Persons voting for and against the Bill shall be entered
on the Journal of each House respectively.  IF ANY BILL SHALL NOT
BE RETURNED BY THE PRESIDENT WITHIN TEN DAYS (SUNDAYS EXCEPTED)
AFTER IT SHALL HAVE BEEN PRESENTED TO HIM, THE SAME SHALL BE A
LAW, in like Manner as if he had signed it, unless the Congress
by their Adjournment prevent its Return, in which Case it shall
                        Doc 1  Pg 6  Ln 23     Pos 13
```

Having two documents in memory makes it easier to cut and copy text from one document to another using Block (ALT-F4), Move (CTRL-F4), and Switch (SHIFT-F3). Remember that you can view the effects in both documents when you use the Windows feature found on Screen (CTRL-F3).

Related Entries

Capitalization

Windows

Tab Align

Tab Align (CTRL-F6) moves the cursor to the next tab setting and aligns text or numbers at a decimal point (period). You can change the alignment character so that text can be aligned at a character other than a decimal point.

Keystrokes

Aligning the Text

1. Set tabs if necessary.

2. Press Tab Align (CTRL-F6). The cursor moves to the next tab setting and "Align Char = ." appears on the status line.

3. Type numbers or text. They are inserted to the left of the cursor until you type the decimal point (period). Any text after the decimal is inserted normally to the right.

Changing the Alignment Character

1. Press Line Format (SHIFT-F8).

2. Type **6** for Align Character.

3. Type the new alignment character. It is not necessary to press ENTER.

There is no immediate indication that the alignment character is changed. For reassurance, you can press Reveal Codes (ALT-F3) to see the code. If the new character is a comma, for example, [Align Char:,] will appear.

Hints

Tab Align is best used when aligning text at a character such as a colon, dash, or a parenthesis (see "Applications"). It can also be effectively used as a quick decimal tab. However, if you are using extensive decimal tabs, it is best to set decimal tabs (see *Tabs, Clear and Set*). The TAB key can then be used rather than Tab Align (CTRL-F6).

You can use any character found on the keyboard for the alignment character, including a space (press SPACEBAR when asked for the alignment character). You cannot use special characters from the extended character set (ASCII decimal values 1 through 31 and 127 through 254).

When text is aligned, the Align On [A] and Align Off [a] codes are inserted, as shown in the following illustration.

```
        5.90              67.80              35.42
      150.34               2.30           3,456.00
       23.32                .54              20.00
         .03             324.18             836.51
                                    Doc 1  Pg 1  Ln 5          Pos  10
[                        ▲                   ▲        ]
▪[A]5[a].90[A]67[a].80[A]35[a].42[HRt]
[A]150[a].34[A]2[a].30[A] 3,456[a].00[HRt]
[A]23[a].32[A][a].54[A]20[a].00[HRt]
[A][a].03[A]324[a].18[A]836[a].51[HRt]
```

These codes are also used for right-aligned tabs, text that is flush right against the margin, and Math's numeric columns.

It takes some patience when making corrections to aligned text because you have to know exactly where to place the cursor when entering or revising text. If deleting aligned text, you might see the message "Delete [Aln/FlshR]? (Y/N) N." To make corrections a little easier, press CTRL-BACKSPACE to delete the word, but leave the alignment codes where they should be. The word or number can then be retyped and aligned correctly.

If you still have problems, press Reveal Codes (ALT-F3) and delete text from the Reveal Codes screen, or position the cursor between the [A] and [a] codes, press ENTER to return to the text, and make the changes. If you have a number of alignments on one line and are having problems, it might be easiest to delete the entire line with Delete to End of Line (CTRL-END) and retype the line.

Applications

Use a colon (:) as the alignment character for a memo heading.

```
                          MEMO

        DATE:

          TO:

        FROM:

     SUBJECT:
```

Align numbers at a comma rather than a decimal point for European-format columns of numbers.

```
3.456,18           427,32               532,36
   87,03             1,98         2.000.000,00
     ,76         2.079,21            7.584,33
  264,00            74,77               49,06
```

Related Entries

Decimal Tabs

Flush Right

Math

Tabs, Clear and Set

TAB Key

Pressing the TAB key moves the cursor to the next tab setting.

Keystrokes

The TAB key is located at the left of the keyboard in relatively the same location as on a typewriter. It may be labeled TAB or with opposite-pointing arrows, as shown in the following keyboard illustration.

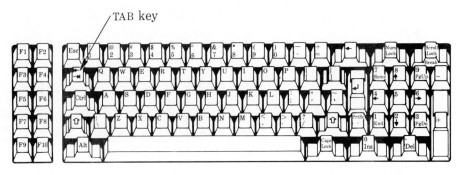

TAB key

Hints

When TAB is pressed, a [TAB] code is inserted; it is visible when you press Reveal Codes (ALT-F3).

If you want to go to an exact position, it is best to use TAB rather than the SPACEBAR. A tab setting is an exact position, but the amount of space produced with the spacebar may vary from printer to printer, especially when using proportional spacing.

Pressing SHIFT-TAB moves the cursor to the previous tab setting. Named Left Margin Release, SHIFT-TAB inserts a code [<-Mar Rel:n] where *n* is the number of spaces moved to the left. You can use the Indent and Left Margin Release features to create a bibliography.

Tab Ruler

A tab ruler can be displayed on the screen showing the current tab and margin settings. Press Screen (CTRL-F3), type **1** for Window, then enter **23** for the number of lines in the window. Tab settings are shown in the ruler line as triangles. If there is a tab setting at the same location as a margin setting, the margin is indicated with a brace rather than a bracket, as in the following illustration.

A ruler line appears temporarily when you press Reveal Codes (ALT-F3). Press ENTER to return to normal editing.

TAB and Typeover

While in Typeover, TAB can be used to move *over* existing text to the next tab setting instead of inserting [Tab] codes. This is especially useful in statistical typing when you want to move quickly from one column to another, or if you want to fill in a form created with Line Draw.

When Typeover is on, pressing TAB moves to the next tab within the text. When you reach the end of a line of text and there are more tab settings, pressing TAB will insert [TAB] codes as it normally does.

Using TAB with Outline

If you are creating an outline with WordPerfect's Outline feature, TAB moves the cursor to the next tab setting and changes the level of numbering. If you want to go back to the previous level, press Left Margin Release (SHIFT-TAB).

Instead of pressing TAB to indent (remember, TAB would result in a new level of numbering), press Indent (F4).

TAB and Indented Text

Use TAB to indent the first line of a paragraph. If all lines in a paragraph are to be indented, use Indent (F4) or Left/Right Indent (SHIFT-F4) instead of TAB. If you use TAB to indent each line manually, extensive editing may be necessary when text is inserted or deleted. See Figure 4-108 for examples.

To create a "hanging indent" (such as those used in bibliographies), press Indent (F4) then Left Margin Release (SHIFT-TAB). All the lines except the first one are aligned at the first tab setting.

As previously mentioned, you can create a form and set tabs on each line if necessary. You can then press INS to turn on Typeover and use the arrow keys to move up and down and TAB to move to the next item to be filled in.

Related Entries

Indent

Left Margin Release

Ruler

Tabs, Clear and Set

```
     When the first line of a paragraph needs to be indented, use
TAB as shown in this example.  A [TAB] code is inserted when TAB
is pressed.

     Indent (F4) was used to indent this paragraph because each
     line should be indented.  When this option is used, you do
     not have to indent each line individually.  Use this option
     for numbered paragraphs.

          To bring both the left and the right margins
          in temporarily, use ->Indent<- (Shift-F4).
          This option is useful for indented paragraphs
          that will return to the normal margins when
          ENTER is pressed.
```

Figure 4-108.   Examples of tabs and indented text

Table of Authorities

The Table of Authorities feature lets you mark citations throughout a document and generate up to 16 sections for cases, statutes, and so on. See Figure 4-109 for a sample Table of Authorities.

While the Table of Authorities feature was designed for the legal field, many others have found uses for this powerful feature. Accountants use the feature to cite tax laws and others have used it to create bibliographies that list the page numbers for each reference.

Each section in the Table of Authorities is sorted alphanumerically (numbers appearing before letters), similar to an index, and each section can have its own format.

Keystrokes

There are four basic steps in creating a Table of Authorities. Each is discussed in detail in the paragraphs that follow the procedure.

TABLE OF AUTHORITIES

Cases   Page(s)

Carlsberg Resources Corp. v. Cambria Savings & Loan Assoc.
554 F.2d 1254 (3d Cir. 1977) 10

Chapman v. Barney
129 U.S. 677 (1889) 6, 10, 11

Coal Co. v. Blatchford
78 U.S. (11 Wall.) 172, 175 (1870) 8

Navarro Savings Association v. Lee
446 U.S. 458 (1980) 7-12, 14, 16

Strawbridge v. Curtiss
7 U.S. (3 Cranch) 267 (1806) 4

Trent Realty Assoc. v. First Federal Savings & Loan Assoc.
657 F.2d 29 (3d Cir. 1981) 10, 11

United Steelworkers v. R.H. Bouligny
382 U.S. 145 (1965) 5, 9

Statutes

28 U.S.C. Section 1332(a)   1
28 U.S.C. Section 1332(c)   4, 5

Fed. R. Civ. P. 17(b)   11
Fed. R. Civ. P. 82   3, 11

Revised Uniform Ltd. Partnership Act
    Section 303, 6 U.L.A. 224 (Supp. 1984)   13
    Section 403, 6 U.L.A. 230 (Supp. 1984)   8

Miscellaneous

C. Wright, The Federal Courts
    Section 7 at 22 (4th ed. 1983)   4

Figure 4-109.   Sample Table of Authorities

1. Decide what each section will be used for: cases, statutes, items from the U.S. Constitution, civil rights acts, and so on.

2. Mark each authority (sometimes referred to as a citation) and indicate the section in which it is to be included. Mark each subsequent occurrence of an authority with the short form.

3. Define the location and format for each section of the Table of Authorities.

4. Generate the table.

Determine What Sections Will Be Used

After typing a document, you will usually know what types of authorities were used in that document. While you can make up the list as you mark items, it is sometimes easier to first list the major sections that will be included in the table. Making the decision beforehand helps speed up the process when marking each item.

Mark Each Authority (Citation)

When you mark an item for the first time, you will be asked to specify the section, the full form (what will actually appear in the table after it is generated), and the short form (a nickname for the full form). When you mark the item again, you only need to specify the short form. See Appendix C for a macro to help automate this procedure.

1. Move the cursor to one end of the authority to be included in the table and press Block (ALT-F4).

2. Move the cursor to the opposite end of the text until the authority is highlighted.

3. Press Mark Text (ALT-F5). The following menu is displayed.

```
Mark for: 1 ToC; 2 List; 3 Redline; 4 Strikeout; 5 Index; 6 ToA: 0
```

4. Type **6** for ToA. A new menu is displayed.

```
ToA section number (Press Enter for short form only):
```

5. Enter the section number. You could also press ENTER to mark the item with a short form. However, if you are marking the first item, the short form has not yet been created. This option is discussed later.

6. The full form (highlighted text) is placed in a separate editing screen. You can then format the text until it looks exactly as it should for the table. You can use bold,

underline, and most other formatting commands. There is an option in the definition menu to delete underlining when the table is generated. Therefore, if underlining should not be included, you do not have to manually delete it.

If you want the authority to appear in a "hanging indent" format, go to the beginning of the citation and press Indent (F4), then Left Margin Release (SHIFT-TAB).

7. Press Exit (F7) when finished editing the full form.

8. You are then asked to enter the short form that will be used to mark subsequent entries. This is an abbreviated form of the full reference. Up to 40 characters of the highlighted block are automatically displayed for the short form, as in the following illustration.

```
Enter Short Form:   17 U.S.C. 4516(f)
```

Edit the displayed text and press ENTER or enter a new short form. Each short form must be unique or you will see an error message when the table is generated.

You can use Search (F2) or Extended Search (HOME,F2) to search for the next occurrence of the authority. Extended Search includes headers, footers, footnotes, and endnotes in the search, but Search does not. When the next occurrence of the authority is found, it should be marked with the short form only.

1. Press Mark Text (ALT-F5).

2. Type **4** for Short Form. The last short form used is displayed.

3. Press ENTER to use the displayed short form.

4. Continue searching and marking all subsequent occurrences of the authority.

**Define the Location and Format
of the Sections**

1. Move the cursor to the point in the document where the Table of Authorities is to be generated.

2. Press Hard Page (CTRL-ENTER) if you want to generate the table on a separate page.

3. The major heading and each section heading must be entered manually. Press Center (SHIFT-F6) and enter the title for the table, then type the headings for each section at the left margin, as shown in Figure 4-110.

4. Move the cursor below the first section heading (where the first section should be generated) and press Mark Text (ALT-F5). The following menu appears.

```
1 Outline; 2 Para #; 3 Redline; 4 Short Form; 5 Index; 6 Other Options: 0
```

```
                          TABLE OF AUTHORITIES


     Cases



     Statutes



     Miscellaneous
```

Figure 4-110.   Major headings for Table of Authorities

```
Other Mark Text Options

    1 - Define Paragraph/Outline Numbering

    2 - Define Table of Contents

    3 - Define List

    4 - Define Table of Authorities

    5 - Define Index

    6 - Remove all Redline Markings and all Strikeout text from document

    7 - Edit Table of Authorities Full Form

    8 - Generate Tables and Index




Selection: 0
```

Figure 4-111.   Other Mark Text Options menu

5. Type **6** for Other Options. The menu shown in Figure 4-111 is displayed.

6. Type **4** to Define Table of Authorities.

7. Enter the number of the section being defined. The Table of Authorities menu is displayed, as shown in Figure 4-112, with the number of the section displayed at the top of the screen.

8. Change any of the options necessary for that section. Remember that all sections are defined separately and each can have its own selections.

9. Press ENTER to return to the document.

10. Repeat the steps for each section under each section title.

11. Press Hard Page (CTRL-ENTER) after the sections if you want the text in the document to start on a separate page.

12. To make sure the page numbers are accurate when the table is generated, press Page Format (ALT-F8), type

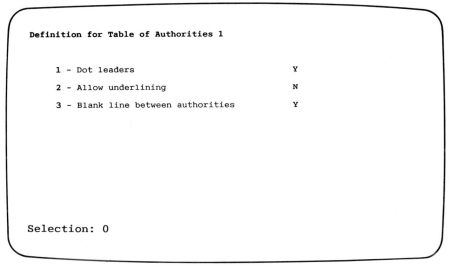

```
Definition for Table of Authorities 1


    1 - Dot leaders                        Y

    2 - Allow underlining                  N

    3 - Blank line between authorities     Y






Selection: 0
```

Figure 4-112.   Table of Authorities menu

2 for New Page Number, enter the page number for the first page of text (usually 1), and choose the style of numbering to be used (arabic or roman). If you neglect this step, you will see a message informing you of this when the table is generated. You can insert the new page number at that time and generate the table again.

Generate the Table of Authorities

1. Press Mark Text (ALT-F5) from anywhere in the document.

2. Type **6** for Other Options. Figure 4-111 displays the options listed.

3. Type **8** to Generate Tables and Index.

4. The message "Existing tables, lists, and indexes will be replaced. Continue? (Y/N): Y" is displayed. Type **Y** to continue or **N** to return to the document if necessary.

A counter is displayed on the status line showing you that progress is being made. Since the process may take sev-

eral passes through the document, the counter will incre-
ment at varying rates. The Table of Authorities, Table of
Contents, lists, and the index are all generated at the same
time.

Hints

When you mark the first authority, the code [ToA:n;short-
form;<Full Form>] is inserted at the cursor location, with *n*
being the number of the section in the table. When only the
short form is used, the code [ToA:;shortform;] is displayed.
The section number and "<Full Form>" are not displayed in
this code because the short form is all that is needed.

When you define the location and format for each section, the code [DefMark:ToA,n] is inserted, with *n* again
being the number of the section. After a section is generated,
an [EndDef] code is placed at the end of each section. If the
table is generated a second time, these codes are used to
block and delete the previous section so the newly generated
table can be displayed in its place.

When you generate a Table of Authorities, all full forms
are found and their page numbers noted. WordPerfect then
searches for the authorities marked with a short form,
matches them up with the applicable full form, and combines
all the page numbers. If the same authority was marked on
three or more consecutive pages, the page numbers are
shown as a range rather than as single pages.

You can edit the table after it has been created. If you
chose the "dot leader" option for listing page numbers, a dot
leader is placed between the text and the page number. If
text is added or deleted, the dot leader is automatically
adjusted as needed.

Editing the Full Form or Short Form

You can always edit the full form in the table after it is
generated. However, if you plan to regenerate the table at
any time, you should edit the full form code in the document.
Then, you would not have to change the entry in the table
each time it is generated.

It is not possible to edit a short form. Instead, you must delete the previous [ToA] code and mark the entry again with the correct short form.

Use Search (F2) or Extended Search (HOME,F2) to help find the [ToA] codes. Both the full form and short forms are considered [ToA] codes. When one is found, you can press Reveal Codes (ALT-F3) to see the code and determine if it is the one for which you are searching.

To make changes to the full form or change the section number, use the following steps.

1. Move the cursor just after the authority to be edited.

2. Press Mark Text (ALT-F5).

3. Type **6** for Other Options.

4. Type **7** to Edit Table of Authorities Full Form. The last authority marked with a full form (just to the left of the cursor) is displayed. If an authority is not found before the cursor, the next full form is found.

5. Make the changes and press Exit (F7) when finished.

6. Enter the section number for the item.

If you have not assigned a unique short form to a full form, you should delete the entire [ToA:n;shortform;<Full Form>] code and mark the item again. If you want to change the short form for any particular item, delete the [ToA:; shortform;] code and mark it with a new short form.

When marking each item, the last short form entered is displayed. This makes it easier to mark each item by just pressing ENTER when that short form is displayed. However, when changing short forms, the appropriate short form is not usually displayed. You can use the standard method already listed, enter the short form manually, or block and mark the text for the short form (if it is found in the document).

1. Move to one end of the text to be used in the short form and press Block (ALT-F4).

2. Move to the opposite end of the short form to highlight the text.

3. Press Mark Text (ALT-F5).

4. Type **6** for ToA.

5. Press ENTER for short form only.

6. The highlighted block is displayed as the short form to be used.

7. Press ENTER to use the displayed short form or edit the text and press ENTER when finished.

After making changes to full forms and short forms, generate the table again.

Error Messages

"Not Enough Memory"   WordPerfect uses document 2 (if available) to generate the tables, lists, and index. If it is not available, document 3 is used. If you get the error message "Not Enough Memory," exit document 2 so the memory for that document can be used. If you still get the message, retrieve the document into document 2 and leave the document 1 screen clear. Table generation can then use the additional memory in document 1 (twice as much memory as allotted to document 2).

"No [DefMark] Found"   If you forget to define the location and format of the table, you will see the error message "No [DefMark] Found." Correct the situation and regenerate the table.

"Can't Find End of Table of Contents, . . ."   When you first generate a table, an [EndDef] code is placed at the end of the table. Each [DefMark] code then has a corresponding [End Def] code. If you regenerate a table and the [DefMark:ToA,n] mark is accidentally deleted but the [EndDef] code is found, the message "Can't find end of table of contents, lists, or index text" is displayed.

If the [EndDef] code is deleted, that section of the table will be generated again, without deleting the first table. You would then get duplicate tables in the same location. If more than one [DefMark] code exists for the same section, the table will be generated in both locations.

"New Page# Not Found"   If you neglect to insert a New Page Number code between the Table of Authorities and the first authority marked, this message will be displayed as a warning that page number listings may not be accurate. Go to the first page of the text after the Table of Authorities, press Page Format (ALT-F8), type **2** for New Page Number, and assign a new number to that page. Regenerate the table.

"Non-Unique Short Form(s) Found"   If you use the same short form for more than one full form, this error message will be displayed to remind you that there must be a unique short form for each full form. The table will still be generated, but asterisks will appear instead of page numbers in the entries that are affected.

   If you use a short form that is not assigned to a full form, the short form will be displayed in the table with an asterisk marking that item.

Related Entries

Block

Search

See also Appendix C, "Macro Library"

Table of Contents

The Table of Contents feature can be used to mark up to five levels of headings or titles and generate a Table of Contents that lists the page numbers for each item. Figure 4-113 shows a sample Table of Contents.

```
                        TABLE OF CONTENTS


THE CONSTITUTION OF THE UNITED STATES . . . . . . . . . . . .     1
      PREAMBLE  . . . . . . . . . . . . . . . . . . . . . . .     1
      ARTICLE I . . . . . . . . . . . . . . . . . . . . . . .     1
            Section 1  . . . . . . . . . . . . . . . . . . . .    1
            Section 2  . . . . . . . . . . . . . . . . . . . .    1
            Section 3  . . . . . . . . . . . . . . . . . . . .    2
            Section 4  . . . . . . . . . . . . . . . . . . . .    4
            Section 5  . . . . . . . . . . . . . . . . . . . .    4
            Section 6  . . . . . . . . . . . . . . . . . . . .    5
            Section 7  . . . . . . . . . . . . . . . . . . . .    5
            Section 8  . . . . . . . . . . . . . . . . . . . .    6
            Section 9  . . . . . . . . . . . . . . . . . . . .    8
            Section 10 . . . . . . . . . . . . . . . . . . . .    9
      ARTICLE II  . . . . . . . . . . . . . . . . . . . . . .    10
            Section 1  . . . . . . . . . . . . . . . . . . . .   10
            Section 2  . . . . . . . . . . . . . . . . . . . .   12
            Section 3  . . . . . . . . . . . . . . . . . . . .   13
            Section 4  . . . . . . . . . . . . . . . . . . . .   13
      ARTICLE III . . . . . . . . . . . . . . . . . . . . . .    13
            Section 1  . . . . . . . . . . . . . . . . . . . .   14
            Section 2  . . . . . . . . . . . . . . . . . . . .   14
                                Doc 1   Pg 46   Ln 1     Pos 51
```

Figure 4-113.   Sample Table of Contents

Keystrokes

The procedure for creating a Table of Contents includes three basic functions.

Block each item and mark it for a specific Table of Contents level.

Define the location and format for the Table of Contents.

Generate the table.

Mark Each Item

1. Move the cursor to one end of the text to be included in the Table of Contents and press Block (ALT-F4). If you include any codes in the block (such as Bold, Underline, or Centering), they will be included in the table as well. Press Reveal Codes (ALT-F3) if you need to check the location of the codes.

2. Move the cursor to the opposite end to highlight the text.

3. Press Mark Text (ALT-F5).

4. Type **1** for ToC.

5. Enter the number of the ToC Level (1 = major heading, 2 = heading, 3 = subheading, and so on). Each level can have its own type of page numbering and will be indented according to the level (level 1 would not be indented, level 2 would be indented to the first setting, level 3 to the second setting, and so on).

Define the Location and Format of the Table

1. Move the cursor to the location where the table should be generated.

2. Press Hard Page (CTRL-ENTER) if you want the Table of Contents to appear on a separate page. Type a heading for the page if desired.

3. Move the cursor to the line where the first line of the Table of Contents should appear.

4. Press Mark Text (ALT-F5). The following menu appears.

```
Mark for: 1 ToC; 2 List; 3 Redline; 4 Strikeout; 5 Index; 6 ToA: 0
```

5. Type **6** for Other Options. See Figure 4-111 to view the options listed on the menu.

6. Type **2** to Define Table of Contents. The menu shown in Figure 4-114 is displayed.

7. Type the number of levels that will be included in the Table of Contents (type a number indicating the number of the highest level marked).

8. A second question, "Display last level in wrapped format? (Y/N) N," appears. Type **N** to leave each entry on a line by itself or **Y** if you want the entries to follow each other and wrap when the end of the line is reached. The following example shows the last level being wrapped.

```
                        TABLE OF CONTENTS

THE CONSTITUTION OF THE UNITED STATES  . . . . . . . . . . .    1
     PREAMBLE  . . . . . . . . . . . . . . . . . . . . . . .    1
     ARTICLE I . . . . . . . . . . . . . . . . . . . . . . .    1
          Section 1 (1); Section 2 (1); Section 3 (2);
          Section 4 (4); Section 5 (4); Section 6 (5);
          Section 7 (5); Section 8 (6); Section 9 (8);
          Section 10 (9)
```

9. When you typed the number of levels to be included in the Table of Contents, a page number listing style is inserted as the default, as shown in Figure 4-115. Option 5, Flush Right Page Numbers with Leaders, is displayed for all levels, unless you answered Y to the question "Display last level in wrapped format? (Y/N) N." In that case, option 3, "(Page Numbers) follow Entries," is displayed as the default option.

If you have chosen to display the last level in a wrapped format, the page number cannot be flush against the right margin. Therefore, only the first three options are displayed as choices for the last level if it is wrapped.

```
Table of Contents Definition

   Number of levels in table of contents (1-5): 0


                              Page Number Position
        Level 1
        Level 2
        Level 3
        Level 4
        Level 5


     Page Number Position
     1 - No Page Numbers
     2 - Page Number Follow Entries
     3 - (Page Numbers) follow Entries
     4 - Flush Right Page Numbers
     5 - Flush Right Page Numbers with Leaders
```

Figure 4-114.   Table of Contents Definition menu

```
Table of Contents Definition

    Number of levels in table of contents (1-5): 3

    Display last level in wrapped format? (Y/N) N

                              Page Number Position
    Level 1                          5
    Level 2                          5
    Level 3                          5
    Level 4
    Level 5


    Page Number Position
    1 - No Page Numbers
    2 - Page Number Follow Entries
    3 - (Page Numbers) follow Entries
    4 - Flush Right Page Numbers
    5 - Flush Right Page Numbers with Leaders
```

Figure 4-115.   Table of Contents Definition menu showing default
page number style after selecting number of levels

The following example shows how each number listing style would appear when the table is generated.

```
No Page Numbers
Page Numbers Follow Entries 1; Entry 4; Entry 10
(Page Numbers) Follow Entries (1); Entry (4); Entry (10)
Flush Right Page Numbers                              1, 4, 10
Flush Right Page Numbers with Leaders . . . . . . . .  1, 4, 10
```

Press ENTER to accept the page number style shown
or enter a new number.

10. Press Hard Page (CTRL-ENTER) after the Table of
Contents definition mark if you want the text of the document to start on a new page.

11. Because the Table of Contents itself will create an
inaccurate count of pages, you can choose the New Page
Number option from the Page Format (ALT-F8) menu to
assign a new number to the first page of the text. See
New Page Number for details.

Generate the Table of Contents

1. Press Mark Text (ALT-F5).

2. Type **6** for Other Options.

3. Type **8** to Generate Tables and Index.

4. The message "Existing tables, lists, and indexes will be replaced. Continue? (Y/N): Y" is displayed. Type **Y** to continue or **N** to return to the document if necessary.

A counter is displayed to let you know that progress is being made.

Hints

When you mark an entry to be included in a Table of Contents, the codes [Mark:ToC,n] and [EndMark:ToC,n] are inserted at the beginning and end of the block. The n indicates the level number for that item.

When you define the location of a Table of Contents, the code [DefMark:ToC,n] is inserted at the cursor location. The n in this code indicates the number of levels chosen. After a section is generated, an [EndDef] code is placed at the end of the table. If the table is generated a second time, these codes are used to block and delete the previous section so the newly generated table can be displayed in its place.

If you have used automatic paragraph numbering for the headings in your document, you can search for a paragraph number, block the entry, and mark it for the Table of Contents rather than manually scrolling through the document.

When a Table of Contents is generated, each item will appear in the order in which it appears in the document. You can mark additional items or delete the [Mark:ToC] codes and regenerate the table. The Table of Contents, Table of Authorities, lists, and index are all generated at once.

After the Table of Contents is generated, each entry will be preceded by the codes [->Indent] and [<-Mar Rel:n]. These codes help create a hanging indent style for those entries that are longer than one line. Each succeeding level has one additional [->Indent] code to move it to the next tab setting. If the table is not aligned correctly, you may need to adjust the tab settings. See *Tabs, Clear and Set* for more information.

You can edit the table after it has been created. If you choose the dot leader option for page number listing, a dot leader is placed between the text and the page number. If text is added or deleted, the dot leader is automatically adjusted as needed.

Error Messages

"Not Enough Memory"   WordPerfect uses document 2 (if available) to generate the tables, lists, and index. If it is not available, document 3 is used. If you get the error message "Not Enough Memory," exit document 2 so the memory for that document can be used. If you still get the message, retrieve the document into document 2 and leave the document 1 screen clear. Table Generation can then use the additional memory in document 1 (twice as much memory as allotted to document 2).

"No [DefMark] Found"   If you forget to define the location and format of the table, you will see the error message "No [DefMark] Found." Correct the situation and regenerate the table.

"Can't Find End of Table of Contents, . . ."   When you first generate a table, an [EndDef] code is placed at the end of the table. Each [DefMark] code then has a corresponding [EndDef] code. If you regenerate a table and the [DefMark: ToC,n] mark is accidentally deleted but the [EndDef] code is found, the message "Can't find end of table of contents, lists, or index text" is displayed.

If the [EndDef] code is deleted, the Table of Contents will be generated again, without deleting the first table. You would then get duplicate tables in the same location. If more than one [DefMark] code exists for the Table of Contents, it will be generated in both locations.

Related Entries

Block

Search

Tabs, Clear and Set

Tabs are preset every five spaces. WordPerfect lets you clear and set individual or multiple tabs.

Keystrokes

1. Press Line Format (SHIFT-F8).

2. Type **1** for Tabs.

3. The cursor remains in the same column position. For example, if the cursor was at position 45, it is placed at position 45 on the Tabs menu, as the following example shows.

```
L....L....L....L....L....L....L....L....L....L....L....L....L....L....L....L...
01234567890123456789012345678901234567890123456789012345678901234567890123456 78
         10        20        30        40        50        60        70
Delete EOL (clear tabs); Enter number (set tab); Del (clear tab);
Left; Center; Right; Decimal; .= Dot leader; Press EXIT when done. 45
```

4. Clear or set tabs. (See the following discussions of types of tab setting/clearing options for further instruction.)

5. Press Exit (F7) when finished.

Clear Individual Tab Settings

1. If the cursor is not on the tab setting you want cleared, enter the position of the tab setting or use → and ← to move the cursor to the tab setting.

2. Press DEL or BACKSPACE to delete the tab.

Clear All Tabs

1. Press HOME,HOME,← to move to the beginning of the line.

2. Press Delete to End of Line (CTRL-END) to delete all tab settings.

Set Individual Tabs

1. Clear tabs if necessary.

2. If the cursor is not where you want the tab to be set, enter the position number, or use → and ← to move the cursor to the correct position.

3. If you entered the exact position, an "L" is automatically inserted for a normal, left-aligned tab. The following list shows the types of tabs that can be set. Enter one of the letters listed if desired.

T or L	Normal, left-aligned tab
R	Right-aligned tab
C	Centered tab (text is centered at the tab setting)
D	Decimal tab (text is aligned at the decimal at the tab setting)

After setting a tab, you have the option of typing a period (.) if you want a dot leader to appear between that tab and the previous tab. You cannot have a dot leader to a centered tab. The following illustration shows examples of different tab settings.

```
Richard L. Anderson    Training          $500.00 . . . . .Daily
Howard Bankett, Jr.    Consultant        $100.00 . . . . Hourly
Sharon F. Day          Programmer             . . . . Negotiable
Jason Weeks            Training          $150.00 . . . . Hourly
Elaine Johnson         Systems Analyst $2,000.00 . . . . Weekly
```

Set Multiple Tabs

1. Clear tabs first if necessary.

2. Enter the position for the first tab stop, a comma, and the interval. For example, 12,5 would set tabs every five spaces beginning at position 12.

Hints

When you set tabs, a Tab Set code similar to the following is inserted into the document.

```
[Tab Set:L5,L10,D50,R74]
```

If you enter the Tabs menu and decide not to make changes, pressing Exit (F7) will still enter the Tab Set code into the document. To exit the menu without inserting a code, press Cancel (F1) instead of Exit.

A ruler can be displayed on the screen to show you the relative position of the tab settings without entering the Tabs menu. See *Ruler* for more information. You can also press Reveal Codes (ALT-F3) to see the ruler temporarily.

Creating Macros to Set and Clear Tabs

If you work with tabs extensively, you might want to create macros to obtain the tab settings that apply to your work. Procedures for three useful macros are included here; the macros are designed to:

Clear all tabs

Set a tab at the current position

Restore the previous tab settings

Clear All Tabs

1. Press Macro Def (CTRL-F10) to define a macro.

2. Name the macro (CLEAR or CLEARTAB could be used).

3. Press Line Format (SHIFT-F8).

4. Type **1** for Tabs.

5. Press HOME,HOME,← to move to the beginning of the line.

6. Press Delete to End of Line (CTRL-END) to delete all tabs.

7. Press Exit (F7).

8. Press Macro Def (CTRL-F10) to end the macro definition.

Set Tab at Current Position   If you are accustomed to moving to a position on a typewriter and pressing a Tab Set key, you might want to define this macro.

1. Press Macro Def (CTRL-F10).

2. Name the macro (SETAB is a suggestion).

3. Press Line Format (SHIFT-F8).

4. Type **1** to set tabs. Note that the cursor remains in the same position.

5. Type **L** for a normal, left-aligned tab.

6. Press Exit (F7).

7. Press Macro Def (CTRL-F10).

You would probably want to execute the "clear tabs" macro before executing this one. While you could combine the two into one macro, it is more advantageous to keep them separate so you can set more than one tab.

Before you execute this macro, be sure to move the cursor to the position where the tab is to be set.

If you often use another type of tab such as decimal tabs, consider defining a macro to set that type of tab as well (type **D** instead of **L** in the previous steps).

Restore Previous Tab Settings   If you have several tables placed throughout a document, you will most likely be changing tabs for a particular table and changing them back after the table. You can create a macro that searches for the previous tab settings and inserts them at the current location so that you don't have to remember the previous settings and manually reinsert them.

Before defining this macro, you need to set tabs at least twice and move the cursor *after* the tab settings.

1. Press Macro Def (CTRL-F10) and enter the name of the macro (RESETABS could be used).

2. Type *** (or other unused characters) to mark your place.

3. Press Reverse Search (SHIFT-F2).

4. Press Line Format (SHIFT-F8), then **1** for Tab Set; [Tab Set:] is displayed as the search string.

5. Press Reverse Search (SHIFT-F2) to begin the search. The last tab setting that was used for the table is found.

6. Press Reverse Search (SHIFT-F2) twice to find the next previous tab setting.

7. Press Block (ALT-F4) to turn on Block.

8. Press ← twice to "mark" the Tab Set code. (You need to press ← twice to move over both the Block and Tab Set codes.)

9. Press Move (CTRL-F4), then **2** to Copy the Block.

10. Press Search (F2), type *** (or other characters used to mark your place), then press Search again.

11. Delete the characters by pressing BACKSPACE as many times as necessary.

12. Press Move (CTRL-F4) and **5** to Retrieve Text. The [Tab Set:] code is retrieved at that point.

13. Press → once to move over the Tab Set code.

14. Press Macro Def (CTRL-F10) to end the macro.

Changing the Spacing Between Tabbed Columns

You can change the spacing between tabbed columns by readjusting the tabs. Move the cursor *after* the original tab setting and enter the Tabs menu. As shown in the following illustration, the tab settings in the menu line up with the columns on the screen.

```
Richard L. Anderson     Training          $500.00 . . . . .Daily
Howard Bankett, Jr.     Consultant        $100.00 . . . . Hourly
Sharon F. Day           Programmer             . . . . Negotiable
Jason Weeks             Training          $150.00 . . . Hourly
Elaine Johnson          Systems Analyst $2,000.00 . . . . Weekly


L...........................C...............D...............R.............
01234567890123456789012345678901234567890123456789012345678901234567890123456789012345678
        20          30          40          50          60          70          80
Delete EOL (clear tabs); Enter number (set tab); Del (clear tab);
Left; Center; Right; Decimal; .= Dot leader; Press EXIT when done.
```

Clear and set tabs as needed. As soon as you exit the menu, the columns are readjusted to fit the new tab settings.

Related Entries

Decimal Tabs

Ruler

Tab Align

Text In/Out

Text In/Out (CTRL-F5) is used to save and retrieve files in a different format and create a document summary or comments for the current document.

Options

When you press Text In/Out (CTRL-F5), the menu shown in Figure 4-116 is displayed. The options listed are explained in the following paragraphs.

DOS Text File Format

You can save a file in DOS text format with the first option listed. While all WordPerfect codes are removed, the format

```
Document Conversion, Summary and Comments

     DOS Text File Format
          1 - Save
          2 - Retrieve  (CR/LF becomes [HRt])
          3 - Retrieve  (CR/LF in H-Zone becomes [SRt])

     Locked Document Format
          4 - Save
          5 - Retrieve

     Other Word Processor Formats
          6 - Save in a generic word processor format
          7 - Save in WordPerfect 4.1 format

     Document Summary and Comments
          A - Create/Edit Summary
          B - Create Comment
          C - Edit Comment
          D - Display Summary and Comments


  Selection: 0
```

Figure 4-116.   Document Conversion menu after pressing Text In/Out

is retained by adding spaces. Paragraph numbers are converted to text. Tab settings are converted to spaces and both hard returns and soft returns are converted to a carriage return/line feed (CR/LF).

Options 2 and 3 let you retrieve a DOS text file and either convert a CR/LF (carriage return/line feed) to a hard return [HRt] or to a [SRt] if it falls within the hyphenation zone. The second option helps retain word wrap. You can also retrieve a DOS text file with the Text In option on the List Files menu. See *DOS Text Files* for more information.

If you want to print a file to disk, you can retain all the text that is included in WordPerfect codes, such as line numbering, headers, footers, and footnotes. See *Print to Disk* for details.

Locked Document Format

You can lock and unlock documents with a password. These documents cannot be retrieved, viewed in List Files, or printed without the correct password. You can also retrieve a locked document using the conventional methods, Retrieve (SHIFT-F10) and the Retrieve option on the List Files menu. When saving or retrieving the file, you are asked to enter the password.

Other Word Processor Formats

The Convert program lets you convert a WordPerfect document to and from WordStar, MultiMate, DCA, and Navy DIF formats. If you have a different word processor, option 6 could be used to save the current document in a generic word processor format.

Actually, the only differences between saving a file as a DOS text file or in a generic word processor format, are that tabs are kept intact and each soft return [SRt] is converted to a space (this feature aids in word wrap for the other word processor). Hard returns are converted to a CR/LF (carriage return/line feed).

You can retrieve a document created with WordPerfect 4.1 into WordPerfect 4.2 without any problems. However, before retrieving a document created with 4.2 into WordPerfect 4.1, you should save it with option 7 first. All 4.2 features are removed from the document so it will not create problems for version 4.1.

Document Summary and Comments

A document summary can be created for each document to identify the author, typist, and date it was created, and to include notes about the document. You can also create any number of nonprinting comments throughout the document. See *Document Summary* or *Comments* for more details.

Related Entries

Comments

Convert Program

Document Summary

DOS Text Files

Lock and Unlock Documents

Print to Disk

Thesaurus

WordPerfect's Thesaurus can display and substitute alternate words that have the same or opposite meaning (synonyms and antonyms). Many of the alternatives themselves also have groups of synonyms associated with them. These groups, too, can be displayed and used as possible alternatives.

Keystrokes

If you have two disk drives, remove the data disk from drive B and insert the Thesaurus disk.

1. If you want to list the alternatives for a word on the screen, move the cursor to that word.

2. Press Thesaurus (ALT-F1). See "Hints" if you get an error message.

3. If the cursor is not on a word, you are prompted to enter a word. If the cursor is on a word, but that word is not found in the Thesaurus, the message "Word not found" is displayed and you are prompted to enter another word.

   The list of alternatives is displayed on the screen in three columns, as shown in Figure 4-117. There are groups of nouns, verbs, adjectives, or antonyms, with each group being divided further into various possible meanings. Each subgroup is numbered consecutively.

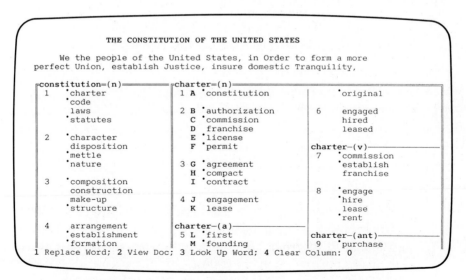

Figure 4-117. Using the Thesaurus to choose word alternatives

4. The following options are available.

Use → and ← to move from column to column. The bolded letters that label the words in the thesaurus list indicate which column is the current one. Press ↑ and ↓ to scroll up and down within a column.

If you cannot find an acceptable alternative, find the next best word which has a bullet (•) by its side and type the letter for that word. (A bullet indicates that the word has its own set of alternatives.)

After moving to the column with the correct alternative, type **1** to Replace the Word in the text. If the cursor was not on a word when Thesaurus (ALT-F1) was pressed, option 1 can be used to insert a word into the document. After choosing option 1, type the letter for the word to be inserted.

Up to four lines of the document are displayed above the Thesaurus screen. If you need to see more of the document, type **2** to View the document. Press Exit (F7) to return to the thesaurus or move the cursor to another word in the document and press Thesaurus (ALT-F1) to display alternatives for that word.

Type **3** to Look Up another Word.

When you choose to display other alternatives, the last column is used. To clear any of the columns, move to that column with ← or → and type **4** to Clear Column. BACKSPACE and DEL will also clear the current column.

5. If you choose option 1 to Replace a Word, you will automatically leave the Thesaurus. Otherwise, press ENTER to leave Thesaurus and return to the document.

Hints

A word having its own group of alternatives is sometimes referred to as a *headword*. Each word listed in the Thesaurus with a bullet (•) is a headword. There are approximately 10,000 headwords in the thesaurus with an overall word count of approximately 150,000.

The following abbreviations are used to identify different types of words in the thesaurus.

n	Noun
a	Adjective
v	Verb
ant	Antonym

Each numbered group of words on the menu is referred to as a subgroup.

The following cursor keys perform the listed functions while in Thesaurus.

← and →	Move from column to column
↑ and ↓	Scroll up and down within a column
Screen Up (-) and Down (+) Page Up (PGUP) and Down (PGDN)	Move the contents of a column up or down one screenful
HOME,HOME, ↑ HOME,HOME, ↓	Scroll to the top or bottom of the list of alternatives in a column
Go To (CTRL-HOME),n	Type the number of a specific subgroup to move to it

Error Messages

"Thesaurus Not Found"   If you are using two disk drives and press Thesaurus (ALT-F1) without inserting the Thesaurus disk into the default drive, you will see the message, "Thesaurus not found. Enter name: B:TH.WP." Insert the disk in drive B and press ENTER or enter the full pathname where the TH.WP can be found.

If you have a hard disk, you should have the Thesaurus file (TH.WP) in the same directory as WP.EXE. Enter the name of the drive, directory, and filename (TH.WP) when you see the message to tell WordPerfect where to look. If you have not yet copied the file to the hard disk, do so before continuing.

If you plan to keep the Thesaurus file in a directory other than where WP.EXE is located, you should use the Setup menu to tell WordPerfect where it can be found so you can avoid the question each time.

"Not Enough Memory"   The Thesaurus takes a large amount of memory when it is started. If you see the error message "Not Enough Memory," check to make sure that document 2 is clear so the additional memory allotted for that document can be used by Thesaurus.

Related Entries

Setup Menu

Timed Backup

See *Backing Up Files*

Top Margin

The top margin can be set in half-line increments. It is preset for 12 half-lines, or 1 inch.

Keystrokes

1. Move to the beginning of the document or to the top of the page to be affected.

2. Press Page Format (ALT-F8).

3. Type **5** for Top Margin. The following prompt appears at the bottom of the Page Format menu.

```
Set half-lines (12/inch) from 12 to
```

4. Enter the number of half-lines for the top margin (12 half-lines equal 1 inch).

5. Press ENTER to leave the Page Format menu and return to the document.

Hints

When the top margin is changed, a code similar to [Top Mar:6] is inserted and will affect the document from that point forward until another Top Margin code is encountered.

When you change the top margin, you should also change the page length and adjust the number of text lines allowed on the page. When you decrease the top margin, you should increase the number of text lines and vice versa. Remember that top margin adjustments you make have an effect on the bottom margin. The following formula is useful.

Form length − Number of text lines − Top margin = Bottom margin

If you change lines per inch to eight lines per inch, the number of lines in the top margin and form length are still figured at six lines per inch.

Headers and page numbers will never print in the top margin. If you want them to print higher on the page, decrease the top margin and increase the number of lines on the page.

Hand-Fed Paper

If you choose continuous forms or select a sheet feeder, the specified top margin is automatically fed by the printer. If you choose hand-fed paper, however, WordPerfect assumes that you will feed at least 1 inch of the page into the printer.

If the top margin is set at less than 1 inch, you should feed that amount into the printer. If the top margin is greater than 1 inch, feed the paper in only 1 inch. WordPerfect will feed down the additional number of lines.

If you are hand-feeding envelopes into a printer (laser printers excluded), you do not have to adjust the top margin or the page length. Instead, feed the envelope to the point where printing should begin and send the printer a "Go."

Related Entries

Bottom Margin

Lines per Inch

Page Length

Totals

See *Addition* or *Math*

Tutorial

WordPerfect includes an on-line, interactive tutorial found on the Learning disk.

Keystrokes

Two Disk Drives

Place the WordPerfect disk in drive A and the Learning disk in drive B.

1. Enter **B:** to change the default drive to drive B.

2. Enter **LEARN** at the B> DOS prompt.

3. Follow the instructions on the screen.

Hard Disk Drive

The following steps help you copy the files found on the Learning disk to a directory called LEARNING on the hard disk (if you have not already done so).

1. Insert the Learning disk in drive A.

2. Type **CD ** to change to the root directory on the hard disk.

3. Type **MD LEARNING** to make a directory called LEARNING on the hard disk. (LEARNING is only a suggestion; use a different name if you wish.)

4. Type **CD \LEARNING** to change to that directory.

5. Type **COPY A:*.*.**

To start the tutorial:

1. From DOS, enter **CD \LEARNING** to go to that directory if you are not already there.

2. Enter **TUTOR** at the C: \LEARNING> DOS prompt.

3. Follow the instructions on the screen.

If the tutorial is not started, you probably do not have a path telling DOS where WordPerfect is located. If this is the case, and assuming you have WordPerfect in a directory named WP, you should enter **PATH C:\WP** before entering **TUTOR.** See Chapter 1 for more information about the PATH command.

Hints

The tutorial will not run if WordPerfect is found in a directory that has an extension (for example, WP4.2). To correct the problem, make a new directory (WP42 is acceptable), copy all the files from the old directory to the new directory, remove the old directory, and edit the path to include the new directory.

The tutorial needs at least 320Kb of memory to run and will not work on some computers that arc not 100-percent IBM compatible.

Typeover

WordPerfect is set to insert characters as they are typed. You can type over existing characters by pressing INS to turn on Typeover.

You can easily make corrections to a document by typing over text instead of inserting some characters and deleting others. This method works especially well if characters are transposed within a word. However, when making corrections, you will most likely use both Typeover and Insert.

Keystrokes

Press INS to switch between Typeover and Insert. "Typeover" appears in the lower left corner of the screen when Typeover is on. The following keys react differently when Typeover is on.

SPACEBAR	Replaces text to the right with spaces
BACKSPACE	Replaces text to the left with spaces
TAB	Moves the cursor over text to the next tab setting without inserting a [TAB] code

Hints

You cannot type over codes. If you encounter a code, text will be inserted instead. If you insert a code when Typeover is on, it will not replace text.

When you type over text, it is considered a "deletion" and can be restored with Cancel (F1).

When in Line Draw, Typeover is automatically turned on. This lets you draw lines around existing text (or through existing text if you are not careful). If you have become accustomed to using Typeover in another word processor, you can change the Setup menu so that WordPerfect is set for Typeover rather than Insert.

Related Entries

INS Key

Line Draw

Type-thru

Most daisy-wheel and some dot-matrix printers allow printing directly from the screen as each character or line is typed. Type-thru is not supported by laser printers.

Keystrokes

1. Press Print (SHIFT-F7). The following menu appears.

```
1 Full Text; 2 Page; 3 Options; 4 Printer Control; 5 Type-thru; 6 Preview: 0
```

2. Type 5 for Type-thru. The next prompt appears.

```
Type-thru printing: 1 by line; 2 by character: 0
```

3. Type **1** to print each line when ENTER is pressed or **2** to print as each character is typed. If you type-thru by line, you can edit a line before it is printed; with character type-thru, you cannot correct mistakes after they are typed.

The menu shown in Figure 4-118 is displayed with either "Line Type-thru Printing" or "Character Type-thru Printing," depending on your choice.

4. Type the characters or line to be printed and press ENTER. The last line printed and the current line are displayed at the top of the screen. See "Options" for information about the other options listed on the menu.

5. Press Exit (F7) or Cancel (F1) to exit the Type-thru menu and return to the document.

```
Line Type-thru Printing

Function Key        Action

Move                Retrieve the previous line for editing
Print Format        Do a printer command
Enter               Print the line
Exit/Cancel         Exit without printing
```

Figure 4-118.   Line Type-thru Printing menu

Options

Move

Press Move (CTRL-F4) to move the previous line back down to the current line. You can then edit the line and send it to the printer by pressing ENTER.

Print Format

Bold, underline, and other formatting changes are not supported in the Type-thru screen. However, you can press Print Format (CTRL-F8) and enter any printer command to control these and other options.

After pressing Print Format (CTRL-F8), "Cmnd:" is displayed. Enter the printer command (found in the printer manual) in decimal form. If you see ESC listed among the commands, convert it to its decimal equivalent (27) and enter it between a less than and greater than symbol, as in <27>. Another command that might be helpful is <12>, which will send a form feed to the printer. When sending a printer command, you can press Retrieve (SHIFT-F10) and enter the name of a file to be downloaded to the printer (a soft font, for example). See *Printer Commands* for complete information on the acceptable format for printer commands.

When you insert a printer command, an ▇ is displayed, indicating the presence of a printer command. As soon as you press ENTER, the command is sent to the printer.

ENTER

Press ENTER to send each line or command to the printer. If character Type-thru was chosen but not supported, press ENTER to print the characters in each line.

Exit/Cancel

Press Exit (F7) or Cancel (F1) to leave the Type-thru screen and return to the document.

Hints

If your printer fully supports Type-thru, the print head will move as you press SPACEBAR or any of the arrow keys ↑, ↓, →, and ←.

You can use most of the delete and cursor keys to edit lines before they are printed. If you want to delete an entire line when using either character or line Type-thru, press Delete to End of Page (CTRL-PGDN). If you are using line Type-thru, you can press Delete to End of Line (CTRL-END) to delete from the cursor to the end of the line.

Applications

Type-thru is most often used for filling in preprinted forms and typing envelopes.

If you find you are often filling in the same pre-printed form, you can set up the form, fill in each item, then print it. See *Merge* for details.

Type-thru is useful for typing envelopes. However, if you have typed a letter that includes the address, you might want to create a macro that would copy and format the address for printing on an envelope. The macro could be used each time an envelope is needed to save time and keystrokes. See Appendix C for a suggested macro.

Related Entries

Merge

Print

See also Chapter 6, "Printer Specifics"

"Unable to Save Printer Selections on WP Disk"

This error message could appear during printer selection and indicates that the WordPerfect disk is full.

Reasons

As you select each printer definition, it is copied into the file WPRINTER.FIL and all associated fonts are copied into WPFONT.FIL. You can select up to 32 printer definitions if there is sufficient room on the WordPerfect disk.

If you are using the Printer program to create a new printer definition, you might see the message "Can't create new printer files on WP disk" if there is not enough room.

Solutions

First, delete any unnecessary files from the WordPerfect disk. If you still do not have enough room for all the printer definitions, use the Printer program to delete the standard printer, DOS text printer, or any other printer definitions not needed. See Chapter 7, "Printer Program," for details on working with the Printer program.

Undelete

Cancel (F1) can be used to restore any or all of the last three deletions. You can also use Undelete to cut and move text with fewer keystrokes than the conventional Move method. However, you should undelete the text as soon as possible because only the last three deletions are remembered.

Keystrokes

1. Move the cursor to the location where the deletion is to be restored.

2. Press Cancel (F1). The most recent deletion is highlighted and displayed, along with the Undelete menu, as shown in Figure 4-119.

3. Type **1** to Restore the deletion, **2** to Show the Previous Deletion, or ENTER to leave the menu without making a choice.

```
    State of New Hampshire shall be entitled to choose three,

Massachusetts eight, Rhode-Island and Providence Plantations one,

Connecticut five, New York six, New Jersey four, Pennsylvania

eight, Delaware one, Maryland six, Virginia ten, North Carolina

five, South Carolina five, and Georgia three.

    When vacancies happen in the Representation from any State,

the Executive Authority thereof shall issue Writs of Election to

fill such Vacancies.

    The House of Representatives shall choose their speaker and

Officers; and shall have the sole Power of Impeachment.

    Section 3.  The Senate of the United States shall be

composed of two Senators from each state, (chosen by the

Undelete: 1 Restore; 2 Show Previous Deletion: 0
```

Figure 4-119.   Pressing Cancel enables you to restore a previous
deletion

Hints

Each "deletion" is understood by WordPerfect to be a consecutive deletion consisting of any amount of text. For example,
you can press BACKSPACE, DEL, delete a block of text, and
Delete to the End of the Page, and it would all be considered
as one deletion. As soon as you press a cursor key or type a
character, the deletion is ended.

If you are using BACKSPACE or DEL to delete and encounter a code, you are asked to confirm the deletion. If you type **Y**
the deletion continues. If you ignore the question or type **N** to
leave the code, the deletion is ended there.

When you are in Typeover mode and type over existing
text, that text is saved as a deletion and can be restored with
Cancel (F1).

In the Undelete menu, instead of typing 2 to Show the
Previous Deletion, you can press ↑ or ↓ to move through the
three deletions.

You cannot undelete a file that has been deleted through the List Files menu. You should use a file recovery program such as Norton's Utilities or Mace Utilities.

Delete Without Saving

Each deletion is saved in memory until memory is filled. It then goes to temporary files on disk named {WP}0.UND, {WP}1.UND, and {WP}2.UND, with the most recent deletion being saved in {WP}0.UND.

If you run out of disk space, the message "Delete without saving for Undelete? (Y/N) N" appears. Type **N** to cancel the deletion and leave the text on the screen. If you do not care about restoring the text later, type **Y**. The deletion will not be saved in this case.

Related Entries

Cancel

Restore Deleted Text

Underline

Underline (F8) is used to <u>underline</u> text before or after it is typed.

Keystrokes

Underline Text as You Type

1. Press Underline (F8) to turn on Underlining. Note that the position number on the status line is underlined (it may be displayed in reverse video or in a different color on a color monitor).

2. Type the text.

3. Press Underline (F8) again to turn off Underlining.

Underline Text After It Has Been Typed

1. Move the cursor to one end of the text to be under-lined.

2. Press Block (ALT-F4) to turn on Block.

3. Move the cursor to the opposite end of the text to be underlined (the text is highlighted as you move the cursor through it).

4. Press Underline (F8).

Remove Underlining

1. Move to the beginning or end of the underlined text.

2. Press Reveal Codes (ALT-F3) to view the text and codes.

3. Locate the Underline On code [U] or Underline Off code [u].

4. Press BACKSPACE if the code is to the left of the cursor or DEL if the code is to the right of the cursor. Deleting either the [U] or [u] will remove the underlining.

After you become more familiar with WordPerfect codes, you can tell where the underline code is by watching the position number on the status line, as shown in Figure 4-120.

Options

Continuous Versus Non-continuous

The spaces between words are automatically underlined. If you do not want the spaces between words underlined, you

a)

```
    If you are at the beginning of an underlined word and the
    position number is not underlined, the underline on code is to
    the right of the cursor.  If the position number is underlined,
    the underline on code is to the left of the cursor.


                                    Doc 1  Pg 1  Ln 1      Pos 44
    [  ▲    ▲    ▲    ▲    ▲    ▲    ▲    ▲    ▲    ▲    ]▲      ▲
    If you are at the beginning of an [U]underlined[u] word and the[SRt]
    position number is [U]not[u] underlined, the underline on code is to[SRt]
    the right of the cursor.  If the position number [U]is[u] underlined,[SRt]
    the underline on code is to the left of the cursor.[HRt]
```

b)

```
    If you are at the beginning of an underlined word and the
    position number is not underlined, the underline on code is to
    the right of the cursor.  If the position number is underlined,
    the underline on code is to the left of the cursor.


                                    Doc 1  Pg 1  Ln 1      Pos 44
    [  ▲    ▲    ▲    ▲    ▲    ▲    ▲    ▲    ▲    ▲    ]▲      ▲
    If you are at the beginning of an [U]underlined[u] word and the[SRt]
    position number is [U]not[u] underlined, the underline on code is to[SRt]
    the right of the cursor.  If the position number [U]is[u] underlined,[SRt]
    the underline on code is to the left of the cursor.[HRt]
```

Figure 4-120.   The position number on the status line indicates the location of the Underline code

will need to turn Underline on and off at the beginning and end of each word. You could create the following macro that will change a solid underline to a broken underline. Before defining the macro, place the cursor in a section of under-lined text.

1. Press Macro Def (CTRL-F10) and enter the name of the macro (BROKENUL for broken underline is a suggestion).

2. Press Reverse Search (SHIFT-F2), Underline (F8) to insert the Underline On [Undrline] code, then Search (F2) to begin the search.

3. Press Block (ALT-F4) to turn on Block.

4. Press Search (F2), Underline (F8), BACKSPACE, then Underline again to insert the Underline Off [u] code.

5. Press Search (F2) again to search for the end of underlining.

6. With the underlined block highlighted, press Replace (ALT-F2), and type **N** for no confirmation.

7. Press SPACEBAR once, then Search (F2) to enter a space as the search string.

8. Press Underline (F8), BACKSPACE, Underline, SPACEBAR, and Underline again. The replacement string should appear as "[u] [Undrline]."

9. Press Search (F2) to complete the operation; then press Macro Def (CTRL-F10) to end the macro definition.

Continuous underlining (as defined by WordPerfect) underlines the text at tabs and the spaces between tabs, as shown in Figure 4-121. The default is non-continuous. To make changes, press Print Format (CTRL-F8) and choose either 7 or 8 for continuous single or double underlining. A code similar to [Undrl Style:7] is placed in the document at the cursor location.

January	February	March	April	May	June
3	5	10	12	17	22
4	8	22	20	31	38
<u>10</u>	<u>12</u>	<u>17</u>	<u>26</u>	<u>37</u>	42
<u>17</u>	<u>25</u>	<u>49</u>	<u>58</u>	<u>85</u>	102

◄—Continuous

Non-continuous

Figure 4-121.   Examples of continuous and non-continuous underlining

Double Underlining

Double underlining is not as easy to get as single underlining. Instead of pressing a single function key, you need to go through the Print Format menu.

1. Press Print Format (CTRL-F8).

2. Type **6** or **8** depending on whether you want non-continuous double underlining.

3. Press ENTER to leave the menu.

4. Press Underline (F8), type the text, then press Underline again to turn off underlining.

5. Press Print Format (CTRL-F8).

6. Type **5** or **7** to return to non-continuous or continuous single underlining.

7. Press ENTER to leave the menu.

You could, of course, change the underlining style after text has been underlined. Remember that a code similar to [Undrl Style:6] is placed in the document; the style of underlining from that point forward will be changed until it encounters another Underline style code.

If you use double underlining often, consider putting the steps into a macro. The exact steps can be found in *Double Underlining* and Appendix C.

Hints

When you press Underline (F8) to turn on underlining, the Underline On and Underline Off codes are actually both inserted at the same time. The cursor remains between the two codes. When Underline is pressed again to turn off Underlining, no code is inserted; instead, the cursor is moved over the code. Therefore, you could use a cursor key such as →, END, or ↓ to move the cursor past the Underline Off code and accomplish the same purpose.

Removing a Section of Underlining

If you have a section of underlined text and decide that you only want part of it to remain underlined, move the cursor to the end of the text you want to remain underlined and press Underline (F8). An Underline Off [u] and Underline On [U] code are inserted with the cursor remaining between the two, as shown in Figure 4-122. WordPerfect automatically inserts the [U] code because it senses that the text to the right is underlined text and assumes you want to keep it that way.

Immediately press DEL to delete the [U] code to the right and type **Y** when asked to confirm the deletion. Underlining is removed from the text to the right of the cursor.

"Writer's Underline"

Usually a writer has to convert his or her files to ASCII (see *DOS Text Files*) before submitting them for publication. When this conversion takes place, however, all WordPerfect codes (including underlining) are lost. To work around this problem, most writers have become accustomed to typing an underscore at the beginning and end of text that should be _underlined_.

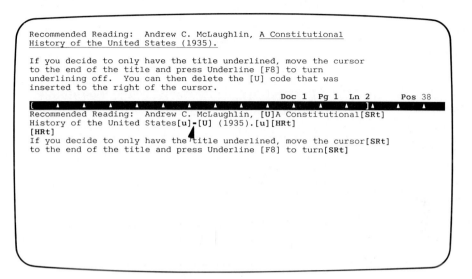

```
Recommended Reading:  Andrew C. McLaughlin, A Constitutional
History of the United States (1935).

If you decide to only have the title underlined, move the cursor
to the end of the title and press Underline [F8] to turn
underlining off.  You can then delete the [U] code that was
inserted to the right of the cursor.
                                         Doc 1  Pg 1  Ln 2       Pos 38

Recommended Reading:  Andrew C. McLaughlin, [U]A Constitutional[SRt]
History of the United States[u]-[U] (1935).[u][HRt]
[HRt]
If you decide to only have the title underlined, move the cursor[SRt]
to the end of the title and press Underline [F8] to turn[SRt]
```

Figure 4-122.   Using the Underline Off [u] and Underline On [U] codes to remove a section of underlining

If you want to use regular underlining throughout the document, you can write the following macro that will change WordPerfect underline codes to an underscore character after the document is completed.

1. Press Macro Def (CTRL-F10).

2. Name the macro (US, for *underscore*, is a suggestion).

3. Press HOME,HOME,↑ to move to the beginning of the document.

4. Press Replace (ALT-F2) and type **N** for no confirmation.

5. Press Underline (F8) twice to insert the Underline On [Undrline] and Underline Off [u] codes.

6. Move the cursor to the left and delete the [Undrline] code.

7. Press Search (F2) to enter the search string.

8. Replace with the underscore character (＿) and the Underline Off code [u] (get the [u] the same way you did

in steps 4 and 5). The replacement string should appear as — [u].

9. Press Search (F2) to start the procedure.

10. Press HOME,HOME,↑ to return to the beginning of the document.

11. Press Replace (ALT-F2) and type **N** for no confirmation.

12. Press Underline (F8) once to insert the Underline On code [Undrline] as the search string.

13. Press Search (F2) and type the underscore character (_) as the replacement string.

14. Press Search (F2) to complete the operation.

15. Press Macro Def (CTRL-F10) to end the macro definition.

You can start the macro anywhere in the document and all underlining is replaced with underscore characters.

Adjusting Underlining on the Screen

Single-Color/Graphics Monitor   If the underlined text is almost invisible or is displayed in reverse video, you probably have a single-color/graphics monitor. Press Screen (CTRL-F3), type **4** for Colors, type **2** for a single-color monitor, type **Y** for fast text display, then choose to have underlining displayed as reverse video or as underline. Some single-color monitors, such as the AT&T, can display the underline. Others, such as some Compaqs, will use reverse video unless you run the MODE UND ON command or switch a hardware switch. If you see flickering on the screen, repeat the steps, but type **N** when asked if you want fast text display.

Color Monitor   Underlined text is displayed in a different color when using a color monitor. If you want to change the color, press Screen (CTRL-F3), type **4** for Colors, type **1** for a color monitor, then type **Y** or **N** for fast text display. One of the options listed is "Underlined Background." This option gives you some indication if there are underlined spaces on the screen. After choosing the desired colors, press Switch (SHIFT-F3) to choose the colors for document 2, then press Exit (F7) when finished.

Moving Underlined Text

If text is moved from an underlined sentence or paragraph, Underline On and Off codes are inserted at the beginning and end of the block so the text will remain underlined when it is retrieved. However, if you retrieve the block into another underlined section of text, Underlining will be turned off after the inserted block. This is because the Underline Off code at the end of the block supersedes the Underline Off code at the end of the original section.

Using Typeover and Line Draw
with Underline

Typeover will not type over codes, nor are codes allowed to type over another character. If the cursor is in a section of underlined text and Typeover is on, regular characters are replaced. However, as soon as the Underline Off code is encountered, characters are inserted. Accordingly, if you turn on Underlining, the typed characters are inserted.

Because of this, if you want underlined text within a box (see *Line Draw*), it is best to type the underlined text first, then draw the box around it. If you want to underline text that is already inside a box, use Block (ALT-F4) to highlight the text, then press Underline.

Some printers cannot do a second pass to get underlining when printing a special character on the same line, as shown in the following example.

```
┌─────────────────────────────────────────┐
│  This is how underlining might look       │
│             underlining                   │
│                                           │
└─────────────────────────────────────────┘
```

If this happens, note that it is a printer limitation and you probably will not be able to get bold or underlined text within a box.

Underlining at the Printer

Some printers print underlining as a solid line, but others can only produce a broken line. If you are not satisfied with the way underlined text is printed, check the printer manual for options so you can try modifying the printer driver (see Chapter 8). See Chapter 7 for specific printer limitations.

Printer Switch Settings

If the underlined text prints out like the following illustration, check the internal switch settings (sometimes referred to as DIP switches) and make sure the switch for Auto LF (automatic line feed) is OFF. If it is turned on, both Word-Perfect and the printer are sending line feeds.

```
If your underlined text looks like this when it prints, check the
LF switch and make sure it is off.
```

Related Entries

Block

Print Format

Unlock a Document

See *Lock and Unlock Documents*

Uppercase Text

See *Capitalization* and *Switch*

Widows and Orphans

Widows and *orphans* are terms for single lines of a paragraph at the bottom and top of a page. Most style books advise against having widows and orphans in a printed document.

WordPerfect is not set to prevent these single lines automatically, but they can be avoided by turning on Widow/Orphan Protect for each document or invoking the feature permanently through the Setup menu.

Keystrokes

1. Move the cursor to the beginning of the document or to the point where widows and orphans should be prevented.

2. Press Page Format (ALT-F8).

3. Type **A** for Widow/Orphan. The following prompt appears on the Page Format menu.

```
    7 - Page Number Column Positions

    8 - Suppress for Current page only

    9 - Conditional End of Page

    A - Widow/Orphan

Widow/Orphan Protect (Y/N): N
```

4. Type **Y** to protect against having widows and orphans, or **N** to allow them.

5. Press ENTER to leave the Page Format menu and return to the document.

Use the Setup menu to turn on Widow/Orphan Protect permanently.

Hints

When you choose the Widow/Orphan option, [W/O On] or [W/O Off] is inserted depending on your selection. Text is affected from that point forward.

WordPerfect protects against widows by moving a widow to the next page with the rest of the paragraph. Orphans are protected against by moving the second to the last line of a paragraph to the next page with the orphan.

Widow/Orphan Protect will not keep a paragraph or section headings with the first two lines of the paragraph. The Conditional End of Page feature (also found on the Page Format menu) should be used instead because it can keep a specific number of lines together.

The Widow/Orphan option also cannot protect three-line paragraphs. The Block Protect feature would be best used in this type of situation because it can protect a specific block of text regardless of the number of lines. To use this option, define a Block (ALT-F4), press Page Format (ALT-F8), and type **Y** to protect the block.

Related Entries

Block Protect

Conditional End of Page

Keep Text Together

Windows

WordPerfect lets you have two documents in memory and switch between them with Switch (SHIFT-F3). You can use the Windows feature to display both documents at once on the screen. You can easily cut and paste text from one document to the other using Windows and Switch.

Keystrokes

1. Press Screen (CTRL-F3).

2. Type **1** for Window. The following message appears.

```
# Lines in this Window: 24
```

The number of lines in the current window are displayed; in the example, "24" represents the number of lines that can usually be displayed on the screen. If you have already split the screen or created the ruler, you will see a different number. Also, if you changed the number of lines that can be displayed on the screen (through the Setup menu), you will see that number.

3. Press ↑ and ↓ to move the ruler until it is in the desired position, then press ENTER. You can also enter the number of lines. The screen will look something like Figure 4-123.

4. Press Switch (SHIFT-F3) to move between the two windows.

Hints

To return the screen to its full size, follow the steps listed above. Enter **24** (or the appropriate number of lines for your

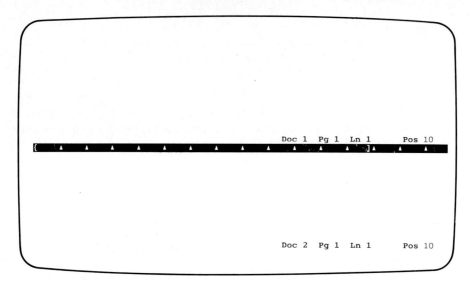

Figure 4-123.   Two documents opened at once

screen) when asked for the number of lines in the window. You can also press ↓ until the ruler moves off the screen, then press ENTER.

   The ruler displays the current margin and tab settings for each document. Tabs are marked with a triangle and the left and right margins are indicated by a square bracket [or]. If both a tab and margin setting are in the same location, the margin is indicated by a brace { or }. When you press Switch (SHIFT-F3), the triangles point to the document being edited.

   If you need to see different parts of the same document, you can retrieve the document in both screens and scroll to the desired locations. However, you should only make editing changes in one version of the document because changes in both cannot be written to the same file. If you need to edit both parts of the document, save them under two different names and combine the edited parts later.

Related Entries

> Ruler
>
> Screen
>
> Switch

Word Count

The number of words in a block, on a page, or in the document is automatically displayed when you check the spelling of a block, page, or document. An option on the Spell menu lets you check the number of words in a document without checking the spelling.

Keystrokes

1. Press Spell (CTRL-F3) from anywhere in the document.

2. Type **6** for Count.

3. When finished counting, a message similar to the following is displayed in the bottom left corner of the screen.

```
Word Count: 2517        Press any key to continue
```

4. Press any key to return to the document.

Hints

Words appearing in headers, footers, footnotes, and endnotes are included in a word count.

Applications

Authors often need an accurate count of the number of words in an article or chapter before submitting it for publication.

If you change the margins or tabs in a document after creating headers, footers, footnotes, or endnotes, they are not automatically updated. If you want the current settings to be reflected in headers, footers, and all notes, do a Word Count.

Related Entries

Spell

Word Search

If you want to search for a word in the current document, see *Search.*

Word Search is a feature included on the List Files menu that lets you search multiple files for a unique word or phrase. This feature could also be called "file search" because it is helpful in locating specific files.

Keystrokes

1. Press List Files (F5). The name of the current drive/ directory is displayed.

2. Press ENTER to see a list of files in that drive/directory, edit the directory name, or enter the name of a different drive/directory. See "Hints" for other options.

3. Type **9** for Word Search. The following prompt appears.

```
Word Pattern:
```

4. Enter up to 20 characters, including wildcard characters and logical AND/OR operators if desired. Use quotation marks around a phrase if it contains a space, semicolon, comma, or single or double quotation marks. See "Hints" for all options.

5. All files containing the word(s) are displayed.

If more than one file is displayed, you can do another Word Search to reduce the number of files, if necessary.

Hints

When entering a word pattern, you can use the following wildcard characters.

?   Represents any single character

*   Represents any number of characters, up to a hard return [HRt]

You can combine words with the AND/OR operators to limit the search, as shown in the following.

; or a space   Search for files containing both x AND y

,   Search for files containing either x OR y

Remember to enclose a phrase in quotation marks if it contains a space, comma, semi-colon, or other quotation marks; otherwise, it will be considered an operator.

The more files listed, the longer it takes Word Search to search through each file. To limit the number of files to be searched, use the following suggestions.

After pressing List Files (F5), you can enter a filename pattern to limit the files displayed. For example, enter *.**LTR** to view all the files ending with a .LTR extension. If you have several files for a specific client, enter *.**JONES***.* to list all documents containing that name.

After you enter the List Files menu, you can mark files by typing an asterisk (∗) while the cursor is on the file. When you do the Word Search, only those files that are marked will be included in the search.

After finding a group of files with the same unique word or phrase, you can delete, print, or copy those files by marking them (press Mark Text (ALT-F5)) and then choosing the applicable item from the menu.

Related Entries

Copy Files

Delete Files

List Files

Look at a File

Print

Search

WordPerfect Files

Table 4-7 shows the files that are found on each WordPerfect disk. Chapter 1 discusses where each file should be copied during installation.

Table 4-8 lists all the temporary overflow files that can be created during the operation of WordPerfect. They are ordinarily created where WP.EXE is located, but can be redirected to another drive/directory with the /d option (enter **WP/D-DIRECTORY** to start WordPerfect). See *Start WordPerfect* and Chapter 3 for more details.

Disk	Filename	Function
WordPerfect	WP.EXE	WordPerfect program
	WPRINTER.FIL	Contains selected printer definitions
	WPFONT.FIL	Contains corresponding character tables
Speller	LEX.WP	Dictionary containing 115,000 words
	SPELL.EXE	Spell program used to customize main dictionary
Thesaurus	TH.WP	Thesaurus file
Learning	WPHELP.FIL	Help information for function keys
	WPHELP2.FIL	Help information for letters A through Z
	TUTOR.COM	Tutorial program
	*.TUT	Files used in the Tutorial
	*.LRN	Files used in the Learning section of the WordPerfect manual
	*.MAC	Macros used in the WordPerfect manual. Two macros, FONT-TEST.MAC and FNTTEST1.MAC, are used to simplify the testing of character tables (fonts).

Table 4-7.　Files on Each WordPerfect Disk

Disk	Filename	Function
Learning (*continued*)	*.TST	Printer test files
	CONVERT.EXE	Convert program for converting documents for use with other software programs
	CURSOR.COM	Cursor program that lets you customize the style of the cursor
	WP.TBL	File to be used with TopView
	MAC.MEX	Macro information for the Macro Editor
	README	File used to test the printer
Printer 1	WPPRINT1.ALL	Contains printer definitions from A through N
	WPFONT1.ALL	Contains corresponding character tables
	WPFEED.FIL	Contains sheet feeder definitions
	PSCRIPT.PS	Used with PostScript printers such as the Apple Laserwriter. The file, once named LASERWRT.PS, is automatically copied to a disk/directory when the Apple Laserwriter printer definition is selected.

Table 4-7.   Files on Each WordPerfect Disk (*continued*)

Disk	Filename	Function
Printer 1 (*continued*)	INITLWRT.PS	File to be copied to Apple Laserwriter once to change the protocol from XON/XOFF to hardware handshaking. See Chapters 5 and 6 for more information.
Printer 2	WPPRINT2.ALL	Contains definitions from O through Z and limited-support printers
	WPFONT2.ALL	Contains corresponding character tables
	WPFEED.FIL	Contains sheet feeder definitions (same as file on Printer 1 disk)
	PRHELP.EXE	Printer Help program for more printer information
	PRINTER.EXE	Printer program used to create or modify printer definitions, character tables, or sheet feeder definitions
	XONXOFF.PS	File used to change the Apple Laserwriter from hardware handshaking back to XON/XOFF

Table 4-7.   Files on Each WordPerfect Disk (*continued*)

Filename	Function
{WP}.TV1	Top virtual file for document 1. Text above the cursor is stored in this overflow file if needed.
{WP}.BV1	Bottom virtual file for document 1. Text below the cursor is stored in this overflow file if needed.
{WP}.TV2	Top virtual file for document 2. See {WP}.TV1 above.
{WP}.BV2	Bottom virtual file for document 2. See {WP}.BV1 above.
{WP}.CHK	Keeps track of the overflow files
{WP}SYS.FIL	WordPerfect system file containing user-definable attributes such as colors and key mapping for special characters
{WP}.SPC	Used to reserve 4Kb of space on the disk in case of a "disk full" error
{WP}0.UND	Contains the most recent deletion
{WP}1.UND	Contains the second most recent deletion
{WP}2.UND	Contains the third most recent deletion
{WP}LEX.SUP	Supplementary dictionary containing user-added words
{WP}BACK.1	Backup file for document 1 (if backup is specified)
{WP}BACK.2	Backup file for document 2
{WP}.Q	Printer queue that lists the documents waiting to be printed
{WP}.#	When printing from the screen rather than disk, files are given a temporary number instead of using the filename

Table 4-8.   Temporary Overflow Files

Related Entries

Start WordPerfect

See also Chapter 1, "Getting Started"

See also Chapter 3, "The Next Step"

WordPerfect Startup Options

See *Start WordPerfect*

WordStar

The Convert program can convert WordStar version 3.3 files to WordPerfect format and back again. If you are accustomed to using WordStar, you might want to check Appendix B for a terminology comparison table to make the conversion to WordPerfect a little easier.

Keystrokes

1. Start the Convert program found on the Learning disk by entering **CONVERT** at the applicable DOS prompt. See *Convert Program* if you need assistance.

2. When prompted for the name of the input file, enter the name of the file to be converted. Include the drive and directory if necessary. If you need to convert more than one file at a time, use the wildcard characters * and ? (*.WS would convert all files with the extension .WS).

3. Enter the name of the file that will be used to hold the converted file when asked for the output file. If the file already exists, you will be asked if you want to replace the previous file. Type **Y** to replace the file or **N** to enter a different filename. Use a similar file pattern with wildcard characters if applicable. The menu in Figure 4-124 is displayed.

4. If the file to be converted is in WordStar format, type **3** to convert the WordStar 3.3 file to WordPerfect. If the file is in WordPerfect format, type **1** to convert WordPerfect to another format. If you type **1**, the following menu appears at the bottom of the screen.

```
1 Revisable-Form-Text (IBM DCA Format)
2 Final-Form-Text (IBM DCA Format)
3 Navy DIF Standard
4 WordStar 3.3
5 MultiMate 3.22
6 Seven-bit transfer format

Enter number of output file format desired
```

Type **4** to convert the WordPerfect file into WordStar 3.3 format.

Hints

If you have WordStar 2000, convert the 2000 file to WordStar 3.3 format, then use WordPerfect's Convert program to convert to WordPerfect format.

When converting files from WordStar to WordPerfect, the following features are not converted.

Doublestrike (only Bold is supported in WordPerfect)

Margins

Merge commands

Paper length

Right justification on screen

Spacing

```
Name of Input File? c:\writing\article.25
Name of Output File? a:article.ws


1 WordPerfect to another format
2 Revisable-Form-Text (IBM DCA Format) to WordPerfect
3 Navy DIF Standard to WordPerfect
4 WordStar 3.3 to WordPerfect
5 MultiMate 3.22 to WordPerfect
6 Seven-bit transfer format to WordPerfect
7 Mail Merge to WordPerfect Secondary Merge
8 WordPerfect Secondary Merge to Spreadsheet DIF
9 Spreadsheet DIF to WordPerfect Secondary Merge

Enter number of Conversion desired
```

Figure 4-124.   Convert Program menu

The features not converted from WordPerfect to Word-Star include the following.

Center

Flush right

Footnotes and endnotes

Hard spaces

Line spacing

Margins

Mark text

Paper length

Right justification

Top margin

Center and Flush Right are not converted as features but spaces are used to retain the format. Only one header and one footer will convert from WordPerfect because WordStar only allows one per document. Many of the features will not convert because WordStar has no corresponding features.

Applications

If you are switching word processors, you can save hours of retyping by converting all WordStar files to WordPerfect. Remember that you can use wildcard characters (B:*.* would convert all files from the disk in drive B).

Some publishers require that files be submitted in ASCII (DOS text) or WordStar format. Use Text In/Out to convert the file to the DOS text format and Convert to convert the document to WordStar format.

Related Entries

Convert Program

DOS Text Files

See also Appendix B, "Conversion Tables for Microsoft Word, WordStar, MultiMate, and DisplayWrite"

"WP Disk Full"

The error message "WP Disk full," or "Not enough room on WP disk to retrieve text," can appear when retrieving a large file.

Reasons

When a file is retrieved, WordPerfect loads as much as possible into memory (up to 64Kb is allowed for document 1 and up to 32Kb is allowed for document 2, but less is used if the maximum amount is not available). When memory is filled, the remaining text spills into overflow files where WP.EXE is located. This feature lets you swap data disks or use the disk drive for the Speller or Thesaurus disks.

If the WordPerfect disk does not have enough room when using two disk drives, or if you have redirected the overflow files to a RAM drive and it runs out of available memory, you will see the error message.

Solutions

Delete all unnecessary files from the WordPerfect disk. Leave WP.EXE, WPRINTER.FIL, and WPFONT.FIL on the disk. If you do not have a sheet feeder, delete the WPFEED.FIL from the disk.

If you formatted the WordPerfect disk with the DOS system files by specifying (FORMAT/S), the extra files are taking up space. Consider using a separate "boot" disk with the DOS system files so you can free up that much space on the WordPerfect disk.

You can usually add more memory to your system at a minimal cost. If you work with large documents regularly, consider purchasing a hard disk. If you have a RAM drive, you could redirect the overflow files there, but remember that a RAM drive takes some of the memory, therefore forcing the large document to go to the overflow files prematurely.

You could redirect the overflow files to the data disk itself with the /d option (enter **WP/D-DRIVE/DIRECTORY** to start WordPerfect). The command WP/D-B: would direct the overflow files to the disk in drive B. If you redirect the overflow files, you cannot remove the disk in that drive.

If you still cannot retrieve the file, make a backup copy of the WordPerfect disk, then delete the two files needed for printing (WPRINTER.FIL and WPFONT.FIL). Retrieve the file and divide it into smaller files (block each section and save it under different names). After this is finished, copy WPRINTER.FIL and WPFONT.FIL back to the WordPerfect disk.

Related Entries

Start WordPerfect

Printing

This printing section includes three chapters. Chapter 5 offers hints about effective use of a laser printer with Word-Perfect. Chapter 6 provides tips on printing and lists each printer supported, as well as its fonts, attributes, suggested pitch settings, and limitations. Proportional spacing, line draw, and sheet feeder information are included where applicable. Chapter 7 introduces you to the Printer program. After reading it, you'll be comfortable looking at, editing, or creating a printer definition. In addition, the chapter includes tips for working with character tables and sheet feeder definitions.

Laser Printers

In this chapter you will learn how to take advantage of the power and speed that has made the laser printer so popular. Specifically, you will find information about downloading soft fonts, changing fonts within a document, printing on envelopes and legal-size paper, and using sheet feeders, along with information on printing special characters and accessing more than eight fonts.

How Laser Printers Work

Laser is an acronym for Light Amplification by Stimulated Emission of Radiation. To create characters or images, a laser beam is reflected with mirrors onto a photosensitive drum, the image is then transferred to paper.

Laser printers are quiet and fast. Most laser printers can print approximately eight pages per minute, although it takes slightly longer for legal-size or manually fed sheets. Print resolution is usually 300×300 dots per inch, thus creating high-quality documents.

Selecting a Printer Definition

When you go through the process of selecting printers, you would usually choose from one to six printer definitions. However, if you have a laser printer with several cartridges

or soft fonts, you should choose *all* applicable printer definitions without regard to the printer number. Up to 32 can be
selected (depending on available disk space). After they have
been selected, you can reassign the six most often used printer definitions to the six printers. See *Select Printers* in Chapter 4 for complete details.

Some laser printers have special requirements that must
be met when they are first installed. These are discussed in
the following paragraphs, according to the type of printer.

Apple LaserWriter

When you select printers, you will not find the Apple Laser-
Writer definitions under *A* in the list of printers; instead,
they are listed under *L* for LaserWriter. There are currently
four printer definitions (Helvetica and Times Roman in both
portrait and landscape orientations); no soft fonts are supported. If you want a Courier font, choose the TI 2115 printer
definitions (Courier portrait and Courier landscape). These
printer definitions are interchangeable because both printers
run under PostScript.

The LaserWriter is a serial printer. Therefore, COM1 (or
another serial port) should be selected. Select 9600 for the
baud rate, no parity, 1 stop bit, and 8 for the character length
(data bits). Make sure that the four-position switch on the
back of the printer is switched to 9600 baud.

When asked to specify the type of forms, select sheet
feeder. Enter **0** for the number of extra lines between pages,
0 as the column position of the left edge of the paper, and **2**
for the number of bins (the second bin is used for hand-fed
paper). Choose the Apple LaserWriter from the list of sheet
feeders.

The Apple LaserWriter is a PostScript printer that
defaults to Xon/Xoff protocol. In order to work with Word-
Perfect, it must be changed to DTR (data terminal ready),
otherwise known as "hardware handshaking," by copying the
INITLWRT.PS file from the Printer 1 disk to the printer.
This only needs to be done *once*, when the printer is first
installed. If you need to return to Xon/Xoff for other pro-

grams, you can copy the XON/XOFF.PS file from the Printer 2 disk to the printer.

To copy the INITLWRT.PS file to the printer, place the Printer 1 disk in drive A and enter the following command at the DOS prompt.

>COPY A:INITLWRT.PS COM1

If the printer is connected to a different serial port, substitute that port for COM1 in the command. The file is written to a nonerasable memory chip and needs to be copied again only if the XON/XOFF.PS file was sent to the printer in the meantime.

When you select the LaserWriter definition, a file named PSCRIPT.PS, found on both printer disks, is also copied with the printer definition. If you have a problem when printing, verify that PSCRIPT.PS is in the same directory as WPRINTER.FIL. This file is sent to the printer at the beginning of each print job and loads a routine called PtrEmulate. This helps the printer accept commands from WordPerfect.

If you have printing problems, confirm that your ROM is version 2.0 or later. You can find the version number in the lower left corner of the first page of the printer self-test.

Hewlett Packard LaserJet Printers

There are currently four HP laser printers supported by WordPerfect: LaserJet, LaserJet+, LaserJet 500+, and Series II. All of the printer definitions are listed under *L* for LaserJet, except for the Series II which is listed as the "HP LaserJet Series II" under *H* for HP. All "+" definitions can also be used for the Series II printer.

The laser printers from Hewlett Packard are usually defined as serial printers. All but the original LaserJet can be set up as a parallel printer. If you are using the serial interface, set the baud rate at 9600, no parity, 1 stop bit, and 8 as the character length.

Select continuous forms or sheet feeder for the type of

form, depending on how your printer is set up. If you have a single paper tray, select continuous forms. If you want to feed the paper into the printer manually, you can do so by taking the printer off line, selecting manual feed, then putting the printer back on line. The printer will then accept hand-fed paper until returned to the normal setting.

If you choose a sheet feeder, enter **0** for the number of extra lines between pages and **0** for the column position of the left edge of the paper. Enter the number of bins (remember that manual feed is considered a bin) and select the LaserJet+ definition. Additional information about specific sheet feeders is included later in this chapter.

Texas Instruments 2115 (OmniLaser)

Also known as the OmniLaser, the TI 2115 is another Post-Script printer supported by WordPerfect. You do not have to send the INITLWRT.PS file to the printer as you do with the Apple LaserWriter.

With the July 10, 1987 release of WordPerfect, the PSCRIPT.PS file was included on the Printer 2 disk so it would be copied when the TI 2115 printer definitions were selected. If you are using a version of WordPerfect released before that date, you will have to copy the file manually from the Printer 1 disk to the same drive and directory where WPRINTER.FIL is located.

The TI 2115 printer definitions include both a Courier portrait and Courier landscape font. If you want Times Roman and Helvetica in both portrait and landscape orientations, you can select the LaserWriter printer definitions for this printer.

Select a serial port (usually COM1), 9600 baud, no parity, 1 stop bit, and 8 for the character length. Select sheet feeder as the type of forms to be used, with **0** for the number of extra lines and **0** for the column position from the left edge of the paper. Enter 3 as the number of sheet feeder bins (manual feed is considered a bin) and select the Texas Instruments 2115 sheet feeder definition from the list.

Xerox Laser Copier/Printer

The Xerox Laser Copier/Printer can use the Xerox 2700 II, 4045 Laser CP (630), and all other printer definitions listed for the Xerox 4045 printer. The 2700 and CP definitions use the internal fonts only. All others use downloaded fonts.

Fonts

One advantage of using a laser printer is the ability to combine many fonts on a single page. A font is a set of characters that look alike. For instance, Helvetica 12 or Courier 10I (italics) are two different types of fonts. Each has its own size, slant, and typeface. Table 5-1 identifies the different characteristics of a font.

When you choose which fonts (cartridges or soft fonts) to purchase, you will usually look for the desired typeface and the characters that are included in that font (commonly called a character set or character table). Some of the most common character sets are U.S. or Standard ASCII, Roman Eight or Extension, and IBM. Most character sets are a variation of the U.S. ASCII character set, which contains the U.S. English alphabet in upper and lowercase as well as punctuation characters. The Roman Eight (or Extension) contains the U.S. characters and a collection of foreign characters. The IBM character set includes all the characters available with the IBM Personal Computer (including Line Draw and text graphics characters).

When a character set does not contain a particular character, WordPerfect will usually print a space to help maintain the right margin. If a space appears where you expected

Typeface	The "name" of the font is the typeface used. Some examples are Courier, Prestige Elite, Letter Gothic, Times Roman, Helvetica, and Presentation.
Orientation	Orientation refers to the direction of printing. Portrait (normal) prints across the width of the page. Landscape or rotated fonts print sideways down the length of the page. The abbreviations denoting the orientation vary from printer to printer. For instance, the HP LaserJet uses P for portrait and L for landscape while Canon uses N for normal and R for rotated.
Spacing	The width of the characters are either fixed or proportional. Fixed characters are given equal widths. In a proportionally spaced font, each character is given a specific width so letters fit together.
Pitch	Pitch or CPI indicates the number of characters printed per inch. Proportionally spaced fonts are not given a set pitch, but can be adjusted to the user's taste.
Point size	A character's size or height is measured in "points." There are approximately 72 points per inch. Some common point sizes are 8, 10, 12, 14, and 24.
Style	Style determines whether the characters will be printed upright or in italics.
Weight	Weight (sometimes called stroke weight) indicates how thick the characters are. The choices are usually light, medium, or bold.
Character set	Each font is made up of a specific set of characters referred to as the symbol set. Some of the choices available are U.S. ASCII, Roman Eight, IBM U.S., Danish/Norwegian, UK, French, German Italian, Swedish/Finnish, Spanish, and Math.

Table 5-1. Characteristics of Fonts

a character to print, the character set for that font probably does not include that character.

Types of Fonts

A laser printer contains built-in, resident fonts. The default resident font (usually Courier 10) is used if a cartridge is not placed in the slot. Fonts are also stored in cartridges that plug into the printer. Cartridges usually contain several related fonts. For instance, the Garland 10N cartridge for the Canon printer contains four fonts: regular, bold, italics, and small print in the Garland typeface.

A *soft font* is stored on software (diskettes) rather than hardware (printer or cartridges). When you want to use soft fonts, they must first be downloaded, or transferred into the printer's memory.

There are advantages and disadvantages to each type of font. If you use the fonts in a cartridge, there is no download-ing time (soft fonts need to be copied to the printer each time it is turned on) and you don't need to be concerned with the amount of memory available in the printer. However, soft fonts are usually less expensive than cartridges and you can usually download as many as will fit in memory.

Although a dot-matrix printer will let you combine fonts, it does not provide the quality of print available with the laser printer. If you had a daisy-wheel printer and your work required the use of many fonts, the print wheel would need to be changed constantly.

Accessing Fonts

WordPerfect supports eight fonts for every printer definition. Chapter 6 has a complete list of printers and the fonts defined for each, including the character table, characteris-tics, and suggested pitch.

After you have identified the number of the desired font (and downloaded any soft fonts), you can change to that font at the cursor location by using the following procedure.

1. Press Print Format (CTRL-F8).

2. Type **1** for Pitch/Font.

3. Enter the desired pitch. (If it is a proportionally spaced font, include an asterisk after the pitch.)

4. Enter the font number.

5. Press ENTER to return to the document.

Most fonts are identified by point size rather than pitch. If you are using a proportionally spaced font, a suggested pitch is given that can be adjusted to your taste.

If you change from one pitch to another, you will usually change the margins at the same time. Consider using macros that will change the pitch, font, margins, and perhaps tab settings at once instead of spending the extra time and keystrokes changing each one separately.

When you choose Bold (F6) in a document, a boldface font is usually used. For example, if font 3 is a boldface font, it will be used for bolding text. Therefore, bolded text would be treated as if there were a font change. You should be aware of this if you have problems bolding in a larger or smaller font or when printing in landscape orientation.

Four laser printers are discussed individually in the following sections because each printer uses a different method of accessing fonts.

Apple LaserWriter

The Apple LaserWriter contains 35 resident fonts, which are listed in Table 5-2. Only the first eight (variations of Helvetica and Times Roman) are accessed by changing fonts in Print Format (CTRL-F8).

One of the most exciting features of a PostScript printer is the ability to scale resident fonts to any point size. If you want to change the point size or font in the printer, you can do so by inserting a printer command. Keep in mind that any font change, including boldface text, will override the printer command. Therefore, you might want to customize your

Identifier	Font Name
A	Helvetica
B	*Helvetica-Oblique*
C	**Helvetica-Bold**
D	***Helvetica-BoldOblique***
E	Times-Roman
F	*Times-Italic*
G	**Times-Bold**
H	***Times-BoldItalic***
I	AvantGarde-Book
J	*AvantGarde-BookOblique*
K	**AvantGarde-Demi**
L	***AvantGarde-DemiOblique***
M	**Bookman-Demi**
N	***Bookman-DemiItalic***
O	Bookman-Light
P	*Bookman-LightItalic*
Q	Helvetica-Narrow
R	*Helvetica-Narrow-Oblique*
S	**Helvetica-Narrow-Bold**
T	***Helvetica-Narrow-BoldOblique***
U	NewCenturySchlbk-Roman
V	*NewCenturySchlbk-Italic*
W	**NewCenturySchlbk-Bold**
X	***NewCenturySchlbk-BoldItalic***
Y	Palatino-Roman
Z	*Palatino-Italic*
a	**Palatino-Bold**
b	***Palatino-BoldItalic***
c	*ZapfChancery-MediumItalic*
u	Courier
v	*Courier-Oblique*
w	**Courier-Bold**
x	***Courier-BoldOblique***
y	Symbol
z	ZapfDingbats

Table 5-2.   Resident Fonts for Apple LaserWriter

printer definition by putting the following command in the "Shift into font" string. See Chapter 7, "Printer Program," for details.

To insert a printer command, use the following steps.

1. Press Print Format (CTRL-F8).

2. Type **A** to Insert Printer Command.

3. Enter the command **<16>?#<32>** where ? is the font identifier (see Table 5-2) and # is the number indicating the size of the font.

The font size is determined by calculating the number of dots required.

$$# = \frac{300 \times pt}{72}$$

In the formula, *pt* is the desired point size (point size indicates the height of a character and is different from pitch). The result should be rounded to the nearest whole number. The following table lists several common point sizes and the result (#) of the calculation for each point size. Use the result in the printer command.

Point Size	*Result*
5	21
8	33
9	38
10	42
11	46
12	50
14	58
16	67
17	71
18	75
20	83

If you want proportional spacing and right justification with these fonts, you will have to create a customized printer definition that includes the widths for each character. You can find out more about this procedure in Chapter 7, "Printer Program."

Hewlett Packard LaserJet Printers

If you have a LaserJet+, 500+, or Series II printer, you can download soft fonts to the printer's memory. During the procedure, you will assign an ID number to the font. WordPerfect can select a font by means of the ID number or by the font's attributes.

   If you plan to use soft fonts, you should become familiar with the Printer program discussed in Chapter 7. You can use the Printer program to look at the printer definitions and see how the fonts are being selected. An example of a printer command that will change fonts is

<27>&l0O<27>(0U<27>(s0p10h12v1s0b3T

This is actually several commands in one. Each command searches for a specific attribute in the following order. The orientation (portrait or landscape) is specified first and the typeface is last.

<27>&l0O	Portrait orientation
<27>(0U	US ASCII character set
<27>(s0p	Fixed pitch
10h	10 pitch
12v	12 points
1s	Italicized
0b	Medium stroke weight
3T	Courier typeface

   The advantage to using this method rather than calling a font by the ID number is that if a font matching all the attributes is not found, the closest match will be used for printing. If you select a font by the ID number and the exact font is not found, the printer will usually default to the resident font.

To call a portrait font by an ID number, enter the following command.

    <27>&l0O<27>(#X

In this command, # is the font ID number. The first character after the ampersand (&) is an *l* (not the numeral 1) and the second a zero, and the third is an uppercase *O*. The command for a landscape font is similar, but adds the number 1 between the *l* and *O*. Again, # represents the ID number in the sample command.

    <27>&l1O<27>(#X

You will learn more about creating a custom printer definition with these commands after reading about downloading fonts and assigning ID numbers.

Downloading Soft Fonts   There are several ways to download fonts. The first option is to use the PCLPak provided by Hewlett Packard. All fonts to be downloaded are copied and compressed into one file. The command to copy the file can be included in the AUTOEXEC.BAT file so that when the computer and printer are turned on, the file is automatically downloaded. If you choose this method, follow the instructions included with the PCLPak.

You can also use WordPerfect to download the fonts and assign an ID number with printer commands. An HP Utility disk that automates the process of creating a customized printer definition and provides character tables for approximately 200 additional soft fonts is available from WordPerfect Corporation at a minimal cost.

If you use the HP Utility disk, you can create a custom printer definition and select the fonts from a list of font definitions. Because this is such an accurate process, each font is called by its ID number instead of being selected by attributes. The fonts to be downloaded should be assigned the ID numbers 1 through 8 in the same order that they appear in the printer definition.

If you do not wish to purchase the HP Utility disk, you can use the following procedure for customizing printer definitions.

1. Select the applicable soft font printer definition(s) from the print list. The following are included on the Printer 2 disk.

LaserJt+,500+ Soft AC: Helv P

LaserJt+,500+ Soft AC: Tms P

LaserJt+,500+ Soft AE: Helv P

LaserJt+,500+ Soft AE: Tms P

LaserJt+,500+ Soft DA: LG,Prs

LaserJt+,500+ Soft EA: PElite

If you are using AD or AF soft fonts, you should select the AC definition and make a small change to the printer definition. See "Creating a Custom Printer Definition for Soft Fonts" later in this chapter.

2. Use option 2 on the Printer Control menu to display the list of soft fonts assigned to each of the eight available fonts. Your screen will look similar to the following.

```
1:  LaserJt+,500+ Soft AC: Tms P Continuous

       1 HP  AD  TmsRmn10R      2 HP  AD  TmsRmn10I
       3 HP  AD  TmsRmn6R       4 HP  AD  TmsRmn8R
       5 HP  AD  TmsRmn8I       6 HP  AD  TmsRmn12R
       7 HP  AD  TmsRmn18B      8 HP  AD  TmsRmn30B
```

These are the fonts that will be searched for when changing fonts. However, remember that if the listed font is not available, the next closest font will be used.

3. List the filenames on the Hewlett Packard SoftFont disk(s) with List Files (F5) and make a list of the soft fonts to be downloaded. For example, HV120IPN.USP contains the Helvetica 12 point italics font in portrait orientation using the U.S. ASCII character set.

4. If you have a hard disk, make a separate directory (FONTS is a suggested name) and copy each soft font file into that directory. Option 7 on the List Files menu will let you create a new directory from within Word-Perfect.

If you have two disk drives, copy the soft font files to a separate "font" disk. Do not use the original disks.

5. Press Print Format (CTRL-F8).

6. Type **A** to Insert Printer Command.

7. Enter the command **<27>*C#D**, where # is the ID number for the font to be downloaded. Any number between 0 and 32,000 can be entered, but the numbers 1 through 8 are most commonly used because you can more easily associate the font number with the ID number.

8. After entering the printer command, you will remain in the Print Format menu. Type **A** to Insert another Print Command.

9. Press Retrieve (SHIFT-F10). You are prompted for the document name.

10. Enter the drive, directory, and name of the file to be downloaded (for example, enter **b:HV120IPN.USP** if the disk containing the soft fonts will be in drive B when the downloading takes place or **C:\FONTS\HV120IPN. USP** if the font is in a "font" directory in drive C).

11. Type **A** to Insert another Printer Command.

12. Enter **<27>*C5F** to make the font "permanent" until the printer is turned off. Permanent fonts will not be affected by a printer reset.

13. Repeat steps 6-12 until all fonts have been selected.

When you press ENTER to return to the WordPerfect screen, it will appear blank. Press Reveal Codes (ALT-F3) and your screen will look similar to the following (a [HRt] was added after each set of codes for aesthetic purposes).

```
                                              Doc 1  Pg 1  Ln 7        Pos 10
[Cmnd:<27>*c1D][Cmnd:<126>c:\fonts\TR12N#US.SFP][Cmnd:<27>*c5F][HRt]
[Cmnd:<27>*c2D][Cmnd:<126>c:\fonts\TR12I#US.SFP][Cmnd:<27>*c5F][HRt]
[Cmnd:<27>*c3D][Cmnd:<126>c:\fonts\TR12B#US.SFP][Cmnd:<27>*c5F][HRt]
[Cmnd:<27>*c4D][Cmnd:<126>c:\fonts\TR18R#US.SFL][Cmnd:<27>*c5F]-[HRt]
```

There should be eight sets of codes (all eight sets might not
be visible at the same time). The first code in the set assigns
the ID number, the next indicates that the named file should
be retrieved to the printer (shown with the <126> for
Retrieve), and the last makes the font permanent until the
printer is turned off. Press ENTER to return to the regular
screen.

Print the file (press Print (SHIFT-F7) and type **1** for Full
Text). The data light on the printer will flash and a blank
page will be ejected after several minutes (it sometimes
takes up to 10 minutes to download the fonts to the printer).
If any characters are printed, you have made a mistake when
entering the printer commands. Press Reveal Codes (ALT-F3)
and check each code for accuracy. Make changes where
needed.

Before saving the file, insert a document summary to
identify the contents of the file. See *Document Summary* in
Chapter 4 for details. If you are using two disk drives, save
the file on the WordPerfect disk. If you have a hard disk, you
can save the file in the WordPerfect directory. Print the file
each time the fonts are to be downloaded.

Even though you can usually download more than eight
fonts, you can access only eight at a time through the font
selections. If you have additional fixed-pitch fonts, you can
access them with a printer command that calls the appropriate ID number—**<27>&lO<27>(#X** for a portrait font and
<27>&l1O<27>(#X for a landscape font, where # is the ID
number. You cannot use the same method for a proportionally spaced font because PS fonts require a character table in
order to print correctly.

Many printers will not download to permanent memory
unless you tell them to. Loading to permanent memory
means that a reset will not erase them from memory. Turn-

ing the printer off will always erase them whether they are permanent or not.

Creating a Custom Printer Definition for Soft Fonts   If you have downloaded the soft fonts listed in the Display Printers and Fonts screen, you should not have to make any adjustments to the printer definition.

If you have made any substitutions, you will need to customize the printer definition so the correct character table will be used and the printer command that changes fonts is accessing the correct soft font.

After you start the Printer program and enter the printer definition area, you can choose to create a new printer definition (using one that is already created as a model) or edit an existing one. The main menu appears as shown in Figure 5-1.

Options 8, 9, and A display submenus that contain the commands to change fonts and select character tables for those fonts. If you choose option 8, you will see the commands

```
         Edit:       LaserJt+,500+ Soft AC: Tms P

1. Printer Initialization

2. Carriage Return/Backspace Control

3. Line Spacing and Vertical Motion Control (VMI)

4. Microspacing and Horizontal Motion Control (HMI)

5. Subscript/Superscript/Underline/Bold

6. Special Text Markings

7. Pitch/Miscellaneous

8. Selecting Fonts (Fonts 1 - 4)

9. Selecting Fonts (Fonts 5 - 8)

A. Character Tables for Fonts


Select Item Number: 0
```

Figure 5-1.   Printer program main menu

Figure 5-2.   Menu to select fonts 1-4

to change into and out of fonts 1 through 4, as shown in Figure 5-2. Option 9 lets you select the commands to change into and out of fonts 5 through 8.

Figure 5-3 shows the menu that is displayed when option A is chosen. If you want to change the character table being used for one of the fonts, select that font's number. A list of predefined character tables is displayed. If the desired tables are not listed, you can use the ones provided on the HP Utility disk or create your own.

The most common change made to submenus 8 and 9 is when a Roman Eight font is used instead of U.S. ASCII. For example, if the AD or AF soft fonts are being used, you would select the AC definition, but change "0U" to "8U" in the "Change into font" string. The following shows the string before and after it has been edited.

<27>&l0O<27>(0U<27>(s0p10h12v1s0b3T

<27>&l0O<27>(8U<27>(s0p10h12v1s0b3T

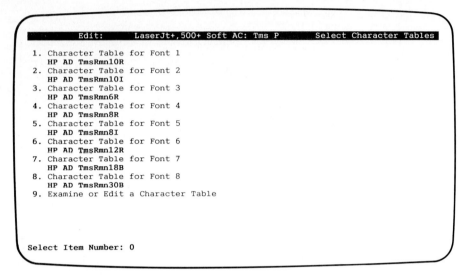

```
    Edit:        LaserJt+,500+ Soft AC: Tms P        Select Character Tables
1. Character Table for Font 1
   HP AD TmsRmn10R
2. Character Table for Font 2
   HP AD TmsRmn10I
3. Character Table for Font 3
   HP AD TmsRmn6R
4. Character Table for Font 4
   HP AD TmsRmn8R
5. Character Table for Font 5
   HP AD TmsRmn8I
6. Character Table for Font 6
   HP AD TmsRmn12R
7. Character Table for Font 7
   HP AD TmsRmn18B
8. Character Table for Font 8
   HP AD TmsRmn30B
9. Examine or Edit a Character Table




Select Item Number: 0
```

Figure 5-3.   Character tables for fonts

When using landscape fonts, you should add a numeral 1 between the *l* and *O* in the "Change into font" string. Another change might be necessary if you used different ID numbers than 1 through 8 for the downloaded soft fonts. The appropriate ID number would then have to be substituted in the string.

If the printer is not printing correctly with the soft fonts, check the following items.

Was the correct soft font disk in the designated drive when the download file was printed? Were the correct soft font filenames used?

Is the correct printer definition selected?

Is the appropriate character table being used for the font?

Has the correct orientation (portrait or landscape) been selected for the font?

Quadram Laser Printer

There are two definitions for the Quadram Laser Printer: standard and optional. See Chapter 6 or use PRHELP (on the Printer 2 disk) to list the fonts to be downloaded for each definition. You might want to consider purchasing the Quadram Utility disk, available from WordPerfect Corporation. The disk contains macros that help with the downloading process as well as character tables for additional soft fonts.

Another option for downloading soft fonts is to use the FONT.EXE utility program included with the Quadram soft fonts. The order in which the soft fonts are downloaded should be the same order in which they are defined in the Display Printers and Fonts screen.

Xerox 4045

If you are using the Xerox 4045 Laser CP (630) or Xerox 2700 II printer definitions, the printer should be set for Diablo 630 emulation. Two resident fonts, Titan and a landscape font, are assigned to fonts 1 and 8 in the Xerox 4045 printer definition and fonts 1 and 2 in the Xerox 2700 II printer definition. All other fonts are left undefined.

Each of the other printer definitions require that specific fonts be downloaded. You will find the list of fonts for each in Chapter 6 and in the PRHELP program (found on the Printer 2 disk).

Soft fonts are downloaded at the DOS level and can be done with a batch file. The following batch file is used to download the fonts for the Century Schoolbook definition. Note the beginning and ending statements in the batch file. The /b indicates that it is a binary transfer.

```
>copy con csb.bat

copy load.1 prn

copy csb6n.p prn/b

copy append.1 prn

copy csb10n.p prn/b

copy append.1 prn

copy csb10i.p prn/b

copy append.1 prn

copy csb12n.p prn/b
```

```
copy append.1 prn

copy csb12i.p prn/b

copy append.1 prn

copy csb14n.p prn/b

copy append.1 prn

copy csb18n.p prn/b

copy append.1 prn

copy csb24n.p prn/b

copy finish.1 prn
^Z
```

The Xerox 4045 Laser Titan printer definition should use the printer in 2700 mode to access the internal Titan fonts. All other definitions should use the printer in Diablo 630 mode.

The Unprintable Region

The laser printing process necessitates an unprintable region around the outer perimeter of the paper to ensure that toner does not reach the transfer unit. The unprintable region on most printers is about 1/4 to 1/3 of an inch.

The printer manufacturer normally has designed the printer to take into account the unprintable region when enforcing top and left margins. If this has not been incorporated into the design of your printer, however, your margin settings will be off by 1/4 to 1/3 of an inch, the width of the unprintable region. On a standard WordPerfect document with 1-inch settings, the document will print with a top margin of 1 1/4 inch, a bottom margin of 3/4 inch, a left margin of 1 1/4 inch, and a right margin of 3/4 inch. Even if the printer has been designed to make it possible for WordPerfect to correct the margin problem, you cannot print at positions within the unprintable region. Any attempts to do so will result in the loss of partial or whole characters.

On the HP LaserJet printers, the top margin will be off by 1/4 inch. WordPerfect can adjust for the left margin, so it will remain at 1 inch. The Canon laser printer lets WordPerfect adjust for both the top and left margins, so both will remain at the standard 1 inch. Most other laser printers add the extra 1/4 or 1/3 inch space. If you find that your laser printer is adding the extra space, you adjust the top and left margins in each document or change the default settings in the Setup menu.

When setting text length and margins, remember to take the laser printer's unprintable region into account. Always leave the page length at 66 lines for letter-size paper and 84 for legal-size paper. The maximum number of text lines (on most laser printers) would be 63 for letter-size and 81 for legal-size paper with a minimum of a 2-line top margin.

Sheet Feeders and Manual Feeding

Several types of sheet feeders can be purchased and attached to a laser printer. When using any printer which has more than one paper tray or a multiple-bin sheet feeder, you should specify the type of forms as a sheet feeder when selecting printers. After you choose a sheet feeder, you are asked several questions. Enter **0** as the number of extra lines to insert between pages and **0** as the column position for the left edge of the paper. You should usually indicate that you have an extra bin that can be used for hand-fed paper.

If you use a mechanical sheet feeder or your printer has only one paper tray, you should probably specify continuous forms when defining the type of forms. Single-bin mechanical sheet feeders usually work by sending a form feed to eject one sheet and insert the next. This setting works fine with most sheet feeders and laser printers.

Refer to your printer manual for additional information

about printing with hand-fed paper. On the HP LaserJet, you should take the printer off line, press the manual feed button, put the printer back on line, and feed the pages as the printer requires them.

Most laser sheet feeders have one additional "nonexistent" bin defined for manually fed paper. If this is the case, go to the top of the page to be affected (or to the top of the document), press Print Format (CTRL-F8), and choose option 9 to change the sheet feeder bin.

Hewlett Packard LaserJet+ Sheet Feeder

The printer can be placed in any of three modes: Auto Upper Tray mode, Lower Cassette mode, and Upper Cassette mode. The type of form selected (continuous or sheet feeder) determines the type of mode that should be used.

If you have selected continuous forms, place the printer in Auto Upper Tray mode. Paper automatically feeds from bin 1. Bin 2 is accessed when bin 1 is empty or when there is a legal-size paper tray in bin 2 and the document has a legal-size page length code.

If you have selected the sheet feeder definition, place the printer in Upper Cassette mode. Bins are accessed through bin changes in the document. Do not use the Auto Upper Tray mode or bin select codes will be ignored.

If you want to use legal-size paper with the 500+ printer, use a legal-size paper tray or manually feed the paper. Although legal-size paper can be placed in a regular letter-size paper tray, the HP recognizes it as letter size and will show a paper jam error when printing. A legal-size paper tray looks very similar to a letter-size tray, but is constructed in such a way that the printer can determine which tray has been inserted.

The A4 metric paper tray will hold paper that measures 11 3/4 × 8 1/4 inches. The form length should be set at 70 when using this type of tray.

Ziyad PaperJet 400 Sheet Feeder

WordPerfect defines the sheet feeder bins for the Ziyad PaperJet definition as follows.

1	Bottom tray of the sheet feeder labeled 1
2	Tray labeled 2 just above bin 1
3	Envelope bin
4	Internal paper tray
5	Feeds from bin 1 until empty, then feeds from bin 2
6	Manual feed on the printer

When printing with this type of sheet feeder, the bin change code needs to follow all other formatting codes (font change, page length, top margin, left and right margins, and so on).

Landscape Printing

When printing in a landscape or rotated font, leave the form length as it is but change the number of text lines (39 will usually give you a 1-inch bottom margin). If your laser printer adds extra space to compensate for the unprintable region, decrease the top margin setting.

The number of text lines and top margin are the same for both letter- and legal-size paper. The form lengths should remain at their respective settings of 66 and 84. Remember that, when printing in landscape orientation, the text will be printed along the length of the paper; thus, the number of lines is the same for letter- and legal-size paper, but the lines themselves can occupy more column positions on legal-size paper.

Place the code for a font change at the beginning of the

document, change the number of text lines (and top margin if necessary), and print as you normally would using a legal-size paper tray or manually feeding the paper. Some printers allow both orientations to be printed on the same page and others send an automatic form feed when the orientation is changed.

Legal-Size Paper

Printing on legal-size paper with a landscape font requires some special considerations. If you have a tray specifically for legal-size paper, most of the difficulties can be avoided with a bin change. If you do not have a legal-size paper tray, use the following suggestions for printing on legal-size paper (either in landscape or portrait).

Apple LaserWriter

To hand feed legal-size paper, you need to create a special printer definition. Enter the Printer program and choose to create a new definition. Choose the applicable LaserWriter printer definition to use as a pattern.

Change the "Initialize printer before print job" string by replacing 3300 with 4200. The string would then appear as:

<X>pscript.ps<X>PtrEmulate<10>300<32>2550
<32>4200<10>

Verify that the string is correct because, unlike most printers, you can actually damage a PostScript printer by sending the wrong command.

Return to WordPerfect and select that new printer definition. Specify sheet feeder as the type of form with **0** as the number of extra lines between pages, **0** as the column position of the left edge of the paper, and **2** for the number of sheet feeder bins. Select the Apple LaserWriter sheet feeder definition.

When using the legal-size paper definition, the bin change code for bin 2 must be the first command at the top of the page. You should then change the page length for legal-size paper. Insert the paper into the manual feed slot and print the document. If there is more than one page, the printer will pause briefly for the next sheet of paper.

Hewlett Packard LaserJet Printers

Although the order of formatting codes does not usually matter, you should always place the page length setting at the beginning of the document when printing with legal-size paper (84 for the form length and a suggested 39 for the number of text lines). Next, change the top margin if necessary, remembering to allow for the unprintable region.

The next command should be to change to the landscape font. Any other formatting and bin change codes should come next. When the document is printed and a legal-size page length code is encountered, it looks for a legal-size paper tray. If the printer does not have one, it may stop and take itself off line.

Choose manual feed on the control panel and press the on-line button to put the printer back on line. Feed the legal-size paper into the manual feed slot until the printer takes the paper.

Xerox 4045 Laser Copier/Printer

If you have the Xerox 4045 laser printer and want to print on legal-size paper, you should create a new printer definition (using an existing definition for the pattern) and add the commands that will recognize legal-size paper.

Enter the Printer program and add the following command to the end of the "Initialize printer before print job" string.

    <27>zg

Also add a second command

<27>m840,0,0,0,510<10>

to the end of each "Shift into font" string. Reenter WordPerfect and select the new printer definition. See Chapter 7 for
more information about working with the Printer program.

Printing with Envelopes and Labels

Once the format is set, printing envelopes and labels is relatively easy. Envelopes can be created with a macro that
searches for and blocks the address on the screen, then formats it for the envelope. The macro could be defined as a
conditional macro so that if no address is found on the screen,
it sets up the format, then stops for you to manually enter the
name and address. See Appendix C for the steps in defining
this type of macro.

To format the address for an envelope, use a landscape
font but do not change the paper length or number of text
lines. The top margin can be changed to a setting of approximately 76 half-lines (or use Advance to tell the printer to
advance to line 32) and set the left and right margins to
approximately 50 and 100. All settings should be adjusted to
suit your needs and particular font. If you have an envelope
bin with your sheet feeder, insert the bin change command at
the top of the page.

If you are manually feeding the envelope, check the
printer manual to see how the envelope should be fed. Most
envelopes are fed into the printer face up either in the center
or with the bottom of the envelope against the right margin.

When printing on a sheet of labels with a laser printer,
each address must contain the same number of lines and the
labels should be fed into the printer manually. The exact
procedure is outlined in the "Labels" entry in Chapter 4.

The format settings should be in the following order: bin
number selection, page length, top margin, left and right
margins, then columns. If you want to print eight lines per

inch, the number of text lines would need to be increased. The number of lines in the form length should not be changed.

Possible Problems and Solutions

Proportionally Spaced Fonts

If you are printing with a proportionally spaced font, always include an asterisk after the pitch number when specifying the pitch. If you forget the asterisk, features such as bold, underlining, and tabs will not print correctly.

Use tab settings rather than spaces to align text. If you use spaces, the text will most likely not line up properly and editing changes may cause further misalignment.

Bold Text Problems

If you want to use the internal font and don't get boldface printing, your printer is most likely trying to use a boldface font from a cartridge. If you want bolding with the internal font, you must delete the Bold codes found in the printer definition program so WordPerfect can control the printing of bolded characters. You cannot bold text when already printing in a boldface font.

If you attempt to bold when in a landscape or rotated font, bolded text may be printed on a page by itself in a portrait font because the printer definition usually calls for a portrait boldface font for bolding.

Line Draw

You cannot usually mix Line Draw and text when in a proportionally spaced font. To get around this limitation, you can draw the lines, use the Advance feature to move back up the page to the appropriate line, change to the proportional font, then enter the text. Although the lines and text will not appear on the screen, they will appear together when printed. See *Advance the Printer to a Specific Line* in Chapter 4 for more information.

Double Underline

An equal sign (=) is used in most fonts for double underlining (the printer moves down during the printing of the double underline). If the double underline prints as a broken line, the equal sign is not wide enough in that font to create a solid line. You can use the Printer program to change how double underlining is accomplished.

If you are using an HP LaserJet printer and encounter the problem (usually in a Roman Eight font), you can substitute the following command for character 255 in the font's character table.

<27>&dD<32><8><27>&a+15V<32><27>&d@<27>
&a−15V

You should then enter the submenu that controls special text markings (option 6 on the Printer Definitions menu). Delete the codes to move up and down and change the double underline character to 255.

HP LaserJet

If you use the original HP LaserJet with the cartridges G, H, J, K, R, U, V, W, or Y, and are having problems with incorrect characters printing, the wrong fonts being used, or other irregular problems (such as not shifting out of the Line Draw font), the problem might lie with the hardware.

On the back of the affected cartridge boxes is a notice that explains how to test for the ROM chip (referred to as a date code). If you find that you need the enhancement, contact your dealer or call (800) 835-HPHP for the nearest authorized Hewlett Packard repair center.

Conclusion

After reading the examples and tips in this chapter, you should see ways that you can customize your printer definitions to fit your particular applications. The most important thing to remember is that you can combine fonts from all sources (internal, more than one cartridge font, and soft fonts) by creating your own printer definitions with the Printer program. If several different fonts work well for you, copy those font definition strings into new printer definitions and select the appropriate character tables. See Chapter 7 for a more in-depth introduction to the Printer program.

Printer Specifics

This chapter lists each printer supported by WordPerfect Corporation as of July 1987. The information is a compilation of display printers and fonts, PRHELP, and the printer tests for each printer.

While you can also refer to all of the above for the information yourself, this chapter gives you the information in one location and supplements it with special notes gleaned from WordPerfect's Customer Support group.

Uses for This Chapter

If you have more than one type of printer in your office and need a specific typeface or capability not available with your printer, you can refer to this chapter to find out how other printers are defined and format your document accordingly. The document can then be printed on the other printer with very few surprises.

Consultants and dealers who support a wide variety of printers can see the capabilities and limitations of a printer at a glance. This chapter also provides possible solutions to problems that might occur with proportional spacing, line drawing, a sheet feeder, or printer switches.

General Terms and Abbreviations

The following is a key to the abbreviations used in this chapter:

```
CR     = Carriage Return
Land   = Landscape
LF     = Line Feed
N      = Normal (portrait)
N/R    = Normal and Rotated on the same
           laser font cartridge
ND     = Not Defined
NLQ    = Near Letter Quality
Port   = Portrait
PS     = Proportional Spacing
Pt     = Point
R      = Rotated (landscape)
RJ     = Right Justification
Rmn    = Roman
Tms    = Times
```

The following is a small glossary of terms:

Baud   Rate at which data is sent to the printer (BPS or bits per second). If you have a question about setting the baud rate for your printer, refer to the printer manual. Sometimes the internal printer switches determine the baud, parity, and other settings.

Character Length or Data Bits   Each character is made up of seven or eight bits. Every serial printer is set up to accept either seven or eight bits. Check the printer manual if you have specific questions.

DIP Switches   A printer usually has internal switches (sometimes referred to as DIP switches) to control auto line feeds, sheet feeders, baud, and parity. They can also be used to choose between a serial or parallel interface if the printer has both capabilities. DIP switch settings are listed in the printer manual. In some cases they are listed in this chapter as well as under the description of the individual printer.

As a rule, leave the DIP switches at the factory settings.

However, some switches *must* be changed for WordPerfect to work correctly.

Download   Some printers have the capability of downloading fonts from a disk to the printer's RAM. If you turn off the printer, memory is erased, making it necessary to download the soft fonts each time you need them.

Your printer should have specific instructions on how to download fonts. If not, refer to Chapter 5 if you have a laser printer, or to *Printer Commands* in Chapter 4 to see how you can download the file to the printer using WordPerfect.

Hardware Handshaking Versus Xon/Xoff   WordPerfect in most cases supports only hardware handshaking for serial printers. However, the hardware handshaking capability was not built into DEC computers, so the version of WordPerfect for the DEC Rainbow supports Xon/Xoff.

Xon/Xoff means that WordPerfect has to scan the signals from the printer to see when to send characters to the printer and when to pause because the printer's buffer is full. Hardware handshaking (also known as DTR or DSR) lets the computer, printer, and cable control (rather than the software) know when data should be sent.

Parallel Versus Serial   A parallel interface sends a byte of information to the printer all at once. The bits that make up each byte travel parallel to each other. The port used for a parallel cable is known as an LPT (line printer) port.

A serial interface sends the data bit by bit, one after another. The most common serial interface is the RS232, which was originally designed to connect computers via the telephone. A port used for a serial interface is referred to as a COM (communications) port.

Parity   Parity is a method of error checking. Parity can be either odd, even, or no parity. In general, if you use eight data bits (character length), you will have no parity.

Pitch   Pitch indicates the number of characters that will be printed per inch.

Point Size   The point size indicates the height of a character (72 points = 1 inch).

Stop Bits   A stop bit signals the end of a character.

Solving Printer Problems

The following are common problems that might occur and
some possible solutions. You should also check under the
individual printer listing in this chapter for more specific
suggestions.

Printer Will Not Print

If the printer has printed before, there is usually a good
explanation as to why it isn't currently printing. Check the
following items and correct them if necessary:

1. Make sure the printer is "on-line." If the on-line light
is not on, press the on-line button to turn it on.

2. Check to see if there is paper in the printer.

3. Check the ribbon.

4. Make sure the cables are securely fastened to both the
computer and printer.

5. Look in the Printer Control menu (press Print
(SHIFT-F7) and type **4** for Printer Control) to see if there
are print jobs waiting and to check the status of the current job. You may have to give the printer a "go" (type **G**
from the menu) or cancel the print job(s), turn the printer off and on, then send the print job again.

If the printer has never printed, check the following
items in addition to the ones listed above:

1. Check the printer selection and make sure it is correct. Try the Standard Printer definition if yours is not listed.

2. Make sure you have selected the correct port from within WordPerfect. Parallel printers use the LPT port and serial printers use the COM port. If a printer has both a parallel and serial interface, they will not work simultaneously. Check the printer DIP switches to make certain that the correct interface has been chosen.

3. Make sure the printer cable is attached to the correct port.

4. Check the cable to make sure it is the correct type. Tandy printers usually need Tandy cables.

5. See if it will print from DOS. If you have a parallel printer, press SHIFT-PRTSC to print the contents of the screen. If you have a serial printer, exit to DOS, insert the Learning Disk in drive A, and enter the following at the DOS prompt: **copy a:readme com1**. If the file does not print, enter **com2**, **com3**, and **com4** in place of **com1** to check all the serial ports.

6. If you have a serial printer, make sure you selected the correct baud, parity, stop bits, and character length.

7. Refer to the printer manual and check all internal DIP switches.

Printer Prints Random or Stray Characters

Check the following items if your printer prints random characters or if it stops after printing part of a document:

1. Make sure cables are securely attached. If they are loose, some bits can be lost.

2. If a serial printer stops at approximately the same point in each document, it could be the result of a buffer overflow. Make sure you have the correct cabling.

3. Make sure the printer accepts hardware handshaking instead of Xon/Xoff. See "General Terms and Abbreviations" earlier in this chapter for more information.

4. If you have chosen proportional spacing on a daisy wheel printer, you should be using a PS print wheel.

5. If the same characters are being printed at the top and/or bottom of a page, you might have defined a sheet feeder when you really don't have one, or you may have selected the wrong sheet feeder. Consequently, the codes for the sheet feeder would not be interpreted correctly, and would be printed as characters.

Printer Double Spaces or Prints Everything on the Same Line

Turn off the Auto Line Feed switch on the printer if bold text and underline characters are not printed on the correct line or if everything prints in double spacing.

If everything prints on the same line, the printer is sending a carriage return without a line feed. If this happens, you might need to do the following:

1. Check the switch settings.

2. Enter the Printer program and choose the Carriage Return/Backspace screen. As shown in Figure 6-1, Options 2 and 3 control the carriage return/line feed combination. Try all four combinations of *yes* and *no* answers until you find the solution.

Paper Not Feeding Correctly

Check the following items if the paper is not feeding into the printer correctly.

1. Make sure you have chosen the correct type of forms (hand-fed, continuous, or sheet feeder). If you chose a sheet feeder, make sure the definition is correct. See

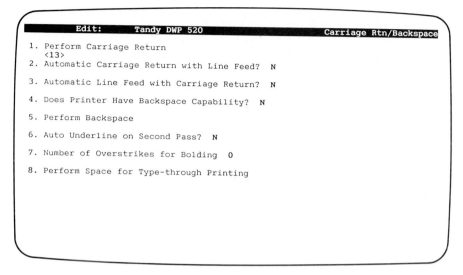

Figure 6-1. Carriage Return/Backspace screen

"Types of Forms and Sheet Feeders," below, for suggestions.

2. Set the forms length on the printer to the correct length.

3. Confirm the page length setting in WordPerfect.

Types of Forms and Sheet Feeders

Hand-Fed   If you use hand-fed paper, remember that WordPerfect assumes that the print head is down 1 inch on the page. If you set the top margin within WordPerfect to anything less, you should roll the paper in accordingly. If you set the top margin to more than 1 inch, you should still roll the paper in just 1 inch. WordPerfect will feed the correct amount of space after 1 inch.

Also, remember that when selecting hand-fed forms, you need to send the printer a "go" for each page (including the first page) before it will print. The computer should "beep," indicating that it is ready for you to insert a new page and type **G** in the Printer Control menu.

Continuous Versus Sheet Feeders If you have a non-supported sheet feeder, or if your printer has a paper tray like those on copy machines (as some laser printers do), then you should define the type of forms as Continuous when selecting printers.

If that definition does not work properly, try the closest definition listed. You can use the Printer program to create a new sheet feeder definition or adjust an existing one. The codes for inserting and ejecting pages should be found with the printer or sheet feeder manuals. See Chapter 7 for more information about working with the Printer program.

When you select Sheet Feeder as the type of forms, you are asked how many extra lines to insert between pages, the column position for the left edge of the paper, and the number of bins. Leave the first two answers at the default unless you have a laser printer. In this case, answer "0" to both questions. Fill in the correct number of bins, then adjust if necessary after testing. This chapter also gives a few specific settings you can try with each type of printer and its sheet feeder.

Proportional Spacing Problems

If you have problems with proportional spacing (PS), check the following items:

1. Make sure your printer has PS capability. Look for your printer in this chapter, refer to *Display Printers and Fonts* in Chapter 4, or run PRHELP from the Printer 2 disk.

2. Choose the correct font. Most proportionally spaced character tables have been assigned to font 3.

3. Choose the correct pitch. As a rule, daisy wheel printers use 13* pitch and dot matrix printers use 11* pitch for PS. Remember to enter the asterisk (*) after the pitch number; this indicates that it is a proportionally spaced font.

4. Check the switch settings on the printer. The general rule is to turn off any PS switches and let WordPerfect control the printer.

If you can get proportional spacing, but there is an unacceptable amount of space between words, you can do one or more of the following:

1. Turn on hyphenation.

2. Decrease the hyphenation zone to create a more even right margin.

3. Turn off right justification.

4. See Chapter 7 for more information about changing Maximum Width of Space Character and Minimum Width of Space Character in the Pitch/Miscellaneous screen.

Printers either adjust for proportional spacing and right justification by using HMI (horizontal motion index) or by microspacing a specific number of units at a time, so printing with PS and/or right justification will be slower and sometimes more "jumpy" than with non-justified, non-proportionally spaced text.

Line Drawing

Check the listing in this chapter for your printer to see which font is best used to draw lines. You may have to use eight lines per inch, found under Print Format (CTRL-F8), or half-line spacing. If you have your choice, you might want to use half-line spacing, because the page length will need to be adjusted if you use eight lines per inch or combine six and eight lines per inch. For eight lines per inch, set the number of single-spaced text lines to 72.

Advance and Superscript/Subscript Problems

If Advance, Superscript, or Subscript are not working correctly, detach the tractor feeder and test the printer. Sometimes the tractor feeder will not let the paper advance. You might be able to partially solve this by releasing the tension on the tractor feeder.

Type-thru

All laser printers do not have type-thru capability. A dot matrix printer, whether you choose to type-thru by line or character, waits until a carriage return is received before it will print.

Text Wrapping to the Next Line Prematurely

If you have an 80-column printer, but have margins exceeding that, text past column 80 will wrap to the next line when printing. To solve the problem change the margins in WordPerfect so they don't go beyond position 80.

Testing the Printer's Capabilities

As mentioned at the beginning of this chapter, the specific printer information was compiled from several sources. The following tools have been provided with WordPerfect to help you test your own printer.

Printer Tests

PRINTER.TST tests many of WordPerfect's printing features such as Redline, Overstrike, Double Underlining, Advance, and others. PRINTER2.TST prints each font in various pitches and tests line drawing in each font both in six lines per inch and eight lines per inch. Remember that if you are using a daisy-wheel printer, you need to send the printer a "go" each time a font change is encountered.

Supported Characters

If you want to see the character tables that are used for each font, press Print (SHIFT-F7), type **4** for Printer Control, then **2** for Display Printers and Fonts.

The file FONT.TST on the Learning Disk can be used to print the characters that are defined for each font. The file should be printed in each font. A macro that has been included on the Learning Disk to help accomplish this is FONTTEST.MAC. With a clear screen, press Macro (ALT-F10) and enter **fonttest** as the macro name. Specify the drive/directory if necessary. Follow the instructions included in the macro.

Printer Help (PRHELP) Program

PRHELP.EXE is a program included on the Printer 2 disk that lists the attributes for each printer and font. When in DOS (not WordPerfect), place the Printer 2 disk in a floppy disk drive and enter **prhelp** at the appropriate DOS prompt. When you select your printer from the list, you are shown a screen similar to the one shown in Figure 6-2.

Non-Supported Printers

WordPerfect includes several non-supported printers on the printer disks. These printers are marked with asterisks.

Non-supported simply means that WordPerfect does not have the printer in-house and cannot test specific problems. They have either created the definition from a user's printer manual or have received the printer definition from users

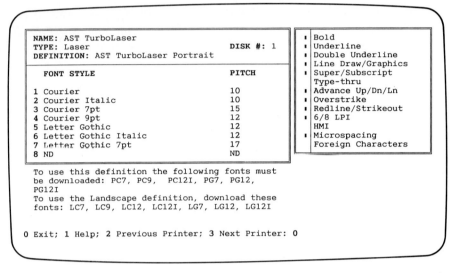

```
NAME: AST TurboLaser                           ▪ Bold
TYPE: Laser                      DISK #: 1      ▪ Underline
DEFINITION: AST TurboLaser Portrait            ▪ Double Underline
                                               ▪ Line Draw/Graphics
  FONT STYLE                     PITCH         ▪ Super/Subscript
                                                 Type-thru
1 Courier                        10            ▪ Advance Up/Dn/Ln
2 Courier Italic                 10            ▪ Overstrike
3 Courier 7pt                    15            ▪ Redline/Strikeout
4 Courier 9pt                    12            ▪ 6/8 LPI
5 Letter Gothic                  12              HMI
6 Letter Gothic Italic           12            ▪ Microspacing
7 Letter Gothic 7pt              17              Foreign Characters
8 ND                             ND

To use this definition the following fonts must
be downloaded: PC7, PC9,  PC12I, PG7, PG12,
PG12I
To use the Landscape definition, download these
fonts: LC7, LC9, LC12, LC12I, LG7, LG12, LG12I


0 Exit; 1 Help; 2 Previous Printer; 3 Next Printer: 0
```

Figure 6-2.   PRHELP.EXE screen showing attributes for selected printer

who created it themselves.

As of July 1987, WordPerfect Corporation provides three printer diskettes. Printer 1 and Printer 2 disks contain all supported printers and Printer 3 contains all non-supported printers. WordPerfect Corporation provides the Printer 3 disk under a separate order only; it does not come with WordPerfect. Call (800) 321-4566 to order the complimentary disk within one month of purchasing WordPerfect if your printer is among those listed. The non-supported printers listed on this disk as of this writing are listed here:

Abati LQ-20

Adler/Royal 1020/5020

Anadex DP 9000/9001/9500/9501

Anadex Silent Scribe DP-9625B

Anadex SS Color DP-9725B

Anadex Word Scribe WP-6000

Anderson Jacobson 833

AT&T 455/457/458

Brother 2024L

Brother 50/60/65/70 Typewriter

Brother DM40

Brother EM-100/EM-200

Brother EM-711 (w/IF-300)

Brother M-1509

C.Itoh 7500 EP

C.Itoh A 10-20

Canon Color Printer A-1210

Centronics 737-1

Centronics GLP

Commodore 6400

Comrex ComRiter

Diablo Advantage D25

Digital LN03 Laser

Digital LQP02

Epson SQ-2000

Facit 4560/8560

Fujitsu DPL24I

Genicom 3304

Hermes PC-4

IBM Proprinter XL24

IBM Quietwriter 7

IBM WheelWriter 3/5

IDS-460/560

Imagen imPRESS Laser

Minolta SP-50B Laser

NEC PC-8023A-C

Olivetti DY-450

Olivetti PR 2300 Ink Jet

Panasonic KX-P1090

Panasonic RK-P400C

Printek 900 Series

Royal Alpha 2015

Sharp ZX-415

Smith Corona Fastext 80

Smith Corona L-1000

Smith-Corona TP1

Smith-Corona Typetronic III

Tandy DMP 120

Tandy DWP 50/210/220/410/510

Tandy DWP II

Teletex TTX-1014

Texas Instruments 810

Texas Instruments 865

Texas Instruments 880

Uchida Color Printer CP-1018

Uchida DWX-305

Vista V300

Xerox 610C/6010/6015 MW

Xerox 620C Memorywriter

If you have a daisy-wheel printer that is not listed as a supported or non-supported printer, try the Diablo 620/630 definition. If you have a dot matrix printer that is not listed, try the Epson FX or IBM Graphics definition. If these suggestions do not work, you can select the Standard Printer definition or customize a printer definition to fit your printer. See Chapter 7 for details.

Printers Supported by WordPerfect

The remainder of this chapter presents an alphabetical list of the printers supported by WordPerfect, along with essential technical information for each machine.

Alphapro 101

Type: Daisy Wheel

Defined as: Alphapro 101

Fonts Assigned:

Character Table		Attributes	Pitch
1	Standard ASCII	Depends on wheel used	10,12,15
2	Standard ASCII	Depends on wheel used	10,12,15
3	Standard ASCII	Depends on wheel used	10,12,15
4	Standard ASCII	Depends on wheel used	10,12,15
5	Standard ASCII	Depends on wheel used	10,12,15
6	Standard ASCII	Depends on wheel used	10,12,15
7	Standard ASCII	Depends on wheel used	10,12,15
8	Standard ASCII	Depends on wheel used	10,12,15

Features Not Suppported: Line Draw, Type-thru, Foreign Characters, Proportional Spacing

Sheet Feeder Information: Define as continuous forms instead of sheet feeder. Turn Mode A and B switches off.

Alps P2000

Type: Dot Matrix

Defined as: Alps P2000

Fonts Assigned:

Character Table		Attributes	Pitch
1	Alps PS	NLQ	10,12,15
2	Alps PS	Emphasized	10,12,15

Character Table	Attributes	Pitch
3 Alps PS	PS	12*
4 Alps PS	Italic	10,12,15
5 Alps PS	Double-Wide	10,12,15
6 Alps PS	Double-High	10,12,15
7 Alps PS	Superscript	10,12,15
8 Alps PS	Draft	10,12,15

Features Not Supported: Type-thru

Proportional Spacing Information:

Font(s) to be used: 3

Pitch to be used: 12*

Limitations: PS is a little jumpy. In order to get PS in near letter quality, right justification must be turned off.

Line Draw Information:

Fonts(s) to be used: All but Font 4.

Limitations: Font 6 vertical lines extend too far. Font 7 requires half-line spacing.

Special Notes: Turn all DIP switches off.

AMT Office Printer

Type: Dot Matrix

Defined as: AMT Office Printer (IBM Color)

Emulating: IBM Color

Fonts Assigned:

Character Table	Attributes	Pitch
1 IBM Graphics	NLQ	10
2 IBM Graphics	Compressed	17
3 AMT Office Printer	Pica PS	11*
4 IBM Graphics	Elite PS	13*
5 IBM Graphics	Italic	12
6 IBM Graphics .	Double-Wide, Double-High	6
7 IBM Graphics	Double-High	12
8 AMT Office Printer	Draft	12

Proportional Spacing Information:

Font(s) to be used: 3,4

Pitch to be used: 11*,13*

Line Draw Information:

Font(s) to be used: 1,2,4,6,7,8

Apple DMP and Apple Imagewriter

Type: Dot Matrix

Defined as: Apple Imagewriter/DMP

Fonts Assigned:

	Character Table	Attributes	Pitch
1	Apple Line Draw	Internal	10,12,15
2	IBM Graphics	Headline (Double-Wide) 5 pitch	10
3	Apple Elite PS	Apple Elite PS	13*
4	IBM Graphics	Pica PS	11
5	IBM Graphics	9 pitch	10
6	IBM Graphics	13.4 pitch	10
7	IBM Graphics	17 pitch	10
8	Apple Line Draw	ND	ND

Features Not Supported: Double Underline, Type-thru

Proportional Spacing Information:

Font(s) to be used: 3,4

Pitch to be used: 13*,11

Limitations: Font 4 Pica PS will not right justify. Do not use an asterisk after the pitch with font 4.

Line Draw Information:

Font(s) to be used: All

Limitations: Must use half-line spacing.

Apple Imagewriter II

Type: Dot Matrix

Defined as: Apple Imagewriter II

Fonts Assigned:

Character Table	Attributes	Pitch
1 Apple Line Draw	NLQ	10,12,15
2 IBM Graphics	Draft (standard)	10,12,15
3 Apple Elite PS	Elite PS	13*
4 IBM Graphics	Half-High	10
5 IBM Graphics	Semi-Condensed	10
6 IBM Graphics	Headline (Double-Wide)	10
7 IBM Graphics	Extended	10
8 Apple Line Draw	High Speed Draft	10,12,15

Features Not Supported: Double Underline, Type-thru

Proportional Spacing Information:

Font(s) to be used: 3

Pitch to be used: 13*

Line Draw Information:

Font(s) to be used: 1,8

Limitations: Must use half-line spacing.

Apple LaserWriter Helvetica Portrait or Landscape

Type: Laser — Postscript

Defined as: LaserWriter Helvetica Portrait or Landscape — 9600 Baud

Fonts Assigned:

Character Table	Attributes	Pitch
1 Helvetica 11pt	Helvetica 11pt	13*
2 Helvetica Oblique 11pt	Helvetica-Oblique 11pt	13*
3 Helvetica Bold 11pt	Helvetica-Bold 11pt	13*
4 Helvetica Bold Oblique 11pt	Helvetica-Bold Oblique 11pt	13*
5 Helvetica 8pt	Helvetica 8pt	18*
6 Helvetica Oblique 8pt	Helvetica-Oblique 8pt	18*
7 Helvetica 5pt	Helvetica 5pt	22*
8 Helvetica Bold 17pt	Helvetica-Bold 17pt	8*

Features Not Supported: Double Underline, Line Draw, Type-thru

Proportional Spacing Information:

Font(s) to be used: All

Pitch to be used: See above

Special Notes: Must copy INITLWRT.PS file to the printer to set it for hardware handshaking. The printer must have ROM Rev 2 and be hooked to an IBM with a serial cable to use the file. (Check printer status sheet for Rev #). The file only needs to be run once unless you change the printer from hardware handshaking. See Chapter 5 for more information.

Apple LaserWriter Times Roman Portrait or Landscape

Type: Laser — Postscript

Defined as: LaserWriter Times Portrait or Landscape — 9600 Baud

Fonts Assigned:

	Character Table	Attributes	Pitch
1	Times 12pt	Times Roman 12pt	13*
2	Times Italic 12pt	Times-Italic 12pt	13*
3	Times Bold 12pt	Times-Bold 12pt	13*
4	Times Bold Italic 12pt	Times-Bold Italic 12pt	13*
5	Times 9pt	Times Roman 9pt	18*
6	Times Italic 9pt	Times-Italic 9pt	18*
7	Times 5pt	Times Roman 5pt	22*
8	Times Bold 18pt	Times-Bold 18pt	8*

Features Not Supported: Double Underline, Line Draw, Type-thru

Proportional Spacing Information:

Font(s) to be used: All

Pitch to be used: See above

Special Notes: Must copy INITLWRT.PS file to the printer to set it for hardware handshaking. The printer must have ROM Rev 2 and be hooked to an IBM with a serial cable to use the file. (Check printer status sheet for Rev #.) The file only needs to be run once unless you change the printer from hardware handshaking. See Chapter 5 for more information.

AST TurboLaser

Type: Laser

Defined as: AST TurboLaser Portrait/Landscape

Fonts Assigned:

	Character Table	Attributes	Pitch
1	AST Line Draw	Courier	10
2	AST Line Draw	Courier Italic	10
3	AST Line Draw	Courier 7pt	15
4	AST Line Draw	Courier 9pt	12
5	AST Line Draw	Letter Gothic	12
6	AST Line Draw	Letter Gothic Italic	12
7	AST Line Draw	Letter Gothic 7pt	17
8	AST Line Draw	ND	ND

Features Not Supported: Type-thru, Foreign Characters

Proportional Spacing Information: Not supported with Line Draw.

Line Draw Information:

Font(s) to be used: All

Special Notes: To use this definition the following fonts must be downloaded: PC7, PC9, PC12I, PG7, PG12, PG12I. To use the Landscape definition, download these fonts: LC7, LC9, LC12, LC12I, LG7, LG12, LG12I.

AST TurboLaser Dutch

Type: Laser

Defined as: AST TurboLaser Dutch PS

Fonts Assigned:

	Character Table	Attributes	Pitch
1	AST Dutch 10 PS	Dutch 10pt	14*
2	AST Dutch10I PS	Dutch 10pt Italic	14*
3	AST Dutch 8 PS	Dutch 8pt	16*/18*
4	AST Dutch14B PS	Dutch 14pt Bold	10*
5	AST Dutch24B PS	Dutch 24pt Bold	7*
6	AST Dutch24B PS	6th font downloaded	ND
7	Standard ASCII	ND	ND
8	Standard ASCII	ND	ND

Features Not Supported: Double Underline, Line Draw, Type-thru, Foreign Characters

Proportional Spacing Information:

Font(s) to be used: 1,2,3,4,5

Pitch to be used: See above

Special Notes: To use this definition, download the following fonts: PD10, PD10I, PD8, PD14B, PD24B.

AST TurboLaser Swiss

Type: Laser

Defined as: AST TurboLaser Swiss PS

Fonts Assigned:

	Character Table	Attributes	Pitch
1	AST Swiss 10 PS	Swiss 10pt	13*/14*
2	AST Swiss10I PS	Swiss 10pt Italic	13*/14*
3	AST Swiss 8 PS	Swiss 8pt	16*/18*
4	AST Swiss12B PS	Swiss 12pt Bold	12*
5	AST Swiss14B PS	Swiss 14pt Bold	10*
6	AST Swiss18B PS	Swiss 18pt Bold	7*/8*
7	AST Swiss24B PS	Swiss 24pt Bold	7*
8	AST Swiss24B PS	Swiss 36pt Bold	5*

Features Not Supported: Double Underline, Line Draw, Type-thru, Foreign Characters

Proportional Spacing Information:

Font(s) to be used: All

Pitch to be used: See above

Limitations: No right justification in font 8.

Special Notes: To use this definition, download the following fonts: PS10, PS10I, PS8, PS12B, PS14B, PS18B, PS24B, PS36B.

Brother HR-1

Type: Daisy Wheel

Defined as: Brother HR-1

Fonts Assigned:

Character Table	Attributes	Pitch
1 Bro HR-1 AmEng	Depends on wheel used	10,12,15
2 Bro HR-1 AmEng	Depends on wheel used	10,12,15
3 Bro HR-1 AmEng	Depends on wheel used	10,12,15
4 Bro HR-1 AmEng	Depends on wheel used	10,12,15
5 Bro HR-1 AmEng	Depends on wheel used	10,12,15
6 Bro HR-1 AmEng	Depends on wheel used	10,12,15
7 Bro HR-1 AmEng	Depends on wheel used	10,12,15
8 Bro HR-1 AmEng	Depends on wheel used	10,12,15

Features Not Supported: Double Underline, Line Draw, Type-thru, 6/8 LPI, Foreign Characters, Proportional Spacing

Brother HR-15XL

Type: Daisy Wheel

Defined as: Brother HR15XL/20/Dynax DX-15

Fonts Assigned:

Character Table	Attributes	Pitch
1 Standard ASCII	Depends on wheel used	10,12,15
2 Standard ASCII	Depends on wheel used	10,12,15
3 BR Anelia PS	Anelia PS	12*
4 Standard ASCII	Depends on wheel used	10,12,15
5 Standard ASCII	Depends on wheel used	10,12,15
6 Standard ASCII	Depends on wheel used	10,12,15
7 Standard ASCII	Depends on wheel used	10,12,15
8 Standard ASCII	Depends on wheel used	10,12,15

Features Not Supported: Line Draw, Foreign Characters

Proportional Spacing Information:

Font(s) to be used: 3

Pitch to be used: 12*

Limitations: Must have the BR Anelia PS wheel. PS is very slow.

Sheet Feeder Information: If you have a CF100 sheet feeder you may have problems with the top margin. In Setup Menu (WP/S), change top margin to "0" and choose the Brother sheet feeder definition. Number of extra lines = 0, position of left edge of paper = 6, bins = 1. These settings may vary. Also check the DIP switches: Left Bank—all closed. Right Bank—5 and 7 open, all others closed. You cannot have less than a 1 inch top margin when using the sheet feeder.

Brother HR-35

Type: Daisy Wheel

Defined as: Dynax DX25/Brother HR-35

Fonts Assigned:

	Character Table	Attributes	Pitch
1	ASCII Backspace	Depends on wheel used	10,12,15
2	ASCII Backspace	Depends on wheel used	10,12,15
3	BR Anelia PS	Anelia PS	13*
4	ASCII Backspace	Depends on wheel used	10,12,15
5	ASCII Backspace	Depends on wheel used	10,12,15
6	ASCII Backspace	Depends on wheel used	10,12,15
7	ASCII Backspace	Depends on wheel used	10,12,15
8	ASCII Backspace	Depends on wheel used	10,12,15

Features Not Supported: Line Draw, Foreign Characters

Proportional Spacing Information:

Font(s) to be used: 3

Pitch to be used: 13*

Limitations: Must have BR Anelia PS wheel.

Brother Twinwriter

Try: Dynax Fortis DH-45 definition

C.Itoh 8510 Prowriter

Type: Dot Matrix

Defined as: C.Itoh 8510 Prowriter

Fonts Assigned:

	Character Table	Attributes	Pitch
1	C.Itoh 8510 PS	Draft	10,12,15
2	C.Itoh 8510 PS	Draft	10,12,15
3	C.Itoh 8510 PS	PS	13*-15*
4	C.Itoh 8510 PS	Draft	10,12,15
5	C.Itoh 8510 PS	Draft	10,12,15
6	C.Itoh 8510 PS	Double-Wide (5,6,8)	10,12,15
7	C.Itoh 8510 PS	Draft	10,12,15
8	C.Itoh 8510 PS	Draft	10,12,15

Features Not Supported: Double Underline, Type-thru, Foreign Characters

Proportional Spacing Information:

Font(s) to be used: 3

Pitch to be used: 13*-15*

Line Draw Information:

Font(s) to be used: 1,2,4,5,6,7,8

Limitations: No double-line draw. Requires half-line spacing in all fonts.

Special Notes: Setting 15 pitch actually selects condensed mode (17 pitch). Printing pauses between lines when using proportional spacing or right justification because it calculates the microspacing before it prints.

C.Itoh C-310 P

Type: Dot Matrix

Defined as: C.Itoh C-310 P

Fonts Assigned:

	Character Table	Attributes	Pitch
1	C.Itoh Extended	LQ	10,12,15
2	C.Itoh Extended	NLQ Italic	10,12,15
3	C.Itoh Extended	PS	11*
4	C.Itoh Extended	NLQ Double-Wide	10,12,15
5	C.Itoh Extended	LQ Blue	10,12,15
6	C.Itoh Extended	LQ Green	10,12,15
7	C.Itoh Extended	LQ Red	10,12,15
8	C.Itoh Extended	Draft	10,12,15

Features Not Supported: Type-thru

Proportional Spacing Information:

Font(s) to be used: 3

Pitch to be used: 11*

Line Draw Information:

Font(s) to be used: All

Limitations: Fonts 5, 6, and 7 require half-line spacing.

C.Itoh C-310 XP

Type: Dot Matrix

Defined as: C.Itoh C-310 XP

Fonts Assigned:

	Character Table	Attributes	Pitch
1	IBM Proprinter	NLQ	10,12,15
2	IBM Proprinter	NLQ Red	10,12,15
3	C.Itoh 310 XP	NLQ PS	11*
4	IBM Proprinter	NLQ Double-Wide	10,12,15
5	IBM Proprinter	NLQ Violet	10,12,15
6	IBM Proprinter	NLQ Blue	10,12,15
7	IBM Proprinter	NLQ Green	10,12,15
8	IBM Proprinter	Draft	10,12,15

Features Not Supported: Type-thru, Line Draw

Proportional Spacing Information:

Font(s) to be used: 3

Pitch to be used: 11*

C.Itoh C310EP

Type: Dot Matrix

Defined as: C.Itoh C310EP

Fonts Assigned:

	Character Table	Attributes	Pitch
1	C.Itoh Extended	NLQ	10,12,15
2	C.Itoh Extended	Draft	10,12,15
3	C.Itoh Extended	NLQ PS	11*
4	C.Itoh Extended	Emphasized	10,12,15
5	C.Itoh Extended	NLQ Double-Wide (5,6,9)	10,12,15
6	C.Itoh Extended	Draft Double-Wide (5,6,9)	10,12,15
7	C.Itoh Extended	Condensed	12,15
8	C.Itoh Extended	Draft	10,12,15

Features Not Supported: Type-thru

Proportional Spacing Information:

Font(s) to be used: 3

Pitch to be used: 11*

Line Draw Information:

Font(s) to be used: All

Limitations: Fonts 5, 6, and 7 require half-line spacing.

C.Itoh C-715

Type: Dot Matrix

Defined as: C.Itoh C-715

Emulating: Epson LQ-1000 identity card (v-1.31)

Fonts Assigned:

Character Table	Attributes	Pitch
1 C.Itoh C-715 PS	LQ	10,12,15
2 C.Itoh C-715 PS	LQ Italic	10,12,15
3 C.Itoh C-715 PS	LQ PS	11*
4 C.Itoh C-715 PS	LQ Double-High	10,12,15
5 C.Itoh C-715 PS	LQ Red	10,12,15
6 C.Itoh C-715 PS	LQ Blue	10,12,15
7 C.Itoh C-715 PS	LQ Violet	10,12,15
8 C.Itoh C-715 PS	Draft	10,12,15

Features Not Supported: Line Draw, Type-thru, Foreign Characters

Proportional Spacing Information:

Font(s) to be used: 3

Pitch to be used: 11*

Special Notes: Double underline will only work in 10 pitch, LQ., non-PS. and regular height. For other colors insert code: <27>r(n) n= 0—black, 1—red, 2—blue, 3—violet, 4—yellow, 5— orange, 6—green. Most features require paper to be fed using either the "push tractor feed" or "friction" method.

C.Itoh C-815

Type: Dot Matrix

Defined as: C.Itoh C-815

Fonts Assigned:

Character Table	Attributes	Pitch
1 C.Itoh C-815 PS	NLQ	10,12,15
2 C.Itoh C-815 PS	Superscript	10,12,15
3 C.Itoh C-815 PS	NLQ PS	10*
4 C.Itoh C-815 PS	NLQ Italic	10,12,15
5 C.Itoh C-815 PS	NLQ Double-Wide (5,6)	10,12
6 C.Itoh C-815 PS	NLQ Double-High	10,12,15
7 C.Itoh C-815 PS	NLQ Double-Wide, Double-High (5)	10
8 C.Itoh C-815 PS	Draft	10,12,15

Features Not Supported: Type-thru, Line Draw

Proportional Spacing Information:

Font(s) to be used: 3

Pitch to be used: 10*

C.Itoh D10-40

Type: Daisy Wheel

Defined as: C.Itoh D10-40

Fonts Assigned:

	Character Table	*Attributes*	*Pitch*
1	ASCII Backspace	Depends on wheel used	10,12,15
2	ASCII Backspace	Depends on wheel used	10,12,15
3	Diablo 630 Bold PS	Diablo 630 Bold PS	13*
4	Diablo Goth PS	Diablo Gothic PS	13*
5	Diablo Rom PS	Diablo Roman PS	13*
6	Diablo Multi-L	Diablo Multi-Lingual	10,12,15
7	Diablo Cubic PS	Diablo Cubic PS	13*
8	ASCII Backspace	Depends on wheel used	10,12,15

Features Not Supported: Line Draw, Type-thru

Proportional Spacing Information:

Font(s) to be used: 3,4,5,7

Pitch to be used: 13*

Limitations: Must use correct print wheel. See above.

C.Itoh Prowriter Jr. Plus

Type: Dot Matrix

Defined as: C.Itoh Prowriter Jr. Plus

Fonts Assigned:

	Character Table	*Attributes*	*Pitch*
1	IBM Graphics	NLQ	10
2	Dot Matrix 1/60	Enhanced	10
3	Epson FX NorPS	PS	11*

Character Table	Attributes	Pitch
4 Epson FX&Type3	Italic	10
5 IBM Graphics	Expanded (5)	10
6 Epson FX&Type3	Expanded Italic (5)	10
7 IBM Graphics	Footnote	15
8 IBM Graphics	Draft	10,12,15

Features Not Supported: Type-thru

Proportional Spacing Information:

Font(s) to be used: 3

Pitch to be used: 11*

Limitations: PS is slow and jerky when right justified. Better to turn off right justification.

Line Draw Information:

Font(s) to be used: 1,2,5,8

Limitations: Some fonts need 8 lines per inch or half-line spacing.

Special Notes: 15 pitch returns 17 pitch.

C.Itoh Starwriter/Printmaster

Type: Daisy Wheel

Defined as: C.Itoh Starwriter/Printmaster

Fonts Assigned:

Character Table	Attributes	Pitch
1 ASCII Backspace	Depends on wheel used	10,12,15
2 ASCII Backspace	Depends on wheel used	10,12,15
3 Standard PS	Depends on wheel used	13*
4 ASCII Backspace	Depends on wheel used	10,12,15
5 ASCII Backspace	Depends on wheel used	10,12,15
6 ASCII Backspace	Depends on wheel used	10,12,15
7 ASCII Backspace	Depends on wheel used	10,12,15
8 ASCII Backspace	Depends on wheel used	10,12,15

Features Not Supported: Line Draw

Proportional Spacing Information:

Font(s) to be used: 3

Pitch to be used: 13*

Sheet Feeder Information: Define a sheet feeder as continuous with the page length set at 90 lines.

Canon A1 Courier

Type: Laser

Defined as: Canon A1 Courier 10 N

Fonts Assigned:

	Character Table	Attributes	Pitch
1	A1 Normal	Courier	10
2	A1 Normal	Double-High Footnote	15
3	A1 Normal	Courier Italic	10
4	A1 Normal	Footnote	15
5	A1 Normal	Double-High, Double-Wide	5
6	A1 Normal	Double-High	10
7	A1 Line Draw	Courier Line Draw	10
8	A1 Normal	Double-High, Double-Wide Footnote	8

Features Not Supported: Type-thru, Proportional Spacing

Line Draw Information:

Font(s) to be used: 7

Limitations: Amount of line draw text is limited by printer RAM. No double-line draw.

Special Notes: Use Canon A1 Courier 10 R for the same font rotated.

Canon A1 Courier N/R

Type: Laser

Defined as: Canon A1 Courier 10 N/R

Fonts Assigned:

	Character Table	Attributes	Pitch
1	A1 Normal N/R	Courier Port	10
2	A1 Normal N/R	Courier Italic Port	10
3	A1 Normal N/R	Courier Footnote Port	17
4	A1 Normal N/R	ND	ND
5	A1 Normal N/R	Courier Land	10
6	A1 Normal N/R	Courier Italic Land	10
7	A1 Normal N/R	Courier Footnote Land	17
8	A1 Normal N/R	ND	ND

Features Not Supported: Type-thru, Proportional Spacing

Line Draw Information:

Font(s) to be used: All

Canon A1 Elite

Type: Laser

Defined as: Canon A1 Elite 12 N

Fonts Assigned:

	Character Table	Attributes	Pitch
1	A1 Normal	Elite	12
2	A1 Normal	Double-High Footnote	15
3	A1 Normal	Elite Italic	12
4	A1 Normal	Footnote	15
5	A1 Normal	Double-High, Double-Wide	6
6	A1 Normal	Double-High	12
7	A1 Line Draw	Elite Line Draw	12
8	A1 Normal	Double-High, Double-Wide Footnote	8

Features Not Supported: Type-thru, Proportional Spacing

Line Draw Information:

Font(s) to be used: 7

Limitations: No double-line draw.

Special Notes: Use Canon A1 Elite 12 R for the same font rotated.

Canon A1 Elite N/R

Type: Laser

Defined as: Canon A1 Elite 12 N/R

Fonts Assigned:

	Character Table	*Attributes*	*Pitch*
1	A1 Normal N/R	Elite Port	12
2	A1 Normal N/R	Elite Italic Port	12
3	A1 Normal N/R	Elite Footnote Port	17
4	A1 Normal N/R	ND	ND
5	A1 Normal N/R	Elite Land	12
6	A1 Normal N/R	Elite Italic Land	12
7	A1 Normal N/R	Elite Footnote Land	17
8	A1 Normal N/R	ND	ND

Features Not Supported: Type-thru, Proportional Spacing

Line Draw Information:

Font(s) to be used: All

Canon A1 Garland

Type: Laser

Defined as: Canon A1 Garland PS N

Fonts Assigned:

	Character Table	*Attributes*	*Pitch*
1	A1 Garland PS	Garland PS 10pt	12*
2	A1 Garland Footnote	Double-High Footnote	15*
3	A1 Garland PS	Garland PS Italic 10pt	12*
4	A1 Garland Footnote	Footnote	15*
5	A1 Garland PS DW	Double-High, Double-Wide	5*/6*
6	A1 Garland PS	Double-High	12*
7	A1 Line Draw	Courier Line Draw	10
8	A1 Garland Footnote DW	Double-High, Double-Wide Footnote	10*

Features Not Supported: Type-thru

Proportional Spacing Information:

Font(s) to be used: 1,2,3,4,5,6,8

Pitch to be used: See above

Line Draw Information:

Font(s) to be used: 7

Limitations: No double-line draw.

Special Notes: Use Canon A1 Garland PS R for the same fonts rotated.

Canon A1 Line Printer

Type: Laser

Defined as: Canon A1 Line Printer N/R

Fonts Assigned:

	Character Table	Attributes	Pitch
1	A1 Normal N/R	Line Printer Land	13.6
2	A1 Normal N/R	Courier Bold Land	10
3	A1 Normal N/R	Courier Footnote Land	15
4	A1 Normal N/R	Courier Footnote Land	17
5	A1 Normal N/R	Courier Footnote Land	20
6	A1 Normal N/R	Line Printer Port	13.6
7	A1 Normal N/R	Courier Bold Port	10
8	A1 Normal N/R	Courier Footnote Normal	20

Features Not Supported: Type-thru, Proportional Spacing

Line Draw Information:

Font(s) to be used: All

Canon A1 Pica

Type: Laser

Defined as: Canon A1 Pica 10 N

Fonts Assigned:

Character Table	Attributes	Pitch
1 A1 Normal	Pica	10
2 A1 Normal	Double-High Footnote	15
3 A1 Normal	Pica Italic	10
4 A1 Normal	Footnote	15
5 A1 Normal	Double-High, Double-Wide	5
6 A1 Normal	Double-High	10
7 A1 Line Draw	Pica Line Draw	10
8 A1 Normal	Double-High, Double-Wide Footnote	8

Features Not Supported: Type-thru, Proportional Spacing

Line Draw Information:

Font(s) to be used: 7

Limitations: No double-line draw.

Special Notes: Use Canon A1 Pica 10 R for the same fonts rotated.

Canon A1 Pica N/R

Type: Laser

Defined as: Canon A1 Pica 10 N/R

Fonts Assigned:

Character Table	Attributes	Pitch
1 A1 Normal N/R	Pica Port	10
2 A1 Normal N/R	Pica Italic Port	10
3 A1 Normal N/R	Pica Footnote Port	17
4 A1 Normal N/R	ND	ND
5 A1 Normal N/R	Pica Land	10
6 A1 Normal N/R	Pica Italic Land	10
7 A1 Normal N/R	Pica Footnote Land	17
8 A1 Normal N/R	ND	ND

Features Not Supported: Type-thru, Proportional Spacing

Line Draw Information:

Font(s) to be used: All

Canon LBP-8 II

Type: Laser

Defined as: Canon LBP-8 II

Fonts Assigned:

	Character Table	Attributes	Pitch
1	A1 Normal N/R	Courier 10pt	10,12
2	A1 Normal N/R	Courier Italic 10pt	10,12
3	A1 Normal N/R	Courier Footnote 8pt	12,15,17
4	A1 Normal N/R	Double-High	10,12
5	A1 Normal N/R	Double-Wide	7
6	A1 Normal N/R	Double-High Double-Wide	7
7	A1 Normal N/R	ND	ND
8	A1 Normal N/R	ND	ND

Features Not Supported: Type-thru, Proportional Spacing

Line Draw Information:

Font(s) to be used: All (but 3 is limited)

Canon LBP-8 II Swiss 721 P

Type: Laser

Defined as: Canon LBP-8 II Swiss721 P

Fonts Assigned:

	Character Table	Attributes	Pitch
1	Canon Swiss721N	Swiss721 10pt	13*
2	Canon Swiss721I	Swiss721 Italic 10pt	13*
3	Canon Swiss721B	Swiss721 Bold 10pt	13*
4	Canon 721 24B	Swiss721 24pt	7*
5	Canon 721 24B	Swiss721 30pt	5*
6	Canon Swiss721N	Swiss721 Double-High	13*
7	Canon Swiss721N	Swiss721 Double-Wide	8*
8	Canon Swiss721N	Swiss721 Double-High, Double-Wide	8*

Features Not Supported: Type-thru

Proportional Spacing Information:

Font(s) to be used: All

Pitch to be used: See previous page

Line Draw Information:

Font(s) to be used: 1,3

Special Notes: Fonts 5, 7, and 8 have no right justification. Be sure to turn off right justification when using these fonts. Turning bold on uses font 3 (Bold 10pt), so you cannot use bold in fonts 4 through 8. If you bold in font 2 (italics), bold will be Roman.

Center Piece Accounting & Tax HP

Type: Laser

Defined as: CenterPiece Acct / Tax for HP

Fonts Assigned:

	Character Table	Attributes	Pitch
1	LaserJet-B Normal	Tms Rmn 10	13*
2	LaserJet-B Italic	Tms Rmn Italic 10	14*
3	ManTal Swiss 14	Helvetica 14 Bold	10*
4	ManTal Swiss 12	Helvetica 12 Bold	12*
5	ManTal Swiss 8N	Helvetica 8	19*
6	ManTal Swiss 6	Helvetica 6	24*
7	Center Piece	Prestige Elite Land	12
8	Center Piece	Prestige Line Draw	12

Features Not Supported: Type-thru, Foreign Characters

Proportional Spacing Information:

Font(s) to be used: 1-6

Pitch to be used: See above

Line Draw Information:

Font(s) to be used: 7,8

Limitations: Font 7 line draw is in landscape.

Centronics 351

Type: Dot Matrix

Defined as: Centronics 351

Fonts Assigned:

Character Table	Attributes	Pitch
1 Centronics 351	Draft Elite	10,12,15
2 Centronics 351	Draft Pica	10,12,15
3 Centronics 351	PS	11*
4 Centronics 351	Double-Wide	10
5 Centronics 351	Double-Wide Compressed	10
6 Centronics 351	Double-Wide Enhanced	10
7 Centronics 351	Enhanced Elite	10
8 Centronics 351	Double-Wide Compressed	10

Features Not Supported: Double Underline, Line Draw, Type-thru, Advance

Proportional Spacing Information:

Font(s) to be used: 3

Pitch to be used: 11*

Centronics GLP II

Type: Dot Matrix

Defined as: Centronics GLP II

Fonts Assigned:

Character Table	Attributes	Pitch
1 Epson FX&Type3	NLQ	10
2 Dot Matrix 1/60	Emphasized	10
3 Epson FX Normal PS	Emphasized PS	11*
4 Epson FX Italic PS	Emphasized Italic	10
5 Epson FX&Type3	Emphasized Double-Wide (5)	10
6 Epson FX&Type3	Emphasized Double-Wide Italic (5)	10
7 Epson FX&Type3	Double-Strike	10,12,15
8 Epson FX&Type3	Draft	10,12,15

Features Not Supported: Double Underline, Type-thru, Advance, Overstrike

Proportional Spacing Information:

Font(s) to be used: 3

Pitch to be used: 11*

Limitations: No right justification in PS.

Line Draw Information:

Font(s) to be used: 2

Limitations: Must use half-line spacing.

Special Notes: NLQ cannot have bold and superscript/subscript on the same line.

Citizen 120D

Type: Dot Matrix

Defined as: Citizen 120D

Fonts Assigned:

	Character Table	Attributes	Pitch
1	Epson FX&Type3	NLQ	10,12
2	Dot Matrix 1/60	Emphasized	10,12,15
3	Epson Normal PS	PS	11*
4	Epson FX&Type3	Italic	10,12,15
5	Epson FX&Type3	NLQ Expanded (5,6,8.5)	10,12,15
6	Epson FX&Type3	NLQ Expanded Italic (5,6,8.5)	10,12,15
7	Epson FX&Type3	Footnote	10,12,15
8	Epson FX&Type3	Draft	10,12,15

Features Not Supported: Double Underline, Type-thru

Proportional Spacing Information:

Font(s) to be used: 3

Pitch to be used: 11*

Line Draw Information:

Font(s) to be used: 2

Limitations: Use half-line spacing.

Special Notes: Setting 15 pitch returns 17 pitch.

Citizen MSP-15

Type: Dot Matrix

Defined as: Citizen MSP-15

Fonts Assigned:

Character Table	Attributes	Pitch
1 IBM Graphics	NLQ	10,12,15
2 Dot Matrix 1/60	NLQ Italic	10,12,15
3 IBM Graphics	Emphasized	10,12,15
4 IBM Graphics	Double-Strike	10,12,15
5 IBM Graphics	NLQ Expanded	5,6,7
6 IBM Graphics	Expanded	5,6,7
7 IBM Graphics	Subscript	10,12,15
8 IBM Graphics	Draft	10,12,15

Features Not Supported: Type-thru, Foreign Characters, Proportional Spacing

Line Draw Information:

Font(s) to be used: 2,3,6,8,

Limitations: Use half-line spacing for font 2.

Citizen MSP-25

Type: Dot Matrix

Defined as: Citizen MSP-25

Fonts Assigned:

Character Table	Attributes	Pitch
1 IBM Graphics	NLQ	10,12,15
2 Dot Matrix 1/60	Enhanced	10,12,15
3 Epson FX NorPS	NLQ PS	13*
4 IBM Graphics	NLQ Italics	10,12,15
5 IBM Graphics	NLQ Double-Wide, Double-High (5,6,8)	10,12,15
6 IBM Graphics	NLQ Double-High	10,12,15
7 IBM Graphics	Footnote	10,12,15
8 IBM Graphics	Draft	10,12,15

Features Not Supported: Type-thru, Foreign Characters

Proportional Spacing Information:

Font(s) to be used: 3

Pitch to be used: 13*

Line Draw Information:

Font(s) to be used: 2,7,8

Limitations: Use half-line spacing for fonts 2 and 8.

Special Notes: 15 pitch returns 17 characters per inch. Do not use 8 lines per inch with font 5 or 6. Bold may be fuzzy when using a tractor feeder.

Citizen Premiere 35

Type: Daisy Wheel

Defined as: Citizen Premiere 35

Fonts Assigned:

	Character Table	Attributes	Pitch
1	Standard ASCII	Depends on wheel used	10,12,15
2	Standard ASCII	Depends on wheel used	10,12,15
3	Dia630 Bold PS	Diablo 630 Bold PS	13*
4	Standard ASCII	Depends on wheel used	10,12,15
5	Standard ASCII	Depends on wheel used	10,12,15
6	Standard ASCII	Depends on wheel used	10,12,15
7	Standard ASCII	Depends on wheel used	10,12,15
8	Daisy Line Draw	Depends on wheel used	10,12,15

Features Not Supported: Type-thru, Foreign Characters

Proportional Spacing Information:

Font(s) to be used: 3

Pitch to be used: 13*

Limitations: Must use the Diablo Bold PS Print Wheel.

Line Draw Information:

Font(s) to be used: 8

Limitations: Heavy single-line draw only.

Sheet Feeder Information: Define the sheet feeder as Diablo Single/Dual/Envl. Number of extra lines = 0, Position of left edge of paper = 5, Number of bins = 2.

Special Notes: The sheet feeder gives a 1-inch top margin so set top margin at 0 in WordPerfect.

Citizen Tribute 224

Type: Dot Matrix

Defined as: Citizen Tribute 224

Fonts Assigned:

	Character Table	Attributes	Pitch
1	Citizen 224	NLQ Courier	10
2	Citizen 224	NLQ Prestige Elite	12
3	Citizen 224	NLQ Courier PS	11*
4	Citizen 224	NLQ Courier Italic	10
5	Citizen 224	NLQ Courier Double-Wide	10
6	Citizen 224	NLQ Courier Double-Wide Italic	10
7	Citizen 224	Condensed (17)	10
8	Citizen 224	Draft	10,12

Features Not Supported: Line Draw, Type-thru, Foreign Characters

Proportional Spacing Information:

Font(s) to be used: 3

Pitch to be used: 11*

Cordata LP300X Bookman

Type: Laser

Defined as: Cordata LP300X Bookman PS

Fonts Assigned:

Character Table	Attributes	Pitch
1 Cordata Bookman9P	Bookman 9pt	13*,14*
2 Cordata Bookman9I	Bookman 9pt Italic	13*,14*
3 Cordata Bookman12P	Bookman 12pt	11*,12*
4 Cordata Bookman12B	Bookman 12pt Bold	11*,12*
5 Cordata Bookman12I	Bookman 12pt Italic	11*,12*
6 Cordata Bookman18B	Bookman 18pt Bold	7*,8*
7 Cordata Laser	PC Sans Serif	19
8 Cordata Bookman9B	Bookman 9pt Bold	13*,14*

Features Not Supported: Double Underline, Type-thru, Advance

Proportional Spacing Information:

Font(s) to be used: 1,2,3,4,5,6,8

Pitch to be used: See above

Line Draw Information:

Font(s) to be used: 7

Cordata LP300X Courier

Type: Laser

Defined as: Cordata LP300X Courier

Fonts Assigned:

Character Table	Attributes	Pitch
1 Cordata Laser	Courier 9pt	12
2 Cordata Laser	Courier 10pt	10
3 Cordata Laser	Courier 10pt Bold	10
4 Cordata Laser	Gothic 9pt	12
5 Cordata Laser	PC 7	18
6 Cordata MX9M	MX 9 Medium	12
7 Cordata Laser	Pi 10pt	10
8 Cordata Laser	Courier 9pt Bold	12

Features Not Supported: Type-thru, Advance, Proportional Spacing

Line Draw Information:

Font(s) to be used: 5,6

Special Notes: Every font is pitch-specific. For 1-inch margins: 12 pitch use 12,90; 10 pitch use 10,74; 18 pitch use 18,135.

Cordata LP300X Karena

Type: Laser

Defined as: Cordata LP300X Karena PS

Fonts Assigned:

	Character Table	Attributes	Pitch
1	Cordata KR10	Karena PS 10pt	12*/13*
2	Cordata KR6	Karena PS 6pt	19*
3	Cordata KR8	Karena PS 8pt	14*
4	Cordata KR12	Karena PS 12pt	12*
5	Cordata KR14B	Karena PS 14pt Bold	9*/10*
6	Cordata KR18B	Karena PS 18pt Bold	7*-9*
7	Cordata KR18B	Karena PS 24pt Bold	6*
8	Cordata KR10B	Karena PS 10pt Bold	12*/13*

Features Not Supported: Double Underline, Line Draw, Type-thru, Advance, Foreign Characters

Proportional Spacing Information:

Font(s) to be used: All

Pitch to be used: See above

Limitations: No right justification in font 7.

Cordata LP300X Swiss

Type: Laser

Defined as: Cordata LP300X Swiss PS

Fonts Assigned:

Character Table	Attributes	Pitch
1 Cordata SW10	Swiss PS 10pt	13*
2 Cordata SW10I	Swiss PS 10pt Italic	13*
3 Cordata SW6	Swiss PS 6pt	20*
4 Cordata SW8	Swiss PS 8pt	18*
5 Cordata SW14B	Swiss PS 14pt Bold	9*/10*
6 Cordata SW18B	Swiss PS 18pt Bold	7*/8*
7 Cordata SW24B2	Swiss PS 24pt Bold	6*
8 Cordata SW10B	Swiss PS 10pt Bold	13*

Features Not Supported: Double Underline, Line Draw, Type-thru, Advance, Foreign Characters

Proportional Spacing Information:

Font(s) to be used: All

Pitch to be used: See above

Cordata LP300X Taylor

Type: Laser

Defined as: Cordata LP300X Taylor

Fonts Assigned:

Character Table	Attributes	Pitch
1 Cordata Laser	Taylor 10pt	10
2 Cordata Laser	Taylor 8pt	12
3 Cordata Laser	Taylor 9pt Bold	12
4 Cordata SW18B	Swiss 18pt Bold	8*
5 Cordata SW18B	Swiss Outline 18pt	8*
6 Cordata SW18B	Swiss Display 20pt	8*
7 Cordata Laser	Casual 10pt	13*
8 Cordata Laser	Taylor 10pt Bold	10

Features Not Supported: Type-thru, Advance, Foreign Characters

Proportional Spacing Information:

Font(s) to be used: 4,5,6,7

Pitch to be used: See above

Limitations: Cannot get right justified PS text.

Line Draw Information:

Font(s) to be used: 1,2,3,8

Special Notes: The fixed-pitch fonts are pitch-specific. For 1-inch margins: for 10 pitch use 10,74; for 12 pitch use 12,90.

Cordata LP300X Text

Type: Laser

Defined as: Cordata LP300X Text PS

Fonts Assigned:

Character Table	Attributes	Pitch
1 Cordata TX10	Text PS 10pt	12*/13*
2 Cordata TX10I	Text PS 10pt Italic	12*/13*
3 Cordata TX6	Text PS 6pt	19*/20*
4 Cordata TX8	Text PS 8pt	14*/15*
5 Cordata TX8B	Text PS 8pt Bold	14*/15*
6 Cordata TX12	Text PS 12pt	11*/12*
7 Cordata TX18M	Text PS 18pt Medium-Bold	8*/9*
8 Cordata TX18B	Text PS 10pt Bold	12*/13*

Features Not Supported: Type-thru, Advance, Foreign Characters, Line Draw

Proportional Spacing Information:

Font(s) to be used: All

Pitch to be used: See above

Cosmo World Adeus CP-2000

Type: Daisy Wheel

Defined as: Cosmo World Adeus

Fonts Assigned:

Character Table	Attributes	Pitch
1 Standard ASCII	Depends on wheel used	10,12,15
2 Standard ASCII	Depends on wheel used	10,12,15
3 Standard ASCII	Depends on wheel used	13* or 12*

Character Table	Attributes	Pitch
4 Standard ASCII	Depends on wheel used	10,12,15
5 Standard ASCII	Depends on wheel used	10,12,15
6 Standard ASCII	Depends on wheel used	10,12,15
7 Standard ASCII	Depends on wheel used	10,12,15
8 Standard ASCII	Depends on wheel used	10,12,15

Features Not Supported: Line Draw, Type-thru, Foreign Characters

Proportional Spacing Information:

Font(s) to be used: 3

Pitch to be used: 13* or 12*

Daisy Systems' M45-Q (Qume)

Type: Daisy Wheel

Defined as: Daisy Systems' M45-Q (Qume)

Emulating: Qume

Fonts Assigned:

Character Table	Attributes	Pitch
1 Daisy Systems	Depends on wheel used	10,12,15
2 Daisy Systems	Depends on wheel used	10,12,15
3 Standard PS	Standard PS	13*
4 Diablo Gothic PS	Diablo Gothic PS	13*
5 Diablo Roman PS	Diablo Roman PS	13*
6 Diablo Cubic PS	Diablo Cubic PS	13*
7 ASCII Backspace	Depends on wheel used	10,12,15
8 Daisy Line Draw	Daisy Line Draw	10,12,15

Proportional Spacing Information:

Font(s) to be used: 3,4,5,6

Pitch to be used: 13*

Line Draw Information:

Font(s) to be used: 8

Limitations: No double-line draw.

Daisywriter

Type: Daisy Wheel

Defined as: Daisywriter

Fonts Assigned:

	Character Table	*Attributes*	*Pitch*
1	ASCII Backspace	Depends on wheel used	10,12,15
2	ASCII Backspace	Depends on wheel used	10,12,15
3	Dia630 Bold PS	Depends on wheel used	13*
4	Diablo Gothic PS	Depends on wheel used	13*
5	Diablo Roman PS	Depends on wheel used	13*
6	Diablo Multi-L	Depends on wheel used	10,12,15
7	ASCII Backspace	Depends on wheel used	10,12,15
8	ASCII Backspace	Depends on wheel used	10,12,15

Features Not Supported: Line Draw, Type-thru, Foreign Characters

Proportional Spacing Information:

Font(s) to be used: 3,4,5

Pitch to be used: 13*

Data General 6321

Type: Daisy Wheel

Defined as: Data General 6321

Fonts Assigned:

	Character Table	*Attributes*	*Pitch*
1	Standard ASCII	Depends on wheel used	10,12,15
2	Standard ASCII	Depends on wheel used	10,12,15
3	Standard ASCII	Depends on wheel used	10,12,15
4	Standard ASCII	Depends on wheel used	10,12,15
5	Standard ASCII	Depends on wheel used	10,12,15
6	Standard ASCII	Depends on wheel used	10,12,15
7	Standard ASCII	Depends on wheel used	10,12,15
8	Standard ASCII	Depends on wheel used	10,12,15

Features Not Supported: Line Draw, Foreign Characters, Proportional Spacing

Special Notes: The baud rate must be set to 300 or lower for use on a personal computer.

Data General Laser

Type: Laser

Defined as: Data General Laser

Fonts Assigned:

Character Table	Attributes	Pitch
1 A1 Normal	Courier	10
2 A1 Normal	Courier Italic	10
3 A1 Normal	Double-High Footnote	15
4 A1 Normal	Footnote	15
5 A1 Normal	Double-High, Double-Wide	5
6 A1 Normal	Double-High	10
7 A1 Normal	Courier Line Draw	10
8 A1 Normal	Double-High, Double-Wide Footnote	8

Features Not Supported: Type-thru, Redline/Strikeout, Proportional Spacing

Line Draw Information:

Font(s) to be used: 7

Limitations: Double-line draw is actually a heavy single line. The corners will not line up well.

Data General Courier 10 Normal/Rotated

Type: Laser

Defined as: Data General Courier 10 N or R

Fonts Assigned:

Character Table	Attributes	Pitch
1 A1 Normal	Courier	10
2 A1 Normal	Courier Italic	10
3 A1 Normal	Double-High Footnote	15
4 A1 Normal	Footnote	15

Character Table	Attributes	Pitch
5 A1 Normal	Double-High, Double-Wide	5
6 A1 Normal	Double-High	10
7 A1 Line Draw	Courier Line Draw	10
8 A1 Normal	Double-High, Double-Wide Footnote	8

Features Not Supported: Type-thru, Proportional Spacing

Line Draw Information:

Font(s) to be used: All

Limitations: Corners do not line up well with font 7. No double-line draw.

Sheet Feeder Information: Define as continuous.

Special Notes: Bold only in fonts 1, 5, and 6.

Data General Elite 12 Normal/Rotated

Type: Laser

Defined as: Data General Elite 12 N or 12 R

Fonts Assigned:

Character Table	Attributes	Pitch
1 A1 Normal	Elite	12
2 A1 Normal	Elite Italic	12
3 A1 Normal	Double-High, Footnote	15
4 A1 Normal	Footnote	15
5 A1 Normal	Double-High, Double-Wide	6
6 A1 Normal	Double-High	12
7 A1 Line Draw	Elite Line Draw	12
8 A1 Normal	Double-High Double-Wide Footnote	8

Features Not Supported: Type-thru, Proportional Spacing

Line Draw Information:

Font(s) to be used: 7

Special Notes: Bold only in fonts 1, 5, and 6.

Data General Garland PS Normal/Rotated

Type: Laser

Defined as: Data General Garland PS N or R

Fonts Assigned:

Character Table	Attributes	Pitch
1 A1 Garland PS	Garland PS 10pt	13*
2 A1 Garland PS	Garland PS Italic 10pt	13*
3 A1 Garland Footnote	Double-High Footnote	19*
4 A1 Garland Footnote	Footnote	19*
5 A1 Garland PS DW	Double-High, Double-Wide	7*
6 A1 Garland PS	Double-High	13*
7 A1 Line Draw	Courier Line Draw	10
8 A1 Garland Footnote D	Double-High, Double-Wide Footnote	10*

Features Not Supported: Type-thru

Proportional Spacing Information:

Font(s) to be used: 1,2,3,4,5,6,8

Pitch to be used: See above

Line Draw Information:

Font(s) to be used: 7

Special Notes: Bold only in fonts 1, 5, and 6.

Data General Line Printer

Type: Laser

Defined as: Data General Line Printer N/R

Fonts Assigned:

Character Table	Attributes	Pitch
1 A1 Normal N/R	Line Printer Land	13
2 A1 Normal N/R	Courier Bold Land	10

Character Table	Attributes	Pitch
3 A1 Normal N/R	Courier Footnote Land	15
4 A1 Normal N/R	Courier Footnote Land	17
5 A1 Normal N/R	Courier Footnote Land	20
6 A1 Normal N/R	Courier Bold Port	10
7 A1 Normal N/R	Line Printer Port	12
8 A1 Normal N/R	Courier Footnote Port	20

Features Not Supported: Double Underline, Line Draw, Type-thru, Proportional Spacing

Data General Pica 10 N

Type: Laser

Defined as: Data General Pica 10 N

Fonts Assigned:

Character Table	Attributes	Pitch
1 A1 Normal	Pica 10pt	10
2 A1 Normal	Pica Italic 10pt	10
3 A1 Normal	Double-High Footnote	15
4 A1 Normal	Footnote	15
5 A1 Normal	Double-High, Double-Wide	5
6 A1 Normal	Double-High	10
7 A1 Line Draw	Pica Line Draw	10
8 A1 Normal	Double-High, Double-Wide Footnote	8

Features Not Supported: Type-thru, Proportional Spacing

Line Draw Information:

Font(s) to be used: 7

Special Notes: Bold only in fonts 1, 5, 6, and 7.

Dataproducts DP

Type: Daisy Wheel

Defined as: Dataproducts DP Series

Fonts Assigned:

	Character Table	Attributes	Pitch
1	Standard ASCII	Depends on wheel used	10,12,15
2	Standard ASCII	Depends on wheel used	10,12,15
3	Dia630 Bold PS	Diablo 630 Bold PS	13*
4	Diablo Gothic PS	Diablo Gothic PS	13*
5	Diablo Roman PS	Diablo Roman PS	13*
6	Diablo Multi-L	Diablo Multi-Lingual	10,12,15
7	Standard ASCII	Depends on wheel used	10,12,15
8	Standard ASCII	Depends on wheel used	10,12,15

Features Not Supported: Type-thru, Foreign Characters, Line Draw

Proportional Spacing Information:

Font(s) to be used: 3,4,5

Pitch to be used: 13*

Limitations: Must have correct print wheel.

Dataproducts 8072

Type: Try SPG 8050 definition.

Dataproducts LZR-1230

Type: Laser

Defined as: Dataproducts LZR-1230

Fonts Assigned:

	Character Table	Attributes	Pitch
1	A1 Normal N/R	Courier	10
2	LaserJet Roman 8	Courier Italic	10
3	Dataproducts Dutch 10	Dutch PS 10pt	15*
4	LaserJet Roman 8	Prestige Elite	12
5	LaserJet Roman 8	Line Printer	17
6	A1 Normal N/R	Courier Land	10
7	A1 Line Draw	Prestige Elite Land	12
8	LaserJet Roman 8	Line Printer Land	17

Features Not Supported: Type-thru

Proportional Spacing Information:

Font(s) to be used: 3

Pitch to be used: 15*

Line Draw Information:

Font(s) to be used: 1,6,7

Special Notes: For manual feed, press off-line, answer paper-source and paper-type questions (letter/legal), and press on-line.

Dataproducts P132 (Color)

Type: Dot Matrix

Defined as: Dataproducts P132 (Color)

Fonts Assigned:

	Character Table	Attributes	Pitch
1	Standard ASCII	Correspondence	10,12,15
2	Standard ASCII	Normal	10,12,15
3	Standard ASCII	PS	11*
4	Standard ASCII	Expanded (5,6,8)	10,12,15
5	Standard ASCII	Blue	10,12,15
6	Standard ASCII	Red	10,12,15
7	Standard ASCII	Yellow	10,12,15
8	Standard ASCII	Draft	10,12,15

Features Not Supported: Double Underline, Line Draw, Type-thru, Foreign Characters

Proportional Spacing Information:

Font(s) to be used: 3

Pitch to be used: 11* or 13*

Limitations: PS will not right justify.

Dataproducts SPG 8050

Type: Dot Matrix

Defined as: Dataproducts SPG 8050

Fonts Assigned:

	Character Table	Attributes	Pitch
1	Dataproducts 8050 PS Foreign	NLQ	10, 12, 15
2	Standard ASCII	Correspondence	10, 12, 15
3	Dataproducts 8050 PS Foreign	PS	13*
4	Dataproducts 8050 Line D	NLQ	10, 12, 15
5	Dataproducts 8050 Line D	Blue	10, 12, 15
6	Dataproducts 8050 Line D	Green	10, 12, 15
7	Dataproducts 8050 Line D	Red	10, 12, 15
8	Standard ASCII	Draft	10, 12, 15

Features Not Supported: Type-thru

Proportional Spacing Information:

Font(s) to be used: 3

Pitch to be used: 13*

Limitations: Footnote line will not appear in font 3, PS.

Line Draw Information:

Font(s) to be used: 4,5,6,7

Special Notes: 15 pitch will return 17 pitch. You can get additional colors if you have the process color ribbon. Insert the following codes as Printer Commands:

Yellow —<27>Q,1,$ Cyan —<27>Q,3,$
Magenta —<27>Q,2,$

You can mix the colors by typing a line in one color, using Advance to go back up to the line and type the line again in a different color.

Diablo 620/630

Type: Daisy Wheel

Defined as: Diablo 620/630

Fonts Assigned:

Character Table	Attributes	Pitch
1 ASCII Backspace	Depends on wheel used	10,12,15
2 Dia620 Bold PS	Diablo 620 Boldface PS	13*
3 Dia630 Bold PS	Diablo 630 Bold PS	13*
4 Diablo Gothic PS	Diablo Gothic PS	13*
5 Diablo Roman PS	Diablo Roman PS	13*
6 Diablo Multi-L	Diablo Multi-Lingual	10*
7 Diablo Cubic PS	Diablo Cubic PS	13*
8 Daisy Line Draw	Depends on wheel used	10,12,15

Proportional Spacing Information:

Font(s) to be used: 2-7

Pitch to be used: See above

Limitations: If there are problems with proportional spacing, turn the second rotary switch to "0."

Line Draw Information:

Font(s) to be used: 8 (limited)

Diablo 630 ECS/ECS IBM

Type: Daisy Wheel

Defined as: Diablo 630 ECS/ECS IBM

Fonts Assigned:

Character Table	Attributes	Pitch
1 ECS Multi-10	ECS Multi 10	10,12,15
2 ECS Teletex	ECS Teletex	10,12,15
3 Dia630 Bold PS	Diablo 630 Bold PS	13*
4 Diablo Gothic PS	Diablo Gothic PS	13*
5 Diablo Roman PS	Diablo Roman PS	13*
6 ECS IBM 12	ECS IBM 12	10,12,15
7 ECS Scientific 12	ECS Scientific 12	10,12,15
8 ASCII Backspace	Depends on wheel used	10,12,15

Features Not Supported: Line Draw, Foreign Characters

Proportional Spacing Information:

Font(s) to be used: 3,4,5

Pitch to be used: 13*

Limitations: You must use a PS wheel and turn PS off at the printer. Change the left rotary switch to "1" and the right rotary switch to "2."

Diablo Advantage D25

Defined as: Try using the Diablo 630 definition.

Sheet Feeder Information: Check the definition in the Printer program for the printer and verify that the Form Length Setting Type is set at "2." In the Setup Menu (WP/S), change the page length from 66 to 90 for the form length and choose 54 text lines. Define as continuous forms. If this does not work, or if you have a problem with the paper tearing, define it as the Qume Single bin sheet feeder. Number of extra lines = 24, column position of left edge of paper = 10. You must then physically slide the sheet feeder to the right until the left side of the paper lines up with column on the paper-guide bar.

Special Notes: If you see random characters printing at the top of the page, go to the first screen in the Printer program titled "Printer Installation" and delete all codes but <12> under the "Reset Printer at End of Page" option.

Diablo Advantage D80IF

Type: Daisy Wheel

Defined as: Diablo Advantage D80IF

Fonts Assigned:

Character Table	Attributes	Pitch
1 ASCII Backspace	Depends on wheel-primary set	10,12,15
2 ASCII Backspace	Depends on wheel-secondary set	10,12,15

Character Table	Attributes	Pitch
3 Dia620 Bold PS	Boldface PS	13*
4 Dia620 Bold PS	Bold Italic PS	13*
5 ASCII Backspace	Depends on wheel- primary set	10,12,15
6 ASCII Backspace	Depends on wheel- secondary set	10,12,15
7 ASCII Backspace	Depends on wheel- primary set	10,12,15
8 ASCII Backspace	Depends on wheel- secondary set	10,12,15

Features Not Supported: Line Draw, Foreign Characters

Proportional Spacing Information:

Font(s) to be used: 3,4

Pitch to be used: 13*

Sheet Feeder Information: Diablo D80IF should be defined as a Diablo sheet feeder. Extra lines = 0, column position of left edge of paper = 0, and bins = 3.

Diconix 150

Type: Inkjet

Defined as: Diconix 150

Fonts Assigned:

Character Table	Attributes	Pitch
1 IBM Graphics	NLQ	12
2 IBM Graphics	Script	12
3 IBM Graphics	Enhanced PS	12
4 IBM Graphics	Expanded Script (6)	12
5 IBM Graphics	Enhanced Expanded (6)	12
6 IBM Graphics	Draft Expanded (6,10)	12,15
7 IBM Graphics	Footnote (12,20)	12,15
8 IBM Graphics	Draft (12,20)	12,15

Features Not Supported: Double Underline, Type-thru, Advance, Proportional Spacing

Line Draw Information:

Font(s) to be used: All

Limitations: Best in 8 lines per inch or half-line spacing.

Special Notes: 15 pitch returns a pitch of 20. PS will not right justify. Printer switch #6 must be on.

Digital LA-50

Type: Dot Matrix

Defined as: Digital LA-50/LA-100

Fonts Assigned:

	Character Table	Attributes	Pitch
1	DEC Complete	Enhanced	10,12
2	DEC Complete	Enhanced GL Set G3	10,12
3	DEC Complete	ND	ND
4	DEC Complete	ND	ND
5	DEC Complete	Double-Wide 5 pitch	10
6	DEC Complete	Double-Wide 6 pitch	10
7	DEC Complete	Double-Wide 8.25 pitch	10
8	DEC Complete	Draft	10,12,15

Features Not Supported: Double Underline, Proportional Spacing

Line Draw Information:

Font(s) to be used: All

Limitations: 8 lines per inch or half-line spacing must be used.

Special Notes: Select LPT for port in WordPerfect even though it is a serial printer.

Digital LA-100

Type: Dot Matrix

Defined as: Digital LA-50/LA-100

Fonts Assigned:

	Character Table	Attributes	Pitch
1	DEC Complete	Enhanced	10
2	DEC Complete	Enhanced GL set G3	10
3	DEC Complete	ND	ND
4	DEC Complete	ND	ND
5	DEC Complete	Double-Wide 5 pitch	10
6	DEC Complete	Double-Wide 5 pitch	10
7	DEC Complete	Double-Wide 5 pitch	10
8	DEC Complete	Draft	10,12,15

Features Not Supported: Double Underline, Proportional Spacing

Line Draw Information:

Font(s) to be used: All but font 8

Limitations: 8 lines per inch or half-line spacing must be used.

Special Notes: 8 LPI works only in draft mode. Select LPT for port in WordPerfect even though it is a serial printer.

Dynax DX-15

Type: Daisy Wheel

Defined as: Brother HR15XL/20/Dynax DX-15

Fonts Assigned:

	Character Table	Attributes	Pitch
1	Standard ASCII	Depends on wheel used	10,12,15
2	Standard ASCII	Depends on wheel used	10,12,15
3	BR Anelia PS	Anelia PS	12*
4	Standard ASCII	Depends on wheel used	10,12,15
5	Standard ASCII	Depends on wheel used	10,12,15
6	Standard ASCII	Depends on wheel used	10,12,15
7	Standard ASCII	Depends on wheel used	10,12,15
8	Standard ASCII	Depends on wheel used	10,12,15

Features Not Supported: Line Draw, Foreign Characters

Proportional Spacing Information:

Font(s) to be used: 3

Pitch to be used: 12*

Limitations: PS is very slow.

Dynax DX-25

Type: Daisy Wheel

Defined as: Dynax DX-25/Brother HR-35

Fonts Assigned:

	Character Table	Attributes	Pitch
1	ASCII Backspace	Depends on wheel used	10,12,15
2	ASCII Backspace	Depends on wheel used	10,12,15
3	BR Anelia PS	Anelia PS	11* or 12*
4	ASCII Backspace	Depends on wheel used	10,12,15
5	ASCII Backspace	Depends on wheel used	10,12,15
6	ASCII Backspace	Depends on wheel used	10,12,15
7	ASCII Backspace	Depends on wheel used	10,12,15
8	ASCII Backspace	Depends on wheel used	10,12,15

Features Not Supported: Line Draw, Foreign Characters

Proportional Spacing Information:

Font(s) to be used: 3

Pitch to be used: 11* or 12*

Sheet Feeder Information: See the information listed under Brother HR-15 if you have a CF100 sheet feeder.

Dynax Fortis DH45

Type: Dual Head

Defined as: Dynax Fortis DH45 (Dual Head)

Fonts Assigned:

	Character Table	Attributes	Pitch
1	Dual Head	NLQ	10,12,15
2	IBM Graphics	Emphasized	10,12,15
3	IBM Graphics	PS Emphasized	13*
4	IBM Graphics	Double-Strike	10,12,15
5	IBM Graphics	Double-Wide (5,6,8)	10,12,15
6	IBM Graphics	Double-Wide Emphasized (5,6,8)	10,12,15
7	IBM Graphics	Superscript	10,12,15
8	IBM Graphics	Draft	10,12,15

Features Not Supported: Type-thru

Proportional Spacing Information:

Font(s) to be used: 3

Pitch to be used: 13*

Line Draw Information:

Font(s) to be used: 1,2,3,4,8

Special Notes: Entering 15 pitch returns 17 pitch.

Epson EX-800

Type: Dot Matrix

Defined as: Epson EX-800

Fonts Assigned:

	Character Table	Attributes	Pitch
1	Epson EX-800	NLQ Roman	10,12,15
2	Epson EX-800	Red	10,12,15
3	Epson EX-800	NLQ Sans Serif PS	11*
4	Epson EX-800	Blue	10,12,15
5	Epson EX-800	Italic	10,12,15
6	Epson EX-800	Double-Wide	6,10
7	Epson EX-800	Double-Wide Italic	6,10
8	Epson EX-800	Draft	10,12,15

Features Not Supported: Type-thru

Proportional Spacing Information:

Font(s) to be used: 3

Pitch to be used: 11*

Line Draw Information:

Font(s) to be used: All

Epson EX-800 Color

Type: Dot Matrix

Defined as: Epson EX-800(Color)

Fonts Assigned:

	Character Table	Attributes	Pitch
1	Epson EX-800	Black	10,12,15
2	Epson EX-800	Red	10,12,15
3	Epson EX-800	Blue PS	13*
4	Epson EX-800	Violet	10,12,15
5	Epson EX-800	Yellow	10,12,15
6	Epson EX-800	Orange	10,12,15
7	Epson EX-800	Green	10,12,15
8	Epson EX-800	Black	10,12,15

Features Not Supported: Type-thru

Proportional Spacing Information:

Font(s) to be used: 3

Pitch to be used: 13*

Line Draw Information:

Font(s) to be used: All

Epson FX-80, FX-85, and FX-100

Type: Dot Matrix

Defined as: Epson FX

Fonts Assigned:

	Character Table	Attributes	Pitch
1	Epson FX&Type3	Draft	10,12,15
2	Dot Matrix 1/60	Enhanced	10,12
3	Epson FX Normal PS	PS	11*
4	Epson FX Italic PS	Enhanced Italic	10,12
5	Epson FX&Type3	Double-Wide	10,12
6	Epson FX&Type3	Double-Wide Italic	10,12
7	Epson FX&Type3	Double-Strike	10,12,15
8	Epson FX&Type3	Draft	10,12,15

Features Not Supported: Double Underline, Type-thru, Advance, Foreign Characters

Proportional Spacing Information:

Font(s) to be used: 3

Pitch to be used: 11*

Limitations: PS is slow and jumpy.

Line Draw Information:

Font(s) to be used: 2

Limitations: Half-line spacing must be used.

Special Notes: To print Greek and math characters with the FX-85, set internal switches to print the IBM character set and define as the IBM Proprinter.

Epson GQ-3500

Type: Laser

Defined as: Epson GQ-3500

Fonts Assigned:

	Character Table	Attributes	Pitch
1	Epson Laser PS	Courier	10
2	Epson Laser PS	EDP 13	15
3	Epson Laser PS	Modern PS	11*
4	Epson Laser PS	EDP 13 Double-High, Double-Wide	8

Character Table	Attributes	Pitch
5 Epson Laser PS	Courier Double-High, Double-Wide	5
6 Epson Laser PS	Courier Landscape	10
7 Epson Laser PS	EDP 13 Landscape	15
8 Epson Laser PS	EDP 13 Double-High, Double-Wide Landscape	8

Features Not Supported: Double Underline, Superscript/Subscript, Type-thru, Advance

Proportional Spacing Information:

Font(s) to be used: 3

Pitch to be used: 11*

Line Draw Information:

Font(s) to be used: 1,2,3,4,6,7,8

Epson GQ-3500 (Card 5400)

Type: Laser

Defined as: Epson GQ-3500 (5400)

Fonts Assigned:

Character Table	Attributes	Pitch
1 Epson Laser PS	Prestige	12
2 Epson Laser PS	Prestige Italic	12
3 Epson Laser PS	Modern PS	11*
4 Epson Laser PS	Prestige 8pt	15
5 Epson Laser PS	Prestige Landscape	12
6 Epson Laser PS	Modern PS Landscape	11*
7 Epson Laser PS	Prestige Landscape	15
8 Epson Laser PS	ND	ND

Features Not Supported: Double Underline, Type-thru, Advance

Proportional Spacing Information:

Font(s) to be used: 3,6

Pitch to be used: 11*

Line Draw Information:

Font(s) to be used: All

Special Notes: Card #5400 can be in either slot A or B.

Epson GQ-3500 (Card 5401)

Type: Laser

Defined as: Epson GQ-3500 (5401)

Fonts Assigned:

	Character Table	*Attributes*	*Pitch*
1	Epson Laser PS	Letter Gothic	12
2	Epson Laser PS	Letter Gothic Italic	12
3	Epson Laser PS	Modern PS	11*
4	Epson Laser PS	Letter Gothic Bold	12
5	Epson Laser PS	Letter Gothic	10
6	Epson Laser PS	Letter Gothic Italic	10
7	Epson Laser PS	Letter Gothic Bold	10
8	Epson Laser PS	Letter Gothic Double-Wide, Double-High (5)	10

Features Not Supported: Double Underline, Type-thru, Advance

Proportional Spacing Information:

Font(s) to be used: 3

Pitch to be used: 11*

Line Draw Information:

Font(s) to be used: 1-7

Special Notes: Card #5401 must be in slot A.

Epson GQ-3500 (Cards 5402/5406)

Type: Laser

Defined as: Epson GQ-3500 (5402/5406)

Fonts Assigned:

Character Table	Attributes	Pitch
1 Epson Helvetica 12R	Helvetica 12pt	11*
2 Epson Helvetica 12I	Helvetica 12pt Italic	11*
3 Epson Helvetica 10R	Helvetica 10pt	13*
4 Epson Helvetica 10I	Helvetica 10pt Italic	13*
5 Epson Helvetica 8R	Helvetica 8pt	15*
6 Epson Helvetica 18B	Helvetica 18pt	7*
7 Epson Helvetica 24B	Helvetica 24pt	6*
8 Epson Laser PS	Courier	10

Features Not Supported: Double Underline, Type-thru, Advance

Proportional Spacing Information:

Font(s) to be used: 1-7

Pitch to be used: See above

Line Draw Information:
Font(s) to be used: 8

Special Notes: Card #5402 must be in slot A and card #5406 must be in slot B.

Epson GQ-3500 (Cards 5403/5407)

Type: Laser

Defined as: Epson GQ-3500 (5403/5407)

Fonts Assigned:

Character Table	Attributes	Pitch
1 Epson Times 12R	Times Roman 12pt	11*
2 Epson Times 12I	Times Roman 12pt Italic	11*
3 Epson Times 10R	Times Roman 10pt	13*
4 Epson Times 10I	Times Roman 10pt Italic	13*
5 Epson Times 8R	Times Roman 8pt	15*
6 Epson Times 18B	Times Roman 18pt	7*
7 Epson Times 24B	Times Roman 24pt	6*
8 Epson Laser PS	Courier	10

Features Not Supported: Double Underline, Type-thru, Advance

Proportional Spacing Information:

Font(s) to be used: 1-7

Pitch to be used: See previous page

Line Draw Information:

Font(s) to be used: 8

Special Notes: Card #5403 must be in slot A and card #5407 must be in slot B.

Epson GQ-3500 (Cards 5404/5408)

Type: Laser

Defined as: Epson GQ-3500 (5404/5408)

Fonts Assigned:

	Character Table	Attributes	Pitch
1	Epson Helvetica 12R	Helvetica 12pt Landscape	11*
2	Epson Helvetica 12I	Helvetica 12pt Italic Landscape	11*
3	Epson Helvetica 10R	Helvetica 10pt Landscape	13*
4	Epson Helvetica 10I	Helvetica 10pt Italic Landscape	13*
5	Epson Helvetica 8R	Helvetica 8pt Landscape	15*
6	Epson Helvetica 18B	Helvetica 18pt Bold Landscape	7*
7	Epson Helvetica 24B	Helvetica 24pt Bold Landscape	6*
8	Epson Laser PS	Courier Landscape	10

Features Not Supported: Double Underline, Type-thru, Advance

Proportional Spacing Information:

Font(s) to be used: 1-7

Pitch to be used: See above

Line Draw Information:

Font(s) to be used: 8

Special Notes: Card #5404 must be in slot A and #5408 must be in slot B.

Epson GQ-3500 (Cards 5405/5409)

Type: Laser

Defined as: Epson GQ-3500 (5405/5409)

Fonts Assigned:

	Character Table	Attributes	Pitch
1	Epson Times 12R	Times Roman 12pt Landscape	11*
2	Epson Times 12I	Times Roman 12pt Italic Landscape	11*
3	Epson Times 10R	Times Roman 10pt Landscape	13*
4	Epson Times 10I	Times Roman 10pt Italic Landscape	13*
5	Epson Times 8R	Times Roman 8pt Landscape	15*
6	Epson Times 18B	Times Roman 18pt Bold Landscape	7*
7	Epson Times 24B	Times Roman 24pt Bold Landscape	6*
8	Epson Laser PS	Courier Landscape	10

Features Not Supported: Double Underline, Superscript/Subscript, Type-thru, Advance, Redline/Strikeout

Proportional Spacing Information:

Font(s) to be used: 1-7

Pitch to be used: See above

Line Draw Information:

Font(s) to be used: 8

Special Notes: Card #5405 must be in slot A and #5409 must be in slot B.

Epson LQ-800 and LQ-1500

Type: Dot Matrix

Defined as: Epson LQ-800/LQ-1500 (2. ROM)

Fonts Assigned:

	Character Table	Attributes	Pitch
1	Dot Matrix 1/60	NLQ	10,12,15
2	Epson LQ 800/1500	Draft Elite	10,12,15
3	Epson LQ 800/1500	NLQ PS	11*
4	Epson LQ 800/1500	Italic	10,12,15
5	Epson LQ 800/1500	Double-Wide	10,12,15
6	Epson LQ 800/1500	Double-Wide Italic	10,12,15
7	Epson LQ 800/1500	Subscript	10,12,15
8	ASCII Line Printer	Draft Pica	10,12,15

Features Not Supported: Double Underline, Type-thru, Advance

Proportional Spacing Information:

Font(s) to be used: 3

Pitch to be used: 11* or 13*

Line Draw Information:

Font(s) to be used: 1

Limitations: Half-line spacing must be used.

Sheet Feeder Information: Define as continuous forms. Printer switch 8 must be on for the sheet feeder.

Epson LQ-2500

Type: Dot Matrix

Defined as: Epson LQ-2500

Fonts Assigned:

	Character Table	Attributes	Pitch
1	Epson LQ-2500	NLQ Roman	10,12,15
2	Epson LQ-2500	NLQ Script	10,12,15
3	Epson LQ-2500	NLQ Sans Serif	13*
4	Epson LQ-2500	NLQ Italic	10,12,15
5	Epson LQ-2500	NLQ Double-Wide	10,12,15
6	Epson LQ-2500	NLQ Courier	10,12,15
7	Epson LQ-2500	NLQ Prestige	10,12,15
8	Epson LQ-2500	Draft	10,12,15

Features Not Supported: Type-thru

Proportional Spacing Information:

Font(s) to be used: 3

Pitch to be used: 13∗

Line Draw Information:

Font(s) to be used: All

Epson LQ-2500 Color

Type: Dot Matrix

Defined as: Epson LQ-2500 (Color)

Fonts Assigned:

Character Table	Attributes	Pitch
1 Epson LQ 2500	Black	10,12,15
2 Epson LQ 2500	Red	10,12,15
3 Epson LQ 2500	Blue PS	13∗
4 Epson LQ 2500	Violet	10,12,15
5 Epson LQ 2500	Yellow	10,12,15
6 Epson LQ 2500	Orange	10,12,15
7 Epson LQ 2500	Green	10,12,15
8 Epson LQ 2500	Black	10,12,15

Features Not Supported: Type-thru

Proportional Spacing Information:

Font(s) to be used: 3

Pitch to be used: 13∗

Line Draw Information:

Font(s) to be used: All

Special Notes: If the printer resets to draft after each print job, enter the Printer program and delete <27>X<0> from the "Reset Printer after Print Job" option leaving <27>2<27>P (found in the Printer Initialization screen). You could also change the option "Shift into Font 1" by adding <27>X<1> to the end of the string so it looks like <27>4<0><27>X<1>.

Epson LX-80

Type: Dot Matrix

Defined as: Epson LX

Fonts Assigned:

	Character Table	Attributes	Pitch
1	Dot Matrix 1/60	Emphasized	10
2	Dot Matrix 1/60	NLQ	10
3	Epson FX&Type3	Compressed	15
4	Epson FX&Type3	Emphasized Italic	10
5	Epson FX&Type3	Double-Wide	5
6	Epson FX&Type3	Double-Wide Italic	5
7	Dot Matrix 1/60	Double-Strike	10,12,15
8	Epson FX&Type3	Draft	10,12,15

Features Not Supported: Double Underline, Type-thru, Advance, Foreign Characters, Proportional Spacing

Line Draw Information:

Font(s) to be used: 1,2,7

Limitations: Half-line spacing must be used.

Epson MX-80

Type: Dot Matrix

Defined as: Epson MX-Graftrax/MX Type III

Fonts Assigned:

	Character Table	Attributes	Pitch
1	Dot Matrix 1/60	Draft	10
2	Epson Graftrax	Italic	10
3	Epson Graftrax	Compressed	10
4	Epson Graftrax	Compressed Italic	10
5	Epson FX&Type3	Double-Wide Compressed	10
6	Epson FX&Type3	Double-Wide Compressed Italic	10
7	Epson FX&Type3	Double-Wide	10
8	Epson FX&Type3	Double-Wide Italic	10

Features Not Supported: Double Underline, Type-thru, Advance, Foreign Characters, Proportional Spacing

Line Draw Information:

Font(s) to be used: 1

Limitations: Half-line spacing must be used.

Facit 4512

Type: Dot Matrix

Defined as: Facit 4512

Fonts Assigned:

	Character Table	Attributes	Pitch
1	ASCII Backspace	NLQ (10)	10
2	ASCII Backspace	Condensed (12)	10
3	Facit 4512 PS	NLQ PS	12*
4	ASCII Backspace	Compressed (16)	10
5	ASCII Backspace	Draft (10)	10
6	ASCII Backspace	Double-Wide (5)	10
7	Dot Matrix 1/60	ND	ND
8	Dot Matrix 1/60	ND	ND

Features Not Supported: Double Underline, Type-thru, Foreign Characters, Limited Line Draw

Proportional Spacing Information:

Font(s) to be used: 3

Pitch to be used: 12*

Line Draw Information:

Font(s) to be used: 7,8 (limited)

Florida Data Office Systems 130

Type: Dot Matrix

Defined as: Florida Data Office Systems 130

Fonts Assigned:

	Character Table	Attributes	Pitch
1	FD Courier PS 3 23	Draft	10,12,15
2	FD Pump-up PS	Correspondence	10,12,15
3	FD Computer PS	NLQ	10,12,15

Character Table	Attributes	Pitch
4 FD Future PS	Compressed	10,12,15
5 FD Old English PS	Draft	10,12,15
6 FD Resume PS	Correspondence	10,12,15
7 FD Gothic PS	NLQ	10,12,15
8 FD Line Draw	NLQ	10,12,15

Features Not Supported: Double Underline, Type-thru, Foreign Characters, Proportional Spacing

Line Draw Information:

Font(s) to be used: 8 (limited)

Sheet Feeder Information: Define as continuous and change the top margin to "0" in the Setup menu (WP/S).

Special Notes: Printer has downloadable font capability. See *download* definition below. Selecting 15 pitch returns 17 pitch at the printer.

Florida Data Office Systems 130 (Download)

Type: Dot Matrix

Defined as: Florida Data Office Systems 130

Fonts Assigned:

Character Table	Attributes	Pitch
1 FD Courier PS 3 23	Draft	11*
2 FD Pump-up PS	Correspondence	11*
3 FD Computer PS	NLQ	11*
4 FD Future PS	Compressed	11*
5 FD Old English PS	Draft	11*
6 FD Resume PS	Correspondence	11*
7 FD Gothic PS	NLQ	11*
8 FD Line Draw	NLQ	10,12,15

Features Not Supported: Double Underline, Type-Thru, Foreign Characters

Proportional Spacing Information:

Font(s) to be used: 1-7

Pitch to be used: 11*

Line Draw Information:

Font(s) to be used: 8

Special Notes: In order to get these styles, the following fonts must be downloaded:

1: #22693.01 Disk 3	2: #22785.01 Disk 3
3: #22684.01 Disk 1	4: #22446.01 Disk 1
5: #22640.01 Disk 1	6: #22688.01 Disk 1
7: #22695.01 Disk 3	8: #22745.01 Disk 3

Fortis DM1310

Type: Dot Matrix

Defined as: Fortis DM1310

Fonts Assigned:

	Character Table	Attributes	Pitch
1	Fortis DM PS	NLQ Courier	10,12
2	Fortis DM PS	NLQ Italic	10,12
3	Fortis DM PS	NLQ PS	10*
4	Fortis DM PS	Emphasized	10,12
5	Fortis DM PS	Enhanced	10,12,15
6	Fortis DM PS	NLQ Double-Wide (5,6)	10,12
7	Fortis DM PS	Draft Double-Wide (5,6,7.5)	10,12,15
8	Fortis DM PS	Draft	10,12,15

Features Not Supported: Line Draw, Type-thru, Foreign Characters

Proportional Spacing Information:

Font(s) to be used: 3

Pitch to be used: 10*

Limitations: Footnote line will not appear in font 3, nor will continuous underline work in that font. Tractor feeding may cause problems.

Special Notes: Bi-directional printing is only available in draft because otherwise the margins stagger. Entering 15 pitch returns 17 pitch.

Fortis DM2015

Type: Dot Matrix

Defined as: Fortis DM2015

Fonts Assigned:

	Character Table	Attributes	Pitch
1	Fortis DM PS	NLQ	10,12
2	Fortis DM PS	Italicized	10,12,15
3	Fortis DM PS	PS	10*
4	Fortis DM PS	Emphasized	10,12,15
5	Fortis DM PS	Enhanced	10,12,15
6	Fortis DM PS	NLQ Double-Wide (5,6)	10,12
7	Fortis DM PS	Double-Wide (5,6,7.5)	10,12,15
8	Fortis DM PS	Draft	10,12,15

Features Not Supported: Double Underline, Line Draw, Type-thru, Foreign Characters

Proportional Spacing Information:

Font(s) to be used: 3

Pitch to be used: 10*

Limitations: Footnote line and continuous underline are not available in font 3.

Special Notes: Entering 15 pitch returns 17 pitch.

Fortis DX21

Type: Daisy Wheel

Defined as: Fortis DX21

Fonts Assigned:

	Character Table	Attributes	Pitch
1	Standard ASCII	Depends on wheel used	10,12,15
2	Standard ASCII	Depends on wheel used	10,12,15
3	Standard ASCII	Depends on wheel used	10,12,15
4	Standard ASCII	Depends on wheel used	10,12,15
5	Standard ASCII	Depends on wheel used	10,12,15
6	Standard ASCII	Depends on wheel used	10,12,15
7	Standard ASCII	Depends on wheel used	10,12,15
8	Standard ASCII	Depends on wheel used	10,12,15

Features Not Supported: Line Draw, Foreign Characters, Proportional Spacing

Fujitsu DL 3400

Type: Dot Matrix

Defined as: Fujitsu DL 3400

Fonts Assigned:

	Character Table	Attributes	Pitch
1	IBM Graphics	NLQ (Courier)	10,12
2	IBM Graphics	Italic	10,12
3	Fujitsu DL3400	PS	11*
4	IBM Graphics	Prestige Elite	12,15
5	IBM Graphics	Compressed	15
6	IBM Graphics	Double-Wide (6)	12
7	IBM Graphics	Double-Wide, Double-High (5,6)	10,12
8	IBM Graphics	Draft	10,12

Features Not Supported: Type-thru

Proportional Spacing Information:

Font(s) to be used: 3

Pitch to be used: 11*

Limitations: Underlines will be broken in PS.

Line Draw Information:

Font(s) to be used: 1,2,3,4,6,8

Limitations: Cannot use font 3 to draw lines and get PS.

Special Notes: Panel mode set to defaults. For color options, insert these printer commands to select the desired color:

Black—<27>r<0>	Magenta—<27>r<1>
Cyan—<27>r<2>	Violet—<27>r<3>
Yellow—<27>r<4>	Orange—<27>r<5>
Green—<27>r<6>	

Fujitsu DL2400C

Type: Dot Matrix

Defined as: Fujitsu DL2400C

Fonts Assigned:

Character Table	Attributes	Pitch
1 IBM Graphics	NLQ	10,12,15
2 IBM Graphics	Shadow Print	10,12,15
3 Fujitsu DPL 12 PS	PS	13*
4 IBM Graphics	Italic	10,12,15
5 IBM Graphics	Double-Wide (5,6,8)	10,12,15
6 IBM Graphics	Double-Wide, Double-High (5,6,8)	10,12,15
7 IBM Graphics	Condensed	10,12,15
8 IBM Graphics	Draft	10,12,15

Features Not Supported: Type-thru

Proportional Spacing Information:

Font(s) to be used: 3

Pitch to be used: 13*

Line Draw Information:

Font(s) to be used: 1,2,4,5,6,8

Special Notes: If WordPerfect loses the left margin, go into the Printer's setup menu (not WordPerfect's Setup Menu), and change the LF CODE from LF & CR to LF ONLY.

Fujitsu DPL24D

Type: Dot Matrix

Defined as: Fujitsu DPL24D

Fonts Assigned:

Character Table	Attributes	Pitch
1 ASCII Backspace	NLQ Courier	10,12,15
2 ASCII Backspace	NLQ Elite	10,12,15
3 Standard PS	NLQ Boldface	12* or 13*
4 ASCII Backspace	Compressed	10,12,15
5 ASCII Backspace	Double-Wide Boldface (5,6,8)	10,12,15
6 ASCII Backspace	Double-Wide Compressed (5,6,8)	10,12,15
7 ASCII Backspace	Correspondence	10,12,15
8 ASCII Backspace	Draft	10,12,15

Features Not Supported: Line Draw, Type-thru, Foreign Characters

Proportional Spacing Information:

Font(s) to be used: 3

Pitch to be used: 12* or 13*

Fujitsu DX2200 (Type F)

Type: Dot Matrix

Defined as: Fujitsu DX2200 (Type F)

Fonts Assigned:

	Character Table	*Attributes*	*Pitch*
1	Fortis DM PS	NLQ	10,12,10*
2	Fortis DM PS	NLQ Italic	10,12,10*
3	Fortis DM PS	PS	10*
4	Fortis DM PS	Compressed (15,17,20)	10,12,15
5	Fortis DM PS	Emphasized	10,10*
6	Fortis DM PS	Enhanced	10,12,15
7	Fortis DM PS	Double-Wide (5,6)	10,12
8	Fortis DM PS	Draft	10,12,15

Features Not Supported: Line Draw, Type-thru, Foreign Characters

Proportional Spacing Information:

Font(s) to be used: 1,2,3,5

Pitch to be used: See above

Limitations: Printer will not right justify in PS.

Special Notes: Double underlining is slow. To access the colors, insert the following as a Printer Command:

<27>r<n> n=color #

0=Black	2=Cyan	4=Yellow	6=Green
1=Magenta	3=Violet	5=Orange	

Fujitsu DX2200 (Type I)

Type: Dot Matrix

Defined as: Fujitsu DX2200 (Type I)

Fonts Assigned:

Character Table	Attributes	Pitch
1 IBM Graphics	NLQ Black	10,12,15
2 IBM Graphics	NLQ Red	10,12,15
3 IBM Graphics	NLQ Blue	10,12,15
4 IBM Graphics	NLQ Purple	10,12,15
5 IBM Graphics	NLQ Orange	10,12,15
6 IBM Graphics	NLQ Green	10,12,15
7 IBM Graphics	Expanded NLQ (5,6,8)	10,12,15
8 IBM Graphics	Draft	10,12,15

Features Not Supported: Type-thru, Proportional Spacing

Line Draw Information:

Font(s) to be used: All

Limitation: Character #182 (╢) prints the single horizontal line up a little too high (╢). This is a printer problem.

Special Notes: Entering 15 pitch returns 17 pitch. There is no bi-directional printing because it is unacceptable with a tractor feeder.

Fujitsu SP 320

Type: Daisy Wheel

Defined as: Fujitsu SP 320

Fonts Assigned:

Character Table	Attributes	Pitch
1 Standard ASCII	Depends on wheel used	10,12,15
2 Standard ASCII	ASCII Line Printer	10,12,15
3 Standard PS	Standard PS	12*
4 Diablo Roman PS	Diablo Roman PS	12*

Character Table	*Attributes*	*Pitch*
5 Diablo Cubic PS	Diablo Cubic PS	12*
6 Dia630 Bold PS	Diablo 630 Bold PS	12*
7 Diablo Multi-L	Diablo Multi-L	10,12,15
8 Standard ASCII	Standard ASCII	10,12,15

Features Not Supported: Line Draw, Foreign Characters

Proportional Spacing Information:

Font(s) to be used: 3,4,5,6

Pitch to be used: See above

GTC Blaser:Portrait/Landscape

Type: Laser

Defined as: GTC Blaser:Portrait/Landscape

Fonts Assigned:

Character Table	*Attributes*	*Pitch*
1 IBM Graphics	Courier	10,12
2 IBM Graphics	Double-Wide (5)	10
3 IBM Graphics	Compressed	12,15
4 IBM Graphics	Courier Landscape	10
5 Standard ASCII	Font #5 depends on cartridge	ND
6 Standard ASCII	Font #6 depends on cartridge	ND
7 Standard ASCII	Font #7 depends on cartridge	ND
8 Standard ASCII	Font #8 depends on cartridge	ND

Features Not Supported: Type-thru, Advance, Overstrike

Line Draw Information:

Font(s) to be used: 1,2,3,4

Limitations: Font 2 requires half-line spacing or 8 lines per inch.

Sheet Feeder Information: Define as continuous forms.

Special Notes: This definition will work with any cartridge, but the PS on the cartridge will not be supported.

GTC Blaser:Roman

Type: Laser

Defined as: GTC Blaser:Roman

Fonts Assigned:

	Character Table	*Attributes*	*Pitch*
1	IBM Graphics	Courier Internal	10,12,15
2	IBM Graphics	Double-Wide	10,12,15
3	IBM Graphics	Compressed	10,12,15
4	IBM Graphics	Subscript	10,12,15
5	Standard ASCII	Font #5 on cartridge	10,12,15
6	Standard ASCII	Font #6 on cartridge	10,12,15
7	Standard ASCII	Font #7 on cartridge	10,12,15
8	Blaser Roman PS	Roman PS	13*

Features Not Supported: Type-thru, Advance

Proportional Spacing Information:

Font(s) to be used: 8

Pitch to be used: 13*

Line Draw Information:

Font(s) to be used: 1,2,3,4

Limitations: Font 2 requires half-line spacing.

GTC Blaser:Swiss/Apollo

Type: Laser

Defined as: GTC Blaser:Swiss/Apollo

Fonts Assigned:

	Character Table	*Attributes*	*Pitch*
1	IBM Graphics	Courier Internal	10,12,15
2	IBM Graphics	Double-Wide	10,12,15
3	IBM Graphics	Compressed	10,12,15
4	IBM Graphics	Subscript	10,12,15
5	Standard ASCII	Font #5 on cartridge	10,12,15

Character Table	Attributes	Pitch
6 Blaser Apollo PS	Apollo PS	13*
7 Standard ASCII	Font #7 on cartridge	10,12,15
8 Blaser Swiss PS	Swiss PS	13*

Features Not Supported: Type-thru, Advance

Proportional Spacing Information:

Font(s) to be used: 6,8

Pitch to be used: 13*

Line Draw Information:

Font(s) to be used: 1,2,3,4

Limitations: Font 2 requires half-line spacing.

HP 2603A Daisywheel

Type: Daisy Wheel

Defined as: HP 2603A Daisywheel

Fonts Assigned:

Character Table	Attributes	Pitch
1 Standard ASCII	Depends on wheel used	10,12,15
2 Standard ASCII	Depends on wheel used	10,12,15
3 Standard ASCII	Modern PS	13*
4 Standard ASCII	Kent PS	13*
5 Standard ASCII	Depends on wheel used	10,12,15
6 Standard ASCII	Depends on wheel used	10,12,15
7 Standard ASCII	Depends on wheel used	10,12,15
8 Standard ASCII	Depends on wheel used	10,12,15

Features Not Supported: Line Draw, Foreign Characters

Proportional Spacing Information:

Font(s) to be used: 3,4

Pitch to be used: 13*

Limitations: Modern PS and Kent PS print wheels must be used with corresponding font.

Sheet Feeder Information: Define as Diablo Single/Dual/ Envl. Extra lines = 0, column position of left edge of paper = 0, number of bins = 3.

HP LaserJet A

Type: Laser

Defined as: LaserJt Reg,+,500+ A: Courier

Fonts Assigned:

	Character Table	Attributes	Pitch
1	LaserJet Roman 8	Courier Port	10
2	LaserJet Roman 8	Courier Italic Port	10
3	LaserJet Roman 8	Line Printer Land	17
4	LaserJet Roman 8	Courier Land	10
5	LaserJet Roman 8	Line Printer Port	17
6	LaserJet+ Graph	ND	ND
7	LaserJet+ Box	ND	ND
8	LaserJet-Box	ND	ND

Features Not Supported: Type-thru, Proportional Spacing

Line Draw Information:

Font(s) to be used: 6,7,8

Limitations: Fonts 6 and 7 for LaserJet+ and Series II. Font 6 returns solid lines. Use font 8 for regular LaserJet.

Special Notes: Font 5 only available on LaserJet+ and Series II.

HP LaserJet B

Type: Laser

Defined as: LaserJt Reg,+,500+ B: Tms Rmn1

Fonts Assigned:

	Character Table	Attributes	Pitch
1	LaserJet-B Normal	Times Roman 10pt	13*
2	LaserJet-B Italic	Times Roman Italic 10pt	13*
3	LaserJet-B Helvetica	Helvetica 14.4pt Bold	10*
4	LaserJet-B Footnote	Times Roman 8pt	18*
5	LaserJet Roman 8	Line Printer Land	17
6	LaserJet+ Box	Courier	10
7	LaserJet Roman 8	Courier Land	10
8	LaserJet-B Bold	Times Roman 10pt Bold	13*

Features Not Supported: Line Draw, Type-thru

Proportional Spacing Information:

Font(s) to be used: 1,2,3,4,8

Pitch to be used: See above

Line Draw Information:

Font(s) to be used: 6

Limitations: LaserJet+ and Series II only.

Special Notes: Bold uses font 8. Redline uses font 2. Super-script/subscript uses font 4. Fonts 2, 4, and 8 will remain in the same orientation as the previous font used.

HP LaserJet C

Type: Laser

Defined as: LaserJt Reg,+,500+ C: Intl 1

Fonts Assigned:

Character Table	Attributes	Pitch
1 LaserJet Roman 8	Courier Port	10
2 LaserJet Roman 8	Courier Italic Port	10
3 LaserJet Roman 8	Line Printer Port	17
4 LaserJet Roman 8	Line Printer Land	17
5 LaserJet Roman 8	Courier Land	10
6 LaserJet+ Graph	ND	ND
7 LaserJet+ Box	ND	ND
8 LaserJet-Box	ND	ND

Features Not Supported: Type-thru, Foreign Characters, Proportional Spacing

Line Draw Information:

Font(s) to be used: 6,7,8

Limitations: Fonts 6 and 7 for the LaserJet+ and Series II. Font 6 gives solid lines. Use font 8 for regular LaserJet.

HP LaserJet D

Type: Laser

Defined as: LaserJt Reg,+,500+ D: P Elite

Fonts Assigned:

	Character Table	Attributes	Pitch
1	LaserJet Roman 8	Prestige Elite Port	12
2	LaserJet Roman 8	Prestige Elite Italic Port	12
3	LaserJet Roman 8	Courier Port	10
4	LaserJet Roman 8	Courier Land	10
5	LaserJet Roman 8	ND	ND
6	LaserJet+ Graph	ND	ND
7	LaserJet+ Box	ND	ND
8	LaserJet-Box	ND	ND

Features Not Supported: Type-thru, Foreign Characters, Proportional Spacing

Line Draw Information:

Font(s) to be used: 6,7,8

Limitations: Fonts 6 and 7 for the LaserJet+ and Series II. Font 6 gives solid lines. Use font 8 for regular LaserJet.

HP LaserJet E

Type: Laser

Defined as: LaserJt Reg,+,500+ E: Gothic

Fonts Assigned:

	Character Table	Attributes	Pitch
1	LaserJet Roman 8	Gothic Port	12
2	LaserJet Roman 8	Gothic Italic Port	12
3	LaserJet Roman 8	Courier Port	10
4	LaserJet Roman 8	Courier Land	10
5	LaserJet Roman 8	ND	ND
6	LaserJet+ Graph	ND	ND
7	LaserJet+ Box	Line Draw	12
8	LaserJet-Box	ND	ND

Features Not Supported: Type-thru, Proportional Spacing

Line Draw Information:

Font(s) to be used: 6,7,8

Limitations: Fonts 6 and 7 only for LaserJet+ and Series II. Font 6 gives solid lines. Use font 8 for regular LaserJet.

HP LaserJet F

Type: Laser

Defined as: LaserJt Reg,+,500+ F: Tms Rmn2

Fonts Assigned:

	Character Table	Attributes	Pitch
1	LaserJet-F Normal	Times Roman 10pt	14*
2	LaserJet-F Italic	Times Roman 10pt Italic	14*
3	LaserJet-F Helvetica	Helvetica 14.4pt Bold	10*
4	LaserJet-F Footnote	Times Roman 8pt	18*
5	LaserJet Roman 8	Line Printer	17
6	LaserJet+ Box	Courier	10
7	LaserJet Roman 8	Courier Land	10
8	LaserJet-F Bold	Times Roman 10pt Bold	14*

Features Not Supported: Type-thru

Proportional Spacing Information:

Font(s) to be used: 1,2,3,4,8

Pitch to be used: See above

Line Draw Information:

Font(s) to be used: 6

Limitations: LaserJet+ only.

Special Notes: Bold uses font 8. Redline uses font 2. Super-script/subscript uses font 4.

HP LaserJet G

Type: Laser

Defined as: LaserJt Reg,+,500+ G: Legal E

Fonts Assigned:

	Character Table	Attributes	Pitch
1	LaserJet Legal	Prestige Legal Port	12
2	LaserJet Legal	Prestige Legal Italic Port	12
3	LaserJet Legal	Prestige Legal Port	17
4	Standard ASCII	Prestige Elite Port	12
5	Standard ASCII	Prestige Elite Port	12
6	Standard ASCII	Prestige Elite Port	17
7	LaserJet Legal	Prestige Legal Land	17
8	LaserJet Line Draw	Line Draw Port	12

Features Not Supported: Type-thru, Proportional Spacing

Line Draw Information:

Font(s) to be used: 8

HP LaserJet H

Type: Laser

Defined as: LaserJt Reg,+,500+ H: Legal C

Fonts Assigned:

	Character Table	Attributes	Pitch
1	LaserJet Legal	Courier Port	10
2	LaserJet Legal	Courier Italic Port	10
3	LaserJet Legal	Prestige Legal Port	17
4	Standard ASCII	Courier Port	10
5	Standard ASCII	Courier Port Italic	10
6	Standard ASCII	Prestige Elite Port	17
7	LaserJet Legal	Prestige Legal Land	17
8	LaserJet Line Draw	Line Draw Port	10

Features Not Supported: Type-thru, Proportional Spacing

Line Draw Information:

Font(s) to be used: 8

HP LaserJet J

Type: Laser

Defined as: LaserJt Reg,+,500+ J: Math E

Fonts Assigned:

	Character Table	Attributes	Pitch
1	LaserJet Roman 8	Prestige Elite Port	12
2	LaserJet Roman 8	Prestige Elite Italic Port	12
3	LaserJet Roman 8	Prestige Elite Port	17
4	LaserJet Math 7	Math 7 Elite Port	12
5	LaserJet Math 8	Math 8 Elite Port	12
6	LaserJet Math 8	Math 8 Elite Port	17
7	LaserJet Pi Font	Line Draw	12
8	LaserJet-Box	Courier Port	10

Features Not Supported: Type-thru, Proportional Spacing

Line Draw Information:

Font(s) to be used: 7,8

Limitations: Use font 7 for LaserJet+ and Series II. Use font 8 for regular LaserJet.

Special Notes: Text cannot be typed while in font 7—it should only be used for lines (this is a special pi font).

HP LaserJet K

Type: Laser

Defined as: LaserJt Reg,+,500+ K: Tms Math

Fonts Assigned:

	Character Table	Attributes	Pitch
1	LaserJet-F Normal	Times Roman 10pt	14*
2	LaserJet-F Italic	Times Roman Italic 10pt	14*
3	LaserJet-F Footnote	Times Roman 8pt	18*
4	LaserJet-K Math7 10	Times Roman Math 7	14*
5	LaserJet-K Math8 10	Times Roman Math 8	14*
6	LaserJet-K Math8 8	Times Roman 8pt Math 8	18*
7	LaserJet-K Pi 10	Pi	14*
8	LaserJet-F Bold	Times Roman 10pt Bold	14*

Features Not Supported: Line Draw, Type-thru

Proportional Spacing Information:

Font(s) to be used: All

Pitch to be used: See above

HP LaserJet L

Type: Laser

Defined as: LaserJt Reg,+,500+ L:Cou P&L

Fonts Assigned:

	Character Table	Attributes	Pitch
1	LaserJet Roman 8	Courier Port	10
2	LaserJet Roman 8	Courier Port Italic	10
3	LaserJet Roman 8	Courier Land	10
4	LaserJet Roman 8	Courier Land Italic	10
5	LaserJet Roman 8	Line Printer Port	17
6	LaserJet+Graph	Line Printer Land	17
7	LaserJet+Box	ND	10
8	LaserJet-Box	ND	10

Features Not Supported: Type-thru, Proportional Spacing

Line Draw Information:

Font(s) to be used: 6,7,8

Limitations: Use fonts 6 and 7 for the LaserJet+ and Series II. Use font 8 for regular LaserJet.

HP LaserJet M

Type: Laser

Defined as: LaserJt Reg,+,500+ M: P E P&L

Fonts Assigned:

	Character Table	Attributes	Pitch
1	LaserJet Roman 8	Prestige Elite Port	12
2	LaserJet Roman 8	Prestige Elite Italic Port	12
3	LaserJet Roman 8	Prestige Elite Land	12
4	LaserJet Roman 8	Prestige Elite Italic Land	12
5	LaserJet Roman 8	Courier Port	10
6	LaserJet+ Graph	Courier Land	10
7	LaserJet+ Box	ND	ND
8	LaserJet− Box	ND	ND

Features Not Supported: Type-thru, Proportional Spacing

Line Draw Information:

Font(s) to be used: 6,7,8

Limitations: Use fonts 6 and 7 for the LaserJet+ and Series II. Use font 8 for regular LaserJet.

HP LaserJet N

Type: Laser

Defined as: LaserJt Reg,+,500+ N: L G P&L

Fonts Assigned:

	Character Table	Attributes	Pitch
1	LaserJet Roman 8	Letter Gothic Port	12
2	LaserJet Roman 8	Letter Gothic Italic Port	12
3	LaserJet Roman 8	Letter Gothic Land	12
4	LaserJet Roman 8	Letter Gothic Italic Land	12
5	LaserJet Roman 8	Courier Port	10
6	LaserJet+ Graph	Courier Land	10
7	LaserJet+ Box	ND	ND
8	LaserJet-Box	ND	ND

Features Not Supported: Type-thru, Proportional Spacing

Line Draw Information:

Font(s) to be used: 6,7,8

Limitations: Use fonts 6 and 7 for the LaserJet+ and Series II. Use font 8 for regular LaserJet.

HP LaserJet P

Type: Laser

Defined as: LaserJt Reg,+,500+ P: Tms P&L

Fonts Assigned:

	Character Table	Attributes	Pitch
1	LaserJet-F Normal	Times Roman 10pt	14*
2	LaserJet-F Italic	Times Roman Italic 10pt	14*
3	LaserJet-F Normal	Times Roman 10pt Land	14*
4	LaserJet-F Italic	Times Roman Italic 10pt Land	14*
5	LaserJet-F Normal	ND	ND
6	LaserJet+ Box	Courier	10
7	LaserJet+ Box	Courier Land	10
8	LaserJet-F Bold	Times Roman 10pt Bold	14*

Features Not Supported: Type-thru

Proportional Spacing Information:

Font(s) to be used: 1,2,3,4,5,8

Pitch to be used: See above

Line Draw Information:

Font(s) to be used: 6,7

Limitations: Supported on the LaserJet+ only.

Special Notes: Fonts 6 and 8 will print in the same orientation as the previously selected font.

HP LaserJet Q

Type: Laser

Defined as: LaserJt Reg,+,500+ Q: Cour,LG

Fonts Assigned:

	Character Table	Attributes	Pitch
1	LaserJet Roman 8	Courier Port	10
2	LaserJet Roman 8	Courier Italic Port	10
3	LaserJet Roman 8	Courier Land	10
4	LaserJet Roman 8	Courier Italic Land	10
5	LaserJet Roman 8	Letter Gothic Port	12
6	LaserJet+ Graph	ND	ND
7	LaserJet+ Box	ND	ND
8	LaserJet-Box	ND	ND

Features Not Supported: Type-thru, Proportional Spacing

Line Draw Information:

Font(s) to be used: 6,7,8

Limitations: Use fonts 6 and 7 for the LaserJet+ and Series II. Use font 8 for regular LaserJet.

HP LaserJet R

Type: Laser

Defined as: LaserJt Reg,+,500+ R: Present

Fonts Assigned:

	Character Table	Attributes	Pitch
1	LaserJet-R Present	Present Bold 14pt Port	10
2	LaserJet-R Present	Present Bold 16pt Port	8.1
3	LaserJet-R Present	Present Bold 18pt Port	6.5
4	LaserJet-R Present	Letter Gothic 14pt Port	10
5	LaserJet-R Present	Present Bold 14pt Land	10
6	LaserJet-R Present	Present Bold 16pt Land	8.1
7	LaserJet-R Present	Present Bold 18pt Land	6.5
8	LaserJet-R Present	Letter Gothic 14pt Land	10

Features Not Supported: Type-thru, Foreign Characters

Line Draw Information:

Font(s) to be used: All

HP LaserJet T

Type: Laser

Defined as: LaserJt Reg,+,500+ T: Helv Tax

Fonts Assigned:

	Character Table	Attributes	Pitch
1	LaserJet Helvetica 10	Helvetica Bold 10pt	13*
2	LaserJet Helvetica 12	Helvetica Bold 12pt	11*
3	LaserJet Helvetica 14	Helvetica Bold 14pt	10*
4	LaserJet Helvetica 8B	Helvetica Bold 8pt	16*
5	LaserJet Helvetica 8N	Helvetica 8pt	16*
6	LaserJet Helvetica 6	Helvetica 6pt	19*
7	LaserJet Roman 8	Courier	10
8	LaserJet Tax Form	Tax Line Draw	10

Features Not Supported: Type-thru

Proportional Spacing Information:

Font(s) to be used: 1-6

Pitch to be used: See above

Line Draw Information:

Font(s) to be used: 8

Special Notes: Foreign characters available with fixed pitch, only in font 7.

HP LaserJet U

Type: Laser

Defined as: LaserJt Reg,+,500+ U: Form Port

Fonts Assigned:

	Character Table	*Attributes*	*Pitch*
1	LaserJet Helvetica2 14B	Helvetica Bold 14pt	10*
2	LaserJet Helvetica2 12B	Helvetica Bold 12pt	11*
3	LaserJet Helvetica2 10B	Helvetica Bold 10pt	13*
4	LaserJet Helvetica2 8N	Helvetica 8pt	18*
5	LaserJet Helvetica2 6N	Helvetica 6pt	22*
6	LaserJet Roman 8	Letter Gothic	17
7	LaserJet Line Draw	Line Draw	10
8	LaserJet Roman 8	Courier	10

Features Not Supported: Type-thru

Proportional Spacing Information:

Font(s) to be used: 1-5

Pitch to be used: See above

Line Draw Information:

Font(s) to be used: 7

HP LaserJet V

Type: Laser

Defined as: LaserJt Reg,+,500+ U: Forms Portrait

Fonts Assigned:

	Character Table	*Attributes*	*Pitch*
1	LaserJet Helvetica2 14B	Helvetica Bold 14pt Land	10*
2	LaserJet Helvetica2 12B	Helvetica Bold 12pt Land	12*
3	LaserJet Helvetica2 10B	Helvetica Bold 10pt Land	13*
4	LaserJet Helvetica2 8N	Helvetica 8pt Land	18*
5	LaserJet Helvetica2 6N	Helvetica 6pt Land	22*
6	LaserJet Roman 8	Letter Gothic Land	17
7	LaserJet Line Draw	Line Draw Land	10
8	LaserJet Roman 8	Courier Land	10

Features Not Supported: Type-thru

Proportional Spacing Information:

Font(s) to be used: 1-5

Pitch to be used: See above

Line Draw Information:

Font(s) to be used: 7

Special Notes: Note that the LaserJt Reg,+,500+ U: Forms Portrait definition is being used. If you want a true V definition, enter the Printer program and create the V definition using the U printer as a pattern. The only change that needs to be made is to change "Initialize Printer Before Print Job" to <27>&ll1T<27>&ll0<27>(8U). This option is found in the first screen, Printer Initialization.

HP LaserJet W

Type: Laser

Defined as: LaserJt Reg,+,500+ W: Bar Code

Fonts Assigned:

	Character Table	Attributes	Pitch
1	LaserJet Roman 8	Courier Port	10
2	LaserJet Roman 8	Gothic Port	10
3	LaserJet Roman 8	Gothic Port	17
4	Standard ASCII	OCR A	10
5	LaserJet Roman 8	Courier Land	10
6	Standard ASCII	Bar Code	4.6
7	Standard ASCII	Bar Code	9.3
8	LaserJet Line Draw	Line Draw	10

Features Not Supported: Double Underline, Type-thru

Line Draw Information:

Font(s) to be used: 8

Special Notes: Turn right justification off when using the bar code fonts.

HP LaserJet Y

Type: Laser

Defined as: LaserJt Reg,+,500+ Y: PC Cour

Fonts Assigned:

	Character Table	Attributes	Pitch
1	LaserJet PC Set	Courier PC Port	10
2	LaserJet PC Set	Courier Italic PC Port	10
3	LaserJet PC Set	Courier PC Port	17
4	LaserJet PC Set	Courier PC Land	17
5	LaserJet Roman 8	Courier Roman Port	10
6	LaserJet Roman 8	Courier Roman Land	10
7	LaserJet Roman 8	ND	ND
8	LaserJet PC Set	Courier PC Bold Port	10

Features Not Supported: Type-thru

Line Draw Information:

Font(s) to be used: 1,4

Limitations: Font 4 requires 8 lines per inch

HP LaserJet Z Helv

Type: Laser

Defined as: LaserJt+,500+ Z: Helv

Fonts Assigned:

	Character Table	Attributes	Pitch
1	HP AD Helvetica 10R	Helvetica 10pt	15*
2	HP AD Helvetica 10I	Helvetica 10pt Italic	15*
3	HP AD Helvetica 12R	Helvetica 12pt	13*
4	HP AD Helvetica 12I	Helvetica 12pt Italic	13*
5	HP AD Helvetica 14B	Helvetica 14pt Bold	10*
6	HP AD Helvetica 8R	Helvetica 8pt	19*
7	Standard ASCII	Line Printer Landscape	17
8	LaserJet Roman 8	Courier Landscape	10

Features Not Supported: Line Draw, Type-thru, Overstrike, Foreign Characters

Proportional Spacing Information:

Font(s) to be used: 1-6

Pitch to be used: See above

HP LaserJet Z Times Roman

Type: Laser

Defined as: LaserJt+,500+ Z: Times Roman

Fonts Assigned:

	Character Table	*Attributes*	*Pitch*
1	HP AD Times Roman 10R	Times Roman 10pt	15*
2	HP AD Times Roman 10I	Times Roman 10pt Italic	15*
3	HP AD Times Roman 12R	Times Roman 12pt	13*
4	HP AD Times Roman 12I	Times Roman 12pt Italic	13*
5	HP AD Times Roman 14B	Times Roman 14pt Bold	11*
6	HP AD Times Roman 8R	Times Roman 8pt	20*
7	Standard ASCII	Line Printer Landscape	17
8	LaserJet Roman 8	Courier Landscape	10

Features Not Supported: Line Draw, Type-thru, Overstrike, Foreign Characters

Proportional Spacing Information:

Font(s) to be used: 1-6

Pitch to be used: See above

HP LaserJet Series II

Type: Laser

Defined as: HP LaserJet Series II

Fonts Assigned:

	Character Table	Attributes	Pitch
1	IBM Graphics	Courier	10
2	IBM Graphics	Courier Bold	10
3	IBM Graphics	Line Printer	17
4	IBM Graphics	Courier Land	10
5	IBM Graphics	Courier Bold Land	10
6	IBM Graphics	Line Printer Land	17
7	IBM Graphics	Courier	10
8	IBM Graphics	Line Printer	17

Features Not Supported: Type-thru, Proportional Spacing

Line Draw Information:

Font(s) to be used: All

Special Notes: Fonts 1 through 6 use the IBMUS symbol set. Fonts 7 and 8 use the IBM Danish/Norwegian symbol set. This printer will also work with all the LaserJet+, 500+ drivers.

HP LaserJet Soft AC Helvetica

Type: Laser

Defined as: LaserJt+,500+ Soft AC: Helv P

Fonts Assigned:

	Character Table	Attributes	Pitch
1	HP AD Helvetica 10R	Helvetica 10pt	14*
2	HP AD Helvetica 10I	Helvetica 10pt Italic	14*
3	HP AD Helvetica 6R	Helvetica 6pt	20*-22*
4	HP AD Helvetica 8R	Helvetica 8pt	18*
5	HP AD Helvetica 8I	Helvetica 8pt Italic	18*
6	HP AD Helvetica 12R	Helvetica 12pt	11*
7	HP AD Helvetica 18B	Helvetica 18pt Bold	8*
8	HP AD Helvetica 30B	Helvetica 30pt Bold	5*

Features Not Supported: Line Draw, Type-thru, Foreign Characters

Proportional Spacing Information:

Font(s) to be used: All

Pitch to be used: See above

Special Notes: This definition uses the US ASCII symbol set. For the Roman 8 symbol set (HP AD soft font disks) change 0U to 8U in the "shift into font" strings using the Printer program. See Chapter 7 for instructions.

HP LaserJet Soft AC Times Roman

Type: Laser
Defined as: LaserJt+,500+ Soft AC: Tms P

Fonts Assigned:

Character Table	Attributes	Pitch
1 HP AD Times Roman 10R	Times Roman 10pt	14*
2 HP AD Times Roman 10I	Times Roman 10pt Italic	14*
3 HP AD Times Roman 6R	Times Roman 6pt	20*-22*
4 HP AD Times Roman 8R	Times Roman 8pt	18*
5 HP AD Times Roman 8I	Times Roman 8pt Italic	18*
6 HP AD Times Roman 12R	Times Roman 12pt	11*
7 HP AD Times Roman 18B	Times Roman 18pt Bold	8*
8 HP AD Times Roman 30B	Times Roman 30pt Bold	5*

Features Not Supported: Line Draw, Type-thru, Foreign Characters

Proportional Spacing Information:

Font(s) to be used: All

Pitch to be used: See above

Special Notes: This definition uses the US ASCII symbol set. For the Roman 8 symbol set (HP AD soft font disks) change 0U to 8U in the "shift into font" strings using the Printer program. See Chapter 7 for instructions.

HP LaserJet Soft AE Helvetica Portrait

Type: Laser

Defined as: LaserJt,+,500+ Soft AE: Helv P

Fonts Assigned:

	Character Table	Attributes	Pitch
1	HP AF Helvetica 11	Helvetica 11pt	14*
2	HP AF Helvetica 11I	Helvetica Italic 11pt	14*
3	HP AF Helvetica 9	Helvetica 9pt	18*
4	HP AF Helvetica 9I	Helvetica Italic 9pt	18*
5	HP AF Helvetica 7	Helvetica 7pt	21*
6	HP AF Helvetica 18	Helvetica 18pt	8*
7	HP AF Helvetica 24	Helvetica 24pt	6*
8	HP AF Helvetica 30	Helvetica 30pt	5*

Features Not Supported: Line Draw, Type-thru, Overstrike

Proportional Spacing Information:

Font(s) to be used: All

Pitch to be used: See above

Special Notes: To print these fonts in landscape orientation, insert a "1" between the "l" and "O" in the "shift into font" strings. To get double underlining in all fonts, copy the string sent to the printer for character 255 in the Times Roman 11 character table to the desired character table. See Chapter 7 for instructions.

HP LaserJet Soft AE Times Roman Port

Type: Laser

Defined as: LaserJt+,500+,Soft AE: Tms P

Fonts Assigned:

	Character Table	Attributes	Pitch
1	HP AF Times Roman 11	Times Roman 11pt	14*
2	HP AF Times Roman 11I	Times Roman Italic 11pt	14*
3	HP AF Times Roman 9	Times Roman 9pt	18*
4	HP AF Times Roman 9I	Times Roman Italic 9pt	18*

Character Table	Attributes	Pitch
5 HP AF Times Roman 7	Times Roman 7pt	25*
6 HP AF Times Roman 18	Times Roman 18pt	9*
7 HP AF Times Roman 24	Times Roman 24pt	6*
8 HP AF Times Roman 30	Times Roman 30pt	5*

Features Not Supported: Line Draw, Type-thru, Overstrike

Proportional Spacing Information:

Font(s) to be used: All

Pitch to be used: See above

Special Notes: To print these fonts in landscape orientation, insert a "1" between the "l" and "O" in the "shift into font" strings. To get double underlining in all fonts, copy the string sent to the printer for character 255 in the Times Roman 11 character table to the desired character table. See Chapter 7 for instructions.

HP LaserJet Soft DA L Gothic,Present

Type: Laser

Defined as: LaserJt+,500+,Soft DA: LG,Prs

Fonts Assigned:

Character Table	Attributes	Pitch
1 LaserJet Roman 8	Letter Gothic 12pt	12
2 LaserJet Roman 8	Letter Gothic Italic 12pt	12
3 LaserJet Roman 8	Letter Gothic 14pt	10
4 Standard ASCII	Presentation Bold 16pt	8
5 Standard ASCII	Presentation Bold 18pt	6
6 Standard ASCII	Presentation Bold 24pt	5
7 LaserJet Math 8	Letter Gothic Math 12pt	12
8 LaserJet-R Present	Line Draw 12pt	12

Features Not Supported: Type-thru, Proportional Spacing

Line Draw Information:

Font(s) to be used: 8

Limitations: 12 pitch must be used.

Special Notes: To print these fonts in landscape orientation, insert a "1" between the "l" and "O" in the font strings. Download these fonts:

Font 1 LG120R12.R8P	Font 2 LG120I12.R8P
Font 3 LG140R10.R8P	Font 4 PS160B08.USP
Font 5 PS180B06.USP	Font 6 PS240B05.USP
Font 7 LG120R12.M8P	Font 8 LP120R12.PLP

HP LaserJet Soft EA Prestige Elite

Type: Laser

Defined as: LaserJt+,500+ Soft EA: P Elite

	Character Table	Attributes	Pitch
1	LaserJet Roman 8	Prestige Elite 10pt	12
2	LaserJet Roman 8	Prestige Elite Italic 10pt	12
3	LaserJet Roman 8	Prestige Elite Bold 10pt	12
4	LaserJet Roman 8	Prestige Elite 7pt	16
5	LaserJet Legal	Prestige Elite Legal 10pt	12
6	LaserJet Math 8	Prestige Elite Math 8 10pt	12
7	LaserJet Pi Font	Prestige Elite Pi Font 10p	12
8	LaserJet-R Present	Line Draw 10pt	12

Features Not Supported: Type-thru, Proportional Spacing

Line Draw Information:

Font(s) to be used: 8

Limitations: 12 pitch must be used.

Special Notes: To print these fonts in landscape orientation, insert a "1" between the "l" and "O" in the font strings. Download these fonts:

Font 1 PR100R12.R8P	Font 2 PR100I12.R8P
Font 3 PR100B12.R8P	Font 4 PR070R16.R8P
Font 5 PR100R12.LGP	Font 6 PR100R12.M8P
Font 7 PR100R12.PIP	Font 8 LP120R12.PLP

HP PaintJet

Type: Inkjet

Defined as: HP PaintJet

Fonts Assigned:

Character Table	Attributes	Pitch
1 LaserJet Roman 8	Black	10,12,15
2 LaserJet Roman 8	Red	10,12,15
3 LaserJet Roman 8	Green	10,12,15
4 LaserJet Roman 8	Yellow	10,12,15
5 LaserJet Roman 8	Blue	10,12,15
6 LaserJet Roman 8	Magenta	10,12,15
7 LaserJet Roman 8	Cyan	10,12,15
8 LaserJet Roman 8	Black	10,12,15

Features Not Supported: Type-thru, Advance, Proportional Spacing, Line Draw

Special Notes: 15 pitch returns 18 pitch.

HP QuietJet Plus

Type: Inkjet

Defined as: HP QuietJet Plus

Fonts Assigned:

Character Table	Attributes	Pitch
1 IBM Graphics	Draft	10,12,15
2 IBM Graphics	Draft	10,12,15
3 IBM Graphics	NLQ	10,12
4 IBM Graphics	Enhanced	10
5 IBM Graphics	NLQ 6 pitch	10
6 IBM Graphics	NLQ 5 pitch	10
7 IBM Graphics	Draft 5 pitch	10
8 IBM Graphics	Draft	10

Features Not Supported: Type-thru, Proportional Spacing

Line Draw Information:

Font(s) to be used: All

Special Notes: 15 pitch returns a pitch of 21.

HP Thinkjet

Type: Inkjet

Defined as: HP ThinkJet

Fonts Assigned:

	Character Table	Attributes	Pitch
1	HP ThinkJet	Draft	10
2	HP ThinkJet	Double-Wide	10
3	HP ThinkJet	Compressed	10
4	HP ThinkJet	Double-Wide Compressed	10
5	ASCII Backspace	ND	ND
6	ASCII Line Printer	ND	ND
7	ASCII Backspace	ND	ND
8	ASCII Line Printer	ND	ND

Features Not Supported: Double Underline, Line Draw, Superscript/Subscript, Type-thru, Advance, Proportional Spacing

Special Notes: Turn all switches off.

IBM Color Jetprinter

Type: Inkjet

Defined as: IBM Color Jetprinter

Fonts Assigned:

	Character Table	Attributes	Pitch
1	IBM Graphics	Black	10,15
2	IBM Graphics	Magenta	10,15
3	IBM Graphics	Cyan	10,15
4	IBM Graphics	Red	10,15
5	IBM Graphics	Green	10,15
6	IBM Graphics	Blue	10,15
7	IBM Graphics	Double-Wide Compressed	10
8	IBM Graphics	Double-Wide	10,15

Features Not Supported: Double Underline, Type-thru, Advance, Proportional Spacing

Line Draw Information:

Font(s) to be used: All

IBM Color Printer

Type: Dot Matrix

Defined as: IBM Color Printer

Fonts Assigned:

Character Table	Attributes	Pitch
1 IBM Graphics	NLQ Band 4	10,12,15
2 IBM Graphics	Draft Band 4	10,12,15
3 IBM Graphics	NLQ Band 3	10,12,15
4 IBM Graphics	Draft Band 3	10,12,15
5 IBM Graphics	NLQ Band 2	10,12,15
6 IBM Graphics	Draft Band 2	10,12,15
7 IBM Graphics	NLQ Band 1	10,12,15
8 IBM Graphics	Draft Band 1	10,12,15

Features Not Supported: Double Underline, Type-thru, Proportional Spacing

Line Draw Information:

Font(s) to be used: All

IBM Convertible

Type: Dot Matrix

Defined as: IBM Convertible

Fonts Assigned:

Character Table	Attributes	Pitch
1 IBM Graphics	Draft	10,15
2 IBM Graphics	Draft	10,15
3 IBM Graphics	Emphasized	10
4 IBM Graphics	Double-Strike	10,15
5 IBM Graphics	Double-Wide Emphasized	10
6 IBM Graphics	Double-Wide	10,15
7 IBM Graphics	Superscript	15
8 IBM Graphics	Draft	10,15

Features Not Supported: Double Underline, Type-thru, Advance, Proportional Spacing

Line Draw Information:

Font(s) to be used: All

Limitations: Fonts 5, 6, and 7 should have half-line spacing.

Special Notes: Make sure printer is on-line with the slide switch.

IBM Graphics Printer

Type: Dot Matrix

Defined as: IBM Graphics Printer

Fonts Assigned:

	Character Table	Attributes	Pitch
1	IBM Graphics	Draft	10,15
2	IBM Graphics	Draft	10,15
3	IBM Graphics	Enhanced	10
4	IBM Graphics	Double-Strike	10,15
5	IBM Graphics	Double-Wide Enhanced (5)	10
6	IBM Graphics	Draft Double-Wide (5,9)	10,15
7	IBM Graphics	Superscript	10,15
8	IBM Graphics	Draft Line Draw	10,15

Features Not Supported: Double Underline, Type-thru, Advance, Proportional Spacing

Line Draw Information:

Font(s) to be used: All

Limitations: Fonts 5, 6, 7 and 8 require half-line spacing.

Special Notes: If all footnotes are double-spaced after the first one, you should enter the Printer program and delete the codes to set VMI <27>A<K><27>2. The code is used to adjust the amount of space for a line feed or reverse line feed, but conflicts with superscript/subscript. If the code is deleted, you cannot get 8 lines per inch.

IBM Pageprinter Courier

Type: Pageprinter

Defined as: IBM Pageprinter Courier

Fonts Assigned:

	Character Table	Attributes	Pitch
1	IBM Pageprinter MLP	Courier	10
2	IBM Pageprinter MLP	Courier Italic	10
3	IBM Pageprinter MLP	Courier	12
4	IBM Pageprinter MLP	Courier	17
5	IBM Pageprinter MLP	Courier Double-Wide	5
6	IBM Pageprinter MLP	Printer's Font #6	ND
7	IBM Pageprinter MLP	Condensed	15
8	IBM Pageprinter MLP	Math Symbol	10

Features Not Supported: Double Underline, Type-thru, Advance, Proportional Spacing

Line Draw Information:

Font(s) to be used: All

Special Notes: Must use specified pitch.

IBM Pageprinter Essay

Type: Pageprinter

Defined as: IBM Pageprinter Essay PS

Fonts Assigned:

	Character Table	Attributes	Pitch
1	IBM Pageprinter MLP	Essay	12*
2	IBM Pageprinter MLP	Essay Italic	12*
3	IBM Pageprinter MLP	Essay Bold	12*
4	IBM Pageprinter MLP	Essay Light	12*
5	IBM Pageprinter MLP	Boldface	12*
6	IBM Pageprinter MLP	Boldface Italic	12*
7	IBM Pageprinter MLP	Document	12*
8	IBM Pageprinter MLP	ND	ND

Features Not Supported: Double Underline, Line Draw, Type-thru, Advance

Proportional Spacing Information:

Font(s) to be used: 1-7

Pitch to be used: See above

Special Notes: Must use specified pitch.

IBM Pageprinter Gothic

Type: Pageprinter

Defined as: IBM Pageprinter Gothic-text

Fonts Assigned:

	Character Table	*Attributes*	*Pitch*
1	IBM Pageprinter MLP	Gothic-text	12
2	IBM Pageprinter MLP	Gothic-text Italic	12
3	IBM Pageprinter MLP	Gothic-text	10
4	IBM Pageprinter MLP	Gothic-text	13
5	IBM Pageprinter MLP	Gothic-text semi-condensed	15
6	IBM Pageprinter MLP	Gothic-text	27
7	IBM Pageprinter MLP	ND	ND
8	IBM Pageprinter MLP	ND	ND

Features Not Supported: Double Underline, Line Draw, Type-thru, Advance, Foreign Characters, Proportional Spacing

Special Notes: Must use specified pitch.

IBM Pageprinter Prestige

Type: Pageprinter

Defined as: IBM Pageprinter Prestige

Fonts Assigned:

	Character Table	*Attributes*	*Pitch*
1	IBM Pageprinter MLP	Prestige	12
2	IBM Pageprinter MLP	Prestige Italic	12
3	IBM Pageprinter MLP	Prestige	10
4	IBM Pageprinter MLP	Letter Gothic	12

Character Table		Attributes	Pitch
5	IBM Pageprinter MLP	Orator	10
6	IBM Pageprinter MLP	Script	12
7	IBM Pageprinter MLP	ND	ND
8	IBM Pageprinter MLP	Math Symbol	12

Features Not Supported: Double Underline, Line Draw, Type-thru, Advance, Proportional Spacing

Special Notes: Must use specified pitch.

IBM Pageprinter Serif

Type: Pageprinter

Defined as: IBM Pageprinter Serif-text

Fonts Assigned:

Character Table		Attributes	Pitch
1	IBM Pageprinter MLP	Serif-text	12
2	IBM Pageprinter MLP	Serif-text Italic	12
3	IBM Pageprinter MLP	Serif-text	10
4	IBM Pageprinter MLP	Serif-text Italic	10
5	IBM Pageprinter MLP	Serif-text	15
6	IBM Pageprinter MLP	ND	ND
7	IBM Pageprinter MLP	ND	ND
8	IBM Pageprinter MLP	ND	ND

Features Not Supported: Double Underline, Line Draw, Type-thru, Advance, Foreign Characters, Proportional Spacing

Special Notes: Must use specified pitch.

IBM Pageprinter Sonoran

Type: Pageprinter

Defined as: IBM Pageprinter Sonoran PS

Fonts Assigned:

	Character Table	Attributes	Pitch
1	Sonoran 10 Point PS	Sonoran 10pt	14*
2	Sonoran Italic PS	Sonoran Italic 10pt	14*
3	Sonoran 8 Point PS	Sonoran 8pt	18*
4	Sonoran 12 Point PS	Sonoran 12pt	12*
5	Sonoran 16 Point PS	Sonoran 16pt	10*
6	Sonoran 24 Point PS	Sonoran 24pt	7*
7	IBM Pageprinter MLP	ND	ND
8	IBM Pageprinter MLP	ND	ND

Features Not Supported: Double Underline, Line Draw, Type-thru, Advance, Overstrike

Proportional Spacing Information:

Font(s) to be used: 1-6

Pitch to be used: See above

Special Notes: Must use specified pitch.

IBM Proprinter

Type: Dot Matrix

Defined as: IBM Proprinter

Fonts Assigned:

	Character Table	Attributes	Pitch
1	IBM Proprinter	NLQ	10,12,15
2	IBM Proprinter	Draft	10,12,15
3	IBM Proprinter	NLQ Emphasized	10,12
4	IBM Proprinter	Draft Emphasized	10,12
5	IBM Proprinter	NLQ Double-Wide	10,12
6	IBM Proprinter	Draft Double-Wide	10,12
7	IBM Proprinter	Draft	10,12,15
8	IBM Proprinter	Draft	10,12,15

Features Not Supported: Double Underline, Type-thru, Advance, Proportional Spacing

Line Draw Information:

Font(s) to be used: All

Limitations: Font 2 requires half-line spacing.

IBM Proprinter II

Type: Dot Matrix

Defined as: IBM Proprinter II

Fonts Assigned:

	Character Table	*Attributes*	*Pitch*
1	IBM Proprinter XL	NLQ II	10,12
2	IBM Proprinter XL	Subscript	10,12,15
3	IBM Proprinter XL	NLQ I	11*
4	IBM Proprinter XL	Double-Wide	10,12,15
5	IBM Proprinter XL	Double-High	10
6	IBM Proprinter XL	Double-Wide, Double-High (5)	10
7	IBM Proprinter XL	Draft 12 pitch	12
8	IBM Proprinter XL	Draft	10,12,15

Features Not Supported: Double Underline, Type-thru, Advance

Proportional Spacing Information:

Font(s) to be used: 3

Pitch to be used: 11*

Line Draw Information:

Font(s) to be used: All

Limitations: Font 2 requires half-line spacing.

IBM Proprinter XL

Type: Dot Matrix

Defined as: IBM Proprinter XL

Fonts Assigned:

Character Table	Attributes	Pitch
1 IBM Proprinter XL	NLQ	10,12,15
2 IBM Proprinter XL	Subscript	10,12,15
3 IBM Proprinter XL	NLQ PS	11*
4 IBM Proprinter XL	Continuous Overscore	10,12,15
5 IBM Proprinter XL	Double-Wide	10,12,15
6 IBM Proprinter XL	Double-High	10
7 IBM Proprinter XL	Double-Wide, Double-High	10
8 IBM Proprinter XL	Draft	10,12,15

Features Not Supported: Type-thru, Advance, Double Underlining

Proportional Spacing Information:

Font(s) to be used: 3

Pitch to be used: 11*

Limitations: Cannot print a footnote line in PS.

Line Draw Information:

Font(s) to be used: All

Limitations: Font 2 requires half-line spacing.

IBM Quietwriter I/II

Type: Thermal

Defined as: IBM Quietwriter I/II

Fonts Assigned:

Character Table	Attributes	Pitch
1 IBM Quietwriter	Font Holder A	Depends on Font
2 IBM Quietwriter	Font Holder A Double-Wide	Depends on Font
3 IBM Quietwriter	Font Holder A—PS	12*
4 IBM Quietwriter	Font Holder A	Depends on font
5 IBM Quietwriter	Font Holder *	Depends on font

Character Table	Attributes	Pitch
6 IBM Quietwriter	Font Holder * Double-Wide	Depends on font
7 IBM Quietwriter	Font Holder *—PS	12*
8 IBM Quietwriter	Font Holder *	Depends on font

Features Not Supported: Advance when using a sheet feeder

Proportional Spacing Information:

Font(s) to be used: 3 or 7

Pitch to be used: 12*

Limitations: For PS, you must use a PS cartridge in slot A if font 3 is selected, and slot * if font 7 is selected.

Line Draw Information:

Font(s) to be used: All

Limitations: Most 12 pitch cartridges do not support line draw. Line draw is not supported with PS cartridges. Some may require 8 lines per inch or half-line spacing.

Sheet Feeder Information: Define as continuous forms. If you hand feed the paper, you must have a top margin of 24 half-lines instead of 12 because you cannot roll the sheet into the correct location. The printer automatically feeds the paper in and needs the extra inch to feed it around the roller.

Special Notes: Cartridges can be used in either holder. DIP switches 3 and 4 must be on to get the extended character set and to use the full carriage width.

IBM Quietwriter III

Type: Thermal

Defined as: IBM Quietwriter III

Fonts Assigned:

Character Table	Attributes	Pitch
1 IBM Quietwriter	Resident Courier 10	10
2 IBM Quietwriter	Resident Courier 12	12

Character Table	Attributes	Pitch
3 IBM Quietwriter	Resident Boldface PS	12*
4 IBM Quietwriter	Pluggable Font PS	12*
5 IBM Quietwriter	Resident Courier 10 Double-Wide (5)	10
6 IBM Quietwriter	Pluggable Font 10 pitch	10
7 IBM Quietwriter	Pluggable Font 12 pitch	12
8 IBM Quietwriter	Resident 17.1 pitch	17

Features Not Supported: Type-thru

Proportional Spacing Information:

Font(s) to be used: 3,4

Pitch to be used: 12*

Limitations: Only supported with internal Bold PS and PS title on cartridge.

Line Draw Information:

Font(s) to be used: All

Limitations: No line draw with PS.

Sheet Feeder Information: Define as continuous forms.

IBM Wheelprinter

Type: Daisy Wheel

Defined as: IBM Wheelprinter

Fonts Assigned:

Character Table	Attributes	Pitch
1 ASCII Backspace	Depends on wheel used	10,12,15
2 ASCII Backspace	Depends on wheel used	10,12,15
3 IBM 5218 Bold PS	IBM 5218 Bold PS	13*
4 ASCII Backspace	Depends on wheel used	10,12,15
5 ASCII Backspace	Depends on wheel used	10,12,15
6 ASCII Backspace	Depends on wheel used	10,12,15
7 ASCII Backspace	Depends on wheel used	10,12,15
8 ASCII Backspace	Depends on wheel used	10,12,15

Features Not Supported: Double Underline, Line Draw, Type-thru, Foreign Characters

Proportional Spacing Information:

Font(s) to be used: 3

Pitch to be used: 13*

Limitations: Must use the IBM 5218 PS print wheel.

Sheet Feeder Information: Define as continuous forms.

IBM Wheelprinter E

Type: Daisy Wheel

Defined as: IBM Wheelprinter E

Fonts Assigned:

	Character Table	Attributes	Pitch
1	ASCII Backspace	Depends on Wheel Used	10,12,15
2	ASCII Backspace	Depends on Wheel Used	10,12,15
3	IBM 5218 Bold PS	IBM 5218 Bold PS	13*
4	ASCII Backspace	Depends on Wheel Used	10,12,15
5	ASCII Backspace	Depends on Wheel Used	10,12,15
6	ASCII Backspace	Depends on Wheel Used	10,12,15
7	ASCII Backspace	Depends on Wheel Used	10,12,15
8	ASCII Backspace	Depends on Wheel Used	10,12,15

Features Not Supported: Line Draw, Type-thru, Foreign Characters

Proportional Spacing Information:

Font(s) to be used: 3

Pitch to be used: 13*

Limitations: Must have IBM 5218 Bold PS print wheel.

Sheet Feeder Information: Define as continuous forms.

Kyocera F-1010 Landscape

Type: Laser

Defined as: Kyocera F-1010 Fixed Landscape

Emulating: HP LaserJet

Fonts Assigned:

	Character Table	Attributes	Pitch
1	LaserJet+ Box	Courier	10
2	LaserJet Roman 8	Courier Italic	10
3	LaserJet Roman 8	Prestige Elite	12
4	LaserJet Roman 8	Prestige Elite Italic	12
5	LaserJet Roman 8	Letter Gothic	12
6	LaserJet Roman 8	Letter Gothic Italic	12
7	LaserJet Roman 8	Line Printer	17
8	LaserJet+ Box	Line Printer	17

Features Not Supported: Type-thru, Proportional Spacing

Line Draw Information:

Font(s) to be used: 1,8

Special Notes: Because of the unprintable region, the laser cursor cannot be positioned to the far left of the paper. Bold and underline will sometimes cause characters to overlap when in landscape. Kyocera is aware of the problem.

Kyocera F-1010 Portrait

Type: Laser

Defined as: Kyocera F-1010 Fixed Portrait

Emulating: HP LaserJet

Fonts Assigned:

	Character Table	Attributes	Pitch
1	LaserJet Roman 8	Courier	10
2	LaserJet Roman 8	Prestige Elite	12
3	LaserJet Roman 8	Prestige Elite	17
4	LaserJet Roman 8	Letter Gothic	12
5	LaserJet Roman 8	Letter Gothic Bold	12
6	LaserJet Roman 8	Line Printer	17
7	LaserJet Roman 8	Line Printer	21
8	LaserJet+ Box	Courier Line Draw	10

Features Not Supported: Type-thru, Proportional Spacing

Line Draw Information:

Font(s) to be used: 8

Special Notes: Because of the unprintable region, the laser cursor cannot be positioned to the far left of the paper.

Kyocera F-1010 Proportional

Type: Laser

Defined as: Kyocera F-1010 TmsRm/Helvetica

Emulating: HP LaserJet

Fonts Assigned:

	Character Table	Attributes	Pitch
1	Kyocera Times 10	Times Roman 10pt	15*
2	Kyocera Times 10I	Times Roman Italic 10pt	15*
3	Kyocera Helvetica 14B	Helvetica 14.4pt Bold	10*
4	Kyocera Times 8	Times Roman 8pt	19*
5	Kyocera Helvetica 12B	Helvetica 12pt Bold	12*
6	Kyocera Helvetica 10B	Helvetica 10pt	15*
7	Kyocera Helvetica 8	Helvetica 8pt	19*
8	Kyocera Helvetica 6	Helvetica 6pt	26*

Features Not Supported: Line Draw, Type-thru, Overstrike

Proportional Spacing Information:

Font(s) to be used: All

Pitch to be used: See above

Special Notes: Because of the unprintable region, the laser cursor cannot be positioned to the far left of the paper.

Mannesmann Tally MT180

Type: Dot Matrix

Defined as: Mannesmann Tally MT180

Fonts Assigned:

	Character Table	Attributes	Pitch
1	Standard ASCII	NLQ	10,12
2	Standard ASCII	Draft	10,12
3	Standard ASCII	Draft	10,12
4	Standard ASCII	Draft	10,12
5	Standard ASCII	Draft	10,12
6	Standard ASCII	Draft	10,12
7	Standard ASCII	Draft	10,12
8	Standard ASCII	Draft	10,12

Features Not Supported: Double Underline, Type-thru, Advance, Foreign Characters, Proportional Spacing, Line Draw

Mannesmann Tally MT290

Type: Dot Matrix

Defined as: Mannesmann Tally MT290 with IBM ROM

Fonts Assigned:

	Character Table	Attributes	Pitch
1	Mannesmann 290	NLQ	10,12,15
2	Mannesmann 290	Emphasized	10,12,15
3	Mannesmann 290	NLQ PS	10*,12*,15*
4	Mannesmann 290	Draft Double-Wide 5 pitch	10
5	Mannesmann 290	Draft Double-Wide 6 pitch	12
6	Mannesmann 290	Draft Double-Wide 7.5 pitch	15
7	Mannesmann 290	Subscript	12,15
8	Mannesmann 290	Draft	10,12,15

Features Not Supported: Double Underline, Line Draw, Type-thru, Advance

Proportional Spacing Information:

Font(s) to be used: 3

Pitch to be used: See above

Special Notes: Entering 15 pitch returns 17 pitch.

Mannesmann Tally MT910

Type: Laser

Defined as: Mannesmann Tally MT910

Emulating: HP LaserJet

Fonts Assigned:

	Character Table	Attributes	Pitch
1	LaserJet Roman 8	Courier	10
2	LaserJet Roman 8	Courier Italic	10
3	LaserJet Roman 8	Line Printer	17
4	LaserJet Roman 8	Courier Land	10
5	LaserJet Roman 8	Courier Italic Land	10
6	LaserJet Roman 8	Line Printer Land	17
7	LaserJet+ Graph	Courier	10
8	LaserJet+ Box	Courier	10

Features Not Supported: Type-thru, Proportional Spacing

Line Draw Information: Font(s) to be used: 7,8

Special Notes: No double underline in fonts 7 and 8.

Mannesmann Tally MT910 (11)

Type: Laser

Defined as: Mannesmann Tally MT910 (11)

Fonts Assigned:

	Character Table	Attributes	Pitch
1	ManTal Dutch 10N	Dutch 10pt	13*
2	ManTal Dutch 10B	Dutch Bold	13*
3	ManTal Dutch 10I	Dutch Italic	13*
4	ManTal Dutch 10BI	Dutch Italic Bold	13*

Character Table	Attributes	Pitch
5 ManTal Dutch 10N	Dutch 10pt Land	13*
6 ManTal Dutch 10B	Dutch Bold Land	13*
7 ManTal Dutch 10I	Dutch Italic Land	13*
8 ManTal Dutch 10BI	Dutch Italic Bold Land	13*

Features Not Supported: Type-thru

Proportional Spacing Information:

Font(s) to be used: All

Pitch to be used: 13*

Sheet Feeder Information: Extra lines = 0, left edge of paper = 0, bins = 3 (bin 1—upper cassette, bin 2—lower cassette, bin 3—manual feed). Try using the HP LaserJet 500+ sheet feeder definition.

Mannesmann Tally MT910 (12/16)

Type: Laser

Defined as: Mannesmann Tally MT910 (12/16)

Fonts Assigned:

Character Table	Attributes	Pitch
1 ManTal Swiss 10	Swiss721 10pt	13*
2 ManTal Swiss 12	Swiss721 12pt	11*
3 ManTal Swiss 14	Swiss721 14pt	10*
4 ManTal Swiss 8B	Swiss721 8pt Bold	18*
5 ManTal Swiss 8	Swiss721 8pt	18*
6 ManTal Swiss 6	Swiss721 6pt	22*
7 LaserJet Roman 8	Swiss721 10pt Land	13*
8 ManTal Tax Form	Swiss721 12pt Land	11*

Features Not Supported: Line Draw, Type-thru

Proportional Spacing Information:

Font(s) to be used: All

Pitch to be used: See above

Sheet Feeder Information: Extra lines = 0, left edge of paper = 0, bins = 3 (bin 1—upper cassette, bin 2—lower cassette, bin 3—manual feed). Try the HP LaserJet 500+ sheet feeder definition.

Special Notes: Definition is for cartridges #12 and #16. Fonts 4 through 6 are for #16.

Mannesmann Tally MT910 (13)

Type: Laser

Defined as: Mannesmann Tally MT910 (13)

Fonts Assigned:

	Character Table	Attributes	Pitch
1	ManTal Swiss 10B	Letter Gothic 12pt	10,12,15
2	ManTal Swiss 10B	Letter Gothic 12pt Italic	10,12,15
3	ManTal Swiss 10B	Letter Gothic 12pt Bold	10,12,15
4	ManTal Swiss 10B	Letter Gothic 12pt Bold Italic	10,12,15
5	ManTal Swiss 10B	Letter Gothic 12pt Land	10,12,15
6	ManTal Swiss 10B	Letter Gothic 12pt Italic Land	10,12,15
7	ManTal Swiss 10B	Letter Gothic 12pt Bold Land	10,12,15
8	ManTal Swiss 10B	Letter Gothic 12pt Bold Italic Land	10,12,15

Features Not Supported: Line Draw, Type-thru, Proportional Spacing

Sheet Feeder Information: Extra lines = 0, left edge of paper = 0, bins = 3 (bin 1—upper casette, bin 2—lower cassette, bin 3—manual feed). Try the HP LaserJet 500+ sheet feeder definition.

Special Notes: Panel set at defaults.

Mannesmann Tally MT910 (15)

Type: Laser

Defined as: Mannesmann Tally MT910 (15)

Fonts Assigned:

Character Table	Attributes	Pitch
1 ManTal Swiss 10	Swiss721 10pt	13*
2 ManTal Swiss 12	Swiss721 12pt	11*
3 ManTal Swiss 14	Swiss721 14pt	10*
4 ManTal Swiss 8b	Swiss721 8pt Bold	18*
5 ManTal Swiss 8	Swiss721 8pt Normal	18*
6 ManTal Swiss 6	Swiss721 6pt	22*
7 LaserJet Roman 8	Courier	10
8 ManTal Tax Form	Courier/Tax Line Draw	10

Features Not Supported: Type-thru

Proportional Spacing Information:

Font(s) to be used: 1-6

Pitch to be used: See above

Line Draw Information:

Font(s) to be used: 8

Limitations: Text not recommended.

Sheet Feeder Information: Extra lines = 0, left edge of paper = 0, bins = 3 (bin 1—upper cassette, bin 2—lower cassette, bin 3—manual feed). Try using the HP LaserJet 500+ sheet feeder definition.

Special Notes: Panel set for default.

MPI Printmate 150

Type: Dot Matrix

Defined as: MPI Printmate 150

Fonts Assigned:

Character Table	Attributes	Pitch
1 Standard ASCII	Draft	10,12,17
2 Standard ASCII	Sans Serif	10,12,17
3 Standard ASCII	Condensed	17
4 Standard ASCII	Double-Wide	5,6,7
5 Standard ASCII	Draft	10,12,17

Character Table	Attributes	Pitch
6 Standard ASCII	Draft	10,12,17
7 Standard ASCII	Draft	10,12,17
8 Standard ASCII	Draft	10,12,17

Features Not Supported: Double Underline, Line Draw, Superscript/Subscript, Type-thru, Advance, Foreign Characters, Proportional Spacing

NEC 2050

Type: Thimble

Defined as: NEC 2050

Fonts Assigned:

Character Table	Attributes	Pitch
1 ASCII Backspace	Depends on thimble used	10,12,15
2 ASCII Backspace	Depends on thimble used	10,12,15
3 NEC Bold PS	Bold PS	13*
4 NEC 3550 Technical	Math Technical	10,12,15
5 NEC Multi-L A	Multi-Lingual A	10,12,15
6 NEC Emperor PS	Emperor PS	13*
7 NEC OCR-B	OCR-B	10,12,15
8 NEC German	German	10,12,15

Features Not Supported: Line Draw, Foreign Characters

Proportional Spacing Information:

Font(s) to be used: 3,6

Pitch to be used: 13*

Limitations: Must have correct PS print wheel.

Sheet Feeder Information: Use the NEC 3550 definition. Sheet feeder must be disengaged to use Type-thru.

NEC 3510, 3530, and 7730

Type: Thimble

Defined as: NEC 3510/3530/7730

Fonts Assigned:

Character Table	Attributes	Pitch
1 ASCII Backspace	Depends on thimble used	10,12,15
2 ASCII Backspace	Depends on thimble used	10,12,15
3 NEC Bold PS	Bold PS	13*
4 NEC 3550 Technical	Depends on thimble used	10,12,15
5 NEC Multi-L A	Depends on thimble used	10,12,15
6 NEC Emperor PS	Emperor PS	13*
7 NEC OCR-B	Depends on thimble used	10,12,15
8 NEC German	Depends on thimble used	10,12,15

Features Not Supported: Line Draw, Foreign Characters

Proportional Spacing Information:

Font(s) to be used: 3,6

Pitch to be used: 13*

NEC 3550

Type: Thimble

Defined as: NEC 3550

Fonts Assigned:

Character Table	Attributes	Pitch
1 ASCII Backspace	Depends on thimble used	10,12,15
2 NEC Line draw	NEC Line Draw	10,12,15
3 NEC Bold PS	Bold PS	13*
4 NEC 3550 Technical	Math Technical	10,12,15
5 NEC Multi-L A	Multi-Lingual A	10,12,15
6 NEC Emperor PS	Emperor PS	13*
7 NEC OCR-B	OCR-B	10,12,15
8 NEC German	German	10,12,15

Features Not Supported: Line Draw, Type-thru, Foreign Characters

Proportional Spacing Information:

Font(s) to be used: 3,6

Pitch to be used: 13*

Limitations: Must use correct print wheel.

Line Draw Information:

Font(s) to be used: 2

Limitations: Platen moves a great deal.

Sheet Feeder Information: Use NEC 3550 definition and leave settings at the default. Switch SW1-6 should be on if you have a sheet feeder attached.

Special Notes: Line draw is very slow and does not use actual line draw characters. Switch SW2-5 must be on for superscript (and footnote numbers) to print properly. SW1-1 should be off (auto CR).

NEC 5515

Type: Thimble

Defined as: NEC 5515/7715

Fonts Assigned:

	Character Table	Attributes	Pitch
1	ASCII Backspace	Depends on thimble used	10,12,15
2	ASCII Backspace	Depends on thimble used	10,12,15
3	NEC Bold PS	Depends on thimble used	13*
4	NEC French	Depends on thimble used	10,12,15
5	NEC Multi-L A	Depends on thimble used	10,12,15
6	NEC Emperor PS	Depends on thimble used	10,12,15
7	NEC OCR-B	Depends on thimble used	10,12,15
8	NEC German	Depends on thimble used	10,12,15

Features Not Supported: Line Draw, Type-thru, Foreign Characters

Proportional Spacing Information:

Font(s) to be used: 3

Pitch to be used: 13*

NEC 8830

Type: Thimble

Defined as: NEC 8830

Fonts Assigned:

Character Table	Attributes	Pitch
1 ASCII Backspace	Depends on thimble used	10,12,15
2 NEC Line Draw	NEC Line Draw	10,12,15
3 NEC MS Bold	MS Bold	13*
4 NEC MS Souvenir	MS Souvenir	13*
5 NEC MS Emperor	MS Emperor	13*
6 NEC OCR-B	OCR-B	10,12,15
7 NEC Multi-L A	Multi-Lingual A	10,12,15
8 NEC 3550 Technical	3550 Technical	10,12,15

Features Not Supported: Type-thru, Foreign Characters

Proportional Spacing Information:

Font(s) to be used: 3,4,5

Pitch to be used: 13*

Limitations: Must use correct print wheel.

Line Draw Information:

Font(s) to be used: 2

Limitation: Does not use actual line draw characters.

NEC 8850

Type: Thimble

Defined as: NEC 8850

Fonts Assigned:

Character Table	Attributes	Pitch
1 ASCII Backspace	Depends on thimble used	10,12,15
2 NEC Line Draw	NEC Line Draw	10,12,15
3 NEC MS Bold	Bold PS	13*

Character Table	Attributes	Pitch
4 NEC MS Souvenir	Souvenir PS	13*
5 NEC MS Emperor	Emperor PS	13*
6 NEC OCR-B	OCR-B	10,12,15
7 NEC Multi-L A	Multi-Lingual A	10,12,15
8 NEC 3550 Technical	Math Technical	10,12,15

Features Not Supported: Type-thru, Foreign Characters

Proportional Spacing Information:

Font(s) to be used: 3,4,5

Pitch to be used: 13*

Limitations: Must use correct print wheel.

Line Draw Information:

Font(s) to be used: 2

Limitations: No double-line draw. Does not use actual line draw characters.

NEC Spinwriter ELF 350

Defined as: Use the NEC 3550 definition, not the ELF 360 definition.

NEC Elf 360

Type: Thimble

Defined as: NEC Elf 360

Fonts Assigned:

Character Table	Attributes	Pitch
1 ASCII Backspace	Depends on thimble used	10,12,15
2 ASCII Backspace	Depends on thimble used	10,12,15
3 NEC Bold PS	Bold PS	13*
4 NEC 3550 Technical	Math Technical	10,12,15
5 NEC Multi-L A	Multi-Lingual A	10,12,15
6 NEC Emperor PS	Emperor PS	13*
7 NEC OCR-B	OCR-B	10,12,15
8 NEC German	German	10,12,15

Features Not Supported: Line Draw, Foreign Characters

Proportional Spacing Information:

Font(s) to be used: 3,6

Pitch to be used: 13*

Limitations: Must have correct print wheel.

NEC Pinwriter P2

Type: Dot Matrix

Defined as: NEC Pinwriter P2/P3-3

Fonts Assigned:

	Character Table	Attributes	Pitch
1	NEC P2/P3-3	NLQ Pica	10
2	NEC P2/P3-3	NLQ Elite	10
3	NEC P2/P3-3	NLQ PS	11*
4	NEC P2/P3-3	Draft Pica	10
5	NEC P2/P3-3	Condensed	10
6	NEC P2/P3-3	Double-Wide	10
7	NEC P2/P3-3	Enhanced	10
7	NEC P2/P3-3	High-Speed Pica	10

Features Not Supported: Double Underline, Type-thru, 6/8 LPI

Proportional Spacing Information:

Font(s) to be used: 3

Pitch to be used: 11*

Line Draw Information:

Font(s) to be used: All (5, 6, and 7 are limited).

Special Notes: The last number on the interface module determines definition to be used.

NEC Pinwriter P3

Type: Dot Matrix

Defined as: NEC Pinwriter P2/P3-2,P2/P3-7

Fonts Assigned:

Character Table	Attributes	Pitch
1 NEC P2/P3-2,7	NLQ Pica	10
2 NEC P2/P3-2,7	NLQ Elite	10
3 NEC P2/P3-2,7	NLQ PS	11*
4 NEC P2/P3-2,7	Draft Pica	10
5 NEC P2/P3-2,7	Condensed	10
6 NEC P2/P3-2,7	NLQ Double-Wide	10
7 NEC P2/P3-2,7	High-Speed Pica	10
8 NEC P2/P3-2,7	Draft Elite	10

Features Not Supported: Double Underline, Type-thru

Proportional Spacing Information:

Font(s) to be used: 3

Pitch to be used: 11*

Line Draw Information:

Font(s) to be used: All

NEC Pinwriter P5 and P7

Type: Dot Matrix

Defined as: NEC Pinwriter P5/P7

Fonts Assigned:

Character Table	Attributes	Pitch
1 NEC P5	NLQ	10,12,15
2 NEC P5 Superscript/ Subscript PS	Condensed	10,12,15
3 NEC P5	PS	13*
4 NEC P5 Italic PS	Italic	10,12,15
5 NEC P5	Double-Wide	10,12,15
6 NEC P5	Double-High	10,12,15
7 NEC P5	Double-High, Triple-Wide	10,12,15
8 NEC P5	Draft	10,12,15

Features Not Supported: Type-thru

Proportional Spacing Information:

Font(s) to be used: 3

Pitch to be used: 13*

Line Draw Information:

Font(s) to be used: 1,3-8

NEC P565

Defined as: Try the NEC P5 definition.

Nissho NP-910

Type: Dot Matrix

Defined as: Nissho NP-910

Fonts Assigned:

	Character Table	Attributes	Pitch
1	IBM Graphics	NLQ Courier 10	10,12,15
2	IBM Graphics	NLQ Courier 12	12,15
3	IBM Graphics	NLQ Courier 15	12,15
4	IBM Graphics	NLQ Courier 18	12,15
5	IBM Graphics	NLQ Courier 10 Italic	10,12,15
6	IBM Graphics	Double-Wide	10,12,15
7	IBM Graphics	Plug-in ROM 10 pitch	10,12,15
8	IBM Graphics	Draft	10,12,15

Features Not Supported: Type-thru, Advance, Proportional Spacing

Line Draw Information:

Font(s) to be used: 1-6,8

Sheet Feeder Information: Define as continuous forms.

Nissho NP-2410

Type: Dot Matrix

Defined as: Nissho NP-2410

Fonts Assigned:

	Character Table	Attributes	Pitch
1	IBM Graphics	NLQ Courier 10	10,12
2	NP 2410 Superscript/ Subscript Compressed PS	Superscript	10,12,15
3	Nissho Century PS	Century PS	13*
4	IBM Graphics	NLQ Courier 10 Italic	10,12
5	IBM Graphics	NLQ Courier 10 Double-Wide	10,12
6	IBM Graphics	Plug-in Cartridge Font 1	n/a
7	Nissho Script PS	Plug-in Cartridge Font 2	n/a
8	IBM Graphics	Draft	10,12,15

Features Not Supported: Type-thru

Proportional Spacing Information:

Font(s) to be used: 3,7

Pitch to be used: 13*

Limitations: The script PS cartridge will do PS in font 7 with pitch at 13*.

Line Draw Information:

Font(s) to be used: 1,4,5,8

Sheet Feeder Information: Try the Diablo Single/Dual/ Envl definition. Extra lines = 0, left edge of paper = 2.

Okidata Laserline 6 (Cartridge L)

Type: Laser

Defined as: Okidata Laserline 6:Courier (L)

Fonts Assigned:

	Character Table	Attributes	Pitch
1	Okidata Laser Box	Courier	10
2	Okidata Laser Box	Courier Italic	10
3	Okidata Laser Box	Courier Bold	10

Character Table	*Attributes*	*Pitch*
4 Okidata Laser Box	Prestige	15
5 Okidata Laser Box	Courier Landscape	10
6 Okidata Laser Box	Courier Italic Landscape	10
7 Okidata Laser Box	Courier Bold Landscape	10
8 Okidata Laser Box	Prestige Landscape	15

Features Not Supported: Type-thru, Proportional Spacing

Line Draw Information:

Font(s) to be used: All

Limitations: No double-line draw.

Sheet Feeder Information: Define as continuous forms.

Okidata Laserline 6 (Cartridge M)

Type: Laser

Defined as: Okidata Laserline 6:PresE (M)

Fonts Assigned:

Character Table	*Attributes*	*Pitch*
1 Okidata Laser Box	Prestige Elite	12
2 Okidata Laser Box	Prestige Elite Italic	12
3 Okidata Laser Box	Prestige Elite Bold	12
4 Okidata Laser Box	Prestige Elite	17
5 Okidata Laser Box	Prestige Elite Landscape	12
6 Okidata Laser Box	Prestige Elite Italic Landscape	12
7 Okidata Laser Box	Prestige Elite Bold Landscape	12
8 Okidata Laser Box	Prestige Elite Landscape	17

Features Not Supported: Type-thru, Proportional Spacing

Line Draw Information:

Font(s) to be used: All

Limitations: No double-line draw.

Sheet Feeder Information: Define as continuous forms.

Okidata Laserline 6 (Cartridge N)

Type: Laser

Defined as: Okidata Laserline 6:LGoth (N)

Fonts Assigned:

	Character Table	*Attributes*	*Pitch*
1	LaserJet Roman 8	Letter Gothic	12
2	LaserJet Roman 8	Letter Gothic Italic	12
3	LaserJet Roman 8	Letter Gothic Bold	12
4	LaserJet Roman 8	Courier	10
5	LaserJet Roman 8	Letter Gothic Landscape	12
6	LaserJet Roman 8	Letter Gothic Italic Landscape	12
7	LaserJet Roman 8	Letter Gothic Bold Landscape	12
8	LaserJet Roman 8	Courier Landscape	10

Features Not Supported: Line Draw, Type-thru, Proportional Spacing

Sheet Feeder Information: Define as continuous forms.

Okidata Laserline 6 (Cartridge P)

Type: Laser

Defined as: Okidata Laserline 6:Times8 (P)

Fonts Assigned:

	Character Table	*Attributes*	*Pitch*
1	Okidata Times 10R	Times Roman 10pt	13*
2	Okidata Times 8R	Times Roman 8pt	17*
3	Okidata Times 8CR	Times Roman compressed 8pt	19*
4	Okidata Helvetica B	Helvetica Bold 14.4pt	10*
5	Okidata Times 10R	Times Roman 10pt Land	13*
6	Okidata Times 8R	Times Roman 8pt Land	17*
7	Okidata Times 8CR	Times Roman compressed 8pt Land	19*
8	Okidata Helvetica B	Helvetica Bold 14.4pt Land	10*

Features Not Supported: Line Draw, Type-thru

Proportional Spacing Information:

Font(s) to be used: All

Pitch to be used: See above

Sheet Feeder Information: Define as continuous forms.

Special Notes: Bold is only available in fonts 1 and 5. In order to do a shadow print in all fonts, replace bold codes with <27>&a+4H to turn bold on, and <27>&a−4H to turn bold off in the Printer program. However, underline may not line up correctly if you use this method.

Okidata Laserline 6 (Cartridge P)

Type: Laser

Defined as: Okidata Laserline 6:Times10 (P)

Fonts Assigned:

	Character Table	Attributes	Pitch
1	Okidata Times 10R	Times Roman 10pt	13*
2	Okidata Times 10I	Times Roman Italic 10pt	13*
3	Okidata Times 10CR	Times Roman Compressed 10pt	15*
4	Okidata Times 10CI	Times Roman Compressed Italic 10pt	15*
5	Okidata Times 10R	Times Roman 10pt Land	13*
6	Okidata Times 10I	Times Roman Italic 10pt Land	13*
7	Okidata Times 10CR	Times Roman Compressed 10pt Land	15*
8	Okidata Times 10CI	Times Roman Compressed Italic 10pt Land	15*

Features Not Supported: Line Draw, Type-thru, Over-strike, Foreign Characters

Proportional Spacing Information:

Font(s) to be used: All

Pitch to be used: See above

Special Notes: Bold is available in fonts 1, 3, 5, and 7. In order to do a shadow print in all fonts, change the bold codes to <27>&a+4H to turn bold on and <27>&a−4H to turn bold off. Underline may not line up correctly when using this method.

Okidata Laserline 6 (Fixed)

Type: Laser

Defined as: Okidata Laserline 6 (Fixed)

Fonts Assigned:

	Character Table	Attributes	Pitch
1	LaserJet Roman 8	Courier 10pt Port	10
2	LaserJet Roman 8	Courier 10pt Italic Port	10
3	LaserJet Roman 8	Courier 10pt Bold Port	10
4	LaserJet Roman 8	Line Printer Port	17
5	LaserJet Roman 8	Courier 10pt Land	10
6	LaserJet Roman 8	Line Printer Land	17
7	LaserJet-Box	Courier 10pt Port	10
8	LaserJet-Box	Courier 10pt Port	10

Features Not Supported: Type-thru, Foreign Characters, Proportional Spacing

Line Draw Information:

Font(s) to be used: 7,8

Limitations: No double-line draw.

Okidata Laserline 6 (PS)

Type: Laser

Defined as: Okidata Laserline 6 (PS)

Fonts Assigned:

	Character Table	Attributes	Pitch
1	LaserJet-B Normal	Times Roman 10pt	13*
2	LaserJet-B Italic	Times Roman 10pt Italic	13*
3	Okidata Times CR	Times Roman 10pt Compressed	14*
4	Okidata Times CI	Times Roman 10pt Compressed Italic	14*
5	Okidata Times CB	Times Roman 10pt Compressed Bold	14*

	Character Table	Attributes	Pitch
6	Okidata Times 8R	Times Roman 8pt	15*
7	Okidata Times 8CR	Times Roman 8pt Compressed	15*
8	LaserJet-B Helvetica	Helvetica 14.4pt Bold	10*

Features Not Supported: Line Draw, Type-thru, Foreign Characters

Proportional Spacing Information:

Font(s) to be used: All

Pitch to be used: See above

Okidata ML 84

Type: Dot Matrix

Defined as: Okidata ML 84

Emulating: With standard Okidata (Step 2 ROM)

Fonts Assigned:

	Character Table	Attributes	Pitch
1	Standard ASCII	NLQ	10,12,15
2	Standard ASCII	ND	10,12,15
3	Standard ASCII	Emphasized	10,12,15
4	Standard ASCII	Emphasized	10,12,15
5	Standard ASCII	Double-Wide	10
6	Standard ASCII	Emphasized/Enhanced Double-Wide	10
7	Standard ASCII	Emphasized/Enhanced	10,12,15
8	Standard ASCII	Draft	10,12,15

Features Not Supported: Double Underline, Line Draw, Type-thru, Advance, Foreign Characters, Proportional Spacing

Special Notes: 15 pitch returns 17 pitch on the printer.

Okidata ML 84 Plug & Play

Type: Dot Matrix

Defined as: Okidata ML 84/93 (IBM ROM)

Fonts Assigned:

Character Table	Attributes	Pitch
1 IBM Graphics	Draft	10,12,15
2 IBM Graphics	NLQ	10
3 IBM Graphics	Emphasized	10
4 IBM Graphics	Double-Strike	10,15
5 IBM Graphics	Double-Wide Emphasized	10
6 IBM Graphics	Double-Wide Draft	10
7 IBM Graphics	Draft	10,12,15
8 Dot Matrix 1/60	Draft	10,12,15

Features Not Supported: Double Underline, Type-thru, Advance, Foreign Characters, Proportional Spacing

Line Draw Information:

Font(s) to be used: All

Limitations: Font 8 requires half-line spacing. Double-line draw in font 8 only.

Special Notes: Printer cannot bold and superscript/subscript at the same time.

Okidata ML 93 (and 82A)

Type: Dot Matrix

Defined as: Okidata ML 93

Fonts Assigned:

Character Table	Attributes	Pitch
1 Okidata 93	Enhanced	10,12,15
2 Okidata 93	Correspondence	10,12
3 Okidata 93	Emphasized	10,12,15
4 Okidata 93	Enhanced	10,12,15
5 Standard ASCII	Double-Wide	10
6 Standard ASCII	Double-Wide Enhanced Emphasized	10
7 Standard ASCII	Enhanced Emphasized	10,12,15
8 Standard ASCII	Draft	10,12,15

Features Not Supported: Double Underline, Line Draw, Type-thru, Advance, Foreign Characters, Proportional Spacing

Special Notes: Printer cannot bold and superscript/subscript at the same time. Also, it cannot overstrike a superscript/subscript.

Okidata ML 192

Type: Dot Matrix

Defined as: Okidata ML 192/192 Plus

Fonts Assigned:

Character Table		Attributes	Pitch
1	IBM Graphics	NLQ	10,12
2	IBM Graphics	Emphasized Enhanced	10,12,15
3	IBM Graphics	Emphasized	10,12,15
4	IBM Graphics	Italic	10,12
5	IBM Graphics	NLQ Double-Wide	10
6	IBM Graphics	Double-Wide Italic	10
7	IBM Graphics	Subscript	10,12,15
8	IBM Graphics	Draft	10,12,15

Features Not Supported: Double Underline, Type-thru, Advance, Proportional Spacing

Line Draw Information:

Font(s) to be used: 1-4,7,8

Limitations: No double-line draw.

Special Notes: Printer cannot bold and superscript/subscript at the same time.

Okidata ML 192 (IBM)

Type: Dot Matrix

Defined as: Okidata ML 192/Okimat20 (IBM)

Fonts Assigned:

Character Table		Attributes	Pitch
1	IBM Graphics	NLQ	10,12,15
2	IBM Graphics	Emphasized	10,12
3	IBM Graphics	Enhanced	10,12,15
4	IBM Graphics	Italic	10,12,15

Character Table	Attributes	Pitch
5 IBM Graphics	Double-Wide (5,6,8.5)	10,12,15
6 IBM Graphics	Double-Wide Italic (5,6,8.5)	10,12,15
7 IBM Graphics	Superscript	10,12,15
8 Dot Matrix 1/60	Draft	10,12,15

Features Not Supported: Double Underline, Type-thru, Advance, Foreign Characters, Proportional Spacing

Line Draw Information:

Font(s) to be used: All

Limitations: Fonts 5 and 6 require half-line spacing. No double-line draw.

Special Notes: Printer cannot bold and superscript/subscript at the same time.

Okidata ML 192 Plus

Type: Dot Matrix

Defined as: Okidata ML 192/192 Plus

Fonts Assigned:

Character Table	Attributes	Pitch
1 IBM Graphics	NLQ	10,12
2 IBM Graphics	Emphasized Enhanced	10,12,15
3 IBM Graphics	Emphasized	10,12,15
4 IBM Graphics	Italic	10,12
5 IBM Graphics	NLQ Double-Wide	10
6 IBM Graphics	Double-Wide Italic	10
7 IBM Graphics	Subscript	10,12,15
8 IBM Graphics	Draft	10,12,15

Features Not Supported: Double Underline, Type-thru, Advance, Proportional Spacing

Line Draw Information:

Font(s) to be used: 1-4,7,8

Limitations: No double-line draw.

Special Notes: For high speed, 200 CPS draft, change codes in definition as shown here:

Screen 9   Option 7: <27>#0

Screen 9   Option 8: <27>0

Okidata ML 292 (IBM)

Type: Dot Matrix

Defined as: Okidata ML 292 (IBM)

Fonts Assigned:

	Character Table	Attributes	Pitch
1	Okidata ML 292	NLQ Black	10,12,15
2	Okidata ML 292	NLQ Black	10,12,15
3	Okidata ML 292	NLQ PS	11*
4	Okidata ML 292	NLQ Italic	10,12
5	Okidata ML 292	NLQ Double-Wide	10,12,15
6	Okidata ML 292	Double-High	10,12
7	Okidata ML 292	Double-Wide, Double-High	10,12
8	Okidata ML 292	Draft	10,12,15

Features Not Supported: Type-thru

Proportional Spacing Information:

Font(s) to be used: 3

Pitch to be used: 11*

Limitations: PS is slow and jumpy.

Line Draw Information:

Font(s) to be used: All

Okidata ML 292 Standard

Type: Dot Matrix

Defined as: Okidata Microline 292

Fonts Assigned:

	Character Table	Attributes	Pitch
1	Okidata ML 292	NLQ	10,12,15
2	Okidata ML 292	Italic	10,12
3	Okidata ML 292	PS	11*
4	Okidata ML 292	Subscript	15
5	Okidata ML 292	Double-Wide (5)	10
6	Okidata ML 292	Double-High	10,12,15
7	Okidata ML 292	Double-Wide, Double-High (5)	10
8	Okidata ML 292	Draft	10,12,15

Features Not Supported: Type-thru, Foreign Characters

Proportional Spacing Information:

Font(s) to be used: 3

Pitch to be used: 11*

Limitations: PS will not right justify.

Line Draw Information:

Font(s) to be used: All

Limitations: Fonts 5 and 7 require half-line spacing.

Special Notes: Entering 15 pitch returns 17 pitch. For colors use the following command:

<27>r[n] n=color #

0=Black	4=Yellow	8=Maroon	12=Dk. Brown
1=Red	5=Orange	9=Olive	13=Charcoal
2=Blue	6=Green	10=Purple	
3=Violet	7=Dk. Blue	11=Dk. Green	

Okidata 293

Defined as: Try the IBM Graphics printer definition.

Okidata Okimate 20 (IBM)

Type: Thermal

Defined as: Okidata ML 192/Okimat20 (IBM)

Fonts Assigned:

Character Table	Attributes	Pitch
1 IBM Graphics	NLQ	10,12,15
2 IBM Graphics	Emphasized	10,12
3 IBM Graphics	Enhanced	10,12
4 IBM Graphics	Italics	10,12,15
5 IBM Graphics	Double-Wide	10,12,15
6 IBM Graphics	Double-Wide Italics	10,12,15
7 IBM Graphics	Condensed (Subscript)	10,12,15
8 Dot Matrix 1/60	Draft	10,12,15

Features Not Supported: Double Underline, Type-thru, Advance, Proportional Spacing

Line Draw Information:

Font(s) to be used: All

Limitations: No double-line draw. Fonts 5 and 6 must have half-line spacing.

Okidata Pacemark 2410

Type: Dot Matrix

Defined as: Okidata Pacemark 2410 (IBM)

Fonts Assigned:

Character Table	Attributes	Pitch
1 IBM Graphics	NLQ	10,12
2 IBM Graphics	Emphasized	10,12
3 IBM Graphics	Enhanced	10,12,15
4 IBM Graphics	Draft	10,12,15
5 IBM Graphics	Double-Wide Enhanced (5,6)	10,12
6 IBM Graphics	Double-Wide Draft (5,6)	10,12,15
7 IBM Graphics	Subscript	15
8 Dot Matrix 1/60	Draft	10,12,15

Features Not Supported: Type-thru, Advance, Proportional Spacing

Line Draw Information:

Font(s) to be used: All

Limitations: Double-line draw in font 8 only. Half-line spacing for fonts 5 and 6.

Olympia Compact RO

Type: Daisy Wheel

Defined as: Olympia Compact RO

Fonts Assigned:

Character Table	Attributes	Pitch
1 Standard ASCII	Depends on wheel used	10,12,15
2 Standard ASCII	Depends on wheel used	10,12,15
3 Standard ASCII	Depends on wheel used	10,12,15
4 Standard ASCII	Depends on wheel used	10,12,15
5 Standard ASCII	Depends on wheel used	10,12,15
6 Standard ASCII	Depends on wheel used	10,12,15
7 Standard ASCII	Depends on wheel used	10,12,15
8 Standard ASCII	Depends on wheel used	10,12,15

Features Not Supported: Double Underline, Line Draw, Type-thru, 6/8 LPI, Foreign Characters, Proportional Spacing

Olympia ESW 2000

Type: Daisy Wheel

Defined as: Olympia ESW 2000

Fonts Assigned:

Character Table	Attributes	Pitch
1 Standard ASCII	Depends on wheel used	10,12,15
2 OE Colony PS	OE Colony PS	13*
3 OE Sterling PS	OE Sterling PS	13*
4 OE Professional PS	OE Professional PS	13*
5 Standard ASCII	Depends on wheel used	10,12,15
6 Standard ASCII	Depends on wheel used	10,12,15
7 Standard ASCII	Depends on wheel used	10,12,15
8 Standard ASCII	Depends on wheel used	10,12,15

Features Not Supported: Line Draw, Type-thru, Foreign Characters

Proportional Spacing Information:

Font(s) to be used: 2,3,4

Pitch to be used: 13*

Olympia Startype

Type: Daisy Wheel

Defined as: Olympia Startype

Fonts Assigned:

	Character Table	Attributes	Pitch
1	Standard ASCII	Depends on wheel used	10,12,15
2	OE Colony PS	Colony PS	13*
3	Sterling PS	Sterling PS	13*
4	Professional PS	Professional PS	13*
5	Standard ASCII	Depends on wheel used	10,12,15
6	Standard ASCII	Depends on wheel used	10,12,15
7	Standard ASCII	Depends on wheel used	10,12,15
8	Standard ASCII	Depends on wheel used	10,12,15

Features Not Supported: Line Draw, Foreign Characters

Proportional Spacing Information:

Font(s) to be used: 2,3,4

Pitch to be used: 13*

Special Notes: Press [Code][O] to put printer on-line. Cannot print beyond position 80 (even in DOS) if on-line. It can type beyond position 80 if off-line and being used as a typewriter.

Panasonic KX-P1091 and KX-P1093

Type: Dot Matrix

Defined as: Panasonic KX-P1091/1093

Fonts Assigned:

	Character Table	Attributes	Pitch
1	IBM Graphics	NLQ	10
2	IBM Graphics	12 Pitch Draft	10
3	IBM Graphics	Double-Wide Compressed	10
4	IBM Graphics	NLQ Italic	10
5	IBM Graphics	NLQ Double-Wide	10
6	IBM Graphics	NLQ Double-Wide Italic	10
7	IBM Graphics	Compressed	10
8	IBM Graphics	Draft	10

Features Not Suported: Double Underline, Type-thru, Advance, Proportional Spacing

Line Draw Information:

Font(s) to be used: All.

Limitations: Switches 1 and 2 must be off to get line draw (also affects IBM character set). No double-line draw. No solid lines with fonts 3 and 7.

Panasonic KX-P1092

Type: Dot Matrix

Defined as: Panasonic KX-P1092

Fonts Assigned:

	Character Table	Attributes	Pitch
1	Dot Matrix 1/60	Emphasized Pica	10
2	Panasonic	Emphasized Elite	10
3	Panasonic	NLQ PS	10
4	Panasonic	Italic	10
5	Panasonic	Double-Wide	10
6	Panasonic	Double-Wide Italic	10
7	Panasonic	Compressed	10
8	Panasonic	Draft	10

Features Not Supported: Type-thru, Proportional Spacing

Line Draw Information:

Font(s) to be used: All

Panasonic KX-P1080i

Type: Dot Matrix

Defined as: Panasonic KX-P1080i

Fonts Assigned:

	Character Table	Attributes	Pitch
1	KX-P 1080i	NLQ PS	10,11*,12,15
2	KX-P 1080i	Compressed (17)	10
3	KX-P 1080i	NLQ PS	10,11*,12,15

Character Table	Attributes	Pitch
4 KX-P 1080i	NLQ Italic	10,12,15
5 KX-P 1080i	NLQ Double-Wide	10,12,15
6 KX-P 1080i	NLQ Double-Wide Italic	10,12,15
7 KX-P 1080i	Draft 12 pitch	12
8 KX-P 1080i	Draft 10 pitch	10

Features Not Supported: Double Underline, Type-thru, Advance

Proportional Spacing Information:

Font(s) to be used: 1,3

Pitch to be used: 11*

Line Draw Information:

Font(s) to be used: All (font 2 not solid)

Special Notes: In order to get 1-inch margins in font 2, margins of 17 and 127 must be used.

Panasonic KX-P1091i and P1092i

Type: Dot Matrix

Defined as: Panasonic KX-P1092i

Fonts Assigned:

Character Table	Attributes	Pitch
1 KX-P 1091i/1092i	NLQ PS	10,11*,12,15
2 KX-P 1091i/1092i	Compressed (17)	10
3 KX-P 1091i/1092i	NLQ PS	10,11*,12,15
4 KX-P 1091i/1092i	NLQ Italic	10,12,15
5 KX-P 1091i/1092i	NLQ Double-Wide	10,12,15
6 KX-P 1091i/1092i	NLQ Double-Wide Italic	10,12,15
7 KX-P 1091i/1092i	Draft 12 pitch	12
8 KX-P 1091i/1092i	Draft 10CPI	10

Features Not Supported: Line Draw, Type-thru

Proportional Spacing Information:

Font(s) to be used: 1,3

Pitch to be used: 11*

Panasonic KX-P1592 and 1595

Type: Dot Matrix

Defined as: Panasonic KX-P1592/1595

Fonts Assigned:

	Character Table	Attributes	Pitch
1	IBM Graphics	NLQ	10,12,15
2	Dot Matrix 1/60	Italic	10,12,15
3	KX-P 1080i	NLQ PS	11*
4	IBM Graphics	NLQ Double-Wide	10,12,15
5	IBM Graphics	Draft Double-Wide	10,12,15
6	IBM Graphics	Double-Wide Italic	10,12,15
7	IBM Graphics	Condensed	10,12,15
8	IBM Graphics	Draft	10,12,15

Features Not Supported: Type-thru

Proportional Spacing Information:

Font(s) to be used: 3

Pitch to be used: 11*

Line Draw Information:

Font(s) to be used: 1,2,4,5,6,8

Panasonic KX-P3131 and 3151

Type: Daisy Wheel

Defined as: Panasonic KX-P3131/3151

Fonts Assigned:

	Character Table	Attributes	Pitch
1	Standard ASCII	Depends on wheel used	10,12,15
2	Standard ASCII	Depends on wheel used	10,12,15
3	Dia630 Bold PS	Bold PS	13*
4	DiaGoth PS	Depends on wheel used	10,12,15
5	Diablo Roman PS	Depends on wheel used	10,12,15
6	Standard ASCII	Depends on wheel used	10,12,15
7	Standard ASCII	Depends on wheel used	10,12,15
8	Standard ASCII	Depends on wheel used	10,12,15

Features Not Supported: Line Draw, Foreign Characters

Proportional Spacing Information:

Font(s) to be used: 3

Pitch to be used: 13*

Primage 90-GT

Type: Daisy Wheel

Defined as: Primage 90-GT

Fonts Assigned:

Character Table	Attributes	Pitch
1 Standard ASCII	Depends on wheel used	10,12,15
2 Standard ASCII	Depends on wheel used	10,12,15
3 Standard ASCII	Depends on wheel used	10,12,15
4 Standard ASCII	Depends on wheel used	10,12,15
5 Standard ASCII	Depends on wheel used	10,12,15
6 Standard ASCII	Depends on wheel used	10,12,15
7 Standard ASCII	Depends on wheel used	10,12,15
8 Standard ASCII	Depends on wheel used	10,12,15

Features Not Supported: Line Draw, Foreign Characters, Proportional Spacing

Special Notes: If you have the Tile PS wheel, you can use the Diablo Bold PS table for proportional spacing (font 3, 13*). This printer has Epson FX emulation, which will give line draw, but it's very slow.

Printronix S7024

Type: Dot Matrix

Defined as: Printronix S7024

Fonts Assigned:

Character Table	Attributes	Pitch
1 IBM Proprinter	NLQ	10,12,15
2 IBM Proprinter	Draft	10,12,15
3 IBM Proprinter	NLQ Emphasized	10,12
4 IBM Proprinter	Draft Emphasized	10,12
5 IBM Proprinter	NLQ Double-Wide (5,6)	10,12

Character Table	Attributes	Pitch
6 IBM Proprinter	Draft Double-Wide (5,6,8)	10,12,15
7 IBM Proprinter	Superscript	15
8 IBM Proprinter	Draft	10,12,15

Features Not Supported: Type-thru, Proportional Spacing

Line Draw Information:

Font(s) to be used: All

Limitations: Fonts 5 and 6 should be printed in half-line spacing.

QMS Kiss

Type: Laser

Defined as: QMS Kiss Laser

Fonts Assigned:

Character Table	Attributes	Pitch
1 QMS Kiss ECS	Courier	10
2 Talaris Line Draw	Q-Format	7
3 QMS Epson Pica	Epson Pica	10
4 QMS Epson Pica Italic	Epson Pica Elite	10
5 QMS Epson Pica	Epson Pica Italic	15
6 QMS Kiss ECS	Epson Compressed	12
7 Talaris Line Draw	Prestige Elite Courier	12
8 Talaris Line Draw	Courier Landscape	10

Features Not Supported: Type-thru, Proportional Spacing

Line Draw Information:

Font(s) to be used: All

Quadram Quadlaser (Standard)

Type: Laser

Defined as: Quadram Quadlaser Standard

Fonts Assigned:

Character Table	Attributes	Pitch
1 Quadlaser Standard	Courier Port	10
2 Quadlaser Standard	Italic Port	10

	Character Table	Attributes	Pitch
3	Quadlaser Standard	Prestige Elite Land	14
4	Quadlaser Standard	Prestige Elite Port	14
5	Quadlaser QTR 8	Times Roman 8pt Port	15*
6	Quadlaser QH 12	Helvetica 12pt Port	13*
7	Quadlaser Standard	Helvetica 16pt Port	8*
8	Quadlaser Standard	Quadlaser Spreadsheet	19

Features Not Supported: Type-thru

Proportional Spacing Information:

Font(s) to be used: 5,6,7

Pitch to be used: See above

Line Draw Information:

Font(s) to be used: 1,2,4,7,8

Limitations: No double-line draw.

Special Notes: For Epson Emulation mode use Epson FX driver. Font 7 will not right justify so turn off within document. Download fonts in this order:

Font 1—QC10F.FNT	Font 2—QCI10F.FNT
Font 3—QPRESF.FNT	Font 4—QPREF.FNT
Font 5—QTR8P.FNT	Font 6—QH12P.FNT
Font 7—QH16P.FNT	Font 8—QSPRF.FNT

Quadram Quadlaser Optional

Type: Laser

Defined as: Quadram Quadlaser Optional

Fonts Assigned:

	Character Table	Attributes	Pitch
1	Quadlaser Standard	Courier	10
2	Quadlaser Standard	Courier Italic	10
3	Quadlaser Standard	Greek/Math	10
4	Quadlaser Standard	Quadlaser Profile 24pt	10
5	Quadlaser Profile 24	Prestige	12
6	Quadlaser Standard	Spreadsheet	17
7	Quadlaser Standard	Courier Bold	10
8	Quadlaser Standard	IBM Extended Line Draw	10

Features Not Supported: Type-thru, Proportional Spacing

Line Draw Information:

Font(s) to be used: 1,5,6,7,8

Limitations: Double-line draw in font 8. No solid lines in fonts 5 and 6.

Special Notes: Font 4 will not right justify. Turn right justification off when using font 4. Download the fonts from their disk #13 in this order:

Font 1 — QCRN12F.FNT	Font 5 — QPEN12F.FNT
Font 2 — QCRI12F.FNT	Font 6 — QSPN08F.FNT
Font 3 — QGRN12P.FNT	Font 7 — QCRB12F.FNT
Font 4 — QPRN24P.FNT	Font 8 — QPCN12F.FNT

Additional character tables are available from WordPerfect Corporation on the Quadlaser Utility disk.

Qume LaserTen Plus (v1.3)

Type: Laser

Defined as: Qume LaserTen Plus (v1.3)

Fonts Assigned:

	Character Table	Attributes	Pitch
1	IBM Graphics	Courier 10pt	10
2	Qume-188	(#5) Courier 12pt	10
3	Qume-188	(#5) Courier 12pt Italic	10
4	Qume-188	(#29) Courier 10pt	10
5	Qume-188	(#29) Courier 7pt	10
6	Qume-188	(#32) Prestige Elite 10pt	10
7	Qume-188	(#33) Letter Gothic 10pt	10
8	Qume-188	(#34) Gothic 7pt	10

Features Not Supported: Type-thru, Proportional Spacing

Line Draw Information:

Font(s) to be used: All

Limitations: Font 1 is the only font with double-line draw. Font 8 has broken lines.

Special Notes: This definition applies specifically to printers with ROM version 1.3.7. Each font is selected by font description. If an exact match is not found in the resident fonts or the three font slots, the closest font is used.

Qume LetterPro Plus and Sprint 11/11+

Type: Daisy Wheel

Defined as: Qume Sprint11/11+/LetterPro Plus

Fonts Assigned:

	Character Table	Attributes	Pitch
1	Standard ASCII	Depends on wheel used	10,12,15
2	Qume Bilingual	Qume Bilingual	10,12,15
3	Qume Bold PS	Qume Bold PS	13*
4	Standard ASCII	Depends on wheel used	10,12,15
5	Standard ASCII	Depends on wheel used	10,12,15
6	Standard ASCII	Depends on wheel used	10,12,15
7	Standard ASCII	Depends on wheel used	10,12,15
8	Standard ASCII	Depends on wheel used	10,12,15

Features Not Supported: Line Draw, Foreign Characters

Proportional Spacing Information:

Font(s) to be used: 3

Pitch to be used: 13*

All Ricoh LP4080R Laser Printers

Special Notes: To switch between portrait and landscape, insert a Hard Page, then enter these codes as printer commands:

```
Landscape = <27><18>D2<32>
Portrait   = <27><18>D1 <32>
```

PRINTER2.TST has more line draw than the buffer can hold, so it spills to the next page. This is not an error, just a limitation.

Ricoh LP4080R Bold

Type: Laser

Defined as: Ricoh LP4080R Bold

Fonts Assigned:

	Character Table	Attributes	Pitch
1	Ricoh	Courier 10 Bold Port	10
2	Ricoh	Prestige Elite 12 Bold Port	12
3	Ricoh	Letter Gothic 15 Bold Port	15
4	Ricoh Century Bold	Century PS Bold Port	13*
5	Ricoh	Courier 15 Bold Land	10
6	Ricoh	Prestige Elite 12 Bold Land	12
7	Ricoh	Letter Gothic 15 Bold Land	15
8	Ricoh Century Bold	Century PS Bold Land	13*

Features Not Supported: Line Draw, Type-thru

Proportional Spacing Information:

Font(s) to be used: 4,8

Pitch to be used: 13*

Ricoh LP4080R Courier

Type: Laser

Defined as: Ricoh LP4080R Courier 10

Fonts Assigned:

	Character Table	Attributes	Pitch
1	Ricoh Courier 10	Courier 10 Port	10
2	Ricoh	Courier 10 Bold Port	10
3	Ricoh Courier 10	Courier 10 Italic Port	10
4	Ricoh Courier 10	Courier 10 Bold Italic Port	10
5	Ricoh Line 1	Courier 10 Land	10
6	Ricoh Line 2	Courier 10 Bold Land	10
7	Ricoh Line 3	Courier 10 Italic Land	10
8	Ricoh Courier 10	Courier Bold Italic Land	10

Features Not Supported: Type-thru, Proportional Spacing

Line Draw Information:

Font(s) to be used: 1,3,4,5,6,7,8

Limitations: Amount of line draw is contingent upon the printer's RAM.

Ricoh LP4080R Letter Gothic

Type: Laser

Defined as: Ricoh LP4080R Letter Gothic

Fonts Assigned:

	Character Table	Attributes	Pitch
1	Ricoh Letter Gothic	Letter Gothic 12 Port	12
2	Ricoh	Letter Gothic 12 Bold Port	12
3	Ricoh Letter Gothic	Letter Gothic 15 Port	15
4	Ricoh Letter Gothic	Letter Gothic 15 Bold Port	15
5	Ricoh Line 1	Letter Gothic 12 Land	12
6	Ricoh Line 2	Letter Gothic 12 Bold Land	12
7	Ricoh Line 3	Letter Gothic 15 Land	15
8	Ricoh Letter Gothic	Letter Gothic 15 Bold Land	15

Features Not Supported: Type-thru, Proportional Spacing

Line Draw Information:

Font(s) to be used: 1,3,4,5,6,7,8

Limitations: Amount of line draw is contingent upon the printer's RAM.

Ricoh LP4080R Prestige Elite

Type: Laser

Defined as: Ricoh LP4080R Prestige Elite

Fonts Assigned:

	Character Table	Attributes	Pitch
1	Ricoh Prestige Elite 12	Prestige Elite 12 Port	12
2	Ricoh	Prestige Elite 12 Bold Port	12
3	Ricoh Prestige Elite 12	Prestige Elite 12 Italic Port	12
4	Ricoh Prestige Elite 12	Prestige Elite 12 Bold	12

Character Table	Attributes	Pitch
5 Ricoh Line 1	Prestige Elite 12 Land	12
6 Ricoh Line 2	Prestige Elite 12 Bold Land	12
7 Ricoh Line 3	Prestige Elite 12 Italic Land	12
8 Ricoh Prestige Elite 12	Prestige Elite 12 Bold Italic Land	12

Features Not Supported: Type-thru, Proportional Spacing

Line Draw Information:

Font(s) to be used: 1,3,4,5,6,7,8

Limitations: Amount of line draw is contingent upon the printer's RAM.

Ricoh LP4080R Standard

Type: Laser

Defined as: Ricoh LP4080R Standard

Fonts Assigned:

Character Table	Attributes	Pitch
1 Ricoh Bold PS	Courier 10 Port	10
2 Ricoh	Prestige Elite 12 Port	12
3 Ricoh Bold PS	Letter Gothic 15 Port	15
4 Ricoh Bold PS	Boldface PS Port	13*
5 Ricoh Line 1	Courier 10 Land	10
6 Ricoh Line 2	Prestige Elite 12 Land	12
7 Ricoh Line 3	Letter Gothic 15 Land	15
8 Ricoh Bold PS	Boldface PS Land	13*

Features Not Supported: Type-thru

Proportional Spacing Information:

Font(s) to be used: 4,8

Pitch to be used: 13*

Line Draw Information:

Font(s) to be used: 1,3,4,5,6,7,8

Limitations: Amount of line draw is contingent upon the printer's RAM.

Ricoh LP4080R Times Roman

Type: Laser

Defined as: Ricoh LP4080R Times Roman

Fonts Assigned:

	Character Table	Attributes	Pitch
1	Ricoh Times Roman	Times Roman 11P Port	15*
2	Ricoh Times Roman 8	Times Roman 11P Bold Port	15*
3	Ricoh Times Roman I	Times Roman 11P Italic Port	15*
4	Ricoh Times Roman BI	Times Roman 11P Bold Italic Port	15*
5	Ricoh Times Roman	Times Roman 11P Land	15*
6	Ricoh Times Roman 8	Times Roman 11P Bold Land	15*
7	Ricoh Times Roman I	Times Roman 11P Italic Land	15*
8	Ricoh Times Roman BI	Times Roman 11P Bold Italic Land	15*

Features Not Supported: Line Draw, Type-thru

Proportional Spacing Information:

Font(s) to be used: All

Pitch to be used: 15*

Ricoh PC LASER 6000 Bold Portrait

Type: Laser

Defined as: Ricoh 6000 : Bold Port

Fonts Assigned:

	Character Table	Attibutes	Pitch
1	Ricoh 6000	Courier 10 Bold Port	10
2	Ricoh 6000	Prestige Elite 12 Bold Port	12
3	Ricoh 6000	Letter Gothic 15 Bold Port	15
4	Ricoh Century PS	Century PS Bold Port	13*
5	Ricoh 6000	Courier 10 Port	10
6	Ricoh 6000	Prestige 12 Elite Port	12
7	Ricoh 6000	Letter Gothic 15 Port	15
8	Ricoh Century PS	Century PS Port	13*

Features Not Supported: Line Draw, Type-thru

Proportional Spacing Information:

Font(s) to be used: 4,8

Pitch to be used: 13*

Ricoh PC LASER 6000 Courier 10

Type: Laser

Defined as: Ricoh 6000 : Courier 10

Fonts Assigned:

	Character Table	Attributes	Pitch
1	Ricoh 6000	Courier 10 Port	10
2	Ricoh 6000	Courier 10 Bold Port	10
3	Ricoh 6000	Courier 10 Italic Port	10
4	Ricoh 6000	Courier 10 Bold Italic Port	10
5	Ricoh 6000	Courier 10 Port	10
6	Ricoh 6000	Prestige Elite 12 Port	12
7	Ricoh 6000	Letter Gothic 15 Port	15
8	Ricoh Century PS	Century PS Port	13*

Features Not Supported: Line Draw, Type-thru

Proportional Spacing Information:

Font(s) to be used: 8

Pitch to be used: 13*

Ricoh PC LASER 6000 Helvetica Landscape

Type: Laser

Defined as: Ricoh 6000 : Helvetica Land

Fonts Assigned:

	Character Table	Attributes	Pitch
1	Ricoh Helvetica	Helvetica 10P Land	15*
2	Ricoh Helvetica B	Helvetica 10P Bold Land	15*
3	Ricoh Helvetica I	Helvetica 10P Italic Land	15*
4	Ricoh Helvetica BI	Helvetica 10P Bold Italic Land	15*

Character Table	Attributes	Pitch
5 Ricoh 6000	Courier 10 Land	10
6 Ricoh 6000	Prestige Elite 12 Land	12
7 Ricoh 6000	Letter Gothic 15 Land	15
8 Ricoh Century PS	Century PS Land	13*

Features Not Supported: Line Draw, Type-thru

Proportional Spacing Information:

Font(s) to be used: 1,2,3,4,8

Pitch to be used: See above

Ricoh PC LASER 6000 Helvetica Portrait

Type: Laser

Defined as: Ricoh 6000 : Helvetica Port

Fonts Assigned:

Character Table	Attributes	Pitch
1 Ricoh Helvetica	Helvetica 10P Port	15*
2 Ricoh Helvetica B	Helvetica 10P Bold Port	15*
3 Ricoh Helvetica I	Helvetica 10P Italic Port	15*
4 Ricoh Helvetica BI	Helvetica 10P Bold Italic Port	15*
5 Ricoh 6000	Courier 10 Port	10
6 Ricoh 6000	Prestige Elite 12 Port	12
7 Ricoh 6000	Letter Gothic 15 Port	15
8 Ricoh Century PS	Century PS Port	13*

Features Not Supported: Line Draw, Type-thru

Proportional Spacing Information:

Font(s) to be used: 1,2,3,4,8

Pitch to be used: See above

Ricoh PC LASER 6000 Italic Portrait

Type: Laser

Defined as: Ricoh 6000 : Italic Port

Fonts Assigned:

Character Table	Attributes	Pitch
1 Ricoh 6000	Courier 10 Italic Port	10
2 Ricoh 6000	Prestige Elite Italic Port	12
3 Ricoh 6000	Letter Gothic Italic Port	15
4 Ricoh Century PS	Century PS Italic Port	13*
5 Ricoh 6000	Courier 10 Port	10
6 Ricoh 6000	Prestige Elite 12 Port	12
7 Ricoh 6000	Letter Gothic 15 Port	15
8 Ricoh Century PS	Century PS Port	13*

Features Not Supported: Line Draw, Type-thru

Proportional Spacing Information:

Font(s) to be used: 4,8

Pitch to be used: 13*

Ricoh PC LASER 6000 Letter Gothic

Type: Laser

Defined as: Ricoh 6000 : Letter Gothic

Fonts Assigned:

Character Table	Attributes	Pitch
1 Ricoh 6000	Letter Gothic 12 Port	12
2 Ricoh 6000	Letter Gothic 12 Bold Port	12
3 Ricoh 6000	Letter Gothic 15 Port	15
4 Ricoh 6000	Letter Gothic 15 Bold Port	15
5 Ricoh 6000	Courier 10 Port	10
6 Ricoh 6000	Prestige Elite 12 Port	12
7 Ricoh 6000	Letter Gothic 15 Port	15
8 Ricoh Century PS	Century PS Port	13*

Features Not Supported: Line Draw, Type-thru

Proportional Spacing Information:

Font(s) to be used: 8

Pitch to be used: 13*

Ricoh PC LASER 6000 Line Printer Landscape

Type: Laser

Defined as: Ricoh 6000 : Line Printer Land

Fonts Assigned:

	Character Table	Attributes	Pitch
1	Ricoh 6000	Courier 16.7 Land	17
2	Ricoh 6000	Prestige Elite 16.7 Land	17
3	Ricoh 6000	Letter Gothic 16.7 Land	17
4	Ricoh Century PS	Century PS Land	13*
5	Ricoh 6000	Courier 10 Land	10
6	Ricoh 6000	Prestige Elite 12 Land	12
7	Ricoh 6000	Letter Gothic 15 Land	15
8	Ricoh Century PS	Century PS Land	13*

Features Not Supported: Line Draw, Type-thru

Proportional Spacing Information:

Font(s) to be used: 4,8

Pitch to be used: 13*

Ricoh PC LASER 6000 Line Printer Portrait

Type: Laser

Defined as: Ricoh 6000 : Line Printer Port

Fonts Assigned:

	Character Table	Attributes	Pitch
1	Ricoh 6000	Courier 16.7 Port	17
2	Ricoh 6000	Prestige Elite 16.7 Port	17
3	Ricoh 6000	Letter Gothic 16.7 Port	17
4	Ricoh Century PS	Century PS Port	13*
5	Ricoh 6000	Courier 10 Port	10
6	Ricoh 6000	Prestige Elite 12 Port	12
7	Ricoh 6000	Letter Gothic 15 Port	15
8	Ricoh Century PS	Century PS Port	13*

Features Not Supported: Line Draw, Type-thru

Proportional Spacing Information:

Font(s) to be used: 4,8

Pitch to be used: 13*

Ricoh PC LASER 6000 PC-1 Landscape

Type: Laser

Defined as: Ricoh 6000 : PC-1 Land

Fonts Assigned:

	Character Table	Attributes	Pitch
1	Ricoh Century PS PC	Courier 10 PC Land	10
2	Ricoh Century PS PC	Prestige Elite 12 PC Land	12
3	Ricoh 6000	Letter Gothic 15 Land	15
4	Ricoh Century PS	Century PS Land	13*
5	Ricoh 6000	Courier 10 Land	10
6	Ricoh 6000	Prestige Elite 12 Land	12
7	Ricoh 6000	Letter Gothic 15 Land	15
8	Ricoh Century PS	Century PS Land	13*

Features Not Supported: Type-thru

Proportional Spacing Information:

Font(s) to be used: 4,8

Pitch to be used: 13*

Line Draw Information:

Font(s) to be used: 1,2

Special Notes: Fonts 1 and 2 have the entire IBM character set.

Ricoh PC LASER 6000 PC-1 Portrait

Type: Laser

Defined as: Ricoh 6000 : PC-1 Port

Fonts Assigned:

	Character Table	Attributes	Pitch
1	Ricoh Century PS PC	Courier 10 PC Port	10
2	Ricoh Century PS PC	Prestige Elite 12 PC Port	12
3	Ricoh 6000	Letter Gothic 15 Port	15
4	Ricoh Century PS	Century PS Port	13*
5	Ricoh 6000	Courier 10 Port	10
6	Ricoh 6000	Prestige Elite 12 Port	12
7	Ricoh 6000	Letter Gothic 15 Port	15
8	Ricoh Century PS	Century PS Port	13*

Features Not Supported: Type-thru

Proportional Spacing Information:

Font(s) to be used: 4,8

Pitch to be used: 13*

Line Draw Information:

Font(s) to be used: 1,2

Special Notes: Fonts 1 and 2 have the full IBM character set.

Ricoh PC LASER 6000 Prestige Elite

Type: Laser

Defined as: Ricoh 6000 : Prestige Elite

Fonts Assigned:

	Character Table	Attributes	Pitch
1	Ricoh 6000	Prestige Elite 12 Port	12
2	Ricoh 6000	Prestige Elite 12 Bold Port	12
3	Ricoh 6000	Prestige Elite 12 Italic Port	12
4	Ricoh 6000	Prestige Elite 12 Bold Italic Port	12
5	Ricoh 6000	Courier 10 Port	10
6	Ricoh 6000	Prestige Elite 12 Port	12
7	Ricoh 6000	Letter Gothic 15 Port	15
8	Ricoh Century PS	Century PS Port	13*

Features Not Supported: Line Draw, Type-thru

Proportional Spacing Information:

Font(s) to be used: 8

Pitch to be used: 13*

Ricoh PC LASER 6000 Standard Landscape

Type: Laser

Defined as: Ricoh 6000 : Standard Land

Fonts Assigned:

	Character Table	Attributes	Pitch
1	Ricoh 6000	Courier 10 Land	10
2	Ricoh 6000	Prestige Elite 12 Land	12
3	Ricoh 6000	Letter Gothic 15 Land	15
4	Ricoh Century PS	Century PS Land	13*
5	Ricoh 6000	Courier 10 Land	10
6	Ricoh 6000	Prestige Elite 12 Land	12
7	Ricoh 6000	Letter Gothic 15 Land	15
8	Ricoh Century PS	Century PS Land	13*

Features Not Supported: Line Draw, Type-thru

Proportional Spacing Information:

Font(s) to be used: 4,8

Pitch to be used: 13*

Ricoh PC LASER 6000 Standard Portrait

Type: Laser

Defined as: Ricoh 6000 : Standard Port

Fonts Assigned:

	Character Table	Attributes	Pitch
1	Ricoh 6000	Courier 10 Port	10
2	Ricoh 6000	Prestige Elite 12 Port	12
3	Ricoh 6000	Letter Gothic 15 Port	15
4	Ricoh Century PS	Century PS Port	13*

Character Table	*Attributes*	*Pitch*
5 Ricoh 6000	Courier 10 Port	10
6 Ricoh 6000	Prestige Elite 12 Port	12
7 Ricoh 6000	Letter Gothic 15 Port	15
8 Ricoh Century PS	Century PS Port	13*

Features Not Supported: Line Draw, Type-thru

Proportional Spacing Information:

Font(s) to be used: 4,8

Pitch to be used: 13*

Ricoh PC LASER 6000 Times Roman Landscape

Type: Laser

Defined as: Ricoh 6000 : Times Roman Land

Fonts Assigned:

Character Table	*Attributes*	*Pitch*
1 Ricoh Times Roman	Times Roman 11P Land	15*
2 Ricoh Times Roman B	Times Roman 11P Bold Land	15*
3 Ricoh Times Roman I	Times Roman 11P Italic Land	15*
4 Ricoh Times Roman BI	Times Roman 11P Bold Italic Land	15*
5 Ricoh 6000	Courier 10 Land	10
6 Ricoh 6000	Prestige Elite 12 Land	12
7 Ricoh 6000	Letter Gothic 15 Land	15
8 Ricoh Century PS	Century PS Land	13*

Features Not Supported: Line Draw, Type-thru

Proportional Spacing Information:

Font(s) to be used: 1,2,3,4,8

Pitch to be used: See above

Ricoh PC LASER 6000 Times Roman Portrait

Type: Laser

Defined as: Ricoh 6000 : Times Roman Port

Fonts Assigned:

	Character Table	Attributes	Pitch
1	Ricoh Times Roman	Times Roman 11P Port	15*
2	Ricoh Times Roman B	Times Roman 11P Bold Port	15*
3	Ricoh Times Roman I	Times Roman 11P Italic Port	15*
4	Ricoh Times Roman BI	Times Roman 11P Bold Italic Port	15*
5	Ricoh 6000	Courier 10	10
6	Ricoh 6000	Prestige Elite 12	12
7	Ricoh 6000	Letter Gothic 15	15
8	Ricoh Century PS	Century PS	13*

Features Not Supported: Line Draw, Type-thru

Proportional Spacing Information:

Font(s) to be used: 1,2,3,4,8

Pitch to be used: See above

Seikosha SP 1000I

Type: Dot Matrix

Defined as: Seikosha SP 1000I

Fonts Assigned:

	Character Table	Attributes	Pitch
1	IBM Graphics	NLQ	10,12,15
2	Dot Matrix 1/60	ND	ND
3	IBM Graphics	NLQ PS	10,12
4	IBM Graphics	Italic	10,12,15
5	IBM Graphics	Double-Wide	5,6,10
6	IBM Graphics	Double-Wide Italic	5,6,10
7	IBM Graphics	Superscript	10,12,15
8	IBM Graphics	Draft	10,12,15

Features Not Supported: Double Underline, Type-thru, Advance, Foreign Characters, Proportional Spacing

Line Draw Information:

Font(s) to be used: All

Seimens PT88 Whisperjet

Type: Inkjet

Defined as: Seimens PT88 Whisperjet

Fonts Assigned:

	Character Table	Attributes	Pitch
1	Seimens Matrix	Draft	10, 12, 15
2	Seimens Matrix	Draft	10, 12, 15
3	Seimens Matrix	Draft	10, 12, 15
4	ASCII Line Printer	Draft	10, 12, 15
5	ASCII Line Printer	Double-Wide	10, 12, 15
6	ASCII Line Printer	Draft	10, 12, 15
7	ASCII Line Printer	Draft	10, 12, 15
8	ASCII Line Printer	Draft	10, 12, 15

Features Not Supported: Double Underline, Type-thru, Foreign Characters, Proportional Spacing

Line Draw Information:

Font(s) to be used: 1,2,3

Silver-Reed EXP 500/550/800

Type: Daisy Wheel

Defined as: Silver-Reed EXP 500/550/800

Fonts Assigned:

	Character Table	Attributes	Pitch
1	Daisy Line Draw	Depends on wheel used	10, 12, 15
2	Daisy Line Draw	Depends on wheel used	10, 12, 15
3	Modern PS	Modern PS	13*
4	Daisy Line Draw	Depends on wheel used	10, 12, 15
5	Daisy Line Draw	Depends on wheel used	10, 12, 15
6	Daisy Line Draw	Depends on wheel used	10, 12, 15
7	Daisy Line Draw	Depends on wheel used	10, 12, 15
8	Daisy Line Draw	Depends on wheel used	10, 12, 15

Features Not Supported: Foreign Characters, no PS for Silver Reed EXP 500

Proportional Spacing Information:

Font(s) to be used: 3

Pitch to be used: 13*

Line Draw Information:

Font(s) to be used: 1,2,4-8

Limitations: Line Draw characters depend on print wheel being used.

Sheet Feeder Information: If using the CF 130 or CF 131, turn DIP switch #3 on. Define as Qume Single Bin or Continuous. Column position of the left edge of paper = 0. The margins must be moved 1/2 inch to the left in WordPerfect because 0 is not enough.

Special Notes: If printing "garbage," turn switch #1 off.

Smith Corona XE6100 Typewriter

Type: Daisy Wheel

Defined as: Smith Corona XE6100

Fonts Assigned:

	Character Table	Attributes	Pitch
1	Standard ASCII	Depends on wheel used	10,12
2	Standard ASCII	Depends on wheel used	10,12
3	Standard ASCII	Depends on wheel used	10,12
4	Standard ASCII	Depends on wheel used	10,12
5	Standard ASCII	Depends on wheel used	10,12
6	Standard ASCII	Depends on wheel used	10,12
7	Standard ASCII	Depends on wheel used	10,12
8	Standard ASCII	Depends on wheel used	10,12

Features Not Supported: Double Underline, Line Draw, Superscript/Subscript, Type-thru, Advance, 6/8 LPI, Foreign Characters, Proportional Spacing

Star Gemini 10X

Type: Dot Matrix

Defined as: Star Radix/Gemini 10X

Fonts Assigned:

	Character Table	Attributes	Pitch
1	Star Radix	Draft	10, 12, 15
2	Star Radix	Italic	10, 12, 15
3	Star Radix	Draft	10, 12, 15
4	Star Radix	Italic	10, 12, 15
5	Star Radix	Double-Wide	10, 12, 15
6	Star Radix	Double-Wide Italic	10, 12, 15
7	Star Radix	Double-Wide	10, 12, 15
8	Double Line	Draft	10, 12, 15

Features Not Supported: Double Underline, Type-thru, Advance, Foreign Characters, Proportional Spacing

Line Draw Information:

Font(s) to be used: All

Limitations: Should use half-line spacing for all.

Star Gemini 10X PC

Type: Dot Matrix

Defined as: Star Gemini 10X PC Printer

Fonts Assigned:

	Character Table	Attributes	Pitch
1	IBM Graphics	Emphasized	10
2	IBM Graphics	Superscript	10, 12, 15
3	IBM Graphics	Double-Strike	10, 12, 15
4	IBM Graphics	Emphasized Double-Strike	10
5	IBM Graphics	Subscript	10, 12, 15
6	IBM Graphics	Emphasized Double-Strike	10, 12, 15
7	IBM Graphics	Double-Wide	10, 12, 15
8	IBM Graphics	Draft	10, 12, 15

Features Not Supported: Double Underline, Type-thru, Advance, Proportional Spacing

Line Draw Information:

Font(s) to be used: All

Limitations: Fonts 2, 5, 6, and 7 require half-line spacing. No solid lines with font 5.

Special Notes: Full character set, but no italics.

Star NB-15

Type: Dot Matrix

Defined as: Star NB-15

Fonts Assigned:

	Character Table	Attributes	Pitch
1	IBM Graphics	NLQ	10,12
2	IBM Graphics	NLQ Italic	10,12
3	Star NB PS	PS	11*
4	IBM Graphics	Font cartridge #1	10,12,15
5	IBM Graphics	Font cartridge #2	10,12,15
6	IBM Graphics	Double-Wide, Double-High	10,12,15
7	IBM Graphics	Quad-Wide, Quad-High	10,12,15
8	IBM Graphics	Draft	10,12,15

Features Not Supported: Type-thru

Proportional Spacing Information:

Font(s) to be used: 3

Pitch to be used: 11*

Limitations: Footnote line will not appear in font 3, PS. Continuous single underline is not available in PS.

Line Draw Information:

Font(s) to be used: All but font 3.

Limitations: May need to adjust to half-line spacing in font 7.

Star NB24-15

Type: Dot Matrix

Defined as: Star NB24-15

Fonts Assigned:

	Character Table	Attributes	Pitch
1	Star NB24 PS	NLQ	10,12
2	Star NB24 PS	Italic	10,12,15
3	Star NB24 PS	PS	11*
4	Star NB24 PS	Subscript	15
5	Star NB24 PS	Double-Wide (5,6,7.5)	10,12,15
6	Star NB24 PS	Double-Wide, Double-High (5,6,7.5)	10,12,15
7	Star NB24 PS	Quad-Wide, Quad-High 2.5,3,3.75	10,12,15
8	Star NB24 PS	Draft	10,12,15

Features Not Supported: Double Underline, Line Draw, Type-thru, Foreign Characters

Proportional Spacing Information:

Font(s) to be used: 3

Pitch to be used: 11*

Limitations: Footnote line is broken in all but PS. No continuous underline in PS.

Star ND-15

Type: Dot Matrix

Defined as: Star ND-15 (IBM mode)

Fonts Assigned:

	Character Table	Attributes	Pitch
1	IBM Graphics	NLQ	10,12
2	IBM Graphics	Double-Wide	10,12,15
3	Star NL/NX PC	Emphasized PS	10*
4	IBM Graphics	Italic	10,12,15
5	IBM Graphics	Emphasized	10,12
6	IBM Graphics	Double-Wide, Double-High 5,6,8.5	10,12,15
7	IBM Graphics	Quad-Wide, Quad-High 2.5,3,4.25	10,12,15
8	IBM Graphics	Draft	10,12,15

Features Not Supported: Type-thru

Proportional Spacing Information:

Font(s) to be used: 3

Pitch to be used: 10*

Line Draw Information:

Font(s) to be used: All but font 3

Limitations: May need to adjust to half-line spacing in fonts 6 and 7. Font 8 prints a broken line.

Special Notes: Entering 15 pitch returns 17 pitch. No footnote line in font 3.

Star NL-10

Type: Dot Matrix

Defined as: Epson FX
Emulating: Epson FX

Fonts Assigned:

	Character Table	Attributes	Pitch
1	Epson FX&Type 3	NLQ	10
2	Dot Matrix 1/60	Emphasized	10,12,15
3	Epson FX Normal PS	Draft PS	11*
4	Epson FX Italic PS	Enhanced Italic	10,12,15
5	Epson FX&Type 3	Draft Double-Wide (5,6,7.5)	10,12,15
6	Epson FX&Type 3	Emphasized Double-Wide Italic	10
7	Epson FX&Type 3	Enhanced	10,12,15
8	Epson FX&Type 3	Draft	10,12,15

Features Not Supported: Double Underline, Line Draw, Type-thru, Foreign Characters

Proportional Spacing Information:

Font(s) to be used: 3

Pitch to be used: 11*

Special Notes: PS will not right justify on this printer. To use Star NL-10 "parallel" module, use Epson FX definition.

Star NL-10 (IBM)

Type: Dot Matrix

Defined as: Star NL/NX-10 (IBM)

Fonts Assigned:

	Character Table	Attributes	Pitch
1	IBM Graphics	NLQ	10
2	IBM Graphics	Double-Wide	10, 12, 15
3	Star NL/NX PS	PS	11*
4	IBM Graphics	Emphasized	10
5	IBM Graphics	Emphasized	10
6	IBM Graphics	Double-High, Double-Wide	10
7	IBM Graphics	Quad-Wide, Quad-High	10
8	IBM Graphics	Draft	10, 12, 15

Features Not Supported: Double Underline, Type-thru

Proportional Spacing Information:

Font(s) to be used: 3

Pitch to be used: 11*

Line Draw Information:

Font(s) to be used: All but font 3.

Limitations: Need to adjust spacing (half-line or 8 LPI) with fonts 2, 6, and 7.

Special Notes: To use Star NL-10 "Parallel" module, use Epson FX definition.

Star NX-10

Type: Dot Matrix

Defined as: Epson FX

Emulating: Epson FX

Fonts Assigned:

	Character Table	Attributes	Pitch
1	Epson FX&Type 3	NLQ	10
2	Dot Matrix 1/60	Double-Wide	10, 12, 15
3	Epson FX Normal PS	NLQ PS	10*

Character Table	Attributes	Pitch
4 Epson FX Italic PS	Italic	10,12,15
5 Epson FX&Type 3	Emphasized Enhanced	10,12,15
6 Epson FX&Type 3	Double-Wide, Double-High	10
7 Epson FX&Type 3	Quad-Wide, Quad-High	10
8 Epson FX&Type 3	Draft	10,12,15

Features Not Supported: Type-thru

Proportional Spacing Information:

Font(s) to be used: 3

Pitch to be used: 10*

Limitations: Footnote line will not appear in font 3, PS. Continuous single underline is not available in PS.

Line Draw Information:

Font(s) to be used: All

Limitations: Fonts 2, 6, and 7 require half-line spacing.

Star Powertype

Type: Daisy Wheel

Defined as: Star Powertype

Fonts Assigned:

Character Table	Attributes	Pitch
1 Standard ASCII	Depends on wheel used	10,12,15
2 Standard ASCII	Depends on wheel used	10,12,15
3 Standard ASCII	Depends on wheel used	10,12,15
4 Standard ASCII	Depends on wheel used	10,12,15
5 Standard ASCII	Depends on wheel used	10,12,15
6 Standard ASCII	Depends on wheel used	10,12,15
7 Standard ASCII	Depends on wheel used	10,12,15
8 Standard ASCII	Depends on wheel used	10,12,15

Features Not Supported: Line Draw, Type-thru, Redline/Strikeout, Foreign Characters, Proportional Spacing

Star SG-10

Type: Dot Matrix

Defined as: Star SG-10

Fonts Assigned:

Character Table		Attributes	Pitch
1	IBM Graphics	NLQ	10
2	IBM Graphics	Emphasized Italic	10
3	IBM Graphics	Emphasized PS	10*
4	IBM Graphics	Emphasized	10
5	IBM Graphics	Emphasized/Enhanced	10,12,15
6	IBM Graphics	Emphasized Double-Wide 5,6,7.5	10,12,15
7	IBM Graphics	Double-Wide (5,6,7.5)	10,12,15
8	IBM Graphics	Draft	10,12,15

Features Not Supported: Double Underline, Type-thru, Advance, Overstrike

Proportional Spacing Information:

Font(s) to be used: 3

Pitch to be used: 13*

Limitations: Right justification with PS not supported.

Line Draw Information:

Font(s) to be used: All

Limitations: Fonts 6 and 7 require half-line spacing.

Special Notes: Entering 15 pitch returns 17 pitch on printer. Turn DIP switch SW2-2 off.

Talaris T810 Dutch PWP

Type: Laser

Defined as: Talaris T810 Dutch PWP

Fonts Assigned:

Character Table	Attributes	Pitch
1 Talaris 17304	Dutch 10pt	14*
2 Talaris 17335	Dutch Italic 10pt	14*
3 Talaris 17306	Dutch 12pt	13*
4 Talaris 17337	Dutch Italic 12pt	13*
5 Talaris 17300	Dutch 6pt	25*
6 Talaris 17331	Dutch Italic 6pt	25*
7 Talaris 17312	Dutch 18pt	8*
8 Talaris Line Draw	Line Draw	10,12,15

Features Not Supported: Type-thru, Foreign Characters

Proportional Spacing Information:

Font(s) to be used: 1-7

Pitch to be used: See above

Line Draw Information:

Font(s) to be used: 8

Talaris T810 Roman PWP

Type: Laser

Defined as: Talaris T810 Roman PWP

Fonts Assigned:

Character Table	Attributes	Pitch
1 Talaris 7009	Roman 10pt	16*
2 Talaris 7010	Roman 12pt	13*
3 Talaris 7011	Roman 18pt	9*
4 Talaris 7014	Roman 6pt	20*
5 Talaris 7016	Roman 8pt	18*
6 Talaris 7027	Roman Italic 10pt	16*
7 Talaris 7028	Roman Italic 12pt	13*
8 Talaris 7032	Roman Italic 6pt	20*

Features Not Supported: Line Draw, Type-thru, Foreign Characters

Proportional Spacing Information:

Font(s) to be used: All

Pitch to be used: See above

Talaris T810 Sans Serif PWP

Type: Laser

Defined as: Talaris T810 Sans Serif PWP

Fonts Assigned:

	Character Table	Attributes	Pitch
1	Talaris 7036	Sans Serif 10pt	14*
2	Talaris 7037	Sans Serif 12pt	14*
3	Talaris 7038	Sans Serif 18pt	9*
4	Talaris 7041	Sans Serif 6pt	25*
5	Talaris 7043	Sans Serif 8pt	20*
6	Talaris 7054	Sans Serif Italic 10pt	14*
7	Talaris 7055	Sans Serif Italic 12pt	14*
8	Talaris 7059	Sans Serif Italic 6pt	25*

Features Not Supported: Type-thru, Foreign Characters

Proportional Spacing Information:

Font(s) to be used: All

Pitch to be used: See above

Talaris T810 Standard

Type: Laser

Defined as: Talaris T810 Standard

Fonts Assigned:

	Character Table	Attributes	Pitch
1	Talaris Port Standard	Courier	10,12,15
2	Talaris Line Draw	Orator	10,12,15
3	Talaris Epson Standard	Epson Normal	10,12,15
4	Talaris Epson Italic	Epson Italic	10,12,15
5	Talaris Epson Standard	Epson Compressed	10,12,15
6	Talaris DT 6xx	Technical Symbols	10,12,15
7	Talaris DT 6xx	Line Draw Symbols	10,12,15
8	Talaris Line Draw	Courier Landscape	10,12,15

Features Not Supported: Type-Thru, Foreign Characters, Proportional Spacing, Line Draw

Line Draw Information:

Font(s) to be used: All except font 6

Talaris T810 Swiss PWP

Type: Laser

Defined as: Talaris T810 Swiss PWP

Fonts Assigned:

Character Table	Attributes	Pitch
1 Talaris 17001	Swiss 10pt	16*
2 Talaris 17002	Swiss 12pt	13*
3 Talaris 17000	Swiss 6pt	25*
4 Talaris 17004	Swiss 18pt	9*
5 Talaris 011	Swiss Italic 10pt	15*
6 Talaris 012	Swiss Italic 12pt	13*
7 Talaris 17010	Swiss Italic 6pt	25*
8 Talaris Line Draw	Line Draw	10,12,15

Features Not Supported: Type-thru, Foreign Characters

Proportional Spacing Information:

Font(s) to be used: 1-7

Pitch to be used: See above

Line Draw Information:

Font(s) to be used: 8

All Tandy Computers/Printers

If you are having problems printing, check the CONFIG.SYS file to see if it contains the command "device=lpdrvr.sys." This command needs to be deleted for WordPerfect to run correctly. However, other programs need this command. Consider placing it in a batch file for the other software programs, but remove it from the batch file used to start WordPerfect.

When using the Tandy 2000 computer and defining a printer in WordPerfect that uses LPT1, choose "8" for the port and enter **prn** for the device or file pathname.

Tandy DMP 130

Type: Dot Matrix

Defined as: Tandy DMP 130

Fonts Assigned:

	Character Table	Attributes	Pitch
1	Tandy DMP 130	NLQ	10
2	Tandy DMP 130	Draft (17)	15
3	Tandy DMP 130	NLQ PS	11*
4	Tandy DMP 130	NLQ Italic	10
5	Tandy DMP 130	Double-Wide	10
6	Tandy DMP 130	Double-Wide Italic	10
7	Tandy DMP 130	NLQ	12
8	Tandy DMP 130	Draft	10

Features Not Supported: Double Underline, Type-thru

Proportional Spacing Information:

Font(s) to be used: 3

Pitch to be used: 11*

Line Draw Information:

Font(s) to be used: All

Limitations: No double-line draw. Fonts 5 and 6 need half-line spacing. Font 2 does not give a solid line.

Special Notes: Must use a Tandy cable.

Tandy DMP 430

Type: Dot Matrix

Defined as: Tandy DMP 430

Fonts Assigned:

	Character Table	Attributes	Pitch
1	TRS DMP 430	NLQ	10
2	TRS DMP 430	Draft Elite	12

Character Table	Attributes	Pitch
3 TRS 430 PS	PS	11*
4 TRS DMP 430	Italic	10
5 TRS DMP 430	NLQ Double-Wide	10
6 TRS DMP 430	Double-Wide Italic	10
7 TRS DMP 430	Condensed	15
8 TRS DMP 430	Draft Pica	10

Features Not Supported: Type-thru, 6/8 LPI, Foreign Characters

Proportional Spacing Information:

Font(s) to be used: 3

Pitch to be used: 11*

Line Draw Information:

Font(s) to be used: 7,8

Limitations: Half-line spacing must be used.

Tandy DMP 2100

Type: Dot Matrix

Defined as: Tandy DMP 2100 (Aux Sw 5&6 on)

Fonts Assigned:

Character Table	Attributes	Pitch
1 TRS DMP 2100	NLQ Pica	10
2 TRS DMP 2100	NLQ Elite	12
3 TRS DMP 2100	PS	12*
4 TRS DMP 2100	Draft Pica	10
5 TRS DMP 2100	Draft Elite	12
6 TRS DMP 2100	Condensed	15
7 TRS DMP 2100	NLQ Double-Wide	10
8 TRS DMP 2100	NLQ Double-Wide	10

Features Not Supported: Double Underline, Type-thru, Foreign Characters

Proportional Spacing Information:

Font(s) to be used: 3

Pitch to be used: 12*

Line Draw Information:

Font(s) to be used: All with half-line spacing.

Special Notes: Must use a Tandy cable.

Tandy DMP 2100P

Type: Dot Matrix

Defined as: Tandy DMP 2100P

Fonts Assigned:

	Character Table	Attributes	Pitch
1	2100 P Elite PS	NLQ Pica	10
2	2100 P Elite PS	NLQ Elite	12
3	2100 P Elite PS	NLQ PS	13*
4	2100 P Elite PS	Draft Elite	12
5	2100 P Elite PS	NLQ Double-Wide (5)	10
6	2100 P Elite PS	Draft Double-Wide (5)	10
7	2100 P Elite PS	Condensed	17
8	2100 P Elite PS	Draft Pica	10

Features Not Supported: Double Underline, Type-thru, 6/8 LPI

Proportional Spacing Information:

Font(s) to be used: 3

Pitch to be used: 13*

Line Draw Information:

Font(s) to be used: All

Limitations: Requires half-line spacing.

Tandy DMP 2110

Type: Dot Matrix

Defined as: Tandy DMP 2110

Fonts Assigned:

	Character Table	Attributes	Pitch
1	DMP 2110 Elite	NLQ Elite PS	13*
2	DMP 2110 Elite	Microfont	10
3	DMP 2110 Courier	NLQ Courier PS	11*
4	DMP 2110 Courier	NLQ Italic	10,12,15
5	DMP 2110 Courier	Double-Wide	10,12,15
6	DMP 2110 Courier	Double-High	10,12
7	DMP 2110 Courier	Double-Wide, Double-High	10
8	IBM Graphics	IBM Character Set	10

Features Not Supported: Type-thru

Proportional Spacing Information:

Font(s) to be used: 1,3

Pitch to be used: See above

Line Draw Information:

Font(s) to be used: All

Limitations: Fonts 1 through 7 require half-line spacing.

Tandy DMP 2200 in IBM Mode

Defined as: Try the IBM Graphics printer definition.

Tandy 210

Defined as: Try the DWP II B definition.

Tandy DWP 230

Type: Daisy Wheel

Defined as: Tandy DWP 230/520

Fonts Assigned:

	Character Table	Attributes	Pitch
1	Standard ASCII	Depends on wheel used	10,12,15
2	Standard ASCII	Depends on wheel used	10,12,15
3	TRS DWP Bold PS	Bold PS	13*
4	Standard ASCII	Depends on wheel used	10,12,15
5	Standard ASCII	Depends on wheel used	10,12,15
6	Standard ASCII	Depends on wheel used	10,12,15
7	Standard ASCII	Depends on wheel used	10,12,15
8	Standard ASCII	Depends on wheel used	10,12,15

Features Not Supported: Line Draw, 6/8 LPI, Foreign Characters

Proportional Spacing Information:

Font(s) to be used: 3

Pitch to be used: 13*

Limitations: No underscore or footnote line in font 3.

Special Notes: Underline will not underline spaces.

Tandy DWP 520

Type: Daisy Wheel

Defined as: Tandy DWP 230/520

Fonts Assigned:

	Character Table	Attributes	Pitch
1	Standard ASCII	Depends on wheel used	10,12,15
2	Standard ASCII	Depends on wheel used	10,12,15
3	TRS Bold PS	Bold PS	13*
4	Standard ASCII	Depends on wheel used	10,12,15
5	Standard ASCII	Depends on wheel used	10,12,15
6	Standard ASCII	Depends on wheel used	10,12,15
7	Standard ASCII	Depends on wheel used	10,12,15
8	Standard ASCII	Depends on wheel used	10,12,15

Features Not Supported: Line Draw, 6/8 LPI, Foreign Characters

Proportional Spacing Information:

Font(s) to be used: 3

Pitch to be used: 13*

Limitations: No underscore or footnote line in font 3.

Special Notes: Underline will not underline spaces.

Tandy DWP II B

Type: Daisy Wheel

Defined as: Tandy DWP II B

Fonts Assigned:

	Character Table	Attributes	Pitch
1	ASCII Line Printer	Depends on wheel used	10,12,15
2	ASCII Line Printer	Depends on wheel used	10,12,15
3	TRS DWP Bold PS	Depends on wheel used	13*
4	ASCII Line Printer	Depends on wheel used	10,12,15
5	ASCII Line Printer	Depends on wheel used	10,12,15
6	ASCII Line Printer	Depends on wheel used	10,12,15
7	ASCII Line Printer	Depends on wheel used	10,12,15
8	ASCII Line Printer	Depends on wheel used	10,12,15

Features Not Supported: Line Draw, 6/8 LPI, Foreign Characters

Proportional Spacing Information:

Font(s) to be used: 3

Pitch to be used: 13*

Texas Instruments 850

Type: Dot Matrix

Defined as: TI 850

Fonts Assigned:

	Character Table	Attributes	Pitch
1	Standard ASCII	Draft	10
2	Standard ASCII	Quality Print Mode	10

Character Table	Attributes	Pitch
3 Standard ASCII	Compressed	10
4 Standard ASCII	Double-Strike	10
5 Standard ASCII	Emphasized	10
6 Standard ASCII	Double-Wide	10
7 Single Line	Draft	10
8 Double Line	Draft	10

Features Not Supported: Double Underline, Type-thru, Advance, Foreign Characters, Proportional Spacing

Line Draw Information:

Font(s) to be used: 7,8 in half-line spacing.

Special Notes: Expanded print can be accessed by inserting a Printer command (<27>W1), but will be canceled at the end of a line (printer limitation).

Texas Instruments 855 and 857

Type: Dot Matrix

Defined as: TI 855/857

Fonts Assigned:

Character Table	Attributes	Pitch
1 ASCII Backspace	Draft	10,12,15
2 ASCII Backspace	Cartridge 1 Quality	ND
3 ASCII Backspace	Cartridge 1 Draft	ND
4 ASCII Backspace	Cartridge 2 Quality	ND
5 ASCII Backspace	Cartridge 2 Draft	ND
6 TI 855 Modern PS	Cartridge 3 Quality	13*
7 TI 855 Modern PS	Cartridge 3 Draft	13*
8 TI 855 Bold PS	Draft	10,12,15

Features Not Supported: Double Underline, Line Draw, Type-thru, Foreign Characters

Proportional Spacing Information:

Font(s) to be used: 6,7

Pitch to be used: 13*

Limitations: PS available only when using the modern PS cartridge in slot 3.

Special Notes: Pitch in fonts 2 through 7 depends on the cartridge installed. If you want to print extended characters in bold, you must delete the Bold On and Bold Off codes in the Printer program.

Texas Instruments 857 Color

Type: Dot Matrix

Defined as: TI 857 (Color)

Fonts Assigned:

Character Table	Attributes	Pitch
1 ASCII Backspace	Black	10,12,15
2 ASCII Backspace	Blue	10,12,15
3 ASCII Backspace	Red	10,12,15
4 ASCII Backspace	Yellow	10,12,15
5 ASCII Backspace	Green	10,12,15
6 TI 855 Modern PS	Purple	10,12,15
7 TI 855 Modern PS	Orange	10,12,15
8 TI 855 Bold PS	Black	10,12,15

Features Not Supported: Double Underline, Line Draw, Type-thru, Foreign Characters, Proportional Spacing

Texas Instruments 2015

FType: Laser

Defined as: TI 2015

Fonts Assigned:

Character Table	Attributes	Pitch
1 IBM Graphics	Courier 10 Port	10
2 IBM Graphics	Courier 12 Port	12
3 IBM Graphics	Courier 15 Port	15
4 IBM Graphics	Courier 10 Port	10
5 IBM Graphics	Courier 10 Land	10
6 IBM Graphics	Courier 12 Land	12
7 IBM Graphics	Courier 15 Land	15
8 IBM Graphics	Courier 10 Land	10

Features Not Supported: Type-thru, Proportional Spacing

Line Draw Information:

Font(s) to be used: All

Limitations: No solid lines with fonts 2, 3, 6, and 7.

Sheet Feeder Information: Define as Texas Instruments 2015 sheet feeder. Extra lines = 0, column position of left edge of paper = 0, bins = 3.

Texas Instruments 2115 Courier Portrait or Landscape

Type: Laser — Postscript

Defined as: TI 2115 Courier Portrait or Landscape

Fonts Assigned:

	Character Table	Attributes	Pitch
1	Helvetica 11 pt	Courier	10
2	Helvetica 11 pt	Courier Italic	10
3	Helvetica 11 pt	Courier Bold	10
4	Helvetica 11 pt	Courier	12
5	Helvetica 11 pt	Courier Bold	12
6	Helvetica 11 pt	Courier	15
7	Helvetica 11 pt	Courier	20
8	Helvetica 11 pt	Courier	5

Features Not Supported: Double Underline, Line Draw, Type-thru, Proportional Spacing

Special Notes: Printer needs to be set to postscript emulation to run with this driver.

Texas Instruments 2115 Helvetica Portrait or Landscape

Type: Laser — Postscript

Defined as: LaserWriter Helvetica Portrait or Landscape

Fonts Assigned:

Character Table	Attributes	Pitch
1 Helvetica 11 pt	Helvetica 11pt	13*
2 Helvetica Oblique 11 pt	Helvetica-Oblique 11pt	13*
3 Helvetica Bold 11 pt	Helvetica-Bold 11pt	13*
4 Helvetica Bold Oblique 11 pt	Helvetica-Bold Oblique 11pt	13*
5 Helvetica 8 pt	Helvetica 8pt	18*
6 Helvetica Oblique 8 pt	Helvetica-Oblique 8pt	18*
7 Helvetica 5 pt	Helvetica 5pt	22*
8 Helvetica 17 pt	Helvetica-Bold 17pt	8*

Features Not Supported: Double Underline, Line Draw, Type-thru

Proportional Spacing Information:

Font(s) to be used: All

Pitch to be used: See above

Special Notes: Printer needs to be set to postscript emulation to run with this driver.

Texas Instruments 2115 Times Roman Portrait or Landscape

Type: Laser — Postscript

Defined as: LaserWriter Times Portrait or Landscape

Fonts Assigned:

Character Table	Attributes	Pitch
1 Times 12 pt	Times Roman 12pt	13*
2 Times Italic 12 pt	Times Italic 12pt	13*
3 Times Bold 12 pt	Times Bold 12pt	13*
4 Times Bold Italic 12 pt	Times Bold Italic 12pt	13*
5 Times 9 pt	Times Roman 9pt	18*
6 Times Italic 9 pt	Times Italic 9pt	18*
7 Times 5 pt	Times Roman 5pt	22*
8 Times Bold 18pt	Times Bold 18pt	8*

Features Not Supported: Double Underline, Line Draw, Type-thru

Proportional Spacing Information:

Font(s) to be used: All

Pitch to be used: See above

Special Notes: Printer needs to be set to postscript emulation to run with this driver.

Toshiba P321, P351, and P351C

Type: Dot Matrix

Defined as: Toshiba P321/P351/P351C

Fonts Assigned:

	Character Table	Attributes	Pitch
1	P321/P351/P351C	NLQ Courier PS	11*
2	P321/P351/P351C	NLQ Elite PS	13*
3	P321/P351/P351C	NLQ Courier PS	11*
4	P321/P351/P351C	Italic	10,12,15
5	P321/P351/P351C	Double-Wide	10,12,15
6	P321/P351/P351C	Double-Wide Italic	10,12,15
7	P321/P351/P351C	Condensed	10,12,15
8	P321/P351/P351C	Draft Courier	10,12,15

Features Not Supported: Type-thru, Foreign Characters

Proportional Spacing Information:

Font(s) to be used: 1,2,3

Pitch to be used: See above

Line Draw Information:

Font(s) to be used: All

Limitations: Must use half-line spacing. No solid lines with font 7.

Special Notes: If the printer has an IBM ROM, define as an IBM Proprinter, not as an IBM Graphics Printer. Colors must be inserted as a Printer command:

Band 1 = <27><121>   Band 2 = <27><109>

Band 3 = <27><99>   Band 4 = <27><98>

Toshiba P1340

Type: Dot Matrix

Defined as: Toshiba P1340

Fonts Assigned:

Character Table	Attributes	Pitch
1 Toshiba P1340	Draft	10,12,15
2 Toshiba P1340	NLQ	10,12,15
3 Toshiba P1340	High-Speed PS	13*
4 Toshiba P1340	NLQ PS	10,12,15
5 Toshiba P1340	Double-Wide	10,12,15
6 Toshiba P1340	NLQ Double-Wide	10,12,15
7 Toshiba P1340	Condensed	10,12,15
8 Toshiba P1340	Double-Wide Condensed	10,12,15

Features Not Supported: Double Underline, Type-thru, Foreign Characters

Proportional Spacing Information:

Font(s) to be used: 3

Pitch to be used: 13*

Line Draw Information:

Font(s) to be used: All

Limitations: Must use half-line spacing.

Special Notes: If Superscript/subscript does not work, it may be a result of tight pinch rollers, not the tension lever.

Toshiba P1350 and P1351

Type: Dot Matrix

Defined as: Toshiba P1350/P1351

Fonts Assigned:

Character Table	Attributes	Pitch
1 Toshiba 1350/1	NLQ Font 2	10,12,15
2 Toshiba 1350/1	NLQ Font 1 PS	13*
3 Toshiba 1350/1	NLQ Font 1 PS	13*
4 Toshiba 1350/1	ND	ND
5 Toshiba 1350/1	ND	ND

Character Table		*Attributes*	*Pitch*
6	Toshiba 1350/1	NLQ Double-Wide	10,12,15
7	Toshiba 1350/1	Draft High-Speed	10,12,15
8	Toshiba 1350/1	ND	ND

Features Not Supported: Double Underline, Type-thru, Foreign Characters

Proportional Spacing Information:

Font(s) to be used: 2,3

Pitch to be used: 13*

Line Draw Information:

Font(s) to be used: All

Limitations: Half-line spacing must be used.

Xerox 2700 II

Type: Laser

Defined as: Xerox 2700 II

Emulating: Diablo 630

Fonts Assigned:

Character Table		*Attributes*	*Pitch*
1	Xerox ISO	Titan 10 Port	10
2	Xerox ISO	XCP14 Land	14
3	Xerox ISO	ND	ND
4	Xerox ISO	ND	ND
5	Xerox ISO	ND	ND
6	Xerox ISO	ND	ND
7	Xerox ISO	ND	ND
8	Xerox ISO	ND	ND

Features Not Supported: Line Draw, Type-thru, Foreign Characters, Proportional Spacing

Xerox 4045

Type: Laser

Defined as: Xerox 4045 Laser CP (630)

Emulating: Diablo 630

Fonts Assigned:

	Character Table	Attributes	Pitch
1	Xerox ISO	Titan 10	10
2	Xerox ISO	ND	ND
3	Xerox ISO	ND	ND
4	Xerox ISO	ND	ND
5	Xerox ISO	ND	ND
6	Xerox ISO	ND	ND
7	Xerox ISO	ND	ND
8	Xerox ISO	XCP14 Land	14

Features Not Supported: Line Draw, Type-thru, 6/8 LPI, Proportional Spacing

Xerox 4045 Century School Book

Type: Laser

Defined as: Xerox 4045 Century School Book

Emulating: Diablo

Fonts Assigned:

	Character Table	Attributes	Pitch
1	Xerox CSB 300 12 MR	Century School Book 12pt	12*
2	Xerox CSB 300 12 MI	Century School Book 12pt Italic	12*
3	Xerox CSB 300 10 MR	Century School Book 10pt	14*
4	Xerox CSB 300 10 MI	Century School Book 10pt Italic	14*
5	Xerox CSB 300 14 MR	Century School Book 14pt	10*
6	Xerox CSB 300 18 MR	Century School Book 18pt	8*
7	Xerox CSB 300 24 MR	Century School Book 24pt	6*
8	Xerox CSB 300 6 MR	Century School Book 6pt	22*

Features Not Supported: Line Draw, Type-thru

Proportional Spacing Information:

Font(s) to be used: All

Pitch to be used: See above

Special Notes: For Printer Rev. #2.1, download these fonts:

22697.FNT	23603.FNT	22681.FNT	22685.FNT
23607.FNT	23615.FNT	23737.FNT	23649.FNT

Xerox 4045 Helvetica

Type: Laser

Defined as: Xerox 4045 Laser Helvetica

Fonts Assigned:

	Character Table	Attributes	Pitch
1	Xerox Helvetica 11	Helvetica 11pt	13*
2	Xerox Helvetica 11I	Helvetica 11pt Italic	13*
3	Xerox Helvetica 10	Helvetica 10pt	15*
4	Xerox Helvetica 10I	Helvetica 10pt Italic	15*
5	Xerox Helvetica 7	Helvetica 7pt	20*
6	Xerox Helvetica 14B	Helvetica 14pt Bold	10*
7	Xerox Helvetica 18B	Helvetica 18pt Bold	8*
8	Xerox Helvetica 24B	Helvetica 24pt Bold	6*

Features Not Supported: Line Draw, Type-thru, Overstrike

Proportional Spacing Information:

Font(s) to be used: All

Pitch to be used: See above

Special Notes: For printer Rev. # 2.1, download these fonts:

22497.FNT	22536.FNT	22489.FNT	22493.FNT
22465.FNT	22553.FNT	22595.FNT	23763.FNT

Xerox 4045 Titan

Type: Laser

Defined as: Xerox 4045 Laser Titan

Emulating: 2700

Fonts Assigned:

	Character Table	Attributes	Pitch
1	Xerox ISO	Titan 10	10
2	Xerox ISO	Titan 10 Italic	10
3	Xerox ISO	Titan 12	12
4	Xerox ISO	Titan 12 Italic	12
5	Xerox ISO	Titan 15	15
6	Xerox ISO	Vintage 10	10
7	Xerox ISO	Vintage 12	12
8	Xerox ISO	XCP14 Land	14

Features Not Supported: Type-thru, Proportional Spacing

Line Draw Information:

Font(s) to be used: 1,2,3,4,6,7

Limitations: Corners do not line up in fonts 2, 3, 4, and 7.

Special Notes: Configure your printer for 2700 mode to use this driver. Download these fonts from the Xerox word processing font set:

22503.FNT	TITN12P.FNT	22507.FNT
TITN15P.FNT	22581.FNT	TITN12IP.FNT

Printer Program

The Printer program included with WordPerfect lets you customize printer definitions to fit your needs and applications. Although you may never need to change a printer definition, you can look in this chapter for insights into how WordPerfect communicates with your printer.

Only the basics of the program are discussed in this chapter. For in-depth information on every option in every menu, consult the booklet, *Defining a Printer Driver*, provided with the WordPerfect package.

Introduction

A printer definition is a preprogrammed set of instructions that tell the printer how to perform various features in WordPerfect. For example, when you create a document and choose formatting options such as page length, bold, or right justification, codes are inserted into the text. When the document is printed, the current printer definition is used to "translate" those WordPerfect codes into commands that can be understood by the printer. All the codes necessary to drive the printer are included with the printer definition and can be viewed and changed with the Printer program.

WordPerfect has included hundreds of printer definitions so that a user can, by selecting his or her printer, call up the set of instructions that will control the printer correctly. Moreover, the user can do this without ever having to know anything about printer codes.

973

If your printer is not among those supported by Word-Perfect, you will need to use the standard printer definition or create your own printer driver using the Printer program. In addition to changing a printer definition, you can send printer commands from within WordPerfect by using the Insert Printer Command option on the Print Format (CTRL-F8) menu. See *Printer Commands* in Chapter 4 for more information. In either case, the commands can be found in the owner's manual furnished with the printer.

If you have a laser printer, you can create one or more printer definitions with a combination of internal fonts, cartridge fonts, or soft fonts. You can have more than eight fonts by using redline, strikeout, and double underlining as font choices. You can create character tables for print wheels and fonts not yet supported. These are all options that can be implemented by using the Printer program.

If you have a question as to which characters can be printed with a particular character table, you can examine and change the table if necessary.

Most electronic sheet feeders are already supported by WordPerfect. If you want to reassign bin numbers or create a sheet feeder definition for one that is not supported, the Printer program can also be used for this purpose.

Starting the Printer Program

When you first receive WordPerfect, you will find three files on the WordPerfect program disk: WP.EXE, WPRINTER. FIL, and WPFONT.FIL. Only a DOS Text Printer and a Standard Printer definition are found in the WPRINTER. FIL file.

When you select printers (see *Select Printers* in Chapter 4), the definitions are copied to WPRINTER.FIL from the WPRINT1.ALL and WPRINT2.ALL files located on the Printer 1 and Printer 2 disks, respectively. The fonts (character tables) assigned to those printer definitions are copied to WPFONT.FIL from FONT1.ALL and FONT2.ALL, also found on the Printer 1 and Printer 2 disks. If you have selected a sheet feeder, the file WPFEED.FIL is copied to the WordPerfect disk.

Only those printer definitions, character tables, and sheet feeder definitions in WPRINTER.FIL, WPFONT.FIL, and WPFEED.FIL can be viewed and edited in the Printer program. Therefore, it is important that you select the appropriate printer definitions before beginning.

After you have selected printers, use the following procedure to start the Printer program. Choose the appropriate set of steps, depending on whether you have a two disk-drive system or are using a hard disk.

Two Disk Drives

1. Place the WordPerfect disk containing WPRINTER. FIL, WPFONT.FIL, and WPFEED.FIL (if applicable) in drive A.

2. Place the Printer 2 disk in drive B.

3. Enter **A:** to change the default drive to drive A if not already there.

4. Enter **B:PRINTER** to start the Printer program.

Hard Disk

1. Change to the directory where WP.EXE is located (enter **CD \WP** if WP is the name of the WordPerfect directory).

2. If the PRINTER.EXE file is in the same directory, enter **PRINTER** at the DOS prompt.

If you have not copied the PRINTER.EXE file to the hard disk, consider doing so. If you cannot spare the disk space and do not plan to use the Printer program often, insert the Printer 2 disk in drive A and enter **A:PRINTER**.

If you see the error message "WPRINTER.FIL not found on current drive," the WPRINTER.FIL is not on the default drive/directory. Make sure you change to the proper drive and directory (as outlined in the steps above) before attempting to start the Printer program.

```
┌────────────────────────────────────────────────────────────────┐
│  ████████████████████████████████████████████████████████████   │
│  PRINTER:  WordPerfect Printer Definition Program                │
│  ████████████████████████████████████████████████████████████   │
│                                                                  │
│                                                                  │
│      Please Choose One:                                          │
│                                                                  │
│              1. General Information and Help                     │
│                                                                  │
│              2. Explanation of Special Codes Used in This Program│
│                                                                  │
│              3. Printer Definitions (Examine, Change)            │
│                                                                  │
│              4. Character Tables (Examine, Change)               │
│                                                                  │
│              5. Sheet Feeder Definitions (Examine, Change)       │
│                                                                  │
│              0. Exit                                             │
│                                                                  │
│      Selection: 0                                                │
│                                                                  │
│                                                                  │
└────────────────────────────────────────────────────────────────┘
```

Figure 7-1.   Initial Printer program screen

Organization of the Printer Program

When you start the Printer program, you will see the menu shown in Figure 7-1. The first option on the menu introduces the Printer program and provides general instructions for editing printer definitions and character tables. Both the first and second options list the special codes created at WordPerfect Corporation to help with some of the printer definitions.

Option 3 shows you which printers are currently selected from within WordPerfect and gives you an opportunity to create, edit, delete, or rename printer definitions. The fourth menu option lets you create or edit character tables used for the fonts, while the fifth option controls the sheet feeder definitions.

Figure 7-2 shows the underlying organization for the

1. General Information and Help

2. Explanation of Special Codes Used in This Program

3. Printer Definitions (Examine, Change)

    Create   Delete

    Edit   Rename

    Main Menu

    1. Printer initialization

    2. Carriage return/backspace control

    3. Line spacing and vertical motion control (VMI)

    4. Microspacing and horizontal motion control (HMI)

    5. Subscript/superscript/underline/bold

    6. Special text markings

    7. Pitch/miscellaneous

    8. Selecting fonts (fonts 1-4)

    9. Selecting fonts (fonts 5-8)

    A. Character tables for fonts ─────┐

4. Character Tables (Examine, Change) ◄─┘

    Create   Delete

    Edit   Rename

Figure 7-2.   Organization of options presented in the Printer program screen

Main Menu

A. String sent to printer

B. Character width

C. Adjust factor (for printers with HMI)

5. Sheet Feeder Definitions (Examine, Change)

Create   Delete

Edit   Rename

Figure 7-2.   Organization of options presented in the Printer Program screen (*continued*)

initial Printer program screen. When you choose to create or edit a printer definition, a "main menu" appears. Each option on the main menu calls a submenu that contains a group of related items and their corresponding printer commands. You can get to the character tables through a printer definition or skip right to them with the fourth option on the initial Printer program menu.

Entering Codes

Because WordPerfect accepts codes in decimal format only, you will need to translate a code into its decimal equivalent first and place it between angle brackets ($<$ and $>$). Characters between 33 and 126 can be entered as themselves without being translated.

For example, most printer manuals give printer commands as Escape sequences such as "ESC W." The ESC key has 27 as its decimal equivalent. Characters between 33 and 126 can be entered as themselves without being translated. Therefore, to enter ESC W as a code into WordPerfect, you would enter $<27>$W (you could also enter $<27><87>$, but it is not necessary to translate the W into decimal format).

Other commands and their decimal equivalents include the following.

BACKSPACE	<8>
Line feed	<10>
Carriage return	<13>
ESC	<27>
SPACEBAR	<32>

You can use the ESC key to enter the <27> and SPACE-BAR to enter a <32>.

If your printer manual lists the commands in BASIC (such as CHR$(27)"W"), change the parentheses to brackets, leave whatever is inside quotation marks, and delete all other characters (including the quotation marks). CHR$(27)"W" would then become <27>W.

Other special codes created by WordPerfect Corporation that are used throughout the program are shown in Table 7-1. These can be entered by holding down the ALT key and

Code	Meaning
<A>	Shift into *alternate character set* for next character, then shift back
<B>	Send *current line spacing* code to the printer (use this to restore line spacing if you had to change it to perform a certain task)
<C>	Send *current pitch* codes to the printer (similar to <B>)
<D>	Do a *carriage return,* then *space forward* to the current column (allows overstriking, or realigns print position after a font/pitch change)

Table 7-1. Special Codes Used in the Printer Program

Code	Meaning
<E>	Repeat these codes on *every line* (any codes which contain <E> will be sent to the printer at the start of every line of printed text)
<F>	Beep, and make printing *wait for a "Go"* (for changing print wheels)
<G>	Replace this code with an *HMI* value in *binary* form (1 = <001>, 2 = <002>, . . .)
<H>	Replace this code with an *HMI* value in *ASCII* form (1 = "1", 2 = "2", . . .)
<I>	Change *bolding* from triple overstrike to double overstrike on HMI-controlled printers (this code may be placed anywhere). Note: Code produces shadow printing on some printers.
<J>	Identifies *Tandy DWP IIB* type printers (printer initialization code)
<K>	Replace this code with a *VMI* value in *binary* form (1 = <001>, 2 = <002>, . . .)
<L>	Replace this code with a *VMI* value in *ASCII* form (1 = "1", 2 = "2", . . .)
<M>	Turn *proportional spacing on*
<N>	Turn *proportional spacing off*
<O>	Switch to a *new font* (font number must follow: 1 = <001>, 2 = <002>, . . .)
<P>	Return to the *previous font* (use this to return to whichever font was active before the last <O> command)
<Q>	Define *character width* for a fixed-pitch font (if included among the "Shift into font" codes). The byte which follows must indicate the exact pitch value ×10 (10 pitch = <100>, 12 pitch = <120>).

Table 7-1.   Special Codes Used in the Printer Program (*continued*)

Code	Meaning
<R>	*Remove extra error checking* during printing. If your printer will print from DOS but not from WordPerfect this code may help. It must be the first code entered in the "Initialize printer before print job" string.
<S>	Replace this code with an *MS* value in *binary* form (1 = <001>, 2 = <002>, . . .)
<T>	Replace this code with an *MS* value in *ASCII* form (1 = "1", 2 = "2", . . .)
<U>	Usage: <U><f><c>: sends the mapping of character *c* from font number *f.* Useful for sharing complex character mappings between fonts in order to save font string storage space.
<V>	Usage: <V><c>: Same as <U>, but assumes the current font.
<W>	Usage: <W><f>: Same as <U>, but assumes the character number is the same as the character number that is being mapped.
<X>	*File download.* Any filename bracketed within <X> will be sent to the printer. The file will be searched for on the unshared and shared WP drives.

Table 7-1.   Special Codes Used in the Printer Program (*continued*)

typing the letter of the code. For example, to insert <A>, you would press ALT-A. You do not have to completely understand these codes to work with the Printer program.

Printer Definitions

Choose option 3 from the initial menu for Printer Definitions (Examine, Change). The menu in Figure 7-3 appears, listing

```
┌─────────────────────────────────────────────────────────────┐
│          ███████████ Printers Currently Defined ███████████   │
│                                                               │
│  1   Standard Printer              2   DOS Text Printer        │
│  3   LaserJt Reg,+,500+ B:Tms Rmn1 4   LaserJt Reg,+,500+ K:Tms Math│
│  5   LaserJt+,500+ Soft AC: Tms P  6   LaserJt Reg,+,500+ F:Tms Rmn2│
│  7   Epson FX                      8   Diablo 620/630          │
│                                                               │
│                                                               │
│                                                               │
│                                                               │
│                                                               │
│                                                               │
│                                                               │
│  A.  Create  B.  Edit  C.  Delete  D.  Rename  E.  Exit  E    │
└─────────────────────────────────────────────────────────────┘
```

Figure 7-3.   Printers Currently Defined menu

all the printer definitions that were selected from within WordPerfect. The options below the list let you create, edit, delete, or rename printer definitions, or exit the menu.

Choose the Delete option if you have selected printer definitions by mistake and want them removed from the list. You can also delete the Standard or DOS Text Printer definitions that are automatically included with the WPRINTER.FIL if you need more room.

If you plan to edit a printer definition, it is advisable that you choose the option to create a printer definition instead. When you ask to create a new printer definition from the menu, you are asked to enter the name of the new printer definition and which printer should be used as a pattern. You can enter the number of the printer to be edited. If there are problems with the new definition, the original will remain unchanged, letting you return to it and start the process over again.

After choosing to create or edit a printer definition, the next screen (which we will call the main menu) appears, as shown in Figure 7-4. The ten options on the menu are used to group different aspects of printing together into sub-menus. Choose each option if you want to see the commands being sent to the printer when a specific feature is needed.

```
        Edit:        LaserJt Reg,+,500+ B:Tms Rmn1
  1. Printer Initialization

  2. Carriage Return/Backspace Control

  3. Line Spacing and Vertical Motion Control (VMI)

  4. Microspacing and Horizontal Motion Control (HMI)

  5. Subscript/Superscript/Underline/Bold

  6. Special Text Markings

  7. Pitch/Miscellaneous

  8. Selecting Fonts (Fonts 1 - 4)

  9. Selecting Fonts (Fonts 5 - 8)

  A. Character Tables for Fonts


  Select Item Number: 0
```

Figure 7-4.   Printer Program main menu

For example, the listed items in Figure 7-5, which would be displayed if option 5 of the main menu were chosen, include some of the commands used for superscript, subscript, and underlining.

Just looking through the submenus will help you get a feel for how your printer is defined. Keep in mind, though, that if a command is not entered for a specific item, it does not mean that the item is not supported. Instead, WordPerfect is probably controlling the feature automatically within the software rather than sending the command specifically for that printer.

Character Tables

Option A on the printer definition main menu lets you select the character tables being used for each font. Figure 7-6 shows the character tables assigned to each of the eight fonts. The ninth item listed is an option to examine or edit a character table. This gives you a list of currently selected fonts and a menu that lets you create, edit, delete, or rename those character tables.

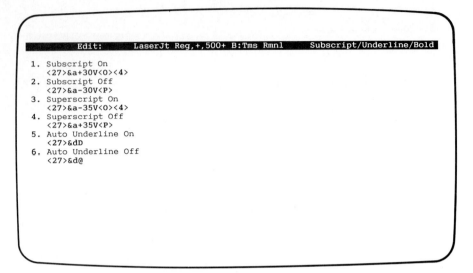

Figure 7-5. Commands for superscript, subscript, and underlining

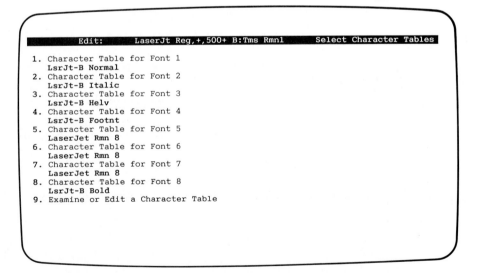

Figure 7-6. Character tables for fonts 1 through 8

If you do not want to go through the printer definition menus to reach the character tables, you can choose option 4 from the initial Printer program screen to examine or change the character tables.

When you choose to create or edit one of the listed character tables, you will see a screen similar to the one shown in Figure 7-7. When you first enter the screen, only the first 55 of the 255 characters available are displayed; you can use any of the cursor keys to move through the list or type the decimal value to go directly to a specific character.

When a <32> is mapped to a character, as in the case of the ¦ symbol (number 124 in the table), it means that the character is not available with that font and a space will be inserted instead to help maintain the right margin. The file FONT.TST found on the Learning disk can be printed in each of the eight fonts so you can see which characters have been defined for that font. If you see an asterisk instead of the decimal value that is being sent to the printer, it means that the command to be sent to the printer would not fit in the space.

```
                            Diablo Multi-L
Dsply Ptr Wd,Ad      Dsply Ptr Wd,Ad      Dsply Ptr Wd,Ad      Dsply Ptr Wd,Ad

p 112 112 10,+0      q 113 113 10,+0      r 114 114 09,+0      s 115 115 09,+0
t 116 116 10,+0      u 117 117 10,+0      v 118 118 10,+0      w 119 119 10,+0
x 120 120 10,+0      y 121 121 10,+0      z 122 122 10,+0      { 123 032 10,+0
¦ 124 032 06,-2      } 125 032 10,+0      ~ 126 032 10,+0      о 127 032 12,+0
Ç 128  *  10,+0      ü 129  *  10,+0      é 130  *  10,+0      â 131  *  09,+0
ä 132  *  09,+0      à 133  *  09,+0      å 134 032 09,+0      ç 135  *  10,+0
ê 136  *  10,+0      ë 137  *  10,+0      è 138  *  10,+0      ï 139  *  08,-1
î 140  *  08,-1      ì 141  *  08,-1      Ä 142  *  10,+0      Å 143 032 10,+0
É 144  *  10,+0      æ 145 032 12,+0      Æ 146 032 12,+0      ô 147  *  10,+0
ö 148  *  10,+0      ò 149  *  10,+0      û 150  *  10,+0      ù 151  *  10,+0
ÿ 152  *  10,+0      Ö 153  *  10,+0      Ü 154  *  10,+0      ¢ 155  *  10,+0
£ 156  *  12,+0      ¥ 157  *  10,+0      ₧ 158 032 12,+0      ƒ 159 032 12,+0
á 160  *  09,+0      í 161  *  08,-1      ó 162  *  10,+0      ú 163  *  10,+0
ñ 164 126 10,+0      Ñ 165 125 10,+0      ª 166 032 12,+0      º 167 032 12,+0

         Information About: î (Decimal Code is: 140)
A. String Sent to Printer: i<8>^
B. Character Width: 08
C. Adjust Factor: -1
E. Exit
```

Figure 7-7.   Screen for creating or editing a character table

As you move the cursor through the characters, you can see information about each character at the bottom of the screen. The highlighted bar displays the decimal value and the character as you see it on the screen. The information below the bar includes the "string," or printer command, sent to the printer, character width, and, in the case of a printer that has HMI (horizontal motion index), the adjust factor for deciding how far to the left or right the character should be printed (used for proportionally spaced fonts). The following example illustrates how Epson FX printers will print ë.

```
          Information About: ë (Decimal Code is: 137)
A. String Sent to Printer: e<8><27>R<1>¯<27>R<0>
B. Character Width: 12
C. Adjust Factor: +0
E. Exit
```

The *e* is printed first, a BACKSPACE is performed, the ESC code <27>R<1> is sent to change to the French international character set, the character in the place of the "~" is printed (..), then another ESC code <27>R<0> is sent to return to the original character set.

With daisy-wheel printers, each character is in a different location on the print wheel and each location is assigned a position number. If you have a print wheel containing the ¶ and § characters, they will most likely be taking the place of other characters normally printed in that location.

Some printers can have an alternate character set defined so you can use the <A> code to switch to the alternate character set, print the special character, then switch back to the original character set. The advanced printer commands <U> and <W> can be used to combine characters from other fonts.

Sheet Feeder Definitions

When you choose option 5 for Sheet Feeder Definitions, you will see a list of all sheet feeders currently supported. These do not have to be selected from within WordPerfect because they are all automatically included in WPFEED.FIL.

All sheet feeders with more than three bins are given more than one menu option for the "extended" bin support. However, if you want to edit, rename, or delete a sheet feeder definition, only the first menu option should be chosen; the other is automatically edited, renamed, or deleted as a matter of course.

When you choose to create or edit a sheet feeder definition, you will see a menu similar to the one shown in Figure 7-8. You can assign the commands to any bin number, keeping in mind that the bin number is the number indicated in the Print Format (CTRL-F8) menu within WordPerfect.

Important Notes Concerning HMI and MS

When defining a printer or character table, it is important to know if your printer supports horizontal motion indexing (HMI) or microspacing (MS). Most daisy-wheel printers support HMI while most laser printers support microspacing.

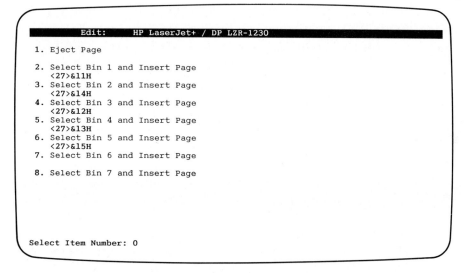

```
        Edit:       HP LaserJet+ / DP LZR-1230

 1. Eject Page

 2. Select Bin 1 and Insert Page
    <27>&l1H
 3. Select Bin 2 and Insert Page
    <27>&l4H
 4. Select Bin 3 and Insert Page
    <27>&l2H
 5. Select Bin 4 and Insert Page
    <27>&l3H
 6. Select Bin 5 and Insert Page
    <27>&l5H
 7. Select Bin 6 and Insert Page

 8. Select Bin 7 and Insert Page




Select Item Number: 0
```

Figure 7-8.   Menu for creating or editing a sheet feeder definition

Some printer definitions use a combination of both to get the desired effect for proportional spacing or right justification.

HMI is a common way of controlling pitch and was introduced with some of the first daisy-wheel printers. Its function is to set the distance to be moved for each character. With a fixed-pitch font in 10 pitch, WordPerfect sets the distance to one-tenth of an inch; at 12 pitch it would be set to one-twelfth of an inch. To right justify the line it merely counts the characters on a line (including spaces), calculates the additional distance necessary to bring the last character to the right margin, and divides that distance evenly among all the characters in the line, excluding spaces. This additional distance may be negative, in which case the characters would actually be moved closer together.

When using proportionally spaced fonts with HMI, the basic formula is still the same. However, WordPerfect looks at the character table assigned to the font you are using to see how far each character should be moved, either to the left or right. Thus, character tables for HMI-type printers have an adjust factor. If you feel a character is printing too close or too far away from another character, you can change the adjust factor in the character table.

Microspacing is a relative type of movement similar to a graphics movement. In other words, it will move a specific amount of space from the current position. When using MS for a fixed-pitch font in 10 pitch, it counts the characters in the line not including spaces between words, calculates the additional distance needed to reach the right margin, divides the additional distance by the number of spaces between words, and sends the resulting distance in place of the spaces between the words. Each printed character would retain the space it occupies, one-tenth of an inch. With 12 pitch the printed characters would be one-twelfth of an inch.

When MS is used for right justifying a proportionally spaced font, an entirely different situation occurs. Rather than consulting the character table to determine the distance to move for each character, as HMI does, the character table serves as a reference to tell WordPerfect how far the printer has already moved when it printed the character. Therefore, there is no adjust factor for MS character tables; only the width of a character is considered. To calculate the space to send between words in order to right justify the line, Word-Perfect measures how far the printer will move when it prints the characters, obtaining the exact distance for each character from the character table. It then calculates the additional distance needed to reach the right margin, divides that distance by the number of spaces between words, and sends that distance in place of the spaces between words.

Since all measurements are positive, (no negative distances, right to left, allowed in the formula), only movements in the positive direction (from left to right) can be performed. When using MS, bi-directional printing is impossible. Also, a pitch too small will cause the right margin to not justify, and a pitch too large will cause the spaces between words to look too wide.

If your printer does not have MS or HMI, right justification is accomplished by adding extra spaces between words where necessary. This process is referred to as *space fill*. If these "double spaces" are undesirable it may be necessary to turn off right justification. Right-justified PS on a printer that uses space fill is usually accomplished through micro-spacing and requires that a microspacing character table be used.

As you can see, it is essential that the correct character table be used when using a proportionally spaced font with either MS or HMI. If proportional fonts do not have the proper character table assigned, all functions performed on a second pass (such as underline, bold, superscripts/subscripts, advance up/down), as well as those features which need calculations from left or right margins (tabs, indenting, centering) will not work correctly.

Tips for Determining Character Widths

When defining a proportionally spaced character table, you will need to determine each character's width. You can usually request the character widths for each font from the printer manufacturer. An alternate method for determining the character width, used by the development staff at Word-Perfect Corporation, is outlined here. It is tedious and slow, but extremely accurate.

Because most character tables are figured in widths of 1/120, 1/300, or 1/720 inch, you can use the common denominator of 60 to help determine the width of a character.

1. Create a document that enters each character 60 times on a single line ending with a period and a hard return as shown in Figure 7-9. To enter the characters quickly, press ESC, type **60**, then press the character to enter it 60 times.

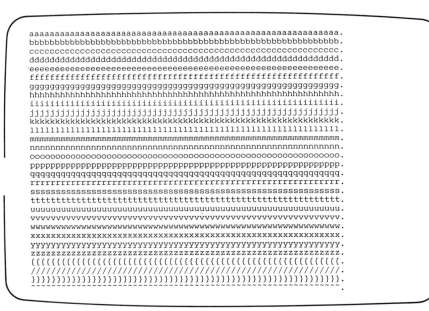

Figure 7-9.   Document for determining character widths

2. Go to the beginning of the document and insert a font change for a proportionally spaced font. The pitch setting will not affect the document, but remember to add the asterisk after the pitch setting. Choose any existing PS font listed as the font number.

3. Print the document. It should look something like the document shown in Figure 7-10.

4. Measure each line from the beginning of the first character to the period at the end of the line.

5. Use the following formula to determine each character's width. If you are not sure of the HMI or MS units, consult your printer manual or refer to the fourth option

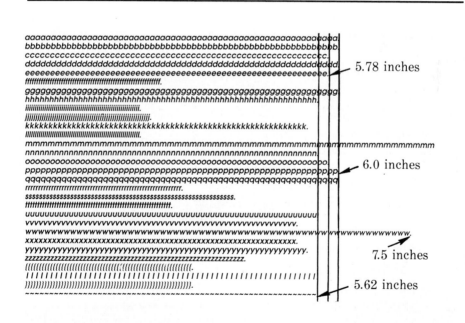

Figure 7-10.   Printout of document determining character widths

on the main menu in the Printer program, Microspacing and Horizontal Motion Control (HMI).

$$\frac{\text{Length of line}}{\text{Number of characters in line}} \times \text{HMI or MS units} = \text{width}$$

For example, as shown in Figure 7-10, the characters a, b, d, g, p, and q each have a line length of 6 inches. Because it was printed with a laser printer that uses 300 dots per inch, the formula would be:

$$\frac{6}{60} \times 300 = 30$$

Therefore, 30 is the character width for the characters a, b, d, g, p, and q.

To determine the adjust factor for printers using HMI, print the document PS.TST on the Learning disk in order to determine whether a character should be placed to the left or right in order to fit nicely with surrounding characters.

Conclusion

The Printer program lets you have control over how a document will be printed. The possibilities are endless, so experiment as much as you wish. Just be sure to always keep a backup of the printer definitions provided with WordPerfect just in case.

This chapter should have helped you get a feel for how the program is organized and how it can be used in specific situations. Again, please refer to the booklet, *Defining a Printer Driver*, for complete details about each option in the program.

Integration

This section gives you tips on integrating WordPerfect with other popular software programs. You will learn how to share data and transfer files with programs such as dBASE III PLUS, PlanPerfect, and Library. Information about other products that help extend WordPerfect, such as For Comment, Ready!, PRD+, KeyNotes, and Inset, is also provided.

Software Integration

Data from practically any software program can be used with WordPerfect. The first section of this chapter presents the options for saving and retrieving ASCII text files and converting documents created with Wang, DisplayWrite, MultiMate, WordStar, Volkswriter, Samna, Microsoft Word, dBASE II and III, R:BASE, and Lotus 1-2-3.

WordPerfect Corporation has developed other software programs that are fully integrated with WordPerfect: Word-Perfect Library, PlanPerfect (formerly called MathPlan), and Repeat Performance. This chapter gives specifics about how these programs can be used effectively with WordPerfect.

Also included is information about extending WordPerfect with add-on products such as ForComment, KeyNotes, PRD+, Ready!, and Inset.

Converting Documents

There are several methods of converting documents created with other programs for use with WordPerfect. Text In/Out (CTRL-F5) can be used for some formats from within WordPerfect, while other file formats require the Convert program included on the Learning disk.

ASCII Files

ASCII is an abbreviation for American Standards Committee for Information Interchange. To ensure compatibility with other software programs, most programs (including WordPerfect) can save or retrieve an ASCII *text* file. This is a file that contains only text, with all unique program codes removed. WordPerfect Corporation calls this type of file a DOS text file rather than an ASCII file because a normal WordPerfect file with codes is also an ASCII file; it just uses the eight-bit characters (those with a decimal value greater than 127) as program codes.

Text In/Out (CTRL-F5) lets you save and retrieve DOS text files from within WordPerfect. Figure 8-1 shows the Text In/Out menu.

Save a DOS Text File

Option 1 on the Text In/Out menu is used to save the current document on the screen as a text file on disk. Some WordPerfect codes are converted to characters that can be saved in a text file (such as with paragraph numbering). Hard and soft returns are converted to carriage return/line feeds (CR/LF) and most of the format (tabs, indents, centering, flush right, and so on) is maintained with spaces.

```
Document Conversion, Summary and Comments

     DOS Text File Format
          1 - Save
          2 - Retrieve   (CR/LF becomes [HRt])
          3 - Retrieve   (CR/LF in H-Zone becomes [SRt])

     Locked Document Format
          4 - Save
          5 - Retrieve

     Other Word Processor Formats
          6 - Save in a generic word processor format
          7 - Save in WordPerfect 4.1 format

     Document Summary and Comments
          A - Create/Edit Summary
          B - Create Comment
          C - Edit Comment
          D - Display Summary and Comments



Selection: 0
```

Figure 8-1.   Text In/Out menu

After a file is saved as a DOS text file, the original file remains on the screen. Do not save it again with the same name. Either clear the screen without saving if you don't want the original file, or save it with a different name. Consider entering a name with an extension .TXT for the DOS text file.

Retrieve a DOS Text File

Option 2 retrieves a DOS text file with all carriage return/line feeds converted to hard returns, while option 3 retrieves a DOS text file and converts any carriage return/line feeds falling within the hyphenation zone to soft returns. In general, you should choose option 2 if you want the lines to remain as they were in the ASCII file, or 3 if you want to take advantage of wordwrap. In either case, set your margins in WordPerfect to correspond to the number of characters per line.

The List Files menu also has an option to retrieve an ASCII text file.

1. Press List Files (F5).

2. Press ENTER to view the displayed directory, or enter a different drive/directory.

3. Highlight the ASCII text file to be retrieved.

4. Type **5** for Text In instead of 1 for Retrieve.

This method is the same as option 2 on the Text In/Out menu where carriage return/line feeds are converted to hard returns rather than soft returns.

Save in a Generic Word Processor Format

Option 6 on the Text In/Out menu lets you save a file in a generic word processor format. There are only two differences between this option and the option to save a DOS text file: tabs are preserved as tabs (not converted to spaces), and a soft return is converted to a space (helping with wordwrap when the file is retrieved into another word processor).

Another option is to print a document to disk using the DOS text printer definition. This option removes WordPerfect codes, but retains such formatting as centering, spacing, columns, headers/footers, footnotes, endnotes, and paragraph and line numbering. Even though the WordPerfect codes are removed, the text found within codes (as in the case of headers/footers, footnotes, and line numbering) is included. Spaces and extra lines are included when necessary to make the document look like the printed version. See *Print to Disk* in Chapter 4 for details.

The Perfect Exchange program, discussed later in this chapter, can also be used for converting ASCII files. Even though the conversion takes place outside of WordPerfect, Perfect Exchange looks at the layout of an ASCII file and inserts applicable WordPerfect codes such as margin settings, line spacing changes, boldface, underlining, centering, tabs, and indents.

Another option on the Text In/Out menu that should be mentioned here is saving a document in 4.1 format. WordPerfect documents are always upward-compatible so there is no problem if you retrieve a document created with an earlier version of WordPerfect. However, if you want to use a 4.2 document with an earlier version of WordPerfect, you may have problems because the 4.2 document would contain some unrecognizable codes.

WordPerfect's Convert Program

Convert is a stand-alone program produced by WordPerfect Corporation that is used to convert documents to and from DCA (document content architecture, used by IBM mainframes and DisplayWrite), WordStar, MultiMate, Navy DIF, Mail Merge (format used by data base programs), DIF (for spreadsheet files), and a seven-bit transfer format.

Starting Convert

The Convert program is included on the WordPerfect Learning disk. Place the Learning disk in drive A (or go to the directory on your hard disk where CONVERT.EXE is located) and type **convert** at the appropriate DOS prompt.

You are asked to enter the input filename—the name of the file to be converted. Use a single filename or a template such as B:*.* or C: \MM *.DOC to convert multiple files. You are then asked to enter the filename for the output document. The input and output filenames must be different or you will get an error message. If you are converting multiple files, enter a template for the output file with an unused extension, such as *.CNV.

Convert Options

After the input and output filenames have been entered, the menu shown in Figure 8-2 appears. Type the number from the menu that represents the format of the input file. If you type 1 to convert a WordPerfect document to another format, the second part of the menu is displayed, asking you to designate the type of conversion desired (see Figure 8-3).

Options 2 through 6 of the initial menu automatically convert the documents to WordPerfect. Option 7 converts data base

```
Name of Input File? chapter.1
Name of Output File? chapter.lws

1 WordPerfect to another format
2 Revisable-Form-Text (IBM DCA Format) to WordPerfect
3 Navy DIF Standard to WordPerfect
4 WordStar 3.3 to WordPerfect
5 MultiMate 3.22 to WordPerfect
6 Seven-bit transfer format to WordPerfect
7 Mail Merge to WordPerfect Secondary Merge
8 WordPerfect Secondary Merge to Spreadsheet DIF
9 Spreadsheet DIF to WordPerfect Secondary Merge

Enter number of Conversion desired
```

Figure 8-2.   Convert Options screen

```
Name of Input File? chapter.1
Name of Output File? chapter.1ws


1 WordPerfect to another format
2 Revisable-Form-Text (IBM DCA Format) to WordPerfect
3 Navy DIF Standard to WordPerfect
4 WordStar 3.3 to WordPerfect
5 MultiMate 3.22 to WordPerfect
6 Seven-bit transfer format to WordPerfect
7 Mail Merge to WordPerfect Secondary Merge
8 WordPerfect Secondary Merge to Spreadsheet DIF
9 Spreadsheet DIF to WordPerfect Secondary Merge

Enter number of Conversion desired 1

1 Revisable-Form-Text (IBM DCA Format)
2 Final-Form-Text (IBM DCA Format)
3 Navy DIF Standard
4 WordStar 3.3
5 MultiMate 3.22
6 Seven-bit transfer format

Enter number of output file format desired
```

Figure 8-3.   Screen to convert WordPerfect to another format

or WordStar data files to a WordPerfect merge file. Fields are separated by ^R and a hard return and records are separated by ^E and a hard return.

Option 8 converts a WordPerfect merge file to DIF format, transferring records and fields to rows and columns accordingly. However, there is a limit of 80 characters per field. If you cannot work with this limitation, consider transferring the file through PlanPerfect. The number of characters allowed in each field is then raised to 250. Option 9 accomplishes the reverse, changing a DIF file to a WordPerfect secondary merge file.

If you choose option 7 (Mail Merge to WordPerfect secondary merge), you are asked for the field and record delimiters as well as any characters to be stripped or removed from the file. You can enter a character or the ASCII decimal value within braces. Usually a data base manager uses a comma (no space) between fields and a carriage return and line feed between records. Often, a character or text field is surrounded by quotation marks as well as a comma because a comma may fall within the field, as in "City, State." This type of comma is almost always followed by a space whereas the comma used as a field delimiter is not. In this case, you should specify a comma (,) as the field delimiter, {13}{10} (carriage return/line feed) as the record delimiter, and the quotation marks (") as the character to be stripped from the file.

Remember to use braces, { and }, rather than the angle brackets, < and >. This might be slightly confusing because you would normally use the angle brackets < and > for decimal values when entering printer commands.

If you know the menu selections by heart, you can enter the commands at the DOS prompt rather than going through the Convert program menus. Enter each item separated by spaces (without parentheses) at the DOS prompt, as shown in the following format illustration.

> CONVERT (input filename) (output filename) (option number from the input menu) (option number from the output menu — optional) (field delimiter — optional) (record delimiter — optional) (characters to be stripped — optional)

You only need to enter the menu number for the output file if you are using option 1 for the input file (WordPerfect to another format). Also, you do not need to enter the field and record delimiters and characters to be stripped unless you are using option 7 (Mail Merge to WordPerfect). A few examples follow.

> CONVERT B:LETTERS.WS B:LETTERS.WP 4 converts the LETTERS.WS (WordStar format) file to LETTERS.WP (WordPerfect format).

> CONVERT *.* *.MDM 1 6 converts all the files found on the default drive from WordPerfect to seven-bit transfer format and gives the converted files a .MDM (modem) extension.

> CONVERT MAILING.DBF MAILLIST.WP 7 , {13}{10} " converts the MAILING.DBF file, where fields are delimited with a comma and double quotes, and records are delimited with a carriage return/line feed, to a WordPerfect merge file MAILLIST.WP. During the process, the quotation marks are stripped from the file.

Converting dBASE, R:BASE, and Lotus 1-2-3 Files

Because of the popularity of dBASE, R:BASE, and Lotus 1-2-3, the following suggestions are included for converting files from these programs.

dBASE

While in dBASE, enter the following command.

USE (NAME) INDEX (INDEX FILES TO BE USED)

This command opens a data base file and sorts the records according to the specified index. If you don't care if the files are sorted, you would only need to enter:

USE (NAME)

After this process is finished, enter:

COPY TO (FILENAME) DELIMITED

The new filename should be different from the original filename and can include the drive and directory where the new file is to be stored. The extension .DBF is automatically added to the filename. Fields are delimited with commas (character fields are further delimited with quotation marks), and records are delimited with a carriage return/line feed. If you want to specify a different field delimiter, you can enter the following command.

COPY TO (FILENAME) DELIMITED WITH (DELIM-ITER)

If you want to specify which fields are to be included, enter a command like the following.

COPY TO (FILENAME) FIELDS (FIELD LIST) DE-LIMITED

There are also options for selecting the records to be included in the copy. See "COPY" in your dBASE manual for further information.

Exit dBASE and enter the following command at the DOS prompt where Convert is found.

> CONVERT (FILENAME) (FILENAME) 7 , {13}{10} "

If necessary, enter the full pathname specifying the drive/directory for the input and output files. The number 7 indicates that the input file is in Mail Merge format. Substitute another character for the field delimiter if you are not using a comma. A carriage return/line feed is always used as the record delimiter.

If you want to retrieve a dBASE report (not data list) into WordPerfect for advanced formatting before printing, you will need to print the report to disk first. Open the data base file with the dBASE USE command.

USE (NAME)

Next, give dBASE the following command.

REPORT FORM (REPORT NAME) TO FILE (FILE-NAME)

The extension .TXT is assigned unless you specify a different one. You can then enter WordPerfect and use Text In/Out (CTRL-F5) to retrieve the file.

R:BASE

R:BASE comes with a program called FileGateway that is used to import and export data. Start FileGateway and complete the following steps.

1. Type **2** to Export data to a file.

2. Type **1** for ASCII delimited.

3. Select a data base from those listed. If it is not found on

the current drive/directory, choose "Other" and enter the full pathname for the desired data base.

4. Choose a table from those listed.

5. The columns (fields) are listed. Move to each field to be included and press ENTER. If you want to include all fields, move to "All" and press ENTER. The fields will be exported in the order in which you select them.

6. The next menu lets you choose how the records are to be sorted. Move the cursor to the first column by which the records will be sorted, press ENTER, then choose Ascending or Descending for the order. Continue with up to ten columns. Records will be sorted accordingly during the export. If you don't care about sorting, press ESC.

7. Use the next menu to specify conditions to limit the rows (records) that will be exported. If you do not want to specify conditions, press ESC.

8. Enter the filename that is to receive the data. If the file already exists, you are asked if you want to overwrite it.

9. When prompted for the parameters, type a comma (,) for the field delimiter (or other unused character) and answer **Y** when asked if each record is to end with a carriage return/line feed. R:BASE automatically places quotation marks around text fields, so using a comma within a text field will not create a problem.

Exit from R:BASE and enter the following command at the DOS prompt where Convert is located.

> CONVERT (FILENAME) (FILENAME) 7 , {13}{10} "

The file is converted to a WordPerfect secondary merge file.

Lotus 1-2-3

As in dBASE, you have two options for converting Lotus files into WordPerfect. You can either convert a Lotus DIF file into a WordPerfect secondary merge file, or you can print all or part of a spreadsheet to a file on disk and retrieve it as text into WordPerfect.

The first option is for those who have a Lotus data base file, or even a regular spreadsheet, and want to convert it to a WordPerfect merge file. To begin the process, choose the "Translate" option from the Lotus access menu and answer the prompts that follow. Choose DIF as the format for the target or destination file. After leaving Lotus, enter the following at the appropriate DOS prompt.

> CONVERT (FILENAME) (FILENAME) 9

The first filename in this command is the name of the target or destination file that was created when using Lotus's Translate option. The second filename is the name used for the converted file. Each row becomes a record and each cell within that row becomes a field in WordPerfect secondary merge format. If you had titles and column headings in the 1-2-3 worksheet, retrieve the file into WordPerfect and delete as many records as necessary until you reach the first complete record.

The second way of converting a Lotus spreadsheet is to print the entire file or a range of cells to disk using the \PRINT command. The following commands should be used in Lotus to prepare a spreadsheet for WordPerfect.

1. Type **\PF (FILENAME)**. This command prints to a file with the name FILENAME (or any chosen name). The extension .PRN is automatically added to the filename. If a file with the same name already exists, you are asked if you want to cancel and enter a new filename or replace and confirm the replacement of the existing file.

2. Type **R** if specifying a range. Move the cursor to one corner of the range and press the period (.). Move to the opposite corner of the range and press ENTER.

3. Type **O** for the Options menu.

4. Type **O** again to go into "Other" options.

5. Type **U** to select "Unformatted" for the format. This option eliminates page breaks and headers and footers.

6. Type **Q** to return to the Print File menu.

7. Type **G** to start the process (Go).

8. Type **Q** to Quit the Print File menu. The file is printed to disk.

When in WordPerfect, change the margins to accept the spreadsheet and press Text In/Out (CTRL-F5). Type **2** to Retrieve a DOS text file with each CR/LF converted to a hard return, and enter the name of the file with the .PRN extension.

When you retrieve a spreadsheet file that has been printed to disk, spaces (rather than tabs) are used to separate columns. If you plan to print the document with proportional spacing, the columns will be misaligned because of the spaces. To solve this problem, you could create a macro that searches for an appropriate number of spaces and replaces them with a tab. However, the number of spaces between text columns will vary, making it necessary to do more than one search and replace in the macro.

Another option would be to use PlanPerfect in the conversion process. Columns would then be separated by tabs.

Using PlanPerfect to Convert Files

If you have PlanPerfect by WordPerfect Corporation, you can press Text In/Out (CTRL-F5), then type **3** to Select an Import/Export Format. The menu shown in Figure 8-4 appears.

As you can see, PlanPerfect allows you to import/export in dBASE, Lotus 1-2-3, and WordPerfect formats. This is possibly the simplest way of importing and exporting data to and from each program.

If a Lotus worksheet is converted to a PlanPerfect worksheet, then converted to WordPerfect (not WordPerfect Merge), the appropriate margins and tabs are automatically set and columns are separated by Tab Align codes so that text and numbers line up correctly. If you use this option, the file does not need to be converted to DIF first and you can use Retrieve (SHIFT-F10) rather than Text In/Out (CTRL-F5) to retrieve the spreadsheet.

```
Import/Export Format              [WP Doc]

    1 - WordPerfect Document

    2 - WordPerfect Merge File

    3 - DOS Text File (space-filled)

    4 - DOS Text File (with tabs)

    5 - Lotus 1-2-3 Worksheet

    6 - Dbase II/III File

    7 - DIF File

    8 - Other
            Row Delimiter
            Column Delimiter
            Spaced-Filled (Y/N)     N


   Selection: 0
```

Figure 8-4.   Import/Export Format menu

If you have a WordPerfect merge (or Notebook) file and want to import it into Lotus or dBASE, you can send it through PlanPerfect first. PlanPerfect knows which fields are character fields and which are numeric and inserts the necessary quotation marks correctly. If you have tried to write macros within WordPerfect to convert a file to dBASE, or have been faced with the limit of characters per record, you will enjoy this option.

Documents from Other Word Processors

If you cannot find a direct conversion for products such as Volkswriter and Samna, you will either have to work with ASCII files or use option 6 on the Text In/Out menu to save the document in a generic word processor format.

Even though WordPerfect or the supplemental Convert program does not offer direct conversion for MultiMate Advantage, WordStar 2000, and Microsoft Word files, you can use another option on the Convert menu as an intermediate format. This is much more desirable than using the ASCII or generic word processing option because you will be able to retain more of the formatting.

MultiMate Advantage

From MultiMate Advantage, you should save the file as a regular MultiMate file (not as a MultiMate Advantage file), then use the MultiMate option on the WordPerfect's Convert menu.

WordStar 2000

Because WordStar 2000 can convert files to WordStar 3.3 format, you can use this to your advantage when converting files from WordStar to WordPerfect and back again.

Microsoft Word

Both Microsoft Word and WordPerfect can save and retrieve files in DCA format. First convert the Microsoft Word document to DCA format (Revisable-Form-Text), then use Convert to transfer it to WordPerfect format using option 2.

Perfect Exchange Program

Perfect Exchange is a good, inexpensive conversion program that can convert MultiMate, DisplayWrite (DCA/RFT), Wang PC, ASCII, Samna, Microsoft Word, Volkswriter, and Word-Star files to and from WordPerfect.

When converting ASCII files, Perfect Exchange will look for lines that should be centered or tabbed and insert the appropriate WordPerfect codes. It even inserts line spacing and margin set codes where applicable. Indents, boldfacing, and underlining are also supported in the conversion process. Some features such as footnotes and columns are converted as separate pages of text.

Perfect Exchange is a product of Systems Compatibility, One East Wacker Drive, Chicago, IL 60601. Call (312) 329-0700 for information on price and features.

Camson Disc Conversion

Camson Disc Conversion, a company providing a conversion series, can convert documents saved on 8-inch diskettes with a dedicated word processor such as Wang to WordPerfect format and back again. Not only will it convert word processing codes, but it can convert documents from one disk format to another. The company can work with the following formats.

DEC

IBM (Display Writer, OS/6, and 5520)

Lanier (No Problem, Super No Problem, and Multi Plus)

MICOM (2000 Series and 3000 Series)

NBI (3000 Series)

Wang (WPS, OIS, and VS)

Xerox (810 and 860)

MS DOS (DisplayWrite II/III, MultiMate, Office Writer, Word-Star, and WordPerfect)

CPM (WordStar)

Camson Disc Conversion is located at 4148 Norse Way, Long Beach, CA 90808. Call (213) 421-3055 for information.

Other WordPerfect Corporation Software

WordPerfect Corporation has developed other software products that work well with WordPerfect. Every attempt has been made to keep the programs as similar as possible in keystrokes, look, and feel. You will find important keys such as Cancel, Help, Exit, Save, Shell, Switch, and Search assigned to the same function keys for each program. In any WordPerfect program, Help (F3) will give assistance for the particular program and, in most cases, you can press Help (F3) twice to display a template on the screen to help identify function keys.

The following sections contain descriptions of the products and their features, in order to introduce you to how they work with WordPerfect.

WordPerfect Library

WordPerfect Library is a compilation of several desktop utilities (calendar, calculator, file manager, notebook with automatic dialing, program editor, and macro editor) with a shell (menu system) to manage them. Shell lets you keep more than one program in memory at a time and switch between them with very few keystrokes. The shell's clipboard feature can be used to copy information from one product to another. Although WordPerfect Library can be used on a dual floppy system, it is far more effective when used on a hard disk.

Shell

The initial menu that you see when you start WordPerfect Library is shown in Figure 8-5. This menu can be customized to include any software product or DOS command.

One of the advantages in using the shell is that you do not have to deal directly with DOS unless you want to. When you create the AUTOEXEC.BAT file, you can include the command **SHELL** and the Shell menu is automatically displayed on the screen each time your computer is started. Each option can be customized to set a default directory and start a program with startup options so that you don't have to worry about pathnames and changing directories. See Figure 8-6 for an example of how you might set up the menu option for WordPerfect.

If you press Shell (CTRL-F1) while in WordPerfect, then type **1** to Go to Shell, the current document is suspended in memory and the Shell menu appears. You can then enter a different program or go to DOS and perform a DOS command. A program held in memory is indicated by an asterisk (*) on the Shell menu.

```
┌──────────────────────────────────────────────────────────────┐
│ WordPerfect Library          Wednesday, November 25, 1987, 11:52am │
├────────────────────────────────┬───────────────────────────────┤
│ A - WordPerfect                │                               │
│                                │                               │
│ B - PlanPerfect                │                               │
│                                │                               │
│ C - Calculator                 │                               │
│                                │                               │
│ D - DOS Command                │                               │
│                                │                               │
│ E - Calendar                   │                               │
│                                │                               │
│ F - File Manager               │                               │
│                                │                               │
│ G - NoteBook                   │                               │
│                                │                               │
│ H - Program Editor             │                               │
│                                │                               │
│ I - Macro Editor               │                               │
│                                │                               │
│ J - Beast (Game)               │                               │
├────────────────────────────────┴───────────────────────────────┤
│ 1 Go to DOS; 2 Clipboard; 3 Change Dir; 4 Setup; 5 Memory Map:   (F7 = Exit) │
└──────────────────────────────────────────────────────────────┘
```

Figure 8-5.   WordPerfect Library initial menu

```
┌──────────────────────────────────────────────────────────────┐
│                        Program Information                     │
│ Menu description:  WordPerfect                                 │
│                                                                │
│ Program name:  c:\wp\wp.exe                                    │
│                                                                │
│ Default directory:  c:\letters                                │
│                                                                │
│ Clipboard  Filename:                                           │
│           End-Of-Line Macro Name:  EOLW.SHM                    │
│                                                                │
│ Startup options:  /m-startup                                  │
│                                                                │
│ Prompt for startup options?  YES                              │
│                                                                │
│ DOS command or batch file?  NO                                │
│                                                                │
│ WordPerfect Corp. Program?  YES                               │
│                                                                │
│ Start resident?  NO                                           │
│                                                                │
│    Enter the message you want displayed on the shell menu for  │
│    this program.                                               │
│                                (F7 = Exit, F3 = Help)          │
└──────────────────────────────────────────────────────────────┘
```

Figure 8-6.   Example of a customized menu

Not only can you hold many programs in memory, but you can pop back and forth between them with just one keystroke. For instance, if you were in the calculator and wanted to go directly to WordPerfect, you could press ALT-SHIFT-W if W were used for WordPerfect, then ALT-SHIFT-C to move back to the calculator if C is used for the Calculator option.

Clipboard

The clipboard is used as a holding place for copying information from one program to another. It uses memory and overflow files if necessary to hold the data until it is retrieved into a program running under Shell, or saved as an ASCII text file.

Regardless of the program you are using (Shell-compatible or not), you can capture all or part of a screen and save or append it to the clipboard. In fact, all the screens in this book were created with this feature.

Memory Map

Option 5 of the Shell menu lets you view a memory map (shown in Figure 8-7) that displays the names of programs loaded into memory, the order in which they were loaded, how much RAM each is using, and the total amount of memory remaining.

Calendar

The calendar can be used to schedule appointments, make prioritized to-do lists, set alarms, and enter memos reminding you of important events.

When you enter the calendar, you see a screen similar to the one shown in Figure 8-8. The current date is highlighted. A ↓ is used to indicate that a memo has been entered, a → lets you know that you have appointments on that date, and a • is used to indicate a to-do list.

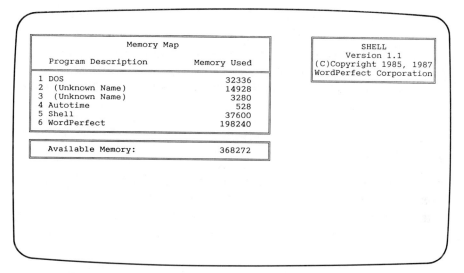

Figure 8-7.   WordPerfect Library memory map

```
CALENDAR.FIL              Wednesday, November 25, 1987          8:05am

 1987            November               1987    Appointments
 Sun   Mon   Tue   Wed   Thu   Fri   Sat       Wednesday, November 25, 1987

   1     2     3     4     5     6     7        8:00am
                                                9:00am
   8     9    10    11    12    13    14       10:00am Meet with John to
                                                       approve art work for
  15    16    17    18    19    20    21                new ad campaign
                                               11:00am
  22    23    24  ↓→ 25    26    27    28      12:00pm Lunch with Marketing
                                                       group
  29    30                                      1:00pm
                                                2:00pm
            ↓ Memo    → Appt    • To-Do         3:00pm
                                                4:00pm
 ┌─┬──────────────────────────────┐            5:00pm Leave for Bobby's
 │M│ Bobby's birthday.             │                   birthday party
 │e│                               │            6:00pm
 │m│                               │
 │o│                               │
 └─┴──────────────────────────────┘

 Ins Add;   Backspace Delete;   * Alarm on/off;   F6 Adjust;   F9 Outline;   F7 Exit;
```

Figure 8-8.   WordPerfect Library calendar

You can use the one-line menu on the status line to go into the appointments schedule or to-do list, enter a memo, go to a different date, choose from several setup options, or print the calendar.

A few of the most useful features in the calendar follow.

You can mark an appointment with an alarm so that, while working in any program, a message is displayed reminding you of the appointment.

Any unmarked items on the to-do list are automatically placed in the next day's list as a type of "tickler" file.

Several calendars can be merged together to find the times that are available for meetings and appointments that involve more than one person.

Memos of up to 255 characters can be entered for each day.

A variety of print options let you print the appointments, to-do lists, and memos for the day, week, month, or year.

You can send also send data from the calendar to WordPerfect via the clipboard.

Calculator

The calculator can be used to give quick calculations that can be sent to the clipboard. It has a "tape" similar to a desktop calculator that can be reviewed, sent to a file or clipboard, or printed.

The calculator template used to label the function keys is displayed directly on the screen (see Figure 8-9). Note that the ALT key is used with the numbered keys across the top for additional functions such as displaying numbers in decimal, hex, binary, octal, fixed, or exponential mode, or using degrees or radians in trigonometric functions. You can also choose whether or not to display the comma in a number, change the value of n, change the sign (+/−), or calculate a grand total.

Several scientific, programmer, financial, and statistical functions are available, as well as options for setting colors,

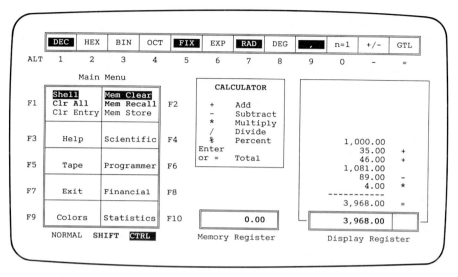

Figure 8-9.   Calculator template

storing numbers in the memory register, and sending results to the clipboard, which can then be retrieved into WordPerfect.

Notebook

The notebook organizes lists of information in a field/record format. The most obvious use is a list for names, phone numbers, and addresses, but many other applications can also be defined, such as using Notebook to keep notes or memos. If you have a modem, the notebook can automatically dial phone numbers for you.

The notebook can display lists and single records. The list display, as shown in the following illustration, displays a limited number of fields, while the record display, shown in Figure 8-10, displays the information in the entire record.

```
Name                    Home Phone   Work Phone   Address
Bobby James             879-5656     982-2376     P.O. Box 2321
John B. Allen           555-2222     555-3456     345 N. Pacific View Drive
Keith Jensen            474-2309     987-5353     20456 Crestview Drive
Susan K. Sullivan       393-6789     202-6521     9877 West Valley Road
```

```
                              N O T E B O O K

  Name: John B. Allen                  Salutation: John

  Address: 345 N. Pacific View Drive   Home Phone: 555-2222
           San Francisco, CA  84848
                                       Work Phone: 555-3456

  Birthday: June 3, 1943

  Notes:    Purchasing agent for several large corporations




 |◄-- Previous field;   --►| Next field;    F7 Exit;           Record 2
```

Figure 8-10.   Notebook record display

You can have alphanumeric fields (a single line of text) or text fields that allow up to 2,000 characters. Records are sorted alphanumerically by the first field. The Line Draw feature (similar to WordPerfect's) can be used to draw lines and boxes around fields, as shown in Figure 8-10.

One of the biggest advantages to using Notebook is that the files are already stored in a WordPerfect merge format. Rather than having to convert the file or transfer it through the clipboard, you can use the notebook file as the secondary file in a merge. You can mark records in the notebook and save them to a separate file that could also be used as a secondary merge file.

If you retrieve the notebook file into WordPerfect, you will notice that there is a "file header" that contains all the setup information. If you do a merge with the file, the header information is ignored because it contains ^N merge codes that make WordPerfect skip to the next record.

Another advantage to using notebook files in a merge, is that instead of specifying fields by a number, you can use the actual name of the field. For example, rather than seeing

"^F3^" in the primary merge file, you can specify a name so that you would see "^Faddress^."

If you plan to use the Notebook file with Merge, you need to have version 4.1 dated 01/10/86 or later. Press Help (F3) to see the version and date of your copy of WordPerfect.

File Manager

The file manager is similar to List Files in WordPerfect; it lets you mark, delete, rename, look, copy, and search through files. However, functions such as deleting and copying are much faster in the file manager.

A few additional options in the file manager are not available in WordPerfect's List Files; these include displaying the amount of free memory and the total size of a directory in the header at the top of the screen. You can also lock more than one file at once. Files can be sorted by extension or date and time in addition to the standard listing by filename.

Program Editor

The program editor was actually created before WordPerfect because the developers at WordPerfect Corporation (then SSI) wanted a better program editor than what was available. WordPerfect uses the same concepts and ideas as the program editor, making it extremely easy to switch between the two programs.

Program or text files can be edited easily because there is no automatic wordwrap feature. There are also specific functions to make programming easier. Among those is a Codes key (ALT-F3) that displays the text in hexadecimal code format, as shown in Figure 8-11.

Help (F3) gives you several Help screens in addition to the standard help files found in other WordPerfect Corporation programs. A list of cursor keys, an ASCII code chart, character code table, formatting characters, and a small macro library can all be displayed through the Help menu.

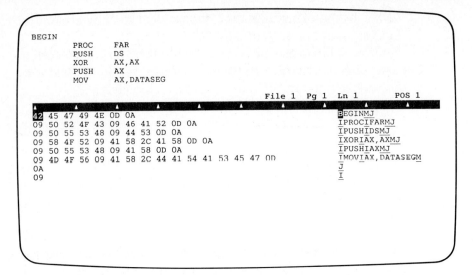

Figure 8-11.   Program Editor Codes key function

Macro Editor

The macro editor is similar to the program editor and is important to anyone who writes macros. The only alternative to using the macro editor is to redefine a macro when changes are needed.

The macro editor can be used to retrieve and edit macros created in WordPerfect, PlanPerfect, the program editor, the macro editor, and the shell. When you retrieve a macro, you will need to enter the filename extension so the macro editor will know what translation table to use for interpreting the function codes. The following shows the macro filename extensions assigned by each program.

.MAC   WordPerfect macros

.PPM   PlanPerfect macros

.PEM   Program Editor macros

.MEM   Macro Editor macros

.SHM   Shell macros

There are features that let you add, move, and delete keystrokes and functions, or insert comments to describe a certain macro or function. A sample macro might look like the following, with the functions shown in bold and all other keystrokes shown as regular text.

```
<Line Format>315 70
<Line Format>42
<Line Format>1<Delete To EOL>42
<Exit><Print Format>3
<Page Format>ay
<Center><Bold><Date>1
```

When editing a macro, you can switch between using the macro editor's function keys and inserting function keystrokes from the appropriate program. For example, if you are editing a macro created in WordPerfect, you can press Function, then use the function keys as they would be used from within Word-Perfect. The macro editor knows which program was used to create a macro and which function keys are assigned to each function because of the extension on the macro file.

Shell Macros

As mentioned previously, you can have shell macros that can be started in one program and move across programs. Shell macros can be used in any program lacking a macro feature (such as the calculator or calendar) to automate an often-repeated function.

PlanPerfect

Formerly called MathPlan, PlanPerfect is a spreadsheet program that is fully compatible with WordPerfect. Keystrokes and menus are very similar, and even the same printing files can be shared by the two programs.

You can create large spreadsheets because of the virtual memory design (similar to WordPerfect's). PlanPerfect has text graphics that can be imported directly into a WordPerfect document through the clipboard. Text graphics use the graphics characters available in your computer's ROM, such as:

▓ ▓ ▊ ▉

This lets text graphs be viewed on a monochrome monitor and printed with a text printer that has those characters.

Bit-mapped graphics for pie charts, line charts, scatter graphs, high-low charts, and so on, are also available in Plan-Perfect. However, bit-mapped graphics cannot be retrieved into a WordPerfect document.

While in PlanPerfect, you can press Text In/Out (CTRL-F5) and choose to import or export a WordPerfect document or WordPerfect merge file. In a regular WordPerfect document, the appropriate margins and tabs are set and columns are separated by Tab Align codes rather than spaces.

The clipboard can be used to move text and graphics from PlanPerfect to WordPerfect. After blocking a section, you can press Shell (CTRL-F1) and choose to save or append the block to the clipboard. While viewing a graph on the screen, you can press Shell and choose the option to send the graph to the clipboard.

Repeat Performance

Repeat Performance is a keyboard enhancement program that accelerates the speed of the cursor when scrolling and deleting text. You can also adjust the delay time so that a key will begin repeating almost instantly. The increase in speed for both operations is very noticeable.

With Repeat Performance, you can also increase the type-ahead buffer so you can continue typing during *Please Wait* messages without losing characters (during a backup, for example). Especially noted for its easy installation, Repeat Performance is fully compatible with WordPerfect.

Extending WordPerfect with Add-On Products

Many programs on the market integrate well with WordPerfect; most of them are memory-resident programs that can be called to the screen while creating a document. Although there are no apparent problems when using popular programs such as Sidekick and other TSR (terminate stay resident) programs, you may run into some problems. If you are using more than one program at once, be aware that the order in which you load programs into memory may be important. You should load memory-resident programs (other than those produced by WordPerfect Corporation) before loading Shell. If you have WordPerfect Library, check the memory map in the shell for verification. WordPerfect can be used with TopView and DesqView, but you will most likely lose some speed in WordPerfect.

The following discussions cover a few products that work well with WordPerfect.

ForComment

ForComment is a program that lets you send drafts of your documents to several reviewers for comments and revisions. It goes beyond the Comment feature in WordPerfect by stamping each comment and suggested revision with the date and reviewer's initials. You can "swap" pieces of the original document with suggested revisions to see how the final document would look before making the changes permanent. Reviewers can view and comment on each other's comments and revisions. There is also a "notepad" feature for creating short documents within ForComment. A sample document in ForComment is shown in Figure 8-12.

ForComment works well with most local area networks (LANs), as does WordPerfect. Thus, you can send documents to

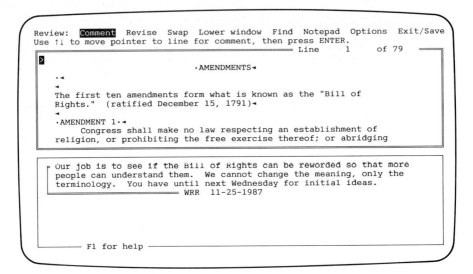

```
Review:  Comment  Revise  Swap  Lower window  Find  Notepad  Options  Exit/Save
Use ↑↓ to move pointer to line for comment, then press ENTER.
═══════════════════════════════════════════════ Line    1    of 79 ═══
▓
                          ·AMENDMENTS◄
  ·◄

  ◄
  The first ten amendments form what is known as the "Bill of
  Rights."  (ratified December 15, 1791)◄
  ◄
  ·AMENDMENT 1·◄
        Congress shall make no law respecting an establishment of
  religion, or prohibiting the free exercise thereof; or abridging
┌─────────────────────────────────────────────────────────────────┐
│ Our job is to see if the Bill of Rights can be reworded so that more │
│ people can understand them.  We cannot change the meaning, only the  │
│ terminology.  You have until next Wednesday for initial ideas.       │
│ ════════════════════════ WRR   11-25-1987                            │


        ── F1 for help ──
```

Figure 8-12.   ForComment sample document

those on the network and receive their comments and revisions quickly.

ForComment can import a WordPerfect file directly into the program, keeping all formatting codes intact. The codes appear as a raised period (·) in ForComment and are restored when the file is exported back into WordPerfect.

The format of the imported document is much like the original; however, bold and underline do not appear on the screen in ForComment because they are codes. Columns are displayed one after another rather than side by side, but the column definition codes are retained. Any math definitions are kept, but the results of the calculations are not. Footnotes are preceded and followed by a ForComment formatting line within the regular text of the document so you can revise and comment on footnotes.

Before importing a WordPerfect file, make sure the length of the line is not more than 71 characters or it will wrap incorrectly in ForComment. If you are using the default 1-inch left and right margins, you shouldn't have any problems. Use Line Format (SHIFT-F8) to change the margins if necessary.

From within ForComment, choose Import from the menu (enter date, author's name, reviewers' names, and so on), then choose WordPerfect format. When you are finished and want to export the document back to WordPerfect, select Options from the main menu, then Export, and enter the name for the exported file. After entering WordPerfect, press Retrieve (SHIFT-F10) and enter the name of the document. Move the cursor through the document to reformat if necessary.

ForComment is a product of Broderbund Software, Inc., 17 Paul Drive, San Rafael, CA 94903. Call (415) 479-1170 for further information.

KeyNotes

KeyNotes is a memory-resident program that can be used to display information through an on-screen window. You can call it to the screen to see common abbreviations, postal codes, or a summary of DOS commands, as well as other information provided with KeyNotes. The text editor for KeyNotes can be used to create your own information files and a key word search is available to search for non-indexed information.

KeyNotes requires approximately 35Kb of RAM. After it is loaded into memory, press ALT \when in WordPerfect, and a window appears letting you select from the information files or search for a key word. Press ESC to close the window and return to WordPerfect.

KeyNotes is produced by Digital Learning Systems, Inc., 4 Century Drive, Parsippany, NJ 07054. Call (201) 538-6640 for further information.

PRD+

You can use PRD+ (Productivity Plus) as a type of "shorthand." After PRD+ and a word list are loaded into memory, you can enter an abbreviation, and the long form is automatically displayed. For example, typing FYI (in upper- or lowercase) will display "for your information," ASAP for "as soon as possible," and CA for "California." You can enter your own abbreviations for names, addresses, openings and closings of letters, and much more.

An abbreviation can contain up to eight characters, and the long form that is attached to the abbreviation can contain up to 240 characters. Although similar to macros, PRD+ can be used without breaking your normal typing speed. As soon as the abbreviation is typed and SPACEBAR or ENTER is pressed, the long form is typed out.

While in WordPerfect, ALT-ESC is used to enable or disable PRD+. Even when disabled, the program remains in memory so that you can enable it and use it again without reloading it.

PRD+ is produced by Productivity Software International, L.P., 1220 Broadway, New York, NY 10001. Call (212) 967-8666 for information.

Ready!

Ready! is an outline processor from the makers of ThinkTank. It is a memory-resident program that occupies approximately 127Kb of memory and can be used for outlines up to 32Kb in size. If you want larger outlines, you should use another program such as ThinkTank.

Ready! can compress and expand outlines to hide or show levels of detail as shown in Figure 8-13. If you move headings, the following levels of detail are automatically moved.

While in WordPerfect, press CTRL-5 (use the 5 found on the numeric keypad) to switch between the WordPerfect and Ready! programs.

If you want to transfer an outline into WordPerfect, you will need to set up Ready! so that the transferred outline will use WordPerfect's outline numbering. This is a little difficult and involves retrieving the CONFIG.RDY file into Ready!, finding the WordPerfect definition, and moving the WordPerfect heading from "Setups Library" to the beginning of "Current Setups." After this step, you need to save the CONFIG.RDY file, type S for Setup, and select the WordPerfect option.

When in WordPerfect, press SHIFT-CTRL-5 to transfer the outline currently in memory to WordPerfect. (Do not try to

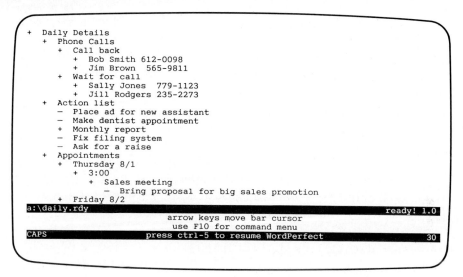

```
+   Daily Details
    +  Phone Calls
       +  Call back
          +  Bob Smith 612-0098
          +  Jim Brown  565-9811
       +  Wait for call
          +  Sally Jones  779-1123
          +  Jill Rodgers 235-2273
    +  Action list
       -  Place ad for new assistant
       -  Make dentist appointment
       +  Monthly report
       -  Fix filing system
       -  Ask for a raise
    +  Appointments
       +  Thursday 8/1
          +  3:00
             +  Sales meeting
                -  Bring proposal for big sales promotion
       +  Friday 8/2
a:\daily.rdy                                                 ready! 1.0
                      arrow keys move bar cursor
                      use F10 for command menu
CAPS                  press ctrl-5 to resume WordPerfect            30
```

Figure 8-13.   Example of a Ready! outline

retrieve the CONFIG.RDY outline into WordPerfect. It contains Ready! codes that produce unpredictable results.) A paragraph numbering code [Par#] is inserted at each item. After the outline is transferred, you will need to do some editing. For instance, the first item is usually not numbered (no hard return is found at the beginning) and there is an extra outline number at the end (because of an extra hard return at the end). Also, there are no spaces or indent codes between the paragraph number and the text, but these can be inserted with a macro.

Ready! is a product of Living Videotext, Inc., 2432 Charleston Road, Mountain View, CA 94043. Call (415) 964-6300 for information.

Inset

Inset is a graphics and text integrator that will let you capture a graphics image from one product and insert it into a WordPerfect document.

After Inset is loaded into memory, you can cut an image from any graphics program and give it a filename (the extension .PIX is automatically attached). Upon entering WordPerfect, move the cursor to the place where the graphics image is to appear. According to the Inset documentation, enter the filename for the graphics image within square brackets, as in:

[PIECHART]

It is best, however, to enter it as a printer command. Press Print Format (CTRL-F8), type **A** to Insert a Printer Command, then enter the filename within brackets. If the file is found in a drive/directory other than the default, include the drive/directory with the filename, as in:

[C:\MATHPLAN \PIECHART]

Before printing the document, make sure that Inset is loaded into memory. During printing or preview (using the Inset preview command), Inset will search for the file named in the brackets and insert it at that location. If you are printing with proportional spacing, specify the exact column position as in:

[PIECHART 20]

Keep in mind that the column number indicates the number of spaces from the left side of the paper, not the left margin.

Inset is a product of American Programmers Guild, Ltd., 12 Mill Plain Road, Danbury, CT 06811. Call (203) 794-0396 for information.

ASCII and Extended Character Set

Dec	Hex	CHR	Dec	Hex	CHR	Dec	Hex	CHR
000	00	NUL	038	26	&	076	4C	L
001	01	SOH	039	27	'	077	4D	M
002	02	STX	040	28	(	078	4E	N
003	03	ETX	041	29	)	079	4F	O
004	04	EOT	042	2A	*	080	50	P
005	05	ENQ	043	2B	+	081	51	Q
006	06	ACK	044	2C	,	082	52	R
007	07	BEL	045	2D	−	083	53	S
008	08	BS	046	2E	.	084	54	T
009	09	HT	047	2F	/	085	55	U
010	0A	LF	048	30	0	086	56	V
011	0B	VT	049	31	1	087	57	W
012	0C	FF	050	32	2	088	58	X
013	0D	CR	051	33	3	089	59	Y
014	0E	SO	052	34	4	090	5A	Z
015	0F	SI	053	35	5	091	5B	[
016	10	DLE	054	36	6	092	5C	\
017	11	DC1	055	37	7	093	5D	]
018	12	DC2	056	38	8	094	5E	^
019	13	DC3	057	39	9	095	5F	_
020	14	DC4	058	3A	:	096	60	`
021	15	NAK	059	3B	;	097	61	a
022	16	SYN	060	3C	<	098	62	b
023	17	ETB	061	3D	=	099	63	c
024	18	CAN	062	3E	>	100	64	d
025	19	EM	063	3F	?	101	65	e
026	1A	SUB	064	40	@	102	66	f
027	1B	ESCAPE	065	41	A	103	67	g
028	1C	FS	066	42	B	104	68	h
029	1D	GS	067	43	C	105	69	i
030	1E	RS	068	44	D	106	6A	j
031	1F	US	069	45	E	107	6B	k
032	20	SPACE	070	46	F	108	6C	l
033	21	!	071	47	G	109	6D	m
034	22	"	072	48	H	110	6E	n
035	23	#	073	49	I	111	6F	o
036	24	$	074	4A	J	112	70	p
037	25	%	075	4B	K	113	71	q

Dec	Hex	CHR		Dec	Hex	CHR		Dec	Hex	CHR
114	72	r		161	A1	í		208	D0	╨
115	73	s		162	A2	ó		209	D1	╤
116	74	t		163	A3	ú		210	D2	╥
117	75	u		164	A4	ñ		211	D3	╙
118	76	v		165	A5	Ñ		212	D4	╘
119	77	w		166	A6	ª		213	D5	╒
120	78	x		167	A7	º		214	D6	╓
121	79	y		168	A8	¿		215	D7	╫
122	7A	z		169	A9	⌐		216	D8	╪
123	7B	{		170	AA	¬		217	D9	┘
124	7C	¦		171	AB	½		218	DA	┌
125	7D	}		172	AC	¼		219	DB	█
126	7E	~		173	AD	¡		220	DC	▄
127	7F	DEL		174	AE	«		221	DD	▌
128	80	Ç		175	AF	»		222	DE	▐
129	81	ü		176	B0	░		223	DF	▀
130	82	é		177	B1	▒		224	E0	α
131	83	â		178	B2	▓		225	E1	β
132	84	ä		179	B3	│		226	E2	Γ
133	85	à		180	B4	┤		227	E3	π
134	86	å		181	B5	╡		228	E4	Σ
135	87	ç		182	B6	╢		229	E5	σ
136	88	ê		183	B7	╖		230	E6	µ
137	89	ë		184	B8	╕		231	E7	τ
138	8A	è		185	B9	╣		232	E8	Φ
139	8B	ï		186	BA	║		233	E9	θ
140	8C	î		187	BB	╗		234	EA	Ω
141	8D	ì		188	BC	╝		235	EB	δ
142	8E	Ä		189	BD	╜		236	EC	∞
143	8F	Å		190	BE	╛		237	ED	Ø
144	90	É		191	BF	┐		238	EE	∈
145	91	æ		192	C0	└		239	EF	∩
146	92	Æ		193	C1	┴		240	F0	≡
147	93	ô		194	C2	┬		241	F1	±
148	94	ö		195	C3	├		242	F2	≥
149	95	ò		196	C4	─		243	F3	≤
150	96	û		197	C5	┼		244	F4	⌠
151	97	ù		198	C6	╞		245	F5	⌡
152	98	ÿ		199	C7	╟		246	F6	÷
153	99	Ö		200	C8	╚		247	F7	≈
154	9A	Ü		201	C9	╔		248	F8	°
155	9B	¢		202	CA	╩		249	F9	•
156	9C	£		203	CB	╦		250	FA	·
157	9D	¥		204	CC	╠		251	FB	√
158	9E	₧		205	CD	═		252	FC	ⁿ
159	9F	ƒ		206	CE	╬		253	FD	²
160	A0	á		207	CF	╧		254	FE	■
								255	FF	blank 'FF'

Terminology Reference

Some say WordPerfect is easy to learn if you have never used another word processor because the transition from a typewriter to WordPerfect is very natural.

If you have used a different word processor and are learning WordPerfect, it can be somewhat difficult to adapt to the new environment and terminology. The tables in this appendix have been prepared to help with that adjustment period.

A table of comparable terms is provided for WordPerfect and each of the leading word processors: WordStar (Table B-1), MultiMate (Table B-2), Microsoft Word (Table B-2), and IBM DisplayWrite (Table B-4). WordStar keystrokes are included in the WordStar table because they are as familiar as the feature name to many users of WordStar.

All features in each program are listed in alphabetical order with the comparable WordPerfect feature and keystrokes listed in parallel columns. You will find that in all but a few instances, WordPerfect matches the other programs feature for feature. "Extra" features that are available with WordPerfect but not with the other word processors have not been listed.

Transferring Files

You can use the Convert program provided on the Learning disk to transfer data created with these word processors to WordPerfect format. There are options for converting Word-Star 3.3 and MultiMate files directly to WordPerfect. After converting IBM DisplayWrite and Microsoft Word documents to revisable-form text (DCA), you can use the Revisable-Form Text option in Convert to transfer the documents to WordPerfect. See Chapter 8 and the *Convert Program* entry in Chapter 4 for more details.

WordStar Professional	WS Keystrokes	WordPerfect	WP Keystrokes
Abandon file	^KQ	Exit	F7
Abort last command	^U	Cancel	F1
Alternate character pitch	^PA	Pitch	Print Format (CTRL-F8), 1
Begin block	^KB	Block	ALT-F4
Beginning of document	^QR		HOME,HOME↑
Block menu	^K	Block	ALT-F4
Block column	^KN	Rectangle	Block (ALT-F4), Move (CTRL-F4), 5
Boldface	^PB	Bold	F6
Bottom of screen	^QX	Screen down	+ on numeric keypad
Center text	^OC	Center	SHIFT-F6
Change logged disk	^KL or L on Main Menu	Default drive	List Files (F5), =, new drive/directory
Character left	^S	Character left	←
Character right	^D	Character right	→
Character Width	.CW	Pitch	Print Format (CTRL-F8), 1
Clear tab	^ON	Tabs	Line Format (SHIFT-F8), 1 or 2
Conditional page	.CP	Conditional End of Page	ALT-F8, 9
		Block Protect	ALT-F4, ALT-F8
		Widow/Orphan Protect	ALT-F8, A
Copy a block	^KC	Move	CTRL-F4, 2
Copy a file	^KO or O from Main Menu	Copy file	List Files (F5), 8
Cursor keys			
Character left	^S		←
Character right	^D		→
Line up	^X		↑

Table B-1.   WordStar Professional/WordPerfect 4.2 Conversion Table

WordStar Professional	WS Keystrokes	WordPerfect	WP Keystrokes
Cursor keys			
Line down	^E		↓
Word left	^A		CTRL←
Word right	^F		CTRL→
Top of screen	^QE		HOME↑
Bottom of screen	^QX		HOME↓
Scroll up	^R or PGUP		− on numeric keypad
Scroll down	^C or PGDN		+ on numeric keypad
Left side of screen	^QS		HOME, ←
Right side of screen	^QD		HOME, →
Beginning of file	^QR		HOME.HOME,↑
End of file	^QC		HOME.HOME,↓
Delete	^KJ	Delete	DEL
Delete a block	^KY	Delete block	Block (ALT-F4), BACKSPACE or DEL
Delete a file	Y from Main Menu	Delete a file	List Files (F5), 2
Delete character at cursor	^G	Delete character	DEL
Delete character left	DEL	Delete character left	BACKSPACE
Delete entire line	^Y	N/A	Write a macro: Home, ←, CTRL-END, and DEL if deleting [HRt]
Delete line left	^Q DEL	N/A	Write a macro: Block (ALT-F4), HOME,←, DEL, Y
Delete line right	^QY	Delete to end of line	CTRL-END
Delete word right	^T	Delete word right	CTRL-BACKSPACE
Directory	^KF	List Files	F5
Double strike	^PD	Bold	F6
Down a line	^Z	Line down	↓

Table B-1.   WordStar Professional/WordPerfect 4.2 Conversion Table (*continued*)

WordStar Professional	WS Keystrokes	WordPerfect	WP Keystrokes
Down screen	^C	Screen down	+ on numeric keypad
End of block	^KK	Block	ALT-F4 and highlight to end of block
End of file	^QC	End of file	HOME,HOME,↓
Exit to operating system	X from Main Menu	Exit	F7
		Go to DOS temporarily	Shell (CTRL-F1), 1, 1
File directory	F on Main Menu	List Files	F5
Find and replace	^QA	Replace	ALT-F2
Find misspelling	^QL	Spell	CTRL-F2
Find text in file	^QF	Search	F2
Footing	.FO	Footer	Page Format (ALT-F8), 6
Heading	.HE	Header	Page Format (ALT-F8), 6
Help menu	^J	Help	F3
Hide/display block	^KH	N/A	Block does not use markers; Cancel (F1) or Block (ALT-F4) will turn off Block
Hyph-help	^OH	Aided hyphenation	Line Format (SHIFT-F8), 5, 4
Insert/overwrite	^V	Insert/Typeover	INS
Install		Setup menu	Enter WP/S at DOS instead of WP
Justify	^OJ	Right justification	Print Format (CTRL-F8), 3 to turn off, 4 to turn on
Last find or block	^QV	Go to original position	CTRL-HOME, CTRL-HOME
		Go to block	CTRL-HOME, ALT-F4
Left side	^QS	Left edge of screen	HOME,HOME, ←
Line down	^X	Line down	↓
Line height	.LH	Lines per inch	Print Format (CTRL-F8), 2

Table B-1.   WordStar Professional/WordPerfect 4.2 Conversion Table (*continued*)

WordStar Professional	WS Keystrokes	WordPerfect	WP Keystrokes
Line up	^E	Line up	↑
MailMerge	M on Main Menu merges to the printer	Merge	CTRL-F9, 1
Ask for variable	.AV	Pause for input from console (keyboard)	^C
Data file in merge	.DF	Secondary merge file	Can call another secondary file with ^Sfilename^S
Display message	.DM	Output message	^Omessage^O^C
Eliminate blank lines	/O	Eliminate blank lines	Use question mark in ^Fn?^ code
Merge report variable	.RV	^Fn^	Merge Codes (ALT-F9), F, number
Margins	^OL and ^OR	Margins	Line Format (SHIFT-F8), 3
Marker	^Q0-9	N/A	
Move Block	^KV	Cut	Block (ALT-F4), Move (CTRL-F4), 1
New page	.PA	Hard page	CTRL-ENTER
Nonbreak space	^PO	Hard space	HOME. SPACEBAR
Nonprinting comment	.IG	Comment or document summary	Text In/Out (CTRL-F5), A and B
Omit page number	.OP	Page numbering set to off	If on, turn off with ALT-F8, 1, 0
On-screen menu	^O	Line Format	SHIFT-F8
		Page Format	ALT-F8
Open a document file	D	Begin typing on screen when program comes up or retrieve an existing file	Retrieve (SHIFT-F10)
Open a nondocument file	N	DOS text or ASCII file	Text In/Out (CTRL-F5)
Other ribbon color	^PY	Font change or insert printer command	Print Format (CTRL-F8), 1 to change font, A to insert printer command

Table B-1.   WordStar Professional/WordPerfect 4.2 Conversion Table (*continued*)

WordStar Professional	WS Keystrokes	WordPerfect	WP Keystrokes
Overprint character	^PH	Overstrike	Superscript/Subscript (SHIFT-F1), 3
Overprint line	^P	Strikeout	Block (ALT-F4), Mark (ALT-F5), 4
Page break	^OP	Hard page or soft page	CTRL-ENTER for hard page; WP enters soft pages automatically
Page length	.PL	Page length	Page Format (ALT-F8), 4
Page numbering	.PN	Page numbering	Page Format (ALT-F8), 1 or ^B in header/footer
Paragraph tab	^OG	Indent	F4
Phantom rubout or phantom space	^PG/^PF	Special characters	Screen (CTRL-F3), 3
Previous position	^QP	Go To, Go To	CTRL-HOME, CTRL-HOME
Print	^KP or ^P	Print	SHIFT-F7, 1 for document or 2 for page
Print display	^OD	Preview	Print (SHIFT-F7), 6
Read file into document	^KR	Retrieve	SHIFT-F10
Reform or reformat	^B	WP automatically reformats the screen after editing changes; Rewrite screen allows manual reformatting	Screen (CTRL-F3), ENTER
Release margins	^OX	Left margin release; expand right margin	SHIFT-TAB; Line Format (SHIFT-F8), 3
Rename	^KE or E on Main Menu	Rename file	List Files (F5), 3
Repeat command or key	^QQ	Repeat keys	ESC, number or character
Repeat last find	^L	Search	F2, F2
Right end of line	^QD	Right side of screen	END or HOME, →
Ruler line	^OT	Ruler	Screen (CTRL-F3), 1, 23

Table B-1. WordStar Professional/WordPerfect 4.2 Conversion Table (*continued*)

WordStar Professional	WS Keystrokes	WordPerfect	WP Keystrokes
Run a program	R on Main Menu	Go to DOS	Shell (CTRL-F1), 1, 1
Run MailMerge	M on Main Menu	Merge	CTRL-F9
Run SpellStar	S on Main Menu	Spell	CTRL-F2
Save (done)	^KD	Exit	F7
Save and resume	^KS	Save	F10
Save and exit	^KX	Exit	F7, Y, name of document, Y
Set left margin or right margin	^OL/^OR	Margins	Line Format (SHIFT-F8), 3
Set line spacing	^OS	Spacing	Line Format (SHIFT-F8), 4
Set tabs	^OI	Tabs	Line Format (SHIFT-F8), 4
Soft hyphen	^OE	Soft hyphen	CTRL-hyphen (-)
Spacing	^OS	Spacing	Line Format (SHIFT-F8), 3
SpellStar	S on Main Menu	Spell	CTRL-F2
Standard pitch	^PN	Pitch	Print Format (CTRL-F8), 1
Stop a command	^U	Cancel	F1
Strikeout	^PX	Strikeout	Block (ALT-F4), Mark Text (ALT-F5), 4
Subscript/ superscript	^PV/^PT	Superscript/ Subscript	SHIFT-F1, 1 for superscript or 2 for subscript
Tab, insert	^I or Tab	TAB key	TAB (or ^I)
Tabs, clear and set	^ON and ^OI	Tabs	Line Format (SHIFT-F8), 3
Top margin	.MT	Top margin	Page Format (ALT-F8), 5
Top of file	^QR	Beginning of file	Home, Home,↑
Top screen	^QE	Screen up	− on numeric keypad
Underscore or underline	^PS	Underline	F8

Table B-1.   WordStar Professional/WordPerfect 4.2 Conversion Table (*continued*)

WordStar Professional	WS Keystrokes	WordPerfect	WP Keystrokes
Up line	^W	Up line	↑
Up screen	^R	Screen up	− on numeric keypad
Vari-tabs	^OV	Tabs	Line Format (SHIFT-F8), 1 or 2
Word left	^A	Word left	CTRL-←
Word right	^F	Word right	CTRL-→
Word wrap	^OW	Automatic	
Write block to file	^KW	Block and Save	ALT-F4, F10

Table B-1.   WordStar Professional/WordPerfect 4.2 Conversion Table (*continued*)

MultiMate Advantage	WordPerfect	WP Keystrokes
Alternate keyboard	CTRL or ALT Key mapping or special characters	Screen (CTRL-F3), 3
Background/foreground printing	Possible to print and edit a document at the same time	
Back up a document automatically	Backup	Setup menu (WP/S), 4
Bold print	Bold	F6
Bound columns	Parallel columns	Math/Columns ALT-F7, 3 and 4
Cancel printing	Stop printing	Printer SHIFT-F7, 4, S
Case significance	Search (uppercase finds only uppercase; lowercase finds both)	Search (F2); Reverse Search (SHIFT-F2); Replace (ALT-F2)
Center	Center text	SHIFT-F6
Clear place marks	N/A	
Column calculations	Math	Math/Columns (ALT-F7), 1 and 2

Table B-2.   MultiMate Advantage/WordPerfect 4.2 Conversion Table

MultiMate Advantage	WordPerfect	WP Keystrokes
Column mode (copy, move, or delete)	Cut, copy, or delete columns	Block (ALT-F4), Move (CTRL-F4), 4
Copy (within document)	Copy text	Block (ALT-F4), Move (CTRL-F4), 2
Copy (external) from one document to another	Copy text	Block (ALT-F4), Move (CTRL-F4), 2
Create an ASCII file	DOS text or ASCII file	Text In/Out (CTRL-F5), 1
Create a new document	In WP, begin typing on a clear screen or change an existing document and save it as a new document. You do not have to name a document until you save it.	
Create a print file	DOS text or ASCII file	Text In/Out (CTRL-F5), 1; Print (SHIFT-F7), send document to printer 6 (print to disk)
Cursor movement	Cursor control or arrow keys	
Custom dictionary	Spell	CTRL-F2, 4, name of new dictionary
Data file	Secondary merge file (created or a Notebook file from WordPerfect Library)	
Decimal tab	Tab Align or Tab Set	(CTRL-F6) or Line Format (SHIFT-F8), 1
Default pitch	Pitch	Print Format (CTRL-F8), 1
Delete	Block delete	ALT-F4, DEL, Y
Delete character	Delete character	DEL
Delete a document	Delete files	List Files (F5), 2, Y
Delete underline	Delete codes	Delete [U] or [u] code in Reveal Codes
Display directory	List Files	F5
Document handling utilities	List Files	F5

Table B-2.   MultiMate Advantage/WordPerfect 4.2 Conversion Table (*continued*)

MultiMate Advantage	WordPerfect	WP Keystrokes
Document summary screen	Document summary	Text In/Out (CTRL-F5), A
Double underscore	Double Underline	Print Format (CTRL-F8), 6 or 8
Draft print	Change font	Print Format (CTRL-F8), 1
Edit an old Document	Retrieve	Retrieve (SHIFT-F10); List Files (F5), 1
End of page	Bottom of page	CTRL-IIOME, ↓
End of screen	Screen down	+ on numeric key pad
Enhanced print	Pitch/font	Print Format (CTRL-F8), 1
Escape	ESC key (to cancel a function, set a variable number for a function, or position a hyphen)	
Footer setup	Footer	Page Format (ALT-F8), 6
Footnotes	Footnotes	CTRL-F7
Format change	Line Format	SHIFT-F8
	Page Format	ALT-F8
	Print Format	CTRL-F8
Format line	Line Format	SHIFT-F8
Format page	Page Format	ALT-F8
Forms fill-in	Forms fill-in (merge)	Merge (CTRL-F9), 1
Go To	Go To	CTRL-HOME
Hard space	Hard space (required space)	HOME-SPACEBAR
Header setup	Header	Page Format (ALT-F8), 6
Help	Help	F3
Highlighting	Block	ALT-F4
Hot print	Page print	Print (SHIFT-F7), 2
Hyphen, soft	Soft hyphen inserted by WP during automatic hyphenation	
Indent	Left indent	F4
	Left/right indent	SHIFT-F4

Table B-2. MultiMate Advantage/WordPerfect 4.2 Conversion Table *(continued)*

MultiMate Advantage	WordPerfect	WP Keystrokes
Insert (drop-down or push), usually in Typeover mode	Automatic Insert/Type-over; preset default is Insert mode (inserts text and pushes existing text to the right) INS (to turn on Typeover, which writes over existing text), WP/S at start-up (to change default to Typeover)	
Insert character	Automatic	
Justification	Right justification	Print Format (CTRL-F8), 3 and 4
Key procedures		
Build	Macro Def	CTRL-F10
Execute	Macro	ALT-F10 to invoke
Pause	Pause	Text In/Out (CTRL-F5)
Prompt	Comments (use for messages)	CTRL-PGUP, ENTER, ENTER
Library	Boilerplates/merge	Merge/Sort (CTRL-F9) or Retrieve (SHIFT-F10)
Line and box drawing	Line Draw	Screen (CTRL-F3), 2
Line length	Margins	Line Format (SHIFT-F8), 3
Line spacing	Spacing	Line Format (SHIFT-F8), 4
Merge	Merge	Merge/Sort (CTRL-F9)
Merge document	Primary file	
Move	Move	CTRL-F4
Next page	Page down	PGDN
Next word	Word right	CTRL-→
Number of lines per page	Page length	Page Format (ALT-F8), 4
Omit line if blank (in merge)	Merge (primary file)	Merge Codes (ALT-F9), F, number of field, ?
Page break	Hard page or soft page	Hard Page (CTRL-ENTER); soft page break automatically entered by WP

Table B-2.   MultiMate Advantage/WordPerfect 4.2 Conversion Table *(continued)*

MultiMate Advantage	WordPerfect	WP Keystrokes
Page combine	N/A	
Page down	Page down	PGDN
Page length	Page length	Page Format (ALT-F8), 4
Page numbering	Page numbering in document or in header/footer	Page Format (ALT-F8), 1 or 6
Page up	Page up	PGUP
Pound symbol (£)	CTRL- or ALT-key mapping	Screen (CTRL-F3), 3
Previous word	Word left	CTRL-←
Print	Print	SHIFT-F7
Print pitch	Pitch	Print Format (CTRL-F8), 1
Printer control codes	Insert printer command	Print Format (CTRL-F8), A
Proportional spacing	Proportional spacing	Print Format (CTRL-F8), 1, pitch, **
Remove a document from the queue	Cancel a print job	Print (SHIFT-F7), 4, C
Rename a document	Rename a file	List Files (F5), 3
Repaginate	Automatic	
Replace	Replace	ALT-F2
	Search and replace	F2, ALT-F2
Required page break	Hard page	CTRL-ENTER
Restart the document currently printing	"Go" (resume printing)	Print (SHIFT-F7), 4, G
Restore a backed-up document	Original backup; set in WP/S; retrieved with .BK! extension	
Return	Enter	ENTER
Save	Save	F10
Save/Exit	Exit	F7
Screen print	Print screen	SHIFT-PRTSC
Search	Search	F2
	Reverse Search	SHIFT-F2
	Replace	ALT-F2

Table B-2. MultiMate Advantage/WordPerfect 4.2 Conversion Table (*continued*)

MultiMate Advantage	WordPerfect	WP Keystrokes
Search document summary screens	Word search or Look	List Files (F5), 9 or 6
Section numbering	Outline or Table of Contents	Mark Text (ALT-F5), 1
Shadow print	Bold	F6
Spacing	Spacing	Line Format (SHIFT-F8), 4
Spell check a document	Spell	CTRL-F2
Spell check a section of a document	Spell check a block	Block (ALT F4), Spell (CTRL-F2)
Status line	Status line at bottom of screen; displays document, page, line, and position of cursor	
Strikeout	Strikeout	Block (ALT-F4), Mark Text (ALT-F5), 4
Strikeover	Typeover (the default in WP is Insert mode)	INS
Subscript	Superscript/Subscript	SHIFT-F1, 2 for subscript
Superscript	Superscript/Subscript	SHIFT-F1, 1 for superscript
System print commands	Date	SHIFT-F5
	Current Page Number	CTRL-B
Tab locations	Tabs	Line Format (SHIFT-F8), 1
Table of Contents	Table of Contents	Block (ALT-F4), Mark Text (ALT-F5), 1
Thesaurus	Thesaurus	ALT-F1
Top margin	Top margin	Page Format (ALT-F8), 5
Typewriter mode	Type-thru	Print (SHIFT-F7), 5
Underline	Underline	F8
Widows and orphans	Widow/Orphan	Page Format (ALT-F8), A

Table B-2.   MultiMate Advantage/WordPerfect 4.2 Conversion Table *(continued)*

Microsoft Word	WordPerfect	WP Keystrokes
ASCII files, save	DOS text or ASCII files	Text In/Out (CTRL-F5), 1
Autosort	Sort	Merge/Sort (CTRL-F9), 2
Bold	Bold on/off	F6
	Bold block	Block (ALT-F4), F6
Cancel	Cancel	F1
Center	Center	SHIFT-F6
Columns	Columns (newspaper and parallel)	Math/Columns (ALT-F7), 4 to define, 3 to turn on/off
Conyws and Convertd programs (used to convert Wordstar, Delimited, DIF, dBase, and SYLK for use with Microsoft Word)	Convert program on Learning Disk (used to convert WordStar, DIF, Navy DIF, MultiMate, Wang, Mailmerge including dBASE, and DCA files for use with WordPerfect)	
Copies, print	Copies, number of	Print (SHIFT-F7), 3; Print (SHIFT-F7), 4, 1
Copy	Copy	Block (ALT-F4), Move (CTRL-F4), 2
Copy, retrieve	Copy, retrieve	Retrieve (SHIFT-F10), ENTER ; Move (CTRL-F4), 5
Delete	Delete block	Block (ALT-F4), Del, Y
	Move	Block (ALT-F4), Move (CTRL-F4), 1
Double underline	Underline style	Print Format (CTRL-F8), 6 or 8
Feed, paper	Forms, type of	Print (SHIFT-F7), 4, 3 to select printers
	Sheet feeder	Print Format (CTRL-F8), type 9 for bin number
Format command	Line Format	SHIFT-F8
	Page Format	ALT-F8
	Print Format	CTRL-F8
Font name and size	Pitch/font change	Print Format (CTRL-F8), 1
Footnote (create)	Footnote (create)	CTRL-F7, 1

Table B-3.   Microsoft Word/WordPerfect 4.2 Conversion Table

Microsoft Word	WordPerfect	WP Keystrokes
Footnote (jump to)	Footnote (edit)	CTRL-F7) 2, footnote number
Footnotes/endnotes (select one option)	Fooootnotes/endnotes	CTRL-F7, 1 for footnote, 5 for endnote
Gallery	Use macros; Change settings in the Setup menu; or Save commonly used settings in a regular file	Macro Def (CTRL-F10) and Invoke Macro (ALT-F10); WP/S at the DOS prompt for Setup menu; Save (F10)
Gutter width	Binding width (under printer options)	Print (SHIFT-F7), 4, 1 or Print (SHIFT-F7), 3
Hanging indent	Hanging indent	Indent (F4), Left Margin Release (SHIFT-TAB)
Help	Help	F3
Highlight	Cursor	
Hyphenate	Hyphenation	Line Format (SHIFT-F8), 5
Indent first line	Tab	TAB
Index, define	Index, define	Mark Text (ALT-F5), 6, 5
Index, mark for	Index, mark for	Mark Text (ALT-F5), 5
Insert deleted/ copied text	Restore deleted text; Retrieve Cut/Copy file	Cancel (F1), 1; Retrieve (SHIFT-F10), ENTER
Italic	Font change	Print Format (CTRL-F8), 1, usually defined as font 2 or 4
Jump to footnote	Footnote (edit)	CTRL-F7, 2, footnote number
Jump to page	Go to page	CTRL-HOME, page number
Keep paragraph together	Conditional End of Page	Page Format (ALT-F8), 9
	Block Protect	Block (ALT-F4), Y
	Widow/Orphan Protect	Page Format (ALT-F8), A
Left indent	Indent	F4

Table B-3.   Microsoft Word/WordPerfect 4.2 Conversion Table *(continued)*

Microsoft Word	WordPerfect	WP Keystrokes
Left/right indent	Left/right indent	SHIFT-F4
Library	Sort	Merge/Sort (CTRL-F9)
	Hyphenate	Line Format (SHIFT-F8)
	Indexing	Mark Text (ALT-F5)
	Paragraph numbering	Mark Text (ALT-F5)
	Outlining	Mark Text (ALT-F5)
	Go to DOS	Shell (CTRL-F1)
	Spell	Spell (CTRL-F2)
	Table of Contents	Mark Text (ALT-F5)
Load, transfer	Retrieve a document	SHIFT-F10
Margins (top, bottom, left, and right)	Margins (left and right)	Line Format (SHIFT-F8), 3
	Margins (top and bottom) (Bottom margin controlled by setting page length and number of text lines)	Page format (ALT-F8), 4 and 5
New page	Hard Page	CTRL-ENTER
Nonbreaking hyphen	Dash	HOME-hyphen (-)
Non-breaking Space	Hard Space	HOME-SPACEBAR
Number, Library	Outline numbering	Mark Text (ALT-F5), 1
	Paragraph Numbering	Mark Text (ALT-F5), 2
	Define numbering style	Mark Text (ALT-F5), 6, 1
Optional Hyphen	Soft hyphen	CTRL-hyphen (-)
Options (used to show invisible codes, use printer display, turn off command menu, set the default tab width, measurement, and mute alarms	Setup menu (used to set program defaults, control "beep," screen size, and other options)	WP/S at DOS prompt
Overtype on/off	Typeover on/off	INS
Page length	Page length	Page Format (ALT-F8), 4
Page number	Page number	Page Format (ALT-F8), 1

Table B-3. Microsoft Word/WordPerfect 4.2 Conversion Table *(continued)*

Microsoft Word	**WordPerfect**	**WP Keystrokes**
Page numbers, print	Page numbers, print	Print (SHIFT-F7), 4, P, filename, page numbers
Page width	N/A	
Print direct	Type-thru	Print (SHIFT-F7), 5
Print file	Print to disk (sends the current print job to predefined printer 6, which prints to a file called DOS.TXT)	Print (SHIFT-F7), 3, 1, 6, ENTER, 1
Print glossary	N/A	
Print merge	Merge	Merge/Sort (CTRL-F9), 1 begins the merge, use ^R (F9) and ^E (SHIFT-F9) to create secondary (data) file; use Merge Codes (ALT-F9) to insert merge codes in primary document (form)
Print Options	Printer Control	Print (SHIFT-F7), 4
Print Printer (print active document)	Print full text	Print (SHIFT-F7), 1
	Print current page	Print (SHIFT-F7), 2
Printer display	Automatic	
Queued, print jobs	Automatic	
Quit	Exit	F7
Range, print	Range, print	Print (SHIFT-F7), 4, P, filename, range
Rename document	Rename document	List Files (F5), ENTER, 3
Repaginate, print	Automatic	
Replace	Replace	ALT-F2
Required hyphen	Hard hyphen	Hyphen key
Return to standard paragraph settings	Delete codes	Reveal Codes (ALT-F3)
Right indent	Left/right indent	SHIFT-F4
Ruler	Ruler	Screen (CTRL-F3), 1, 23
Run, library	Go to DOS	Shell (CTRL-F1), 1

Table B-3.   Microsoft Word/WordPerfect 4.2 Conversion Table (*continued*)

Microsoft Word	WordPerfect	WP Keystrokes
Running head	Headers/footers	Page Format (ALT-F8), 6
Save document	Save a document	F10
Scrap	Delete buffer	Last three deletions are kept in delete buffer. Restore by pressing Cancel (F1).
	Cut/copy buffer	Block (ALT-F4), Move (CTRL-F4) stores most recent cut/copied text in file "named" with ENTER key. You can Save (F10) to or Retrieve (SHIFT-F10) from this file by pressing ENTER rather than entering a filename
Scrolling	Moving the cursor	Cursor movement keystrokes (see Chapter 4 for list)
Search	Search	F2
	Search	SHIFT-F2
Select text (highlight)	Block	ALT-F4
Setup, printer port	Port, printer	Print (SHIFT-F7), 4, 3, to select printers and ports
Small caps	N/A	
Space before paragraph	Blank lines	ENTER
Spell	Spell (checks spelling and allows correction at the same time rather than in separate passes)	CTRL-F2
Strikethrough	Strikeout	Block (ALT-F4), Mark Text (ALT-F5), 4
	Overstrike (to over-strike a single character with another)	Super/Subscript (SHIFT-F1), 3
Style	Define macros that contain format settings	Macro Def (CTRL-F10), name macro, enter format settings, CTRL-F10 again
Style bar	Reveal Codes	ALT-F3

Table B-3. Microsoft Word/WordPerfect 4.2 Conversion Table
(continued)

Microsoft Word	WordPerfect	WP Keystrokes
Subscript	Subscript or block subscript	Superscript/Subscript (SHIFT-F1), 2 or Block first
Superscript	Superscript or block superscript	Superscript/Subscript (SHIFT-F1), 1 or Block first
Table, define	Table of Contents, define	Mark Text (ALT-F5), 6, 2
Table, mark	Table of Contents, mark (basic procedure also used for lists and Tables of Authorities)	Block (ALT-F4), Mark Text (ALT-F5), 1
Tabs, clear	Tab, clear	Line Format (SHIFT-F8), 1, Del
Tabs, reset all	Tabs, clear all	Line Format (SHIFT-F8), 1, CTRL-END
Tabs, set	Tabs, set	Line Format (SHIFT-F8), 1
Transfer clear	Exit	F7
Transfer delete	Delete files	List Files (F5), ENTER, 2
Transfer glossary	N/A	
Transfer load	Retrieve a document	SHIFT-F10
Transfer merge	Retrieve one document into another	Retrieve (SHIFT-F10)
Transfer options	View and change default directory	List Files (F5), =, directory name to change default
Transfer rename	Rename documents	List Files (F5), ENTER, 3
Transfer save	Save a document	F10
Underline	Underline on/off	F8
	Underline block	Block (ALT-F4), (F8)
Undo	Undelete	Cancel (F1)
Widow/Orphan control	Widow/Orphan, Protect	Page Format (ALT-F8), A
Windows (up to eight)	Windows (two documents)	Screen (CTRL-F3), 1
Window close	Window	Screen (CTRL-F3), 1
Window Move	Window	Screen (CTRL-F3), 1

Table B-3.   Microsoft Word/WordPerfect 4.2 Conversion Table
(*continued*)

DisplayWrite 4	WordPerfect	WP Keystrokes
ASCII copy to file	DOS text or ASCII file	Text In/Out (CTRL-F5), 1
Begin/end keep	Conditional End of Page or Block Protect	Page Format (ALT-F8), 9 or, while Block is on, Page Format (ALT-F8), Y
Block edit	Cut, copy, delete, or move text	Block (ALT-F4), Move (CTRL-F4)
Bold	Bold	F6
Carriage return or required carriage return	Hard return or soft return	Hard Return (ENTER); soft return automatically entered by WP
Center	Center	SHIFT-F6
Codes, display all	Reveal Codes	ALT-F3
Compress documents	N/A	
Copy documents	Copy files	List Files (F5), 8
Create comment	Document summary or comments	Text In/Out (CTRL-F5), A-D
Create document	In WP, begin typing on a clear screen	Text In/Out (CTRL-F5), A-D
Cursor draw	Line Draw	Screen (CTRL-F3), 2
Cursor	Cursor control or arrow keys	
Default drive	List Files	F5, =
Defaults	Default settings	WP/S, 2 (to change preset program defaults)
Display options	Colors or set colors	Screen (CTRL-F3), 4
Document assembly	Boilerplates or document assembly (merge)	Retrieve (SHIFT-F10) or Merge/Sort (CTRL-F9)
Document comment	Document summary or comments	Text In/Out (CTRL-F5), A through D
DOS commands	Go to DOS	Shell (CTRL-F1), 1
Erase documents	Delete files	List Files (F5), 2
Final-form text conversion	Convert	Enter CONVERT at DOS prompt
Footnotes	Footnotes	CTRL-F7, 1 and 2

Table B-4.   DisplayWrite 4/WordPerfect 4.2 Conversion Table

DisplayWrite 4	WordPerfect	WP Keystrokes
Format	Line Format	SHIFT-F8
	Page Format	ALT-F8
	Print Format	CTRL-F8 WP/S (to change preset defaults)
Get	Retrieve and Text In/Out	SHIFT-F10, CTRL-F5
Go to page	Go To	CTRL-HOME, page number
Headers and footers	Headers/footers	Page Format (ALT-F8), 6
Hyphenation	Hyphenation	Line Format (SHIFT-F8), 5
Indent	Indent	F4
	Left/right indent	SHIFT-F4
Keyboard extensions	Special characters or CTRL or ALT-key mapping	Screen (CTRL-F3), 3
Keystroke programming	Macros	Macro Def (CTRL-F10); Macro (ALT-F10) to start
Line adjust	Automatic	
List services	List Files	F5
Margins	Margins	Line Format (SHIFT-F8), 3
Math	Math	Math/Columns (ALT-F7), 1 and 2
Merge	Merge	CTRL-F9, 1
Notepad	Switch	SHIFT-F3
Outline appearance	Change paragraph/outline numbering	Mark Text (ALT-F5), 6, 1
Outlines	Outlines	Mark Text (ALT-F5), 1
Overstrike characters	Overstrike	Superscript/Subscript (SHIFT-F1), 3
Page ends	Hard and soft page breaks	Hard Page (CTRL-ENTER); soft page breaks are automatically entered
Page numbers	Page numbering in document or in header/footer	Page Format (ALT-F8), 1 or 6 for header/footer

Table B-4.   DisplayWrite 4/WordPerfect 4.2 Conversion Table (*continued*)

DisplayWrite 4	WordPerfect	WP Keystrokes
Paginate	Widows/Orphans	Page Format(ALT-F8), A
Paper clip	N/A	
Print (background/ foreground)	Print (always background)	SHIFT-F7
Profiles	Setup menu	WP/S at DOS prompt
Recover documents	Backup	WP/S
Reference areas, tables	N/A	
Rename documents	Rename Files	List Files (F5), 3
Required hyphen	Hard hyphen	HOME-hyphen (-)
Required space	Hard space	HOME-SPACEBAR
Required tab	Indent	F4
Revisable-form text conversion	Convert	Enter CONVERT at DOS prompt
Revise document	Retrieve	SHIFT-F10
Revision marking	Redline/Strikeout	Block Text (ALT-F4), Mark Text (CTRL-F4), 3 and 4
Save document	Save document or Save and Exit	F10 or F7
Scale line	Ruler	Screen (CTRL-F3), 1, 23
Search	Search	F2
	Reverse Search	SHIFT-F2
	Replace	ALT-F2
Skip to line	Advance to line	Superscript/Subscript (SHIFT-F1), 6
Spell	Spell	CTRL-F2
Subscripts and superscripts	Superscripts/subscripts	SHIFT-F1, 1 or 2
Supplement	Change dictionary	Spell (CTRL-F2), 4
Tables	Columns	ALT-F7, 3 and 4
Tabs	Tabs	Line Format (SHIFT-F8), 1

Table B-4. DisplayWrite 4/WordPerfect 4.2 Conversion Table (*continued*)

DisplayWrite 4	WordPerfect	WP Keystrokes
Typestyle	Pitch/font	Print Format (CTRL-F8), 1
Underline	Underline	F8
Utilities	List Files	F5
	Convert program	Enter CONVERT at DOS prompt
View document	Preview	Print (SHIFT-F7), 6
Working copy	Original backup file is named with .BK!	Set in WP/S

Table B-4.   DisplayWrite 4/WordPerfect 4.2 Conversion Table (*continued*)

General Suggestions
for Macros

Any keystrokes in this book can be placed into a macro, especially if the keystrokes for a specific feature are too involved or you have a hard time remembering them.

Usually you would not create a macro for features that require only a few keystrokes. However, if you would prefer pressing Alt-P to print the document on the screen instead of pressing Print (Shift-F7) and typing 1, then you could define an Alt-P macro to do so.

If a macro will depend on certain situations, you will need to create those conditions before defining the macro. For example, if the macro is to search for a [Margin Set] code, you should insert a [Margin Set] code into the document defining the macro. You should also remember to place the proper "positioning" keystrokes into a macro. For example, if you should be at the beginning of a document before doing a forward search, you should include a (HOME, HOME, ↑) as the first step in the macro.

You should not have a macro that clears the screen without saving the document. If you insist on using this type of macro, name it with a full name instead of using an Alt-key combination. This would require more keystrokes to start the macro, but would guard against accidentally clearing the screen and losing the current document if the Alt-key combination was accidentally pressed.

If you often delete whole lines, sentences, or paragraphs when editing, you might want to create macros that delete them for you. These types of macros are not quite as dangerous because you can restore deleted text with Cancel (F1).

The macro names given are only suggestions. You should name them according to your personal preferences. If you want the macros to be accessible from any directory, save them in the drive/directory where WP.EXE is located. Precede the name of the macro with the full pathname (**a:** or **c:\wp** are examples). If the macros are to be used for documents in a specific directory, save them in that directory (for example, a macro that sets up the format for letters would be saved in a "LETTER" directory). Remember that the default directory is searched first.

Do not worry about making mistakes while defining a macro. Remember that corrections will also be recorded.

Macros in Chapter 4 includes an explanation of how you can set up a macro library that would list the names and descriptions of each macro. By using a macro library, you can pick a macro from the list rather than trying to remember the name and exactly what it does.

ARCHIVE

An archive macro would let you keep all memos or letters in one file instead of several separate files. You could create daily, weekly, or monthly archive files, and you could have different archive macros for different types of documents.

- First, the archive file needs to be created. Because an empty file cannot be saved, you need to insert some type of codes that will not affect the document. Clear the screen and press Bold (F6), Underline (F8), Bold (F6), and Underline (F8).
- Save the archive file (MEMO.ARC or LETTER.ARC are suggested filenames). Clear the screen.
- With a letter or memo on the screen, press Macro Def (Ctrl-F10) and name the macro (**archive** is a suggestion).
- Press HOME, HOME, ↓ to go to the end of the document and press Hard Page (Ctrl-ENTER) to insert a page break (this will be used to separate documents in the archive file).
- Press Block (Alt-F4) and press HOME, HOME, ↑ to highlight the entire document.
- Press Move (Ctrl-F4) and type **3** to Append. Enter the name of the archive file.
- Optional Step: Clear the screen. If you do not include this step, the document will remain on the screen after the macro is finished.
- Press Macro Def (Ctrl-F10) to end the macro definition.

After creating and printing a letter or memo, start the macro.

DELETE

Delete Whole Line

Pressing Ctrl-Y in WordStar and other programs deletes the entire line, including the Hard or Soft Return at the end of the line. You can do the same thing in WordPerfect using a macro.

- Press Macro Def (Ctrl-F10) and name the macro (Alt-Y is a suggestion).
- Press HOME, HOME, ← to go to the beginning of the line.
- Press Delete to End of Line (Ctrl-End).
- Press DEL to delete the Hard Return or space created by the Soft Return.
- Press Macro Def (Ctrl-F10) to end the macro definition.

Delete Sentence or Paragraph

While WordPerfect has a delete sentence and paragraph feature, it takes a few keystrokes that could easily be put into a macro. After naming the macro, press Move (Ctrl-F4) and type **1** for Sentence or **2** for Paragraph, then **3** to Delete.

DISPLAY

Change from 4.2 to 4.1 Display

WordPerfect 4.2 displays the text at the far left of the screen so you can see more of the text at the right. WordPerfect 4.1 displayed the text away from the left side of the screen, giving you an imaginary left margin. If you prefer the 4.1 display, invoke this macro anywhere in the document (it is not a permanent change so must be invoked for each document).

- Press Macro Def (Ctrl-F10) and name the macro (Alt-D for Display is a suggestion).
- Press Ctrl-PgUp, type **0**, and press ENTER to make the macro visible (it needs the automatic screen rewrite to work properly).
- Press HOME, HOME, ← to go to the beginning of the line.

- Press Left Margin Release (Shift-TAB) twice to force the text to the right.
- Press BACKSPACE twice to delete the [←Mar Rel:] codes.
- Press Go To (Ctrl-HOME) twice to return to your original location.
- Press Macro Def (Ctrl-F10) to end the macro definition.

FOOTNOTES

To convert footnotes to endnotes, define Newspaper Columns at the beginning of the document and turn on Columns. All footnotes are automatically converted to endnotes. Delete the [Col Def:] and [Col on] codes to return the text to regular text (not in columns).

The following macro can be used to convert endnotes to footnotes. With appropriate changes, you can change footnotes to endnotes if you do not want to use the columns suggestion above.

- Move the cursor to the beginning of the document. The document needs to have at least one endnote before defining the macro.
- Press Macro Def (Ctrl-F10) and name the macro (**footnote** is a suggestion).
- Press Footnote (Ctrl-F7) and type **6** to Edit an Endnote. The next endnote found is displayed. Press ENTER to edit that endnote.
- Press DEL and type **y** to confirm the deletion of the endnote number or press → to skip over the number.
- Press Block (Alt-F4), then HOME, HOME, ↓ to highlight the text in the endnote.
- Press Move (Ctrl-F4) and type **1** to cut the text.
- Press Exit (F7) to exit the endnote.
- Press BACKSPACE, then type **y** to delete the endnote number from the text.
- Press Footnote (Ctrl-F7) and type **1** to Create a footnote.
- Press Move (Ctrl-F4) and type **5** to retrieve the endnote text into the footnote.
- Press Exit (F7) to exit the footnote.
- Press Macro (Alt-F10) and enter the name of this macro (**footnote** was the suggested name) to create a repeating macro.
- Press Macro Def (Ctrl-F10) to end the macro definition.

Start the macro at the beginning of the document.

FORMAT

You can define macros for the different types of formats you commonly use. For example, if you change pitch and font often, create a macro that changes the pitch, font, margins, and tabs all at once. If it seems easier to use a macro to change the spacing or other fairly simple tasks, do so. If you use right justification for all documents except letters, create a "letter" macro that includes turning off right justification as a step in the macro. See Letters and Memos later in this appendix for more suggestions.

Indented paragraphs

The following macro changes from double spacing to single spacing, indents, pauses for you to enter the text for the indented paragraph, then changes back to double spacing.

- Press Macro Def (Ctrl-F10) and name the macro (Alt-I for indent is a suggestion).
- Press ENTER to create the blank space between the text and paragraph.
- Press Line Format (Shift-F8), type **4** for Spacing, and enter **1** for single spacing.
- Press →Indent← (Shift-F4) to indent the paragraph from the left and right margins.
- Press Ctrl-PgUp, then press ENTER twice to insert a pause in the macro.
- Press ENTER twice to create the blank space between the paragraph and the text.
- Press Line Format (Shift-F8), type **4** for Spacing, and enter **2** for double spacing.
- Press Macro Def (Ctrl-F10) to end the macro definition.

Remember that the extra space between the text and the paragraph is part of the macro. When the macro pauses, type the text for the paragraph. As soon as you press ENTER, the macro continues.

Keep Headings with First Two Lines of a Paragraph

WordPerfect's Widow/Orphan feature does not automatically keep a heading with the first two lines of a paragraph. This macro will search for headings preceded by three Hard Returns and insert the proper command for you.

- Press ENTER three times to create the necessary condition, then move to the top of the screen before defining the macro.
- Press Macro Def (Ctrl-F10) and name the macro (**keep** is a suggestion).
- Press Search (F2), press ENTER three times to search for three [HRt] codes, then press Search (F2) again to begin the search.
- Press ↑ once to move to the line before the heading.
- Press Page Format (Alt-F8) and type **9** for Conditional End of Page. Enter **4** if the document is single spaced or **7** if it is double spaced. This number can be adjusted depending on how you usually enter headings and paragraphs.
- Press ENTER to exit the Page Format menu.
- Press Macro (Alt-F10) and enter the name of this macro (**keep** was the suggested name) to create a repeating macro.
- Press Macro Def (Ctrl-F10) to end the macro definition.

When you are finished creating a document, go to the beginning of the document and start the macro. It will search for each heading and insert the Conditional End of Page command until no more headings (three [HRt]s) are found.

LETTERS AND MEMOS

Everyone has their own personal format for letters and memos. Use the suggestions below as a guideline for creating your own.

Begin Letter

- Press Macro Def (Ctrl-F10) and name the macro (**letter** is a suggestion).
- If you have a sheet feeder with letterhead in one bin, press Print Format (Ctrl-F8), type **9** and enter the appropriate bin number.

- While in the Print Format menu, type **3** to turn off right justification if desired. Change pitch and font if necessary and press ENTER to leave the Print Format menu.
- If you usually write short, one-page letters, press Page Format (Alt-F8), type **3** to Center the Page from Top to Bottom, then press ENTER to exit the menu. If they are usually longer than one page, press Super/Subscript (Shift-F1), type **6** to Advance to a Line, then enter the appropriate line number (to avoid printing on the letterhead logo). Pressing ENTER four or more times instead will adversely affect other steps in the macro.
- Change the left and right margins if necessary with Line Format (Shift-F8) option **3**.
- If you do not have letterhead, you might want to create your own. Press Center (Shift-F6) or Flush Right (Alt-F6) and enter your name. Continue with the address and phone number if desired.
- Move the cursor to the position where the date is to appear. Press Date (Shift-F5) and type **1** to insert the current date.
- Press ENTER four times.
- Press Macro Def (Ctrl-F10) to end the macro definition.

End Letter

When finished with a letter, you can have a macro that inserts the closing, creates a header that includes the addressee's name, current date, and page number for multiple-page letters, and starts the macro that is used to address an envelope.

- Create a sample letter with the "letter" macro before defining this macro. Press Macro Def (Ctrl-F10) and name the macro (**close** is a suggestion).
- Press ENTER twice to create space between the body of the letter and the closing.
- If you place the closing next to the left margin (block style), enter the closing (Sincerely yours, Yours truly, etc.). If you use a modified block style, set Tabs, and enter the closing.
- Press HOME, HOME, ↑ to go to the beginning of the document.
- Press Search (F2), press ENTER four times to search for four [HRt] codes, then press Search (F2) again to start the search.
- Press Block (Alt-F4), press Search (F2), press ENTER twice, then press Search (F2) again to highlight the name and address. If you

only want the name to be included in the header, press Block (Alt-F4) and press ↓ once to highlight the name.

- Press Move (Ctrl-F4) and type **2** to Copy the block.
- Press HOME, HOME, ↑ to go to the beginning of the document.
- Press Page Format (Alt-F8), type **6** for Headers or Footers, type **1** for Header A, then type **1** for Every Page.
- Press Move (Ctrl-F4) and type **5** to Retrieve the text.
- Press HOME, HOME, ↓, press Date (Shift-F5), and type **1** to Insert the date.
- Press ENTER to move to the next line, type **Page**, then press Ctrl-B (^B) to insert the current page number at print time.
- Press Exit (F7) to exit the header.
- When you are returned to the Page Format menu, type **8**, then **5** to turn off the header for the first page. Press ENTER to exit the Page Format menu.
- Press Macro (Alt-F10) and enter the name of the envelope macro (**env** is a suggestion) to start an envelope macro.
- If you want to send the letter to the printer, press Print (Shift-F7) and type **1** for Full Text.
- Press Macro Def (Ctrl-F10) to end the macro definition.

Address an Envelope

This macro searches for four [HRt]s (usually signifying a name and address), copies the name and address to a separate page at the end of the document, formats the address, prints it, and finally deletes it. If the four [HRt] codes are not found, the "env1" macro is started instead, setting up the format for an envelope. After you have manually entered the name and address, you can send it to the printer and clear the screen.

When defining the macro, remember how the envelope is to be fed into the printer (hand fed, envelope bin, or manual feed on a laser printer) and set the format accordingly.

- Create a sample letter with the "letter" macro before defining this macro. Press Macro Def (Ctrl-F10) and name the macro (**env** is a suggestion).
- Press Macro (Ctrl-F10) and enter the name of the "not found" macro (**env1** is a suggestion). The "env1" macro will be created later and will set up the envelope format so the name and address can be entered manually if an address is not found on the screen.

- Press HOME, HOME, ↑ to go to the beginning of the document.
- Press Search (F2), press ENTER four times to search for four [HRt] codes, then press Search (F2) again to start the search.
- Press Block (Alt-F4), press Search (F2), press ENTER twice, then press Search (F2) again to highlight the name and address.
- Press Move (Ctrl-F4) and type **2** to Copy the block.
- Press HOME, HOME, ↓ to go to the end of the document and press Hard Page (Ctrl-ENTER) to insert a page break.
- Press Print Format (Ctrl-F8). If you are using a laser printer, type **1** and change to a landscape font. If you have an envelope bin or need to change to manual feed on a laser printer, type **9**, and insert the appropriate bin number. Press ENTER to exit the Print Format menu.
- Press Page Format (Alt-F8), type **5** for Top Margin, and enter the appropriate number of half-lines. Laser printers should use a setting of 72. If you are hand feeding envelopes into a daisy wheel printer, you can control where the printing will begin and do not have to insert a top margin code. In either case, it is not necessary to change the page length. Press ENTER to exit the menu.
- Change the left and right margins so the address will be printed in the center of the envelope. Suggested settings are 50 and 100, but depend on the size of the envelope and the font being used.
- Press Move (Ctrl-F4) and type **5** to retrieve the text (the name and address copied earlier).
- Press Print (Shift-F7) and type **2** to print the Page. If you are using hand-fed envelopes, you might want to insert a delay (press Ctrl-PgUp and enter **10**) and send the printer a "Go" (press Print [Shift-F7], type **4** for Printer Control, then type **g**).
- Press Move (Ctrl-F4), type **3** for Page, then **3** to Delete the page. Press BACKSPACE and type **y** to delete the Hard Page break.
- Press Macro Def (Ctrl-F10) to end the macro definition.

Create the **env1** macro by repeating all formatting commands used in the original "env" macro (font change, bin number, margins, etc.).

Memos

The following macro will set up the format for a memo and pauses for you to fill in each item (TO:, FROM:, etc.).

- Press Macro Def (Ctrl-F10) and name the macro (**memo** is a suggestion).
- Change the margins if necessary with Line Format (Shift-F8), option 3.
- Press Center (Shift-F8), Bold (F6), then type **MEMORANDUM** at the beginning of the page. Press ENTER two or three times to create space.
- Press Line Format (Shift-F8), type **1** to set Tabs, then press Delete to End of Line (Ctrl-End). Enter **20**, then type **R** to set a right aligned tab at position 20. Enter **23** to set a regular tab, then press Exit (F7). (These tab settings are dependent on a left margin of 10; adjust if necessary.)
- With Bold still on, press TAB, and type **DATE:**. Press Bold (F6) to turn off bold.
- Press TAB again, press Date (Shift-F3), then type **1** to insert the date.
- Press ENTER twice and type **TO:** in bold. Press TAB, Ctrl-PgUp, then ENTER twice to insert a pause. Repeat this step for **FROM:** and **SUBJECT:**.
- Press ENTER a few times to add space and draw a line across the page. This can be done by pressing Bold (F6) and Underline (F8), then using SPACEBAR to draw the line. Press Bold (F6) and Underline (F8) to turn them off when you reach the right margin. (You could use Line Draw if it is available on your printer.)
- Press ENTER a few times until you reach the line where the body of the memo is to begin.
- Press Macro Def (Ctrl-F10) to end the macro definition.

When the macro is run, it will pause for each item in the heading, then continue each time ENTER is pressed.

MARK TEXT

Mark Table of Authorities Entries

After you have marked the first occurrence of an authority, you can have this macro mark all future occurrences of the authority with the Short Form. This macro is a repeating conditional macro that involves three different macros.

- Before defining the macro, have at least two identical authorities in the document and mark the first one (the Full Form and Short Form will be entered at that time).
- Press Macro Def (Ctrl-F10) and name the macro (**toa** is a suggestion).
- Press Search (F2) to search for the next occurrence of the authority. Press Delete to End of Line (Ctrl-End) to delete the previous search string (this creates less confusion later).
- Press Ctrl-PgUp, ENTER, type part of the authority to be marked, then press ENTER again. This step creates a pause in the macro. Information is entered between the two ENTER keystrokes because it is necessary when defining the macro.
- Press Search (F2) again to begin the search.
- Press Macro (Alt-F10) and enter the name of the macro that will mark the authority and repeat the search (**mark** is a suggestion). This macro is defined below.
- Press Macro Def (Ctrl-F10) to end the macro definition.

Define the "MARK" macro.

- Press Macro Def (Ctrl-F10) and name the macro (**mark** was the suggested name).
- Press Macro (Alt-F10) and enter the name of the macro that will be started when no future occurrences of an authority are found (**end** is a suggestion). This macro should be defined separately and should include only the keystrokes HOME, HOME, ↑.
- Press Mark Text (Alt-F5), type **4** for Short Form, then press ENTER to accept the last Short Form entered.
- Press Search (F2) twice to continue the search.
- Press Macro (Alt-F10) and enter the name of this macro (**mark** was the suggested name) so the macro will repeat until no further occurrences of the authority are found.
- Press Macro Def (Ctrl-F10) to end the macro definition.

Remember to define the "END" macro containing the keystrokes HOME, HOME, ↑.

The macro assumes that you have just marked an authority with the Full and Short Forms. When the macro is started, it pauses for you to enter part of the authority as the search string. When you press ENTER, it marks each occurrence of the authority, then returns to the beginning of the document so you can begin the process again.

PAGE NUMBERING

Number all Pages Except the First One

- Press Macro Def (Ctrl-F10) and enter the name of the macro (**number** is a suggestion).
- Press HOME, HOME, ↑ to go to the beginning of the document.
- Press Page Format (Alt-F8), type **1** for Page Number Position, then choose the page number position you prefer.
- Type **8**, then enter **1, 2,** or **3** (again depending on your preference) to suppress the page number, headers, and footers on the first page; suppress only the page numbers; or print the page number at the bottom center of the first page only.
- Press ENTER to exit the Page Format menu.
- Press Macro Def (Ctrl-F10) to end the macro definition.

Page n of n

The following macro helps you create a header or footer that indicates the current page number and the total number of pages.

- Press Macro Def (Ctrl-F10) and name the macro (**page#** is a suggestion.
- Press HOME, HOME, ↓ to go to the end of the document.
- Press Ctrl-PgUp and ENTER twice to insert a pause into the macro.
- Press HOME, HOME, ↑ to go to the beginning of the document.
- Press Page Format (Alt-F8), type **6** for Headers or Footers, choose a header or footer, then type **1** to include the header or footer on every page.
- Press Center (Shift-F6) and type **Page ^B of**. (Press Ctrl-B to insert the ^B code.)
- Press Ctrl-PgUp and ENTER twice to insert another pause.
- Press Exit (F7) to exit the header. As an optional step, use option 8 on the Page Format menu to suppress the header or footer on the first page, then press ENTER to exit the Page Format menu.
- Press Macro Def (Ctrl-F10) to end the macro definition.

After a document is created, run the macro. It will pause at the end of the document so you can take note of the last page number. When you press ENTER, it creates the header or footer and pauses again so you can enter the number that was just displayed on the screen.

If the document is edited later and the number of pages change, you should delete the previous header or footer code and repeat the macro. In fact, you could include a step at the beginning of the macro, but an existing header or footer might be inadvertantly deleted.

PARAGRAPH NUMBERING

Number a List

With this macro, you can number a list of items after they have been entered.

- Press ENTER once or twice to create a few [HRt] codes, then go to the beginning of the document.
- Press Macro Def (Ctrl-F10) and name the macro (**list** is a suggestion).
- Press Search (F2), press ENTER once or twice depending on how many [HRt]s are used between each item in the list, then press Search (F2) again to start the search.
- Press Mark Text (Alt-F5), type **2**, and press ENTER to insert a paragraph number.
- Press Indent (F4) to indent the line to the first tab setting.
- Press Macro Def (Ctrl-F10) to end the macro definition.

The cursor should be on the line above the list before you start the macro. Press ESC and type the number of lines to be numbered (do not press ENTER), then start the macro. It will then be repeated that many times or until no more [HRt]s are found. Change the paragraph numbering style at the beginning of the list if necessary.

Align Paragraph Numbers

This macro can be used to align paragraph numbers on the decimal point after they have been entered. It assumes you have used Indent (F4) between each paragraph number and the text. Another macro included in the WordPerfect manual explains how to align paragraph numbers as they are entered.

- You need to have at least one paragraph number after the cursor before defining this macro. Press Macro Def (Ctrl-F10) and name the macro (**align** is a suggestion).
- Press Search (F2), press Mark Text (Alt-F5), type **2** to search for a paragraph number, then press Search (F2) again to start the search.
- Press ← to move to the left of the paragraph number.
- Press Tab Align (Ctrl-F6), then → once to move to the right of the paragraph number.
- Press SPACEBAR twice, type a period (**.**) to end the Tab Align, then press BACKSPACE to delete the period.
- Press Super/Subscript, then type **3** so the Indent that follows will overstrike the second space.
- Press Macro (Alt-F10) and enter the name of this macro (**align** was the suggested name) to create a repeating macro.
- Press Macro Def (Ctrl-F10) to end the macro definition.

PRINT MACROS

Print a Document or Page

You can easily send the current document or page to the printer by pressing Print (Shift-F7) and typing **1** or **2**. These steps can be included in an Alt-P macro if you wish.

Send the Printer a "Go"

With this macro, you can send the printer a "Go" without having to enter the Printer Control menu.

- Press Macro Def (Ctrl-F10) and name the macro (Alt-G is a suggestion).
- Press Print (Shift-F7).
- Type **4** for Printer Control.
- Type **g** to send the printer a "go."
- Press ENTER to exit the menu.
- Press Macro Def (Ctrl-F10) to end the macro definition.

PRODUCTIVITY

Count Total Number of Lines

If you charge a client by the number of lines typed, use this macro to estimate the amount for you.

- Press Macro Def (Ctrl-F10) and name the macro (**count** is a suggestion).
- Press HOME, HOME, ↑ to go to the beginning of the document.
- Press Print Format (Ctrl-F8), type **B** for Line numbering, and **2** to turn on Line Numbering. Type **3** and answer **n** to not Count blank lines, then **6** and answer **n** to not Restart numbering on each page. Press ENTER twice to return to the document.
- Press HOME, HOME, ↓ to go to the end of the document.
- Press Print (Shift-F7), type **6** for Preview, then **2** for Page.
- When the Preview screen appears, press Ctrl-PgUp and ENTER twice to insert a pause in the macro. When the macro is run, you can move the cursor to the last line, take note of the line number, then press ENTER to continue the macro.
- Press Exit (F7) to return to the document.
- Press HOME, HOME, ↑ to go to the beginning of the document, press DEL, they type **y** to delete the Line Numbering code.
- Press Macro Def (Ctrl-F10) to end the macro definition.

SAVE

Save and Resume

This macro assumes that the current document has been saved once. If it has not been saved, the macro will not work and you will have a document named "y" on the disk.

- Press Macro Def (Ctrl-F10) and name the macro (Alt-S is a suggestion).
- Press Save (F10). The name of the document should appear.
- Press ENTER to accept the name and type **y** to replace the previous file.
- Press Macro Def (Ctrl-F10) to end the macro definition.

Save and Clear the Screen

This macro also assumes that the document has been saved once. If it has not been saved, the macro will not work.

- Press Macro Def (Ctrl-F10) and name the macro (Alt-X is a suggestion).
- Press Exit (F7) and type **y** to Save the Document.
- Press ENTER to accept the filename and type **y** to replace the previous file.
- Type **n** to not exit WP and clear the screen.
- Press Macro Def (Ctrl-F10) to end the macro definition.

TABS

Clear All Tabs

- Press Macro Def (Ctrl-F10) and name the macro (**clear** is a suggestion).
- Press Line Format (Shift-F8), type **1** for Tabs, press HOME, HOME, ← to move to the beginning of the line, then press Delete to End of Line (Ctrl-End).
- Press Exit (F7).
- Press Macro Def (Ctrl-F10) to end the macro definition.

Set Tab at Current Position

If you are used to moving the cursor to a position on a typewriter and pressing a Tab Set key, you might want to define this macro.

- Press Macro Def (Ctrl-F10) and name the macro (Alt-T or **setab** are suggestions).
- Press Line Format (Shift-F8), type **1** for Tabs, then **T** or **L** to set a Tab.
- Press Exit (F7).
- Press Macro Def (Ctrl-F10) to end the macro definition.

Before using this macro, you might want to use the "clear all tabs" macro first. When the macro is run, a tab will be set at the cursor's location.

Restore Previous Tab Settings

If you have several tables placed throughout a document, you will most likely change tabs for the table then change them back after the table has been entered. You can create a macro that searches for the previous tab setting and inserts it in the current location rather than trying to remember the previous settings and manually reinserting them.

Before defining this macro, you need to set tabs at least twice and move the cursor <u>after</u> the tab settings.

- Press Macro Def (Ctrl-F10) and name the macro (**reset** is a suggestion).
- Type ******* (or any other unused characters) to mark your place.
- Press ←Search (Shift-F2), Line Format (Shift-F8), then type **1** to search for a [Tab Set] code. Press Search (F2) to begin the search. The last tab setting that was used for the table is found.
- Press ←Search (Shift-F2) twice to find the next previous tab setting.
- Press Block (Alt-F4) to turn on block.
- Press ← twice to "block" the Tab Set code. (You need to press ← twice because it has to move over both the Block and Tab Set codes).
- Press Move (Ctrl-F4) and type **2** to Copy the Block.
- Press Search (F2), type ******* (or other characters that were used to mark your place), then press Search (F2) again.
- Delete the characters by pressing BACKSPACE as many times as necessary.
- Press Move (Ctrl-F4) and type **5** to retrieve the text. The [Tab Set] code is retrieved at that point.
- Press → once to move over the [Tab Set] code.
- Press Macro Def (Ctrl-F10) to end the macro definition.

Realign After Tab Setting Types Have Changed

If you set tabs or enter a table, then change the tab settings, the columns automatically adjust to the new position. However, if you change the <u>type</u> of tab (left, right, decimal, or center), the alignment of each column does not automatically change. The following macro can be used to change a table with regular, left-aligned tab settings to any other type. Similar macros could be used to change other types of tabbed columns.

- Go to the line just below the table and press TAB. This step is necessary for the last item in the table to be aligned properly. Go the beginning of the table and reset the tabs if you have not already done so.
- Press Macro Def (Ctrl-F10) and name the macro (**realign** is a suggestion).
- Press Search (F2), TAB, then Search (F2) again to search for the first [TAB] code.
- Press Block (Alt-F4).
- Press Search (F2) twice to search for the next [TAB] code.
- Press ← once to move the cursor just before the [TAB] code. The text in the first column of the first line should be highlighted.
- Press Move (Ctrl-F4) and type **1** to Cut the Block.
- Press BACKSPACE to delete the previous [TAB] code, then press TAB to insert a new [TAB] code. Align or Center codes will be inserted if applicable.
- Press Move (Ctrl-F5) and type **5** to retrieve the text. The text will be aligned correctly.
- Press Macro (Alt-F10) and enter the name of this macro (**realign** was the suggested name) to create a repeating macro.
- Press Macro Def (Ctrl-F10) to end the macro definition.

The macro will repeat until no further [TAB]s are found.

TRANSPOSE

Transpose Characters

Before defining a transpose macro, you need to decide where the cursor will be placed (on the first or second character to be transposed). This macro assumes the cursor will be on the first character.

- You need at least two characters on the screen before defining the macro. Place the cursor under the first character.
- Press Macro Def (Ctrl-F10) and name the macro (Alt-C to transpose "characters" is a suggestion).
- Press DEL to delete the character.
- Press → to move the cursor one space to the right.
- Press Cancel (F1) and type **1** to Restore the character.
- Press Macro Def (Ctrl-F10) to end the macro definition.

This macro will not work if a code is immediately to the right of the cursor.

Transpose Words

This macro assumes that the cursor is on the first word to be transposed.

- You need at least two words on the screen before defining the macro and the second word must be followed by a space. Place the cursor anywhere in the first word.
- Press Macro Def (Ctrl-F10) and name the macro (Alt-W to transpose Words is a suggestion).
- Press Delete Word (Ctrl-BACKSPACE) to delete the current word.
- Press Search (F2), SPACEBAR, then Search (F2) again to search for the next space.
- Press Cancel (F1) and type **1** to Restore the word.
- Press Macro Def (Ctrl-F10) to end the macro definition.

UNDERLINING

Change Underline to Broken Underline

This macro can be used if you do not want spaces to be underlined.

- Place the cursor within a section of underlined text. Press Macro Def (Ctrl-F10) and enter the name of the macro (**brokenu** for broken underline is a suggestion).
- Press ←Search (Shift-F2), press Underline (F8) to insert the [Undrline] code, then press Search (F2) to begin the search.
- Press Block (Alt-F4) to turn on block.
- Press Search (F2), Underline (F8), BACKSPACE, then Underline again to insert the [u] code. Press Search (F2) again to search for the end of underlining.
- With the underlined block highlighted, press Replace (Alt-F2) and type **n** for no confirmation.
- Press SPACEBAR once, then Search (F2) to enter a space as the search string.

- Press Underline (F8), BACKSPACE, Underline, SPACEBAR, and Underline (F8) again. The replacement string should appear as "[u] [Undrline]."
- Press Search (F2) to start the procedure.
- Press Macro Def (Ctrl-F10) to end the macro definition.

Turn Double Underline On and Off

If you use double underlining often, you can create two macros to turn it on and off for you.

- Press Macro Def (Ctrl-F10) and enter the name of the macro (**don** and **doff** are suggestions).
- Press Print Format (Ctrl-F8) and type **6** or **8** for the "on" macro, and **5** or **7** for the "off" macro.
- Press ENTER to leave the Print Format menu.
- Press Underline (F8) to turn underlining on or off.
- Press Macro Def (Ctrl-F10) when finished.

When you want double underlining, press Macro (F10) and enter the name of the "on" macro. After you have finished typing the text, press Macro (F10) and enter the name of the "off" macro.

Change Underline to the Underscore Character

If you submit articles electronically, you will usually save the WordPerfect document as a DOS Text file first, thus removing all underline codes. This macro will insert an underscore character at the beginning and end of the text that is normally underlined.

- Press Macro Def (Ctrl-F10) and name the macro (**us** for underscore is a suggestion).
- Press HOME, HOME, ↑ to move to the beginning of the document.
- Press Replace (Alt-F2) and type **n** for no confirmation.
- Press Underline (F8), BACKSPACE, then Underline (F8) again to insert the underline off [u] code.
- Press Search (F2) to enter the search string.
- Replace with the underscore character "_" and the underline off [u]

code (display the [u] code the same way you did in the earlier step). The replace string should appear as "_[u]".
- Press Search (F2) to start the procedure.
- Press HOME, HOME, ↑ to return to the beginning of the document.
- Press Replace (Alt-F2) and type **n** for no confirmation.
- Press Underline (F8) once to insert the underline code [Undrline] as the search string.
- Press Search (F2) and type the underscore character (_) as the replace string.
- Press Search (F2) to start the procedure.
- Press Macro Def (Ctrl-F10) to end the macro definition.

You can start the macro anywhere in the document and all underlining is replaced with underscore characters.

UPPERCASE/LOWERCASE

Capitalize the First Letter of a Word

Use the following macro to capitalize the first letter of a word. For example, if you have typed a person's name without capitalizing it, you could use this macro to capitalize the first letter for you.

- The cursor can be anywhere in a word except on the first character. Press Macro Def (Ctrl-F10) and name the macro (Alt-U for uppercase is a suggestion).
- Press Ctrl-← to move to the beginning of the word.
- Press Block (Alt-F4) and press → once to highlight the first letter of the word.
- Press Switch (Shift-F3) and type **1** for Uppercase.
- Press Block (Alt-F4) to turn off block.
- Press Ctrl-→ and → to move into the next word (so the macro could be repeated easily).
- Press Macro Def (Ctrl-F10) to end the macro definition.

The cursor should not be on the first letter of a word when this macro is started.

Lowercase All Except the First Letter

If you have a word in CAPS and want all but the first letter in lowercase, use the following macro.

- The cursor can be anywhere in the word except on the first character. Press Macro Def (Ctrl-F10) and name the macro (Alt-L is a suggestion).
- Press Ctrl-← to move to the beginning of the word, then → once to move past the first letter.
- Press Block (Alt-F4), then press Ctrl-→ to go to the end of the word.
- Press Switch (Shift-F3) and type **2** for Lowercase.
- Press Block (Alt-F4) to turn off block.
- Press → to move into the next word so the macro can be repeated easily if necessary.
- Press Macro Def (Ctrl-F10) to end the macro.

WINDOWS

Open Window

If the keystrokes necessary to split the screen (open a window) and close it again seem complicated, you can use the following macros to do it for you.

- Press Macro Def (Ctrl-F10) and name the macro (**open** is a suggestion).
- Press Screen (Ctrl-F3) and type **1** for Window.
- Enter **12** or any other number for the number of lines in the window.
- Press Macro Def (Ctrl-F10) to end the macro.

Close Window

- Press Macro Def (Ctrl-F10) and name the macro (**close** is a suggestion).
- Press Screen (Ctrl-F3) and type **1** for Window.
- Enter **24** for the number of lines in the window.
- Press Macro Def (Ctrl-F10) to end the macro.

You may need to make adjustments if your monitor can display more or less than 24 lines. The documents in either screen are not affected by these macros. If you want to save the documents when you close a window, add these steps to the macro.

Alphapro 101	Alphacom, Inc.
Alps® P2000™	Alps Electric Co. Ltd.
Amiga®	Commodore Electronics Ltd.
AMT™	Advanced Matrix Technology, Inc.
Apple®	Apple Computer, Inc.
Apple IIc™	Apple Computer, Inc.
Apple IIe™	Apple Computer, Inc.
Apple IIGS™	Apple Computer, Inc.
Atari® ST™	Atari Corporation
BDT™	Buro-und Datentechnik
Brother® Twinwriter™	Brother International Corporation
Canon®	Canon, Inc.
Centronics®	Centronics Data Computer Corporation
Citizen™	Citizen America Corporation
Color Jetprinter™	International Business Machines Corporation
Compact RO®	Olympia USA, Inc.
COMPAQ®	COMPAQ Computer Corporation
COMPAQ DESKPRO 286®	COMPAQ Computer Corporation
COMPAQ PORTABLE III™	COMPAQ Computer Corporation
Convertible™	International Business Machines Corporation
Cordata LP300X™	Cordata
Daisy Systems™	Daisy Systems, An AES Company
Daisywriter™	Computers International
Data General™	Data General Corporation
DataPerfect™	WordPerfect Corporation
Dataproducts®	Dataproducts Corporation
dBASE II®	Ashton-Tate
dBASE III®	Ashton-Tate
DESQview™	Quarterdeck Office Systems
Diablo®	Xerox Corporation
Diconix 150™	Diconix, A Kodak Company
Digital™	Digital Equipment Corporation
Dynax™	Dynax, Inc.
Elf	NEC Corporation
Epson®	Seiko Epson Corporation
Facit™	Facit Data Products
Florida Data™	Florida Data Corporation
Fortis™	Fortis Computer Systems, a Division of Dynax, Inc.
Fujitsu™	Fujitsu Limited
FX-100™	Epson America, Inc.
Graphics™ Printer	International Business Machines Corporation
GTC Blaser™	Blaser Industries
Helvetica®	Linotype Company
HP™ LaserJet™	Hewlett-Packard Company
HP LaserJet PLUS™	Hewlett-Packard Company
Hyperion®	Bytec-Comterm, Inc.
IBM®	International Business Machines Corporation
IBM PC AT™	International Business Machines Corporation

IBM PC XT®	International Business Machines Corporation
ImageWriter®	Apple Computer, Inc.
Kyocera™	Kyocera Corporation
Laserline™	Oki America, Inc.
LaserWriter®	Apple Computer, Inc.
Library™	WordPerfect Corporation
Macintosh™	Apple Computer, Inc.
Mannesmann Tally™	Mannesmann Tally Corporation
Microline® 292 Standard®	Oki America, Inc.
MPI™ Printmate™	Micro Peripherals, Inc.
MS-DOS®	Microsoft Corporation
MultiMate®	MultiMate International Corporation
NEC®	NEC Corporation
Nissho™	Nissho Iwai American Corporation
Okidata®	Oki America, Inc.
Okimate™	Oki America, Inc.
Olympia ESW 2000™	Olympia USA, Inc.
1-2-3®	Lotus Development Corporation
Pacemark™	Oki America, Inc.
Pageprinter™	International Business Machines Corporation
PaintJet™	Hewlett-Packard Company
Palatino®	Linotype Company
Panasonic®	Matsushita Electric Industrial Company
Pinwriter™	NEC Corporation
PlanPerfect™	WordPerfect Corporation
Plug 'N Play™	Oki America, Inc.
Primage 90-GT®	Primages, Inc.
PrintMaster™	Unison World, Inc.
Printronix S7024™	Printronix
ProWriter™	C. Itoh Digital Products, Inc.
QMS® Kiss™	QMS, Inc.
Quadram® Quadlaser™	Quadram
QuietJet™	Hewlett-Packard Company
Quietwriter®	International Business Machines Corporation
Qume® LaserTen™	Qume Corporation
Ricoh™	Ricoh Corporation
Seikosha SP 1000I™	Seikosha Company Ltd.
Silver-Reed EXP 500/550/800™	Silver Seiko Ltd.
Spinwriter®	NEC Corporation
Star™ Gemini™	Star Micronics, Inc.
Star™ Powertype™	Star Micronics, Inc.
Startype™	Olympia USA, Inc.
StarWriter™	C. Itoh Digital Products, Inc.

INDEX

The note program that won the most awards just got a whole lot better!

At Personics we take a personal interest in our products. So, naturally we were honored when PC Magazine cited SmartNotes for technical excellence, and when InfoWorld readers chose SmartNotes as the pop-up program of the year. And SmartNotes was the **ONLY** note program on

PC Magazine's , "The Best of the Best Utilities List." Well, honors are nice, but we knew that SmartNotes could be even better. Here's a look at a few of the new features that we've added to make SmartNotes Version 2 the only note program you'll ever need:

❑ SmartNotes saves and retrieves notes automatically. No fussing with note files.

❑ Notes pop up automatically. You don't have to press a hotkey to see your notes.

❑ Version 2 is more tightly integrated with Lotus 1-2-3 than earlier versions. Notes remain attached even when SmartNotes is not resident in memory. There are NO conditions where notes can become lost.

❑ Four alternatives are offered for note pop-up: ◆ The entire note pops up automatically. ◆ A small marker pops up automatically. ◆ Only the note's context (or spreadsheet cell) is highlighted automatically. ◆ The note pops up only in response to the SmartNotes activation key. (Nothing happens automatically.)

❑ Three note sizes are offered, including a new one line note -- great for annotating file directories!

❑ The note file capacity has been increased from 50 notes to 125 notes per note file.

❑ You can redefine the SmartNotes activation keys to suit your personal preference and avoid conflict with other programs.

❑ SmartNotes now consumes **LESS** memory than earlier versions.

SmartNotes Version 2

The Perfect Attachment for WordPerfect and *All* Your Software

SmartNotes lets you attach notes to Word Perfect, DOS directories, 1-2-3, just about anything on your screen.

Version 2 is remarkably easy to use. Picture this: You've just finished attaching a note to a DOS directory --what the heck is FORMLET3.LTR? You enter WordPerfect, bring in a proposal and, PRESTO, a note pops-up. No buttons to push. No commands to remember. And you don't need to fuss with note files. Everything is automatic.

Use notes to outline revisions, remind yourself to verify a fact or a figure, mark passages that need more work, or comment on a colleague's document. Notes are saved in separate files so they don't alter or modify your documents in any way. And since notes pop-up automatically, they're perfect reminders.

SmartNotes runs on any IBM PC, XT, AT, PS/2 or compatible. Not copy protected. Just $49.95 with this coupon. Regular price is $79.95.

Order now and save $30.

- -

Please send me SmartNotes Version 2 for $49.95. (If paying by credit card, fill in card number and expiration date below. If paying by check, make check payable to Personics. Mass residents add $2.50 sales tax. Personics pays for shipping.)

Payment (circle one) VISA   MC   AMEX   Diners   Check

Card Number_____**Exp**_____

Name_____

Address_____

City_____**State** _____**Zip**_____

Phone (____**)**_____

MAIL TO: **Personics, 2352 Main Street, Concord, MA 01742**

Call Personics at 617-897-1575 for additional information.

WordPerfect Support Group

P.O. Box 1577, Baltimore, MD 21203
Phone (301) 889-7894

Deduct 10% with This Coupon!

The WordPerfect Support Group is an independent users group for owners of all WordPerfect Corporation products. The support group has over 15,000 members worldwide. The full-time WordPerfect Support Group staff researches member questions and publishes solutions through *The WordPerfectionist Newsletter* and the WPSG forum on CompuServe. The entire group benefits from the shared experiences of thousands of fellow users.

The WordPerfectionist Newsletter

The support group newsletter covers a wide range of topics from news and update information to in-depth tutorials. Reviews of books, training materials, and utilities are printed along with articles to help anyone from beginner to expert. A one-year membership includes 12 issues of the newsletter. The WPSG offers a full money back guarantee at any time if you are not satisfied. Back issues of the newsletter are also available. *($36 third class delivery, $48 U.S. dollars for first class delivery and Canada, $68 U.S. dollars for air mail to other countries, Volume I back issues $27, Volume II issues 1-6 $15)*

CompuServe Forum and TAPCIS

You can join in the active discussions between members on the WPSG forum on the CompuServe Information Service. The forum acts as a clearinghouse for WP related news, utilities, printer drivers, and problem solving assistance. This WPSG "meeting place" is open 24 hours a day, and thousands attend over the course of a month. CompuServe subscribers can get to the forum by typing **GO WPSG** online. A completely automated communications package for accessing CompuServe forums called **TAPCIS** is available. This program includes a free IntroPak sign-on kit and $15 of free usage. WPSG members can order **TAPCIS** for $40.

Send your name, company, address, phone number, this coupon, and payment less 10% to the address above. The WordPerfect Support Group accepts checks drawn on U.S. banks, MasterCard, Visa, and company purchase orders.

Perfect for Attorneys, CPAs, Consultants, PR/Advertising agencies, Engineers or ANY Service professional...

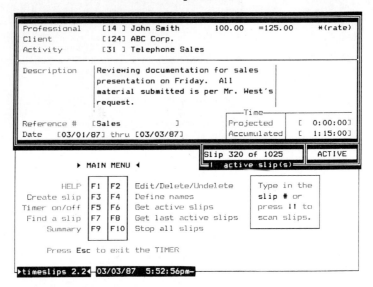

CUSTOM INVOICES, "STOPWATCH" TIMING AND MORE!

Now with just a few keystrokes, you can generate professional-looking invoices that command respect... automatically clock and record every billable minute (or enter from time sheets) and NEVER LOSE ANOTHER BILLABLE CHARGE! And because it's "memory resident," TIMESLIPS is just a keystroke away. Hit a key, write the slip, hit a key again, and return to your work. Use it with your word processor, spreadsheet or by itself.

GET TIMESLIPS UP AND RUNNING ON YOUR SCREEN AND SEE FOR YOURSELF!

TRY IT FOR 30 DAYS...And find out for yourself just how powerful, how versatile, how quick and easy it is. If you're not convinced after 30 days, just return the program for a full and prompt refund. So why wait? Order today and get TIMESLIPS running for your business now!

SYSTEM REQUIREMENTS: IBM PC/XT/AT or compatible with 2 floppy disks or 1 floppy disk and a hard disk and 384 Kb of RAM required. TIMESLIPS uses 49K while memory-resident.

THE REVIEWERS RAVE...

"TIMESLIPS handles an extremely important function elegantly."—**PC WEEK**

"How good is TIMESLIPS?—It's explosively good! AN UNPARALLELED VALUE!"—**JURIS MAGAZINE**

"It offers everything a far more expensive system can do, at a minimum investment."
—**NATIONAL LAW JOURNAL**

239 Western Ave., Essex, MA 01929
(617) 468-7358

Save $50⁰⁰ & a Pile of Headaches

ForComment™:
the perfect way to have a group review your WordPerfect documents

Say goodbye to scribbled comments and sticky notes. ForComment adds an entirely new dimension to writing and editing for users of WordPerfect and other leading wordprocessing programs.

". . . Brøderbund seems to have invented a new application, which might be called shared editing."
Stewart Alsop, PC Letter

Quickly and easily, ForComment lets you (and others in your workgroup) make comments and suggest revisions to a document and then automatically collate them all. Even if you each use a different word processing program!

". . . it's a great timesaver, it's easier on reviewers, and it cuts photocopying expenses considerably."
Alan J. Fridlund
InfoWorld, April 27, 1987

ForComment works directly with WordPerfect, WordStar, MultiMate, MicroSoft Word, and any ASCII file. It allows up to 15 reviewers to use their own computers to make comments and suggest revisions to an imported text. Each comment is automatically stamped with the reviewer's initials and the date.

Then you can use ForComment to collate all the comments, at the same time creating an audit trail. Next, you can review them and decide which ones to adopt, which ones to adapt, . . . and which ones to ignore.

"In short, ForComment is a winner and a unique kind of software. We rate it an excellent value."
Alan J. Fridlund
InfoWorld, April 27, 1987

A revised draft can be produced in a fraction of the time it would take to interpret the usual tangle of chicken-scratched notes.

Who is ForComment designed for?

Just about anyone who needs to have documents reviewed by others can benefit, whether you're on a network, use a modem or pass disks around. It's especially helpful for workgroups and LAN users in such fields as:

Law: contract negotiations and litigation briefs.

Corporate Communications: annual reports, press releases.

Training: updating manuals.

Personnel: maintaining policies and procedures.

Government: RFP's, policy statements.

Publishing: editing, developing multi-author projects.

Education: teaching writing, grant proposals.

SAVE $50 ON THIS SPECIAL OFFER FOR WORDPERFECT USERS ▶

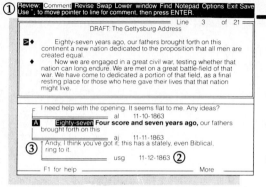

ForComment and WordPerfect fit together perfectly:

WordPerfect files can be imported into ForComment and exported back directly — no need to convert to ASCII.

☞ ForComment preserves all WordPerfect formatting, including footnotes and endnotes.

☞ You can run ForComment from the WordPerfect Library or directly from disk.

☞ On a LAN, ForComment is the perfect companion to the WordPerfect Network Version.

Technical Details

IBM PC/Tandy/and compatibles (256K or more).

Supports IBM® PC Network, Novell Advanced NetWare™ /86 and /286, 3Com EtherSeries™ and 3Com 3+Plus.™

SEND FOR THE $5.95 DEMO DISK . . . OR ORDER NOW AND SAVE $50!

ForComment in action:

1. ForComment is intuitive and easy to learn, with Lotus-like menus and an on-disk tutorial.

2. Date-Stamping creates a detailed audit trail, showing exactly who said what when.

3. Author and reviewers can all comment on each other's comments. So you can dialog without calling a formal meeting.

4. Files can be printed out (with comments and suggestions as footnotes or endnotes) for review away from the computer.

- -

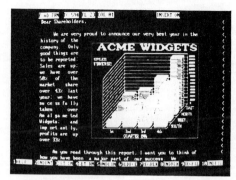

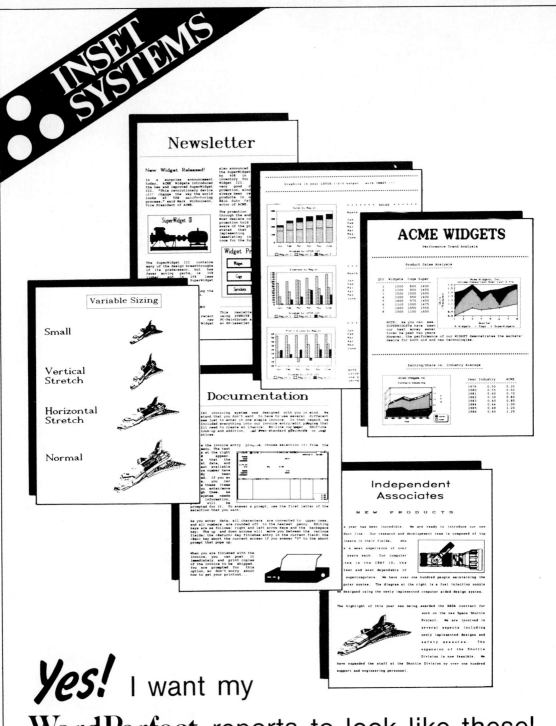

Other related Osborne/McGraw-Hill titles include:

UNIX®: The Complete Reference System V Release 3
by Stephen Coffin

The Complete Reference series now includes a book for all Unix® users! *UNIX®: The Complete Reference* includes expansive coverage of System V Release 3, the version that runs on 386 machines and on the new Macintosh™ II. Stephen Coffin, a UNIX programmer and a member of AT&T's technical staff, approaches UNIX with a perspective that benefits users of microcomputers, minicomputers, and mainframes. There is special, timely coverage of UNIX on the 80386 micros; all code in the book was run on a 386. If you're just beginning UNIX, the first part of the book will help you get started. If you're an experienced UNIX user, this book is an invaluable and extensive reference. *UNIX®: The Complete Reference* offers discussions of commands, text processing, editing, programming, communications, the Shell, and the UNIX file system. Important highlights include running MS-DOS® under UNIX, upgrading to Release 3, and extensive coverage of UNIX on the 386.

$27.95 p, Hardcover Edition
0-07-881333-6, 750 pp., 7⅛ x 9¼
$24.95 p, Paperback Edition
0-07-881299-2, 750 pp., 7⅛ x 9¼

Turbo Pascal®: The Complete Reference
by Stephen O'Brien

Turbo Pascal®: The Complete Reference is an important addition to both the *Borland-Osborne/McGraw-Hill Programming Series* and Osborne's *Complete Reference Series*. *1-2-3®: The Complete Reference* and *dBASE III PLUS™: The Complete Reference* have appeared on best-seller lists across the country. Now programmer Stephen O'Brien has written the first single resource that provides both expert and novice programmers with the entire range of Turbo Pascal's techniques, all illustrated in short examples and applications. Every aspect of Turbo Pascal is thoroughly described, including topics that were previously unavailable in one reference, such as memory-resident programs, DOS and BIOS services, and assembly language routines. *Turbo Pascal®: The Complete Reference* is clear, comprehensive, and organized for quick fact-finding. An ideal desktop resource you can refer to whenever you're programming with Borland's renown Turbo Pascal compiler.

$24.95 p
0-07-881290-9, 640 pp., 7⅜ x 9¼
The Borland-Osborne/McGraw-Hill Programming Series

WordPerfect® Made Easy
by Mella Mincberg

Here's the book that makes learning WordPerfect® quick, easy ... even enjoyable. With Mincberg's follow-along lessons, this IBM® PC compatible word processing software will be at your command in just a couple of hours. Edit text, save and print a document, set tabs, format pages. You'll become a skillful Word-Perfect user as you work through practical applications. When you're ready to explore more sophisticated WordPerfect features, Mincberg is there with detailed instructions to help you run WordPerfect's spell checker and mail merge, manage files, create macros, and use special enhancements like windows and line numbering. Mincberg, author of the ever-so-useful *WordPerfect®: Secrets, Solutions, Shortcuts*, draws on her years of computer training experience to help you become an assured, savvy WordPerfect user. (Includes quick-reference command card.)

$18.95 p
0-07-881297-6, 400 pp., 7⅛ x 9¼

Advanced WordPerfect®: Programming and Techniques, Second Edition
by Eric Alderman and Lawrence J. Magid

"Highly recommended...even I learned some new tricks and I'm a pretty old dog."
RICHARD P. WILKES, Editor of The WordPerfectionist, National Newsletter for the WordPerfect Support Group.

"This is it folks. The WordPerfect book you have been waiting for. I can't imagine a WordPerfect user who couldn't benefit by using this book...I can recommend purchase without reservation..."
ANN KIMBER, President of the Seattle WordPerfect User Group.

"...This one is worth every penny of what turns out to be nearly the lowest-priced WordPerfect book I've seen." RICHARD SHROUT, Librarian, Member of the WordPerfect Support Group.

Make this popular IBM® PC-compatible software work above and beyond the usual word processing procedures with *Advanced WordPerfect,®* now in its second edition. Revised to cover the newly released version 4.2, *Advanced WordPerfect®* shows you how to use macros to perform office automation tasks, control mail-merge operations, produce columnar reports, handle paragraph numbering and outlining, and create indexes. Ambitious WordPerfect users will also learn how to apply WordPerfect's mathematical capabilities and how to integrate WordPerfect with other products, such as Lotus® 1-2-3,® dBASE III,® SideKick,® and ProKey.™ Two well-known columnists, Alderman and Magid have written the *best* WordPerfect book available. Read it and find out why.

$18.95 p
0-07-881271-2, 350 pp., 7⅜ x 9¼

WordPerfect®: Secrets, Solutions, Shortcuts
by Mella Minceberg

Designed specifically with business professionals in mind, *WordPerfect®: Secrets, Solutions, Shortcuts* provides helpful WordPerfect techniques that let you tame this a-maze-ing word processing software. Mella Minceberg, a computer consultant, trainer, and technical writer, has organized the book into three comprehensive sections: basic features, advanced features, and macros and applications. Each chapter focuses on either a specific WordPerfect operation, such as typing and editing text or working with columns of numbers, or on an application such as creating a table or a billing statement. Minceberg offers thorough explanations of procedures, discusses circumstances where certain shortcuts work better, and teaches you to anticipate and avoid pitfalls. With Minceberg's expert tips and practical suggestions, all the power of WordPerfect will be at your fingertips.

$19.95 p
0-07-881261-5, 500 pp., 7-3/8 x 9-1/4

The Osborne/McGraw-Hill Guide to Using Lotus™ 1-2-3,™ Second Edition, Covers Release 2
by Edward M. Baras

Your investment in Lotus™ 1-2-3™ can yield the most productive returns possible with the tips and practical information in *The Osborne/McGraw-Hill Guide to Using Lotus™ 1-2-3.™* Now the second edition of this acclaimed bestseller helps you take full advantage of Lotus' new 1-2-3 upgrade, Release 2. This comprehensive guide offers a thorough presentation of the worksheet, database, and graphics functions. In addition, the revised text shows you how to create and use macros, string functions, and many other sophisticated 1-2-3 features. Step by step, you'll learn to implement 1-2-3 techniques as you follow application models for financial forecasting, stock portfolio tracking, and forms-oriented database management. For both beginners and experienced users, this tutorial quickly progresses from fundamental procedures to advanced applications.

$18.95 p
0-07-881230-5, 432 pp., 7-3/8 x 9-1/4

1-2-3® Made Easy
by Mary Campbell

Osborne's famous "Made Easy" format, which has helped hundreds of thousands of WordStar® users master word processing, is now available to Lotus® 1-2-3® beginners. *1-2-3® Made Easy* starts with the basics and goes step by step through the process of building a worksheet so you can use Lotus' spreadsheet with skill and confidence. Each chapter provides a complete 1-2-3 lesson followed by practical "hands-on" exercises that help you apply 1-2-3 immediately to the job. When you've got worksheets down, you'll learn to create and print graphs, manipulate 1-2-3's data management features, use advanced file features . . . even design keyboard macros. As the author of *1-2-3®: The Complete Reference*, and a columnist for IBM® PC UPDATE, ABSOLUTE REFERENCE, and CPA JOURNAL, Mary Campbell has plenty of experience with 1-2-3. With her know-how, you'll soon be handling 1-2-3 like a pro.

$18.95 p
0-07-881293-3, 400 pp., 7-3/8 x 9-1/4

The Advanced Guide to Lotus™ 1-2-3™
by Edward M. Baras

Edward Baras, Lotus expert and author of *The Symphony™ Book, Symphony™ Master,* and *The Jazz™ Book,* now has a sequel to his best-selling *Osborne/McGraw-Hill Guide to Using Lotus™ 1-2-3.™* For experienced users, *The Advanced Guide to Lotus 1-2-3* delves into more powerful and complex techniques using the newest software upgrade, Release 2. Added enhancements to 1-2-3's macro language, as well as many new functions and commands, are described and thoroughly illustrated in business applications. Baras shows you how to take advantage of Release 2's macro capabilities by programming 1-2-3 to simulate Symphony's keystroke-recording features and by processing ASCII files automatically. You'll also learn to set up your own command menus; use depreciation functions, matric manipulation, and regression analysis; and convert text files to the 1-2-3 worksheet format.

$18.95 p
0-07-881237-2, 325 pp., 7-3/8 x 9-1/4

dBASE III PLUS™ Made Easy
by Miriam Liskin

Liskin's *Advanced dBASE III PLUS™* and Jones' *Using dBASE III PLUS™* have been so successful that we're filling in the gap for beginners with *dBASE III PLUS™ Made Easy*. Learning dBASE III PLUS™ couldn't be simpler. You'll install and run the program, enter and edit data. Discover all the features of using dBASE III PLUS at the dot prompt. Each concept is clearly explained and followed by examples and exercises that you can complete at your own speed. Liskin discusses sorting and indexing, performing calculations, and printing reports and labels. Multiple databases are emphasized, and Liskin presents strategies for working with them. You'll also find chapters on customizing the working environment and exchanging data with other software. If you're curious about higher-level use, Liskin's final chapter shows how to combine the commands you've learned into batch programs so you can begin to automate your applications. (Includes two command cards for quick reference.)

$18.95 p
0-07-881294-1, 350 pp., 7-3/8 x 9-1/4

Using dBASE III® PLUS™
by Edward Jones

Osborne's top-selling title, *Using dBASE III,®* by Edward Jones, has now been updated to include Ashton-Tate's new upgrade, dBASE III® PLUS.™ With Jones' expertise you'll be in full command of all the new features of this powerful database software. Learn to design, create, and display a dBASE III PLUS database, devise entry forms with the dBASE III PLUS screen painter, generate reports, use Query files, and plug into dBASE III PLUS networking. In addition, you'll find out how to install dBASE III PLUS on a hard disk, conduct data searches, and manipulate assistant pull-down menus. *Using dBASE III® PLUS™* is a thorough and practical handbook for both beginning and experienced dBASE III users.

$18.95
0-07-881252-6, 350 pp., 7-3/8 x 9-1/4

Advanced dBASE III PLUS™:
Programming and Techniques
by Miriam Liskin

Liskin's enormously successful *Advanced dBASE III®* has been completely revised to offer comprehensive coverage of dBASE III PLUS.™ Expand your dBASE® skills as you learn programming techniques that let you design and implement more effective dBASE III PLUS business applications. Nationally known columnist and consultant Miriam Liskin addresses the "real world" business environment so you can make the most of dBASE III PLUS modes of operation. Liskin's discussion of new features offers you greater convenience when you work with multiple files at the dot prompt. You'll learn how to write portable, hardware-independent systems and use new error-trapping capabilities so you can work with more flexible on-line help systems. You'll also find out how to benefit from file- and record-locking features that enable you to design a multiuser data base system that can be especially important in networking.

$21.95 p
0-07-881249-6, 816 pp., 7-3/8 x 9-1/4

DOS Made Easy
by Herbert Schildt

If you're at a loss when it comes to DOS, Herb Schildt has written just the book you need, *DOS Made Easy*. Previous computer experience is not necessary to understand this concise, well-organized introduction that's filled with short applications and exercises. Schildt walks you through all the basics, beginning with an overview of a computer system's components and a step-by-step account of how to run DOS for the first time. Once you've been through the initial setup, you'll edit text files, use the DOS directory structure, and create batch files. As you feel more comfortable with DOS, Schildt shows you how to configure a system, handle floppy disks and fixed disks, and make use of helpful troubleshooting methods. By the time you've gone this far, you'll be ready for total system management—using the printer, video modes, the serial and parallel ports, and more. *DOS Made Easy* takes the mystery out of the disk operating system and puts you in charge of your PC.

$18.95 p
0-07-881295-X, 385 pp., 7-3/8 x 9-1/4

WordStar® 4.0 Made Easy
by Walter A. Ettlin

WordStar® Made Easy, the original "Made Easy" guide with 350,000 copies sold worldwide, has been so successful that Osborne has published a companion volume on the new WordStar® version 4.0. All 4.0 commands and features are thoroughly described and illustrated in practical exercises so you can put WordStar to immediate use, even if you've never used a computer before. Walter Ettlin, who has written four books and taught high school for 23 years, guides you from the fundamentals of creating a memo or report to using WordStar's calculator mode, macro commands, and Word Finder™. You'll also learn to use WordStar's latest spelling checker. *WordStar® 4.0 Made Easy* puts you in control of your software with the acclaimed "Made Easy" format now found in 11 Osborne titles. (Includes a handy pull-out command card.)

$16.95 p
0-07-881011-6, 300 pp., 7-3/8 x 9-1/4

DisplayWrite 4™ Made Easy
by Gail Todd

Upgrading from DisplayWrite 3™ to DisplayWrite 4™? Here's the book that provides a thorough introduction to IBM's word processing software. Handle new menus, screens, and options with ease as Todd leads you from basic steps to more sophisticated procedures. The famous "Made Easy" format offers hands-on exercises and plenty of examples so you can quickly learn to produce letters and reports. All of DisplayWrite 4's new features are covered, including printing interfaces; the voice add-on; Paper Clip, the cursor control that lets you take up where you left off; and Notepad, a convenience that enables you to insert notes into documents. Todd, the author of numerous user guides and manuals, has the know-how to get you up and running fast.

$19.95 p
0-07-881270-4, 420 pp., 7-3/8 x 9-1/4

Available at fine bookstores and computer stores everywhere.

For a complimentary catalog of all our current publications contact:
Osborne/McGraw-Hill, 2600 Tenth Street, Berkeley, CA 94710

Phone inquiries may be made using our toll-free number.
Call 800-227-0900 or 800-772-2531 (in California). TWX 910-366-7277.

Prices subject to change without notice.

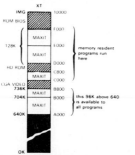
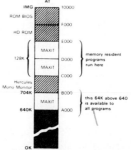